A Guide to

Massachusetts
Public Records

Parishes, Towns, and Counties

A Guide to
Massachusetts Public Records

Parishes, Towns, and Counties

Carroll D. Wright

foreword by

David Curtis Dearborn

Originally published as the *Report on the Custody and Condition of the Public Records of Parishes, Towns, and Counties: 1889*

NEW ENGLAND HISTORIC
GENEALOGICAL SOCIETY

First published in 1889
Foreword copyright © 2014 by the New England Historic Genealogical Society

ISBN: 978-0-88082-317-3
Library of Congress Number: 2014937223

Cover design by Carolyn Oakley Sheppard and Leslie A. Weston
Cover photo: Etching of the Southern View of Fitchburg by John Warner Barber,
from his book *History and Antiquities of Every Town in Massachusetts* (1839)

Printed in the United States of America

NEW ENGLAND HISTORIC GENEALOGICAL SOCIETY
Boston, Massachusetts
AmericanAncestors.org
2014

Foreword

Despite its relatively small size, Massachusetts arguably has the most complete and comprehensive set of records of historical value of any state. Record-keeping began shortly after the first settlements were established, and for the most part the records have survived to a remarkable degree. The records themselves exist at every level of government: state, county and town.

By the mid-nineteenth century, agitation grew for establishing a public records commission, such as existed at the time in England, with the power to bring all the Commonwealth's important records into a single repository. Other parties objected to this idea, both because of the possible expense involved, but mainly because many local officials objected to giving up custody of their records. Despite these objections, interest in the subject grew to the point that in 1884, the Massachusetts Legislature authorized the preparation of a report showing the condition of the public records of the parishes, towns and counties of the Commonwealth. Carroll D. Wright was appointed commissioner to prepare this report.

Wright's *Report on the Custody and Condition of the Public Records of Parishes, Towns and Counties*, published in 1889, is the result of his efforts. This remarkable book brings together under one cover a town-by-town, church-by-church, and county-by-county listing of all the records existing for each jurisdiction. Its 379 pages contain a wealth of information useful not only to the genealogist, but to the local historian as well.

The book is divided into several sections, each prefaced by detailed explanatory notes. The first two deal with laws relating to records, and to proprietors' records, with a listing by town of those that existed in 1889. The next section lists records of surviving and extinct churches. This is divided into two parts: the first lists records of existing and extinct churches arranged by city or town, with the cities and towns grouped under their respective counties. The second part lists the same information, but with the records of existing and extinct churches grouped by denomination. These include records of numerous Protestant denominations, as well as of Roman Catholic churches and Jewish synagogues.

The next section lists city and town records, arranged under their respective counties. For each community, we are given a list of the kinds of records to be found (e.g., town proceedings; births, marriages and deaths; marriage intentions; assessors; selectmen; proprietors, miscellaneous), the number of volumes in each category, in whose custody they reside (usually the town clerk), years covered, whether indexed, and condition. Numerous footnotes alert the reader to gaps in particular record groups, missing volumes, records kept elsewhere, or other special circumstances. For each city and town, we are also provided with a chronology of important dates: date of establishment or incorporation (often citing chapter and verse of the Provincial Laws or Mass. Records), name changes, and dates when parts were annexed from or to other towns.

Following this is a section dealing with the various types of court records: the records of the Supreme Judicial Court (SJC), arranged by county; miscellaneous records held by the SJC [now at the State Archives], including those of the Court of Assistants and the Governor's Council; and the records of the county Superior Courts.

The last section describes county records, and is divided into two parts, the first describing the records in the county registries of probate, and the second those in the county registries of deeds.

Genealogists researching Massachusetts ancestors are fortunate in that for many, but not all towns, the records of birth, marriage and death have been published in book form down to 1850. Other types of records, such as those of selectmen's minutes, town meetings, tax rolls, proprietors' records, etc., often are not in print or are not readily available. In such cases, a trip to the appropriate city or town clerk's office may be advisable. When visiting a city or town hall, it is not unusual to encounter clerks who have little knowledge of (or interest in) their historical records. Armed with the knowledge of what was known to have existed in the clerk's custody in 1889, you should be in a better position to gain access to the particular type of record you desire.

Users of this book should keep in mind that many things have changed since this book was first printed. Many churches that flourished then have merged with other parishes or no longer exist. On 26 April 1927, the four central Massachusetts towns of Dana, Enfield, Greenwich and Prescott were abolished to make way for the Quabbin Reservoir, and the remnants of each were annexed to neighboring towns. Early probate records for a number of counties are no longer held in the local registries, but are now at the State Archives. Those seeking a better understanding of the intricacies of Massachusetts records should also consult several other books. For church records, Harold F. Worthley's *An inventory of the records of the particular (Congregational) churches of Massachusetts gathered 1620-1805* (Cambridge, Harvard University Press, 1970 [Harvard Theological Studies, XXV]) is an excellent, but now somewhat dated, town-by-town listing of each Congregational (many now Unitarian-Universalist) church in the state. William Francis Galvin, *Historical data relating to Counties, Cities and Towns in Massachusetts* (Boston: NEHGS, 1997) incorporates from Wright much of the data relating to the formation, naming, and boundary changes in the state's municipalities, but brings it up to date. Richard LeBaron Bowen's *Massachusetts Records: A Handbook for Genealogists, Historians, Lawyers, and other Researchers* (Rehoboth, Mass., privately printed, 1957) provides a good general discussion of records, with emphasis on those at the county level. The chapter on Massachusetts, by Winifred Lovering Holman Dodge, in vol. 1 of Milton Rubincam, ed., *Genealogical Research: Methods and Sources* (revised ed., Washington, D.C., American Society of Genealogists, 1980) also provides many useful insights into the peculiarities of record-keeping and jurisdictional border-changes in Massachusetts that may trip up the unwary genealogist. Finally, users should consult the Massachusetts chapter of Michael J. Leclerc, ed., *Genealogist's Handbook for New England Research* (5th ed., Boston: NEHGS, 2012) for general information on researching and records in the state, including detailed maps, up-to-date addresses and contact information, and a valuable listing of towns.

Carroll Wright's *Report on the Custody and Condition of the Public Records* has long been out of print, and only a few genealogists have even been aware of its existence. It is my hope that this new printing brings this extraordinarily useful and neglected book to the attention of a much wider audience.

David Curtis Dearborn
Senior Genealogist Emeritus
NEW ENGLAND HISTORIC
GENEALOGICAL SOCIETY

REPORT

ON THE

CUSTODY AND CONDITION OF THE PUBLIC RECORDS

OF

PARISHES, TOWNS, AND COUNTIES.

BY

CARROLL D. WRIGHT,

COMMISSIONER.

BOSTON:

WRIGHT & POTTER PRINTING COMPANY, STATE PRINTERS,

18 POST OFFICE SQUARE,

1889.

INDEX TO SUBJECTS.

INDEX.

Commonwealth of Massachusetts.

OFFICE OF THE COMMISSIONER OF PUBLIC RECORDS
OF PARISHES, TOWNS, AND COUNTIES,
20 BEACON STREET, BOSTON, March 1, 1889.

Hon. W. E. BARRETT, *Speaker of the House of Representatives.*

SIR : — I have the honor to present to the Legislature a report on the custody and condition of the public records of parishes, towns, and counties.

By Chapter 65, Resolves of 1884, the Governor and Council were authorized to appoint a suitable person, to serve without compensation, who should report to the succeeding Legislature upon the condition of the public records of the parishes, towns, and counties of the Commonwealth. Under this resolve, Governor Robinson did me the honor to ask me to make a report to the Legislature, showing, in a general way, the condition of the records referred to in the resolve, and suggested that it might be well, as the decennial census was approaching, to arrange for the collection of preliminary material through the machinery thereof. February 12, 1885, I sent a communication to the honorable Senate and House of Representatives, stating the general difficulties encountered and that no estimate of the condition of the public records of parishes, towns, and counties could be made without information of a specific nature, and asked that the sum of $500 be appropriated for the purpose of carrying out the above mentioned provisions of Chapter 65. In response to this request, the Legislature promptly authorized me, by Chapter 19 of the Resolves of 1885, approved March 11, to expend a sum not exceeding $500 in collecting the necessary information in regard to the records named, such information to be collected so far as possible by means of the Census of 1885, and ordered that the report called for by the Resolve of 1884 be made to the next Legislature, that is, to the Legislature of 1886.

During the progress of the Census of 1885, and under the resolve just referred to, much information was collected, by means of the Census Enumerators, relating to the records of towns and parishes, and, by the employment of special agents, relative to court and county records. The pressure of the work pertaining to the census was such that the information collected in 1885 could not be compiled at once, and it was not until 1888 that the returns made by the enumerators and special agents were critically examined. While a vast deal of information had been collected, and that of a very valuable character, it was evident that much more would be needed to perfect the data in order to enable me to make an intelligent report to the Legislature upon the condition of records. To this end the following resolve was passed February 9, 1888 :

[CHAPTER 9.]

RESOLVE IN RELATION TO PUBLIC RECORDS OF PARISHES, TOWNS AND
COUNTIES.

Resolved, That the commissioner appointed under the provisions of chapter sixty-five of the resolves of the year eighteen hundred and eighty-four, relating to public records of parishes, towns, and counties, is hereby authorized to expend a sum not exceeding fifteen hundred dollars, for the purpose of compiling and tabulating the information relating to such records collected in accordance with the provisions of chapter nineteen of the resolves of the year eighteen hundred and eighty-five, and to make the report in print called for by said resolves. [*Approved February 9, 1888.*

Under this authorization I at once began the work of collecting missing information, and for this purpose appointed Robert T. Swan, Esq., as Secretary of the Commission. Correspondence with town and parish authorities and interviews with clerks of courts developed the necessity of still further and more efficient labors in order to secure what the Legislature originally intended. I, therefore, asked the Legislature to grant further means, and May 18, 1888, near the close of the session, the Legislature passed a Resolve, Chapter 81 of the Resolves of that year, by which the Commissioner appointed under the provisions of Chapter 65 of the Resolves of 1884, relating to public records of parishes, towns, and counties, was authorized to expend a sum not exceeding $2,500, in addition to the sum authorized by Chapter 9, given above. Under this authorization the work has been carried through, and yet it is far from complete ; it is as conclusive as it is possible to make

it, however, when considered on the general basis as contemplated by the Legislature at the time of the passage of the
resolve of 1884, originating the Commission.

For many years the propriety of organizing a public record
commission, after the style and with the powers of the English
record commission, has been agitated, the general intent of
such a commission being to bring into a central depository all
the important records of the Commonwealth. To such an
enterprise various objections have been brought, and on various accounts, both from the economic and the local point of
view. It was urged that under such a commission great
expense would be involved and the records of towns and counties would be taken from the custody of the local officers.
Town and county pride, or better, town and county public spirit,
which has always been fostered in this Commonwealth, seemed
to be opposed to such a measure, and yet Governors and members
of the Legislature from time to time have recognized the necessity of taking some action by which the public records should not
only be properly indexed but thoroughly preserved. By Chapter 60, Resolves of 1884, a commission of five was appointed, to
serve without pay, to investigate the condition of the records,
files, papers, and documents in the State Department. This
commission consisted of the Honorable Secretary of the Commonwealth, Hon. Samuel A. Green, Justin Winsor, Esq., William P. Upham, Esq., and Hon. Augustus E. Scott. This
commission made an exceedingly interesting and valuable report in January, 1885, upon the condition of the records, files,
papers, and documents in the Secretary's Department. In this
report the commissioners say, with respect to such documents
on file at the State House, that they " have found the documents of every kind under his (the Secretary's) charge in as
good condition as he has been permitted, with the clerical
force at his command, to put them ; while at the same time the
commission, as a whole, may report that condition to be far
from what is desirable." As a result of that report there is no
doubt that the archives and all records, files, papers, and documents now in the custody of the State will be brought into
excellent condition in due time.

It seems, then, that the originators of the present investigation had in view the ascertaining of such information as would

indicate the desirability or undesirability of making any effort on the part of the State for not only bringing into proper condition the records of parishes, towns, and counties, but of ascertaining some means of preserving them after they are brought into proper condition. My purpose has been to learn the custody and condition of these records so far as possible, and, having stated them to the Legislature, to offer such suggestions for future efforts as the investigation might indicate.

The difficulties in the way of carrying out the intent of the Legislature were greater than at first appeared. The investigation was the first attempt in the State of the kind contemplated. No appropriation was at first made for the preliminary work, for it was desirable that the condition of the public records should be ascertained at as little cost as possible and without the necessity of establishing the machinery of a great record commission. The preliminary work, however, was done at a small cost, and in fact the whole investigation has been conducted and completed within an expense of $4,500.

It being the first time that an inquiry into the custody and condition of public records has been made, the official custodians of the records had made no examination which would enable them to answer carefully the necessary inquiries. The town clerks and the enumerators during the census divided the responsibility; for in some cases the enumerators left blanks with the clerks, expecting the clerks to fill and return them, but often the enumerator was obliged to make his own examination and report what he happened to find. Church officers were slow to furnish information in a large number of cases, although some of them were very prompt and very assiduous in complying with the request of the government. Oftentimes, however, when the church and parish each had records, either the church or parish records were forgotten, and consequently in many cases but one set of records is reported. All these difficulties necessitated an extensive correspondence.

It is true that much of the data is general and much information is missing, but where it was apparent that information was missing and could probably be supplied, it has been asked for. The neglect to reply to such requests, however, has made it necessary to submit this report with some omissions and apparent inconsistencies. In some cases contradictory infor-

mation has been given by different persons, each presuming to
know the truth, but unless one or the other of these statements
could be confirmed from some other source than the informant
all such information has been omitted from the report rather
than use doubtful statements as to fact. Some information has
been received too late for use in the report, the knowledge that
this work was being prosecuted having led interested persons to
send information of which they only were possessed.

The question asked of all officers having parish, town, or
county records in their custody as to the condition of such
records has been differently understood, some having taken it
to mean the completeness and accuracy of the records, while
others have interpreted it to mean the state of preservation at
the time of the inquiry. The latter has been the more common
understanding, and the answers presented apply generally to
the state of preservation, explanatory foot-notes being used
whenever necessary.

Certain records and papers which by law are required to be
kept in certain depositories are undoubtedly in the proper
place, but from their infrequent use have been forgotten and
not reported. These are the records and papers more likely
than any others to be lost.

All persons of whom inquiry was made in this investigation
were asked if they knew of private records of the particular
kind called for. In response to this question many gave the
names of persons having, or who were supposed to have,
the records sought. In every instance correspondence was
opened with the persons named. The correspondence in this
matter during the early part of the investigation was in the
form of a circular letter, asking if any information could be
given in regard to the records, especially records of extinct
churches; but the replies were so few and unsatisfactory that
the letters sent later to persons reported as having records in
their possession asked for the confirmation or contradiction
of the statement made by others concerning their possession of
the records specified. If the possession was disclaimed, no
name is given; but if the information was confirmed or no reply was received, the name of the party having, or said to have,
possession of such records is stated in the report.

No inquiry has been made in regard to the records kept by

officers outside of the present limits of the State, although in several instances parts of the adjoining States have been at some time embraced within the territorial bounds of the Commonwealth. Neither has any attempt been made to present the legislation by which the United States Government, through any authorization, by commissioners or otherwise, has changed the State lines.

Upon commencing the work of verification of the returns of the various custodians of records, which in fact has been the chief occupation of the Secretary of the Commission and his assistants, perplexing discrepancies in dates appeared, which made it necessary to examine the earlier laws pertaining to the establishment of courts, county offices, and towns, and to the keeping of records. This examination developed so many facts, both interesting and necessary to a complete understanding of apparent peculiarities and discrepancies in the returns referred to, that those laws, which by successive stages of improvement have become the laws of today, are presented in their appropriate places, with references to the authorities from which they are cited.

It would be absurd to claim that all the laws relating to this subject have been found, for the incompleteness of the early records, the absence from the archives of acts and parts of acts, and the imperfect indexing of volumes of records and laws, render it impossible to make such claim. Much legislation must remain in doubt until further research is made. So, only such acts, the final passage of which is established beyond doubt by the records, are presented in this report. The temptation to which many historians yield, of assuming as fact what is undoubtedly fact, though not specifically recorded, has been avoided.

The importance of keeping records seems to have been first recognized in 1634, when "a survey of all improved or enclosed land of every free inhabitant" was ordered, the record of which was to be "a sufficient assurance" of ownership. In 1637 the recording of lands was made compulsory, and in 1639 all courts, magistrates, and commissioners were ordered to record their judgments, and records were to be kept of births, marriages, and deaths. From that time the recording of matters of value to posterity has been a subject of constant legislation.

The authorities cited, and the abbreviations used to denote authorities, are as follows : Copies of proceedings of the Privy Council, in England, in the office of the Commissioner of the Province Laws ; Massachusetts Archives (Mass. Archives) ; Massachusetts Colony Laws, edition of 1660 (Mass. Col. Laws, edit. 1660) ; Massachusetts Council Records (Mass. Council Rec.) ; Massachusetts Laws (Mass. Laws) ; Massachusetts Records (Mass. Rec.) ; New York Record of Town Grants (N. Y. Town Grants) ; Perpetual Laws of Massachusetts, edition of 1789 (Perpet. Laws of Mass., edit. 1789) ; Plymouth Colony Laws, edition of 1836 (Ply. Col. Laws, edit. 1836) ; Plymouth Colony Records (Ply. Col. Rec.) ; Province Laws (Prov. Laws) ; Resolves and orders, unprinted (Resolve) ; Supreme Judicial Court, Suffolk County, Records (S. J. Court, Suffolk County, Records). The reference to volume and page is given in every instance, wherever such reference is possible (except for the Resolves), until January 6, 1779, for legislation relating to towns and until 1784 for legislation relating to courts. This change in reference is made necessary by reason of certain acts relating to courts, passed between 1779 and 1784, being contained in the edition of the Perpetual Laws, and reference being made thereto, whereas certain acts relating to towns are not contained in that edition, and are, therefore, referred to only by the dates of the respective acts. Since 1784, the date of the act is deemed sufficient reference.

The Resolves passed between May 20, 1666, and May 10, 1776, are not yet printed, and the various volumes of written copies being differently arranged, a reference to particular volumes is not practicable. The Commissioner of the Province Laws is preparing a volume of these Resolves, the pages containing those passed prior to 1708 being already in plate, while the material is prepared for presenting all passed subsequent to that time and prior to 1763.

The spelling found in the earlier laws has been modernized, unless for some special reason it has seemed best to quote exactly the original spelling. For instance, the name of a town, as first given in the presentation of the legislation relating to towns, conforms to the spelling as it appears for the first time in the records.

The difficulty of research in the old records of the State (and by records of the State is meant the records of the Colonies, Province, and State) is well stated by Mr. Justin Winsor, in the Memorial History of Boston, in which he says : " In our State House, too, are tier upon tier of volumes labelled ' Massachusetts Archives,' so arranged, indeed, in an attempted classification that it is irksome and unsatisfactory to consult them." Mr. Winsor refers also to Palfrey's History of New England, where the author condemns the condition of things relative to these records. It will be seen, therefore, that the difficulties in making this investigation are great, indeed, and that the omissions in the chain of legislation relative to various records are not only excusable but are such as to involve the necessity on the part of the State of completing them by giving the proper power and authority in this direction.

Difficulty arises in establishing the date of legislation in two ways, first, from the old custom prior to 1752 of double dating in January, February, and March (to the 25th), a custom which has led to much confusion and uncertainty on the part of persons using such dates ; and second, from the fact that until 1831 the legislative year commenced in May and that the legislation is often recorded as of the day and year of the opening of the session, although the time specified was in the next calendar year. This makes the ascertainment of dates exceedingly perplexing to a person unfamiliar with records prior to 1831. The dates given in this report, however, are made to conform to the present method of reckoning the calendar year, that is, from January 1 to December 31.

In the earlier records of the General Court the date of the first day of the session is recorded, and legislation for several days is often entered as of that date. In the printed volumes of the Massachusetts Records, also, a date is often given in the margin which applies to several pages of legislation, when it is apparent from the text that the date should have been changed for successive days ; that is, that the legislation actually took place on a date different from the first date given in the margin. Town records for these reasons give different dates for legislation applying to towns from those found in the records of the State, as, for instance, the Dedham records give September 10, 1636, as the date of incorporation of the town, while September 8, 1636, is given in the records of the State.

One would naturally suppose that there would be at the State House authentic records from which facts relating to the incorporation of towns and counties could be ascertained, and also records of the action of towns and cities which became necessary in order to carry out acts of the Legislature. Diligent search has failed to discover, however, in any records in the possession of the State the record of the incorporation of several of the towns or of the County of Dukes County, or the record, in most cases, of the action of towns or cities relating to the acceptance of certain acts of legislation, which acts without such acceptance would be void.

No record is found of the incorporation of the town of Falmouth or of Succanesset in connection with Falmouth, but the town historian of Falmouth, referring to the incorporation of Succanesset, says: "That record makes a legal title to the existence of this town, but the time and reason of the adoption of its present name is an unsolved mystery"; that is to say, the record of legislation proves that there is such a town, but no citation can be made as to the time of the incorporation of, or the time and reason of the adoption of the name of, Falmouth.

So, nothing can be found as to the incorporation of Bradford further than a resolve passed February 24, 1701, which says: "The line anciently agreed to by Rowley, upon allotting out of Merrimack Lands (so called), being originally a part of their Township, now Bradford, is confirmed." The town records of Rowley may, therefore, throw some light upon "their Township," but no such light is thrown on the subject by any State records.

If it is desired to learn what the record shows of the establishment of "Edgar Towne," "Sharborn" (since Sherburn, and then Nantucket), and "Tisbury-Towne," reference must be had to the New York records.

A resolve which is fixed upon to establish the date of the incorporation of Chilmark uses this language: "That the Mannour of Tisbury, commonly called Chilmark, have all the powers of a town." Under this language it would be more strictly Tisbury, and not Chilmark, that was incorporated.

The lands called New Braintree and a part of the town of Hardwick were by law made a district, but the resolve accomplishing this is fixed upon as the incorporation of New Braintree.

The town records of Sutton show that by an order dated May 15, 1704, a township was granted, but the first mention of Sutton in the State records is October 28, 1714, while the Manual of the General Court gives June 21, 1715, as the date of incorporation.

These instances show the necessity of the collection of accurate data relative to the incorporation of towns.

Reference has been made also to the absence of records relating to the acceptance by towns and cities of legislation referring particularly to them.   Records of the acceptance by towns of city charters from the Legislature are wanting in nearly all cases.   The city of Lynn was incorporated April 10, 1850, provided the act of incorporation was accepted by the town of Lynn within twenty days.   The Manual gives the date of acceptance as May 14, 1850, thirty-four days after.   As a matter of fact, the State has no record of the action of the town of Lynn in this respect, but the town records give the date as April 19, 1850.

Certain acts have been passed by the Legislature which were provisional upon the payment of money by one town to another, some of which acts were to take effect when the agreement to pay was voted and others when the payment was actually made, but the action of the town or towns involved has not been made a matter of State record.

The foregoing statements are general in their character, and indicate the labor required for a presentation of the facts needed by the Legislature upon which to base intelligent action.   They also show the difficulties in the way of carrying out the original intention of the Legislature so far as this preliminary commission is concerned.

It will be seen, as has been stated, that this report is incomplete in many particulars.   The deficiencies, however, are pointed out and can be easily understood.   They are the chief argument, after all, to convince one of the necessity for the exercise of the most rigid oversight of the public records of our State.

The information contained in this report is presented in six divisions, as follows : Laws relating to Records ; Proprietors Records ; Church Records ; Town Records ; Court Records ; and County Records.

For each division there is given the information relative to records and the name of the office, officer, or person having the custody of the records, except in the case of the records of the existing churches, which are in possession of some duly authorized church officer. Various notes explanatory of the information contained in the tabular presentations are also given, but, in addition thereto, certain general statements are necessary. For convenience, these general statements are classified under their respective divisions.

LAWS RELATING TO RECORDS. — The information given under this division relates to the legislation concerning court records, town and city records, and records of births, marriages, and deaths. During the early years of the colonies these records were intermingled and these laws are, therefore, presented in a separate division rather than under the different divisions of court records and town records.

PROPRIETORS OF COMMON LANDS. — Under this division there has been given the citation of laws relating to proprietors. There is little to be said other than what is given in the citations referred to on page 5, or more than appears in the tabular presentation on pages 6–8.

It is to be regretted that more care was not taken to furnish the Commission with the distinctive name of the Common Lands. The information that a town has possession of the records of the proprietors is valuable, but if the name of the proprietors had been supplied it would be much more valuable, especially as there is often a variance between the name found on the records of the State and that in the volumes in possession of the towns.

An attempt was made to present the several proprieties under the names by which they were granted, with a summary of the acts relating to them and by which they were finally merged in the towns ; but the confusion of names in the earlier records, the variance in names before alluded to, and the loose legislation by which such proprieties were established or merged, required far more extensive research than was possible under this preliminary investigation.

CHURCHES. — Many persons interested in church matters have kindly sent to the Commission historical sketches relating to certain churches, but as a history of the churches of the Commonwealth has not been attempted such historical sketches have not been included in the report. These have often been the means of making clear what otherwise would have been doubtful points and of confirming information or clearing up contradictory matters, and have frequently led to further inquiries, the answers to which have in various ways perfected the records. The pains taken by the persons sending such historical sketches is fully recognized and their kindness appreciated.

The terms church, parish, and society are so indiscriminately used that the description of the records, in the column headed " Kind" in the tabular presentations, is undoubtedly wrong in many cases. The establishing of parishes or precincts which afterward became towns, and the keeping of the parish and town records as one record through a long term of years, have led to confusion in this respect. Town clerks returned as the earliest date in the town records the date of the beginning of the parish records, while at the same time church officers have said that the parish records in their possession include the period during which the parish was the town under the old order of things. Such complications have been investigated as far as possible and the erroneous results corrected, so that the years stated to be covered by the parish records are generally those during which the parish was wholly distinct from the town. Owing to the fact that the records which in reality constituted the record of the town in its earliest period of existence were parish records, they have in many cases remained in the possession of the religious society connected with or growing out of the parish, and the town in such cases has no record in its possession prior to the time of the separation of the parish and town. All such records now in the hands of parish or society officers, that is, where the parish was merged into the town or the town erected out of the parish, should be copied by the town and the records kept as a part of the town records.

The indiscriminate use of the terms church, parish, society, and congregation has extended through the records and laws

from the earliest days of the colonies. The following expres-
sions occur in recent laws : " The term religious society and
society in the preceding section shall include parishes";
" every religious society established or organized"; "any
church that may be organized may be incorporated"; "any
religious society connected with a church"; "any church connected with a religious society."

In the ancient records the use of these terms is even more
confusing. No successive acts of legislation establishing the
earliest churches, parishes, precincts, societies, or congregations have been found, but the following terms and phrases
quoted below show the uses of the several terms and give a
slight idea of the difficulty of separating the records of religious
and municipal bodies.

In 1646 the court ordered " that something be done to
maintain the liberties of the churches." Men and women of
orthodox opinions were allowed in the " congregations" which
in 1665 were already gathered. In 1668 the court undertook,
evidently, to prevent confusion in regard to the term church
by ordering that " by the church is meant such as are in full
communion only." By an act passed in 1677 towns and plantations were ordered to raise money by taxation for the support
of " their" respective ministers, and in 1692 it was ordered
that " the minister of the town" should be chosen in town
meeting. As the latter act created difficulty " in divers towns
where there are more churches than one," it was repealed
in 1693 and each church was allowed to choose its own minister, " and the major part of such inhabitants as do there
usually attend on the public worship of God, and are by law
duly qualified for voting in town affairs, concurring in the
church's act, the person thus elected and approved, accepting
and settling with them, shall be the minister." It was provided
" that nothing herein contained is intended or shall be construed to extend to abridge the inhabitants of Boston of their
accustomed way and practice as to their choice of ministers."
Nothing has been found in any records explaining this " way
and practice." Difficulties arose under this act, and in 1695 it
was provided that if the minister chosen by a church was not
approved by the town meeting, if a council of three or five of
the elders and messengers of a neighboring church did approve,

the minister should be settled. In 1681 the "church and society at the North River at Scituate," and, in the same act, the " congregation and society up the river," were mentioned. " District, parish, or precinct," is a phrase used in 1718, while in 1786 " each parish and precinct " is declared to be a body corporate. The Constitution classifies together "towns, parishes, precincts, and other bodies politic, or religious societies," but excludes churches. The failure of the church officers to designate correctly the kind of records in their possession is not strange, therefore, even though it may not be excusable.

The returns from the churches in the small towns usually give the denomination as the distinguishing name of the church, but in cities and the larger towns local names are often given. It being impossible to obtain by any means at our command the corporate or exact names of churches, the names given in the several denominational lists have been adopted. Effort has been made to obtain returns from every church in the State, and such returns have been received from every church of whose existence any information could be obtained. A few new societies, holding meetings in halls, may have been omitted, but being new, their records, if any are kept, would not be of any great value historically at present or in a report of this kind.

Oftentimes there has been a division of a society into two separate bodies, and in some cases the oldest date of organization has been claimed by both, each considering itself the original society. Such a proceeding, of course, is wrong. If the new society has survived and the old has become extinct, the claiming of the original date of organization by the surviving society, as is often done, is historically misleading.

In many cases the only church record is one kept by the pastor, and too often, under such circumstances, he has taken the record away when leaving the church. The records of baptisms, marriages, and births contained in such records have been found often to be the only records kept in very early years.

A classification of churches under denominational names has been a difficult and perplexing work. The general terms Methodist, Episcopal, Congregational, Evangelical, Orthodox,

Liberal, and Christian, given in the returns as received from
church officers, have been carefully examined in connection
with various denominational lists, and if the names of the
several churches did not appear in those lists authority has
been found for classifying them under the denomination, as
given.

The following tabular statement presents the denominations
of the existing churches in the State from which returns have
been received, with the number of churches of each denomination included in this report :

Advent Baptist,	1	Independent Methodist,.	1
African Methodist Episcopal,	7	Jewish, .	6
African Methodist Episcopal		Latter Day Saints, .	7
Zion, .	5	Messiah, .	1
Baptist, .	286	Methodist,	1
Catholic Apostolic,	1	Methodist Episcopal,	347
Christian,	2	New Jerusalem,	15
Christian Baptist, .	1	Presbyterian, .	11
Christian Connection,	15	Primitive Methodist,	2
Congregational,	535	Protestant Episcopal,	133
Disciples of Christ,	2	Reformed Episcopal,	1
Evangelical Congregational,.	1	Reformed Presbyterian,	2
Evangelical Independent,	1	Roman Catholic,	282
Evangelical Lutheran, .	10	Second Advent,	14
Free Baptist, .	14	Seventh Day Advent,	1
Free Congregational,	1	Undenominational,	11
Free Evangelical, .	2	Union Evangelical,	1
French Protestant, .	1	Unitarian,	179
Friends, .	31	United Presbyterian,	3
German Congregational,	1	United Society (Shakers),	3
German Methodist Episcopal,	2	Universalist, .	115
German Reformed,	2	Wesleyan Methodist,	1
Gethsemane Baptist,	1		
Independent Baptist,	1	Total,	2,060

Especial pains was taken in the investigation concerning
church records to ascertain all information possible in regard
to extinct churches, but very many such churches have undoubtedly been forgotten by persons from whom such information was solicited. Some information in regard to their
records, such as the motive for destroying them or the reason
why they are retained by certain persons, has been received
but is not presented in the report.

In many cases nothing more is returned in regard to extinct

churches than the statement that an old edifice is remembered
as having once existed.   In one case the single answer is made
that there are a few persons still living who remember the
church, but nothing is known of any records.   In such cases,
that is, when nothing is known of any records, some date
connected with the church which would serve to identify it
has been given in the tables, with the hope that some interested person, being reminded of it, might furnish information.

The denomination of the church at the time it became extinct
is given, and if it was reported as formerly of a different denomination, such fact is given in a foot-note.   The extinct
churches given as Methodist may have been Methodist Episcopal, but as no list of the churches at the time these severally
became extinct was obtainable, no accurate statement could be
made regarding them.   When a parish or society has given up
its organization but a church still exists, the church is given
as existing, with explanatory notes in regard to the parish or
society.   Sometimes, in answer to inquiries, the clerk of a
society would say that he has the records of an extinct church,
but whether in his official capacity he does not state.   It is
sometimes reported, also, that a church officer has the records
of an extinct church, but whether by any legal right is not
reported.   In most of these cases it is probable that the clerk
or church officer should have deposited the records with the
town or city clerk, in accordance with law.

Some persons have learned through correspondence with the
Commission that there was a legal depository for such records
in their possession and have been glad to place them in the
custody designated by law.   Very many of the churches
reported as extinct were not mentioned by town officers or
persons making returns for existing churches in the same
town, the facts presented regarding them having been learned
from historians or persons interested in the subject.   It is
somewhat strange that town clerks in so many instances should
not know, by virtue of their authority over them, of the existence of such records.

The following table presents the number and denominations
of the extinct churches in the State, so far as ascertained :

African Methodist Episcopal,	1	Protestant Episcopal,	. .	7
African Methodist Episcopal		Reformed Methodist,	. .	3
Zion, ...	1	Roman Catholic,	. . .	2
Baptist, ...	54	Second Advent,	. . .	2
Christian, ...	2	Six Principles Baptist, .	.	1
Congregational, . . .	58	Undenominational, .	. .	1
Dissenting Congregational, .	1	Unitarian, ...		18
Evangelical, ...	2	United Brethren, . .		2
Free Baptist, ...	3	United Society (Shakers),	.	1
Friends, ...	8	Universalist, ...		34
Independent Congregational,	1	Wesleyan, ...		2
Jewish, ...	2	Wesleyan Methodist, .	.	2
Methodist, ...	9	Denomination not given,	.	16
Methodist Episcopal, . .	26			
Methodist Protestant, . .	3	Total, ...	.	266
Presbyterian, ...	4			

TOWN RECORDS. — The omission of records for the years between the date of the establishment of the town and the date given in the return made by the town clerk as the beginning of the oldest volume in his possession indicates, in certain cases, the probable loss of volumes of town records, but no mention was made, however, in very many cases of the loss of such volumes in answer to the specific question, "Have any volumes of your records been lost or destroyed?" Correspondence in such cases has shown that no attention has been given to this matter; yet the conclusion cannot be avoided that many such volumes have either been lost or misplaced. Town clerks are prohibited by law from allowing their records to go out of their custody, except upon a summons, yet town clerks frequently say that records "at present" are in the hands of some unauthorized person.

The dates covered by the records of the doings of selectmen and assessors were, inadvertently, not asked for in the beginning of this investigation, but were given in many cases, especially where the clerks or enumerators were interested in giving the State full information.

The great variation which will be observed relative to the number of volumes of assessors' records is accounted for by the fact that in some cases the volumes of records of proceedings were reported, while in many cases the yearly valuation lists were included. The accumulation of valuation lists has caused the assessors in some instances to remove the older lists from the safes, where by law they should be kept. These lists have become cumbersome and the capacity of the safes is unequal to their preservation.

The returns in regard to the number of volumes of originals and copies of records of births, marriages, and deaths must be incorrect to some extent, but correspondence has failed to correct the errors. Volumes are called "copies" of volumes which are not copies of volumes but are in fact volumes containing copies of records of births, marriages, and deaths which were entered in the volumes of town proceedings or in various church records and which have been copied from those sources. This collecting and copying of such records into separate volumes is, it is gratifying to know, becoming quite common in the towns, and the habit should be universal.

A most valuable record for the use of conveyancers and others was reported by one town clerk, who had an indexed record of the maiden names of women married in the town, with a reference to the record of the marriage.

As has been stated, it became necessary in the work of verification to refer to the acts of legislation in regard to the establishment of the towns and the common lands from which many of them were erected, and so many errors were found in print in various places that it was thought best to present a summary of legislation, so far as ascertained, which affected the territorial limits, change of name, or subsequent incorporation as a city, of each town. So, under the tables giving the facts as to the kind of records, the number of volumes, the custody, the years covered by them, the condition, etc., will be found the summary of legislation referred to. The first mention of the town name which has been found in the body of the early records is given, although the name sometimes appears in the margin of such records against the name of the plantation or common lands many years earlier than the date given as that of the incorporation or establishment of the town, and historians have used the date of the earliest mention, although these marginal names bear evidence of having been inserted after the record was made. Such entries appear, for instance, as against the record concerning "Rexhame," where, at the close of the sentence, indicated by a period, the words "now called Marshfield" are written. As Rexhame is men-

tioned some time later as a town, it is fair to assume that the
marginal note did not belong to the record. So, against a
paragraph relating to a village of Salem, appearing in the
records in 1639, the words " Salem Village now Wenham "
are written, whereas by an act of 1643 it is ordered that " Enon
shalbee called Wennam."   It is confusing to the investigator to
find that the first mention of the town name is sometimes earlier
and sometimes later than the date fixed upon by historians as
that of the incorporation of the town, or than the date first
reported in the first volume of town records.

The presentation made under town records is not a historical summary of legislation relating to the lands which were
first plantations and then towns, much of which, as has been
said, may be a matter of town record only, but it is a presentation of the facts contained in the record in possession of the
State, with a reference to this record covering the first appear-
ance of the town name, and of its successive appearances when
territorial limits, change of name, or change to a city are the
subjects of legislation.   Various conclusions can be drawn
from the records.   The date of the first mention of a town in
a tax act is sometimes fixed upon as the date of incorporation ;
the date of the first mention of the land, which by its location
afterward became the town, is sometimes used to establish the
date of incorporation ; also, the date when the " town " is
given all the privileges of other towns, etc., etc., is sometimes
used as the conclusive date as to the incorporation.   For these
reasons, it may be contended that the dates which are given in
this report as the ones on which certain towns were incorporated are incorrect, as they will not agree with statements in
town histories and in other works.   However, it is believed
that the dates of the establishment of the several towns, or of
the first mention of the town names here given, are the correct
ones.   If a town was named in the tax act of any year, and
this was the first time the town was mentioned in legislation,
it is fair to assume that it was at that time acknowledged as a
town already in existence, and the date of the tax act cannot
justly be considered as the date of incorporation.   If a
" town " by an act was given the privileges of other towns,
it must already have been a town, and the date of such legislation cannot fairly be considered as the date of incorporation.

Again, if a town — A, for instance — had been Plantation No. 2 for forty years, and then the name of Plantation No. 2 was changed to the Town of A, and then the name A was changed to B after another forty years, the Town of B should not date from the establishment of Plantation No. 2, while, as a matter of fact, the records of the Town of B begin eighty years later; but the circumstances of this illustration apply in some cases. So, there are certain towns which, from all that can be ascertained from the records in the possession of the State, never were established, and there are some not now recognized as towns which, so far as the State record is concerned, have never become extinct. "Nashaway," by a single act, was made Prescott, West Towne, and Lancaster. So far as the State records are concerned, West Towne still exists; but granting that it was intended to change the name of West Towne, as well as Prescott, to Lancaster, and that the town historian is correct in saying that it is known that part of the record should bear the date of 1652 instead of 1653 West Towne existed for one year. The Plantation of Arlington, in the county of Hampshire, was made the town of "Winchester," but no further record of the name of Winchester in this connection can be found. It may be that it was absorbed into Connecticut, but the bounds are so indefinite that it cannot be located or traced by any records at hand. It seems hardly possible that the Commonwealth could lose a town, but so it appears from the records at hand.

The inquiry concerning the indexing of volumes was differently understood in the course of the investigation; some town clerks thought it referred to records of births, marriages, and deaths only, while others considered that it applied to all volumes.

The miscellaneous records were too numerous in kind to present in detail by name. The large number in some towns indicates that separate volumes are used more and more for separate subjects. The first date in the oldest volume of miscellaneous records is given in the tables, although the volumes, as a rule, bear different dates of beginning.

It will be observed in the summary of legislation for towns that in many cases part of each town is said to be annexed to the other town. While this is generally true when town lines are run and bounds are established, mention is made of the fact only when the act so specified, it being inferred that enough territory changed ownership to make it worthy of mention in the act.

COURT RECORDS. — The first " Monthly Court, or Court of Assistants," was holden in Charlestown, August 23, 1630 (Mass. Rec., Vol. I., p. 73). This was sometimes called the Great Quarter Court. The first General Court was holden in Boston, October 19, 1630 (Mass. Rec., Vol. I., p. 79). These courts seem to have exercised both legislative and judicial functions and powers until 1636, when the establishment of courts of law was commenced, and it is from the latter courts or their successors that returns have been asked.

In some of the courts, especially in the earlier courts, the volumes of records have no numbers, the dates giving them their consecutive order. For the sake of uniformity, and for convenience in designating certain volumes which contain the records of successive courts, these volumes have been numbered consecutively in the tables giving the facts concerning court records.

The files of papers have not, as a rule, been mentioned by the clerks of the courts in giving information, but in many cases it is learned that they are in such condition as to demand immediate attention. Lack of room has necessitated the packing away in unfit places of the older files, and some have been found which crumble and fall to pieces under the most careful handling. The report from the clerks that the condition of their records is good applies rather to the records in general use, the unused ones having been forgotten or ignored.

The small number of volumes of records of notaries public found in the offices of the clerks of courts indicates that the records of many notaries have not been placed there, as the law directs, or that they have been overlooked and forgotten.

In connection with the tabulated facts relating to court records there will be found valuable citations as to the laws establishing courts and providing for records.

The following report by Mr. John Noble, Clerk of the Supreme Judicial Court of Suffolk County, in relation to the files in that court, is exceedingly interesting, as showing what is best and feasible in the matter of arranging and preserving files :

The files of the Superior Court of Judicature for the several counties, and also of the Supreme Judicial Court prior to the present century, fill in all about three hundred and seventy-five (375) boxes. There are also seventy (70) boxes of executions, twelve (12) boxes of inquests, three (3) boxes of libels for divorce (one of which contains also partitions from 1797 to 1799), and six (6) boxes of Probate files.

There is also a large collection of papers now being arranged and put in a suitable form for preservation and reference under my direction. This collection comprises what were once the files of the various courts held in the county of Suffolk, covering the period from 1629 to 1729, and also a considerable portion of the files from 1730 to 1799. The papers before 1700 number about eighteen thousand (18,000), and the rest number about one hundred and thirty-five thousand (135,000). They have heretofore been deposited in boxes, chests, and drawers in different parts of the Court House, and also for a time in the cellar of the Registry Building, becoming in the course of years utterly confused and much injured by neglect and careless handling. There can be no doubt that very many valuable papers have been wholly lost. Still, what now remains of these files of court constitutes an accumulation of material for historical, genealogical, and topographical inquiry unequalled by any other, unless it be the State Archives at the State House. All those prior to 1730 have now been almost completely restored to their original file arrangement, and where this was impossible they have been arranged chronologically. Those from 1730 to 1799 have been arranged in decades.

COUNTY RECORDS. — The returns concerning county records contain nothing relating to the records of county treasurers, although inquiry was made in regard to them. The records reported were generally books of account, and, as a rule, not of ancient date. Any satisfactory report in regard to the whereabouts of the ancient records of county treasurers, who were among the first persons to keep records, would require special investigation and the most careful search.

The presentation in regard to the registries of deeds contains most important information. The setting off of new counties from old ; the transferring of towns from the jurisdiction of one registry to another, and in some instances the retransferring of such towns ; and the establishing of additional registries in a county, make it difficult for persons wishing to consult the records in the registries to know in which registry the recording for certain years was made. The explanatory notes which precede the returns in regard to the records of each registry, and the table showing the establishment of counties (page xl), will be found of great assistance in obviating this difficulty.

The lists of cities and towns constituting the several districts for the registry of deeds, as given in the explanatory notes, are believed to be the only ones in any State document. The Public Statutes, even, do not recite the cities and towns in each district, but after naming those which shall constitute one district in a county provide that " the remainder of said county " shall constitute the other, excepting in Berkshire county where the towns lying north and south of the towns named as comprising the Middle district are constituted respectively the Northern and Southern districts. As will be seen by reference to the explanatory notes to the returns for the registries in Franklin, Hampden, and Hampshire counties, the omission to name the towns in the act of March 1, 1787, prevents a positive statement as to what towns constituted the Northern and Southern districts at that time.

A few of the registers of deeds report that they have certified copies of records of deeds recorded in other registries of lands now in their districts. The convenience of this system of transferring records is too apparent to need comment further than to suggest that the system be made general.

The following table gives the date of the establishment of each county, and is especially valuable in connection with the examination of county records. No attempt, however, has been made to trace county changes, as upon the establishment of many of the towns county lines were changed.

NAMES OF COUNTIES.	Date of Establishment	Reference to Act
Barnstable, .	June 2, 1685	Ply. Col. Laws, edit. 1836, p. 295.
Berkshire, . .	April 21, 1761[1]	Prov. Laws, Vol. IV., p 432.
Bristol, . .	June 2, 1685	Ply. Col. Laws, edit. 1836, p. 295.
Dukes County, .	June 22, 1695[2]	Prov. Laws, Vol. I., p. 216.[2]
Essex, . .	May 10, 1643	Mass. Rec., Vol. II., p. 38.
Franklin, . .	June 24, 1811[3]	Mass. Laws.
Hampden, . .	February 25, 1812[4]	Mass. Laws.
Hampshire, .	May 7, 1662	Mass. Rec., Vol. IV., Part 2, p. 52.
Middlesex, .	May 10, 1643	Mass. Rec., Vol. II., p. 38.
Nantucket, .	June 22, 1695	Prov. Laws, Vol. I., p. 216.
Norfolk (old), .	May 10, 1643[5]	Mass. Rec., Vol. II., p. 38.
Norfolk, . .	March 26, 1793[6]	Mass. Laws.
Plymouth, . .	June 2, 1685	Ply. Col. Laws, edit. 1836, p. 295.
Suffolk, . .	May 10, 1643	Mass. Rec., Vol. II., p. 38.
Worcester, .	April 2, 1731[7]	Prov. Laws, Vol. II., p. 584.

[1] Act took effect June 30, 1761.

[2] By an act passed by the legislature of New York, November 1, 1683, entitled, " An act to divide this province and dependences into shires and Countyes," the County of Dukes County was established as follows : " Dukes County so contayns the Island of Nantuckett, Martin's Vineyard Elizabeth Island and nomans Land." By the Province Charter in 1692 (Prov. Laws, Vol. I., p. 9) the " Isles of Cappawock and Nantuckett near Cape Cod " were granted to the Province of Massachusetts Bay. June 13, 1693 (Prov. Laws, Vol. I., p. 117), the " Islands of Capawock, alias Martha's Vineyard," are referred to. June 22, 1695 (Prov. Laws, Vol. I., p. 216), it was ordered that " The Islands of Martha's Vineyard, Elsabeth Islands, the islands called Noman's land and all the dependencies formerly belonging to Dukes County (the Island of Nantucket only excepted) shall be and remain, and continue to be one county to all intents and purposes, by the name of Dukes County."

[3] Act took effect December 2, 1811.

[4] Act took effect August 1, 1812.

[5] February 4, 1680, the towns remaining in Norfolk County were re-annexed to Essex County (Mass. Rec. Vol. V., p. 264).

[6] Act took effect June 20, 1793.

[7] Act took effect July 10, 1731.

RECOMMENDATIONS.

From what has been said, and from the perusal of the returns, it is evident that some action should be taken by the State, not only to preserve the records of parishes, towns, and counties which are now in the custody of the officers designated by law, but toward bringing into such custody those records which are improperly in the possession of individuals who for various reasons have seen fit to retain them. Legislation should provide that a church seceding from another should begin new records. Certainly, the new church should not hold the records of the church from which it secedes. So, in cases where churches have been sold and all meetings discontinued, and the society has really become extinct, but the old clerk claims the records, there should be some provision by which the records could be brought into the proper custody.   Proprietors records, which are held in the towns set off from the old town because the town proper often happened to be in that part of the territory set off, should be in the old town and not in the new. Town officers in too many cases have not carried out the laws regarding records.   The State should see to it that they do. It may be well in the future to increase the penalties under the general statutes for neglect relative to the custody and preservation of records, or to increase the penalty for destroying, mutilating, or secreting records.   Also, persons giving up records which they have procured at a cost, for the sake of preserving them, should be compensated in a proper sum.   If these records have been used for profit then no compensation should be allowed and no prospective loss be considered.

The attention of the Legislature is drawn to a report on the Public Records by a committee of the Council of the New England Historic Genealogical Society, made at the annual meeting of the society, held in Boston, January 2, 1889.   I have deemed it expedient to reproduce this report in full, together with a letter sent out to town and city clerks by Francis II. Brown, Corresponding Secretary of the New England Historic Genealogical Society, so that they shall become a part of the documents of the State and be preserved.[1]   These two documents show, taken in connection with the results of this investigation, that the conclusion is inevitable that some action should be taken, and at once, by the State.

I would not recommend the creation of a record commission, to be erected on the model of the English Record Commission, for it seems to me wise to preserve and stimulate local interest in records.   If they were to be brought to a central office, this interest would decline.   The institutions of this State are against such a proceeding.   Everything is done in this Commonwealth to preserve the integrity of the municipality, as represented by towns and cities.   The loss of the custody of their documents would work in an antagonistic way in the mat-

---

[1] See pages xliv–li.

ter of the preservation of such documents ; at least, such result is to be feared.

On studying the whole question, as it has been presented to my mind through this preliminary investigation, I do not hesitate to recommend that the present Commission be continued by the Legislature for a sufficient length of time to enable it to bring all the records available into the custody of the officers designated by law. There seems to be ample legislation, but it is not properly carried out. It cannot be enforced through correspondence. To enforce it there should be the personal attention of some officer of the State, familiar with the subject, and whose business should be not only to look up lost records but to see that the existing records are put in proper shape for preservation and that the law relative to the safe-keeping of such records is observed. Two or three years' service, resulting in an expenditure of from ten to twelve thousand dollars, would accomplish the whole purpose and set the records of parishes, towns, and counties in proper order. The length of time during which such Commission should carry on its work could be easily determined by the Governor and Council, through reports which the Commissioner should make to them. A sufficient salary should be provided, so that the Commissioner could devote his whole time to carrying out the orders of the Legislature. He should also be furnished with the means for the employment of proper clerical assistance and for the payment of necessary travelling expenses.

These are the recommendations which I most urgently make to the Legislature, and they cover the action which in my own judgment appears to be necessary. If beyond these, should the State see fit to adopt them, the Legislature would ask towns and cities to make complete indexes of all their records, and also provide that copies of important records be made and furnished the State, so that they may not be lost through any misfortune which may befall the town records, a most important step would be taken relative to the preservation of valuable documents.

In closing this report, I desire to acknowledge, and most heartily, the very valuable services of Robert T. Swan, Esq., the Secretary of the Commission, to whom has been committed the details of the investigation since the work of the enumerators ceased. It is by his industry and constant care that so many of the errors in past records have been corrected and brought out in this report and that hitherto unknown points of information have been brought to light.

The Commission has also had the assistance of Mr. Frank E. Bradish, whose experience in the line of the work of the Commission has been of great value. The verification of references and citations, the hunting out of records that were not generally known to exist, and the searching for little points of information which are ordinarily overlooked, entitle him to my sincere thanks.

The character of the data from which this report is compiled has made it difficult to arrange the statistical material in compact and readable form; I believe, however, that the various presentations will be found intelligible. In this matter of arrangement I am under obligations to Mr. William C. Hunt, of the Bureau of Statistics of Labor, for valuable suggestions.

I have the honor to be,
Very respectfully,
Your obedient servant,

CARROLL D. WRIGHT,
Commissioner.

[The following report and accompanying letter are referred to on page xli and are appended for the information of the Legislature.]

THE PUBLIC RECORDS.

THE DANGERS TO WHICH THEY ARE EXPOSED AND THE PROPER METHOD OF PRESERVING THEM.

REPORT OF A COMMITTEE OF THE COUNCIL OF THE NEW ENGLAND HISTORIC GENEALOGICAL SOCIETY, MADE AT THE ANNUAL MEETING OF THE SOCIETY, HELD IN BOSTON, JANUARY 2, 1889.

John T. Hassam, A.M., for the Committee, reported as follows:

There is no subject which has a stronger claim to our attention than the preservation of town and county records.

It is greatly to be regretted that when the General Court, in 1639, first made provision for our system of records, it did not require them to be on parchment, as was the case with contemporary records in England, instead of allowing them to be intrusted to such perishable material as paper. Wills in the Principal Registry of Probate in London, handsomely written on parchment, and probated as early as 1373, are, after the lapse of more than five hundred years, just as legible and in just the same condition as they were when they were made. Ancient charters, far ante-dating even these, are just as perfect now as on the day when they were granted. In the first year of the reign of King James the First, anno 1603, it was expressly ordered that the Church records of baptisms, marriages and burials should be on parchment, thereby supplementing the proposed legislation of the fifth year of Queen Elizabeth, anno 1563. Even to this day, in England, wills, deeds, marriage settlements, and other important legal documents continue to be written on parchment. But in this country, parchment, from the very earliest times, seems to have been seldom or never used for municipal or ecclesiastical records, and but very rarely for legal documents. In our own day, even its name is in danger of being lost or rather applied to something quite different. For when the shopkeepers and stationers speak of parchment, they mean parchment-paper — an imitation parchment — not real parchment, the skins themselves, which alone are suitable for the public records and which should have been used for that purpose from the very first.

For paper, even the best of it, cannot be lasting or permanent. Our most ancient records are written on English hand-made paper, far superior in every respect to the machine-made paper of modern times. Whether our dry climate is more injurious to paper than is the moist climate of England is a subject which need not be entered upon here. Some of our public records have resisted decay for more than two hundred and fifty years, but it is only too evident that these powers of resistance are now in many cases nearly at an end, and that the time is not far distant when these records will have entirely disappeared. Perhaps if we had continued in the simple ways of our forefathers the evil day might have been still further postponed, but it is certain that the introduction of modern improvements, like steam heat and gas, into our large public offices has resulted in the rapid deterioration of the records therein contained. In some instances the paper has become too brittle to touch, and it has crumbled into small pieces. In others it has been fairly perforated by the corrosive action of the ink. Some record books long kept in safes have alternately absorbed moisture and then become dry until their leaves, reduced to mere tinder, can hardly be turned at all.

But this hand-made rag paper, perishable as it has proved to be, is far more suitable for record purposes than is the modern machine-made article. With that, the case is still worse. Very little paper is now manufactured entirely from rags. Most of that now in use is made wholly or partly of wood fibre. This adulteration is not due merely to the paper-makers' desire to produce cheaper goods. The enormous increase in the use of paper in modern times compels them to seek new sources of supply for raw materials. All the rags in the world would prove insufficient to enable them to meet the incessant demand for more paper. This wood paper has been known to commerce for less than a score of years — much too short a period to enable us to determine satisfactorily how long it may be expected to last. But in all human probability it will be less able than the other to stand the test of time, and will shortly begin to crumble to pieces. Some experts maintain that the whole literature of this generation will have utterly disappeared before the end of the next century, just as if it had never been, by the decay of the paper on which it is printed.

The introduction of gas has proved destructive to books in great libraries, not only in this country but also in England. And it is probable that new inventions for heating and lighting will, in the future, make no smaller demands on the strength of fabrics.

Not only does paper crumble, but ink loses its color. In some of our public offices, records not half a century old have almost faded out. Are we sure that the writing inks now in use will leave any visible trace of their existence to the searcher of the next century?

But this is not all. To the slow but certain destruction caused by the disintegration of the paper, must be added swift and remorseless annihilation by fire. In the smaller towns generally the records are kept in the house of the town clerk. The provisions of Pub. Stat. ch. 37, § 4, in regard to fire-proof safes, are illusory. In the larger towns and in the cities a perhaps safer place of deposit is found in the town and city halls, but after the experience we have had in the great Boston, Chicago and Portland fires, no such building can be said with confidence to be fire-proof. Some of our ancient towns have lost all their records by fire. And the same is true of many parishes. Indeed, the loss from this cause alone, of town, church and county records, is in the aggregate little short of appalling. Under these circumstances, it is almost criminal negligence to allow any book of record to exist only in a single copy. Its life then hangs by a single thread.

Now what is the remedy for this state of affairs? It is not far to seek, but is manifest to every thinking man. Not even the crumbling of the paper, the corrosion or fading of the ink, not even a sweeping conflagration, can utterly destroy records whose custodians have taken proper means to preserve them. How can this be done? In one way only. Simply by the multiplication of copies. The invention of the art of printing has made great changes in the modern world. In no direction has the advance been greater than in this. Copies, instead of being made toilsomely and laboriously by hand, can now be produced almost with the quickness of thought; and the great reduction in the cost of printing of late years has placed it in the power of every town and parish, however poor and feeble, to put into imperishable form its records, at least the earliest of them. And the work cannot be begun too soon. Nor is this all. The greater use made of stereotyping now-a-days — for now even newspapers are printed from stereotype plates — has given us an additional safeguard. The printed volumes, being widely distributed, could not all be destroyed by fire, and being subject to different atmospheric conditions could not all crumble to pieces at once. Some would certainly survive. But even if they should not, the stereotype plates would remain. From them, other copies could be printed at the mere cost of press-work and paper. This would forever set at rest all fear of a total loss of records, a fate which hangs over most town and county records to-day.

Where an ancient town has remained intact from its first settlement until now, the necessity of preserving in print records of such great historical value is readily apparent. Yet where other towns have been, in more modern times, set off from an ancient town, the need becomes still more evident. The safety of the records and the convenience of the public alike require it. Some towns have been repeatedly subdivided. In one instance, some seventeen or eighteen towns have been, in whole or in part, formed from the territory granted by the General Court to the original town. And other instances, equally as striking, can doubtless be cited. Although the newer municipalities have a history in common with the older towns of which they once formed a part, their records are defective inasmuch as they extend back only to the time of separation, the books prior to that date remaining in the hands of the clerk of the parent town. This works serious inconvenience. Matters are continually coming up which necessitate reference to the earlier records, and they are not at hand. Each new town should have a complete set of the records, prior to separation, of the original town of which it then formed a part. They belong as much to it as to the other. A new town should not be forced to see such invaluable documents placed beyond its control and in the keeping of officials not responsible to it, subjected to all the vicissitudes and dangers which records are continually running. Now the art of printing enables us to obviate all these difficulties. It solves the problem completely. When once the records are in type, extra copies can be had merely for the cost of press-work and paper. And each is an exact duplicate of the other. No copyist's errors need be feared where the work is done with such mechanical accuracy. A printed copy is vastly superior to any manuscript copy that can possibly be made.

But it must not for a moment be supposed that the people who live in any given town are the only persons interested in its records or concerned for the preservation of them. All of our towns, both ancient and modern, have contributed no small portion of their population to build up and develop the other parts of our rapidly growing country. There is hardly a remote corner of any one of the states and territories of the West where representatives of our New England families are not to be found. They naturally feel a peculiar pride in the place of their birth, and the children of these exiles should be encouraged to keep constantly in mind the home of their fathers. The publication of these records, therefore, interests a much larger number of people than are to be found within the limits of any single town, and these printed volumes reach more readers than we can easily imagine.

It is not necessary for the present purpose to go into details. But a few practical suggestions will not be out of place.

Steps should be at once taken to put in print the general records of every town, including, of course, the Selectmen's books, starting with the first volume and bringing the work down to at least the beginning of the present century.

As for the births, deaths and marriages, under the law as it now stands, the clerk of each city and town is required by Pub. Stat. ch. 32, § 10, to annually transmit to the Secretary of the Commonwealth certified copies of the records of births, marriages and deaths which have occurred therein during the preceding year. These certified copies in the Secretary's office would be invaluable in case of the destruction by fire of the original records. Although they begin with the year 1841, and continue up to the present time, the returns for the first few years are very defective. The only official records prior to the passage of the acts in relation to registration returns are in the custody of the various town and city clerks and city registrars and clerks of courts. Many of them are in very bad condition, and they are fast going to decay. Of these no duplicates, except in very rare instances, exist, and when once destroyed they can never be replaced. These records should at once be printed down to at least the year 1845, or better still to 1850. In no town are they very voluminous, and the cost of putting them in print need not be great.

But these town records of births, marriages and deaths need to be supplemented by the Church Records. In many cases the latter will supply important information not to be found in the Town Records. These ecclesiastical records containing baptisms, marriages, deaths, burials, admissions and dismissals, should be printed down to the same date, 1850. They are even more likely to be lost or destroyed than the municipal records, being scattered about in various parishes and in too many cases in hands of persons who are far from appreciating their value. The number of extinct parishes, the records of which have fallen into private possession, is probably much greater than is generally supposed, and the provisions of Pub. Stat. ch. 37, §§ 15 and 16, in such cases have not, it is to be feared, been strictly complied with.

Then there are the inscriptions on the gravestones in ancient cemeteries. These stones are liable to be broken or to crumble away. They are seldom lasting and are not so durable as the printed page. The disappearance of old gravestones is within the experience of every one who has had much to do with them. These inscriptions should be copied and printed down to the same date, 1850. With the general records of the towns, including the selectmen's books and proprietors' records brought down to the beginning of this century, and the records, municipal and ecclesiastical, of births, marriages, deaths, burials, admissions and dismissals brought down to 1850 and all in print, we could rest in confidence that this part of our records would be safe for all time.

As for County and State Records, where the necessity for printing is if possible even more imperative, that subject can be considered at another time.

One more matter of detail may be alluded to here. Of course, it will not do to set up type directly from the original. A copy should be made for the printer. This copy should be written only on one side of the paper, leaving the other blank, and should be carefully collated with the original. But the proof sheets as they come from the printer should be compared not with the copy but with the original record. By this means only, can we be sure to avoid all errors and thus have in print an accurate transcript of the original.

The pagination of the original should be carefully preserved by placing each of its page numbers in brackets in that part of the printed page where each page of the original begins. There is no need of any other numbering, and the index can thus be made to refer directly to the original records.

This index should be an index of places and an index of persons arranged both by Christian and surnames. A miscellaneous or general index will also be found useful, and will greatly facilitate reference to the original.

Small pica will probably be found the most convenient type.

There are many advantages in stereotyping. In the first place, fewer copies need be printed. Others can be struck off at any time afterwards as they are needed. This will effect a saving in many ways. Then too corrections, if errors are discovered, can be made in the plates, and thus the long list of "errata" which used to disfigure books can be avoided. Nothing of this sort will show in the books when printed. Stereotyping is now much cheaper than formerly, and it adds but slightly (all things considered) to the actual cost.

Several towns are now engaged in putting in print their early records. It is desirable therefore to secure unity of action, and to call the attention of such towns as have not yet taken any steps in this direction, to the importance and necessity of prompt action. These are a few of the reasons which might be urged in favor of the immediate undertaking of the good work.

NEW ENGLAND HISTORIC GENEALOGICAL SOCIETY.
SOCIETY'S HOUSE, 18 SOMERSET ST.,
BOSTON, JANUARY 23, 1889.

To the Town or City Clerk.

SIR : — I enclose a copy of a Report made at the Annual Meeting
of this Society, on the proper method of preserving Town Records.
Will you be kind enough to read it carefully, as the subject is an
important one? Several towns and cities are now engaged in printing their records.

BOSTON. — All the Town Records from 1630 to 1778, the Selectmen's Records from 1701 to 1764, the records of Births, Marriages
and Deaths in the City Registrar's Office, and the First Church Baptisms from 1630 to 1700, are now in print. The work is still in
progress. This is done by the Record Commissioners by means of
annual appropriations made by the City Council. Eventually all the
Boston records, from the first settlement of the Town down to the
granting of the City Charter in 1822, will be accessible to the public
in print.

BRAINTREE. — The Town Records from 1640 to 1793, and the Births,
Marriages and Deaths for the same period, are printed in one volume
by vote of the towns of Braintree, Quincy, Randolph and Holbrook,
which formerly comprised the town of Braintree. Quincy and Randolph were set off from Braintree in 1792 and 1793 respectively ; and
Holbrook formed part of Randolph until 1872.

BROOKLINE. — The Town Records from 1634 to 1838 have been
printed in one volume by vote of the town. The Committee were
also instructed to prepare a complete record of Births, Marriages and
Deaths.

DEDHAM. — The Births, Marriages and Deaths recorded in the
Town Clerk's office, from 1635 to 1845, have been printed in one
volume. All the Baptisms, Marriages, Deaths, Burials, Admissions
and Dismissals, found in the Church Records from 1638 to 1845,
have been printed in another volume. The second volume contains
also the first book of records of the First Church, printed in full, all
the inscriptions in the Ancient Burial Place, and all the inscriptions,
prior to 1845, in the other parish cemeteries. All this by votes of
the town.

LANCASTER. — The Town Records from 1643 to 1725, and the
Births, Marriages and Deaths from 1645 to 1700, are printed with
other historical matter, in one volume, by vote of the town.

PROVIDENCE, R. I. — An index, arranged by Christian and surnames, in four volumes, of all Births, Marriages and Deaths, from 1636 to 1870, has been printed by vote of the City Council.

WORCESTER. — The Town Records, from 1722 to 1783, are published in the Collections of the Worcester Society of Antiquity.

Several other cities and towns are about to print their early records,* and we hope that your town — or city — if it has not already done so, may also be induced to enter upon this important and too long neglected work.

This Society is now engaged in gathering statistics on the subject from all the cities and towns in this Commonwealth, and I have been appointed to enter into communication with all Town and City Clerks.

Will you kindly inform me :

I. What, if any, steps have been taken toward this end in your town or city, and what progress has thus far been made?

II. If no such steps have been taken, will you not submit this communication and the accompanying report to the Selectmen, or City Council, to see what action they may be disposed to take in the matter?

III. Will it be advisable to insert an article in the warrant for the next town meeting to see what the town will do in this regard?

IV. Will you kindly give me the names and addresses of a few of your citizens — such as would naturally be interested in this project, well disposed toward it and inclined to favor it, in order that I may communicate with them?

FRANCIS H. BROWN,
Corresponding Secretary.

---

* Not only have the records of several towns and parishes in this Commonwealth been totally destroyed by fire, but the same fate has befallen County Records. All the records in the Registry of Deeds for the County of Barnstable were destroyed by fire, Oct. 22, 1827. All the Probate Records for the County of Cumberland, which, although now in Maine, was formerly a part of Massachusetts, were destroyed in the great Portland fire of July 4, 1866. This fate, however, can never overtake the early records of the County of York, in that State, for four volumes of deeds, from 1642 to 1699, are now in print. And this is true of the early Probate Records, for all the Maine wills from 1640 to 1760 are now printed. The early deeds of Suffolk County, in our own State, are also safe for all time, four volumes having thus far been printed.

LAWS RELATING TO RECORDS.

[This presentation relates to the legislation concerning court records, town and city records, and records of births, marriages, and deaths, which during the early years of the colonies were intermingled. Although births, marriages, and deaths are recorded in town records, they were also recorded for many years in court records. This fact, together with the practice which has prevailed of legislating in regard to records concerning them by separate legislation, has warranted a special presentation of that legislation.

The laws relating to records other than as above named are included as a part of the presentations devoted to such records.]

COURT RECORDS.

1639. **Sept.** **9.** Mass. Rec., Vol. I., pp. 275, 276. Courts, magistrates, and commissioners were ordered to record their judgments with the evidence in each case, "to be kept to posterity." On the same day 'Mr. Stephen Winthrop was chosen to record things at Boston."

1647. **Nov.** **11.** Mass. Rec., Vol. II., p. 208. It was ordered that, to the end that all records of the Colony "may be safely preserved and improved, a strong press made of very firm oak planks be kept in some place convenient at Boston, by direction of the Governor." A press was also to be provided wherever any court of record was holden.

1699. **July** **18.** Prov. Laws, Vol. I., p. 374. Clerks for all courts were to be appointed by the justices.

1763. **Feb.** **25.** Prov. Laws, Vol. IV., p. 618. It was ordered that the clerks of the several courts and the several registers of probate, that were then appointed, should give bonds for keeping up the records of their respective courts, and any clerk who in six months from June 1, 1763, did not have his records completed (unless sickness or some extraordinary casualty prevented), was to forfeit his bond.

1763. **June** **15.** Prov. Laws, Vol. IV., p. 661. It was ordered that the justices of all courts forthwith cause all unrecorded papers in the offices of deceased clerks or registers, ex-clerks, or ex-registers to be recorded by such persons as they may employ for the purpose.

1787. **Feb.** **16.** Perpet. Laws of Mass., edit. 1789, p. 108. It was ordered that the clerks of the several courts who might be appointed should, before entering upon their respective duties, give bonds "for keeping up seasonably and in good order the records of the same court, and also to make and keep convenient and correct alphabets of the records of which they shall respectively be appointed officers and keepers."

1797. Mar. 11. Mass. Laws. Whereas in the practice under the act establishing the Supreme Judicial Court it had been found inconvenient to have the records of the proceedings of the court in the distant counties kept in Boston, it was ordered that on and after August 1, 1797, clerks of the Courts of Common Pleas in their respective counties, excepting those of Lincoln, Hancock, Washington, Dukes County, and Nantucket, shall become clerks of the Supreme Judicial Court and shall keep records. The clerk for Suffolk was to be clerk for Suffolk and Nantucket; the clerk for Barnstable to be clerk for Barnstable and Dukes County. A clerk was to be appointed for Lincoln, Hancock, and Washington counties, the records for which were to be kept in Lincoln County. The files and records of the Supreme Judicial Court, then kept in the office of the clerk of that court in Boston, were to be removed to the office of the Court of Common Pleas in Suffolk County.

1811. June 18. Mass. Laws. Clerks of the courts in the several counties were authorized, who should be clerks of all the judicial courts in their respective counties and have custody of all the records, files, etc., remaining in the respective offices of the clerks of the Supreme Judicial Court and Court of Common Pleas, The court was ordered to provide in each county "as soon as convenient, offices of stone or bricks, which shall be fire proof, well arranged and provided with suitable alcoves, cases, and boxes, for the safe keeping of all records, files, papers, and documents."

TOWN AND CITY RECORDS.

1641. Dec. 10. Mass. Rec., Vol. I., p. 344. It was ordered that in every town a person should be chosen to be called "clerk of the writs."

1692. Nov. 16. Prov. Laws, Vol. I., p. 65. Towns were ordered to choose a town clerk, who should record all "town votes, orders, grants and divisions of land, made by such town, and orders made by the selectmen," and keep records of various minor matters which are named.

1851. May 15. Mass. Laws. County commissioners, city governments, and selectmen were ordered "to have all books of public record or registry," belonging to the counties, cities, or towns "well and strongly bound, and other papers and documents filed and arranged in a careful and orderly manner." They were also ordered to provide at the expense of the county, city, or town "a suitable place for the safe keeping and preservation of the public records and other valuable documents, where they shall be deposited and securely kept." The clerk or register of any county, city, or town was ordered to "keep all records and written documents in his sole custody, and in no case except upon summons in due form of law to have them, or cause or permit them to be removed or taken away."

1857. Apr. 30. Mass. Laws. City governments and selectmen were ordered to provide, at the expense of their respective cities and towns, safes "of ample size for the safe preservation of books of records or registry, and other important documents or papers belonging to said city or town," and it was made the duty of the clerk of each city and town to keep such records and papers in the safe "at all times except when they shall be wanted for use."

1867. **May** **24.** Mass. Laws. County commissioners were authorized and required to have made under their direction copies " of such books of records of proprietors, or town proprietaries, within their respective counties, as in their judgment ought to be preserved and perpetuated," such copies to be deposited in the registry of deeds for the county or division of a county to which said records relate.

1874. **Apr.** **10.** Mass. Laws. The act of May 24, 1867, was amended in the first section, and copies were to be made " of such records or books of records of proprietors, or town proprietaries, or of any city, or town, or county within, or without, the Commonwealth, as relate to titles of land in their respective counties," the copies to be deposited as provided in that act.

RECORDS OF BIRTHS, MARRIAGES, AND DEATHS.

1639. **Sept.** **9.** Mass. Rec., Vol. I., p. 276. It was ordered that records be kept of the days of every marriage, birth, and death of every person within this jurisdiction. (No provision is made for the keeping of these records, unless it be by the paragraph in the record which says " Mr. Stephen Winthrop was chosen to record things at Boston.")

1642. **June** **14.** Mass. Rec., Vol. II., p. 15. By this act, which is called an act in addition to the act of September 9, 1639, clerks of the writs in the several towns were hereafter to record all births and deaths, and deliver a return of the same yearly to the recorder of the court belonging to the jurisdiction in which they live. Persons authorized to marry were to return the names of persons married by them, and the date when married, to the recorder of the court nearest their habitations. Said recorders were faithfully and carefully " to enroll such births, marriages, and deaths as shall thus be committed to their trust."

1692. **Nov.** **3.** Prov. Laws, Vol. I., p. 61. Every justice and minister was ordered to register all marriages solemnized " before any of them," and make a return quarterly to the clerk of the Sessions of the Peace, to be by him registered.

1693 **Feb.** **17.** Prov. Laws, Vol. I., p. 104. Every town clerk was ordered to register all births and deaths.

1695. **June** **19.** Prov. Laws, Vol. I., p. 210. All marriages were to be registered by the town clerk of the town where they were consummated, and every justice and minister was to return within three months the names of all persons married by him, to the clerk of the town.

1716 **Dec.** **1.** Prov. Laws, Vol. II., p. 60. Every town clerk was ordered to give in a list of marriages to the clerk of the Sessions of the Peace, annually in April, and every clerk of the court was to record the same.

1786. **June** **22.** Perpet. Laws of Mass., edit. 1789, p. 14. Every justice and minister was ordered to keep a record of marriages solemnized before him, and annually in April make a return of the same to the clerk of the town, district, or plantation in which he lived. Every such clerk was to record such returns, and return a list or copy to the clerk of the court of General Sessions of the Peace, annually in May, who was also to record these copies. (This act took effect on the last day of December, 1786.)

1796. Feb. 13. Mass. Laws. Town clerks were not in future holden to return certificates of·marriages to the clerks of the courts of General Sessions of the Peace, nor were the clerks of these courts to record them. (This act took effect April 1, 1796, and was to be in force two years. The act was an act to establish fees, and the provision here cited was embodied in an obscure way. It was not intended evidently that the two years' limitation should apply to this provision, and it was not construed so, as the recording of marriages in the records of the Court of General Sessions of the Peace was discontinued in 1796. The act establishing fees was re-enacted June 21, 1798, and annually thereafter, to be in effect for one year, until June 22, 1804, when no limit as to time was fixed, but no legislation in regard to the certifying of marriages to the clerk of the Court of Sessions after 1796 has been found.)

1796. Feb. 26. Mass. Laws. Every town clerk and every "district clerk" was ordered to record all births and deaths, the act to take effect September 1, 1796. The act passed in 1692 (no date being given) for registering births and deaths was repealed.

1834. Apr. 1. Mass. Laws. Every justice and minister was ordered to keep a record of all marriages solemnized before him, and the clerk of each society of Friends was ordered to keep a record of all marriages solemnized in the meeting of which he was clerk; they were also to make a return of these marriages, annually in April, to the city or town clerk and to the clerk of the city or town in which one or both of the persons married resided when neither of them belonged or resided in the same town as the minister or justice. This act took effect May 1, 1834, and repealed the acts relating to marriages passed June 22, 1786 (except the seventh section which did not relate to recording), June 15, 1795, January 27, 1818, February 20, 1818, and February 12, 1821.

1844. Mar. 16. Mass. Laws. The time for making the returns provided for in the act of April 1, 1834, was changed from "annually in April" to "between the first and tenth of each month." School committees were ordered to ascertain the births in the cities and towns and return a record of them to the city or town clerks annually in May, and sextons or others having charge of burial places were to return a record of burials on or before the tenth of each month. The Secretary of the Commonwealth was ordered to furnish blank books of suitable size to be used as books of record, and the city and town clerks were to enter, in separate columns, the births, marriages, and deaths.

1849. May 2. Mass. Laws. Town clerks, city clerks, and city registrars were "authorized and required to obtain, record, and index the information concerning births, marriages, and deaths now required by law."

1855. May 17. Mass. Laws. The superintendents of the State almshouses located at Monson, Tewksbury, and Bridgewater were required to make a record of all births and deaths occurring in the institutions under their care, and make a return of the same annually to the Secretary of the Commonwealth. The town clerks of these towns were exempted from this duty.

PROPRIETORS RECORDS.

LAWS RELATING TO PROPRIETORS.

[The laws relating to proprietors are first presented, in their order chronologically, and are followed by a table which gives, alphabetically, the cities and towns from which information has been received regarding the records of the Proprietors of the Common and Undivided Lands, with the name of the Common Lands, the years covered by the records, and the name or designation of the person or parties having possession of the records. The use of the dash signifies in the column headed "Name of Common Lands," that no distinctive name other than that of the town was given, and in the other columns that the information is wanting.]

1634. May 14. Mass. Rec., Vol. I., p. 117. "None but the General Court hath power to * * * and dispose of lands, viz.: to give and confirm proprieties."

1638. Sept. 6. Mass. Rec., Vol. I., p. 240. "For avoiding the trouble of this Court about granting of land, and the more equal proceeding therein," it was ordered that the Treasurer and four persons, who are named in the act, "or any 4 or 3 of them," shall take the names of all who desire lands, consider and pass upon their demands, having regard "that the country at large be not burdened to provide lands for the inhabitants of such towns as have land enough to supply them, except other consideration require it; and that they consider that, though the first planters were allowed 50 acres for each person, yet this benefit is not to be allowed to all others"; that they "set down the names of all such as they shall find fit to have lands granted them," and "make certificate thereof to the next Court."

1784. Mar. 10. Perpet. Laws of Mass., edit. 1789, p. 61. It was enacted that the last clerk of the proprietors of any common and undivided lands should continue to exercise the duties of such clerk notwithstanding the final and total division of such lands, "until the records shall be lodged with the clerk of the town in which the land lies; and when the land lies in several towns, they may be lodged with the clerk of such town as the Court of Sessions, upon application made to them for that purpose, shall order and direct."

1791. Mar. 9. Mass. Laws. Proprietors who had made final division of lands and had deposited their records with town clerks were empowered to hold meetings for business relating to debts, taxes, and contracts dated before the division, recall their records, and cause the clerk *then chosen*, or the town clerk, to record votes and proceedings at such meetings. No such meetings could be held more than ten years after the division.

1851. May 15. Mass. Laws. It was enacted that the books of record and other documents of the ancient proprietors of townships or common lands, in case said proprietors have ceased to be a body corporate, shall when not otherwise legally disposed of or provided for by such proprietary body before its dissolution, be vested and held to be in the clerk for the time being of the city or town in which the lands or larger part of them lie. And it shall be the duty of the clerk to claim them.

[5]

PROPRIETORS RECORDS.

Cities and Towns.	Counties	Name of Common Lands	Records Years covered	Records In Possession of—
Adams, . .	Berkshire .	–	–	Unknown[1]
Agawam, . .	Hampden .	Agawam Meadows . . .	–	–
Andover, . .	Essex . .	Cochickewicke and Andover .	1643 –	Town Clerk
Ashburnham, .	Worcester .	–	1736–1780	Town Clerk
Ashfield, . .	Franklin .	–	1738–1802	Town Clerk
			1746–1792	Town Clerk
Athol, . .	Worcester .	Payquage	1749–1824[2]	Town Clerk
Attleborough, .	Bristol . .	Rehoboth North Purchase	1666–1839	Town Clerk
Barnstable, .	Barnstable .	–	1703–1795	Town Clerk[3]
Becket, . .	Berkshire .	Old Number Four . . .	1737–1765	Town Clerk
Bellingham, .	Norfolk .	–	1713–1813	Town Clerk
Bernardston, .	Franklin .	–	1735–1819	Town Clerk[4]
Beverly, . .	Essex . .	The Common Lands . .	1698–1750	Town Clerk
		Snake Hill Pasture . . .	1728–1817	Town Clerk
BOSTON, . .	Suffolk .	–	1634–1728	City Clerk
		Common Lands of Dorchester	1713–1793	[5]_
Bridgewater, .	Plymouth .	–	1675–1827[6]	Town Clerk[6]
Brimfield, . .	Hampden .	–	1731–1824[7]	Town Clerk
Brookfield, .	Worcester .	–	1702–1767	Town Clerk
CAMBRIDGE, .	Middlesex .	–	1634–1829	City Clerk[8]
Chester, . .	Hampden .	Murrayfield	–	J. Merrick Bell
Cohasset, . .	Norfolk .	–	1636–1813	Town Clerk
Cummington, .	Hampshire .	Number Five . . .	1762–1804	Town Clerk[9]
Danvers, . .	Essex . .	The Neck of Land . .	1772–1841	Town Clerk
Dartmouth, .	Bristol . .	Dartmouth Lands . . .	–	[10]_
Dedham, . .	Norfolk .	–	1636–1720	Town Clerk[11]
Deerfield, . .	Franklin .	Pocomtuck . . .	1699–1801	[12]_
		The Common Fields . .	1734–1858	[12]_
Dighton, . .	Bristol . .	–	1674–1740	Town Clerk[9]
Dracut, . .	Middlesex .	–	1715–1733	Gayton M. Hall
Duxbury, . .	Plymouth .	–	1709–1730	Town Clerk
E. Bridgewater,	Plymouth .	Bridgewater	1675–1827	Town Clerk[13]
Eastham, . .	Barnstable .	The Seventy Seven Proprietors of Town of Eastham . .	1743–1885	Peter Higgins
Edgartown, .	Dukes County	–	1676–1827	Town Clerk
Easton, . .	Bristol . .	Taunton North Purchase Company . . .	1668–1885	{ Edward D. Williams[14]
Egremont, .	Berkshire .	–	1756–1862	Town Clerk
Essex, . .	Essex . .	Chebacco Eighth of Common Lands of Ipswich . . .	1722–1747	Town Clerk
Falmouth, . .	Barnstable .	–	1661–1805	Town Clerk[9]
FITCHBURG, .	Worcester .	–	–	[15]_
Freetown, . .	Bristol . .	–	–	[16]_
GLOUCESTER, .	Essex . .	–	1707–1820	City Clerk[17]
Grafton, . .	Worcester .	–	1728–1742	Town Clerk[18]
Granby, . .	Hampshire .	–	–	Town Clerk
Greenwich, .	Hampshire .	Narragansett Township . .	1733–1783	Town Clerk

[1] There is a copy in possession of C. F. Sayles.

[2] The records from 1734 to 1749 were carried away by the proprietors' clerk in 1759.

[3] There is a copy also in possession of Allen H. Bearse, Hyannis, and one in the Registry of Probate at Barnstable.

[4] There is a copy also in possession of the Pocomtuck Valley Memorial Association.

[5] Registry of Deeds at Dedham.

[6] These are copies of the original records, and the town clerks of East Bridgewater and West Bridgewater have each a copy in their possession.   [7] The records prior to 1731 were burned.

[8] There is a copy also in possession of the City Clerk.

[9] There is a copy also in possession of the Town Clerk.

[10] Registry of Deeds at New Bedford.

[11] There are records of grants of land scattered through the early town records.

[12] Pocomtuck Valley Memorial Association.

[13] See foot-note [6] on this page.   [14] Present Clerk of the Proprietors.

[15] The records are supposed to be in private possession in Lunenburg.

[16] The first volume commencing about 1659 has not been found; the second volume commencing after 1683 is in the possession of James Winslow.

[17] There are copies also in possession of the City Clerk.

[18] This is a copy of the original records which are lost.

PROPRIETORS RECORDS — Continued.

CITIES AND TOWNS.	Counties	Name of Common Lands	RECORDS	
			Years covered	In Possession of—
Groton,	Middlesex	–	1683–1829	Town Clerk
Hadley,	Hampshire	–	1689–1702	Town Clerk[1]
Hardwick,	Worcester	–	1734–1739	Town Clerk[2]
Harwich,	Barnstable	The Quasson	–	Sidney Brooks
Hatfield,	Hampshire	–	1671–1767	Town Clerk[3]
		Bradstreet and Denison Farms	1712–1735	Town Clerk[5]
HAVERHILL,	Essex	–	1673–1763	City Clerk
Hingham,	Plymouth	–	1635–1788	Town Clerk
Holden,	Worcester	Worcester North Half	1722 –	Town Clerk
Hopkinton,	Middlesex	–	–	4_
Hull,	Plymouth	–	5_	Robert Gould[6]
Ipswich,	Essex	–	1638–1680	Town Clerk
Lancaster,	Worcester	–	1653–1818	Town Clerk
Lanesborough,	Berkshire	–	1742–1766	Town Clerk
Leicester,	Worcester	–	1714–1776	Town Clerk
Lenox,	Berkshire	–	1764–1769	Town Clerk
Leominster,	Worcester	–	1701–1847	Town Clerk
Lincoln,	Middlesex	–	1747–1754	–
Littleton,	Middlesex	Nashobah Lands	– 1715	Town Clerk
Longmeadow,	Hampden	The General Fields	–	D. M. Pease[7]
Lunenburg,	Worcester	–	– 1728	Town Clerk
LYNN,	Essex	–	1706 –	City Clerk[8]
Manchester,	Essex	–	1718–1769	Town Clerk[9]
Marion,	Plymouth	Rochester	1679–1885	10_
Marlborough,	Middlesex	Indian Lands	1699–1795	Town Clerk
Marshfield,	Plymouth	–	–	Wendall A. Phillips[11]
Mashpee,	Barnstable	–	1834 –	William H. Simon
Mattapoisett,	Plymouth	Rochester	1679–1885	Town Clerk[10]
Medfield,	Norfolk	–	1719–1800	Town Clerk
Mendon,	Worcester	–	1708–1815	Town Clerk
Middleborough,	Plymouth	–	1675–1704	Town Clerk[9]
Montague,	Franklin	–	–	County Commissioners
Monterey,	Berkshire	Township Number One at Housatonnoc	1737–1762	Town Clerk
Mt. Washington,	Berkshire	–	1750 –	12_
Nantucket,	Nantucket	–	1716–1885	Proprietors Clerk
Natick,	Middlesex	–	1702–1790	Town Clerk[9]
NEW BEDFORD,	Bristol	Dartmouth Lands	–	13_
Newbury,	Essex	–	1635–1828	Town Clerk
New Marlboro',	Berkshire	Eleven Thousand Acres	1767–1790	Town Clerk
			1737–1801	Town Clerk
New Salem,	Franklin	–	–	14_
NORTHAMPTON,	Hampshire	–	1653–1731	City Clerk[1]
		–	1757–1775	City Clerk[1]
		–	1800–1839	City Clerk[1]
No. Brookfield,	Worcester	–	1750–1812	Charles Adams, Jr.[15]
Northfield,	Franklin	–	1685–1723	Town Clerk
Palmer,	Hampden	–	1732–1750	E. B. Gates
		–	1716–1732	J. H. Temple[16]
Pelham,	Hampshire	–	1738–1767	Town Clerk[1]
Petersham,	Worcester	–	–	Selectmen
Plymouth,	Plymouth	–	1702–1713	Town Clerk
Princeton,	Worcester	Rutland	1714–1770	Town Clerk
Reading,	Middlesex	–	–	Town Clerk
Rehoboth,	Bristol	–	–	Solon Carpenter[17]

[1] There are copies also in the Registry of Deeds at Northampton.

[2] This is a bound copy of the original manuscript, which is in possession of the Town Clerk.

[3] There are copies also in the Registry of Deeds at Northampton, and a copy of the volume covering the years from 1702 to 1735 in possession of James M. Crafts of Whately.

[4] Registry of Deeds at East Cambridge.

[5] There are records of grants in the first volume of the town records which begins in 1677.

[6] East Cambridge. [7] Present Clerk of the Proprietors.

[8] This is made up of copies of original records.

[9] There is a copy also in possession of the Town Clerk.

[10] This is a copy of the original records. [11] East Marshfield.

[12] There is a copy which is supposed to be with the original records.

[13] Registry of Deeds at New Bedford; there is a copy in possession of the City Clerk.

[14] The proprietors' records were burned in 1855.

[15] These are copies of the original records. [16] Framingham. [17] Seekonk.

PROPRIETORS RECORDS — Concluded.

CITIES AND TOWNS.	Counties	Name of Common Lands	RECORDS	
			Years covered	In Possession of —
Richmond, .	Berkshire .	Yokum Town and Mount Ephraim	1764–1769	Town Clerk
Rochester, .	Plymouth .	–	1679–1885	Town Clerk[1]
Rowley, .	Essex .	–	1643 –	Town Clerk
		East Ox Pasture in Rowley .	1769–1844	[2]–
Royalston, .	Worcester .	–	1752–1787	Town Clerk
Rutland, .	Worcester .	–	1720–1797	Town Clerk
SALEM, .	Essex .	–	1713–1739	City Clerk[3]
Sandisfield, .	Berkshire .	–	1735–1862	Town Clerk
Sandwich, .	Barnstable .	–	1685–1722	Town Clerk
Savoy, .	Berkshire .	Bullock's Grant . . .	1771–1801[4]	Town Clerk[5]
Scituate, .	Plymouth .	Conihasset Partners . .	1648–1767	Town Clerk[6]
		–	1725–1745	Town Clerk
Sherborn, .	Middlesex .	–	1681–1721	Town Clerk
		–	1715–1730	Town Clerk[7]
Sheffield, .	Berkshire .	Lower Housatonic Propriety .	–	[8]–
		Upper Housatonic Propriety .	–	[9]–
Shrewsbury, .	Worcester .	–	1718–1811	Town Clerk
Shutesbury, .	Franklin .	–	1760–1805	Town Clerk
Somerset, .	Bristol .	–	1680–1830	Town Clerk
SPRINGFIELD, .	Hampden .	Inward Commons . . .	1713–1813	City Clerk[10]
		Outward Commons . . .	1698–1735	City Clerk[10]
		–	1650–1699	City Clerk[10]
Stockbridge, .	Berkshire .	–	1739–1825	Town Clerk
Stow, .	Middlesex .	–	1722–1803	Town Clerk[5]
Sturbridge, .	Worcester .	–	–	Town Clerk
Sudbury, .	Middlesex .	–	1700–1780	Town Clerk
Sunderland, .	Franklin .	–	1673–1718	Town Clerk[5]
Sutton, .	Worcester .	–	1714–1809	Town Clerk
Swansea, .	Bristol .	–	1668–1739	Town Clerk
TAUNTON, .	Bristol .	–	1661–1804	City Clerk[11]
		–	1638–1656	W. K. Watkins[12]
Templeton, .	Worcester .	–	1733 –	Selectmen
Tisbury, .	Dukes County	–	1750–1885	Town Clerk
Topsfield, .	Essex .	–	1715–1779	Town Clerk
		Hassocky Meadow . . .	1711–1779	Town Clerk
		Hassocky Meadow . . .	1816–1850	Town Clerk
		Stickney Meadow . . .	1792–1804	Town Clerk
Townsend, .	Middlesex .	–	–	Selectmen
Truro, .	Barnstable .	–	1699–1800	Town Clerk
WALTHAM, .	Middlesex .	Watertown	1636–1742	City Clerk[13]
Warwick, .	Franklin .	–	1735–1772	Town Clerk
Watertown, .	Middlesex .	–	1644–1742	Town Clerk[14]
W. Bridgewater, .	Plymouth .	Bridgewater	1675–1827	Town Clerk[15]
Westfield, .	Hampden .	–	1667–1830	Town Clerk
Westminster, .	Worcester .	–	1728–1759	Town Clerk[16]
Williamstown, .	Berkshire .	–	–	[17]–
Winchendon, .	Worcester .	Ipswich Canada . . .	1737–1797	Town Clerk
Woburn, .	Middlesex .	–	1738–1765	Town Clerk
WORCESTER, .	Worcester .	–	1667–1788	City Clerk[3]
Wrentham, .	Norfolk .	–	1662–1829	Town Clerk
Yarmouth, .	Barnstable .	–	1669–1706	Town Clerk
		–	1710–1733	Town Clerk[5]

[1] The records are kept in the house of the Town Clerk. There is a copy also in the Registry of Deeds at Plymouth.   [2] Massachusetts State Library.

[3] There is a copy also in possession of the City Clerk.

[4] Dated at Rehoboth.

[5] There is a copy also in possession of the Town Clerk.

[6] There is a copy also in the Registry of Deeds at Plymouth.

[7] This is an attested copy; the original is missing.

[8] Registry of Deeds at Great Barrington.

[9] These records were in the Registry of Deeds at Great Barrington but are now missing.

[10] There are copies also in the possession of the City Clerk.

[11] There are copies also in the Registry of Deeds at Taunton.   [12] Boston.

[13] Part of the records have been copied.

[14] There is a copy also in possession of the City Clerk of Waltham.

[15] See foot-note [6] on page 6.

[16] There is a copy also in possession of the Town Clerk, and one in possession of the Massachusetts Historical Society at Boston.   [17] The Chairman of the Selectmen, temporarily.

CHURCH RECORDS.

[The presentation of church records (including the records of churches, parishes and religious societies) is divided into two parts, the first part relating to the records of existing churches, and the second part to the records of extinct churches. Under each of these divisions the returns concerning church records are presented first by towns and then by denominations.

In all cases where the records of existing churches are not returned as being misplaced or lost, they have been reported to be in the possession of some duly authorized church official from whom the information in regard to their condition was obtained. With few exceptions, however, the records of extinct churches are returned as being either in the possession of persons or organizations probably not the legal custodians, the name of the possessor being given in each case, or no information concerning them could be ascertained, and for these reasons no return as to their condition has been made.]

EXISTING CHURCHES: BY TOWNS.

[In this table the returns concerning records are presented alphabetically by denominations, under the name of each town, the distinguishing names, if any, of the churches of each denomination also being given alphabetically. The names given in the various lists published by authority of the different denominations are adopted as the distinguishing names in this table, and where no published lists could be obtained written lists were supplied and have been used.

The dates of organization are given in the lists published by the Baptist, Congregational New Jerusalem, Unitarian, and Universalist denominations, and those dates are used in this table. For the other denominations the dates of organization are given only when they were returned by the several churches. In many cases where churches have divided both organizations claim the original date of organization, although the records of one or the other must be necessarily of a later date than the reported date of organization. The dates of organization and of legal incorporation are usually different. In some cases the records commenced at an earlier date than the year in which the church was organized, services having been held by the congregation and records kept before the formal organization as a church or society.

When a church has undergone one or more reorganizations but is virtually the same body, it is given under its present name and denomination, with explanatory foot-notes.

The denominations considered in this table number forty-five and are as follows : — Advent Baptist, African Methodist Episcopal, African Methodist Episcopal Zion, Baptist, Catholic Apostolic, Christian, Christian Baptist, Christian Connection, Congregational, Disciples of Christ, Evangelical Congregational, Evangelical Independent, Evangelical Lutheran, Free Baptist, Free Congregational, Free Evangelical, French Protestant, Friends, German Congregational, German Methodist Episcopal, German Reformed, Gethsemane Baptist, Independent Baptist, Independent Methodist, Jewish, Latter Day Saints (abbreviation of the corporate name of the denomination, "The Church of Jesus Christ of Latter Day Saints"), Messiah, Methodist, Methodist Episcopal, New Jerusalem, Presbyterian, Primitive Methodist, Protestant Episcopal, Reformed Episcopal, Reformed Presbyterian, Roman Catholic, Second Advent, Seventh Day Advent, Undenominational, Union Evangelical, Unitarian, United Presbyterian, United Society (Shakers), Universalist, and Wesleyan Methodist.

The use of the dash signifies that the information is wanting, except in the case of the local meetings of Friends, and the Roman Catholic churches which in this table are said to be "attended from" other churches. The information concerning these is explained by the respective foot-notes and by the two following paragraphs.

The Roman Catholic churches " attended from " other churches have no separate records, the records being included in those of the church from which they are attended.

There are no separate records of the local meetings of Friends, the records being included in the records of monthly meetings.]

EXISTING CHURCHES: BY TOWNS — Continued.

COUNTY OF BARNSTABLE.

CITIES, TOWNS, AND NAMES OF CHURCHES.	Date of Organization	RECORDS		
		Kind	Years covered	Condition
Barnstable,				
Baptist:				
Barnstable,	1842	Church	1842–1885	Well kept
Hyannis,	1771	Church	1772–1885	Good
Osterville,	1835	Church	1830–1885	Good
Congregational:				
Centreville,	1840	Church	1816–1885	Well preserved
Hyannis,[1]	1854	Church and Parish	1854–1885	Good
West Barnstable,[2]	1616	Parish	1716–1885	Good
Methodist Episcopal:				
Barnstable,	–	Church[3]	1870–1885[4]	Good
Centreville,	–	Church	1877–1885	Good
Marston's Mills,	–	Church	1812–1885	Good
Osterville,	–	Church	1846–1885	Good
Roman Catholic:				
Hyannis,[5]	–	–	–	–
Unitarian:				
Congregational Church and Society in the East Precinct,[6]	1639	Parish	1725–1885	Good
Universalist:				
Hyannis,	1880	Society	1875–1885	Good
Bourne,				
Baptist:				
Pocasset,	1838	Church	1838–1885	Good
Methodist Episcopal:				
Bourne,	–	Church	1850–1885	Good
Sagamore,	–	Church	1828–1885	Good
Brewster,				
Baptist,	1824	Society	1824–1885	Good
Unitarian:				
First Parish,	1700	Parish	1747–1885	Fair
Universalist,	1824	Society	1824–1885	Good
Chatham,				
Baptist,	1824	Church	1834–1885	Good
Congregational:				
First,	1720	Church	1861–1885[7]	Fair
		Parish	1824–1885[8]	Fair
Methodist Episcopal,	–	Church	1821–1885	Good
Universalist,	1835	Church	1820–1885	Fair
		Society	1822–1885	Fair
Dennis,				
Congregational:				
South Dennis,	1817	Church and Parish	1817–1885	Poor
Union,	1866	Society	1868–1885	Fair
Latter Day Saints,	–	Church	1866–1885	–
Methodist Episcopal:				
Dennis,	–	Church	9–	–
West Dennis,	–	Church	1873–1885	Good

[1] Formed from the Methodist Episcopal and Wesleyan churches.

[2] Organized in England in 1616. Settled in Scituate in 1634; in Barnstable in 1639, and in West Barnstable in 1716.   [4] The earlier records are lost.

[3] There is also a record of the pastors from 1820 to 1885.   [5] Attended from Wood's Holl.

[6] Originally gathered in England in 1639 by Rev. John Lothrop. Accepting his diary, in possession of the Congregational Church at West Barnstable, as a record, together with the records of that church, the records are nearly continuous from 1639 to 1885.

[7] The church records were burned in 1861, in the fire which destroyed the parsonage. There is a summary of the old records up to that time, and a full record since.

[8] Parish reorganized in 1871.   [9] Partial records have been kept but are missing.

Cities, Towns, and Names of Churches.	Date of Organization	Records		
		Kind	Years covered	Condition
Eastham,				
Methodist Episcopal, ...	–	Church	1819–1885	[1]–
Falmouth,				
Congregational:				
East Falmouth, ...	1821	Church	1821–1885	Good
First, ...	1708 {	Church	1731–1885	–
		Parish	1804–1885[2]	–
North Falmouth, ...	1833	Church	1833–1885	Good
Waquoit, ...	1849	Church	1849–1885	Good
Wood's Holl, ...	1880	Church	1881–1885	–
Friends, ...	1709	[3]–	1709–1885	–
Methodist Episcopal:				
East Falmouth, ...	–	Church	1860–1885	Good
Falmouth, ...	–	Church	1811–1885	Good
West Falmouth, ...	–	Church	1854–1885	Imperfect[4]
Wood's Holl, ...	–	Church	1880–1885	Good
Protestant Episcopal:				
Church of Messiah (Wood's Holl), .	–	Church	1851–1885	–
Roman Catholic:				
Falmouth,[5]	–	–	–	–
Wood's Holl, ...	–	Church	1880–1885	–
Harwich,				
Baptist:				
West Harwich, ...	1767	Church	1773–1885	Good
Congregational:				
Harwich, ...	1747	Church	1747–1885	Good
Pilgrim (Harwich Port), . .	1855 {	Church and Parish }	1855–1885	Good
Methodist Episcopal:				
South Harwich, ...	–	Church	1853–1885	Good
Roman Catholic,[5]	–	–	–	–
Mashpee,				
Baptist, ...	1838	Church	1832–1885	Good
Orleans,				
Congregational, ...	1646 {	Church and Society }	1648–1885	Fair
Methodist Episcopal, ...	–	Church	1837–1885	Good
Roman Catholic,[6]	–	–	–	–
Universalist, ...	1876	Society	1835–1885	Good
Provincetown,				
Congregational, ...	1769	Church	1769–1885	Good
Methodist Episcopal:				
Centenary, ...	–	Parish	1860–1885	Good
Centre, ...	1795	Church	1839–1885[7]	Complete
Roman Catholic:				
Saint Peter's, ...	–	Church	1868–1885	Good
Universalist, ...	1843	Parish	1829–1885	Good
Sandwich,				
Congregational, ...	1639	Church	1639–1885	Good
Friends, ...	1672	[3]–	1672–1885	–
Methodist Episcopal, ...	1796	Church	1796–1885	Good

[1] The bound records are in fair condition, but the unbound are dilapidated.
[2] The earlier parish records are lost.
[3] The records are included in the Sandwich Monthly Meeting records.
[4] Imperfect to 1877; in much better condition since that year.   [6] Attended from Sandwich.
[5] Attended from Wood's Holl.   [7] The records from 1795 to 1839 are lost.

Existing Churches: By Towns — Continued.

County of Barnstable — Concluded.

Cities, Towns, and Names of Churches.	Date of Organ- ization	Kind	Years covered	Condition
Sandwich — Con.				
Protestant Episcopal:				
Saint John's, ...	1853	Church	1884–1885[1]	–
Roman Catholic:				
Saint Peter's, ...	1843	Church	1843–1885	Good
Unitarian:				
First Church of Christ, . . .	1638 {	Church Parish	1695–1885 1780–1885	Good Good
Truro,				
Congregational:				
First, ...	1711	Church	1709–1885	–
North Truro, ...	1842	Church	1840–1885	Good
Methodist Episcopal:				
South Truro, ...	–	Church	1794–1885	–
Truro, ...	1826	Parish	1826–1885	Good
Roman Catholic,[2]	–	–	–	–
Wellfleet,				
Congregational:				
First, ...	1723	Church	1723–1885	Good
Second (South Wellfleet), . . .	1833	Church	1834–1885	Good
Methodist Episcopal, ...	–	Church	1818–1885	Good
Roman Catholic,[2]	–	–	–	–
Universalist, ...	1874	Parish	1840–1885	Good
Yarmouth,				
Baptist:				
South Yarmouth, ...	1824	Church	1844–1885	–
Congregational:				
First, ...	1639	Parish	1679–1885[3]	–
West Yarmouth, ...	1844	Church	1840–1885	Good
Friends, ...	1709	4-	1709–1885	–
Methodist Episcopal:				
South Yarmouth, ...	–	Church	1853–1885	Good
Yarmouth Port, ...	–	Parish	1840–1885	–
New Jerusalem, ...	1843	Society	1838–1885	Good
Roman Catholic,[5]	–	–	–	–
Universalist, ...	1867	Society	1836–1885	–

County of Berkshire.

Adams,				
Baptist, ...	1826	Church	1826–1885	Good
Congregational, ...	1840	Church	1840–1885	Good
Methodist Episcopal, ...	–	Church	1871–1885	Good
Protestant Episcopal:				
Saint Mark's, ...	–	Church	1869–1885	Good
Roman Catholic:				
Church of Seven Dolors (South Adams),	–	Church	1882–1885	Good
Saint Charles's (South Adams), . .	–	Church	1875–1885	Good
Universalist, ...	1872	Church	1872–1885	Good

[1] No services were held between 1865 and 1884; there are no records prior to 1884.

[2] Attended from Provincetown.

[3] The records from 1639 to about 1679 were burned.

[4] The records are included in the Sandwich Monthly Meeting records.

[5] Attended from Wood's Holl.

Existing Churches : By Towns — Continued.

County of Berkshire — Continued.

Cities, Towns, and Names of Churches.	Date of Organ- ization	Records		
		Kind	Years covered	Condition
Alford,				
Congregational, ...	1846	Church	1846–1851[1]	Complete
Becket,				
Baptist, ...	1764 {	Church and } Society {	2_	–
Congregational :				
First, ...	1758 }	Church Society	1758–1885 1798–1885	Good Good
North Becket, ...	1840 {	Church and } Society {	1849–1885	Good
Roman Catholic,[3]	–	–	–	–
Cheshire,				
Baptist, ...	1789	Church	1834–1885	Good
Methodist Episcopal, ...	–	Church	1850–1885	Good
Roman Catholic :				
Assumption,[4] .	–	–	–	–
Universalist, ...	1849	Church	1849–1885	Good
Clarksburg,[5]				
Dalton,				
Congregational, ...	1785	Parish	1809–1885	Good
Methodist Episcopal, ...	–	Church	1858–1885	Good
Egremont,				
Baptist, ...	1789	Church	1789–1885	Good
Congregational :				
South Egremont, ...	1816	Society	1833–1885	Good
Methodist Episcopal :				
North Egremont, ...	–	Society	1860–1885	Good
Florida,				
Baptist, ...	1810	Church	1810–1885	Well preserved
Great Barrington,				
African Methodist Episcopal Zion, . .	–	Church	1872–1885	Good
Congregational :				
First, ...	1743	Church	1753–1885	Good
Housatonic, ...	1841 {	Church and } Society {	1841–1885	Good
Methodist Episcopal :				
Great Barrington, ...	1842	Church	1842–1885	Good
Housatonic, ...	–	Church	1868–1885	Good
Protestant Episcopal :				
Saint James's, ...	–	Church	1821–1885	Imperfect
Trinity (Van Deusenville), . . .	–	Church	1873–1885[6]	Good
Roman Catholic :				
Saint Bridget's (Housatonic),[7] .	–	–	–	–
Saint Peter's, ...	–	Church	1855–1885	Good
Hancock,				
Baptist, ...	1772	Church	1830–1885	Good
United Society (Shakers), . . .	1790	Society	1790–1885	–

[1] A few entries were made as late as 1869. The church was reorganized in 1874, since which time partial records have been kept.

[2] For occasional years only.

[3] Attended from Hinsdale.

[4] Attended from South Adams.

[5] There is no church in Clarksburg.

[6] The records from 1845 to 1873 are lost.

[7] Attended from Great Barrington.

EXISTING CHURCHES: BY TOWNS — Continued.

COUNTY OF BERKSHIRE — Continued.

CITIES, TOWNS, AND NAMES OF CHURCHES.	Date of Organ- ization	RECORDS		
		Kind	Years covered	Condition
Hinsdale,				
Baptist, ...	1797	Church	1792–1885	Good
Congregational, ...	1795	Church	1795–1885	Good
		Parish	1833–1885	Good
Roman Catholic:				
Saint Patrick's, ...	1868	Church	1868–1885	Good
Lanesborough,				
Baptist, ...	1818	Church	1833–1885[1]	Good
Congregational, ...	1764	Church	1785–1885	Good
Methodist Episcopal, ...	–	Church	1864–1885[2]	Good
Protestant Episcopal:				
Saint Luke's, ...	–	Church	1823–1885	Good
		Parish	1767–1885	Good
Lee,				
Baptist, ...	1851	Church	1850–1885	Good
Congregational, ...	1780	Church	1780–1885	Good
Methodist Episcopal, ...	–	Church	1839–1885	Good
Protestant Episcopal:				
Saint George's, ...	–	Church	1856–1885	Good
Roman Catholic:				
Saint Mary's, ...	–	Church	1857–1885	Fair
Undenominational:				
Union (South Lee), ...	–	Church	1827–1885	Good
Lenox,				
Congregational, ...	1769	Church[3]	1769–1860	Incomplete
		Church	1860–1885	Complete
Methodist Episcopal, ...	–	Church	1834–1885[4]	Good
Protestant Episcopal:				
Trinity, ...	–	Church	1794–1885	–
Roman Catholic:				
Saint Anne's,[5]	–	–	–	–
Monterey,				
Congregational, ...	1750	Church	1750–1855	Partial records
		Church	1855–1885	Complete
Mount Washington,				
Congregational, ...	1874	Church[6]	1874–1885	–
New Ashford,				
Methodist Episcopal,[7]	–	Church	1825–1885	Incomplete
New Marlborough,				
Baptist, ...	1847	Church	1847–1885	Dilapidated
		Society	1848–1885	Dilapidated
Congregational:				
First, ...	1744	Parish[8]	1861–1885	Good
Mill River, ...	1871	Church	1871–1885	Good

[1] The records prior to 1833 are lost.

[2] The record from 1873 to 1881 is a partial record only.

[3] The first volume of the society records from 1834 to 1876 is in possession of the Town Clerk.

[4] The records prior to 1834 are incomplete.   [5] Attended from Lee.

[6] The first volume of the records of the "Mount Washington Ecclesiastical Society," commencing about 1878, are in possession of William H. Weaver.

[7] The church edifice was never dedicated to any denomination.

[8] Daniel Grant has records from 1826 to 1869. The records prior to 1826 are supposed to have been purposely destroyed.

CITIES, TOWNS, AND NAMES OF CHURCHES.	Date of Organ- ization	RECORDS		
		Kind	Years covered	Condition
New Marlborough — Con.				
Congregational: — Con. Southfield, ...	1794 ⎰	Church and Parish ⎱	1790–1885	Good
Methodist Episcopal: Hartsville, ...	1844	Church	1858–1885[1]	Good
Roman Catholic: Immaculate Conception (Mill River),[2]	–	–	–	–
Saint Mary's, ...	–	Church	1866–1885	–
North Adams,				
Baptist, ...	1808	Church	1808–1885	Good
Congregational, ...	1827	Church	1827–1885	–
Methodist Episcopal, ...	–	Church	1792–1885	[3]–
Protestant Episcopal, ...	–	Church	1855–1885	Complete
Roman Catholic: Notre Dame, ...	–	Church	1871–1885	Good
Saint Francis's, ...	–	Church	1865–1885	Good
Universalist, ...	1861	Parish	1859–1885	Good
Otis,				
Congregational, ...	1779	Church	1812–1885	Good
Protestant Episcopal: Saint Paul's, ...	–	Church	1828–1885	Good
Peru,				
Congregational, ...	1770	Parish	1820–1885	Good
Pittsfield,				
Baptist, ...	1772	Church	1800–1885	Complete
Congregational: First, ...	1764 ⎰	Church Parish	1764–1885[4] 1868–1885[5]	Good Good
Second, ...	1846	[6]–	–	–
South, ...	1850	Church	1848–1885	Complete
Methodist Episcopal, ...	–	Church	1831–1885[7]	Good
Protestant Episcopal: Saint Stephen's, ...	–	Church	1832–1885	–
Roman Catholic: Notre Dame, ...	–	Church	1869–1885	Good
Saint Joseph's, ...	–	Church	1844–1885	Good
Richmond,				
Congregational, ...	1765 ⎰	Church Parish	1784–1885 1824–1885	Good Good
Sandisfield,				
Baptist, ...	1779	Church	1779–1885	–
Congregational: First, ...	1756	Church[8]	1756–1885	–
New Boston, ...	1874 ⎰	Church Society	1874–1885 1876–1885	–

[1] The records from 1844 to 1858 are missing. [2] Attended from Great Barrington.

[3] The records prior to 1802 are meagre.

[4] Minutes of church meetings are omitted between October 30, 1863, and April 23, 1872. A copy of the church records from 1753 to 1845 is in possession of the Town Clerk.

[5] The parish records prior to 1868 were burned. There is a written history of the parish, contained in its record book, covering the period from its organization to the time of the destruction of its records. [6] The church and society records are lost.

[7] The records from about 1791 are lost. William Renne of Pittsfield has valuable private memoranda relating to the early history of this church.

[8] The parish records for the first thirty-eight years are in possession of the Town Clerk.

EXISTING CHURCHES: BY TOWNS — Continued.

COUNTY OF BERKSHIRE — Continued.

CITIES, TOWNS, AND NAMES OF CHURCHES.	Date of Organ- ization	RECORDS		
		Kind	Years covered	Condition
Savoy,				
Baptist, ...	1786	Church	1786–1885	Good
Methodist Episcopal :				
Savoy Circuit, ...	–	Church	1880–1885	Good
Second Advent,[1]	–	–	–	–
Sheffield,				
Congregational :				
Church of Christ, ...	1735	Church	1814–1885[2]	Complete
Methodist Episcopal :				
Ashley Falls, ...	–	Church	1857–1885	Good
Sheffield, ...	–	Church	1848–1885	Good
Protestant Episcopal :				
Christ, ...	–	Church	1866–1885	Good
Roman Catholic,[3]	–	–	–	–
Stockbridge,				
Congregational :				
Curtisville, ...	1824	Church	1824–1885	Fair
First, ... {	1735 {	Church	1850–1885[4]	Good
		Parish	1828–1885	Good
Methodist Episcopal, ...	–	Church	1835–1885	Incomplete
Protestant Episcopal :				
Saint Paul's, ...	–	Church	1839–1885	Good
Roman Catholic :				
Saint Joseph's,[5]	–	–	–	–
Tyringham,				
Baptist, ... {	1827 {	Church and Society {	1878–1885[6]	Good
Methodist Episcopal, ...	–	Church	1852–1885	Good
Washington,				
Methodist Episcopal, ...	–	Church	1843–1885	Good
West Stockbridge,				
Congregational :				
Centre, ...	1789	Parish	1829–1885	–
Village, ...	1833	Society	1833–1885	–
Methodist Episcopal, ... {	– {	Church and Parish {	1838–1885	–
Roman Catholic :				
Saint Patrick's, ...	–	Church	1871–1885	Good
Williamstown,				
Baptist, ...	1805	Church	1805–1885	Fair
Congregational :				
College, ...	1833	Church	1833–1885	Good
First, ...	1765	Church	1843–1885[7]	Good
Second (South Williamstown), . {	1836 {	Church and Parish[8] {	1836–1885	Fair
Methodist Episcopal, ...	–	Church	1855–1885	Good

[1] This church is said to be nearly extinct; no information has been obtained.

[2] The records contain an account of the settlement of the first pastor of the church in 1735, but no records prior to 1814 are reported.　　[4] The earlier church records are lost.

[3] Attended from Great Barrington.　　[5] Attended from West Stockbridge.

[6] The earlier records are in possession of Mrs. Edward Slater.

[7] The records prior to 1843 were burned.

[8] B. F. Mills and Charles A. Mills have private records.

EXISTING CHURCHES: BY TOWNS — Continued.

COUNTY OF BERKSHIRE — Concluded.

CITIES, TOWNS, AND NAMES OF CHURCHES.	Date of Organ- ization	RECORDS		
		Kind	Years covered	Condition
Williamstown — Con.				
Protestant Episcopal:				
Saint John's, ...	–	Church	1870–1885	Fair
Undenominational:				
Church of Christ in the White Oaks, .	–	–	–	–
Windsor,				
Congregational:				
Church of Christ, ...	1772	Society	1846–1885[1]	–

COUNTY OF BRISTOL.

	Date of Organ- ization	Kind	Years covered	Condition
Acushnet,				
Baptist:				
Long Plain, ...	1838	Church	1834–1885	Good
Friends:				
Acushnet Meeting, ...	1709	[2]–	1709–1885	–
Long Plain Meeting, ...	1709	[2]–	1709–1885	–
Methodist Episcopal:				
Acushnet, ...	–	Church	1807–1885	Good
Long Plain, ...	–	Church	1852–1885	Good
Attleborough,				
African Methodist Episcopal Zion, . .	1873	Church	1877–1885	Fair
Baptist:				
North Attleborough, . . .	1769	Church	1769–1885	Good
Congregational:				
First (West Attleborough), . .	1712	Church	1740–1885[3]	Good
		Church	1686–1706[4]	–
Second, ...	1748 {	Church	1866–1885	Complete
		Parish	1743–1885	Good
Third (Attleborough Falls), . .	1874	Church	1874–1885	Good
Free Evangelical (North Attleborough),	–	Church	1860–1885	Good
Gethsemane Baptist:				
North Attleborough, ...	–	Church	1882–1885	Good
Methodist Episcopal:				
Attleborough, ...	1866	Church	1866–1885	Good
Hebronville, ...	–	Church	1876–1885	Good
Protestant Episcopal:				
Grace (North Attleborough), . .	1858	Parish	1858–1885	Good
Roman Catholic:				
Saint John's (East Attleborough), .	1883	Church	1883–1885	–
Saint Mary's (North Attleborough), .	–	Church	1850–1885	Good
Undenominational:				
Union (Hebronville), ...	–	Church	1828–1885	Good
Universalist:				
Attleborough, ...	1874	Church	1874–1885	Good
North Attleborough, ...	–	Church	1816–1885	Good
Berkley,				
Congregational:				
First, ...	1737	Church	1820–1885	Fair

[1] A volume of records prior to 1846 is lost.

[2] The records prior to 1793 are included in the Sandwich Monthly Meeting records; since 1793 in the New Bedford Monthly Meeting records.

[3] The records prior to 1740 are probably lost. The volume from 1743 to 1796 is deposited, for safe keeping, with the Town Clerk.

[4] A part of this volume is lost.

EXISTING CHURCHES: BY TOWNS — Continued.

COUNTY OF BRISTOL — Continued.

CITIES, TOWNS, AND NAMES OF CHURCHES.	Date of Organ- ization	Kind	Years covered	Condition
Berkley — Con.				
Methodist Episcopal :				
Berkley, ...	–	Church	1873–1885	–
Myricksville,[1]	1871	Church	1871–1885	Good[1]
Dartmouth,				
Christian Connection :				
Bakerville, ...	–	Church	1863–1885	Good
Hixville, ...	–	Church	1780–1885	Good
Second Christian, ...	–	Church	1836–1885	–
Smith's Mills, ...	–	Church	1838–1885	Good
Congregational :				
South Dartmouth, .	–	Parish	1858–1885	Good
Friends :				
Allen's Neck Meeting, ...	1807	2–	1807–1885	–
Apponegansett Meeting, . . .	1699	2–	1699–1885	–
Smith's Mills Independent Meeting, .	1845	3–	1845–1885	–
Smith's Neck Meeting, . . .	1819	2–	1819–1885	–
Roman Catholic,[4]	–	–	–	–
Dighton,				
Baptist, ...	1780	Church	1807–1885	5–
Congregational :				
First, ...	1710	Church	1826–1885	Good
Methodist Episcopal :				
Dighton, ...	–	Church	1866–1885	Good
North Dighton, ...	–	Church	1860–1885	Good
Roman Catholic,[6]	–	–	–	–
Unitarian :				
Pedobaptist Congregational Society, .	1797	Parish	1797–1885	Fair
Easton,				
Congregational, ...	1745 {	Church Parish	1747–1885 1839–1885	Good Good
Methodist Episcopal :				
Central (North Easton), . . .	1861 {	Church and Parish	1861–1885	Good
Washington Street (North Easton), .	1795 {	Church Parish	1861–1885[7] 1810–1885	Good Good
Roman Catholic :				
Immaculate Conception (No. Easton),	1840	Church	1840–1885	Good
Unitarian :				
First Parish of Easton, ...	1720	Parish	1792–1885	Good
Unity Church (North Easton), . .	1855	Parish	1868–1885	Good
Fairhaven,				
Congregational, ...	1794	Church	1794–1885	Good
Friends, ...	1849	8–	1849–1885	–
Methodist Episcopal, ...	–	Church	1830–1885	9–
Roman Catholic,[4]	–	–	–	–
Unitarian :				
Washington Street Christian Church,	1832	Church	1819–1885	Good

[1] Originally organized in 1853 under the name of the Protestant Methodist Church. The records prior to 1871 are imperfect.

[2] The records are included in the Dartmouth Monthly Meeting records.

[3] The records are included in the Dartmouth Independent Monthly Meeting records.

[4] Attended from New Bedford.

[5] The records for some of the earlier years are incomplete.

[6] Attended from Taunton.

[7] The church records prior to 1861 were carried away.

[8] The records are included in the New Bedford Monthly Meeting records.

[9] The records from 1830 to 1849 are imperfect.

EXISTING CHURCHES: BY TOWNS — Continued.

COUNTY OF BRISTOL — Continued.

CITIES, TOWNS, AND NAMES OF CHURCHES.	Date of Organ- ization	RECORDS		
		Kind	Years covered	Condition
FALL RIVER,				
African Methodist Episcopal, . . .	–	Church	1878–1885	Irregularly kept
Baptist:				
First, ...	1781 }	Church and } Parish	1781–1885	Good
Second, ...	1846	Church	1846–1885	Good
Christian Connection :				
Bogle Street Christian, ...	–	Church	1880–1885	Good
First Christian, ...	–	Church	1837–1885	Good
North Christian, ...	–	Church	1842–1885	Good
Congregational :				
Central, ...	1842	Church	1842–1885	Good
First, ...	1816 }	Church	1816–1885	Incomplete
		Society	1850–1885	–
Third, ...	1875	Church	1874–1885	Good
Friends, ...	1824	1–	1824–1885	–
Latter Day Saints, ...	1865	Church	1865–1885	Fair
Methodist Episcopal :				
Brayton, ...	–	Church	1860–1885	Good
First, ...	–	Church	1827–1885	Good
North, ...	–	Church	1848–1885	Good
Park, ...	–	Church	1874–1885	Good
Quarry Street, ...	–	Church	1870–1885	Good
Saint Paul's, ...	–	Church	1851–1885	Good
New Jerusalem, ...	1854	Society	1854–1885	Good
Presbyterian, ...	–	Church	1849–1885	–
Primitive Methodist, ...	–	Church	1872–1885	Good
Protestant Episcopal :				
Ascension, ...	–	Church	1837–1885	Good
Saint James's, ...	– {	Church and } Parish	1884–1885	Good
Saint John's, ...	–	Church	1878–1885	Good
Roman Catholic :				
Immaculate Conception, . . .	–	Church	1883–1885	Good
Notre Dame de Lourdes, . . .	–	Church	1872–1885	Good
Sacred Heart, ...	–	Church	1873–1885	Good
Saint Ann's, ...	–	Church	1869–1885[2]	Good
Saint Joseph's, ...	–	Church	1873–1885	Good
Saint Louis's, ...	–	Church	1885 –	Good
Saint Mary's, ...	–	Church	1840–1885	Good
Saint Patrick's, ...	–	Church	1872–1885	Good
Saints Peter and Paul's, . . .	–	Church	1882–1885	Good
Unitarian, ...	1832	Church[3]	1839–1885	Good
Freetown,				
Congregational :				
Assonet, ...	1747 }	Church	1807–1885	Good
		Parish	1852–1885	Good
Friends, ...	1759	4–	1759–1856	–
Mansfield,				
Baptist, ...	1838	Church	1830–1885	Good
Congregational, ...	1838	Church	1838–1885	Good
Friends, ...	1819	5–	1819–1856	–
Methodist Episcopal :				
Emmanuel, ...	–	Church	1860–1885	Good
First, ...	–	Church	1811–1885	Good

[1] The records are included in the Swansea Monthly Meeting records. Meetings were held in 1812 or 1814.

[2] The records of burials are not continued after 1878.

[3] A private record is in possession of J. M. Aldrich.

[4] The records are included in the Swansea Monthly Meeting records. The meeting was discontinued in 1856, and again set up in 1887.

[5] The records are included in the Smithfield (R. I.) Monthly Meeting records.

EXISTING CHURCHES: BY TOWNS — Continued.

COUNTY OF BRISTOL — Continued.

CITIES, TOWNS, AND NAMES OF CHURCHES.	Date of Organ- ization	RECORDS		
		Kind	Years covered	Condition
Mansfield — Con.				
New Jerusalem,[1]	1846	Church	1846–1885	Good
Roman Catholic,[2]	–	–	–	–
Unitarian:				
First Congregational Parish,	1731	Church	1734–1885	Fair
NEW BEDFORD,				
African Methodist Episcopal,	–	Church	1851–1885	Good
African Methodist Episcopal Zion,	–	Church	1840–1885	Good
Baptist:				
First,	1813	Church	1828–1885	Good
Second,	1846	Church	1850–1885	Good
Salem,	1859	Church	1858–1885	Good
North,	1873	Church	1873–1885	Good
Christian:				
Purchase Street,	–	Church and Society	1808–1885	Good
Christian Connection:				
Bonney Street,	–	Church	1850–1885	Good
Middle Street Christian,	–	Church	1848–1885	Good
Spruce Street Christian,	–	Church	1869–1885	Good
Congregational:				
Acushnet,	1696	Church and Parish	1828–1885[3]	Incomplete
North,	1807	Church	1807–1885	Fair
Trinitarian,	1831	Church	1832–1885	Good
Friends:				
New Bedford Independent Meeting,	1845	[4]–	1845–1885	–
New Bedford Meeting,	1785	[5]–	1785–1885	–
Latter Day Saints,	–	Church	1881–1885	Good
Methodist Episcopal:				
Allen Street,	–	Church	1852–1885	Good
County Street,	–	Church	1820–1885	Good
Fourth Street,	–	Church	1835–1885	Good
Pleasant Street,	–	Church	1844–1885	Good
Protestant Episcopal:				
Grace,	–	Church	1833–1885	Good
Saint James's,	–	Parish	1878–1885	Good
Roman Catholic:				
Sacred Heart,	–	Church	1877–1885	Good
Saint John the Baptist's,	–	Church	1875–1885	Good
Saint Lawrence's,	–	Church	1870–1885	Good
Saint Mary's,[6]	–	–	–	–
Second Advent,	–	Church	1854–1885	Good
Undenominational:				
Christian Union,	–	Church	1874–1885	Good
Unitarian:				
Congregational Parish,	1714	Church	1731–1885	Good
First Congregational Society,[7]	1795	Church and Parish	1811–1885	Good
Universalist,	–	Church	1835–1885	Good
Norton,				
Baptist,	1838	Church	1761–1885	Good
Congregational,	1832	Church	1832–1885	Good
Methodist Episcopal:				
Chartley,	–	Church	1876–1885	Good
Roman Catholic:				
Saint Mary's,[8]	–	–	–	–

[1] Originally instituted as the Foxborough and Mansfield Society.

[2] Attended from Attleborough.   [3] The records prior to 1828 are lost.

[4] The records are included in the Dartmouth Independent Monthly Meeting records.

[5] The records from 1785 to 1792 are included in the Dartmouth Monthly Meeting records; since 1792 in the New Bedford Monthly Meeting records.   [6] Attended from Saint Lawrence's.

[7] Papers of the late Rev. Samuel West, relating to the original First Congregational Parish, are in possession of Rev. William J. Potter.   [8] Attended from East Attleborough.

EXISTING CHURCHES: BY TOWNS — Continued.

COUNTY OF BRISTOL — Continued.

CITIES, TOWNS, AND NAMES OF CHURCHES.	Date of Organization	RECORDS		
		Kind	Years covered	Condition
Raynham,				
Baptist,[1]	1839	Church	1831–1885	Fair
Congregational:				
North Raynham, ...	1875 }	Church and } Society	1876–1885	Good
Raynham, '	1731 }	Church Parish	1739–1885 1834–1885	Good Good
Unitarian:				
Second Congregational Society, . .	1828	Church	2_	–
Rehoboth,				
Baptist, ...	1840	Church	1840–1885	Good
Congregational, ...	1721	Church	1721–1885	Good
Methodist Episcopal:				
North Rehoboth, ...	–	Church	1849–1885	Good
Seekonk,				
Baptist, ...	1794	Church	1794–1885	Good
Somerset,				
Baptist, ...	1803	Church	1803–1885	Good
Christian Baptist, ...	– }	Church and } Society	1841–1885	Good
Congregational, ...	1861 }	Church and } Parish	1863–1885	Good
Friends:				
Swansea Meeting, ...	1732	3_	1732–1885	–
Methodist Episcopal:				
Somerset, ...	1842	Church	1842–1885	Good
South Somerset, ...	–	Church	1802–1885	Good
Roman Catholic:				
Saint Patrick's, ...	–	Church	1874–1885	Good
Swansea,				
Baptist, ...	1663	Church	1663–1885[4]	Fair
Christian Connection, ...	–	Church	1680–1885	Good
Free Baptist:				
North Swansea, ...	–	Church	1843–1885	Good
Protestant Episcopal:				
Christ, ...	–	Church	1846–1885	Good
Universalist:				
North Swansea, ...	–	Church	1876–1885	Good
TAUNTON,				
Baptist:				
Winthrop Street, ...	–	Parish	1819–1885	Good
Congregational:				
Evangelical (East Taunton), . .	1853	Church	1853–1885	Good
First (West Taunton), . . .	1637	Church	1792–1885	Good
Trinitarian, ...	1821	Church	1821–1885	Complete
Union, ...	1868 }	Church and } Parish	1868–1885	Good
Winslow, ...	1837	Church	1853–1885	Good
Free Baptist, ...	–	Church	1878–1885[5]	Good

[1] This church has records from 1831 to 1837 of a branch of the Fourth Church of Middleborough.

[2] Twenty or more years. Services were discontinued in 1840, although the society still holds its organization.

[3] The records are included in the Swansea Monthly Meeting records.

[4] There is an interval of forty or fifty years in the earlier records. The oldest volume was brought from Swansea, Wales.

[5] The earlier records were burned.

EXISTING CHURCHES : BY TOWNS — Continued.

COUNTY OF BRISTOL — Concluded.

CITIES, TOWNS, AND NAMES OF CHURCHES.	Date of Organ- ization	RECORDS		
		Kind	Years covered	Condition
TAUNTON — Con.				
Methodist Episcopal :				
Central, ...	–	Church	1852–1885	Good
First, ...	–	Church	1835–1885	Fair
Grace, ...	–	Church	1874–1885	Good
Presbyterian :				
First, ...	–	Church	1883–1885	Good
Protestant Episcopal :				
Saint John's, ...	–	Church	1867–1885	Good
Saint Thomas's, ...	– {	Parish	1750–1790	Mutilated
	{	Parish	1825–1885	Good
Roman Catholic :				
Sacred Heart, ...	–	Church	1873–1885	Good
Saint James's,[1]	–	Church	1883–1885	Good
Saint Mary's, ...	–	Church	1832–1885	–
Unitarian :				
First Congregational Society,[2] . .	1637 {	Church and { Parish	1637–1885	Good
Universalist, ...	– {	Church and { Parish	1841–1885	Good
Westport,				
Congregational :				
Pacific Union, ...	1858	Church	1858–1885	Good
Friends, ...	1766	[3]–	1766–1885	–
Methodist Episcopal :				
Westport Point, ...	–	Church	1840–1885	Fair
Roman Catholic,[4]	–	–	–	–

COUNTY OF DUKES COUNTY.

Chilmark,				
Congregational, ...	1700	[5]–	[5]–	Poor
Methodist Episcopal, ...	–	Church	1810–1885	Well preserved
Cottage City,				
Baptist :				
Oak Bluff, ...	1877	Church	1877–1885	Good
Methodist Episcopal, ...	–	Church	1877–1885	Good
Edgartown,				
Baptist, ...	1823	Church	1823–1885	Good
Congregational, ...	1642	Church	1717–1885	Good
Methodist Episcopal, ...	–	Church	1787–1885	Good
Gay Head,				
Baptist, ...	1832	Church	1693–1885	Good
Gosnold,				
Methodist Episcopal :				
Cuttyhunk, ...	–	Church	1875–1885	Good

[1] Called also Immaculate Conception.

[2] Called the " Pilgrim Church " until about 1821, when it became Unitarian.

[3] The records are included in the Westport Monthly Meeting records.

[4] Attended from Fall River.

[5] No record with the exception of the pastor's private record from 1787 to 1820.

EXISTING CHURCHES : BY TOWNS — Continued.

COUNTY OF DUKES COUNTY — Concluded.

CITIES, TOWNS, AND NAMES OF CHURCHES.	Date of Organization	RECORDS		
		Kind	Years covered	Condition
Tisbury,				
Baptist :				
North Tisbury, ...	1833	Church and Parish	1832–1885	–
Vineyard Haven, ...	1780	Church and Parish	1782–1885	–
Congregational :				
West Tisbury, ...	1673	Church and Parish	1701–1885	–
Methodist Episcopal :				
North Tisbury, ...	–	Church	1857–1885	–
Vineyard Haven, ...	–	Church	1857–1885	–
Protestant Episcopal :				
Grace (Vineyard Haven), . . .	–	Parish	1862–1885	Good

COUNTY OF ESSEX.

CITIES, TOWNS, AND NAMES OF CHURCHES.	Date of Organization	Kind	Years covered	Condition
Amesbury,				
Congregational, ...	1831	Church and Parish	1832–1885[1]	Good
Friends, ...	1701	[2]–	1701–1885	–
Methodist Episcopal, ...	–	Church / Church	1844–1871 / 1871–1885	Incomplete / Good
Protestant Episcopal :				
Saint James's, ...	–	Church	1833–1885	Good
Roman Catholic :				
Saint Joseph's, ...	–	Church	1867–1885	Good
Universalist, ...	–	Church / Church	1833–1871 / 1871–1885	Incomplete / Good
Andover,				
Baptist, ...	1834	Church	1858–1885	Good
Congregational :				
Ballardvale Union, ...	1854	Church	1875–1885	Good
Free Christian, ...	1846	Church	1846–1885	Incomplete
South, ...	1711	Parish	1708–1885	Good
Theological Seminary, ...	1865[3]	Church	1865–1885	–
West, ...	1826	Church and Parish	1826–1885	Good
Methodist Episcopal :				
Ballardvale, ...	–	Church	1863–1885[4]	Good
Protestant Episcopal :				
Christ, ...	–	Church	1835–1885	Good
Roman Catholic :				
Saint Augustine's, ...	–	Church	1851–1885	–
Saint Joseph's (Ballardvale),[5] . .	–	–	–	–
Beverly,				
Baptist :				
First, ...	1801	Church / Parish	1801–1885 / 1817–1885	Good / Good
Second, ...	–	Church	1834–1885	Good
Congregational :				
Dane Street, ...	1802	Church / Parish	1802–1885 / 1868–1885[6]	Good / Good
Second (North Beverly), . . .	1715	Church	1715–1885	Good
Washington Street, ...	1837	Church	1837–1885	Good

[1] A very valuable volume of the church records is missing.
[2] The records are included in the Amesbury Monthly Meeting records.
[3] This church was formed in 1816 but not being strictly Congregational the new church was organized in 1865. The old church is about extinct.
[4] The earlier records are lost.   [5] Attended from Andover.
[6] The first volume of parish records is lost.

EXISTING CHURCHES: BY TOWNS — Continued.

COUNTY OF ESSEX — Continued.

CITIES, TOWNS, AND NAMES OF CHURCHES.	Date of Organ- ization	RECORDS		
		Kind	Years covered	Condition
Beverly — Con.				
Methodist Episcopal, ...	–	Church	1867–1885	Good
Protestant Episcopal :				
Saint Peter's, ...	–	Church	1864–1885	Good
Roman Catholic :				
Star of the Sea, ...	–	Church	1865–1885	Good
Unitarian :				
First Parish, ...	1667	Church[1]	1668–1885	Good
Universalist, ...	1856 {	Parish	1840–1861[2]	Good
		Parish	1867–1885	Good
Boxford,				
Congregational :				
First, ...	1702 {	Church	1702–1885[3]	Good
		Parish	1735–1885	Good
West Boxford, ...	1736 {	Church	1735–1885	Good
		Parish	1829–1885	Good
Bradford,				
Congregational :				
First, ...	1682 {	Church	1682–1885	Good
		Parish	1780–1885	Good
Danvers,				
Baptist, ...	– {	Church	1793–1885	Good
		Society	1781–1885	Good
Congregational :				
First, ...	1689 {	Church	1689–1885[4]	Good
		Parish	1672–1735[4]	Good
		Parish	1766–1885	Good
Maple Street, ...	1844	Church	1844–1885	Good
Methodist Episcopal :				
Tapleyville, ...	–	Church	1871–1885	Good
Protestant Episcopal :				
Calvary, ...	–	Church	1858–1885	Complete
Roman Catholic :				
Church of Annunciation, . . .	–	Church	1862–1885	Good
Unitarian :				
Unitarian Congregational Society, .	1865 {	Church and Parish	1865–1885	Good
Universalist, ...	1877	Parish	1815–1885	Good
Essex,				
Congregational :				
First, ...	1681 {	Church	1665–1885	Good
		Parish	1700–1885[5]	Good
Methodist Episcopal, ...	–	Church	1875–1885	Complete
Universalist, ...	1876	Church	1829–1885	Complete
Georgetown,				
Baptist, ...	1785 {	Church	1785–1885	Good
		Parish	1811–1885	Good
Congregational :				
Georgetown, ...	1732 {	Church and Parish	1732–1885	Good
Orthodox Memorial, ...	1864 {	Church and Parish	1864–1885	–
Roman Catholic :				
Saint Mary's, ...	–	Church	1874–1885	–

[1] There are copies of parish records from 1667 to 1830 in possession of the Town Clerk.

[2] The records from 1862 to 1866 are lost.

[3] There are intervals in the church records, the records for the years from 1749 to 1758 and from 1833 to 1837 being omitted.

[4] The early portions of the first volume of both church and parish records, which were in bad condition, have been printed by the Essex Institute. The volume of parish records from 1735 to 1766 was burned, but there are records of the parish treasurer for those years.

[5] The records for the earlier years are lost.

Existing Churches: By Towns — Continued.

County of Essex — Continued.

CITIES, TOWNS, AND NAMES OF CHURCHES.	Date of Organ- ization	RECORDS Kind	Years covered	Condition.
GLOUCESTER,				
Baptist:				
East Gloucester, ...	–	Church	1863–1885	Good
First, ...	1831	Church	1830–1885	Good
Congregational:				
Evangelical, ...	1829 {	Church and Parish {	1829–1885	Good
Lanesville, ...	1830 {	Church	1830–1885	1–
		Society	1828–1885	1–
West Gloucester, ...	1716 {	Church	1716–1827	–
		Church	1845–1885	–
Methodist Episcopal:				
Bay View, ...	–	Church	1870–1885	Good
Prospect Street, ...	–	Church	1825–1885	Good
Riverdale, ...	–	Church	1850–1885	Good
Protestant Episcopal:				
Saint John's, ...	–	Church	1862–1885	Good
Roman Catholic:				
Sacred Heart (Lanesville),[2] . .	–	–	–	–
Saint Ann's, ...	–	Church	1852–1885	Good
Unitarian:				
First Parish, ...	1642 {	Church	1702–1849	Meagre
		Parish	1728–1885	Good
Universalist:				
East Gloucester, ...	–	Church	1884–1885	Good
Gloucester, ...	1799 {	Church and Parish {	1779–1885	Fair
Lanesville, ...	–	Parish	1876–1885	Good
West Gloucester, ...	1716[3]	Parish	1716–1885	Incomplete
Groveland,				
Congregational, ...	1727	Church[4]	1726–1885	Good
Methodist Episcopal, ...	–	Church	1831–1885	Good
Protestant Episcopal:				
Saint James's (South Groveland), .	–	Parish	1873–1885	Good
Roman Catholic:				
Saint Patrick's (South Groveland),[5] .	–	–	–	–
Hamilton,				
Congregational:				
First, ...	1714 {	Church and Parish {	1712–1885	Good
HAVERHILL,				
Baptist:				
Calvary, ...	1871 {	Church and Parish {	1873–1885	Incomplete
First, ...	1765	Church	1793–1885	Fair
Second, ...	1822	Church	1822–1885	Good
Portland Street, ...	1859	Church	1859–1885	Fair
Christian Connection:				
South Christian, ...	1806 {	Church and Parish {	1806–1885	Incomplete
Congregational:				
Centre, ...	1833 {	Church and Parish {	1833–1885	Good
Fourth, ...	1744[6]	Church	1743–1885	–
North Haverhill, ...	1859	Church	1859–1885	Good
Riverside, ...	–	Church	1884–1885	Good
West, ...	1735 {	Church	1735–1885	Good
		Parish	1799–1885	Good

[1] The records from 1828 to 1864 were irregularly kept; since the legal incorporation in 1864 they are complete.

[2] Attended from Rockport.   [3] Reorganized in 1867 as the Third Universalist.

[4] There is a private record in possession of Gardner P. Ladd.

[5] Attended from Georgetown.   [6] Reorganized in 1883.

EXISTING CHURCHES: BY TOWNS — Continued.

COUNTY OF ESSEX — Continued.

CITIES, TOWNS, AND NAMES OF CHURCHES.	Date of Organ- ization	RECORDS		
		Kind	Years covered	Condition
HAVERHILL — Con.				
Free Baptist,	1859	Church	1859–1885	Good
Methodist Episcopal:				
Grace,	–	Church	1870–1885	Good
Protestant Episcopal:				
Saint John's,	–	Church	1875–1885	Good
Trinity,	–	Parish	1855–1885	1
Roman Catholic:				
Saint James's,	–	Church	1851–1885	Good
Saint Joseph's,	–	Church	1876–1885	Good
Second Advent,	–	Church	1875–1885	Incomplete
Unitarian:				
First Parish,	1645	Church and Parish	1790–1885	Good
Universalist:				
Haverhill,	–	Church	1853–1885	Good
West Haverhill,	–	Church	1844–1885	Good
Wesleyan Methodist,	–	Church	1852–1885	Good
Ipswich,				
Congregational:				
First,	1634	Church	1720–1885[2]	–
Linebrook,	1749	Church	1749–1885	Good
South,	1747	Church	1865–1885[3]	Good
		Parish	1747–1885	Good
Methodist Episcopal,	–	Church	1822–1885	Good
Protestant Episcopal:				
Ascension,	–	Parish	1873–1885	Good
Roman Catholic:				
Saint Joseph's,[4]	–	–	–	–
LAWRENCE,				
Baptist:				
First,	1847	Church	1847–1885	Good
		Society	1856–1885	Good
Second,	1860	Church	1860–1885	Good
Congregational:				
Lawrence Street,	1847	Church and Society	1846–1885	Complete
Riverside,	1878	Church	1878–1885	Good
South,	1868	Church	1868–1885	Good
Tower Hill,	1875	Church and Society	1875–1885	Good
Trinity,[5]	–	Church and Parish	1883–1885	Good
Free Baptist,	–	Church	1847–1885	Good
Methodist Episcopal:				
Bodwell Street,	–	Church	1879–1885	Good
Gardner Street,	–	Church	1853–1885	Good
Haverhill Street,	–	Church	1847–1885	Good
Parker Street,	–	Church	1870–1885	Good
Presbyterian,	–	Church	1868–1885	Good
Protestant Episcopal:				
Grace,	–	Church	1846–1885	Good
Saint John's,	–	Church	1866–1885	Good
Saint Thomas's,	–	Church	1878–1885	Good
Roman Catholic:				
Saint Ann's,	–	Church	1871–1885	Good
Saint Augustine's Chapel,[7]	–	–	–	–
Saint Lawrence O'Toole's,[7]	–	–	–	–

[1] Portions of the records prior to 1873 are lost; since 1873 the records are complete.

[2] The earlier records are lost.

[3] The records for the years from 1865 to 1878 are missing.   [4] Attended from Beverly.

[5] Formed by the union of the Central and Eliot Congregational Churches.

[6] The records from 1874 to 1878 are partial records only.

[7] Attended from Saint Mary's at Lawrence.

EXISTING CHURCHES: BY TOWNS — Continued.

COUNTY OF ESSEX — Continued.

CITIES, TOWNS, AND NAMES OF CHURCHES.	Date of Organ- ization	RECORDS		
		Kind	Years covered	Condition
LAWRENCE — Con.				
Roman Catholic: — Con.				
Saint Mary's, ...	–	Church	1849–1885	Good
Saint Patrick's (South Lawrence), .	–	Church	1872–1885	Good
Second Advent, ...	– {	Church and Parish	1867–1885	Good
Unitarian :				
First Unitarian Society, . .	1847	Society	1847–1885	Good
Universalist, ...	1859 {	Church and Society	1847–1885	Good
LYNN,				
African Methodist Episcopal, . . .	–	Church	1858–1885	[1]–
Baptist :				
East Lynn, ...	1874	Church	1874–1885	–
First, ...	1816	Church	1833–1885	Good
Washington Avenue, . . .	1854	Church	1854–1885	Good
Congregational :				
Central, ...	1850 {	Church Parish	1850–1885[2] 1850–1885[3]	Good Good
Chestnut Street, ...	1860 {	Church and Parish	1857–1885	–
First, ...	1632	Church	1763–1885[4]	Good
North, ...	1869	Church	1869–1885	Good
Free Baptist :				
High Street, ...	–	Church	1871–1885	–
Friends, ...	1677	[5]–	1677–1885	
Methodist Episcopal :				
Boston Street, ...	–	Church	1850–1885	Good
Common Street, ...	–	Church[6]	1794–1885	Good
Maple Street, ...	–	Church	1850–1885	Good
Saint Paul's, ...	–	Church[7]	1811–1885	–
South Street, ...	–	Church	1830–1885	Good
Trinity, ...	–	Church	1873–1885	Good
Protestant Episcopal :				
Saint Stephen's, ...	–	Church	1844–1885	Good
Roman Catholic :				
Saint Joseph's, ...	–	Church	1874–1885	Good
Saint Mary's, ...	–	Church	1849–1885	Good
Unitarian :				
Second Congregational, . .	1822 {	Church Society	1822–1848 1822–1885	Incomplete Complete
Universalist :				
First, ...	– {	Church and Parish	1833–1885	Good
Second, ...	–	Church	1837–1885	Good
Lynnfield,				
Congregational :				
Lynnfield Centre, ...	1720 {	Church and Society	1833–1885	Good
Second (South Lynnfield), . .	1854	Church	1854–1885	Good
Unitarian :				
First Congregational Society, . .	1715	Church	1720–1885	–
Manchester,				
Baptist, ...	1849	Church	1884–1885[8]	–
Congregational :				
Orthodox, ...	1716 {	Church and Parish	1837–1885	Good

[1] From 1858 to 1873 the records are imperfect; for the later years they are good.

[2] The records for 1878 and 1879 are omitted.   [3] The records from 1851 to 1868 are omitted.

[4] The records from 1632 to 1763, with the exception of the records of installations, deaths, and dismissals of pastors, were burned.

[5] The records are included in the Salem Monthly Meeting records.

[6] Church records are known to exist but at present are missing from their proper custody.

[7] There are other records extant but they are missing.

[8] There were no records kept prior to 1884.

EXISTING CHURCHES: BY TOWNS — Continued.

COUNTY OF ESSEX — Continued.

CITIES, TOWNS, AND NAMES OF CHURCHES.	Date of Organization	RECORDS		
		Kind	Years covered	Condition
Manchester — Con.				
Roman Catholic:				
Sacred Heart,[1]	–	–	–	–
Marblehead,				
Baptist, ...	1810	Church	1810–1885	Good
Congregational:				
First, ...	1684	Church	1684–1885	Good
Methodist Episcopal, ...	–	Church	1794–1885	Incomplete[2]
Protestant Episcopal:				
Saint Michael's, ...	– {	Church	1714–1775	–
		Church	1802–1885	–
Roman Catholic:				
Our Lady Star of the Sea, . . .	–	Church	1870–1885	Good
Unitarian:				
Second Congregational Society, . .	1716 {	Church and Parish	1716–1885	Good
Universalist, ...	– {	Church and Parish	1836–1885	Good
Merrimac,				
Baptist:				
Merrimac, ...	1867	Church[3]	1867–1885	Good
Merrimac Port, ...	1849 {	Church	1849–1885	–
		Parish	1806–1834	–
		Parish	1845–1885	–
Congregational, ...	1726 {	Church and Parish	1726–1885	–
Methodist Episcopal.				
Merrimac Port, ...	–	Church	1883–1885	–
Roman Catholic:				
Church of the Nativity,[4] . . .	–	–	–	–
Universalist, ...	1865 {	Church and Parish	1840–1885	–
Methuen,				
Baptist, ...	1815	Church	1815–1885	Good
Congregational:				
First, ...	1729	Parish	1781–1885	5_
Methodist Episcopal, ...	–	Church	1853–1885	Good
Protestant Episcopal:				
Saint Thomas's, ...	–	Church	1885 –	Good
Roman Catholic,[6]	–	–	–	–
Universalist, ...	1840	Church	1832–1885	7_
Middleton,				
Congregational, ...	1729 {	Church	1728–1885	Good
		Parish	1831–1885	Good
Methodist Episcopal, ...	–	Church	1879–1885	–
Universalist, ...	–	Church	1829–1885	–
Nahant,				
Independent Methodist, ...	–	Parish	1850–1885	Good
Roman Catholic:				
Saint Thomas Apostle,[8] . . .	–	–	–	–

[1] Attended from Beverly.

[2] The records for the first fifty years are very imperfect and for the later years are defective.

[3] Mrs. G. S. Hoyt has private records.

[4] Attended from Amesbury.

[5] The records prior to 1820 are meagre; since 1820 they are complete.

[6] Attended from Saint Mary's at Lawrence.

[7] The records prior to 1874 are meagre; since 1874 they are complete.

[8] Attended from Saint Mary's at Lynn.

EXISTING CHURCHES : BY TOWNS — Continued.

COUNTY OF ESSEX — Continued.

CITIES, TOWNS, AND NAMES OF CHURCHES.	Date of Organization	RECORDS		
		Kind	Years covered	Condition
Newbury,				
Congregational :				
Byfield, ...	1706 {	Church	1744–1885	Good
		Parish	1762–1885	Good
First, ...	1635	Church	1674–1885	¹–
Methodist Episcopal :				
Byfield, ...	–	Church	1827–1885	Good
NEWBURYPORT,				
Baptist, ...	1809 {	Church and Parish }	1869–1885	Good
Christian Connection :				
Middle Street, ...	–	Church	1873–1885	Good
Congregational :				
Belleville, ...	1808	Church	1835–1885	Good
Fourth, ...	1793 {	Church	1837–1885²	Good
		Parish	1794–1885	Good
North, ...	1768 {	Church	1767–1885	Good
		Parish	1768–1826	Good
Whitfield, ...	1850	Church	1853–1885	Good
Methodist Episcopal :				
Purchase Street, . . .	–	Church	1835–1885	Good
Washington Street, . . .	–	Church	1865–1885	–
Presbyterian :				
Newburyport, ...	–	Parish	1764–1885	Good
Second, ...	1796	Parish	1796–1885	Good
Protestant Episcopal :				
Saint Paul's, ...	–	Church	1714–1885	Good
Roman Catholic :				
Immaculate Conception, . .	–	Church	1850–1885	–
Second Advent, ...	1846	Parish	1856–1885	Good
Unitarian :				
First Religious Society, . .	1725	Church	1800–1885	Good
North Andover.				
Congregational :				
Evangelical, ...	1834	Church	1834–1885	Good
Methodist Episcopal, . . .	–	Church	1848–1885	Good
Protestant Episcopal :				
Saint Paul's, ...	–	Church	1881–1885	Good
Roman Catholic :				
Saint Michael's,³ . . .	–	–	–	–
Unitarian :				
North Parish Church and Society, .	1645 {	Church and Society }	1686–1885	Well preserved
Peabody,				
Baptist, ...	1843	Church	1844–1885	–
Congregational :				
Peabody, ...	1713 {	Church	1793–1885	–
		⁴–	1793–1885	–
Rockville, ...	1874	Church	1874–1885	Good
Methodist Episcopal, . . .	–	Church	1840–1885	–
Protestant Episcopal :				
Saint Paul's, ...	–	Church	1874–1885	–
Roman Catholic :				
Saint John's, ...	–	Church	1874–1885	–
Unitarian :				
First, ...	1825	Church	1826–1885	–
Universalist, ...	1877	Church	1832–1885	Good

¹ The later records are in good condition, and the earlier records, which were not in good condition, have been copied.

² The church records from 1794 to 1837 were destroyed.

³ Attended from Saint Patrick's at South Lawrence.

⁴ Records of the proprietors of the church property, which contain also the parish records.

EXISTING CHURCHES: BY TOWNS — Continued.

COUNTY OF ESSEX — Continued.

CITIES, TOWNS, AND NAMES OF CHURCHES.	Date of Organ- ization	RECORDS		
		Kind	Years covered	Condition
Rockport,				
Baptist,	1808	Church	1808–1885	–
Congregational:				
First,	1755	Church	1755–1885	1_
Pigeon Cove,	1874	Church	1874–1885	Good
Methodist Episcopal,	–	Church and Parish	1808–1885	–
Roman Catholic:				
Saint Joachim's,	–	Church	1856–1885	Good
Universalist:				
First,	1842	Church	1821–1885	Good
Pigeon Cove,	–	Church	1869–1885	Good
Rowley,				
Baptist,	1830	Church	1830–1885	–
Congregational,	1639	Church	1666–1885[2]	Fair
		Parish	1639–1885	Fair
Universalist,	–	Church	1877–1885	Good
		Society	1858–1869	Good
SALEM,				
Baptist:				
Calvary,	1870	Church	1871–1885	Good
Central,	1826	Church	1826–1885	Good
First,	1804	Church and Parish	1804–1885	Good
Congregational:				
Crombie Street,	1832	Church	1832–1885	Good
		Parish	1832–1885	Good
South,	1735	Church	1774–1885	Good
Tabernacle,	1629	Church	1743–1885	–
Friends,	1677	3_	1677–1885	–
Methodist Episcopal:				
Lafayette Street,	–	Church	1847–1885	–
Wesley Chapel,	–	Church	1871–1885	Good
New Jerusalem,	–	Church and Parish	1869–1885	Good
Protestant Episcopal:				
Grace,	–	Church	1859–1885	Good
Saint Peter's,	–	Parish	1735–1885	4_
Roman Catholic:				
Immaculate Conception,	–	Church	1831–1885	Fair
Saint James's,	–	Church	1848–1885	–
Saint Joseph's,	–	Church	1873–1885	–
Second Advent,	–	Church	1850–1885	Good
Unitarian:				
First Congregational Society,	1629	Church and Society	1829–1885	Good
Independent Congregational in Barton				
Square,	1824	Parish	1824–1885	Good
Second,	1717	Parish	1846–1885	Good
The North Society,	1772	Church and Parish[5]	1772–1885	Good
Universalist,	1810	Church	1805–1885	–
Salisbury,				
Baptist:				
Salisbury and Amesbury,	1780	Church	1780–1885	Good

[1] The records prior to 1805 are incomplete; since 1805 they are good.

[2] The church records prior to 1666 were burned.

[3] The records are included in the Salem Monthly Meeting records. Meetings of Friends were held as early as 1658.

[4] The records from 1735 to 1835 are incomplete; from 1835 to 1885 they are good.

[5] The records of the First Church, from which the North Church was formed, are included in these records.

EXISTING CHURCHES: By Towns — Continued.

COUNTY OF ESSEX — Concluded.

CITIES, TOWNS, AND NAMES OF CHURCHES.	Date of Organ-ization	RECORDS Kind	RECORDS Years covered	RECORDS Condition
Salisbury — Con.				
Christian Connection,	–	Church	1825–1885	Good
Congregational:				
Rocky Hill,	1718	Church	1718–1885	Good
Union,	1835	Church	1835–1885	Good
Methodist Episcopal:				
East Parish,	–	Parish	1793–1885	Good
Pond Street,	–	Church	1847–1885	Good
Universalist,	–	Church	1826–1885	Good
Saugus,				
Congregational:				
Saugus Centre,	1732	Parish	1739–1885	Good
Methodist Episcopal:				
Cliftondale,	–	Church	1854–1885	Good
East Saugus,	– {	Church / Parish	1863–1885 / 1822–1885	Good / Good
Saugus,	–	Church	1877–1885	Good
Universalist,[1]	1876	Parish	1738–1885	Good
Swampscott,				
Baptist,	1872	Society	1875–1885	–
Congregational:				
First,	1846 {	Church / Parish	1846–1885[2] / 1846–1885[3]	Good / Good
Disciples of Christ,	–	Church	1865–1885	Good
Methodist Episcopal,	–	Church	1854–1885	Fair
Roman Catholic,[4]	–	–	–	–
Topsfield,				
Congregational,	1663 }	Church / Parish	1663–1885 / 1824–1885	Good / Good
Methodist Episcopal,	–	Church	1824–1885	Good
Wenham,				
Baptist,	1831 {	Church and Parish	1831–1885	Good
Congregational,	1644 {	Church[5] / Parish	1682–1885 / 1833–1885	Good / Good
West Newbury,				
Baptist,	1867	Church	1867–1878	Good
Congregational:				
First,	1698	Church	1698–1885	Good
Second,[6]	1731 }	Church / Parish	1731–1885 / 1731–1885	Good / Good
Roman Catholic:				
Saint Ann's,[7]	–	–	–	–

[1] From 1738 to 1832 this church was Congregational, since which time it has been Universalist. It was reorganized in 1876.

[2] The records for 1867 and 1868 are omitted.

[3] The records for 1872, 1873, and 1874 are omitted.

[4] Attended from Saint Joseph's at Lynn.

[5] A copy of the private record kept by Rev. John Fiske, pastor of the church from 1644 to 1655, is in possession of the Town Clerk.

[6] Organized in 1731 as the Fourth Church of Newbury; in 1764 name changed to Third Church of Newbury; in 1819, when the town of Newbury was divided, the name was changed to West Church in West Newbury, and in 1821 name changed to Second Church in West Newbury, its present name.

[7] Attended from Georgetown.

EXISTING CHURCHES : BY TOWNS — Continued.

COUNTY OF FRANKLIN.

CITIES, TOWNS, AND NAMES OF CHURCHES.	Date of Organization	RECORDS		
		Kind	Years covered	Condition
Ashfield,				
Baptist, ...	1867	Church	1867–1885	Good
Congregational, ...	1763 {	Church Parish	1763–1885 1820–1885	Good[1] Good
Protestant Episcopal:				
Saint John's, ...	–	Church	1830–1885	–
Bernardston,				
Baptist, ...	1808	Church	1808–1885	Good
Congregational, ...	1824	Church	1833–1885	–
Methodist Episcopal, ...	–	Parish	1857–1873[2]	–
Unitarian:				
First Congregational, ...	1741	Parish	1817–1885	Good
Universalist,[3]	1872 {	Society Society	1820–1839 1845–1885	Good Good
Buckland,				
Congregational, ...	1785 {	Church and Parish	1820–1885	Good
Methodist Episcopal, ...	–	Church	1849–1885	Good
Charlemont,				
Baptist, ...	–	Church	1767–1885	Good
Congregational:				
East Charlemont, ...	1845	Church	1840–1885	Good
First, ...	1788	Church	1791–1885	Good
Methodist Episcopal, ...	–	Church	1831–1885	Good
Unitarian:				
Unitarian Congregational Society, .	–	Society	1826–1885	Incomplete[4]
Colrain,				
Baptist:				
First, ...	– {	Church Society	1780–1885 1818–1867	–
Second, ...	–	Church	1803 [4]–	Incomplete[4]
Congregational, ...	1750	Church	1820–1885	Good
Methodist Episcopal:				
Colrain, ...	–	Church	1833–1885	Good
East Colrain, ...	–	Church	1830–1885	Fair
Conway,				
Baptist, ...	1820 {	Church Parish	1820–1885 1843–1885	Good Good
Congregational, ...	1768 {	Church and Parish	1833–1885	Good
Methodist Episcopal, ...	–	Church	1871–1885	Good
Roman Catholic, ...	–	Church	1883–1885	Good
Deerfield,				
Congregational:				
Orthodox, ...	1835 {	Church Parish	1835–1885 1838–1885	Good Good
South Deerfield, ...	1818 {	Church and Parish	1818–1885	Good
Methodist Episcopal:				
South Deerfield, ...	–	Church	1849–1885	Good
Roman Catholic,[5]	–	–	–	–
Unitarian:				
First Congregational, ...	1688 {	Church and Parish	1820–1885	Good

[1] The first eight pages of the first volume are missing.
[2] The parish records prior to 1857 were burned.
[3] Originally organized in 1820 as The First Restoration Society.
[4] Some of the records were burned.
[5] Attended from Greenfield.

EXISTING CHURCHES: BY TOWNS — Continued.

COUNTY OF FRANKLIN — Continued.

CITIES, TOWNS, AND NAMES OF CHURCHES.	Date of Organ- ization	RECORDS		
		Kind	Years covered	Condition
Erving,				
Baptist, ...	1880	Church	1880–1885	–
Congregational:				
Evangelical, ...	1832	Church	1832–1885	Good
Gill,				
Congregational, ...	1796	Church	1806–1885	Good
Methodist Episcopal, ...	– {	Society Pastor's	1827–1885 1866–1885	Fair –
Greenfield,				
Baptist, ...	1852 {	Church and Parish	1852–1885	Fair
Congregational:				
First, ...	1754 {	Church Parish	1813–1885 1817–1885	Incomplete Good
Second, ...	1817	Parish	1862–1885[1]	–
Evangelical Lutheran:				
German, ...	1877	Church	1877–1885	–
Methodist Episcopal, . . .	–	Church	1831–1885	Good
Protestant Episcopal:				
Saint James's, ...	–	Church	1812–1885	Good
Roman Catholic:				
Holy Trinity, ...	–	Church	1868–1885	Good
Unitarian:				
Third Congregational, . . .	1825	Church	1825–1885	Good
Hawley,				
Congregational:				
First (East Hawley), ...	1778 {	Church Parish	1778–1885[2] 1824–1885	Good Good
West Hawley, ...	1825	Church	1824–1885	Good
Heath,				
Congregational, ...	1785 {	Church Parish	1785–1885 1825–1885	Good Good
Methodist Episcopal, ...	1859	Church	–	–
Leverett,				
Baptist:				
North Leverett, ...	–	Church	1767–1885	Fair
Congregational, ...	1784	Church	1784–1885	Fair
Leyden,				
Methodist Episcopal, ...	–	Church	1860–1885	Good
Universalist, ...	–	Church	1867–1885	Good
Monroe,				
Baptist, ...	1884	Church	1884–1885	–
Montague,				
Baptist (Turner's Falls), . . .	1872	Church	1872–1885	–
Congregational:				
First, ...	1752	Church	1828–1885	Good
Miller's Falls, ...	1872	Church	1870–1885	–
Turner's Falls, ...	1875	Church	1875–1885	Good
German Congregational (Turner's Falls),	–	Church	1879–1885	–
German Methodist Episcopal, . . .	–	Church	1872–1885	–

[1] The records from 1817 to 1862 are missing.   [2] The church records from 1798 to 1803 are lost.

EXISTING CHURCHES: BY TOWNS — Continued.

COUNTY OF FRANKLIN — Continued.

CITIES, TOWNS, AND NAMES OF CHURCHES.	Date of Organization	RECORDS		
		Kind	Years covered	Condition
Montague — Con.				
Roman Catholic:				
French, ...	–	Church	1884–1885	Good
Saint Mary's (Turner's Falls), . .	1872	Church	1872–1885	Good
Unitarian:				
Second Congregational Society, . .	1825	Church	1825–1885	Good
Unitarian Society of Turner's Falls, .	1873	Church	1873–1885	Good
New Salem,				
Congregational, ...	1845	Church	1779–1885	Good[1]
Unitarian:				
Congregational Society, . .	1742	Parish[2]	1742–1885	Fair
Northfield,				
Congregational, ...	1825 }	Church / Parish	1825–1885 / 1825–1885	Good / –
Unitarian:				
First Congregational Society, . .	1718	Parish	1826–1885	Good
Orange,				
Baptist, ...	1870	Church	1870–1885	Complete
Congregational:				
Central, ...	1846 }	Church and Parish	1846–1885	Complete
North Orange, ...	1843	Church	1843–1885	Good
Methodist Episcopal, ...	–	Church	1875–1885	Good
Roman Catholic, ...	–	Church	1882–1885	Good
Universalist:				
North Orange, ...	1878 }	Church and Parish	1878–1885	Complete
Orange, ...	1858 }	Church and Parish	1851–1885	Good
Rowe,				
Baptist, ...	1810	Church	1810–1885	Good
Methodist Episcopal, ...	–	Church	1840–1885	Fair
Unitarian:				
First Congregational, ...	1780	Parish	1804–1885	Good
Shelburne,				
Baptist:				
Shelburne Falls, ...	1833	Church	1833–1885	–
Congregational:				
First, ...	1770	Church	1770–1885	–
Shelburne Falls, . . .	1850	Church	1846–1885	–
Methodist Episcopal:				
Shelburne Falls, ...	–	Church	1870–1885	[3]–
Protestant Episcopal:				
Emmanuel Memorial (Shelburne Falls),	–	Parish	1882–1885	Good
Roman Catholic:				
Shelburne Falls, ...	–	Church	1884–1885	–
Universalist:				
Shelburne Falls, ...	1864	Church	1867–1885	Good
Shutesbury,				
Baptist, ...	1778	Church	1835–1885	Good
Congregational, ...	1742	Church	1804–1885	Good

[1] There are partial records also from 1756 to 1779, in poor condition.

[2] There are also records kept by pastors which commence earlier than the parish records.

[3] The earlier records are incomplete.

EXISTING CHURCHES : BY TOWNS — Continued.

COUNTY OF FRANKLIN — Concluded.

CITIES, TOWNS, AND NAMES OF CHURCHES.	Date of Organ- ization	RECORDS		
		Kind	Years covered	Condition
Sunderland,				
Baptist, ...	1822	Church	1820–1885	Good
Congregational, ...	1718 {	Church[1] Parish	1718–1885 1832–1885	Good Good
Warwick,				
Baptist, ...	1843	Church	1843–1885	Good
Congregational : Trinitarian, ...	1829	Parish	1829–1885	Good
Unitarian : First Congregational Parish, . .	1763	Church	1760–1885	Good
Wendell,				
Baptist, ...	1799	Church	1797–1885	Good
Congregational : First (Wendell Centre), . . .	1774	Church	1774–1885	Good
Whately,				
Congregational, ...	1771 {	Church Parish	1771–1885 1828–1885	Good Good

COUNTY OF HAMPDEN.

Agawam,				
Baptist, ...	1790	Church	1790–1885	–
Congregational : Agawam, ...	1819	Church	1836–1885	–
Feeding Hills, ...	1762 {	Church and Parish	1758–1885[2]	–
Methodist Episcopal : Feeding Hills, ...	–	Church	1803–1885	Good
Blandford,				
Congregational, ...	1735	Parish	1799–1885	Good
Methodist Episcopal : Blandford, ...	–	Church	1814–1885	Good
North Blandford, ...	– {	Church Church Parish	1839–1866 1876–1885 1839–1885	– – –
Brimfield,				
Congregational :				
First, ...	1724 {	Church[3] Parish	1748–1885 1832–1885	– –
Second, ...	1879 {	Church Parish	1879–1885 1881–1885	Good Good
Chester,				
Congregational :				
First (Chester Centre), . . .	1769 {	Church Society	1852–1885 1811–1885	Good Good
Second (Chester Depot), . . .	1844 {	Church and Society	1844–1885	Good
Methodist Episcopal, ...	–	Church	1873–1885	Good
Roman Catholic,[4]	–	–	–	–

[1] Financial records of the church from 1716 to 1831 are in possession of the Town Clerk.

[2] The records from 1758 to 1836 are in possession of the Town Clerk.

[3] The church records prior to 1748 were burned.

[4] Attended from Westfield.

EXISTING CHURCHES: BY TOWNS — Continued.

COUNTY OF HAMPDEN — Continued.

CITIES, TOWNS, AND NAMES OF CHURCHES.	Date of Organ- ization	RECORDS		
		Kind	Years covered	Condition
Chicopee,				
Baptist :				
Central,	1835	Church	1835–1885	Good
First,	1828	Church	1828–1885	Good
Congregational :				
First,	1752	Church	1824–1885[1]	Fair
Second (Chicopee Falls),	1830	Church	1830–1885	Good
Third,	1834	Church	1834–1885	–
Methodist Episcopal :				
Chicopee,	–	Church	1839–1885	–
Chicopee Falls,	–	Church	1838–1885[2]	Good
Protestant Episcopal :				
Grace,	–	Church	[3]–	–
Roman Catholic :				
French,	–	Church	1876–1885	Good
Holy Name of Jesus,	–	Church	1842–1885	Good
Saint Patrick's (Chicopee Falls),	–	Church	1873–1885	Good
Unitarian :				
First Unitarian Society,	1841	Church	1842–1885	Good
Universalist,	1840	Church	1845–1885	Good
Granville,				
Baptist :			Church	1790–1791	–
East Granville,	1790	Church	1802–1816	–
		Church	1852–1885	–
Congregational :				
East Granville,	1747	Church[4]	1747–1885	[5]–
West Granville,	1781	Church and Parish	1781–1885	Complete
Methodist Episcopal,	1879	Church	1879–1885	–
Hampden,				
Baptist,[6]	1794	Church	1794–1885	Fair
Congregational,[7]	1785	Church	1788–1885	Good
Methodist Episcopal,	–	Church	1838–1885	Good
Holland,				
Congregational,	1765	Church	1765–1885	Good
HOLYOKE,				
Baptist :				
First,[8]	1803	Church	1803–1885	Good
Second,	1849	Church	1849–1885	Good
Congregational :				
First,	1799	Church	1799–1885	Good
		Parish	1827–1885	Good
Second,	1849	Church	1849–1885	Good
French Protestant,	1884	Society	–	–
German Reformed,	–	Church	1868–1885	Good
Methodist Episcopal,	–	Church	1853–1885	Good
Protestant Episcopal :				
Saint Paul's,	–	Church	1863–1885	Good
Roman Catholic :				
Precious Blood,	–	Church	1869–1885	Good
Sacred Heart,	–	Church	1878–1885	Good
Saint Jerome's,	–	Church	1854–1885	Good
Unitarian :				
Liberal Christian Congregational Society,	1874	Church	1874–1885	Good

[1] The records prior to 1824 are meagre. [2] The records prior to 1838 are incomplete.
[3] The records cover occasional years from 1846 to 1877.
[4] There is a private record kept by Rev. Mr. Cooley, in possession of John Gillett.
[5] The records prior to 1797 were poorly kept; since 1797 they are good.
[6] Called also South Wilbraham Baptist; formerly Monson and Wilbraham Baptist.
[7] Called also South Wilbraham Congregational.
[8] Formerly within the limits of West Springfield.

EXISTING CHURCHES: BY TOWNS — Continued.

COUNTY OF HAMPDEN — Continued.

CITIES, TOWNS, AND NAMES OF CHURCHES.	Date of Organ- ization	Kind	Years covered	Condition.
Longmeadow,				
Baptist:				
East Longmeadow, ...	1818	Church	1807–1885	Good
Congregational:				
East Longmeadow, ...	1829	Parish	1829–1885	Fair
Longmeadow, ...	1716	Parish	1820–1885	Good
Methodist Episcopal:				
East Longmeadow, ...	–	Church	1853–1885	Good
Roman Catholic:				
Saint Mary's,[1]	–	–	–	–
Ludlow,				
Congregational:				
Church of Christ, ...	1867	Church	1867–1885	Good
First, ...	1790	Church	1850–1885	Good
Methodist Episcopal:				
Ludlow Centre, ...	–	Church	1793–1885	Good
Monson,				
Congregational, ...	1762 {	Church	1807–1885	Good
		Parish	1830–1885	Good
Methodist Episcopal, ...	–	Church	1850–1885	Good
Roman Catholic:				
Saint Patrick's, ...	–	Church	1878–1885	Good
Universalist, ...	–	Church	1883–1885	Good
Montgomery,				
Congregational,[2]	1797	–	–	–
Methodist Episcopal, ...	–	Church	1847–1885	Good
Palmer,				
Baptist:				
Palmer, ...	1852	Church	1852–1885	Good
Three Rivers, ...	1825	Church	1825–1885	–
Congregational:				
First (Thorndike), . . .	1733	Church	1733–1885	Good
Second, ...	1847	Church	1847–1885	Good
Methodist Episcopal:				
Bondsville, ...	–	Church	1866–1885	Good
Palmer, ...	–	Church	1840–1885	Good
Roman Catholic:				
Saint Bartholomew's (Bondsville), .	–	Church	1876–1885	Good
Saint Mary's (Thorndike), . .	–	Church	1874–1885	Good
Saint Thomas's, ...	–	Church	1879–1885	Good
Universalist, ...	1876	Church	1875–1885	Good
Russell,				
Baptist, ...	1816	Church	1816–1885	Good
Methodist Episcopal, . . .	–	Church	1868–1885	Good
Southwick,				
Baptist, ...	1806	Church	1805–1885	Fair
Congregational, ...	1773	Church	1773–1885	[3]–
Methodist Episcopal, . . .	–	Church	1816–1885	[4]–
SPRINGFIELD,				
Baptist:				
First, ...	1811	Church	1819–1885	Good
State Street, ...	1864	Church	1864–1885	Good
Third, ...	1872	Church	1872–1885	Good

[1] Attended from West Springfield. [3] The records for some of the earlier years are missing.
[2] There are no services now held in this church. [4] The records from 1844 to 1858 are incomplete.

EXISTING CHURCHES: BY TOWNS — Continued.

COUNTY OF HAMPDEN — Continued.

CITIES, TOWNS, AND NAMES OF CHURCHES.	Date of Organ- ization	RECORDS		
		Kind	Years covered	Condition
SPRINGFIELD — Con.				
Congregational:				
First,	1637 {	Church and } Parish }	1735–1885	Fair
Hope,	1876	Church	1877–1885	Good
Indian Orchard,	1848	Church	1854–1885[1]	Good
North,	1846	Church	1846–1885	Good
Olivet,	1833	Church	1833–1885	Good
Sanford Street,[2]	1864	Church	1849–1885	Fair
South,	1842	Church	1842–1885	Good
Methodist Episcopal:				
Florence Street,	–	Church	1815–1885	Fair
Grace,	–	Church	1867–1885	Good
State Street,	–	Church	1823–1885	Fair
Trinity,	–	Church	1844–1885	Good
Union American,	–	Church	1865–1885	Good
New Jerusalem,	–	Church	1853–1885	Good
Protestant Episcopal:				
Christ,	–	Church	1821–1885	Good
Roman Catholic:				
Sacred Heart,	–	Church	1874–1885	Good
Saint Aloysius's (Indian Orchard),	–	Church	1874–1885	Good
Saint Joseph's,	–	Church	1876–1885	Good
Saint Matthew's (Indian Orchard),	–	Church	1868–1885	Good
Saint Michael's,	–	Church	1861–1885	Good
Second Advent,	–	Church	1860–1885	Good
Union Evangelical:				
Memorial,	–	Church	1865–1885	Good
Unitarian:				
Third Congregational Society,	1819	Church	1819–1885	Fair
Universalist:				
Saint Paul's,	1825	Church	1827–1885	Fair
Tolland,				
Congregational,	1797	Church	1853–1885[3]	–
Wales,				
Baptist,	1736	Church	1736–1885	–
Methodist Episcopal,	–	Church	1830–1885	–
Westfield,				
Baptist,	1833	Church	1833–1885	Fair
Congregational:				
First,	1679	Church	1679–1885[4]	Fair
Second,	1856 {	Church and } Society }	1856–1885	Good
Methodist Episcopal:				
Westfield,	–	Church	1835–1885	Good
West Parish,	–	Church	1795–1885	Good
Protestant Episcopal:				
Atonement,	–	Church	1873–1885	Good
Roman Catholic:				
Saint Mary's,	–	Church	1862–1885	Good
Second Advent,	–	Church	1869–1885	Good
Universalist,	–	Church	1853–1885	Good
West Springfield,				
Baptist,	1879	Church	1870–1885	–
Congregational:				
First,	1698 {	Church	1720–1885	–
		Parish	1707–1885	–

[1] The record for the year 1864 is omitted.

[2] Originally Methodist; reorganized as Congregational in 1864.

[3] Earlier records are known to be in existence but they are missing.

[4] From 1806 to 1870 the record is simply a list of officers and members.

EXISTING CHURCHES : BY TOWNS — Continued.

COUNTY OF HAMPDEN — Concluded.

CITIES, TOWNS, AND NAMES OF CHURCHES.	Date of Organ- ization	RECORDS		
		Kind	Years covered	Condition
West Springfield — Con.				
Congregational : — Con.				
Second (Mittineague), ...	1850 }	Church and } Parish	1850–1885	–
Park Street, ...	1871	Parish	1871–1885	–
Methodist Episcopal, ...	–	Church	1870–1885	–
Roman Catholic :				
Immaculate Conception, . . .	–	Church	1875–1885	–
Saint Thomas's (Mittineague),[1] . .	–	–	–	–
Wilbraham,				
Congregational, ...	1741 }	Church / Parish	1804–1885 / 1741–1885	– / –
Methodist Episcopal :				
Glendale, ...	– }	Church / Church	1875–1879[2] / 1882–1885	– / –
Wilbraham, . . o . . .	–	Church	1791–1885	–
Roman Catholic :				
North Wilbraham,[3]	–	–	–	–
Undenominational :				
Christian Union Society, . . .	–	Society	1868–1885	–
Grace Chapel Society, ...	–	Parish	1876–1885	–

COUNTY OF HAMPSHIRE.

Amherst,				
Baptist, ...	1832	Church	1827–1885	–
Congregational :				
College, ...	1826	Church	1826–1885	Good
First, ...	1739 }	Church and } Parish	1735–1885	Fair
Second (East Street), . . .	1782	Church	1782–1885	Good
North (North Amherst), . . .	1826	Church	1826–1885	Good
South Amherst, ...	1858	Church	1853–1885	Good
Methodist Episcopal :				
Amherst, ...	–	Church	1875–1885	Good
North Amherst, ...	–	Church	1844–1885	Good
Protestant Episcopal :				
Grace, ...	–	Church	1864–1885	Good
Roman Catholic :				
Saint Patrick's, ...	–	Church	1869–1885	4–
Belchertown,				
Baptist, ...	1795	Church	1795–1885	–
Congregational, ...	1737	Church	1834–1885	Good
Methodist Episcopal, ...	–	Church	1865–1885	–
Chesterfield,				
Congregational, ...	1764	Church	1828–1885	Good
Cummington,				
Congregational :				
East Cummington, . . .	1839	Church	1841–1885	–
West Cummington, o . . .	1840	Church	1840–1885	Fair
Universalist :				
West Cummington, ...	–	Church	1840–1885	Good

[1] Attended from Immaculate Conception at West Springfield.

[2] The records from 1869 to 1874 are in possession of the Town Clerk.

[3] Attended from Palmer.

[4] The records are incomplete and are being reviewed.

Existing Churches: By Towns — Continued.

County of Hampshire — Continued.

Cities, Towns, and Names of Churches.	Date of Organ- ization	Records		
		Kind	Years covered	Condition
Easthampton,				
Congregational:				
First, ...	1785	Church	1835–1885	–
Payson, ...	1852	Church	1852–1885	Good
Methodist Episcopal, ...	1867	1–	–	–
Protestant Episcopal:				
Saint Philip's, ...	–	Church	1871–1885	Good
Roman Catholic ·				
Immaculate Conception, . . .	–	Church	1871–1885	Good
Enfield,				
Congregational, ...	1790	Church	1828–1885[2]	Fair
		So. Parish of Greenwich	1787–1830	Fair
		Parish of Enfield	1830–1885	Fair
Methodist Episcopal, ...	–	Church	1849–1885	Well kept
Roman Catholic,[3]	–	–	–	–
Goshen,				
Congregational, ...	1780	Church	1828–1885	Fair
Granby,				
Congregational, ...	1762	Church	1820–1885	–
Greenwich,				
Congregational, ...	1749	Church	1760–1885	Good
		Parish[4]	1865–1885	Good
Hadley,				
Congregational:				
First, ...	1639	Church[5]	1766–1885	Well preserved
		Parish[5]	1852–1885	Well preserved
Second (North Hadley), . . .	–	Church	1854–1885	Incomplete
Russell, ...	1841	Church	1841–1885	Good
Hatfield,				
Congregational, ...	1670	Church[6]	1670–1885	Good
		Parish	1835–1885	Good
Huntington,				
Baptist, ...	1852	Church	1852–1885	Good
Congregational:				
First, ...	1778	Church	1778–1885	–
		Parish	1832–1885	Incomplete
Second, ...	1846	Church	1846–1885	Good
Middlefield,				
Baptist, ...	1817	Church	1817–1885	Fair
Congregational, ...	1783	Church	1783–1885	Fair

[1] There are no formal records.   [2] The records prior to 1828 are lost.

[3] Attended from Ware.

[4] The Town Clerk has parish records from 1749 to 1782.

[5] The church records prior to 1766 were burned in a fire which destroyed the house of the pastor in 1766; the parish records prior to 1852 were burned in a fire in the paper mill of Smith & Bell in 1852.

[6] There are no complete records prior to 1871.

EXISTING CHURCHES : BY TOWNS — Continued.

COUNTY OF HAMPSHIRE — Continued.

CITIES, TOWNS, AND NAMES OF CHURCHES.	Date of Organ- ization	RECORDS		
		Kind	Years covered	Condition
NORTHAMPTON,				
Baptist, ...	1826 {	Church	1826–1885	Good
		Parish	1847–1885	Good
Congregational :				
Edwards, ...	1833	Church	1832–1885	Good
First, ...	1661	Parish	1826–1885	Good
Florence, ...	1861	Church	1861–1885	Good
Free Congregational, ...	–	Church	1863–1885	Good
Methodist Episcopal :				
Florence, ...	–	Church	1871–1885	Good
Northampton, ...	–	Church	1842–1885	Good
Protestant Episcopal :				
Saint John's, ...	–	Church	1826–1885	–
Roman Catholic :				
Church of the Annunciation (Florence),	–	Church	1878–1885	Good
Saint Mary's, ...	–	Church	1846–1885	Good
Unitarian :				
Second Congregational, . . .	1825	Church	1825–1885	Good
Pelham,				
Congregational :				
Packardville, ...	1869	Church	1869–1885	–
Pelham, ...	1837	Church[1]	1862–1885	–
Methodist Episcopal, ...	–	Church	1831–1885	–
Plainfield,				
Congregational, ...	1786	Parish	1837–1885	Good
Prescott,				
Congregational, ...	1823	Church	1825–1885	–
Methodist Episcopal :				
North Prescott, ...	–	Church	1868–1885	Fair
Southampton,				
Congregational, ...	1743 {	Church	1743–1885	Good
		Parish	1832–1885	Good
Methodist Episcopal, ...	–	Church	1840–1885	Good
South Hadley,				
Congregational :				
First, ...	1733	Church	1733–1885	Fair
South Hadley Falls,[2] . . .	1824 {	Church and Society	1878–1885	Good
		Parish	1824–1885	Good
Methodist Episcopal :				
South Hadley Falls, ...	–	Church	1833–1885	Fair
Roman Catholic :				
Saint Patrick's, ...	–	Church	1877–1885	Well kept
Ware,				
Congregational :				
East Ware, ...	1826	Church	1826–1885	Good
First, ...	1751	Church	1751–1885[3]	–
Methodist Episcopal, ...	–	Church	1843–1885	Incomplete
Roman Catholic :				
Our Lady of Mount Carmel, . .	–	Church	1871–1885	Good
Saint William's, ...	–	Church	1860–1885	Good

[1] The church records prior to 1862 are lost; the parish records from 1738 to 1767 are in possession of the Town Clerk.

[2] Formed from the union of the Religious Society and Congregational Church of South Hadley Falls, and the First Congregational Church and Ecclesiastical Society of South Hadley Falls.   [3] The records from 1754 to 1759 are lost.

EXISTING CHURCHES : BY TOWNS — Continued.

COUNTY OF HAMPSHIRE — Concluded.

CITIES, TOWNS, AND NAMES OF CHURCHES.	Date of Organ- ization	RECORDS		
		Kind	Years covered	Condition
Ware — Con.				
Unitarian :				
First Unitarian Society, . . .	1846	Society	1846–1885	Good
Westhampton,				
Congregational, ...	1779 {	Church Parish	1779–1885 1828–1885	– Fair
Williamsburg,				
Congregational :				
First, ...	1771 {	Church Parish	1771–1885 1842–1885	Good Good
Haydenville, ...	1851 {	Church and Parish }	1851–1885	Good
Methodist Episcopal, ...	–	Church	1851–1885	–
Roman Catholic :				
Saint Mary's (Haydenville),[1] . .	–	–	–	–
Worthington,				
Congregational, ...	1771 {	Church Parish	1771–1885 1865–1885	Good Good
Methodist Episcopal :				
South Worthington, ...	–	Church	1863–1885	Good
West Worthington, ...	–	Church	1877–1885	Good

COUNTY OF MIDDLESEX.

Acton,				
Baptist :				
West Acton, ...	1846	Church	1846–1885	Good
Congregational, ...	1832	Church	1832–1885	–
Universalist :				
South Acton, ...	–	Parish	1866–1885	Good
West Acton, ...	1876	Church	1859–1885	Good
Arlington,				
Baptist, ...	1781	Church[2]	1781–1885	Good
Congregational, ...	1842 {	Church and Parish }	1842–1885	Good
Protestant Episcopal :				
Saint John's, ...	1875	Church	1875–1885	–
Roman Catholic :				
Saint Malachi's, ...	–	Church	1873–1885	–
Unitarian :				
First Congregational Parish, . .	1733 {	Church Parish	1739–1885 1732–1885	Good Good
Universalist, ...	1842	Church	1840–1885	Good
Ashby,				
Congregational, ...	1776 {	Church Parish	1776–1885 1834–1885	Good Good
Unitarian :				
First Parish, ...	1767 {	[3]– Parish	– 1841–1885	– Good
Ashland,				
Baptist, ...	1843	Church	1843–1885	Good
Congregational, ...	1835	Church	1835–1885	Good
Methodist Episcopal, ...	–	Church	1870–1885	Good
Roman Catholic :				
Saint Cecilia's, ...	–	Church	1884–1885	–

[1] Attended from Annunciation at Florence.   [2] The records are being copied.
[3] The pastor has private records from 1868 to 1885.

EXISTING CHURCHES : BY TOWNS — Continued.

COUNTY OF MIDDLESEX — Continued.

CITIES, TOWNS, AND NAMES OF CHURCHES.	Date of Organ- ization	RECORDS		
		Kind	Years covered	Condition.
Ayer,				
Baptist, ...	1851	Church	1851–1885	Good
Congregational, ...	1867	Church	1864–1885	Good
Methodist, ...	–	Church	1876–1885	–
Roman Catholic:				
Saint Mary's, ...	–	Church	1867–1885	Fair
Unitarian :				
First Unitarian Parish,[1] . . .	1864 {	Church and Parish }	1855–1885	Good
Bedford,				
Congregational, ...	1730 {	Church Parish	1730–1885 1832–1885	Good Good
Roman Catholic:				
Saint Michael's,[3]	–	–	–	–
Unitarian :				
First Parish, ...	1730 {	Church Parish	1730–1885 1730–1885	2_ 2_
Belmont,				
Congregational :				
Waverly, ...	1865 {	Church Parish	1868–1885 1861–1885	– –
Roman Catholic :				
Patronage of Saint Joseph,[4] . .	–	–	–	–
Unitarian :				
Christian Union Society, . . .	1882	Society	1882–1885	Good
Congregational Society, . . .	1856 {	Church Parish	1859–1885 1856–1885	Good Good
Billerica,				
Baptist :				
First, ...	1828	Church	1828–1885	Good
North Billerica, ...	– {	Church and Parish }	1869–1885	Good
Congregational, ...	1829 }	Church and Society }	1829–1885	Good
Roman Catholic :				
Saint Andrew's,[5]	–	–	–	–
Unitarian :				
First Congregational Society, . .	1663	Society	1663–1885	Fair
Boxborough,				
Congregational, ...	1784	Church	1783–1885	6_
Evangelical Congregational, . .	–	Church	1833–1885	Fair
Burlington,				
Congregational, ...	1735 {	Church and Parish }	1730–1885	Fair
CAMBRIDGE,				
African Methodist Episcopal :				
Saint Paul's, ...	–	Church	1873–1885	Good
Baptist :				
Broadway, ...	1865	Church	1865–1885	Good
Charles River, ...	–	Church	1870–1885	Good
First, ...	1817	Church	1817–1885	Good
Second, ...	1827	Church	1827–1885	Good
North Avenue, ...	1854	Church	1854–1885	Good
Old Cambridge, ...	1844	Church	1844–1885	Good
Union, ...	–	Church	1877–1885	–

[1] Name changed from South Groton Christian Union in 1864.

[2] The records from 1730 to 1796 are incomplete.

[3] Attended from Lexington.   [5] Attended from Lowell.

[4] Attended from Arlington.   [6] The earlier records are in very poor condition.

EXISTING CHURCHES: BY TOWNS — Continued.

COUNTY OF MIDDLESEX — Continued.

CITIES, TOWNS, AND NAMES OF CHURCHES.	Date of Organ- ization	Kind	Years covered	Condition
CAMBRIDGE — Con.				
Congregational:				
First (Cambridge), ...	1636	Church and Parish	1636–1885	[1]-
First (Cambridgeport), . . .	1827	Church	1827–1885	Good
North Avenue, ...	1857	Church and Society	1857–1885	Good
Pilgrim (Cambridgeport), . . .	1865	Church	1865–1885	Good
Wood Memorial (Cambridgeport),[2] .	1872	Church	1872–1885	Good
Methodist Episcopal:				
Grace Street, ...	—	Church	1873–1885	Good
Harvard Street, ...	—	Church	1823–1885	Good
North Avenue, ...	—	Church	1865–1885	Good
Trinity, ...	—	Church	1822–1885	Good
Protestant Episcopal:				
Ascension, ...	—	Church	1875–1885	[3]-
Christ, ...	—	Church	1862–1885	Good
		Parish	1870–1885	Good
Saint James's, ...	—	Parish	1865–1885	Good
Saint John's Memorial, . . .	—	Church	1868–1885	Good
Saint Peter's (Cambridgeport), . .	—	Church	1863–1885	Good
		Parish	1842–1885	Good
Roman Catholic:				
Sacred Heart of Jesus (East Cambridge), ...	—	Church	1842–1885	Good
Saint Mary's, ...	—	Church	1867–1885	Good
Saint Peter's, ...	—	Church	1842–1885	Good
Unitarian:				
Cambridgeport Parish, . . .	1809	Church and Parish	1808–1885	—
First Parish, ...	1636	Church	1696–1885[4]	Good
		Parish	1733–1771	Poor
		Parish	1782–1885	Good
Lee Street, ...	1846	Church and Parish	1846–1885	—
Third Congregational Society, . .	1827	Parish	1827–1885	Good
Universalist:				
First Universalist Society, . . .	1827	Society	1822–1885	Good
Second, ...	—	Church	1827–1885	Good
Third, ...	1872	Church	1872–1885	Fair
Carlisle,				
Congregational, ...	1830	Church	1830–1885	Good
Unitarian:				
First Religious Society, . . .	1780	Church	1842–1885	Good
Chelmsford,				
Baptist:				
Central, ...	1847	Church	1847–1885	Good
First, ...	1771	Church and Parish	1771–1885	Good
Congregational:				
Chelmsford Central, . . .	1876	Church	1876–1885	Well kept
Second (North Chelmsford), . .	1824	Church	1827–1885	Fair
Methodist Episcopal (West Chelmsford),	—	Church[5]	1870–1885	Good
Protestant Episcopal:				
Saint Ann's, ...	—	Parish	1875–1885	—
Roman Catholic:				
Saint John the Evangelist's,[6] . .	—	—	—	—
Unitarian:				
First Congregational, . . .	1655	Society[7]	1741–1885	Good

[1] The records from 1636 to 1696 and from 1829 to 1867 are incomplete.

[2] Originally incorporated in 1873 as Chapel Congregational Church.

[3] The records prior to 1882 are very meagre.   [4] The earlier church records are lost.

[5] A volume of the records of pastors from 1847 to 1870 was prepared in the latter year.

[6] Attended from Saint Patrick's at Lowell.

[7] There are private records kept by Rev. John Fiske, in possession of David Pulsifer of Boston.

Existing Churches: By Towns — Continued.

County of Middlesex — Continued.

Cities, Towns, and Names of Churches.	Date of Organization	Records		
		Kind	Years covered	Condition
Concord,				
Congregational: Trinitarian, ...	1826	Church	1826–1885	Good
Protestant Episcopal: Trinity, ...	–	Church	1884–1885	Good
Roman Catholic: Saint Bernard's, ...	–	Church	1868–1885	–
Unitarian: First Parish, ...	1636	Parish	1738–1885	Good
Dracut,				
Congregational: Central, ...	1847	Parish	1814–1885	Good
First Evangelical, ...	1721 {	Church	1765–1885	Good
		Society	1834–1885	Complete
Dunstable,				
Congregational, ...	1757 {	Church	1757–1885	–
		Parish	1830–1885	–
Universalist, ...	– {	Parish	1818–1843	Good
		Parish	1876–1885[1]	Good
Everett,				
Baptist, ...	1871	Church	1871–1885	Good
Congregational, ...	1861	Church	1861–1885	Good
Methodist Episcopal, ...	–	Church	1870–1885	Good
Universalist, ...	–	Church	1872–1885	Good
Framingham,				
Baptist: Framingham, ...	1826 {	Church and Parish	1812–1885	Good
South Framingham, ...	1854	Church	1855–1885	Good
Congregational: Edwards (Saxonville), ...	1835 {	Church	1835–1885	Good
		Parish	1827–1885	Good
Plymouth, ...	1701 {	Church and Parish	1830–1885	Good
South Framingham, ...	1873 {	Church and Society	1873–1885	Complete
Methodist Episcopal: Saxonville, ...	–	Church	1834–1885	Good
South Framingham, ...	1869	Parish	1869–1885	Good
Protestant Episcopal: Saint John's, ...	–	Parish	1860–1885	Good
Roman Catholic: Saint Bridget's,[2]	–	–	–	–
Saint George's (Saxonville), . .	–	Church	1840–1885	–
Saint Stephen's (South Framingham),	–	Church	1878–1885	Good
Unitarian: First, ...	1701	Parish	1840–1885	Good
Universalist: South Framingham, . . .	1878	Parish	1878–1885	–
Groton,				
Baptist, ...	–	Church	1832–1885	–
Congregational, ...	1664	Church	1825–1885	–
Protestant Episcopal: Saint John's Chapel, ...	–	Church	1884–1885	–
Unitarian: First Parish, ...	1655	Parish	1815–1885	–
Holliston,				
Baptist, ...	1860	Church	1860–1885	Good

[1] Reorganized in 1876.   [2] Attended from South Framingham.

EXISTING CHURCHES: BY TOWNS — Continued.

COUNTY OF MIDDLESEX — Continued.

CITIES, TOWNS, AND NAMES OF CHURCHES.	Date of Organization	RECORDS		
		Kind	Years covered	Condition
Holliston — Con.				
Congregational:				
First,	1728	Church	1728–1885	Good
Methodist Episcopal,	–	Church	1833–1885	Good
Roman Catholic:				
Saint Mary's,	–	Church	1870–1885	–
Hopkinton,				
Baptist,	1842	Church	1837–1885	Good
Congregational,	1724	Church	1724–1885	Complete
Methodist Episcopal,	–	Church	1835–1885	–
Protestant Episcopal:				
Saint Paul's,[1]	–	Church	1817–1885	–
Roman Catholic:				
Saint John the Evangelist's,	–	Church	1855–1885	Good
Hudson,				
Baptist,	1852	Church	1852–1885	Good
Methodist Episcopal,	–	Church	1865–1885	Good
Roman Catholic:				
Saint Michael's,	–	Church	1871–1885	Good
Unitarian:				
Union Society,	1860	Society	1865–1885	Good
Lexington,				
Baptist,	1834	Church	1830–1885	Good
Congregational:				
Hancock,	1868 {	Church and } Society	1868–1885	Good
Protestant Episcopal:				
Church of our Redeemer,	–	Church	1884–1885	Good
Roman Catholic:				
Saint Bridget's,	–	Church	1874–1885	Good
Unitarian:				
First Congregational Society,	1696	Society	1696–1885[2]	Good
The Church of the Redeemer (East Lexington),	1865	Church	1840–1885	Good
Lincoln,				
Congregational:				
First,	1747	Church	1830–1885	Good
Protestant Episcopal:				
Saint Ann's (South Lincoln),	–	Parish	1874–1885	Good
Unitarian:				
Unitarian Congregational Society,	1841	Parish	1841–1885[3]	–
Littleton,				
Baptist,	1822	Church	1822–1885	–
Congregational,	1840	Church	1840–1885	–
Unitarian:				
First Congregational Society,	1717	Society	1830–1885	–
LOWELL,				
Baptist:				
Branch Street,	1869	Church	1869–1885	Good
Fifth Street,	1874	Church*	1874–1885	Good
First,	1826	Church	1826–1885	Good
Worthen Street,	1831	Church	1831–1885	Good

[1] The church edifice was destroyed by fire in 1865, but the society retains its organization.

[2] There are omissions in the records at times when the society was without a pastor.

[3] The records for 1878, 1879, and 1880 are omitted.

EXISTING CHURCHES: BY TOWNS — Continued.

COUNTY OF MIDDLESEX — Continued.

CITIES, TOWNS, AND NAMES OF CHURCHES.	Date of Organization	RECORDS		
		Kind	Years covered	Condition
LOWELL — Con.				
Congregational :				
Eliot,	1830	Church	1830–1885	Good
First,	1826	Church	1826–1885	Good
French,	1877	Church and Parish	1877–1885	Good
High Street,	1846	Church	1845–1885	Good
		Society	1865–1885	Good
John Street,	1839	Church	1839–1885	Good
Kirk Street,	1845	Church	1845–1885	Fair
Pantucket,	1797	Church and Parish	1797–1885	Good[1]
Evangelical Lutheran :				
Swedish,	–	Church	1882–1885	–
Free Baptist :				
Chelmsford,	–	Church	1883–1885	–
First,	–	Church	1833–1885	Good
Mount Vernon,	–	Church and Society	1874–1885	–
Methodist Episcopal :				
Central,	–	Church	1854–1885	Good
Highland,	–	Church	1879–1885	–
Saint Paul's,	–	Church	1835–1885	Incomplete
Worthen Street,	–	Church	1841–1885	[2]–
Presbyterian :				
First,	1869	Church	1869–1885	Good
Primitive Methodist,	–	Church and Parish	1879–1885	Good
Protestant Episcopal :				
House of Prayer,	1877	Church	1877–1885	Good
Saint Anne's,	–	Church and Parish	1824–1885	Good
Saint John's,	–	Church and Parish	1860–1885	Good
Roman Catholic :				
Immaculate Conception,	–	Church	1868–1885	–
Saint Joseph's,	–	Church	1868–1885	–
Saint Patrick's,	–	Church	1836–1885	–
Saint Peter's,	–	Church	1842–1885	–
Unitarian :				
First Unitarian Society,	1830	Church	1829–1885	Good
Universalist :				
First,	1827	Church and Parish	1827–1885	Good
Second,	–	Church	1838–1885	Good
MALDEN,				
Baptist :				
Malden,	1803	Church	1803–1885	Good
Maplewood,	1871	Church	1820–1885	Good
Congregational :				
Faulkner Evangelical Union,	1882	Church	1882–1885	Good
First,	1649	Church	1770–1885	Good
Linden,	1876	Church	1876–1885	Good
Maplewood,	1874	Church	1874–1885	Good
Methodist Episcopal :				
Malden,	–	Church	1819–1885	Good
Maplewood,	–	Church	1859–1885	Good
Protestant Episcopal :				
Saint Paul's,	–	Church	1864–1885	Good
Saint Luke's (Linden),	–	Church	1883–1885	Good
Roman Catholic :				
Immaculate Conception,	–	Church	[3]–	–
Unitarian :				
First Congregational Unitarian Society,	1875	Church	1875–1885	Good
Universalist,	1826	Church	1828–1885	Good

[1] The records prior to 1847 are incomplete.

[2] The earlier records are in very poor condition.

[3] Records of marriages from 1861 to 1885, and of baptisms from 1868 to 1885.

EXISTING CHURCHES: BY TOWNS — Continued.

COUNTY OF MIDDLESEX — Continued.

CITIES, TOWNS, AND NAMES OF CHURCHES.	Date of Organ- ization	Kind	Years covered	Condition
Marlborough,				
Baptist, ...	1868	Church	1867–1885	Good
Congregational:				
Union, ...	1666	Church[1]	1700–1885	Fair
Methodist Episcopal, ...	–	Church	1854–1885	Good
Roman Catholic:				
Immaculate Conception, . .	1851	Church	1858–1885	Good
Saint Mary's, ...	–	Church	1870–1885	–
Unitarian:				
West Parish, ...	1806	Parish	1804–1885	Good
Universalist, ...	1866	Church	1863–1885	Good
Maynard,				
Congregational, ...	1852	Church	1851–1885	Good
Methodist Episcopal, ...	–	Church	1868–1885	Incomplete
Roman Catholic:				
Saint Bridget's,[2]	–	–	–	–
Medford,				
Baptist, ...	1841	Parish	1856–1885	Good
Congregational:				
Mystic, ...	1847	Church	1847–1885	Good
West Medford, ...	1872 }	Church and Society	1872–1885	Good
Methodist Episcopal:				
Medford, ...	–	Church	1872–1885	Good
West Medford, ...	–	Church	1872–1885	Good
Protestant Episcopal:				
Grace, ...	–	Church	1848–1885	Fair
Roman Catholic:				
Saint Joseph's, ...	–	Church	1883–1885	–
Unitarian:				
First Parish, ...	1713	Church	1712–1885	Fair
Universalist, ...	1834	Church	1831–1885	Good
Melrose,				
Baptist, ...	1856	Church	1856–1885	–
Congregational:				
Melrose, ...	1848 }	Church and Society	1848–1885	–
Melrose Highlands, . . .	1875 }	Church and Parish	1875–1885	Good
Methodist Episcopal, ...	–	Church	1813–1885	–
Protestant Episcopal:				
Trinity, ...	1857	Church	1857–1885	–
Roman Catholic:				
Saint Bridget's,[3]	–	–	–	–
Unitarian:				
Congregational Unitarian Society, .	1867	Parish	1867–1885	Good
Universalist, ...	1882 }	Church and Parish	1867–1885	Good
Natick,				
Baptist, ...	1849	Church	1865–1885	Good
Congregational:				
John Eliot (South Natick), . . .	1859	Church	1859–1885	Good
Natick, ...	1802 }	Church Parish	4– 1820–1885	–
Methodist Episcopal, ...	–	Church	1865–1885[5]	–
Protestant Episcopal:				
Saint Paul's, ...	–	Parish	1871–1885	Good

[1] There are private records kept by Rev. S. A. Houghton, Berlin.

[2] Attended from Concord.

[3] Attended from Stoneham.

[4] The first volume of church records is missing.

[5] The records from 1836 to 1865 are lost.

EXISTING CHURCHES: BY TOWNS — Continued.

COUNTY OF MIDDLESEX — Continued.

CITIES, TOWNS, AND NAMES OF CHURCHES.	Date of Organ- ization	RECORDS		
		Kind	Years covered	Condition
Natick — Con.				
Roman Catholic:				
Sacred Heart (South Natick),[1]	–	–	–	–
Saint Patrick's,	–	Church	1861–1885	Good
Unitarian:				
First Unitarian Parish (South Natick),	1828	Church	1830–1885	Good
Universalist,	1882	Parish	1876–1885	Good
NEWTON,				
Baptist:				
Myrtle (West Newton),	1874	Church	1880–1885[2]	Good
Newton,	–	Church	1863–1885	Good
Newton Centre,	1780	Church	1780–1885	Good[3]
Second (Newton Upper Falls),	1835	Church	1835–1885	Good
West Newton,	–	Church	1866–1885	Good
Congregational:				
Auburndale,	1850	Church	1850–1885	Good
Eliot,	1845	Church / Parish	1845–1885 / 1844–1885	Good
First (Newton Centre),	1664	Church and Parish	1770–1885[4]	Good
Newton Highlands,	1872	Church	1872–1885	Well kept
Newtonville,	1868	Church	1868–1885	Good
North Village,	1866	Church and Society	1866–1885	–
Second (West Newton),	1781	Church	1778–1885	Well preserved
Methodist Episcopal:				
Newton,	1863	Church	1863–1885	Good
Newton Centre,	–	Church	1880–1885	Good
Newton Lower Falls,	–	Church	1861–1885	–
Newton Upper Falls,	–	Church	1828–1885	Good
Newtonville,	–	Church	1870–1885	Good
New Jerusalem,	1869	Church	1857–1885	Good
Protestant Episcopal:				
Grace,	–	Church and Parish	1855–1885	Good
Messiah (Auburndale),	–	Church	1871–1885	Good
Saint Mary's (Newton Lower Falls),	–	Church	1872–1885	Good
Roman Catholic:				
Our Lady, Help of Christians,	–	Church	1868–1885	Good
Saint Bernard's (West Newton),	–	Church	1876–1885	Good
Saint Mary's (Newton Upper Falls),	–	Church	1870–1885	Good
Unitarian:				
Channing Religious Society,	1851	Church	1851–1885	Good
First Unitarian Society,	1848	Society	1854–1885	Good
Unitarian Society (Newton Centre),	1877	Society	–	–
Universalist,	1873	Church	1872–1885	Good
North Reading,				
Baptist,	1817	Church	1817–1885	Fair
Congregational,	1720	Church	1802–1885	Good
Methodist Episcopal,	–	Church	1880–1885	Good
Universalist,	–	Parish	1713–1885	Fair
Pepperell,				
Congregational,	1747	Church / Parish	– / 1832–1885	–
Methodist Episcopal (East Pepperell),	–	Church	1866–1885	–
Roman Catholic:				
Saint Joseph's,	–	Church	1885 –	Good
Unitarian:				
First Parish,	1747	Church / Parish	– / 1833–1885	–

[1] Attended from Natick. [2] The records from 1874 to 1880 are destroyed.
[3] The records of some of the meetings prior to 1830 are omitted.
[4] The records prior to 1770 were burned, but were partially restored from memory.

Existing Churches : By Towns — Continued.

County of Middlesex — Continued.

Cities, Towns, and Names of Churches.	Date of Organ-ization	Records		
		Kind	Years covered	Condition
Reading,				
Baptist, ...	1832	Church	1837–1885	Good
Congregational :				
Bethesda, ...	1849	Church	1849–1885	Good
Old South, ...	1770	Parish	1771–1885	Good
Methodist Episcopal, ...	–	Church	1869–1885	–
Presbyterian, ...	–	Church	1873–1885	Good
Roman Catholic :				
Saint Agnes's,[1]	–	–	–	–
Unitarian :				
Christian Union Society,[2] . . .	1869	Church	1869–1885	Good
Sherborn,				
Congregational, ...	1685 }	Church and Parish }	1830–1885	–
Unitarian :				
First Congregational, ...	1685 }	Church Parish	1734–1885 1685–1885	– –
Shirley,				
Baptist, ...	1853	Church	1852–1885	–
Congregational :				
Shirley Village, ...	1828	Parish	1846–1885	–
Unitarian :				
First Congregational Society, . .	1753	Church	1822–1885	–
United Society (Shakers), . . .	–	Society	1792–1885	Good
Universalist :				
Shirley Village, ...	– }	Church and Parish }	1812–1885	Good
Somerville,				
Baptist :				
Somerville, ...	1853	Church	1852–1885	Good
West Somerville, ...	1874	Church	1874–1885	Good
Perkins Street, ...	–	Church	1845–1885	Good
Congregational :				
Broadway, ...	1864	Church	1864–1885	Good
First, ...	1855	Church	1855–1885	Good
Prospect Hill, ...	1874	Church	1874–1885	Good
West, ...	1874	Church	1875–1885	Good
Free Baptist, ...	–	Church	1872–1885	–
Methodist Episcopal :				
Broadway, ...	–	Church	1873–1885	Good
Flint Street, ...	–	Church	1868–1885	Good
Park Avenue, ...	–	Church	1872–1885	Good
Union Square, ...	–	Church	1857–1885	Good
Protestant Episcopal :				
Emmanuel, ...	–	Church	1866–1885	Good
Saint Thomas's, ...	–	Church	1866–1885	Good
Roman Catholic :				
Patronage of Saint Joseph, . . .	–	Church	1869–1885	Good
Saint Ann's, ...	–	Church	1881–1885	–
Unitarian :				
First Congregational Society, . .	1846 }	Church and Parish }	1844–1885	Good
Universalist :				
Somerville, ...	1861	Church	1864–1885	Fair
Third (West Somerville), . . .	– }	Church and Parish }	1880–1885	Good

[1] Attended from Wakefield.

[2] This society was originally organized as Unitarian, April 2, 1827; in 1838 united with the Second Universalist Society of Reading, which had been organized a few years previously; in 1856 the Second Universalist Society was reorganized as the First Universalist Society of Reading, and in 1869 was again reorganized as Unitarian under its present name. Very meagre records prior to 1869 are in possession of the clerk of the present society.

Existing Churches: By Towns — Continued.

County of Middlesex — Continued.

Cities, Towns, and Names of Churches	Date of Organization	Records		
		Kind	Years covered	Condition
Stoneham,				
Baptist, ...	1870	Church	1868–1885	Good
Congregational, ...	1729 {	Church / Parish	1729–1885 / 1827–1885	Good / Good
Methodist Episcopal, ...	–	Church	1857–1885	Good
Roman Catholic: Saint Patrick's, ...	–	Church	1868–1885	Good
Unitarian: Christian Union, ...	1866	Church	1867–1885	Good
Stow,				
Methodist Episcopal: Rock Bottom,[1]	–	Church	1823–1885	Good
Unitarian: First Parish, ...	1700	Parish	1833–1885	Good
Sudbury,				
Congregational: Union, ...	1640	Church	1840–1885	–
Methodist Episcopal, ...	–	Church	1830–1885	–
Unitarian: First Congregational Society, . .	1636	Church	1785–1885	–
Tewksbury,				
Baptist (North Tewksbury), . . .	1843 {	Church and Society	1843–1885	Fair
Congregational, ...	1735	Church	1736–1885	Good
Roman Catholic,[2]	–	–	–	–
Townsend,				
Baptist (West Townsend), . . .	1827 {	Church / Society[3]	1827–1885 / 1818–1885	Good / Good
Congregational, ...	1734 {	Church and Parish	1830–1885	Good
Methodist Episcopal, ...	–	4–	–	–
Roman Catholic: Saint John's,[5]	–	–	–	–
Tyngsborough,				
Congregational, ...	1868	Church	1868–1885	Good
Unitarian: First Parish, ...	1755	Church	1834–1885	Good
Universalist, ...	1874	Church	1841–1885	Fair
Wakefield,				
Baptist, ...	1804	Church	1800–1885	Good
Congregational, ...	1645	Church	1722–1885	Good
Methodist Episcopal, ...	–	Church	1864–1885	–
Protestant Episcopal: Emmanuel, ...	–	Church	1870–1885	–
Roman Catholic: Saint Joseph's, ...	–	Church	1873–1885	Good
Universalist, ...	1843	Church	1843–1885	Good
Waltham,				
Baptist, ...	1852 {	Church and Society	1852–1885	Good
Congregational, ...	1820 {	Church / Parish[6]	1820–1885 / 1859–1885	Good / Good

[1] Originally the Methodist Religious Society of Marlborough.

[2] Attended by the Oblate Fathers.   [3] The society records from 1818 to 1827 are meagre.

[4] The only record extant is to be found in a history of Townsend.

[5] Attended from East Pepperell.   [6] The records are in possession of Charles Stickney.

EXISTING CHURCHES: BY TOWNS — Continued.

COUNTY OF MIDDLESEX — Continued.

CITIES, TOWNS, AND NAMES OF CHURCHES.	Date of Organ- ization	RECORDS		
		Kind	Years covered	Condition
WALTHAM — Con.				
Methodist Episcopal, .	1837	Church	1837–1885	Good
New Jerusalem, .	1869	Society	1860–1885	Good
Protestant Episcopal:				
Christ, .	–	Parish	1848–1885	Good
Roman Catholic:				
Saint Mary's, .	–	Church	1864–1885	Good
Unitarian:				
First Parish, .	1696	Church and Parish	1837–1885[1]	Fair
Universalist, .	1874	Church Society	1874–1885 1865–1885	Good Good
Watertown,				
Baptist, .	1830	Church	1830–1885	–
Congregational:				
Phillips, .	1855	Church	1855–1885	–
Methodist Episcopal, .	–	Church	1837–1885	Good
Protestant Episcopal:				
Mission, .	–	Parish	1883–1885	Good
Roman Catholic:				
Saint Patrick's, .	–	Church	1855–1885	Good
Unitarian:				
First Congregational Society, .	1630	Church Parish	1686–1885 1835–1885	– –
Wayland,				
Congregational, .	1828	Church Parish	1828–1885 1818–1885	Good Good
Methodist Episcopal:				
Cochituate, .	–	Church	1880–1885[2]	Fair
Unitarian:				
First, .	1722	Church[3] Parish	1803–1885 1834–1885	– –
Westford,				
Congregational, .	1828	Church Parish Proprietors of Meet- ing House	1828–1885 1828–1885 1842–1885	Good Good Good
Methodist Episcopal:				
Graniteville, .	–	Church	1869–1885	–
Unitarian:				
First Congregational Parish, .	1727	Church Parish	1727–1885 1826–1885	– –
Weston,				
Baptist, .	1789	Church	1784–1885	Good
Methodist Episcopal, .	–	Church	1811–1885	Fair
Unitarian,				
First Parish, .	1698	Church and Parish	1709–1885	Good
Wilmington,				
Congregational, .	1733	Church Parish	1733–1885 1865–1885	Good Good
Methodist Episcopal, .	–	Church	1882–1885	–
Winchester,				
Baptist, .	1852	Church and Parish	1852–1885	Complete
Congregational, .	1840	Church and Parish	1840–1885	Complete
Methodist Episcopal, .	1872	Church	1872–1885	Complete

[1] The records prior to 1837 are in possession of the City Clerk.
[2] No records prior to 1880 have been preserved.
[3] There are private records in possession of Horace Heard.

EXISTING CHURCHES: BY TOWNS — Continued.

COUNTY OF MIDDLESEX — Concluded.

CITIES, TOWNS, AND NAMES OF CHURCHES.	Date of Organ- ization	RECORDS		
		Kind	Years covered	Condition.
Winchester — Con.				
Protestant Episcopal :				
Epiphany, ...	1884	Church	1884–1885	Complete
Roman Catholic :				
Saint Mary's, ...	1873	Church	1873–1885	Complete
Unitarian :				
The Winchester Unitarian Society, .	1865	Church	1865–1885	Complete
Woburn,				
Baptist, ...	1781	Church	1781–1885	–
Congregational :				
First, ...	1642	Church	1732–1885	–
North, ...	1849 {	Church	1849–1885	Good
		Parish	1849–1885	Good
Methodist Episcopal, ...	–	Church	1850–1885	Fair
Protestant Episcopal :				
Trinity, ...	–	Church	1867–1885	Good
Roman Catholic :				
Saint Charles's, ...	–	Church	1854–1885	Fair
Saint Joseph's (East Woburn),[1] .	–	–	–	–
Unitarian :				
First Unitarian Parish, ...	1847	Parish	1852–1885	Good

COUNTY OF NANTUCKET.

Nantucket,				
Baptist :				
First, ...	1839 {	Church	1840–1885	Good
		Parish	1839–1885	Good
Congregational, ...	1728	Church	1767–1885	Good
Friends :				
Nantucket Independent Meeting, .	1845	[2]–	1845–1885	–
Nantucket Meeting, ...	1708	[3]–	1708–1885	–
Methodist Episcopal, ...	–	Church	1815–1885	Good
Protestant Episcopal :				
Saint Paul's, ...	–	Parish	1846–1885	Fair
Roman Catholic :				
Our Lady of the Isle,[4] . . .	–	–	–	–
Unitarian :				
Parish of the Second Congregational Meeting House, ...	1808	Parish	1846–1885[5]	–

COUNTY OF NORFOLK.

Bellingham,				
Baptist :				
Bellingham, ...	1737	Church	1737–1885	Good
North Bellingham, ...	1867	Church	1867–1885	Good

[1] Attended from Winchester.

[2] The records are included in the Nantucket Independent Monthly Meeting records. The records of the original Nantucket Meeting from 1708 to 1845 are in possession of the Nantucket Independent Monthly Meeting.

[3] The records prior to 1845 are in possession of the Nantucket Independent Monthly Meeting; from 1845 to 1867 in possession of Matthew Barney ; since 1867 the records of business concerning the Nantucket Meeting are included in the New Bedford Monthly Meeting records.

[4] Attended from Wood's Holl.

[5] The records from 1809 to 1846 were destroyed in the fire of 1846.

EXISTING CHURCHES: BY TOWNS — Continued.

COUNTY OF NORFOLK — Continued.

CITIES, TOWNS, AND NAMES OF CHURCHES.	Date of Organ- ization	RECORDS		
		Kind	Years covered	Condition
Braintree,				
Congregational:				
First, ...	1707 {	Church	1825–1885[1]	Good
		Parish	1838–1885	Good
South Braintree, ...	1829 {	Church and Parish	1830–1885	Good
Methodist Episcopal:				
South Braintree, ...	–	Church	1874–1885	Good
Roman Catholic:				
Saint Francis's (South Braintree),[2] .	–	–	–	–
Brookline,				
Baptist, ...	1828	Church	1828–1885	–
Congregational:				
Harvard, ...	1844 {	Church and Parish	1844–1885	–
Methodist Episcopal, ...	1873	Church	1873–1885	Fair
New Jerusalem, ...	1857	Society	1857–1885	Incomplete
Protestant Episcopal:				
Church of our Saviour (Longwood), .	–	Church	1868–1885	Good
Saint Paul's, ...	–	Church	1861–1885	Good
Roman Catholic:				
Assumption, ...	–	Church	1852–1885	Good
Unitarian:				
First Parish, ...	1717	Parish	1834–1885	Good
Canton,				
Baptist, ...	1814	Church	1814–1885	Good
Congregational:				
Evangelical, ...	1828	Church	1828–1885	Good
Roman Catholic:				
Saint John's, ...	–	Church	1861–1885	Good
Unitarian:		Church[3]	1717–1799	Good
		Church	1808–1819	Good
First Congregational Parish, . .	1717 {	Church	1823–1848	Good
		Church	1853–1885	Good
		Parish[4]	1820–1885	Good
Universalist, ...	1853 {	Parish	1819–1830	Good
		Parish	1849–1885	Good
Cohasset,				
Congregational:				
Beechwood, ...	1863	Church	1863–1885	Good
Second, ...	1824 {	Church and Society	1824–1885	Good
Methodist Episcopal:				
Nantasket, ...	–	Church	1831–1885	[5]–
Unitarian:				
First Parish, ...	1721 {	Church and Parish	1721–1885	Good
Dedham,				
Baptist:				
East Dedham, ...	1843	Church	1843–1885	Good
West Dedham, ...	1824	Church	1824–1885	–
Congregational:				
First, ...	1638 {	Church	1820–1885	Good
		Parish	1822–1885	Good
Islington, ...	1880	Church	1874–1885	Good

[1] The earlier church records are supposed to have been burned.

[2] Attended from Quincy.

[3] The church has copies only of the records from 1717 to 1783. The original records from 1727 to 1783 are in possession of Charles F. Dunbar, Buffalo, N. Y.

[4] The first volume covering the years from 1726 to 1797 is lost.

[5] The records prior to 1844 are incomplete.

EXISTING CHURCHES : BY TOWNS — Continued.

COUNTY OF NORFOLK — Continued.

CITIES, TOWNS, AND NAMES OF CHURCHES.	Date of Organization	RECORDS		
		Kind	Years covered	Condition
Dedham — Con.				
Methodist Episcopal, ...	–	Church	1848–1885	Fair
Protestant Episcopal :				
Good Shepherd, ...	–	Church	1873–1885	Good
Saint Paul's, ...	–	Church	1874–1885	Good
Roman Catholic :				
Saint Mary's, ...	–	Church	1870–1885	Fair
Unitarian :				
First Parish, ...	1638 {	Church / Church	1638–1670[1] / 1724–1885	Good / Good
Third Parish (West Dedham), . .	1735	Parish	1737–1885	Fair
Dover,				
Baptist :				
Springdale, ...	1838	Church	1838–1885	–
Congregational :				
Second, ...	1839	Parish	1838–1885	–
Unitarian :				
First Parish, ...	1749	Parish	1832–1885	–
Foxborough,				
Baptist, ...	1817	Parish	1816–1885	Good
Congregational, ...	1779	Parish	1855–1885	–
Roman Catholic :				
Saint Mary's, ...	–	Church	1878–1885	Good
Universalist, ...	1865	Church	1809–1885[2]	–
Franklin,				
Baptist, ...	– {	Church and Parish	1872–1885	–
Congregational :				
Franklin, ...	1737 {	Church / Parish	1738–1885 / 1846–1885	– / –
South Franklin, ...	1855 {	Church and Parish	1855–1885	–
Methodist Episcopal, ...	–	Church	1854–1885	Good
Roman Catholic :				
Saint Mary's, ...	–	Church	1877–1885	Good
Universalist, ...	1859 {	Church / Parish	1859–1885 / 1856–1885	Good / Good
Holbrook,				
Baptist :				
Brookville, ...	1868	Church	1868–1885	Good[3]
Congregational :				
Winthrop,[4]	1856	Parish	1856–1885	Good
Methodist Episcopal, ...	1879	Church	1879–1885	Good
Hyde Park,				
Baptist, ...	1858	Church	1858–1885	Good
Congregational :				
Clarendon Hills, ...	1880	Church	1880–1885	Good
First, ...	1863	Church	1861–1885	Good
Methodist Episcopal, ...	–	Church	1870–1885	Good
Protestant Episcopal :				
Christ, ...	–	Church	1860–1885	Good
Roman Catholic :				
Most Precious Blood, ...	–	Church	1863–1885	Good
Unitarian :				
First Unitarian Society, . . .	1868	Church	1868–1885	Good

[1] A volume covering the years from 1670 to 1724 is lost.

[2] The records prior to 1809 were burned.

[3] The records from 1870 to 1873 are incomplete.

[4] Formerly the Second Congregational of Randolph.

EXISTING CHURCHES: BY TOWNS — Continued.

COUNTY OF NORFOLK — Continued.

CITIES, TOWNS, AND NAMES OF CHURCHES.	Date of Organization	RECORDS		
		Kind	Years covered	Condition
Medfield,				
Baptist, ...	1776	Church	1776–1885	–
Congregational:				
Second, ...	1828	Church	1828–1885	–
Roman Catholic,[1]	–	–	–	–
Unitarian:				
First Congregational Parish, . .	1650	Parish	1652–1885	–
Medway,				
Baptist:				
West Medway, ...	1832	Church	1819–1885	Good[2]
Congregational:				
Medway Village, ...	1838	Church and Parish	1838–1885	Good
Second (West Medway), . . .	1750	Church	1750–1779	Fair
		Church	1814–1885	Good
		Parish	1748–1885	Fair
Methodist Episcopal:				
West Medway, ...	–	Church	1857–1885	Good
Roman Catholic:				
Saint Joseph's, ...	–	Church	1863–1885	Good
Millis,				
Congregational:				
First Church of Christ in Medway, .	–	Church	1648–1885	Good
First Church of East Medway, . .	1714	Church	1714–1885	[3]–
Milton,				
Baptist, ...	–	Church	1882–1885	Good
Congregational:				
First, ...	1678	Church	1839–1885	Good
Second (East Milton), ...	1843	Church	1843–1885	Good
		Parish	1846–1885	Good
Unitarian:				
First Congregational Society, . .	1662	Church	1678–1885	Incomplete
		Parish	1818–1885	Good
Needham,				
Baptist, ...	1856	Church	1854–1885	Good
Congregational:				
Evangelical, ...	1857	Church	1857–1859	–
		Church	1872–1885	–
Methodist Episcopal:				
Highlandville, ...	–	Church	1865–1885	Incomplete
Unitarian:				
First Congregational Society, . .	1711	Church	–	–
		Parish	1778–1885	–
Norfolk,				
Baptist, ...	1843	Church	1842–1885	–
Congregational, ...	1839	Parish	1796–1885	Good
Norwood,				
Baptist, ...	1858	Church	1858–1885	–
Congregational,[4]	1736	Church	1736–1885	Good[5]
		Parish	1730–1885	Good[5]
Roman Catholic:				
Saint Catherine's,[6]	–	–	–	–
Universalist, ...	1857	Church	1827–1885	Fair

[1] Attended from Foxborough.

[2] The records from 1824 to 1830 are incomplete.

[3] The earlier records are partly illegible.

[4] Formerly the Second Parish in Dedham.

[5] With the exception of the first volume.

[6] Attended from Dedham.

EXISTING CHURCHES: BY TOWNS — Continued.

COUNTY OF NORFOLK — Continued.

CITIES, TOWNS, AND NAMES OF CHURCHES.	Date of Organization	RECORDS		
		Kind	Years covered	Condition
Quincy,				
Baptist:				
Quincy, ...	1867	Church	1867–1885	Good
Wollaston, ...	1871	Church	1871–1885	Good
Congregational:				
Evangelical, . . .	1832	Church	1841–1885	Good
Wollaston, ...	1876	Church	1876–1885	Good
Washington Street, . . .	1883	Church	1883–1885	Good
Methodist Episcopal:				
Wollaston, ...	–	Church	1874–1885	Good
West Quincy, ...	–	Church and Parish	1872–1885	Good
Protestant Episcopal:				
Christ, ...	–	Church	1728–1885	Good
Roman Catholic:				
Sacred Heart (North Quincy),[1] .	–	–	–	–
Saint John's, ...	–	Church	1843–1885	Good
Saint Mary's (West Quincy),[1] .	–	–	–	–
Unitarian:				
First Congregational Society, .	1639	Church[2]	1865–1885	Good
Universalist, ...	1833	Church	1831–1885	Good
Randolph,				
Baptist, ...	1819	Parish	1819–1885	Good
Congregational:				
First, ...	1731	Church and Parish	1728–1885	Good
Roman Catholic:				
Saint Mary's, ...	–	Church	1850–1885	Good
Sharon,				
Baptist, ...	1814	Church	1814–1885	Good
Congregational:				
First, ...	1740	Church	1821–1885	–
Roman Catholic:				
Saint Aloysius's Chapel,[3] . .	–	–	–	–
Unitarian:				
First Congregational Society, . .	1740	Church / Parish	1741–1885 / 1740–1885	Incomplete
Stoughton,				
Baptist:				
East Stoughton, ...	1780	Church	1785–1885	Good
Congregational:				
First, ...	1744	Parish	1743–1885	Good
Methodist Episcopal:				
North Stoughton, ...	–	Church	1817–1885	Good
Stoughton, ...	–	Church	1813–1885	Good
Roman Catholic:				
Immaculate Conception, . . .	–	Church	1858–1885	Good
Saint Michael's (East Stoughton),[4] .	–	–	–	–
Universalist, ...	1831	Church / Parish	1743–1885 / 1743–1885	Incomplete / Good
Walpole,				
Congregational:				
East Walpole, ...	1878	Church	1877–1885	–
Walpole, ...	1826	Church and Society	1826–1885	Good
Methodist Episcopal:				
First (South Walpole), . . .	–	Church	1850–1885	–
Walpole, ...	–	Society	1835–1885	Good

[1] Attended from Quincy.

[2] Edward W. Marsh has a copy of an incomplete record from 1688 to 1832 of the First Church of Braintree (now Quincy).

[3] Attended from Stoughton.   [4] Attended from Holbrook.

Existing Churches : By Towns — Continued.

County of Norfolk — Concluded.

Cities, Towns, and Names of Churches.	Date of Organ- ization	Records		
		Kind	Years covered	Condition
Walpole — Con.				
Roman Catholic :				
Saint Francis's, ...	–	Church	1873–1885	Good
Unitarian :				
First Congregational Society, . .	1730 {	Church Parish	1724–1885 1826–1885	Good Good
Wellesley,				
Congregational :				
Wellesley, ...	1798 {	Church Church	1798–1825 1833–1885	Good Good
Wellesley Hills,[1]	1847	Church	1873–1885	Good
Unitarian :				
Wellesley Hills,[2]	1871	Church	1871–1885	Good
Weymouth,				
Baptist, ...	1854 {	Church and Parish	1854–1885	Good
Congregational :				
East Weymouth, ...	1860	Church	1843–1885	Good
First, ...	1623	Parish	1724–1885	Good
Second (South Weymouth), . .	1723 {	Church and Society	1723–1885	Fair
Pilgrim (North Weymouth), . .	1852	Church	1851–1885	Good
Union (South Weymouth), . .	1842 {	Church and Society	1842–1885	Good
Weymouth and Braintree, . .	1811 {	Church Parish	1811–1885 1810–1885	Complete [3]_
Methodist Episcopal :				
East Weymouth, ...	–	Church	1822–1885	Good
Porter (East Weymouth), . .	–	Church	1878–1885	Good
Protestant Episcopal :				
Trinity, ...	–	Parish	1870–1885	Good
Roman Catholic :				
Immaculate Conception (East Wey- mouth), ...	–	Church	1882–1885	Good
Sacred Heart, ...	–	Church	1866–1885	–
Saint Francis Xavier's (South Wey- mouth),[4]	–	–	–	–
Saint Jerome's (North Weymouth),[5] .	–	–	–	–
Unitarian :				
First Unitarian Society, . . .	1873	Society	1873–1885	Incomplete
Universalist :				
First, ...	1840	Church	1836–1885	Good
Second (South Weymouth), . .	–	Society	1864–1885	Good
Third (North Weymouth), . .	–	Church	1858–1885	Good
Wrentham,				
Baptist, ...	– {	Church and Parish	1823–1885[6]	Fair
Congregational :				
First, ...	1692 {	Church[7] Society	1843–1885 1692–1885	Good Good
Latter Day Saints :				
Plainville, ...	–	Church	1876–1885	Good
Protestant Episcopal :				
Trinity, ...	–	Church	1864–1885	Good
Roman Catholic,[8]	–	–	–	–
Universalist :				
West Wrentham, ...	–	Society	1845–1885	Good

[1] Called also the Grantville Congregational.
[2] Called also the Grantville Unitarian.
[5] Attended from East Weymouth.
[6] The church records prior to 1823 were burned.
[7] The church records prior to 1843 are supposed to have been destroyed.
[8] Attended from Franklin.
[3] The first volume is lost.
[4] Attended from Weymouth.

EXISTING CHURCHES: BY TOWNS — Continued.

COUNTY OF PLYMOUTH.

CITIES, TOWNS, AND NAMES OF CHURCHES.	Date of Organ- ization	Kind	Years covered	Condition
Abington,				
Congregational:				
First,	1712 {	Church	1720–1885	Good
		Parish	1832–1885	Good
Fourth (North Abington),	1839 {	Church and Parish	1839–1885	Good
New Jerusalem,	1835	Society	1833–1885	Good
Roman Catholic:				
Saint Bridget's,	–	Church	1864–1885	–
Universalist:				
First,	1863	Church	1836–1885	Good
Bridgewater,				
Congregational:				
Bridgewater,	1821	Church	1821–1885	Good
Scotland,	1836	Church	1836–1885	Good
Methodist Episcopal,	1874	Church	1874–1885	Good
New Jerusalem,	1833	Church	1833–1885	Good
Protestant Episcopal:				
Trinity,	1747	Church	1747–1885	Good
Roman Catholic:				
Saint Thomas Aquinas's,	1855	Church	1855–1885	Good
Unitarian:				
First Congregational Society,	1716	Society	1716–1885[1]	Good
BROCKTON,				
Baptist:				
Brockton,	1877	Church	1876–1885	Good
Swedish (Campello),	–	Church	1883–1885	Good
Congregational:				
Campello,	1837	Church	1837–1885	Good
First,	1740	Church[2]	1737–1885	–
Porter Evangelical Society,	1850	Society	1850–1885	Good
Evangelical Independent:				
Swedish (Campello),	–	Church	1881–1885	Good
Evangelical Lutheran:				
Swedish (Campello),	–	Church	1867–1885	Good
Free Baptist,	–	Church	1884–1885	Good
Latter Day Saints,	–	Church	1880–1885	–
Methodist Episcopal:				
Campello,	–	Church	1879–1885	Good
Central,	–	Church	1851–1885	–
West,	–	Church	1831–1885	Good
New Jerusalem,	1838	Church	1832–1885	Good
Protestant Episcopal:				
Saint Paul's,	–	Church	1875–1885	Good
Roman Catholic:				
Saint Paul's,	–	Church	1856–1885	Good
Unitarian:				
Unity,	1881	Parish	1881–1885	Good
Universalist,	–	Parish	1884–1885	Good
Carver,				
Baptist,	1791 {	Church 3_	1789–1885	–
			1823–1885	–
Congregational:				
North Carver,	1733 {	Church 3_	1780–1885	Good
			1731–1885	Good
Methodist Episcopal:				
South Carver,	–	Church	1867–1885	Good
Second Advent:				
Advent Christian,	–	Church	1820–1885	–

[1] There is an interval in the records for about twenty years, the years not being specified.

[2] There are private records in possession of J. R. Perkins.

[3] Records of the proprietors of the church property.

EXISTING CHURCHES : BY TOWNS — Continued.

COUNTY OF PLYMOUTH — Continued.

CITIES, TOWNS, AND NAMES OF CHURCHES.	Date of Organization	RECORDS		
		Kind	Years covered	Condition
Duxbury,				
Congregational :				
Pilgrim, ...	1843	Church	1843–1885	–
Friends, ...	1702[1]	[2]–	1702–1885	–
Methodist Episcopal :				
West Duxbury, ...	–	Church	1868–1885	–
Unitarian :				
First, ...	1632 {	Church / Parish	1739–1885 / 1828–1885	Incomplete / Good
East Bridgewater,				
Congregational :				
Union, ...	1826 {	Church and Parish	1826–1885	Good
Methodist Episcopal, ...	–	Church	1857–1885	Fair
New Jerusalem, ...	1838 {	Church and Parish	1838–1885	Good
Roman Catholic :				
Saint John's,[3]	–	–	–	–
Unitarian :				
First Parish, ...	1724 {	Church and Parish	1724–1885	Good
Halifax,				
Congregational, ...	1734	Parish	1824–1885	Good
Hanover,				
Baptist, ...	1806 {	Church / Parish	1806–1885 / 1843–1885	Good / Good
Congregational :				
First, ...	1728 {	Church / Parish	1728–1885 / 1807–1885	Good / Good
Second (Four Corners), . . .	1854 {	Church and Parish	1852–1885	Good
Methodist Episcopal, ...	1850	Church	1849–1885	–
Protestant Episcopal :				
Saint Andrew's,[4]	– {	Church / Church / Parish	1782–1809 / 1819–1885 / 1780–1885	– / – / –
Roman Catholic :				
Our Lady of the Sacred Heart,[5] . .	–	–	–	–
Hanson,				
Baptist :				
South Hanson, ...	1806 {	Church and Society	1812–1885	Good
Congregational, ...	1748 {	Church / Society	1749–1885 / 1746–1885	Incomplete / Good
Hingham,				
Baptist, ...	1831 {	Church and Society	1828–1885	Good
Congregational :				
Evangelical, ...	1847 {	Church and Parish	1847–1885	Fair
Methodist Episcopal, ...	–	Church	1818–1885	Good
Protestant Episcopal :				
Saint John's, ...	–	[6]–	–	–

[1] This is the earliest date recorded, but meetings were undoubtedly held prior thereto.

[2] The records are included in the records of the Pembroke Monthly Meeting, which was attached to the New Bedford Monthly Meeting in 1876.

[3] Attended from Bridgewater.

[4] From 1731 to 1811, Saint Andrew's Church of Scituate.

[5] Attended from Rockland.

[6] There has been no parish organization and there are no records.

EXISTING CHURCHES : BY TOWNS — Continued.

COUNTY OF PLYMOUTH — Continued.

CITIES, TOWNS, AND NAMES OF CHURCHES.	Date of Organization	RECORDS		
		Kind	Years covered	Condition
Hingham — Con.				
Roman Catholic :				
Saint Paul's, ...	–	Church	1872–1885	Good
Unitarian :				
First Parish, ...	1635 {	Church and Parish }	1720–1885[1]	Good
Second Parish (South Hingham), .	1745	Parish	1745–1885	Good
Third Congregational Society, . .	1807	Parish	1807–1885	Good
Universalist, ...	1823	Parish	1861–1885	–
Hull,				
Methodist Episcopal, ...	–	Church	1816–1885	Good[2]
Kingston,				
Baptist, ...	1805	Church	1805–1885	Good
Congregational :				
Mayflower, ...	1828 {	Church and Society }	1828–1885	Good
Roman Catholic :				
Saint Joseph's,[3]	–	–	–	–
Unitarian :				
First Congregational Parish, . .	1717	Parish	1720–1885	[4]–
Lakeville,				
Congregational :				
Lakeville, ...	1725 {	Church	1724–1885	Good
		Parish	1719–1885	Dilapidated
Union Grove, ...	1877	Church	1877–1885	Good
Marion,				
Congregational, ...	1703	Church	1703–1885	Good
Methodist Episcopal, ...	1866	Church	1866–1885	Good
Universalist, ...	1828	Church	1844–1885[5]	Good
Marshfield,				
Baptist :				
Marshfield, ...	1788 {	Church	1788–1885	Good
		Society	1816–1885	Good
North Marshfield, ...	1833	Church	1833–1885	Good
Congregational :				
First, ...	1632 {	Church	1696–1885	Good
		Parish	1814–1885	Good
Second (East Marshfield), . .	1835	Church	1835–1885	Good
Friends, ...	1692[6]	[7]–	1692–1885	–
Methodist Episcopal, ...	1813	Church	1825–1885	Incomplete
Unitarian :				
Grace Chapel, ...	1882	Society	1882–1885	Good
Second Congregational Society, . .	1738	Parish	1738–1885	Good
Mattapoisett,				
Congregational, ...	1736 {	Church and Parish }	1736–1885	Good
Friends, ...	1702[8]	[9]–	1702–1885	–
Universalist, ...	1831	Church	1828–1885	Good

[1] The record kept by Rev. Ebenezer Gay, from 1718 to 1787, and by Rev. Henry Ware from 1787 to 1805, is in possession of the church.

[2] The records prior to 1860 were imperfectly kept.　　　[3] Attended from Plymouth.

[4] The records prior to 1784 are imperfect.　　　[5] The records prior to 1844 are lost.

[6] This is the earliest date recorded, but meetings were undoubtedly held prior thereto.

[7] The records are included in the records of the Pembroke Monthly Meeting, which was attached to the New Bedford Monthly Meeting in 1876.

[8] Originally set up as the Sippican Meeting; afterward the Rochester Meeting.

[9] The records prior to 1793 are included in the Sandwich Monthly Meeting records; since 1793 in the New Bedford Monthly Meeting records.

EXISTING CHURCHES : BY TOWNS — Continued.

COUNTY OF PLYMOUTH — Continued.

CITIES, TOWNS, AND NAMES OF CHURCHES.	Date of Organization	RECORDS		
		Kind	Years covered	Condition
Middleborough,				
Baptist :				
Central, ...	1828 {	Church	1800–1862	Incomplete
		Parish	1828–1885	Good
First, ...	1756	Church	1756–1885	Good
Third, ...	1761 {	Church and Society {	1795–1885	Good
Congregational :				
Central, ...	1847	Parish	1847–1885	Good
First, ...	1694	Parish	1694–1885	Good
North Middleborough, ...	1748	Parish	1743–1885	Complete
Methodist Episcopal :				
Middleborough, ...	–	Church	1865–1885	Good
South Middleborough, ...	–	Church	1858–1885	Good
Pembroke,				
Friends, ...	1708[1]	[2]–	1708–1885	Good
Methodist Episcopal :				
Bryantville, ...	–	Church	1825–1885	Fair
Unitarian :				
First, ...	1712	Parish	1764–1885	Good
Plymouth,				
African Methodist Episcopal, . . .	–	Church	1871–1885	Fair
Baptist, ...	1800	Church	1809–1885	Fair
Congregational :				
Fifth (Chiltonville), ...	1862	Church	1852–1885	Good
Fourth (Chiltonville), ...	1818	Church	1814–1885	Good
Pilgrimage, ...	1606 {	Church	1606–1885	Good
		Parish	1802–1885[3]	Fair
Second (South Plymouth), . . .	1738	Church	1747–1885	Good
Latter Day Saints :				
North Plymouth, ...	–	Church	1882–1885	Good
Methodist Episcopal, ...	1843	Church	1843–1885	–
Protestant Episcopal :				
Christ, ...	–	Church	1844–1885	Good
Roman Catholic :				
Saint Peter's, ...	–	Church	1876–1885	–
Unitarian :				
First Parish, ...	1620	Church	1620–1885	Incomplete
Universalist, ...	1827	Church	1826–1885	Fair
Plympton,				
Congregational, ...	1698	Church	1695–1885	Good
Rochester,				
Congregational :				
First (Rochester Centre), . . .	1703 {	Church	1798–1885	Good
		Parish	1780–1885	Good
North Rochester, ...	1753	Church	1877–1885[4]	Good
Rockland,				
Baptist, ...	1856	Church	1854–1885	Good
Congregational, ...	1813 {	Church	1812–1885	Good
		Parish	1812–1852[5]	Good
		Parish	1872–1885	Good
Methodist Episcopal, ...	–	Church	1832–1885	Good

[1] This is the earliest date recorded, but meetings were undoubtedly held prior thereto.

[2] The records are included in the records of the Pembroke Monthly Meeting, which was attached to the New Bedford Monthly Meeting in 1876.

[3] The records prior to 1802 are kept in Pilgrim Hall.

[4] The records prior to 1841 were burned.

[5] One volume covering the years from 1853 to 1871 was burned in the Boston fire in 1872.

EXISTING CHURCHES: BY TOWNS — Continued.

COUNTY OF PLYMOUTH — Concluded.

CITIES, TOWNS, AND NAMES OF CHURCHES.	Date of Organization	RECORDS		
		Kind	Years covered	Condition
Rockland — Con.				
Roman Catholic:				
Holy Family, ...	1883	Church	1883–1885	Good
Unitarian:				
The Unitarian Society of Rockland, .	1884	Parish	1884–1885	Good
Scituate,				
Baptist (North Scituate), ...	1825	Church	1825–1885	Good
Congregational, ...	1635	Church	1634–1885	Good
Methodist Episcopal, ...	–	Church	1821–1885	Fair
Roman Catholic:				
Church of the Nativity,' . .	–	–	–	–
Unitarian:				
First Parish, ...	1634	Parish	1695–1885	Good
Universalist:				
West Scituate, ...	– {	Society 2_	1812–1885 1772–1885	Good Good
South Abington,				
Baptist, ...	1822 {	Church and Parish	1822–1885	Good
Congregational, ...	1807	Church	1808–1885	Good
Methodist Episcopal, ...	–	Church	1874–1885	Good
Roman Catholic:				
Church of the Holy Ghost,[3] . .	–	–	–	–
South Scituate,				
Methodist Episcopal, ...	–	Parish	1852–1885	Good
Unitarian:				
First Parish, ...	1644 {	Church and Parish	1797–1885	Good
Universalist, ...	– {	Church and Parish	1863–1885	Good
Wareham,				
Congregational, ...	1793	Parish[4]	1739–1885	Good
Methodist Episcopal, ...	–	Church	1843–1885[5]	Good
Protestant Episcopal:				
Good Shepherd, ...	–	Church	1883-1885	–
Roman Catholic:				
Saint Patrick's,[6]	–	–	–	–
West Bridgewater,				
Baptist, ...	1833	Church	1833–1885	Good
Methodist Episcopal (Cochesett), . .	–	Church	1841–1885	–
Unitarian:				
First Congregational Society, . .	1651 {	Church Church Society Society	1721–1808 1836–1885 1726–1806 1821–1885	– – – –

COUNTY OF SUFFOLK.

BOSTON,				
[The churches in the outlying districts of Boston are given under the names of the several districts.]				
African Methodist Episcopal:				
First, ...	1818	Church	1857–1885	Fair
African Methodist Episcopal Zion, . .	–	Church	1836–1885	–

[1] Attended from Cohasset.
[3] Attended from Abington.
[4] The Town Clerk has records from 1830 to 1870.
[2] Records of the proprietors of the meeting-house.
[5] The records from 1826 to 1842 are lost.
[6] Attended from Sandwich.

EXISTING CHURCHES: BY TOWNS — Continued.

COUNTY OF SUFFOLK — Continued.

CITIES, TOWNS, AND NAMES OF CHURCHES.	Date of Organization	RECORDS		
		Kind	Years covered	Condition
BOSTON — Con.				
Baptist:				
Charles Street,[1]	1807	Church	1807–1885	Good
Clarendon Street,[2]	1827	Church	1827–1885[3]	Good
Day Star, ...	1878	Church	1876–1885	–
Ebenezer, ...	1873	Church	1871–1885	Good
First, ...	1664	Church	1665–1885	[4]–
First German, ...	1879	Church	1880–1885	Good
Harvard Street, ...	1839 {	Church	1839–1885	Fair
	{	Parish	1876–1885	Fair
Independent, ...	–	Church	1805–1885	Fair
Mariners, ...	1851	Church	1851–1885	Good'
Twelfth, ...	1848	Church	1848–1885	Fair
Union Temple, ...	1863	Church	1863–1885	Good
Warren Avenue,[5]	1743	Church	1863–1885[6]	Good
Catholic Apostolic, ...	–	Church	1864–1885	Good
Christian Connection:				
First Christian, ...	–	Church	1804–1885	–
Congregational:				
Berkeley Street,[7]	1827	Church	1831–1885	Good
Central,[8]	1835	Church	1841–1885	Complete
Independent, ...	–	Church	1845–1885	Good
Mount Vernon, ...	1842	Church	1843–1885	Good
Old South, ...	1669	Church	1669–1885	Good
Olivet, ...	1876	Church	1875–1885	Good
Park Street, ...	1809	Church	1835–1885	Good
Shawmut, ...	1845	Church	1845–1885	–
Union,[9]	1822	Church	1822–1885	Good
Evangelical Lutheran:				
Boston, ...	1839	Church	1845–1885	Good
Emmanuel (Swedish), . . .	– {	Church	1873–1885	Good
	{	Parish	1877–1885	Good
Norwegian, ...	–	Church	1884–1885	Good
Free Baptist:				
First, ...	–	Church	1844–1885	Good
Friends, ...	1870[10]	[11]–	1870–1885	–
German Reformed, ...	–	Church	1840–1885	Good[12]
Independent Baptist:				
Bowdoin Square, ...	1840	Church	1840–1885	Good
Jewish:				
Mishkan Israel, ...	1879	Society	1879–1885	Good
Ohabei Sholom, ...	1843	Society	1843–1885	Good
Shaare Tefillah, ...	1854	[13]–	–	–
Shomrai Beth Abraham, . . .	1868	Society	1868–1885	–
Temple Adath Israel, . . .	1842	[13]–	–	–
Zion's Holy Prophets of Israel, .	1878	[13]–	–	–
Messiah, ...	–	Society	1881–1885	Good
Methodist Episcopal:				
Bromfield Street,[14]	–	Church	1806–1885	Good
Morgan Memorial, ...	–	Church	1885 –	Good

[1] Formerly the Third Baptist.

[2] Formerly the Federal Street Baptist, and later the Rowe Street Baptist.

[3] The records which were commenced in 1827 pertain to matters in 1821.

[4] The earlier records are in poor condition and need copying.

[5] Formerly the Second Baptist.

[6] The records from 1743 to 1856 are in possession of the City Clerk.

[7] Prior to January 28, 1861, the Pine Street Congregational Society.

[8] Prior to 1841 the Franklin Street Church, the records of which are not accounted for.

[9] Called also the Essex Street.

[10] Originally set up in 1664; became extinct in 1808, and again set up in 1870.

[11] The records from 1870 to 1883 are included in the Salem Monthly Meeting records; since 1883 in the Boston Monthly Meeting records.

[12] The records prior to 1849 are imperfect.

[13] No records are kept.

[14] Formerly the Second Methodist Episcopal.

CITIES, TOWNS, AND NAMES OF CHURCHES.	Date of Organ- ization	RECORDS		
		Kind	Years covered	Condition
BOSTON — Con.				
Methodist Episcopal; — Con.				
People's,	–	Church	1834–1885	Good[1]
Revere Street,	1826	2–	–	–
Swedish,	–	Church	1882–1885	Good
Temple Street,[3]	1792	Church	1873–1885[3]	–
Tremont Street,	–	Church	1862–1885	Good
New Jerusalem,	1818	Church	1817–1885	4–
Presbyterian :				
First,	–	Church	1862–1885	Good
Saint Andrew's,[5]	1860	Church	1882–1885	Good
Protestant Episcopal :				
Advent,	–	Church	1844–1885	Good
Christ,	–	Society	1806–1885[6]	Good
Emmanuel,	–	Church	1860–1885	–
Good Shepherd,	–	Church	1877–1885	Good
Messiah,	1843 {	Parish	1871–1885	Good
	{	Treasurer's	1843–1885	Good
Saint Andrew's,	–	Church	1876–1885	Good
Saint John the Evangelist's,	–	Church	1883–1885	Good
Saint Mark's,	–	Church	1851–1885	Good
Saint Paul's,	–	Church	1820–1885	Good
Trinity,	–	Church[7]	1733–1885	Good
Reformed Episcopal,	–	Church	1882–1885	Good
Reformed Presbyterian :				
First,	–	Church	1854–1885	Good
Second,	–	Church	1871–1885	Good
Roman Catholic :				
Cathedral of the Holy Cross,	–	Church	1803–1885	–
Holy Trinity,	–	Church	1846–1885	Good
Immaculate Conception,	–	Church	1858–1885	Well kept
Notre Dame des Victoires,	–	Church	1880–1885	Good
Saint James's,	–	Church	1853–1885	Well kept
Saint John the Baptist's,	–	Church	1873–1885	Well kept
Saint Joseph's,	–	Church	1862–1885	Good
Saint Leonard of Port Maurice's,	–	Church	1873–1885	Good
Saint Mary's,	–	Church	1836–1885	Good
Saint Stephen's,	–	Church	1862–1885	–
Saint Thomas Aquinas's,	–	Church	1869–1885	–
Second Advent :				
Church of Christ,	–	Church	1866–1885	Good
Unitarian :				
Appleton Street Free Chapel,	1883	Church	1883–1885	Good
Arlington Street,[8]	1730	Church	1786–1885	Good
Church in Brattle Square,[9]	1699	Church[10]	1699–1840	–
Church of the Disciples,	1841	Parish	1841–1885	Good
Church of the Unity,	1857	Church	1857–1885	Good
Hollis Street,[11]	1732	Church	1730–1885	Good
King's Chapel,[12]	1686	Church	1686–1885	Good

[1] The records since 1853 are complete.

[2] All the records disappeared about 1881.

[3] Organized as the First Methodist Episcopal; since 1873 called also Grace Church. Two histories of the church have been written; one in manuscript is in possession of the Methodist Historical Society, and the other is in the church book. If the earlier records are in existence they are in possession of the families of the successive clerks.

[4] The records have been irregularly kept at times.

[5] Prior to 1869 the Springfield Street Congregational.

[6] Formed in 1722; the records prior to 1806 are lost.

[7] There are copies in possession of the City Registrar.

[8] Formed in 1727 as the Presbyterian Church in Long Lane; later the Federal Street Unitarian.

[9] Originally Congregational; the church edifice was sold in 1876.

[10] The parish records were burned in the Boston fire in 1872.

[11] Originally Congregational. The records of meetings prior to 1730 were written in 1730.

[12] Protestant Episcopal prior to 1786.

Existing Churches: By Towns — Continued.

County of Suffolk — Continued.

Cities, Towns, and Names of Churches.	Date of Organization	Records		
		Kind	Years covered	Condition
Boston — Con.				
Unitarian — Con.				
New South,[1]	1867	Parish	1867–1885	Good
Second,[2]	1649	Church	1662–1885	Fair
South Congregational,	1828	Church	1827–1885	Good
The First Church in Boston,[3]	1630	Parish	1630–1885	Good[3]
Warren Street Chapel,	1835	Church	1836–1885	Good[4]
West Boston Society (Independent Congregational),	1737	Church	1806–1885[5]	Good
United Presbyterian,	–	Church	1846–1885	Good
Universalist:				
Second Society,	1837	Church	1817–1885	Good
Shawmut,[6]	1837	Church	1836–1885	–
Brighton,				
Baptist:				
Brighton Avenue,	1853	Church	1853–1885	Good
Congregational,	1827 {	Church	1827–1849[7]	Good
		Church	1873–1885	Good
Methodist Episcopal:				
Allston,	–	Church	1874–1885	Good
Protestant Episcopal:				
Saint Margaret's,	–	Church	1872–1885	Good
Roman Catholic:				
Saint Columbkille's,	–	Church	1870–1885	Good
Unitarian:				
The First Parish of Brighton,[8]	1730	Church	1772–1885	Good
Universalist,	1872	Church	1860–1885	Good
Charlestown,				
Baptist:				
Bunker Hill,	1851	Church	1850–1885	Good
First,	1801	Church	1801–1885	Good
Congregational:				
First,	1632 {	Church	1632–1885	Good
		Parish	1783–1885	Good
Winthrop,	1833	Church	1832–1885	Good
Methodist Episcopal:				
Monument Square,	–	Church	1847–1885	Good
Trinity,	1820	Church	1873–1885[9]	Well preserved
Protestant Episcopal:				
Saint John's,	–	Church	1841–1885	–
Roman Catholic:				
Saint Francis de Sales's,	–	Church	1859–1885	Good
Saint Mary's,	–	Church	1829–1885	Good
Unitarian:				
Harvard,[10]	1815 {	Church	1817–1885	Good
		Parish	1815–1885	Good
Universalist,	1812	Church	1810–1885	Good

[1] Originally organized in 1719 as Congregational; reorganized in 1867. The records from 1815 to 1867, with the exception of a few in possession of the parish clerk, are in possession of the Massachusetts Historical Society.

[2] Organized as the Old North Church, originally Congregational.

[3] Originally Congregational. The earlier records have been copied.

[4] There are occasional intervals in the records.

[5] During the Revolution the earlier records were carried to the British Provinces and the church was disorganized; reorganized in 1806.

[6] Originally the Fifth Universalist Church.

[7] The records from 1850 to 1872 were destroyed in the Boston fire in 1872.

[8] Originally Congregational.

[9] The records prior to 1872 were burned.

[10] Prior to 1818 the Second Congregational Society in Charlestown, and from 1818 to 1837 the New Church in Charlestown.

CITIES, TOWNS, AND NAMES OF CHURCHES.	Date of Organ- ization	RECORDS		
		Kind	Years covered	Condition
BOSTON — Con.				
Dorchester,				
Baptist :				
Neponset Avenue,[1]	1837	Church	1836–1885	Good
Stoughton Street,[2]	1845	Church	1845–1885	Good
Congregational :				
Pilgrim,[3]	1867	Church[4]	1862–1885	Good
Second, ...	1808	Church	1804–1885	Good
Trinity (Neponset), ...	1859	Church	1859–1885	– .
Village, ...	1829 {	Church	1828–1885[5]	Good
		Parish	1839–1885	Good
Methodist Episcopal :				
Appleton,[6]	–	Church	1861–1885	Meagre
Dorchester, ...	–	Church	1809–1885	Good
Howard Avenue, ...	–	Church	1876–1885	Good
Mattapan, ...	–	Church	1874–1885	Fair .
Parkman Street, ...	–	Church	1874–1885	Well kept
Protestant Episcopal :				
All Saints[7], ...	–	Church	1874–1885	Good
Saint Ann's, ...	–	Church	1877–1885	Good
Saint Mary's, ...	–	Church	1847–1885	Good
Roman Catholic :				
Saint Gregory's, ...	–	Church	1864–1885	Good
Saint Peter's, ...	–	Church	1873–1885	–
Unitarian :				
Church of the Unity (Neponset), .	1859	Church	1859–1885	Good
First Parish of Dorchester,[7] .	1630 {	Church	1636–1885	Good
		Parish	1808–1885	Good
Harrison Square Society, . . .	1848	Church	1848–1885	Good
Third Religious Society in Dorchester,	1813	Church	1815–1885	Good
Universalist :				
Grove Hall, ...	1878	Church	1877–1885	Good
Saint John's,[8]	1874 {	Church	1859–1862	Complete
		Church	1876–1885[9]	Complete
East Boston,				
Baptist :				
Central Square, ...	1844	Church	1843–1885	Well kept
Trinity, ...	1878	Church	1878–1885	Complete
Congregational :				
Maverick, ...	1836	Church	1837–1885	Good
Evangelical Lutheran :				
German, ...	–	Church	1871–1885	Good
Methodist Episcopal :				
Meridian Street and Bethel, . .	–	Church	1842–1885	Good
Saratoga Street, ...	–	Church	1853–1885	Good
Presbyterian, ...	–	Church	1859–1885[10]	Good
Protestant Episcopal :				
Saint John's, ...	–	Church	1845–1885	–
Roman Catholic :				
Church of Our Lady of the Assump- tion, ...	–	Church	1869–1885	Good
Church of the Sacred Heart, . .	–	Church	1874–1885	Good
Most Holy Redeemer, . . .	–	Church	1844–1885	Good

[1] Formerly the First Baptist of Dorchester.

[2] Formerly the North Baptist of Dorchester.

[3] Prior to 1877 the Cottage Street Congregational.

[4] The society gathered in 1846; the records prior to 1862 are unaccounted for.

[5] There is a recorded item of 1807.

[6] Prior to 1870 the Second Methodist Episcopal Church of Dorchester.

[7] Originally Congregational. The earlier records since 1636 have been copied; the records prior to 1636 are missing and are supposed to have been carried to Windsor, Conn.

[8] Organized in 1859 as the Dorchester Universalist Society.

[9] There is a record also of one meeting in 1870, and one in 1874.

[10] The earlier records are lost.

EXISTING CHURCHES: BY TOWNS — Continued.

COUNTY OF SUFFOLK — Continued.

CITIES, TOWNS, AND NAMES OF CHURCHES.	Date of Organ- ization	RECORDS		
		Kind	Years covered	Condition
BOSTON — Con.				
East Boston — Con.				
Roman Catholic : — Con.				
Saint Mary's, Star of the Sea, . .	–	Church	1868–1885	Good
Unitarian :				
Church of Our Father, ...	1846	Parish	1846–1885	Fair
Universalist, ...	1865[1]	Church	1865–1885	Good
Roxbury,				
Baptist :				
Dearborn Street, ...	1870	Church	1870–1885	Good
Dudley Street, ...	1821	Church	1819–1885	Good
Ruggles Street, ...	1870	Church	1870–1885	Good
Congregational :				
Eliot, ...	1834	Church	1834–1885	Good
Highland, ...	1869	Church	1869–1885	Good
Immanuel,[2]	1857	Church	1857–1885	–
Walnut Avenue, ...	1870	Church	1870–1885	Good
Evangelical Lutheran :				
Trinity, ...	–	Church	1871–1885	Good
German Methodist Episcopal, . . .	–	Church	1852–1885	Good
Latter Day Saints, ...	–	Church	1867–1885	Good
Methodist Episcopal :				
Egleston Square, ...	–	Church	1877–1885	Good
Highland, ...	–	Church	1869–1885	Fair
Winthrop Street, ...	–	Church	1839–1885	Good
New Jerusalem, ...	1870	Church	1870–1885	–
Protestant Episcopal :				
Saint James's, ...	–	Church	1833–1885	Good
Saint John's, ...	–	Church	1871–1885	Good
Roman Catholic :				
Our Lady of Perpetual Help, . .	–	Church	1883–1885	Good
Saint Francis de Sales's, . . .	–	Church	1855–1885	Good
Saint Joseph's, ...	–	Church	1846–1885	Good
Saint Patrick's, ...	–	Church	1836–1885	Good
Unitarian :				
First Religious Society in Roxbury,[3] .	1631	Church	1641–1885	Good
Mount Pleasant Congregational, . .	1846	Church	1845–1885	Good
Universalist, ...	1822	Church	1820–1885	Good
South Boston,				
Baptist :				
Fourth Street, ...	1858	Church	1864–1885	Good
South, ...	1828	Church	1828–1885	Good
Congregational :				
E Street, ...	1861	Church	1860–1885	Good
Phillips, ...	1823	Church	1823–1885	Good
Methodist Episcopal :				
City Point, ...	–	Church	1883–1885	Good
Dorchester Street, ...	–	Church	1808–1885	Fair
Saint John's, ...	–	Church	1835–1885	–
Washington Village, ...	–	Church	1871–1885	–
Presbyterian, ...	–	Church	1870–1885	Good
Protestant Episcopal :				
Grace, ...	–	Church	1877–1885	Good
Saint Matthew's, ...	–	Church	1816–1885	Fair
Roman Catholic :				
Gate of Heaven, ...	–	Church	1863–1885	Good
Our Lady of the Rosary, . . .	–	Church	1884–1885	Good
Saint Augustine's, ...	–	Church	1868–1885	Good
Saints Peter and Paul's, . . .	–	Church	1847–1885	Good
Saint Vincent de Paul's, . . .	–	Church	1872–1885	Good

[1] Originally organized in 1840, but no records prior to 1865 are in existence
[2] Formerly Vine Street, Roxbury.
[3] Originally Congregational.

EXISTING CHURCHES: BY TOWNS — Continued.

COUNTY OF SUFFOLK — Continued.

CITIES, TOWNS, AND NAMES OF CHURCHES.	Date of Organ- ization	Kind	Years covered	Condition
BOSTON — Con.				
South Boston — Con.				
Unitarian:				
Hawes Place Congregational Society,	1822	Church	1819–1885	Good
Second Hawes Congregational Uni-				
tarian Society, ...	1845	Church	1845–1885	Good
Unity Chapel, ...	1856	Church	1855–1885	Good
Universalist,[1]	1870	Church	1830–1885	–
West Roxbury,				
Baptist:				
Jamaica Plain, ...	1842	Church	1840–1885	Good
Roslindale, ...	1875	Church	1875–1885	Good
Congregational:				
Boylston (Jamaica Plain), . .	1879	Church	1879–1885	Good
Jamaica Plain, ...	1853	Church	1852–1885	Good
South,[2]	1835	Church	1833–1885	Good
Evangelical Lutheran, . . .	..	Church	1874–1885	Good
Methodist Episcopal:				
Jamaica Plain, ...	–	Church	1859–1885	Good
Roslindale, ...	–	Church	1873–1885	Good
Protestant Episcopal:				
Saint John's, ...	–	Church	1841–1885	Good
Unitarian:				
First Congregational Society of Ja-				
maica Plain,[3]	1770	Church	1760–1885	Good
The First Congregational Parish of }	1712 {	Church	1712–1885	Good
West Roxbury,[3] . . . }		Parish	1733–1885	Good
Universalist:				
Jamaica Plain, ...	–	Church	1871–1885	–
CHELSEA,				
African Methodist Episcopal, . .	–	Church	1876–1885	Good
Baptist:				
Cary Avenue, ...	1859	Church	1859–1885	Good
First, ...	1836	Church	1836–1885	Good
Congregational:				
Central, ...	1851 {	Church and Parish }	1851–1885	Good
First, ...	1841	Church	1841–1885	Complete
Third, ...	1877	Church	1877–1885	Good
Methodist Episcopal:				
Bellingham, ...	–	Church	1853–1885	Incomplete
Walnut Street, ...	–	Church	1839–1885	Good
Protestant Episcopal:				
Saint Luke's, ...	–	Church	1842–1885	Good
Roman Catholic:				
Saint Rose's, ...	–	Church	1862–1885	Good
Second Advent, ...	–	Church	1867–1885	Good
Unitarian:				
First Unitarian Society, . .	1837	Church	1838–1885	Good
Universalist, ...	1842	Church	1845–1885	Good
Revere,				
Baptist, ...	1877	Church	1877–1885	Good
Congregational:				
Beachmont, ...	1881	Church	1883–1885	Good
Revere, ...	1828	Church[4]	1828–1885	–
Unitarian:				
First Congregational Society, . .	1715 {	Church	1715–1776	Good
		Church	1783–1885	Good

[1] Organized as the Fourth Universalist.

[2] Prior to 1855 the Spring Street Evangelical Society.

[3] Originally Congregational.

[4] There are copies of private records from 1719 to 1829 in possession of Benjamin H. Dewing.

EXISTING CHURCHES: BY TOWNS — Continued.

COUNTY OF SUFFOLK — Concluded.

CITIES, TOWNS, AND NAMES OF CHURCHES.	Date of Organ- ization	RECORDS		
		Kind	Years covered	Condition
Winthrop,				
Baptist, ...	1871	Church	1872–1885	Good
Methodist Episcopal, ...	–	Church	1835–1885	Good
Roman Catholic:				
Point Shirley,[1]	–	–	–	– •
Saint John the Evangelist's,[1] . .	–	–	–	–

COUNTY OF WORCESTER.

	Date			
Ashburnham,				
Congregational:				
First, ...	1760 {	Church	–	–
		Parish	1824–1885	–
Second, ...	1842	Church	1843–1885	–
Methodist Episcopal, ...	1831 {	Church	1831–1850[2]	Fair
Roman Catholic:		Church	1868–1885	Fair
Saint Dennis's,[3]	–	–	–	–
Athol,				
Baptist, ...	1813 {	Church	1810–1885	Good
		Parish	1858–1885	Good
Congregational, ...	1750 {	Church	1830–1885	Good
Methodist Episcopal:		Parish	1873–1885	Good
Athol, ...	–	Church	1834–1885	–
South Athol, ...	–	Church	1841–1885	Fair
Roman Catholic:				
Saint Catherine's, ...	–	Church	1882–1885	Good
Second Advent, ...	–	Church	1864–1885	Good
Unitarian:				
First Congregational Church,[4] . .	1750	Church	1750–1885	Good[5]
Second Unitarian Society, . . .	1877	Church	1877–1885	Good
Auburn,				
Congregational, ...	1776 {	Church	1776–1885	[6]–
Roman Catholic:		Parish	1824–1885	Good
Saint Joseph's (Stoneville),[7] . .	–	–	–	–
Barre,				
Baptist, ...	1832	Church	1832–1885	–
Congregational:				
Evangelical, ...	1827 {	Church and Parish }	1827–1885	Good
Methodist Episcopal, ...	–	Church	1860–1885[8]	Good
Roman Catholic:				
Saint Joseph's,[9]	–	–	–	–
Unitarian:				
First Parish, ...	1756	Church	1818–1885	Good
Berlin,				
Congregational, ...	1779	Church	1769–1885	Good
Methodist Episcopal, ...	–	Church	1880–1885	Good
Unitarian:				
First Unitarian Society, . . .	1872	Church	1871–1885	Good

[1] Attended from Saint Mary's, Star of the Sea, at East Boston.
[2] The records include facts from 1794.   [4] Originally the Church of Christ of Pergauge.
[3] Attended from Winchendon.   [5] Sixty leaves have been cut out.
[6] The records for twelve years are missing, the years not being designated.
[7] Attended from Oxford.   [8] A volume of earlier records is missing.
[9] Attended from Templeton.

EXISTING CHURCHES: BY TOWNS — Continued.

COUNTY OF WORCESTER — Continued.

CITIES, TOWNS, AND NAMES OF CHURCHES.	Date of Organ- ization	RECORDS		
		Kind	Years covered	Condition
Blackstone,				
Congregational, ...	1841 {	Church Parish	1841–1885 1860–1885	– –
Free Baptist, ...	– {	Church and Parish	1822–1885[1]	Good
Methodist Episcopal:				
East Blackstone, ...	–	Church	1868–1885	Good
Millville, ...	–	Church	1849–1885	Good
Protestant Episcopal:				
Saint John's (Millville), . . .	–	Parish	1851–1885	Good
Roman Catholic:				
Saint Augustine's (Millville), . .	–	Church	1884–1885	–
Saint Paul's, ...	–	Church	1850–1885	Good
Bolton,				
Baptist, ...	1833	Church	1833–1885	Good
Friends, ...	1799	[2]–	1799–1885	–
Unitarian:				
First Congregational Church, . .	1740 {	Church Parish	– 1834–1885	– –
Boylston,				
Congregational:				
Boylston Centre, ...	1743 {	Church[3] Parish Parish	1777–1885 1743–1786 1796–1885	Good Good Good
Brookfield,				
Baptist:				
East Brookfield, ...	1818	Church	1818–1885	Good
Congregational, ...	1756	Church	1827–1885	Good
Methodist Episcopal, ...	–	Church	1847–1885	Good
Roman Catholic:				
Saint Mary's, ...	–	Church	1885	–
Undenominational:				
Union (East Brookfield), . . .	–	Church	1878–1885	Good
Union (Podunk), ...	–	Church	1885	–
Unitarian:				
First Congregational Church, . .	1754	Church	1755–1885	Good
Charlton,				
Congregational, ...	1761	Church	1761–1885	Well preserved
Methodist Episcopal:				
Charlton City,	–	Church[4]	1854–1885	Well preserved
Universalist, ...	1864	Church	1851–1885	Well preserved
Clinton,				
Baptist, ...	1847	Church	1847–1885	Good
Congregational:				
First Evangelical, ...	1844 {	Church Parish	1844–1885 1859–1885	Good Good
Methodist Episcopal, ...	–	Church	1850–1885	Good
Protestant Episcopal:				
Good Shepherd, ...	1879	Church	1879–1885	Good
Roman Catholic:				
Saint John's, ...	–	Church	1845–1885	Good
Second Advent, ...	–	Church	1879–1885	Good
Unitarian:				
First Unitarian Society, . .	1850	Church	1852–1885	Good

[1] The records from 1870 to 1881 are meagre.

[2] The records are included in the Bolton Monthly Meeting records.

[3] A private record kept by Rev. Ebenezer Morse from 1743 to 1777 is supposed to be in existence.

[4] There are records of Methodist Episcopal meetings in Charlton from 1778 in possession of the present pastor.

EXISTING CHURCHES: BY TOWNS — Continued.

COUNTY OF WORCESTER — Continued.

CITIES, TOWNS, AND NAMES OF CHURCHES.	Date of Organ- ization	Kind	Years covered	Condition
Dana,				
Congregational:				
Dana Centre,	1852	Church	1852–1885	Good
Methodist Episcopal:				
North Dana,	–	Church	1853–1885	Poor
Douglas,				
Congregational:				
East Douglas,	1834	Church	1835–1885	Fair
First,	1747	Church	1747–1885	Good
Methodist Episcopal:				
East Douglas,[1]	–	Church	1844–1885	Good[1]
Roman Catholic:				
Saint Patrick's (East Douglas),	–	Church	1865–1885	–
Dudley,				
Congregational,	1732	Church	1 ...	Fair
Methodist Episcopal,	–	Church[2]	18 ...	–
FITCHBURG,				
Baptist,	1833	Church	1831–1885	Good
Congregational:				
Calvinistic,	1768	Church	1823–1885	Good
Rollstone,	1868	Church	1868–1885	Good
Methodist Episcopal:				
Fitchburg,	–	Church	1841–1885	Fair
West Fitchburg,	–	Church	1881–1885	Good
Protestant Episcopal:				
Christ,	–	Church	1883–1885	Good
Roman Catholic:				
Sacred Heart (West Fitchburg),	–	Church	1880–1885	Good
Saint Bernard's,	–	Church	1848–1885	Good
Unitarian:				
First Parish,	1768	Church	1805–1885	Good
Universalist,	1858	Church	1844–1885	Good
Gardner,				
Baptist,	1830	Church	1828–1885	–
Congregational:				
First,	1786	Church	1828–1885	Good
Methodist Episcopal,		Church[3]	1869–1885	Good
Roman Catholic:				
Sacred Heart of Jesus,	–	Church	1879–1885	Good
Unitarian:				
First Unitarian Society,	1884	Church	1884–1885	Good
Universalist,	1868	Church	1868–1885	Good
Grafton,				
Baptist:				
First,	1800	Church	1800–1885	Good
North Grafton,	1836	Church	1836–1885	–
Congregational:				
Grafton,	1731	Church	1731–1885	–
Saundersville,	1860	Church	1860–1885	Good
Free Baptist:				
Farnumsville,	–	Church	1862–1885	Good
Methodist Episcopal:				
North Grafton,	–	Church	1849–1885[4]	Good

[1] Reformed Methodist from 1844 to 1865; the records for this period are imperfect.

[2] The records are in possession of the Webster Methodist Episcopal Church. No services are now held.

[3] Records have been regularly kept by pastors.

[4] The records from 1841 to 1849 are in existence but are missing.

CITIES, TOWNS, AND NAMES OF CHURCHES.	Date of Organization	RECORDS		
		Kind	Years covered	Condition
Grafton — Con.				
Roman Catholic :				
Saint Philip's,	–	Church	1869–1885	Good
Unitarian :				
Congregational Society,	1731	Church	1861–1885	Good
United Presbyterian :				
Sutton United Presbyterian,	–	Church	1856–1885	Good
Hardwick,				
Congregational :				
First Calvinistic,	1736 {	Church	1736–1885	Good
		Parish	1836–1885	Good
Gilbertville,	1867	Church	1864–1885	Good
Roman Catholic :				
Saint Aloysius's (Gilbertville),[1]	–	–	–	–
Undenominational :				
Union,	1842	Church	1842–1885	Good
Harvard,				
Baptist,	1776	Church	1776–1885	[2]–
Congregational,	1733	Church	1820–1885	Good
Unitarian :				
First Congregational Parish,	1733	Church	1733–1885	–
United Society (Shakers),	–	Society	1791–1885	Good
Holden,				
Baptist,	1806 {	Church and { Parish	1804–1885	Good
Congregational,	1742	Church[3]	1852–1885	–
Roman Catholic :				
Saint Mary's,	–	Church	1884–1885	Good
Hubbardston,				
Congregational,	1770 {	Church	1810–1885	Good
		Parish	1827–1885	Good
Methodist Episcopal,	–	Church	1840–1885	[4]–
Unitarian :				
First Congregational Society,	1770 {	Church	1770–1885	Good
		Parish	1835–1885	Good
Lancaster,				
Congregational,	1839	Church	1839–1885	Good
New Jerusalem,	1875	Church	1875–1885	Good
Seventh Day Advent,	–	Church	1864–1885	Good
Unitarian :				
First Congregational Society,	1653	Parish	1836–1885	Good
Leicester,				
Baptist :				
Greenville,	1737 {	Church	1737–1885	Good[5]
		Parish	1856–1885	Good
Congregational :				
First,	1718 {	Church	1797–1885	Good
		Parish	1833–1885	Good
Methodist Episcopal :				
Cherry Valley,	–	Church	1851–1885	Good
Roman Catholic :				
Saint Aloysius's (Rochdale),	–	Church	1855–1885	Good
Saint Joseph's,	–	Church	1855–1885	Good
Unitarian :				
Second Congregational Society,	1833	Church	1833–1885	–

[1] Attended from Ware.

[2] The earlier records are lost, but the main facts from them are on record.

[3] The records prior to 1828 are in the hands of the Town Clerk ; from 1828 to 1852 they are lost.

[4] The records prior to 1884 are incomplete.

[5] The church records prior to 1787 are imperfect.

Existing Churches: By Towns — Continued.

County of Worcester — Continued.

Cities, Towns, and Names of Churches.	Date of Organization	Records		
		Kind	Years covered	Condition
Leominster,				
Baptist, ...	1851	Church	1870–1885	Good
Congregational:				
Leominster, ...	1822	Church	1822–1885	Good
North Leominster, ...	1874	Church	1875–1885	Good
Methodist Episcopal, ...	–	Church	1823–1885	Good
Roman Catholic:				
Saint Leo's, ...	–	Church	1871–1885	Fair
Unitarian:				
First Congregational Society, . .	1835	Church	1743–1885	Good
Lunenburg,				
Congregational, ...	1835	Church	1835–1885	Good
Methodist Episcopal, ...	–	Church	1805–1885	Good
Mendon,				
Methodist Episcopal, ...	–	Church	1741–1885	Good
Unitarian:				
First Parish, ...	1669 {	Church	1728–1885	Good
		Parish	1769–1885	Good
Milford,				
Baptist, ...	1853	Church	1853–1885	Good
Congregational:				
First, ...	1741 {	Church	1741–1885	Good
		Parish	1741–1885	Good
Methodist Episcopal, ...	– {	Church	1848–1885	Good
Protestant Episcopal:		Parish	1870–1885	Good
Trinity, ...	–	Church	1863–1885	Good
Roman Catholic:				
Saint Mary's, ...	–	Church	1848–1885	Good
Unitarian:				
The Hopedale Parish, ...	1867	Parish	1867–1885	Good
Universalist, ...	1851	Church	1785–1885	Good
Millbury,				
Baptist, ...	1836 {	Church and Parish {	1836–1885	Good
Congregational:				
First, ...	1747	Church	1743–1885	–
Second, ...	1827	Church	1828–1885	Good
Methodist Episcopal, ...	–	Church	1877–1885	Good
Roman Catholic:				
French, ...	–	Church	1884–1885	Good
Saint Bridget's, ...	–	Church	1869–1885	Good
Unitarian:				
First Unitarian Society, . . .	1884	Church	1885 –	Good
New Braintree,				
Congregational, ...	1754 {	Church	1779–1885[1]	Good
		Parish	1845–1885	Good
Northborough,				
Baptist, ...	1827	Church	1827–1885	Good
Congregational, ...	1832	Parish	1830–1885	Good
Unitarian:				
First Congregational Church and Society, ...	1746	Parish	1830–1885	Good
Northbridge,				
Congregational:				
First, ...	1782 {	Church	1782–1885	–
		Parish	1834–1885	–
Rockdale, ...	1879	Church	1879–1885	–
Whitinsville, ...	1834	Church	1834–1885	–

[1] There are intervals in the records prior to 1796.

EXISTING CHURCHES: BY TOWNS — Continued.

COUNTY OF WORCESTER — Continued.

CITIES, TOWNS, AND NAMES OF CHURCHES.	Date of Organ- ization	RECORDS		
		Kind	Years covered	Condition.
Northbridge — Con.				
Friends, ...	1730	1—	1730–1885	–
Methodist Episcopal : Whitinsville, ...	1850	Church	1850–1885	Good
Roman Catholic : Saint Patrick's (Whitinsville),[2] . .	–	–	–	–
United Presbyterian : Whitinsville, ...	1871	Church	1871–1885	–
North Brookfield,				
Congregational : First, ...	1752	Church and Society	1752–1885	Good
Union, ...	1854	Church and Society	1854–1885	Good
Methodist Episcopal, ...	–	Church	1830–1885	Good
Roman Catholic : Saint Joseph's, ...	–	3—	–	–
Oakham,				
Congregational, ...	1773	Parish[4]	1829–1885	Good
Oxford,				
Baptist : North Oxford, ...	1837	Church	1837–1885	Good
Congregational, ...	1721	Church Parish	1720–1885 1813–1885	Good Good
Methodist Episcopal, ...	–	Church	1836–1885	Good
Protestant Episcopal : Grace, ...	–	Church	1863–1885	Good
Roman Catholic : Saint Roch's, ...	–	Church	1858–1885	Good
Universalist, ...	–	Church	1785–1885	Good
Paxton,				
Congregational, ...	1767	Church Church Parish	1767–1768 1793–1885 1830–1885	Good Good Good
Petersham,				
Baptist, ...	1849	Church	1849–1885	–
Congregational, ...	1823	Church	1825–1885	–
Unitarian : First Congregational Parish, . .	1738	Parish	1738–1885	–
Phillipston,				
Congregational, ...	1785	Parish	1830–1885	Good
Methodist Episcopal, ...	–	Church Church	1829–1868 1879–1885	Poor Poor
Princeton,				
Congregational : First (Princeton Centre), . . .	1764	Church Parish	1767–1885 1833–1885	Good Good
Methodist Episcopal, ...	–	Church	1840–1885	Good
Royalston,				
Baptist : West Royalston, ...	1768	Parish	1768–1885	Fair

[1] The records are included in the Uxbridge Monthly Meeting records.

[2] Attended from Uxbridge.   [3] There are no records.

[4] The church records from 1773 to 1885 are in possession of the Town Clerk.

EXISTING CHURCHES: BY TOWNS — Continued.

COUNTY OF WORCESTER — Continued.

CITIES, TOWNS, AND NAMES OF CHURCHES.	Date of Organ- ization	RECORDS		
		Kind	Years covered	Condition
Royalston — Con.				
Congregational:				
First, ...	1766 {	Church Parish	1766–1885 1827–1885	Good Good
Second (South Royalston), . . .	1837 {	Church and Parish	1837–1885	Good
Methodist Episcopal:				
South Royalston, ...	–	Church	1845–1885	Good
Rutland,				
Congregational, ...	1727 {	Church Parish	1727–1885 1830–1885	– –
Shrewsbury,				
Congregational, ...	1723	Parish	1742–1885	Good
Methodist Episcopal, ...	–	Church	1846–1885	Fair
Roman Catholic:				
Saint Theresa's,[1]	–	–	–	
Southborough,				
Baptist:				
Fayville, ...	1825	Parish[2]	1823–1885	Incomplete
Congregational:				
Pilgrim, ...	.1831	Church[3]	1831–1885	–
Southville, ...	1865 {	Church and Parish	1865–1885	Good
Protestant Episcopal:				
Saint Mark's, ...	–	Church	1860–1885	–
Southbridge,				
Baptist, ...	1842	Church	1816–1885	Good
Congregational, ...	1801	Church	1816–1885	Good
Free Evangelical (Globe Village), .	–	Parish	1853–1885	Good
Methodist Episcopal, ...	–	Church	1836–1885	Good
Roman Catholic:				
Notre Dame, ...	–	Church	1869–1885	–
Saint Mary's, ...	–	Church	1853–1885	Good
Universalist, ...	1850	Church	1840–1885	Fair
Spencer,				
Baptist, ...	1878	Church	1878–1885	Good
Congregational, ...	1744	Parish	1832–1885	Good
Methodist Episcopal, ...	–	Church	1843–1885	Good
Roman Catholic:				
Saint Mary's, ...	–	Church	1852–1885	Good
Universalist, ...	1878	Church	1876–1885	Good
Sterling,				
Baptist, ...	1837 {	Church and Parish	1837–1885	Good
Congregational, ...	1852 {	Church and Parish	1855–1885	Good
Unitarian:				
First Congregational Society, . .	1742 {	Church Parish	1745–1885 1836–1885	Good Good
Sturbridge,				
Baptist:				
Fiskdale, ...	1749	Church	1785–1885	Good

[1] Attended from West Boylston.

[2] A part of the church and parish records are in possession of Rev. Henry Gay.

[3] There are private records in possession of Daniel B. Johnson.

EXISTING CHURCHES : BY TOWNS — Continued.

COUNTY OF WORCESTER — Continued.

CITIES, TOWNS, AND NAMES OF CHURCHES.	Date of Organ- ization	RECORDS		
		Kind	Years covered	Condition
Sturbridge — Con.				
Congregational, ...	1736 {	Church	1736–1767[1]	Good
		Church	1801–1885	Good
Unitarian :	{	Parish	1831–1885	Good
Unitarian Congregational Society, .	1864	Church	1864–1885	Good
Sutton,				
Baptist :				
First, ...	1785	Church	1785–1885	Good
Manchaug, ...	1842	Church	1842–1885	Good
Second, ...	1792	Church	1792–1885	Good
Congregational :				
First, ...	1720	Church	1720–1885	Good[2]
Protestant Episcopal :	{	Parish	1827–1885[3]	Good
Saint John's (Wilkinsonville), . .	– {	Parish Reg- ister }	1825–1861	Good
Templeton,				
Baptist	1782 {	Church	1783–1885	Good
		Parish	1865–1885	Good
Congregational :				
Baldwinville, ...	1874	Church	1873–1885	Good
Templeton, ...	1832 {	Church	1832–1885	Good[4]
		Parish	1832–1885	Good
Methodist Episcopal :				
East Templeton, ...	–	Church	1843–1885	Good
Roman Catholic :				
Saint Martin's (Otter River), . .	–	Church	1850–1885	–
Unitarian :				
First Parish, ...	1733	Church	1806–1885	Good
Upton,				
Congregational, ...	1735 {	Church	1751–1885	Good[5]
		Parish	1834–1885	Good
Methodist Episcopal, ...	–	Church	1874–1885	Good
Roman Catholic :				
Holy Angels', [6]	–	–	–	–
Unitarian :				
First Unitarian Society, . . .	1848	Church	1848–1885	–
Uxbridge,				
Baptist				
North Uxbridge, ...	1842	Church	1869–1885	Good
Congregational, ...	1730 {	Church	1730–1885	Good
		Parish	1832–1885	Good
Friends	1730	7 –	1730–1885	–
Methodist Episcopal, ...	–	Church	1875–1885	Good
Roman Catholic :				
Saint Mary's, ...	–	Church	1867–1885	–
Unitarian :				
First Congregational Society, . .	1731 {	Church	1833–1885	Good
		Parish	1797–1885	Good
Warren,				
Congregational :				
Warren, ...	1745	Parish	1824–1885	Good
West Warren, ...	1866	Church	1865–1885	Good
Methodist Episcopal :				
Warren, ...	–	Church	1854–1885	Good
West Warren, ...	–	Church	1876–1885	–

[1] The records from 1767 to 1801 are supposed to have been stolen and destroyed.

[2] The records have been recently revised.

[3] Prior to 1861 there are copies only, the original records having been destroyed by the copyist.

[4] The records prior to 1869 are imperfect.

[5] With the exception of the first volume, which was in bad condition and has been copied. The chronological order is somewhat confused.   [6] Attended from Grafton.

[7] The records are included in the Uxbridge Monthly Meeting records.

EXISTING CHURCHES: BY TOWNS — Continued.

COUNTY OF WORCESTER — Continued.

CITIES, TOWNS, AND NAMES OF CHURCHES.	Date of Organ- ization	RECORDS		
		Kind	Years covered	Condition
Warren — Con.				
Roman Catholic:				
Saint Athanasius's, ...	–	Church	1873–1885	–
Saint Thomas's (West Warren),[1] .	–	–	–	
Universalist,[2]	1864	Church	1830–1885	Fair
Webster,				
Baptist, ...	1814 {	Church and } Parish {	1814–1885	–
Congregational, ...	1838	Parish	1838–1885	–
Methodist Episcopal, ...	–	Church	1834–1885	–
Protestant Episcopal:				
Reconciliation, ...	–	Church	1868–1885	–
Roman Catholic:				
Sacred Heart, ...	–	Church	1870–1885	Good
Saint Louis's, ...	–	Church	1853–1885	Good
Second Advent, ...	1885	Church	1885 –	–
Universalist, ...	1860	Church	1866–1885	Good
Westborough,				
Baptist, ...	1814	Church	1815–1885	Good
Christian, ...	–	Church	1858–1885	Good
Congregational, ...	1724	Church	1724–1885	Good
Methodist Episcopal, ...	–	Church	1858–1885	Good
Roman Catholic:				
Saint Luke's, ...	–	Church	1870–1885	Good
Unitarian:				
First Congregational Society, . .	1717	Parish	1825–1885	'–
West Boylston,				
Baptist, ...	1818	Church	1818–1885	Good
Congregational, ...	1796	Parish	1861–1885[3]	Good
Methodist Episcopal:				
Oakdale, ...	–	Church	1860–1885	Good
West Boylston, ...	–	Church	1858–1885	Good
Roman Catholic:				
Saint Luke's, ...	–	Church	1870–1885[4]	Good
Undenominational:				
First Liberal, ...	–	Parish	1830–1885	Good
West Brookfield,				
Congregational:				
First, ...	1717 {	Church	1758–1885	Good
		Parish	1754–1885	Good
Methodist Episcopal, ...	–	Church	1852–1885	Good
Westminster,				
Baptist, ...	1830	Church	1830–1885	Good
Congregational, ...	1742	Parish	1820–1885	Complete
Universalist, ...	–	Church	1820–1885	Good
Winchendon,				
Advent Baptist,[5]	1798	Church	1798–1885	Good
Baptist, ...	1848	Church	1848–1885	Good
Congregational:				
First, ...	1762 {	Church	1800–1885[6]	Good
		Parish	1826–1885	Good
North, ...	1843	Church	1843–1885	Good

[1] Attended from Warren.

[2] Organized in 1830 as the Independent Believers; afterward the Second Universalist of Western.   [3] The records from 1792 to 1860 were burned in 1868.

[4] There were earlier records which were burned.

[5] Originally the Royalston and Winchendon Baptist.

[6] The church records from 1762 to 1799 are said to have been taken away in 1799 by the pastor.

EXISTING CHURCHES: BY TOWNS — Concluded.

COUNTY OF WORCESTER — Concluded.

CITIES, TOWNS, AND NAMES OF CHURCHES.	Date of Organization	RECORDS		
		Kind	Years covered	Condition
Winchendon — Con.				
Methodist Episcopal,	1796	Church	1796–1885	–
Roman Catholic:				
Immaculate Heart of Mary,	–	Church	1871–1885	–
Unitarian:				
Church of the Unity,	1865	Church	1865–1885	Good
WORCESTER,				
African Methodist Episcopal Zion,	–	Church	1848–1885	Good
Baptist:				
Dewey Street,	1872	Church	1872–1885	Good
First,	1812	Church	1831–1885[1]	Good
First Swedish,	1881	Church	1881–1885	Good
Lincoln Square,	1881	Church	1881–1885	Good
Main Street,	1853	Church[2]	1853–1885	Good
Mount Olive,	1885	Church	1885 –	Good
Pleasant Street,	1842	Church	1844–1885	Good
Congregational:				
Central,	1820	Church	1822–1885[3]	Good
First,	1716	Church	1717–1885	Fair
Piedmont,	1872	Church	1872–1885	Good
Pilgrim,	1885	Church	1885 –	Good
Plymouth,	1869	Church	1869–1885	Good
Salem Street,	1848	Church	1848–1885	Good
Summer Street,	1865	Church	1865–1885	Good
Swedish,	1880	Church	1880–1885	Good
Union,	1836	Church	1836–1885	Fair
Disciples of Christ:				
First Church of Christ,	–	Church	1860–1885	Fair
Evangelical Lutheran:				
Gethsemane,	–	Church	1881–1885	Good
Free Baptist,	–	Church	1881–1885	Good
Friends,[4]	1735	[5]–	1735–1885	–
Methodist Episcopal:				
Coral Street,	–	Church	1872–1885	Good
First Swedish Society,	–	Church	1883–1885	Good
Grace,	–	Church	1867–1885	Good
Laurel Street,	–	Church	1845–1885	Good
Trinity,	–	Church	1834–1885	Fair
Webster Square,	–	Church	1860–1885	Good
Protestant Episcopal:				
All Saints',	–	Church	1835–1885	Fair
Saint John's,	–	Church	1884–1885	Good
Saint Matthew's,	–	Church	1871–1885	Fair
Roman Catholic:				
Immaculate Conception,	–	Church	1874–1885	Good
Notre Dame,	–	Church	1869–1885	Good
Sacred Heart,	–	Church	1880–1885	Good
Saint Ann's,	–	Church	1853–1885	Good
Saint John the Apostle and Evangelist's,	–	Church	1846–1885	Good
Saint Paul's,	–	Church	1856–1885	Good
Undenominational:				
Church of the Covenant,	1885	Church	1885 –	Good
Unitarian:				
Second Congregational Church,	1785	Church	1785–1885	Good
The Church of the Unity,	1846	Church	1846–1885	Good
Universalist:				
All Souls,	–	Church	1884–1885	Good
First,	1843	Church	1841–1885	Good

[1] The records prior to 1831 were burned.

[2] The society connected with the church dissolved in 1883; the records of the society to that time are in possession of W. C. Young.

[3] One volume is missing.   [4] Originally established in Leicester.

[5] The records are included in the Uxbridge Monthly Meeting records.

EXISTING CHURCHES: BY DENOMINATIONS.

[In this table, the names of cities and towns are presented alphabetically under the name of each denomination, and are followed respectively by the names of the counties in which they are located. The distinguishing names, if any, of the churches of each denomination are also given alphabetically for each city and town.

For further explanation of the information contained in the table, see the explanatory notes under "Existing Churches: By Towns," on page 9.]

ADVENT BAPTIST.

CITIES AND TOWNS.	Counties	Distinguishing Name	Year in which Organized	RECORDS		
				Kind	Years covered	Condition
Winchendon, .	Worcester	¹–	1798	Church	1798–1885	Good

AFRICAN METHODIST EPISCOPAL.

BOSTON, . .	Suffolk .	First . . .	1818	Church	1857–1885	Fair
CAMBRIDGE, .	Middlesex	Saint Paul's . . .	–	Church	1873–1885	Good
CHELSEA, .	Suffolk .	–	–	Church	1876–1885	Good
FALL RIVER, .	Bristol .	–	–	Church	1878–1885	Irregularly kept
LYNN, .	Essex .	–	–	Church	1858–1885	²–
NEW BEDFORD,	Bristol .	–	–	Church	1851–1885	Good
Plymouth, . .	Plymouth	–	–	Church	1871–1885	Fair

AFRICAN METHODIST EPISCOPAL ZION.

Attleborough, .	Bristol .	–	1873	Church	1877–1885	Fair
BOSTON, . .	Suffolk .	–	–	Church	1836–1885	–
Gt. Barrington,	Berkshire	–	–	Church	1872–1885	Good
NEW BEDFORD,	Bristol .	–	–	Church	1840–1885	Good
WORCESTER, .	Worcester	–	–	Church	1848–1885	Good

BAPTIST.

Acton, . .	Middlesex	West Acton .	1846	Church	1846–1885	Good
Acushnet, . .	Bristol .	Long Plain . .	1838	Church	1834–1885	Good
Adams, .	Berkshire	–	1826	Church	1826–1885	Good
Agawam, . .	Hampden .	–	1790	Church	1790–1885	–
Amherst, . .	Hampshire	–	1832	Church	1827–1885	–
Andover, . .	Essex .	–	1834	Church	1858–1885	Good
Arlington, . .	Middlesex	–	1781	Church³	1781–1885	Good
Ashfield, . .	Franklin .	..	1867	Church	1867–1885	Good
Ashland, . .	Middlesex	–	1843	Church	1843–1885	Good
Athol, . .	Worcester	–	1813 {	Church	1810–1885	Good
				Parish	1858–1885	Good
Attleborough, .	Bristol .	No. Attleborough .	1769	Church	1769–1885	Good
Ayer, . . .	Middlesex	–	1851	Church	1851–1885	Good
Barnstable, .	Barnstable	Barnstable . .	1842	Church	1842–1885	Well kept
		Hyannis . .	1771	Church	1772–1885	Good
		Osterville . .	1835	Church	1830–1885	Good

¹ Originally the Royalston and Winchendon Baptist.

² From 1858 to 1873 the records are imperfect; for the later years they are good.

³ The records are being copied.

EXISTING CHURCHES : BY DENOMINATIONS — Continued.

BAPTIST — Continued.

CITIES AND TOWNS.	Counties	Distinguishing Name	Year in which Organ- ized	RECORDS		
				Kind	Years covered	Condition
Barre, . .	Worcester	–	1832	Church	1832–1885	–
Becket, . .	Berkshire	–	1764 {	Church and Society }	1_	–
Belchertown, .	Hampshire	–	1795	Church	1795–1885	–
Bellingham, .	Norfolk .	Bellingham . .	1737	Church	1737–1885	Good
		North Bellingham	1867	Church	1867–1885	Good
Bernardston, .	Franklin .	–	1808	Church	1808–1885	Good
Beverly, . .	Essex .	First . . .	1801 {	Church	1801–1885	Good
				Parish	1817–1885	Good
		Second . . .	–	Church	1834–1885	Good
Billerica, . .	Middlesex	First . . .	1828	Church	1828–1885	Good
		North Billerica .	– {	Church and Parish }	1869–1885	Good
Bolton, . .	Worcester	–	1833	Church	1833–1885	Good
BOSTON, . .	Suffolk .	Brighton Avenue (Brighton) . .	1853	Church	1853–1885	Good
		Bunker Hill (Charlestown) .	1851	Church	1850–1885	Good
		Central Square (East Boston) .	1844	Church	1843–1885	Well kept
		Charles Street[2] .	1807	Church	1807–1885	Good
		Clarendon Street[3] .	1827	Church	1827–1885[4]	Good
		Day Star . .	1878	Church	1876–1885	–
		Dearborn Street (Roxbury) .	1870	Church	1870–1885	Good
		Dudley Street (Roxbury) .	1821	Church	1819–1885	Good
		Ebenezer . .	1873	Church	1871–1885	Good
		First . . .	1664	Church	1665–1885	5_
		First (Charlestown)	1801	Church	1801–1885	Good
		First German .	1879	Church	1880–1885	Good
		Fourth Street (South Boston) .	1858	Church	1864–1885	Good
		Harvard Street .	1839 {	Church	1839–1885	Fair
				Parish	1876–1885	Fair
		Independent . .	–	Church	1805–1885	Fair
		Jamaica Plain (West Roxbury)	1842	Church	1840–1885	Good
		Mariners . .	1851	Church	1851–1885	Good
		Neponset Avenue (Dorchester)[6] .	1837	Church	1836–1885	Good
		Roslindale (West Roxbury) . .	1875	Church	1875–1885	Good
		Ruggles Street (Roxbury) .	1870	Church	1870–1885	Good
		South (South Bos- ton) . . .	1828	Church	1828–1885	Good
		Stoughton Street (Dorchester)[7] .	1845	Church	1845–1885	Good
		Trinity (East Bos- ton) . . .	1878	Church	1878–1885	Complete
		Twelfth . . .	1848	Church	1848–1885	Fair
		Union Temple .	1863	Church	1863–1885	Good
		Warren Avenue[8] .	1743	Church	1863–1885[9]	Good
Bourne, . .	Barnstable	Pocasset . .	1838	Church	1838–1885	Good
Brewster, . .	Barnstable	–	1824	Society	1824–1885	Good
BROCKTON, .	Plymouth	Brockton . .	1877	Church	1876–1885	Good
		Swedish (Campello)	–	Church	1883–1885	Good
Brookfield, .	Worcester	East Brookfield .	1818	Church	1818–1885	Good
Brookline, .	Norfolk .	–	1828	Church	1828–1885	–

[1] For occasional years only. [2] Formerly the Third Baptist.
[3] Formerly the Federal Street, and later the Rowe Street Baptist.
[4] The records which were commenced in 1827 pertain to matters in 1821.
[5] The earlier records are in poor condition and need copying.
[6] Formerly the First Baptist of Dorchester.
[7] Formerly the North Baptist of Dorchester.
[8] Formerly the Second Baptist.
[9] The records from 1743 to 1856 are in possession of the City Clerk.

EXISTING CHURCHES: BY DENOMINATIONS — Continued.

BAPTIST — Continued.

CITIES AND TOWNS.	Counties	Distinguishing Name	Year in which Organized	RECORDS		
				Kind	Years covered	Condition
CAMBRIDGE, .	Middlesex	Broadway . .	1865	Church	1865–1885	Good
		Charles River	–	Church	1870–1885	Good
		First . . .	1817	Church	1817–1885	Good
		North Avenue .	1854	Church	1854–1885	Good
		Old Cambridge .	1844	Church	1844–1885	Good
		Second . .	1827	Church	1827–1885	Good
		Union . . .	–	Church	1877–1885	–
Canton, . .	Norfolk .	–	1814	Church	1814–1885	Good
Carver, . .	Plymouth	–	1791 {	Church [1]	1789–1885	–
				1823–1885	–
Charlemont, .	Franklin .	–	–	Church	1767–1885	Good
Chatham, . .	Barnstable	–	1824	Church	1834–1885	Good
Chelmsford, .	Middlesex	Central . . .	1847	Church	1847–1885	Good
		First . . .	1771 {	Church and Parish	1771–1885	Good
CHELSEA, . .	Suffolk .	Cary Avenue .	1859	Church	1859–1885	Good
		First . . .	1836	Church	1836–1885	Good
Cheshire, . .	Berkshire	–	1789	Church	1834–1885	Good
Chicopee, . .	Hampden	Central . . .	1835	Church	1835–1885	Good
		First . . .	1828	Church	1828–1885	Good
Clinton, . .	Worcester	–	1847	Church	1847–1885	Good
Colrain, . .	Franklin .	First . . .	– {	Church	1780–1885	–
				Society	1818–1867	–
		Second . . .	–	Church	1803 –	Incomplete[2]
Conway, . .	Franklin .	–	1820 {	Church	1820–1885	Good
				Parish	1843–1885	Good
Cottage City, .	Dukes Co.	Oak Bluff . .	1877	Church	1877–1885	Good
Danvers, . .	Essex .	–	– {	Church	1793–1885	Good
				Society	1781–1885	Good
Dedham, . .	Norfolk .	East Dedham .	1843	Church	1843–1885	Good
		West Dedham .	1824	Church	1824–1885	–
Dighton, . .	Bristol .	–	1780	Church	1807–1885	3_
Dover, . .	Norfolk .	Springdale .	1838	Church	1838–1885	–
Edgartown, .	Dukes Co.	–	1823	Church	1823–1885	Good
Egremont, .	Berkshire	–	1789	Church	1789–1885	Good
Erving, . .	Franklin .	–	1880	Church	1880–1885	–
Everett, . .	Middlesex	–	1871	Church	1871–1885	Good
FALL RIVER, .	Bristol .	First . . .	1781 {	Church and Parish	1781–1885	Good
		Second . . .	1846	Church	1846–1885	Good
FITCHBURG, .	Worcester	–	1833	Church	1831–1885	Good
Florida, . .	Berkshire	–	1810	Church	1810–1885	Well preserved
Foxborough, .	Norfolk .	–	1817	Parish	1816–1885	Good
Framingham, .	Middlesex	Framingham .	1826 {	Church and Parish	1812–1885	Good
		So. Framingham .	1854	Church	1855–1885	Good
Franklin, . .	Norfolk .	–	– {	Church and Parish	1872–1885	–
Gardner, . .	Worcester	–	1830	Church	1828–1885	–
Gay Head, .	Dukes Co.	–	1832	Church	1693–1885	Good
Georgetown, .	Essex .	–	1785 {	Church	1785–1885	Good
				Parish	1811–1885	Good
GLOUCESTER, .	Essex .	East Gloucester .	–	Church	1863–1885	Good
		First . . .	1831	Church	1830–1885	Good
Grafton, . .	Worcester	First . . .	1800	Church	1800–1885	Good
		North Grafton .	1836	Church	1836–1885	–
Granville, . .	Hampden .	East Granville .	1790 {	Church	1790–1791	–
				Church	1802–1816	–
				Church	1852–1885	–
Greenfield, .	Franklin .	–	1852 {	Church and Parish	1852–1885	Fair
Groton, . .	Middlesex	–	–	Church	1832–1885	–
Hampden, . .	Hampden .	4_	1794	Church	1794–1885	Fair
Hancock, . .	Berkshire	–	1772	Church	1830–1885	Good

[1] Records of the proprietors of the church property.
[2] Some of the records were burned.
[3] The records for some of the earlier years are incomplete.
[4] Called also South Wilbraham Baptist; formerly Monson and Wilbraham Baptist.

EXISTING CHURCHES: BY DENOMINATIONS — Continued.

BAPTIST — Continued.

CITIES AND TOWNS.	Counties	Distinguishing Name	Year in which Organized	Kind	Years covered	Condition
Hanover, . .	Plymouth	–	1806	Church / Parish	1806-1885 / 1843-1885	Good / Good
Hanson, . .	Plymouth	South Hanson .	1806	Church and / Society	1812-1885	Good
Harvard, . .	Worcester	–	1776	Church	1776-1885	1-
Harwich, . .	Barnstable	West Harwich	1767	Church	1773-1885	Good
HAVERHILL, .	Essex	Calvary . . .	1871	Church and / Parish	1873-1885	Incomplete
		First . . .	1765	Church	1793-1885	Fair
		Portland Street	1859	Church	1859-1885	Fair
		Second . .	1822	Church	1822-1885	Good
Hingham, . .	Plymouth	–	1831	Church and / Society	1828-1885	Good
Hinsdale, . .	Berkshire	–	1797	Church	1792-1885	Good
Holbrook, .	Norfolk .	Brookville .	1868	Church	1868-1885	Good[2]
HOLYOKE, .	Hampden	First[3] . . .	1803	Church	1803-1885	Good
		Second . .	1849	Church	1849-1885	Good
Holden . .	Worcester	–	1806	Church and / Parish	1804-1885	Good
Holliston, .	Middlesex	–	1860	Church	1860-1885	Good
Hopkinton, .	Middlesex	–	1842	Church	1837-1885	Good
Hudson, .	Middlesex	–	1852	Church	1852-1885	Good
Huntington, .	Hampshire	..	1852	Church	1852-1885	Good
Hyde Park, .	Norfolk .	–	1858	Church	1858-1885	Good
Kingston, . .	Plymouth	–	1805	Church	1805-1885	Good
Lanesborough, .	Berkshire	–	1818	Church	1833-1885[4]	Good
LAWRENCE, .	Essex .	First . . .	1847	Church / Society	1847-1885 / 1856-1885	Good / Good
		Second . .	1860	Church	1860-1885	Good
Lee, . . .	Berkshire	–	1851	Church	1850-1885	Good
Leicester, . .	Worcester	Greenville . .	1737	Church / Parish	1737-1885 / 1856-1885	Good[5] / Good
Leominster, .	Worcester	–	1851	Church	1870-1885	Good
Leverett, . .	Franklin .	North Leverett .	–	Church	1767-1885	Fair
Lexington, .	Middlesex	–	1834	Church	1830-1885	Good
Littleton, . .	Middlesex	–	1822	Church	1822-1885	–
Longmeadow, .	Hampden	East Longmeadow	1818	Church	1807-1885	Good
LOWELL, . .	Middlesex	Branch Street .	1869	Church	1869-1885	Good
		Fifth Street . .	1874	Church	1874-1885	Good
		First . . .	1826	Church	1826-1885	Good
		Worthen Street .	1831	Church	1831-1885	Good
LYNN, . .	Essex .	East Lynn . .	1874	Church	1874-1885	–
		First . . .	1816	Church	1833-1885	Good
		Washington Ave..	1854	Church	1854-1885	Good
MALDEN, . .	Middlesex	Malden . . .	1803	Church	1803-1885	Good
		Maplewood .	1871	Church	1820-1885	Good
Manchester, .	Essex .	–	1849	Church	1884-1885[6]	–
Mansfield, . .	Bristol .	–	1838	Church	1830-1885	Good
Marblehead, .	Essex .	–	1810	Church	1810-1885	Good
Marlborough, .	Middlesex	–	1868	Church	1867-1885	Good
Marshfield, .	Plymouth	Marshfield . .	1788	Church / Society	1788-1885 / 1816-1885	Good / Good
		North Marshfield .	1833	Church	1833-1885	Good
Mashpee, . .	Barnstable	–	1838	Church	1832-1885	Good
Medfield, . .	Norfolk .	–	1776	Church	1776-1885	–
Medford, . .	Middlesex	–	1841	Parish	1856-1885	Good
Medway, . .	Norfolk .	West Medway .	1832	Church	1819-1885	Good[7]
Melrose, . .	Middlesex	–	1856	Church	1856-1885	–
Merrimac, . .	Essex .	Merrimac . .	1867	Church[8]	1867-1885	Good
				Church	1849-1885	–
		Merrimac Port .	1849	Parish / Parish	1806-1834 / 1845-1885	– / –

1 The earlier records are lost, but the main facts from them are on record.
2 The records from 1870 to 1873 are incomplete.
3 Formerly within the limits of West Springfield.   4 The records prior to 1833 are lost.
5 The church records prior to 1787 are imperfect.
6 There were no records kept prior to 1884.
7 The records from 1824 to 1830 are incomplete.   8 Mrs. G. S. Hoyt has private records.

EXISTING CHURCHES: BY DENOMINATIONS — Continued.

BAPTIST — Continued.

CITIES AND TOWNS.	Counties	Distinguishing Name	Year in which Organized	RECORDS		
				Kind	Years covered	Condition
Methuen, . .	Essex .	–	1815	Church	1815–1885	Good
Middleborough,	Plymouth	Central . . .	1828 {	Church Parish	1800–1862 1828–1885	Incomplete Good
		First . . .	1756	Church	1756–1885	Good
		Third . . .	1761 {	Church and Society	1795–1885	Good
Middlefield, .	Hampshire	–	1817	Church	1817–1885	Fair
Milford, . .	Worcester	–	1853	Church	1853–1885	Good
Millbury, . .	Worcester	–	1836 {	Church and Parish	1836–1885	Good
Milton, . .	Norfolk .	–	–	Church	1882–1885	Good
Monroe, . .	Franklin .	–	1884	Church	1884–1885	–
Montague, . .	Franklin .	Turner's Falls .	1872	Church	1872–1885	–
Nantucket, .	Nantucket	First . . .	1839 {	Church Parish	1840–1885 1839–1885	Good Good
Natick, . .	Middlesex	–	1849	Church	1865–1885	Good
Needham, . .	Norfolk .	–	1856	Church	1854–1885	Good
NEW BEDFORD,	Bristol	First . . .	1813	Church	1828–1885	Good
		North . . .	1873	Church	1873–1885	Good
		Salem . . .	1859	Church	1858–1885	Good
		Second . . .	1846	Church	1850–1885	Good
NEWBURYPORT,	Essex .	–	1809 {	Church and Parish	1869–1885	Good
New Marlboro',	Berkshire	–	1847 {	Church Society	1847–1885 1848–1885	Dilapidated Dilapidated
NEWTON, . .	Middlesex	Myrtle (W. Newton) . . .	1874	Church	1880–1885[1]	Good
		Newton . . .	–	Church	1863–1885	Good
		Newton Centre .	1780	Church	1780–1885	Good[2]
		Second (Newton Upper Falls) .	1835	Church	1835–1885	Good
		West Newton .	–	Church	1866–1885	Good
Norfolk, . .	Norfolk .	–	1843	Church	1842–1885	–
North Adams, .	Berkshire	–	1808	Church	1808–1885	Good
NORTHAMPTON,	Hampshire	–	1826 {	Church Parish	1826–1885 1847–1885	Good Good
Northborough, .	Worcester	–	1827	Church	1827–1885	Good
North Reading,	Middlesex	–	1817	Church	1817–1885	Fair
Norton, . .	Bristol .	–	1838	Church	1761–1885	Good
Norwood, . .	Norfolk .	–	1858	Church	1858–1885	–
Orange, . .	Franklin .	–	1870	Church	1870–1885	Complete
Oxford, . .	Worcester	North Oxford .	1837	Church	1837–1885	Good
Palmer, . .	Hampden	Palmer . . .	1852	Church	1852–1885	Good
		Three Rivers .	1825	Church	1825–1885	–
Peabody, . .	Essex .	–	1843	Church	1844–1885	–
Petersham, .	Worcester	–	1849	Church	1849–1885	–
Pittsfield, . .	Berkshire	–	1772	Church	1800–1885	Complete
Plymouth, . .	Plymouth	–	1800	Church	1809–1885	Fair
Quincy, . .	Norfolk .	Quincy . . .	1867	Church	1867–1885	Good
		Wollaston . .	1871	Church	1871–1885	Good
Randolph, . .	Norfolk .	–	1819	Parish	1819–1885	Good
Raynham, . .	Bristol .	3–	1839	Church	1831–1885	Fair
Reading, . .	Middlesex	–	1832	Church	1837–1885	Good
Rehoboth, . .	Bristol .	–	1840	Church	1840–1885	Good
Revere, . .	Suffolk .	–	1877	Church	1877–1885	Good
Rockland, . .	Plymouth	–	1856	Church	1854–1885	Good
Rockport, . .	Essex .	–	1808	Church	1808–1885	–
Rowe, . .	Franklin .	–	1810	Church	1810–1885	Good
Rowley, . .	Essex .	–	1830	Church	1830–1885	–
Royalston, .	Worcester	West Royalston .	1768	Parish	1768–1885	Fair
Russell, . .	Hampden .	–	1816	Church	1816–1885	Good
SALEM, . .	Essex .	Calvary . . .	1870	Church	1871–1885	Good
		Central . . .	1826	Church	1826–1885	Good
		First . . .	1804 {	Church and Parish	1804–1885	Good

[1] The records from 1874 to 1880 are destroyed.

[2] The records of some of the meetings prior to 1830 are omitted.

[3] This church has records from 1831 to 1837 of a branch of the Fourth Church of Middleborough.

EXISTING CHURCHES: BY DENOMINATIONS — Continued.

BAPTIST — Continued.

CITIES AND TOWNS.	Counties	Distinguishing Name	Year in which Organ-ized	RECORDS		
				Kind	Years covered	Condition
Salisbury, . .	Essex .	Salisbury and Amesbury . .	1780	Church	1780–1885	Good
Sandisfield, .	Berkshire	–	1779	Church	1779–1885	–
Savoy, . .	Berkshire	–	1786	Church	1786–1885	Good
Scituate, . .	Plymouth	North Scituate	1825	Church	1825–1885	Good
Seekonk, . .	Bristol .	–	1794	Church	1794–1885	Good
Sharon, . .	Norfolk .	–	1814	Church	1814–1885	Good
Shelburne, .	Franklin .	Shelburne Falls .	1833	Church	1833–1885	–
Shirley, . .	Middlesex	–	1853	Church	1852–1885	–
Shutesbury, .	Franklin .	–	1778	Church	1835–1885	Good
Somerset, . .	Bristol .	–	1803	Church	1803–1885	Good
SOMERVILLE, .	Middlesex	Perkins Street .	–	Church	1845–1885	Good
		Somerville . .	1853	Church	1852–1885	Good
		West Somerville .	1874	Church	1874–1885	Good
South Abington,	Plymouth	–	1822 {	Church and Parish }	1822–1885	Good
Southborough, .	Worcester	Fayville . . .	1825	Parish[1]	1823–1885	Incomplete
Southbridge, .	Worcester	–	1842	Church	1816–1885	Good
Southwick, .	Hampden .	–	1806	Church	1805–1885	Fair
Spencer, . .	Worcester	–	1878	Church	1878–1885	Good
SPRINGFIELD, .	Hampden .	First . . .	1811	Church	1819–1885	Good
		State Street . .	1864	Church	1864–1885	Good
		Third . . .	1872	Church	1872–1885	Good
Sterling, . .	Worcester	–	1837 {	Church and Parish }	1837–1885	Good
Stoneham, . .	Middlesex	–	1870	Church	1868–1885	Good
Stoughton, .	Norfolk .	East Stoughton .	1780	Church	1785–1885	Good
Sturbridge, .	Worcester	Fiskdale . .	1749	Church .	1785–1885	Good
Sunderland, .	Franklin .	–	1822	Church	1820–1885	Good
Sutton, . .	Worcester	First . . .	1785	Church	1785–1885	Good
		Manchaug . .	1842	Church	1842–1885	Good
		Second . . .	1792	Church	1792–1885	Good
Swampscott, .	Essex .	–	1872	Society	1875–1885	–
Swansea, . .	Bristol .	–	1663	Church	1663–1885[2]	Fair
TAUNTON, . .	Bristol .	Winthrop Street .	–	Parish	1819–1885	Good
Templeton, .	Worcester	–	1782 {	Church	1783–1885	Good
				Parish	1865–1885	Good
Tewksbury, .	Middlesex	North Tewksbury	1843 {	Church and Society }	1843–1885	Fair
Tisbury, . .	Dukes Co.	North Tisbury .	1833 {	Church and Parish }	1832–1885	–
		Vineyard Haven .	1780 {	Church and Parish }	1782–1885	–
Townsend, .	Middlesex	West Townsend .	1827 {	Church	1827–1885	Good
				Society[3]	1818–1885	Good
Tyringham, .	Berkshire	–	1827 {	Church and Society }	1878–1885[4]	Good
Uxbridge, . .	Worcester	North Uxbridge .	1842	Church	1869–1885	Good
Wakefield, .	Middlesex	–	1804	Church	1800–1885	Good
Wales, . .	Hampden .	–	1736	Church	1736–1885	–
WALTHAM, .	Middlesex	–	1852 {	Church and Society }	1852–1885	Good
Warwick, . .	Franklin .	–	1843	Church	1843–1885	Good
Watertown, .	Middlesex	–	1830	Church .	1830–1885	–
Webster, . .	Worcester	–	1814 {	Church and Parish }	1814–1885	–
Wendell, . .	Franklin .	–	1799	Church	1797–1885	Good
Wenham, . .	Essex .	–	1831 {	Church and Parish }	1831–1885	Good
Westborough, .	Worcester	–	1814	Church	1815–1885	Good
West Boylston, .	Worcester	–	1818	Church	1818–1885	Good
W. Bridgewater,	Plymouth	–	1833	Church	1833–1885	Good
Westfield, . .	Hampden .	–	1833	Church	1833–1885	Fair
Westminster, .	Worcester	–	1830	Church	1830–1885	Good

[1] A part of the church and parish records are in possession of Rev. Henry Gay.

[2] There is an interval of forty or fifty years in the earlier records. The oldest volume was brought from Swansea, Wales.

[3] The society records from 1818 to 1827 are meagre.

[4] The earlier records are in possession of Mrs. Edward Slater.

EXISTING CHURCHES: BY DENOMINATIONS — Continued.

BAPTIST — Concluded.

CITIES AND TOWNS.	Counties	Distinguishing Name	Year in which Organized	Kind	Years covered	Condition
West Newbury,	Essex .	–	1867	Church	1867–1878	Good
Weston, . .	Middlesex	. –	1789	Church	1784–1885	Good
W. Springfield,	Hampden	–	1879	Church	1870–1885	–
Weymouth, .	Norfolk .	–	1854 }	Church and Parish }	1854–1885	Good
Winchendon, .	Worcester	–	1848	Church	1848–1885	Good
Williamstown, .	Berkshire	–	1805	Church	1805–1885	Fair
Winchester, .	Middlesex	–	1852 }	Church and Parish }	1852–1885	Complete
Winthrop,.	Suffolk .	–	1871	Church	1872–1885	Good
Woburn, . .	Middlesex	–	1781	Church	1781–1885	–
WORCESTER, .	Worcester	Dewey Street .	1872	Church	1872–1885	Good
		First . . .	1812	Church	1831–1885[1]	Good
		First Swedish .	1881	Church	1881–1885	Good
		Lincoln Square .	1881	Church	1881–1885	Good
		Main Street . .	1853	Church[2]	1853–1885	Good
		Mount Olive . .	1885	Church	1885 –	Good
		Pleasant Street .	1842	Church	1844–1885	Good
Wrentham, .	Norfolk .	–	– }	Church and Parish }	1823–1885[3]	Fair
Yarmouth, .	Barnstable	South Yarmouth .	1824	Church	1844–1885	–

CATHOLIC APOSTOLIC.

BOSTON, . .	Suffolk .	–	–	Church	1864–1885	Good

CHRISTIAN.

NEW BEDFORD,	Bristol .	Purchase Street .	– }	Church and Society }	1808–1885	Good
Westborough, .	Worcester	–	–	Church	1858–1885	–

CHRISTIAN BAPTIST.

Somerset, . .	Bristol .	–	– }	Church and Society }	1841–1885	Good

CHRISTIAN CONNECTION.

BOSTON, . .	Suffolk .	First Christian .	–	Church	1804–1885	–
Dartmouth, .	Bristol .	Bakerville . .	–	Church	1863–1885	Good
		Hixville . . .	–	Church	1780–1885	Good
		Second Christian .	–	Church	1836–1885	–
		Smith's Mills .	–	Church	1838–1885	Good
FALL RIVER, .	Bristol .	Bogle Street Christian . . .	–	Church	1880–1885	Good
		First Christian .	–	Church	1837–1885	Good
		North Christian .	–	Church	1842–1885	Good
HAVERHILL, .	Essex .	South Christian .	1806 }	Church and Parish }	1806–1885	Incomplete

[1] The records prior to 1831 were burned.

[2] The society connected with the church dissolved in 1883; the records of the society to that time are in possession of W. C. Young.

[3] The church records prior to 1823 were burned.

EXISTING CHURCHES : BY DENOMINATIONS — Continued.

CHRISTIAN CONNECTION — Concluded.

CITIES AND TOWNS.	Counties	Distinguishing Name	Year in which Organized	RECORDS		
				Kind	Years covered	Condition
NEW BEDFORD,	Bristol	Bonney Street	–	Church	1850–1885	Good
		Middle Street Christian	–	Church	1848–1885	Good
		Spruce Street Christian	–	Church	1869–1885	Good
NEWBURYPORT,	Essex	Middle Street	–	Church	1873–1885	Good
Salisbury, .	Essex	–	–	Church	1825–1885	Good
Swansea, .	Bristol	–	–	Church	1680–1885	Good

CONGREGATIONAL.

CITIES AND TOWNS.	Counties	Distinguishing Name	Year in which Organized	RECORDS		
				Kind	Years covered	Condition
Abington, .	Plymouth	First	1712	Church	1720–1885	Good
				Parish	1832–1885	Good
		Fourth (North Abington)	1839	Church and Parish	1839–1885	Good
Acton,	Middlesex		1832	Church	1832–1885	–
Adams,	Berkshire	–	1840	Church	1840–1885	Good
Agawam, .	Hampden	Agawam	1819	Church	1836–1885	–
		Feeding Hills	1762	Church and Parish	1758–1885[1]	–
Alford,	Berkshire	–	1846	Church	1846–1851[2]	Complete
Amesbury,	Essex	–	1831	Church and Parish	1832–1885[3]	Good
Amherst, .	Hampshire	College	1826	Church	1826–1885	Good
		First	1739	Church and Parish	1735–1885	Fair
		North (North Amherst)	1826	Church	1826–1885	Good
		Second (East Street)	1782	Church	1782–1885	Good
		South Amherst	1858	Church	1853–1885	Good
Andover, .	Essex	Ballardvale Union	1854	Church	1875–1885	Good
		Free Christian	1846	Church	1846–1885	Incomplete
		South	1711	Parish	1708–1885	Good
		Theological Seminary	1865[4]	Church	1865–1885	–
		West	1826	Church and Parish	1826–1885	Good
Arlington, .	Middlesex	–	1842	Church and Parish	1842–1885	Good
Ashburnham, .	Worcester	First	1760	Church	–	–
				Parish	1824–1885	–
		Second	1842	Church	1843–1885	–
Ashby,	Middlesex	–	1776	Church	1776–1885	Good
				Parish	1834–1885	Good
Ashfield, .	Franklin	–	1763	Church	1763–1885	Good[5]
				Parish	1820–1885	Good
Ashland, .	Middlesex	–	1835	Church	1835–1885	Good
Athol,	Worcester	–	1750	Church	1830–1885	Good
				Parish	1873–1885	Good
Attleborough, .	Bristol	First (West Attleborough)	1712	Church	1740–1885[6]	Good
				Church	1686–1706[7]	–
		Second	1748	Church	1866–1885	Complete
				Parish	1743–1885	Good

[1] The records from 1758 to 1836 are in possession of the Town Clerk.

[2] A few entries were made as late as 1869. The church was reorganized in 1874, since which time partial records have been kept.

[3] A very valuable volume of the church records is missing.

[4] This church was formed in 1816 but not being strictly Congregational the new church was organized in 1865. The old church is about extinct.

[5] The first eight pages of the first volume are missing.

[6] The records prior to 1740 are probably lost. The volume from 1743 to 1796 is deposited, for safe keeping, with the Town Clerk.   [7] A part of this volume is lost.

EXISTING CHURCHES: BY DENOMINATIONS — Continued.

CONGREGATIONAL — Continued.

CITIES AND TOWNS.	Counties	Distinguishing Name	Year in which Organized	RECORDS		
				Kind	Years covered	Condition
Attleborough —Con.	Bristol .	Third (Attleborough Falls)	1874	Church	1874–1885	Good
Auburn, . .	Worcester	–	1776	Church / Parish	1776–1885 / 1824–1885	1– / Good
Ayer, . . .	Middlesex	–	1867	Church	1864–1885	Good
Barnstable, .	Barnstable	Centreville . .	1840	Church	1816–1885	Well preserved
		Hyannis[2] . .	1854	Church and Parish	1854–1885	Good
		West Barnstable .	1616[3]	Parish	1716–1885	Good
Barre, . .	Worcester	Evangelical . .	1827	Church and Parish	1827–1885	Good
Becket, . .	Berkshire	First . . .	1758	Church / Society	1758–1885 / 1798–1885	Good / Good
		North Becket .	1840	Church and Society	1849–1885	Good
Bedford, . .	Middlesex	–	1730	Church / Parish	1730–1885 / 1832–1885	Good / Good
Belchertown, .	Hampshire	–	1737	Church	1834–1885	Good
Belmont, . .	Middlesex	Waverly . .	1865	Church / Parish	1868–1885 / 1861–1885	– / –
Berkley, . .	Bristol .	First . . .	1737	Church	1820–1885	Fair
Berlin, . .	Worcester	–	1779	Church	1769–1885	Good
Bernardston, .	Franklin .	–	1824	Church	1833–1885	–
Beverly, . .	Essex .	Dane Street . .	1802	Church / Parish	1802–1885 / 1868–1885[4]	Good / Good
		Second (North Beverly) . .	1715	Church	1715–1885	Good
		Washington Street	1837	Church	1837–1885	Good
Billerica, . .	Middlesex	–	1829	Church and Society	1829–1885	Good
Blackstone, .	Worcester	–	1841	Church / Parish	1841–1885 / 1860–1885	– / –
Blandford, .	Hampden .	–	1735	Parish	1799–1885	Good
BOSTON, . .	Suffolk .	Berkeley Street[5] .	1827	Church	1831–1885	Good
		Boylston (Jamaica Plain) . . .	1879	Church	1879–1885	Good
		Brighton . .	1827	Church / Church	1827–1849[6] / 1873–1885	Good / Good
		Central[7] . . .	1835	Church	1841–1885	Complete
		E Street (South Boston) . .	1861	Church	1860–1885	Good
		Eliot (Roxbury) .	1834	Church	1834–1885	Good
		First(Charlestown)	1632	Church / Parish	1632–1885 / 1783–1885	Good / Good
		Highland (Roxbury) . .	1869	Church	1869–1885	Good
		Immanuel[8] (Roxbury) . .	1857	Church	1857–1885	–
		Independent . .	–	Church	1845–1885	Good
		Jamaica Plain .	1853	Church	1852–1885	Good
		Maverick (East Boston) .	1836	Church	1837–1885	Good
		Mount Vernon .	1842	Church	1843–1885	Good
		Old South . .	1669	Church	1669–1885	Good
		Olivet . . .	1876	Church	1875–1885	Good
		Park Street . .	1809	Church	1835–1885	Good

[1] The records for twelve years are missing, the years not being designated.

[2] Formed from the Methodist Episcopal and Wesleyan churches.

[3] Organized in England in 1616; settled in Scituate in 1634; in Barnstable in 1639, and in West Barnstable in 1716.

[4] The first volume of parish records is lost.

[5] Prior to January 28, 1861, the Pine Street Congregational Society.

[6] The records from 1850 to 1872 were destroyed in the Boston fire in 1872.

[7] Prior to 1841 the Franklin Street Church, the records of which are not accounted for.

[8] Formerly Vine Street.

EXISTING CHURCHES: BY DENOMINATIONS — Continued.

CONGREGATIONAL — Continued.

CITIES AND TOWNS.	Counties	Distinguishing Name	Year in which Organ-ized	RECORDS		
				Kind	Years covered	Condition
BOSTON — Con.	Suffolk	Phillips (South Boston)	1823	Church	1823–1885	Good
		Pilgrim (Dorches-ter)[1]	1867	Church[2]	1862–1885	Good
		Second (Dorches-ter)	1808	Church	1804–1885	Good
		Shawmut	1845	Church	1845–1885	–
		South (West Rox-bury)[3]	1835	Church	1833–1885	Good
		Trinity (Neponset),	1859	Church	1859–1885	–
		Union[4]	1822	Church	1822–1885	Good
		Village (Dorches-ter)	{ 1829 {	Church / Parish	1828–1885[5] / 1839–1885	Good / Good
		Walnut Avenue (Roxbury)	1870	Church	1870–1885	Good
		Winthrop (Charlestown)	1833	Church	1832–1885	Good
Boxborough,	Middlesex	–	1784	Church	1783–1885	6–
Boxford,	Essex	First	{ 1702 {	Church / Parish	1702–1885[7] / 1735–1885	Good / Good
		West Boxford	{ 1736 {	Church / Parish	1735–1885 / 1829–1885	Good / Good
Boylston,	Worcester	Boylston Centre	{ 1743 {	Church[8] / Parish / Parish	1777–1885 / 1743–1786 / 1796–1885	Good / Good / Good
Bradford,	Essex	First	{ 1682 {	Church / Parish	1682–1885 / 1780–1885	Good / Good
Braintree,	Norfolk	First	{ 1707 {	Church / Parish	1825–1885[9] / 1838–1885	Good / Good
		South Braintree	1829	Church and Parish	1830–1885	Good
Bridgewater,	Plymouth	Bridgewater	1821	Church	1821–1885	Good
		Scotland	1836	Church	1836–1885	Good
Brimfield,	Hampden	First	{ 1724 {	Church[10] / Parish	1748–1885 / 1832–1885	–
		Second	{ 1879 {	Church / Parish	1879–1885 / 1881–1885	Good / Good
BROCKTON,	Plymouth	Campello	1837	Church	1837–1885	Good
		First	1740	Church[11]	1737–1885	
		Porter Evangelical Society	1850	Society	1850–1885	Good
Brookfield,	Worcester	–	1756	Church	1827–1885	Good
Brookline,	Norfolk	Harvard	{ 1844 {	Church and Parish	1844–1885	–
Buckland,	Franklin	–	{ 1785 {	Church and Parish	1820–1885	Good
Burlington,	Middlesex	–	{ 1735 {	Church and Parish	1730–1885	Fair
CAMBRIDGE,	Middlesex	First (Cambridge)	{ 1636 {	Church and Parish	1636–1885	12–

[1] Prior to 1877 the Cottage Street Congregational.

[2] The society gathered in 1846; the records prior to 1862 are unaccounted for.

[3] Prior to 1855 the Spring Street Evangelical Society.

[4] Called also the Essex Street.

[5] There is a recorded item of 1807.

[6] The earlier records are in very poor condition.

[7] There are intervals in the church records, the records for the years from 1749 to 1758 and from 1833 to 1837 being omitted.

[8] A private record kept by Rev. Ebenezer Morse from 1743 to 1777 is supposed to be in existence.

[9] The earlier church records are supposed to have been burned.

[10] The church records prior to 1748 were burned.

[11] There are private records in possession of J. R. Perkins.

[12] The records from 1636 to 1696 and from 1829 to 1867 are incomplete.

EXISTING CHURCHES: BY DENOMINATIONS — Continued.

CONGREGATIONAL — Continued.

CITIES AND TOWNS.	Counties	Distinguishing Name	Year in which Organized	Records Kind	Records Years covered	Records Condition
CAMBRIDGE — Con.	Middlesex	First (Cambridgeport)	1827	Church	1827–1885	Good
		North Avenue	1857	Church and Society	1857–1885	Good
		Pilgrim (Cambridgeport)	1865	Church	1865–1885	Good
		Wood Memorial (Cambridgeport)[1]	1872	Church	1872–1885	Good
Canton,	Norfolk	Evangelical	1828	Church	1828–1885	Good
Carlisle,	Middlesex	–	1830	Church	1830–1885	Good
Carver,	Plymouth	North Carver	1733	Church 2–	1780–1885 1731–1885	Good Good
Charlemont,	Franklin	East Charlemont	1845	Church	1840–1885	Good
		First	1788	Church	1791–1885	Good
Charlton,	Worcester	–	1761	Church	1761–1885	Well preserved
Chatham,	Barnstable	First	1720	Church[3] Parish[4]	1861–1885 1824–1885	Fair Fair
Chelmsford,	Middlesex	Chelmsford Central	1876	Church	1876–1885	Well kept
		Second (North Chelmsford)	1824	Church	1827–1885	Fair
CHELSEA,	Suffolk	Central	1851	Church and Parish	1851–1885	Good
		First	1841	Church	1841–1885	Complete
		Third	1877	Church	1877–1885	Good
Chester,	Hampden	First (Chester Centre)	1769	Church Society	1852–1885 1811–1885	Good Good
		Second (Chester Depot)	1844	Church and Society	1844–1885	Good
Chesterfield,	Hampshire	–	1764	Church	1828–1885	Good
Chicopee,	Hampden	First	1752	Church	1824–1885	Fair[5]
		Second (Chicopee Falls)	1830	Church	1830–1885	Good
		Third	1834	Church	1834–1885	–
Chilmark,	Dukes Co.	–	1700	6–		
Clinton,	Worcester	First Evangelical	1844	Church Parish	1844–1885 1859–1885	Good Good
Cohasset,	Norfolk	Beechwood	1863	Church	1863–1885	Good
		Second	1824	Church and Society	1824–1885	Good
Colrain,	Franklin	–	1750	Church	1820–1885	Good
Concord,	Middlesex	Trinitarian	1826	Church	1826–1885	Good
Conway,	Franklin	–	1768	Church and Parish	1833–1885	Good
Cummington,	Hampshire	East Cummington	1839	Church	1841–1885	–
		West Cummington	1840	Church	1840–1885	Fair
Dalton,	Berkshire	–	1785	Parish	1809–1885	Good
Dana,	Worcester	Dana Centre	1852	Church	1852–1885	Good
Danvers,	Essex	First	1689	Church Parish Parish	1689–1885 1672–1735 1766–1885	Good[7] Good[7] Good
		Maple Street	1844	Church	1844–1885	Good
Dartmouth,	Bristol	South Dartmouth	–	Parish	1858–1885	Good
Dedham,	Norfolk	First	1638	Church Parish	1820–1885 1822–1885	Good Good
		Islington	1880	Church	1874–1885	Good

[1] Originally incorporated in 1873 as Chapel Congregational Church.

[2] Records of the proprietors of the church property.

[3] The church records were burned in 1861 in the fire which destroyed the parsonage. There is a summary of the old records up to that time, and a full record since.

[4] Parish reorganized in 1871.

[5] The records prior to 1824 are meagre.

[6] No record, with the exception of the pastor's private record from 1787 to 1820.

[7] The early portions of the first volume of both church and parish records, which were in bad condition, have been printed by the Essex Institute. The volume of parish records from 1735 to 1766 was burned, but there are records of the parish treasurer for those years.

EXISTING CHURCHES: BY DENOMINATIONS — Continued.

CONGREGATIONAL — Continued.

CITIES AND TOWNS.	Counties	Distinguishing Name	Year in which Organized	RECORDS		
				Kind	Years covered	Condition
Deerfield, . .	Franklin .	Orthodox . .	1835	Church	1835–1885	Good
				Parish	1838–1885	Good
		South Deerfield .	1818	Church and Parish	1818–1885	Good
Dennis, . .	Barnstable	South Dennis .	1817	Church and Parish	1817–1885	Poor
		Union . . .	1866	Society	1868–1885	Fair
Dighton, . .	Bristol .	First . . .	1710	Church	1826–1885	Good
Douglas, . .	Worcester	East Douglas .	1834	Church	1835–1885	Fair
		First . .	1747	Church	1747–1885	Good
Dover, . .	Norfolk .	Second . .	1839	Parish	1838–1885	–
Dracut, . .	Middlesex	Central . . .	1847	Parish	1814–1885	Good
		First Evangelical .	1721	Church	1765–1885	Good
				Society	1834–1885	Complete
Dudley, . .	Worcester	–	1732	Church	1744–1885	Fair
Dunstable, .	Middlesex	–	1757	Church	1757–1885	–
				Parish	1830–1885	–
Duxbury, . .	Plymouth	Pilgrim . . .	1843	Church	1843–1885	–
E. Bridgewater,	Plymouth	Union . . .	1826	Church and Parish	1826–1885	Good
Easthampton, .	Hampshire	First . . .	1785	Church	1835–1885	–
		Payson . .	1852	Church	1852–1885	Good
Easton, . .	Bristol .	–	1745	Church	1747–1885	Good
				Parish	1839–1885	Good
Edgartown, .	Dukes Co.	–	1642	Church	1717–1885	Good
Egremont,. .	Berkshire	South Egremont .	1816	Society	1833–1885	Good
				Church	1828–1885[1]	Fair
Enfield, . .	Hampshire	–	1790	So. Parish of Greenwich	1787–1830	Fair
				Parish of Enfield	1830–1885	Fair
Erving, . .	Franklin .	Evangelical . .	1832	Church	1832–1885	Good
Essex, . .	Essex .	First . . .	1681	Church	1665–1885	Good
				Parish[2]	1700–1885	Good
Everett, . .	Middlesex	–	1861	Church	1861–1885	Good
Fairhaven, .	Bristol .	–	1794	Church	1794–1885	Good
FALL RIVER, .	Bristol .	Central . . .	1842	Church	1842–1885	Good
		First . . .	1816	Church	1816–1885	Incomplete
				Society	1850–1885	–
		Third . . .	1875	Church	1874–1885	Good
Falmouth, .	Barnstable	East Falmouth .	1821	Church	1821–1885	Good
		First . . .	1708	Church	1731–1885	–
				Parish[3]	1804–1885	–
		North Falmouth .	1833	Church	1833–1885	Good
		Waquoit . .	1849	Church	1849–1885	Good
		Wood's Holl . .	1880	Church	1881–1885	–
FITCHBURG, .	Worcester	Calvinistic .	1768	Church	1823–1885	Good
		Rollstone . .	1868	Church	1868–1885	Good
Foxborough, .	Norfolk .	–	1779	Parish	1855–1885	–
Framingham, .	Middlesex	Edwards (Saxonville) . .	1835	Church	1835–1885	Good
				Parish	1827–1885	Good
		Plymouth . .	1701	Church and Parish	1830–1885	Good
		South Framingham	1873	Church and Society	1873–1885	Complete
Franklin, . .	Norfolk .	Franklin . .	1737	Church	1738–1885	–
				Parish	1846–1885	–
		South Franklin .	1855	Church and Parish	1855–1885	–
Freetown, . .	Bristol .	Assonet . . .	1747	Church	1807–1885	Good
				Parish	1852–1885	Good
Gardner, . .	Worcester	First . . .	1786	Church	1828–1885	Good
Georgetown, .	Essex .	Georgetown . .	1732	Church and Parish	1732–1885	Good
		Orthodox Memorial	1864	Church and Parish	1864–1885	–
Gill, . . .	Franklin .	–	1796	Church	1806–1885	Good

---

[1] The records prior to 1828 are lost.

[2] The records for the earlier years are lost.

[3] The earlier parish records are lost.

EXISTING CHURCHES: BY DENOMINATIONS — Continued.

CONGREGATIONAL — Continued.

CITIES AND TOWNS.	Counties	Distinguishing Name	Year in which Organized	RECORDS		
				Kind	Years covered	Condition
GLOUCESTER, .	Essex .	Evangelical . .	1829	Church and Parish	1829–1885	Good
		Lanesville . .	1830	Church	1830–1885	1_
				Society	1828–1885	1_
		West Gloucester .	1716	Church	1716–1827	–
				Church	1845–1885	–
Goshen, . .	Hampshire	–	1780	Church	1828–1885	Fair
Grafton, . .	Worcester	Grafton . . .	1731	Church	1731–1885	–
		Saundersville .	1860	Church	1860–1885	Good
Granby, . .	Hampshire	–	1762	Church	1820–1885	–
Granville, . .	Hampden	East Granville .	1747	Church[2]	1747–1885	3_
		West Granville .	1781	Church and Parish	1781–1885	Complete
Gt. Barrington,	Berkshire	First . . .	1743	Church	1753–1885	Good
		Housatonic . .	1841	Church and Society	1841–1885	Good
Greenfield, .	Franklin .	First . . .	1754	Church	1813–1885	Incomplete
				Parish	1817–1885	Good
		Second . . .	1817	Parish	1862–1885[4]	–
Greenwich, .	Hampshire	–	1749	Church	1760–1885	Good
				Parish[5]	1865–1885	Good
Groton, . .	Middlesex	–	1664	Church	1825–1885	–
Groveland, .	Essex .	–	1727	Church[6]	1726–1885	Good
				Church[7]	1766–1885	Well preserved
Hadley, . .	Hampshire	First . . .	1639	Parish[7]	1852–1885	Well preserved
		Russell . . .	1841	Church	1841–1885	Good
		Second (North Hadley) . .	–	Church	1854–1885	Incomplete
Halifax, . .	Plymouth	–	1734	Parish	1824–1885	Good
Hamilton, . .	Essex .	First . . .	1714	Church and Parish	1712–1885	Good
Hampden, . .	Hampden	8_	1785	Church	1788–1885	Good .
Hanover, . .	Plymouth	First . . .	1728	Church	1728–1885	Good
				Parish	1807–1885	Good
		Second (Four Corners) . .	1854	Church and Parish	1852–1885	Good
Hanson, . .	Plymouth	–	1748	Church	1749–1885	Incomplete
				Society	1746–1885	Good
Hardwick, .	Worcester	First Calvinistic .	1736	Church	1736–1885	Good
				Parish	1836–1885	Good
		Gilbertville . .	1867	Church	1864–1885	Good
Harvard, . .	Worcester	–	1733	Church	1820–1885	Good
Harwich, . .	Barnstable	–	1747	Church	1747–1885	Good
		Pilgrim (Harwich Port) . .	1855	Church and Parish	1855–1885	Good
Hatfield, . .	Hampshire	–	1670	Church[9]	1670–1885	Good
				Parish	1835–1885	Good
HAVERHILL, .	Essex .	Centre . . .	1833	Church and Parish	1833–1885	Good
		Fourth . . .	1744[10]	Church	1743–1885	–
		North Haverhill .	1859	Church	1859–1885	Good
		Riverside . .	–	Church	1884–1885	Good
		West . . .	1735	Church	1735–1885	Good
				Parish	1799–1885	Good

[1] The records from 1828 to 1864 were irregularly kept; since the legal incorporation in 1864 they are complete.

[2] There is a private record kept by Rev. Mr. Cooley, in possession of John Gillett.

[3] The records prior to 1797 were poorly kept; since 1797 they are good.

[4] The records from 1817 to 1862 are missing.

[5] The Town Clerk has parish records from 1749 to 1782.

[6] There is a private record in possession of Gardner P. Ladd.

[7] The church records prior to 1766 were burned in a fire which destroyed the house of the pastor in 1766; the parish records prior to 1852 were burned in a fire in the paper mill of Smith & Bell in 1852.   [8] Called also South Wilbraham Congregational.

[9] There are no complete records prior to 1871.   [10] Reorganized in 1883.

EXISTING CHURCHES: BY DENOMINATIONS — Continued.

CONGREGATIONAL. — Continued.

CITIES AND TOWNS.	Counties	Distinguishing Name	Year in which Organized	RECORDS		
				Kind	Years covered	Condition
Hawley, . .	Franklin .	First (East Hawley) .	1778	Church	1778–1885[1]	Good
				Parish	1824–1885	Good
		West Hawley .	1825	Church	1824–1885	Good
Heath, . .	Franklin .	—	1785	Church	1785–1885	Good
				Parish	1825–1885	Good
Hingham, . .	Plymouth	Evangelical . .	1847	Church and Parish	1847–1885	Fair
Hinsdale, . .	Berkshire	—	1795	Church	1795–1885	Good
				Parish	1833–1885	Good
Holbrook, . .	Norfolk	Winthrop[2] .	1856	Parish	1856–1885	Good
Holden, . .	Worcester	—	1742	Church[3]	1852–1885	–
Holland, . .	Hampden	—	1765	Church	1765–1885	Good
Holliston, . .	Middlesex	—	1728	Church	1728–1885	Good
HOLYOKE, . .	Hampden	First . . .	1799	Church	1799–1885	Good
				Parish	1827–1885	Good
		Second . . .	1849	Church	1849–1885	Good
Hopkinton, .	Middlesex	—	1724	Church	1724–1885	Complete
Hubbardston, .	Worcester	—	1770	Church	1810–1885	Good
				Parish	1827–1885	Good
Huntington, .	Hampshire	First . . .	1778	Church	1778–1885	–
				Parish	1832–1885	Incomplete
		Second . .	1846	Church	1846–1885	Good
Hyde Park, .	Norfolk .	Clarendon Hills .	1880	Church	1880–1885	Good
		First . . .	1863	Church	1861–1885	Good
Ipswich, . .	Essex .	First . . .	1634	Church	1720–1885[4]	–
		Linebrook . .	1749	Church	1749–1885	Good
		South . . .	1747	Church	1865–1885[5]	Good
				Parish	1747–1885	Good
Kingston, . .	Plymouth	Mayflower . .	1828	Church and Society	1828–1885	Good
Lakeville, . .	Plymouth	Lakeville . .	1725	Church	1724–1885	Good
				Parish	1719–1885	Dilapidated
		Union Grove .	1877	Church	1877–1885	Good
Lancaster, . .	Worcester	—	1839	Church	1839–1885	Good
Lanesborough, .	Berkshire	—	1764	Church	1785–1885	Good
LAWRENCE, .	Essex .	Lawrence Street .	1847	Church and Society	1846–1885	Complete
		Riverside . .	1878	Church	1878–1885	Good
		South . .	1868	Church	1868–1885	Good
		Tower Hill . .	1875	Church and Society	1875–1885	Good
		Trinity[6] . . .	–	Church and Parish	1883–1885	Good
Lee, . . .	Berkshire	—	1780	Church	1780–1885	Good
Leicester, . .	Worcester	First . . .	1718	Church	1797–1885	Good
				Parish	1833–1885	Good
Lenox, . .	Berkshire	—	1769	Church[7]	1769–1860	Incomplete
				Church	1860–1885	Complete
Leominster, .	Worcester	Leominster . .	1822	Church	1822–1885	Good
		North Leominster	1874	Church	1875–1885	Good
Leverett, . .	Franklin .	—	1784	Church	1784–1885	Fair
Lexington, .	Middlesex	Hancock . .	1868	Church and Society	1868–1885	Good
Lincoln, . .	Middlesex	First . . .	1747	Church	1830–1885	Good
Littleton, . .	Middlesex	—	1840	Church	1840–1885	–
Longmeadow, .	Hampden	East Longmeadow	1829	Parish	1829–1885	Fair
		Longmeadow .	1716	Parish	1820–1885	Good
LOWELL, . .	Middlesex	Eliot . . .	1830	Church	1830–1885	Good
		First . . .	1826	Church	1826–1885	Good
		French . . .	1877	Church and Parish	1877–1885	Good

[1] The church records from 1798 to 1803 are lost.
[2] Formerly the Second Congregational of Randolph.
[3] The records prior to 1828 are in the hands of the Town Clerk; from 1828 to 1852 they are lost.
[4] The earlier records are lost.
[5] The records for the years from 1865 to 1878 are missing.
[6] Formed by the union of Central and Eliot Congregational churches.
[7] The first volume of the society records from 1834 to 1876 is in possession of the Town Clerk.

EXISTING CHURCHES : BY DENOMINATIONS — Continued.

CONGREGATIONAL — Continued.

CITIES AND TOWNS.	Counties	Distinguishing Name	Year in which Organized	Kind	Years covered	Condition
LOWELL — Con.	Middlesex	High Street . .	1846	Church	1845–1885	Good
				Society	1865–1885	Good
		John Street . .	1839	Church	1839–1885	Good
		Kirk Street . .	1845	Church	1845–1885	Fair
		Pantucket . .	1797	Church and Parish	1797–1885	Good[1]
Ludlow, . .	Hampden	Church of Christ .	1867	Church	1867–1885	Good
		First . . .	1790	Church	1850–1885	Good
Lunenburg, .	Worcester	–	1835	Church	1835–1885	Good
LYNN, . .	Essex .	Central . . .	1850	Church	1850–1885[3]	Good
				Parish	1850–1885	Good
		Chestnut Street .	1860	Church and Parish	1857–1885	–
		First . . .	1632	Church	1763–1885[4]	Good
		North . . .	1869	Church	1869–1885	Good
Lynnfield, .	Essex .	Lynnfield Centre .	1720	Church and Society	1833–1885	Good
		Second (South Lynnfield) . .	1854	Church	1854–1885	Good
MALDEN, .	Middlesex	Faulkner Evangelical Union . .	1882	Church	1882–1885	Good
		First . . .	1649	Church	1770–1885	Good
		Linden . . .	1876	Church	1876–1885	Good
		Maplewood . .	1874	Church	1874–1885	Good
Manchester, .	Essex .	Orthodox . .	1716	Church and Parish	1837–1885	Good
Mansfield, . .	Bristol .	–	1838	Church	1838–1885	Good
Marblehead, .	Essex .	–	1684	Church	1684–1885	Good
Marion, . .	Plymouth	–	1703	Church	1703–1885	Good
Marlborough, .	Middlesex	Union . . .	1666	Church[5]	1700–1885	Fair
Marshfield, .	Plymouth	First . . .	1632	Church	1696–1885	Good
				Parish	1814–1885	Good
		Second (East Marshfield) .	1835	Church	1835–1885	Good
Mattapoisett, .	Plymouth	–	1736	Church and Parish	1736–1885	Good
Maynard, . .	Middlesex	–	1852	Church	1851–1885	Good
Medfield, . .	Norfolk .	Second . . .	1828	Church	1828–1885	–
Medford, . .	Middlesex	Mystic . . .	1847	Church	1847–1885	Good
		West Medford .	1872	Church and Society	1872–1885	Good
Medway, . .	Norfolk .	Medway Village .	1838	Church and Parish	1838–1885	Good
		Second (West Medway) . . .	1750	Church	1750–1779	Fair
				Church	1814–1885	Good
				Parish	1748–1885	Fair
Melrose, . .	Middlesex	Melrose . . .	1848	Church and Society	1848–1885	–
		Melrose Highlands	1875	Church and Parish	1875–1885	Good
Merrimac, .	Essex .	–	1726	Church and Parish	1726–1885	–
Methuen, . .	Essex .	First . . .	1729	Parish	1781–1885	6–
Middleborough,	Plymouth	Central . . .	1847	Parish	1847–1885	Good
		First . . .	1694	Parish	1694–1885	Good
		No. Middleborough	1748	Parish	1743–1885	Complete
Middlefield, .	Hampshire	–	1783	Church	1783–1885	Fair
Middleton, .	Essex .	–	1729	Church	1728–1885	Good
				Parish	1831–1885	Good
Milford, . .	Worcester	First . . .	1741	Church	1741–1885	Good
				Parish	1741–1885	Good
Millbury, . .	Worcester	First . . .	1747	Church	1743–1885	–
		Second . . .	1827	Church	1828–1885	Good

[1] The records prior to 1847 are incomplete.   [2] The records for 1878 and 1879 are omitted.
[3] The records from 1851 to 1868 are omitted.
[4] The records from 1632 to 1763, with the exception of the installations, deaths, and dismissals of pastors, were burned.
[5] There are private records kept by Rev. S. A. Houghton, Berlin.
[6] The records prior to 1820 are meagre; since 1820 they are complete.

EXISTING CHURCHES: BY DENOMINATIONS — Continued.

CONGREGATIONAL — Continued.

CITIES AND TOWNS.	Counties	Distinguishing Name	Year in which Organized	RECORDS		
				Kind	Years covered	Condition
Millis, . . :	Norfolk .	First Church of Christ in Medway	–	Church	1648–1885	Good
		First Church of East Medway .	1714	Church	1714–1885	1–
Milton, . .	Norfolk .	First . . .	1678	Church	1839–1885	Good
		Second (East Milton) . . .	1843	Church	1843–1885	Good
				Parish	1846–1885	Good
Monson, . .	Hampden	–	1762	Church	1807–1885	Good
				Parish	1830–1885	Good
Montague, .	Franklin .	First . . .	1752	Church	1828–1885	Good
		Miller's Falls	1872	Church	1870–1885	–
		Turner's Falls .	1875	Church	1875–1885	Good
Monterey, . .	Berkshire	–	1750	Church	1750–1885	Incomplete
				Church	1855–1885	Complete
Montgomery, .	Hampden	2–	1797	–	–	–
Mt. Washington, .	Berkshire	–	1874	Church3	1874–1885	–
Nantucket, .	Nantucket	–	1728	Church	1767–1885	Good
Natick, . .	Middlesex	John Eliot (South Natick) . .	1859	Church	1859–1885	Good
		Natick . . .	1802	Church	–	–
				Parish	1820–1885	–
Needham, . .	Norfolk .	Evangelical . .	1857	Church	1857–1859	–
				Church	1872–1885	–
NEW BEDFORD,	Bristol .	Acushnet . .	1696	Church and Parish	1828–18855	Incomplete
		North . . .	1807	Church	1807–1885	Fair
		Trinitarian . .	1831	Church	1832–1885	Good
New Braintree, .	Worcester	–	1754	Church	1779–18856	Good
				Parish	1845–1885	Good
Newbury, . .	Essex .	Byfield . . .	1706	Church	1744–1885	Good
				Parish	1762–1885	Good
NEWBURYPORT,	Essex .	First . . .	1635	Church	1674–1885	7–
		Belleville . .	1808	Church	1835–1885	Good
		Fourth . . .	1793	Church	1837–18858	Good
				Parish	1794–1885	Good
		North . . .	1768	Church	1767–1885	Good
				Parish	1768–1826	Good
		Whitfield . .	1850	Church	1853–1885	Good
New Marlboro',	Berkshire	First . . .	1744	Parish	1861–18859	Good
		Mill River . .	1871	Church	1871–1885	Good
		Southfield . .	1794	Church and Parish	1790–1885	Good
New Salem, .	Franklin .	–	1845	Church	1779–1885	Good10
NEWTON, . .	Middlesex	Auburndale . .	1850	Church	1850–1885	Good
		Eliot . . .	1845	Church	1845–1885	Good
				Parish	1844–1885	Good
		First (Newton Centre) .	1664	Church and Parish	1770–188511	Good
		Newton Highlands	1872	Church	1872–1885	Well kept
		Newtonville . .	1868	Church	1868–1885	Good
		North Village .	1866	Church and Society	1866–1885	–
		Second (West Newton) .	1781	Church	1778–1885	Well preserved

1 The earlier records are partly illegible.   2 There are no services now held in this church.
3 The first volume of the records of the "Mount Washington Ecclesiastical Society," commencing about 1878, are in possession of William H. Weaver.
4 The first volume of church records is missing.
5 The records prior to 1828 are lost.
6 There are intervals in the records prior to 1796.
7 The later records are in good condition, and the earlier records, which were not in good condition, have been copied.
8 The church records from 1794 to 1837 were destroyed.
9 Daniel Grant has records from 1826 to 1869. The records prior to 1826 are supposed to have been purposely destroyed.
10 There are partial records also from 1756 to 1779, in poor condition.
11 The records prior to 1770 were burned, but were partially restored from memory.

EXISTING CHURCHES : BY DENOMINATIONS — Continued.

CONGREGATIONAL — Continued.

CITIES AND TOWNS.	Counties	Distinguishing Name	Year in which Organ- ized	RECORDS		
				Kind	Years covered	Condition
Norfolk, . .	Norfolk .	–	1839	Parish	1796–1885	Good
North Adams, .	Berkshire	–	1827	Church	1827–1885	–
NORTHAMPTON,	Hampshire	Edwards . .	1833	Church	1832–1885	Good
		First . .	1661	Parish	1826–1885	Good
		Florence . .	1861	Church	1861–1885	Good
North Andover,	Essex .	Evangelical . .	1834	Church	1834–1885	Good
Northborough, .	Worcester	–	1832	Parish	1830–1885	Good
Northbridge, .	Worcester	First . . .	1782 {	Church Parish	1782–1885 1834–1885	– –
		Rockdale . .	1879	Church	1879–1885	–
		Whitinsville . .	1834	Church	1834–1885	–
No. Brookfield,	Worcester	First . . .	1752 {	Church and Society	1752–1885	Good
		Union . . .	1854 {	Church and Society	1854–1885	Good
Northfield, .	Franklin .	–	1825 {	Church Parish	1825–1885 1825–1885	Good Good
North Reading,	Middlesex	–	1720	Church	1802–1885	Good
Norton, . .	Bristol .	–	1832	Church	1832–1885	Good
Norwood, . .	Norfolk .	1–	1736 {	Church Parish	1736–1885 1730–1885	Good[2] Good[2]
Oakham, . .	Worcester	–	1773	Parish[3]	1829–1885	Good
Orange, . .	Franklin .	Central . . .	1846 {	Church and Parish	1846–1885	Complete
		North Orange .	1843	Church	1843–1885	Good
Orleans, . .	Barnstable	–	1646 {	Church and Society	1648–1885	Fair
Otis, . . .	Berkshire	–	1779	Church	1812–1885	Good
Oxford, . .	Worcester	–	1721 {	Church Parish	1720–1885 1813–1885	Good Good
Palmer, . .	Hampden .	First (Thorndike)	1733	Church	1733–1885	Good
		Second . . .	1847	Church	1847–1885	Good
Paxton, . .	Worcester	–	1767 {	Church Church Parish	1767–1768 1793–1885 1830–1885	Good Good Good
Peabody, . .	Essex .	Peabody . .	1713 {	Church 4–	1793–1885 1793–1885	– –
		Rockville . .	1874	Church	1874–1885	Good
Pelham, . .	Hampshire	Packardville .	1869	Church	1869–1885	–
		Pelham . . .	1837	Church[5]	1862–1885	–
Pepperell, .	Middlesex	–	1747 {	Church Parish	– 1832–1885	– –
Peru, . . .	Berkshire	–	1770	Parish	1820–1885	Good
Petersham, .	Worcester	–	1823	Church	1825–1885	–
Phillipston, .	Worcester	–	1785	Parish	1830–1885	Good
Pittsfield, . .	Berkshire	First . . .	1764 {	Church Parish	1764–1885[6] 1868–1885[7]	Good Good
		Second . . .	1846	8–	–	–
		South . . .	1850	Church	1848–1885	Complete
Plainfield, .	Hampshire	–	1786	Parish	1837–1885	Good
Plymouth, .	Plymouth	Fifth (Chiltonville)	1862	Church	1852–1885	Good
		Fourth (Chilton- ville) . . .	1818	Church	1814–1885	Good
		Pilgrimage . .	1606 {	Church Parish	1606–1885 1802–1885[9]	Good Fair
		Second (South Plymouth) . .	1738	Church	1747–1885	Good

[1] Formerly the Second Parish in Dedham.   [2] With the exception of the first volume.

[3] The church records from 1773 to 1885 are in possession of the Town Clerk.

[4] Records of the proprietors of the church property, which contain also the parish records.

[5] The church records prior to 1862 are lost; the parish records from 1738 to 1767 are in posses- sion of the Town Clerk.

[6] Minutes of church meetings are omitted between October 30, 1863, and April 23, 1872. A copy of the church records from 1753 to 1845 is in possession of the Town Clerk.

[7] The parish records prior to 1868 were burned. There is a written history of the parish, contained in its record book, covering the period from organization to the time of the destruction of its records.   [8] The church and society records are lost.

[9] The records prior to 1802 are kept in Pilgrim Hall.

EXISTING CHURCHES: BY DENOMINATIONS — Continued.

CONGREGATIONAL — Continued.

CITIES AND TOWNS.	Counties	Distinguishing Name	Year in which Organized	Kind	Years covered	Condition
Plympton, . .	Plymouth	–	1698	Church	1695–1885	Good
Prescott, . .	Hampshire	–	1823	Church	1825–1885	Good
Princeton, . .	Worcester	First (Princeton Centre) . .	1764 {	Church Parish	1767–1885 1833–1885	Good Good
Provincetown, .	Barnstable	–	1769	Church	1769–1885	Good
Quincy, . .	Norfolk .	Evangelical . .	1832	Church	1841–1885	Good
		Washington Street	1883	Church	1883–1885	Good
		Wollaston . .	1876	Church	1876–1885	Good
Randolph, . .	Norfolk .	First . . .	1731 {	Church and Parish	1728–1885	Good
Raynham, . .	Bristol .	North Raynham .	1875 {	Church and Society	1876–1885	Good
		Raynham . .	1731 {	Church Parish	1739–1885 1834–1885	Good Good
Reading, . .	Middlesex	Bethesda . .	1849	Church	1849–1885	Good
		Old South . .	1770	Parish	1771–1885	Good
Rehoboth, . .	Bristol .		1721	Church	1721–1885	Good
Revere, . .	Suffolk .	Beachmont . .	1881	Church	1883–1885	Good
		Revere . . .	1828	Church[1]	1828–1885	–
Richmond, .	Berkshire	–	1765 {	Church Parish	1784–1885 1824–1885	Good Good
Rochester, .	Plymouth	First (Rochester Centre) . .	1703 {	Church Parish	1798–1885 1780–1885	Good Good
		North Rochester .	1753	Church	1877–1885[2]	Good
Rockland, . .	Plymouth	–	1813 {	Church Parish Parish	1812–1885 1812–1852[3] 1872–1885	Good Good Good
Rockport, . .	Essex .	First . . .	1755	Church	1755–1885	4–
		Pigeon Cove . .	1874	Church	1874–1885	Good
Rowley, . .	Essex .	–	1639 {	Church Parish	1666–1885[5] 1639–1885	Fair Fair
Royalston, .	Worcester	First . . .	1766 {	Church Parish	1766–1885 1827–1885	Good Good
		Second (South Royalston) .	1837 {	Church and Parish	1837–1885	Good
Rutland, . .	Worcester	–	1727 {	Church Parish	1727–1885 1830–1885	– –
SALEM, . .	Essex .	Crombie Street .	1832 {	Church Parish	1832–1885 1832–1885	Good Good
		South . . .	1735	Church	1774–1885	Good
		Tabernacle . .	1629	Church	1743–1885	–
Salisbury, . .	Essex .	Rocky Hill . .	1718	Church	1718–1885	Good
		Union .. .	1835	Church	1835–1885	Good
Sandisfield, .	Berkshire	First . . .	1756	Church[6]	1756–1885	–
		New Boston . .	1874 {	Church Society	1874–1885 1876–1885	–
Sandwich, . .	Barnstable	–	1639	Church	1639–1885	Good
Saugus, . .	Essex .	Saugus Centre .	1732	Parish	1739–1885	Good
Scituate, . .	Plymouth	–	1635	Church	1634–1885	Good
Sharon, . .	Norfolk .	First . . .	1740	Church	1821–1885	–
Sheffield, . .	Berkshire	Church of Christ .	1735	Church	1814–1885[7]	Complete
Shelburne, .	Franklin .	First . . .	1770	Church	1770–1885	–
		Shelburne Falls .	1850	Church	1846–1885	–
Sherborn, . .	Middlesex	–	1685 {	Church and Parish	1830–1885	–
Shirley, . .	Middlesex	Shirley Village .	1828	Parish	1846–1885	–
Shrewsbury, .	Worcester	–	1723	Parish	1742–1885	Good
Shutesbury, .	Franklin .	–	1742	Church	1804–1885	Good
Somerset, . .	Bristol .	–	1861 {	Church and Parish	1863–1885	Good

[1] There are copies of private records from 1719 to 1829 in possession of Benjamin H. Dewing.

[2] The records prior to 1841 were burned.

[3] One volume covering the years from 1853 to 1871 was burned in the Boston fire in 1872.

[4] The records prior to 1805 are incomplete; since 1805 they are good.

[5] The church records prior to 1666 were burned.

[6] The parish records for the first thirty-eight years are in possession of the Town Clerk.

[7] The records contain an account of the settlement of the first pastor of the church in 1735, but no records prior to 1814 are reported.

EXISTING CHURCHES: BY DENOMINATIONS — Continued.

CONGREGATIONAL. — Continued.

CITIES AND TOWNS.	Counties	Distinguishing Name	Year in which Organ-ized	RECORDS		
				Kind	Years covered	Condition
SOMERVILLE, .	Middlesex	Broadway . .	1864	Church	1864–1885	Good
		First . . .	1855	Church	1855–1885	Good
		Prospect Hill .	1874	Church	1874–1885	Good
		West , . .	1874	Church	1875–1885	Good
South Abington,	Plymouth	–	1807	Church	1808–1885	Good
Southampton, .	Hampshire	–	1743 {	Church	1743–1885	Good
				Parish	1832–1885	Good
Southborough, .	Worcester	Pilgrim . . .	1831	Church[1]	1831–1885	–
		Southville . .	1865 {	Church and Parish	1865–1885	Good
Southbridge, .	Worcester	–	1801	Church	1816–1885	Good
South Hadley, .	Hampshire	First . . .	1733	Church	1733–1885	Fair
		South Hadley Falls[2]	1824 {	Church and Society	1878–1885	Good
				Parish	1824–1885	Good
Southwick, .	Hampden .	–	1773	Church	1773–1885	3–
Spencer, .	Worcester	–	1744	Parish	1832–1885	Good
SPRINGFIELD, .	Hampden .	First . . .	1637 {	Church and Parish	1735–1885	Fair
		Hope . . .	1876	Church	1877–1885	Good
		Indian Orchard .	1848	Church	1854–1885[4]	Good
		North . . .	1846	Church	1846–1885	Good
		Olivet . . .	1833	Church	1833–1885	Good
		Sanford Street[5] .	1864	Church	1849–1885	Fair
		South . . .	1842	Church	1842–1885	Good
Sterling, .	Worcester	–	1852 {	Church and Parish	1855–1885	Good
Stockbridge, .	Berkshire	Curtisville . .	1824	Church	1824–1885	Fair
		First . . .	1735 {	Church	1850–1885[6]	Good
				Parish	1828–1885	Good
Stoneham, .	Middlesex	–	1729 {	Church	1729–1885	Good
				Parish	1827–1885	Good
Stoughton, .	Norfolk .	First . . .	1744	Parish	1743–1885	Good
Sturbridge, .	Worcester	–	1736 {	Church	1736–1767[7]	Good
				Church	1801–1885	Good
				Parish	1831–1885	Good
Sudbury, .	Middlesex	Union . . .	1640	Church	1840–1885	–
Sunderland, .	Franklin .	–	1718 {	Church[8]	1718–1885	Good
				Parish	1832–1885	Good
Sutton, .	Worcester	First . . .	1720	Church	1720–1885	Good[9]
Swampscott, .	Essex .	First . . .	1846 {	Church	1846–1885[10]	Good
				Parish	1846–1885[11]	Good
TAUNTON, .	Bristol .	Evangelical (East Taunton) . .	1853	Church	1853–1885	Good
		First (W. Taunton)	1637	Church	1792–1885	Good
		Trinitarian . .	1821	Church	1821–1885	Complete
		Union . . .	1868 {	Church and Parish	1868–1885	Good
		Winslow . .	1837	Church	1853–1885	Good
Templeton, .	Worcester	Baldwinville . .	1874	Church	1873–1885	Good
		Templeton . .	1832 {	Church	1832–1885[12]	Good
				Parish	1832–1885	Good
Tewksbury, .	Middlesex	–	1735	Church	1736–1885	Good
Tisbury, .	Dukes Co.	West Tisbury .	1673 {	Church and Parish	1701–1885	–

[1] There are private records in possession of Daniel B. Johnson.

[2] Formed from the union of the Religious Society and Congregational Church of South Hadley Falls, and the First Congregational Church and Ecclesiastical Society of South Hadley Falls.

[3] The records for some of the earlier years are missing.

[4] The record for the year 1864 is omitted.

[5] Originally Methodist; reorganized as Congregational in 1864.

[6] The earlier church records are lost.

[7] The records from 1767 to 1801 are supposed to have been stolen and destroyed.

[8] Financial records of the church from 1716 to 1831 are in possession of the Town Clerk.

[9] The records have been recently revised.   [11] The records for 1872, 1873, and 1874 are omitted.

[10] The records for 1867 and 1868 are omitted.   [12] The records prior to 1869 are imperfect.

EXISTING CHURCHES: BY DENOMINATIONS — Continued.

CONGREGATIONAL — Continued.

CITIES AND TOWNS.	Counties	Distinguishing Name	Year in which Organized	Records Kind	Years covered	Condition
Tolland, . .	Hampden .	–	1797	Church[1]	1853–1885	–
Topsfield, . .	Essex .	–	1663	Church	1663–1885	Good
				Parish	1824–1885	Good
Townsend, .	Middlesex	–	1734	Church and Parish	1830–1885	Good
Truro, . .	Barnstable	First . . .	1711	Church	1709–1885	–
		North Truro . .	1842	Church	1840–1885	Good
Tyngsborough, .	Middlesex	–	1868	Church	1868–1885	Good
Upton, . .	Worcester	–	1735	Church	1751–1885	Good[2]
				Parish	1834–1885	Good
Uxbridge, . .	Worcester	–	1730	Church	1730–1885	Good
				Parish	1832–1885	Good
Wakefield, .	Middlesex	–	1645	Church	1722–1885	Good
Walpole, . .	Norfolk .	East Walpole .	1878	Church	1877–1885	–
		Walpole . .	1826	Church and Society	1826–1885	Good
WALTHAM, .	Middlesex	–	1820	Church	1820–1885	Good
				Parish[3]	1859–1885	Good
Ware, . .	Hampshire	East Ware . .	1826	Church	1826–1885	Good
		First . . .	1751	Church	1751–1885[4]	–
Wareham, .	Plymouth	–	1793	Parish[5]	1739–1885	Good
Warren, .	Worcester	Warren . . .	1745	Parish	1824–1885	Good
		West Warren .	1866	Church	1865–1885	Good
Warwick, . .	Franklin .	Trinitarian . .	1829	Parish	1829–1885	Good
Watertown, .	Middlesex	Phillips . .	1855	Church	1855–1885	–
Wayland, . .	Middlesex	–	1828	Church	1828–1885	Good
				Parish	1818–1885	Good
Webster, . .	Worcester	–	1838	Parish	1838–1885	–
Wellesley, .	Norfolk .	Wellesley . .	1798	Church	1798–1825	Good
				Church	1833–1885	Good
		Wellesley Hills[6] .	1847	Church	1873–1885	Good
Wellfleet, . .	Barnstable	First . . .	1723	Church	1723–1885	Good
		Second (South Wellfleet) . .	1833	Church	1834–1885	Good
Wendell, . .	Franklin .	First (Wendell Centre) . .	1774	Church	1774–1885	Good
Wenham, . .	Essex .	–	1644	Church[7]	1682–1885	Good
				Parish	1833–1885	Good
Westborough, .	Worcester	–	1724	Church	1724–1885	Good
West Boylston,	Worcester	–	1796	Parish	1861–1885	Good
West Brookfield,	Worcester	First . . .	1717	Church	1758–1885	Good
				Parish	1754–1885	Good
Westfield, . .	Hampden .	First . . .	1679	Church	1679–1885[9]	Fair
		Second	1856	Church and Society	1856–1885	Good
Westford, . .	Middlesex	–	1828	Church	1828–1885	Good
				Parish	1828–1885	Good
				Proprietors of Meeting House	1842–1885	Good
Westhampton, .	Hampshire	–	1779	Church	1779–1885	–
				Parish	1828–1885	Fair
Westminster, .	Worcester	–	1742	Parish	1820–1885	Complete
West Newbury,	Essex .	First . . .	1698	Church	1698–1885	Good
		Second[10] . .	1731	Church	1731–1885	Good
				Parish	1731–1885	Good

[1] Earlier records are known to be in existence but they are missing.

[2] With the exception of the first volume, which was in bad condition and has been copied. The chronological order is somewhat confused.

[3] The records are in possession of Charles Stickney.

[4] The records from 1754 to 1759 are lost.   [5] The Town Clerk has records from 1830 to 1870.

[6] Called also the Grantville Congregational.

[7] A copy of the private record kept by Rev. John Fiske, pastor of the church from 1644 to 1655, is in possession of the Town Clerk.   [8] The records from 1792 to 1860 were burned in 1868.

[9] From 1806 to 1870 the record is simply a list of officers and members.

[10] Organized in 1731 as the Fourth Church of Newbury; in 1764 name changed to Third Church of Newbury; in 1819, when the town of Newbury was divided, the name was changed to West Church in West Newbury, and in 1821 name changed to Second Church in West Newbury, its present name.

EXISTING CHURCHES: BY DENOMINATIONS — Continued.

CONGREGATIONAL. — Concluded.

CITIES AND TOWNS.	Counties	Distinguishing Name	Year in which Organized	RECORDS		
				Kind	Years covered	Condition
Westport, . .	Bristol .	Pacific Union .	1858	Church	1858–1885	Good
W. Springfield, .	Hampden	First . . .	1698	Church	1720–1885	–
				Parish	1707–1885	–
		Park Street . .	1871	Parish	1871–1885	–
		Second (Mittineague) .	1850	Church and Parish	1850–1885	–
W. Stockbridge,	Berkshire	Centre . . .	1789	Parish	1829–1885	–
		Village . . .	1833	Society	1833–1885	–
Weymouth, .	Norfolk .	East Weymouth .	1860	Church	1843–1885	Good
		First . . .	1623	Parish	1724–1885	Good
		Pilgrim (North Weymouth) .	1852	Church	1851–1885	Good
		Second (South Weymouth)	1723	Church and Society	1723–1885	Fair
		Union (South Weymouth)	1842	Church and Society	1842–1885	Good
		Weymouth and Braintree	1811	Church	1811–1885	Complete
				Parish	1810–1885	1–
Whately, . .	Franklin .	–	1771	Church	1771–1885	Good
				Parish	1828–1885	Good
Wilbraham, .	Hampden	–	1741	Church	1804–1885	–
				Parish	1741–1885	–
Williamsburg, .	Hampshire	First . . .	1771	Church	1771–1885	Good
				Parish	1842–1885	Good
		Haydenville . .	1851	Church and Parish	1851–1885	Good
Williamstown, .	Berkshire	College . . .	1833	Church	1833–1885	Good
		First . . .	1765	Church	1843–1885[2]	Good
		Second (South Williamstown)	1836	Church and Parish[3]	1836–1885	Fair
Wilmington, .	Middlesex	–	1733	Church	1733–1885	Good
				Parish	1865–1885	Good
Winchendon, .	Worcester	First . . .	1762	Church	1800–1885[4]	Good
				Parish	1826–1885	Good
		North . . .	1843	Church	1843–1885	Good
Winchester, .	Middlesex	–	1840	Church and Parish	1840–1885	Complete
Windsor, . .	Berkshire	Church of Christ .	1772	Society	1846–1885[5]	–
Woburn, . .	Middlesex	First . . .	1642	Church	1732–1885	–
		North . . .	1849	Church	1849–1885	Good
				Parish	1849–1885	Good
WORCESTER, .	Worcester	Central . . .	1820	Church	1822–1885[6]	Good
		First . . .	1716	Church	1717–1885	Fair
		Piedmont . .	1872	Church	1872–1885	Good
		Pilgrim . . .	1885	Church	1885 –	Good
		Plymouth . .	1869	Church	1869–1885	Good
		Salem Street . .	1848	Church	1848–1885	Good
		Summer Street .	1865	Church	1865–1885	Good
		Swedish . .	1880	Church	1880–1885	Good
		Union . . .	1836	Church	1836–1885	Fair
Worthington, .	Hampshire	–	1771	Church	1771–1885	Good
				Parish	1865–1885	Good
Wrentham, .	Norfolk .	First . . .	1692	Church[7]	1843–1885	Good
				Society	1692–1885	Good
Yarmouth, .	Barnstable	First . . .	1639	Parish	1679–1885[8]	–
		West Yarmouth .	1844	Church	1840–1885	Good

DISCIPLES OF CHRIST.

Swampscott, .	Essex .	–	–	Church	1865–1885	Good
WORCESTER, .	Worcester	First Church of Christ . .	–	Church	1860–1885	Fair

[1] The first volume is lost. [2] The records prior to 1843 were burned.

[3] B. F. Mills and Charles A. Mills have private records.

[4] The church records from 1762 to 1799 are said to have been taken away in 1799 by the pastor.

[5] A volume of records prior to 1846 is lost. [6] One volume is missing.

[7] The church records prior to 1843 are supposed to have been destroyed.

[8] The records from 1639 to about 1679 were burned.

EXISTING CHURCHES: BY DENOMINATIONS — Continued.

EVANGELICAL CONGREGATIONAL.

CITIES AND TOWNS.	Counties	Distinguishing Name	Year in which Organized	RECORDS		
				Kind	Years covered	Condition
Boxborough, .	Middlesex	–	–	Church	1833–1885	Fair

EVANGELICAL INDEPENDENT.

BROCKTON, .	Plymouth	Swedish(Campello)	–	Church	1881–1885	Good

EVANGELICAL LUTHERAN.

BOSTON, . .	Suffolk .	Boston . . .	1839	Church	1845–1885	Good
		Emmanuel (Swedish) . . .	–	Church / Parish	1873–1885 / 1877–1885	Good / Good
		German (East Boston) . . .	–	Church	1871–1885	Good
		Norwegian . .	–	Church	1884–1885	Good
		Trinity (Roxbury)	–	Church	1871–1885	Good
		West Roxbury .	–	Church	1874–1885	Good
BROCKTON, .	Plymouth	Swedish(Campello	–	Church	1867–1885	Good
Greenfield, .	Franklin .	German . . .	1877	Church	1877–1885	–
LOWELL, . .	Middlesex	Swedish . . .	–	Church	1882–1885	–
WORCESTER, .	Worcester	Gethsemane . .	–	Church	1881–1885	Good

FREE BAPTIST.

Blackstone, .	Worcester	–	–	Church and Parish	1822–1885[1]	Good
BOSTON, . .	Suffolk .	First . . .	–	Church	1844–1885	Good
BROCKTON, .	Plymouth	–	–	Church	1884–1885	Good
Grafton, . .	Worcester	Farnumsville .	–	Church	1862–1885	Good
HAVERHILL, .	Essex .	–	1859	Church	1859–1885	Good
LAWRENCE, .	Essex .	–	–	Church	1847–1885	Good
LOWELL, . .	Middlesex	Chelmsford . .	–	Church	1883–1885	–
		First . . .	–	Church	1833–1885	Good
		Mount Vernon .	–	Church and Society	1874–1885	–
LYNN, . .	Essex .	High Street . .	–	Church	1871–1885	–
SOMERVILLE, .	Middlesex	–	–	Church	1872–1885	–
Swansea, . .	Bristol .	North Swansea .	–	Church	1843–1885	Good
TAUNTON, . .	Bristol .	–	–	Church	1878–1885[2]	Good
WORCESTER, .	Worcester	–	–	Church	1881–1885	Good

FREE CONGREGATIONAL.

NORTHAMPTON, .	Hampshire	–	–	Church	1863–1885	Good

FREE EVANGELICAL.

Attleborough, .	Bristol .	No. Attleborough .	–	Church	1860–1885	Good
Southbridge, .	Worcester	Globe Village .	–	Parish	1853–1885	Good

[1] The records from 1870 to 1881 are meagre.

[2] The earlier records were burned.

EXISTING CHURCHES: BY DENOMINATIONS — Continued.

FRENCH PROTESTANT.

CITIES AND TOWNS.	Counties	Distinguishing Name	Year in which Organized	RECORDS		
				Kind	Years covered	Condition
HOLYOKE, . .	Hampden	–	1884	Society	–	–

FRIENDS.

Acushnet, . .	Bristol .	Acushnet Meeting	1709	1–	1709–1885	–
		Long Plain Meeting	1709	1–	1709–1885	–
Amesbury,	Essex .	–	1701	2–	1701–1885	–
Bolton, . .	Worcester	–	1799	3–	1799–1885	–
BOSTON, . .	Suffolk .	–	1870[4]	5–	1870–1885	–
Dartmouth, .	Bristol .	Allen's Neck Meeting . . .	1807	6–	1807–1885	–
		Apponegansett Meeting . .	1699	6–	1699–1885	–
		Smith's Mills Independent Meeting	1845	7–	1845–1885	–
		Smith's Neck Meeting . . .	1819	6–	1819–1885	–
Duxbury, . .	Plymouth	–	1702[8]	9–	1702–1885	–
Fairhaven, .	Bristol .	–	1849	10–	1849–1885	–
FALL RIVER, .	Bristol .	–	1824	11–	1824–1885	–
Falmouth, . .	Barnstable	–	1709	12–	1709–1885	–
Freetown, . .	Bristol .	–	1759	13–	1759–1856	–
LYNN, . .	Essex .	–	1677	14–	1677–1885	–
Mansfield, . .	Bristol .	–	1819	15–	1819–1885	–
Marshfield, .	Plymouth	–	1692[8]	9–	1692–1885	–
Mattapoisett, .	Plymouth	–	1702[16]	1–	1702–1885	–
Nantucket, .	Nantucket	Nantucket Independent Meeting	1845	17–	1845–1885	–
		Nantucket Meeting	1708	18–	1708–1885	–

[1] The records prior to 1793 are included in the Sandwich Monthly Meeting records; since 1793 in the New Bedford Monthly Meeting records.

[2] The records are included in the Amesbury Monthly Meeting records.

[3] The records are included in the Bolton Monthly Meeting records.

[4] Originally set up in 1664; became extinct in 1808, and again set up in 1870.

[5] The records from 1870 to 1883 are included in the Salem Monthly Meeting records; since 1883 in the Boston Monthly Meeting records.

[6] The records are included in the Dartmouth Monthly Meeting records.

[7] The records are included in the Dartmouth Independent Monthly Meeting records.

[8] This is the earliest date recorded, but meetings were undoubtedly held prior thereto.

[9] The records are included in the records of the Pembroke Monthly Meeting, which was attached to the New Bedford Monthly Meeting in 1876.

[10] The records are included in the New Bedford Monthly Meeting records.

[11] The records are included in the Swansea Monthly Meeting records. Meetings were held as early as 1812.

[12] The records are included in the Sandwich Monthly Meeting records.

[13] The records are included in the Swansea Monthly Meeting records. The meeting was discontinued in 1856, and again set up in 1887.

[14] The records are included in the Salem Monthly Meeting records.

[15] The records are included in the Smithfield (R. I.) Monthly Meeting records.

[16] Originally set up as the Sippican Meeting; afterward the Rochester Meeting.

[17] The records are included in the Nantucket Independent Monthly Meeting records. The records of the original Nantucket Meeting from 1708 to 1845 are in possession of the Nantucket Independent Monthly Meeting.

[18] The records prior to 1845 are in possession of the Nantucket Independent Monthly Meeting; from 1845 to 1867 in possession of Matthew Barney; since 1867 the records of business concerning the Nantucket Meeting are included in the New Bedford Monthly Meeting records.

EXISTING CHURCHES : BY DENOMINATIONS — Continued.

FRIENDS — Concluded.

CITIES AND TOWNS.	Counties	Distinguishing Name	Year in which Organized	Kind	Years covered	Condition
NEW BEDFORD,	Bristol .	New Bedford Meeting . .	1785	1–	1785–1885	–
		New Bedford Independent Meeting	1845	2–	1845–1885	–
Northbridge, .	Worcester	–	1730	3–	1730–1885	–
Pembroke, .	Plymouth	–	1708⁴	5–	1708–1885	–
SALEM, . .	Essex .	–	1677	6–	1677–1885	–
Sandwich, . .	Barnstable	–	1672	7–	1672–1885	–
Somerset, . .	Bristol .	Swansea Meeting .	1732	8–	1732–1885	–
Uxbridge, . .	Worcester	–	1730	3–	1730–1885	–
Westport, . .	Bristol .	–	1766	9–	1766–1885	–
WORCESTER, .	Worcester	–	1735¹⁰	3–	1735–1885	–
Yarmouth, .	Barnstable	–	1709	7–	1709–1885	–

GERMAN CONGREGATIONAL.

Montague, . .	Franklin .	Turner's Falls .	–	Church	1879–1885	–

GERMAN METHODIST EPISCOPAL.

BOSTON, . .	Suffolk .	Roxbury . .	–	Church	1852–1885	Good
Montague, .	Franklin .	–	–	Church	1872–1885	–

GERMAN REFORMED.

BOSTON, . .	Suffolk .	–	–	Church	1840–1885	Good¹¹
HOLYOKE, . .	Hampden	–	–	Church	1868–1885	Good

GETHSEMANE BAPTIST.

Attleborough, .	Bristol .	No. Attleborough .	–	Church	1882–1885	Good

INDEPENDENT BAPTIST.

BOSTON, . .	Suffolk .	Bowdoin Square .	1840	Church	1840–1885	Good

[1] The records from 1785 to 1792 are included in the Dartmouth Monthly Meeting records; since 1792 in the New Bedford Monthly Meeting records.

[2] The records are included in the Dartmouth Independent Monthly Meeting records.

[3] The records are included in the Uxbridge Monthly Meeting records.

[4] This is the earliest date recorded, but meetings were undoubtedly held prior thereto.

[5] The records are included in the records of the Pembroke Monthly Meeting, which was attached to the New Bedford Monthly Meeting in 1876.

[6] The records are included in the Salem Monthly Meeting records. Meetings of Friends were held as early as 1658.

[7] The records are included in the Sandwich Monthly Meeting records.

[8] The records are included in the Swansea Monthly Meeting records.

[9] The records are included in the Westport Monthly Meeting records.

[10] Originally established in Leicester.　　　[11] The records prior to 1849 are imperfect.

Existing Churches: By Denominations — Continued.

Independent Methodist.

Cities and Towns.	Counties	Distinguishing Name	Year in which Organ-ized	Records		
				Kind	Years covered	Condition
Nahant, . .	Essex .	–	–	Parish	1850–1885	Good

Jewish.

Boston, . .	Suffolk .	Mishkan Israel .	1879	Society	1879–1885	Good
		Ohabei Sholom .	1843	Society	1843–1885	Good
		Shaare Tefillah .	1854	¹–	–	–
		Shomrai Beth Abraham . .	1868	Society	1868–1885	–
		Temple Adath Is-rael . . .	1842	¹–	–	–
		Zion's Holy Proph-ets of Israel .	1878	¹–	–	–

Latter Day Saints.

Boston, . .	Suffolk .	Roxbury . .	–	Church	1867–1885	Good
Brockton, .	Plymouth .	–	–	Church	1880–1885	–
Dennis, . .	Barnstable .	–	–	Church	1866–1885	–
Fall River, .	Bristol .	–	1865	Church	1865–1885	Fair
New Bedford,	Bristol .	–	–	Church	1881–1885	Good
Plymouth,. .	Plymouth .	North Plymouth .	–	Church	1882–1885	Good
Wrentham, .	Norfolk .	Plainville . .	–	Church	1876–1885	Good

Messiah.

Boston, . .	Suffolk .	–	–	Society	1881–1885	Good

Methodist.

Ayer,. . .	Middlesex	–	–	Church	1876–1885	–

Methodist Episcopal.

Acushnet, .	Bristol .	Acushnet . .	–	Church	1807–1885	Good
		Long Plain . .	–	Church	1852–1885	Good
Adams, . .	Berkshire .	–	–	Church	1871–1885	Good
Agawam, . .	Hampden .	Feeding Hills .	–	Church	1803–1885	Good
Amesbury, .	Essex .	–	– }	Church	1844–1871	Incomplete
				Church	1871–1885	Good
Amherst, . .	Hampshire	Amherst . .	–	Church	1875–1885	Good
		North Amherst .	–	Church	1844–1885	Good
Andover, . .	Essex .	Ballardvale . .	–	Church	1863–1885²	–
Ashburnham, .	Worcester .	–	1831 }	Church	1831–1850³	Fair
				Church	1868–1885	Fair
Ashland, . .	Middlesex .	–	–	Church	1870–1885	Good
Athol, . .	Worcester .	Athol . . .	–	Church	1834–1885	–
		South Athol . .	–	Church	1841–1885	Fair
Attleborough, .	Bristol .	Attleborough .	1866	Church	1866–1885	Good
		Hebronville . .	–	Church	1876–1885	Good

¹ No records are kept.
² The earlier records are lost.
³ The records include facts fr͞ ͞ 1794.

EXISTING CHURCHES : BY DENOMINATIONS — Continued.

METHODIST EPISCOPAL — Continued.

CITIES AND TOWNS.	Counties	Distinguishing Name	Year in which Organ- ized	RECORDS		
				Kind	Years covered	Condition
Barnstable, .	Barnstable	Barnstable . .	–	Church[1]	1870–1885[2]	Good
		Centreville . .	–	Church	1877–1885	Good
		Marston's Mills .	–	Church	1812–1885	Good
		Osterville . .	–	Church	1846–1885	Good
Barre, . .	Worcester	–	–	Church	1860–1885[3]	Good
Belchertown, .	Hampshire	–	–	Church	1865–1885	–
Berkley, . .	Bristol .	Berkley . . .	–	Church	1873–1889	–
		Myricksville . .	1871[4]	Church	1871–1885	Good[5]
Berlin, . .	Worcester	–	–	Church	1880–1885	Good
Bernardston, .	Franklin .	–	–	Parish	1857–1873[5]	–
Beverly, . .	Essex .	–	–	Church	1867–1885	Good
Blackstone, .	Worcester	East Blackstone .	–	Church	1868–1885	Good
		Millville . .	–	Church	1849–1885	Good
Blandford, .	Hampden .	Blandford . .	–	Church	1814–1885	Good
			{	Church	1839–1866	–
		North Blandford .	– {	Church	1876–1885	–
			(	Parish	1839–1885	–
BOSTON, . .	Suffolk .	Allston (Brighton)	–	Church	1874–1885	Good
		Appleton (Dor- chester)[6] . .	–	Church	1861–1885	Meagre
		Bromfield Street[7] .	–	Church	1806–1885	Good
		City Point (South Boston) . .	–	Church	1883–1885	Good
		Dorchester . .	–	Church	1809–1885	Good
		Dorchester Street (South Boston) .	–	Church	1808–1885	Fair
		Egleston Square (Roxbury) . .	–	Church	1877–1885	Good
		Highland (Rox- bury) . . .	–	Church	1869–1885	Fair
		Howard Avenue (Dorchester) .	–	Church	1876–1885	Good
		Jamaica Plain (W. Roxbury) . .	–	Church	1859–1885	Good
		Mattapan (Dor- chester) . .	–	Church	1874–1885	Fair
		Meridian Street and Bethel (East Boston) . .	–	Church	1842–1885	Good
		Monument Square (Charlestown) .	–	Church	1847–1885	Good
		Morgan Memorial	–	Church	1885 –	Good
		Parkman Street (Dorchester) .	–	Church	1874–1885	Well kept
		People's . .	–	Church	1834–1885	Good[8]
		Revere Street .	1826	[9]–	–	–
		Roslindale (West Roxbury) . .	–	Church	1873–1885	Good
		Saint John's (So. Boston) . .	–	Church	1835–1885	–
		Saratoga Street (E Boston) . .	–	Church	1853–1885	Good
		Swedish . .	–	Church	1882–1885	Good
		Temple Street[10] .	1792	Church	1873–1885[10]	–

1 There is also a record of the pastors from 1820 to 1885.

2 The earlier records are lost.   3 A volume of earlier records is missing.

4 Originally organized in 1853 under the name of the Protestant Methodist Church. The records prior to 1871 are imperfect.

5 The parish records prior to 1857 were burned.

6 Prior to 1870 the Second Methodist Episcopal Church of Dorchester.

7 Formerly the Second Methodist Episcopal.

8 The records since 1853 are complete.   9 All the records disappeared about 1881.

10 Organized as the First Methodist Episcopal; since 1873 called also Grace Church. Two histories of the church have been written; one in manuscript is in possession of the Methodist Historical Society, and the other is in the church book. If earlier original records are in exist- ence they are in possession of the families of the successive clerks.

EXISTING CHURCHES: BY DENOMINATIONS — Continued.

METHODIST EPISCOPAL — Continued.

CITIES AND TOWNS.	Counties	Distinguishing Name	Year in which Organized	RECORDS		
				Kind	Years covered	Condition
BOSTON — Con.	Suffolk .	Tremont Street .	–	Church	1862–1885	Good
		Trinity (Charlestown) . . .	1820	Church	1873–1885[1]	Well preserved
		Washington Village (So. Boston)	–	Church	1871–1885	
		Winthrop Street (Roxbury) .	–	Church	1839–1885	Good
Bourne, . .	Barnstable	Bourne . . .	–	Church	1850–1885	Good
		Sagamore .	–	Church	1828–1885	Good
Braintree, . .	Norfolk .	South Braintree .	–	Church	1874–1885	Good
Bridgewater, .	Plymouth	–	1874	Church	1874–1885	Good
BROCKTON, .	Plymouth	Campello .	–	Church	1879–1885	Good
		Central . . .	–	Church	1851–1885	–
		West . . .	–	Church	1831–1885	Good
Brookfield, .	Worcester	–	–	Church	1847–1885	Good
Brookline, . .	Norfolk .	–	1873	Church	1873–1885	Fair
Buckland, . .	Franklin .	–	–	Church	1849–1885	Good
CAMBRIDGE, .	Middlesex	Grace Street .	–	Church	1873–1885	Good
		Harvard Street .	–	Church	1823–1885	Good
		North Avenue .	–	Church	1865–1885	Good
		Trinity . . .	–	Church	1822–1885	Good
Carver, . .	Plymouth	South Carver .	–	Church	1867–1885	Good
Charlemont, .	Franklin .	–	–	Church	1831–1885	Good
Charlton, . .	Worcester	Charlton City .	–	Church[2]	1854–1885	Well preserved
Chatham, . .	Barnstable	–	–	Church	1821–1885	Good
Chelmsford, .	Middlesex	West Chelmsford .	–	Church[3]	1870–1885	Good
CHELSEA, . .	Suffolk .	Bellingham .	–	Church	1853–1885	Incomplete
		Walnut Street .	–	Church	1839–1885	Good
Cheshire, . .	Berkshire	–	–	Church	1850–1885	Good
Chester, . .	Hampden	–	–	Church	1873–1885	Good
Chicopee, . .	Hampden	Chicopee . .	–	Church	1839–1885	–
		Chicopee Falls .	–	Church	1838–1885[4]	Good
Chilmark, . .	Dukes Co.	–	–	Church	1810–1885	Well preserved
Clinton, . .	Worcester	–	–	Church	1850–1885	Good
Cohasset, . .	Norfolk .	Nantasket . .	–	Church	1831–1885	[5]–
Colrain, . .	Franklin .	Colrain . . .	–	Church	1833–1885	Good
		East Colrain .	–	Church	1830–1885	Fair
Conway, . .	Franklin .	–	–	Church	1871–1885	Good
Cottage City, .	Dukes Co.	–	–	Church	1877–1885	Good
Dalton, . .	Berkshire	–	–	Church	1858–1885	Good
Dana, . .	Worcester	North Dana .	–	Church	1853–1885	Poor
Danvers, . .	Essex .	Tapleyville .	–	Church	1871–1885	Good
Dedham, . .	Norfolk .	–	–	Church	1848–1885	Fair
Deerfield, . .	Franklin .	South Deerfield .	–	Church	1849–1885	Good
Dennis, . .	Barnstable	Dennis . .	–	Church	[6]–	–
		West Dennis .	–	Church	1873–1885	Good
Dighton, . .	Bristol .	Dighton . .	–	Church	1866–1885	Good
		North Dighton .	–	Church	1860–1885	Good
Douglas, . .	Worcester	East Douglas[7] .	–	Church	1844–1885	Good[7]
Dudley, . .	Worcester	–	–	Church[8]	1843–1885	–
Duxbury, . .	Plymouth	West Duxbury .	–	Church	1868–1885	–
E. Bridgewater,	Plymouth	–	–	Church	1857–1885	Fair
Eastham, . .	Barnstable	–	–	Church	1819–1885	[9]–

[1] The records prior to 1872 were burned.

[2] There are records of Methodist Episcopal meetings in Charlton from 1778 in possession of the present pastor.

[3] A volume of the records of pastors from 1847 to 1870 was prepared in the latter year.

[4] The records prior to 1838 are incomplete.

[5] The records prior to 1844 are incomplete.

[6] Partial records have been kept, but are missing.

[7] Reformed Methodist from 1844 to 1865; the records for this period are imperfect.

[8] The records are in possession of the Webster Methodist Episcopal Church. No services are now held.

[9] The bound records are in fair condition, but the unbound are dilapidated.

Existing Churches: By Denominations — Continued.

Methodist Episcopal — Continued.

Cities and Towns.	Counties	Distinguishing Name	Year in which Organized	Records		
				Kind	Years covered	Condition
Easthampton, .	Hampshire	–	1867	¹–	–	–
Easton, . .	Bristol .	{ Central (North Easton) . }	1861	{ Church and Parish }	1861–1885	Good
		Washington St. (North Easton)	1795	{ Church² Parish }	1861–1885 1810–1885	Good Good
Edgartown, .	Dukes Co.	–	–	Church	1787–1885	Good
Egremont,. .	Berkshire	North Egremont .	–	Society	1860–1885	Good
Enfield, . .	Hampshire	–	–	Church	1849–1885	Well kept
Essex, . .	Essex .	–	–	Church	1875–1885	Complete
Everett, . .	Middlesex	–	–	Church	1870–1885	Good
Fairhaven, .	Bristol .	–	–	Church.	1830–1885	³–
FALL RIVER, .	Bristol .	Brayton . . .	–	Church	1860–1885	Good
		First . . .	–	Church	1827–1885	Good
		North . . .	–	Church	1848–1885	Good
		Park . . .	–	Church	1874–1885	Good
		Quarry Street .	–	Church	1870–1885	Good
		Saint Paul's .	–	Church	1851–1885	Good
Falmouth, .	Barnstable	East Falmouth .	• –	Church	1860–1885	Good
		Falmouth .	–	Church	1811–1885	Good
		West Falmouth	–	Church	1854–1885	Imperfect⁴
		Wood's Holl .	–	Church	1880–1885	Good
FITCHBURG, .	Worcester	Fitchburg .	–	Church	1841–1885	Fair
		West Fitchburg .	–	Church	1881–1885	Good
Framingham, .	Middlesex	Saxonville .	–	Church	1834–1885	Good
		So. Framingham .	1869	Parish	1869–1885	Good
Franklin, . .	Norfolk .	–	–	Church	1854–1885	Good
Gardner, . .	Worcester	–	–	Church⁵	1869–1885	Good
Gill, . . .	Franklin .	–	{ –	Society	1827–1885	Fair
				Pastor's	1866–1885	Fair
GLOUCESTER, .	Essex .	Bay View . .	–	Church	1870–1885	Good
		Prospect Street .	–	Church	1825–1885	Good
		Riverdale .	–	Church	1850–1885	Good
Gosnold, . .	Dukes Co.	Cuttyhunk .	–	Church	1875–1885	Good
Grafton, . .	Worcester	North Grafton .	–	Church	1849–1885⁶	Good
Granville, . .	Hampden .	–	1879	Church	1879–1885	–
Gt. Barrington,	Berkshire	Gt. Barrington .	1842	Church	1842–1885	Good
		Housatonic .	–	Church	1868–1885	Good
Greenfield, .	Franklin .	–	–	Church	1831–1885	Good
Groveland, .	Essex . .	–	–	Church	1831–1885	Good
Hampden, . .	Hampden. .	–	–	Church	1838–1885	Good
Hanover, . .	Plymouth	–	1850	Church	1849–1885	–
Harwich, . .	Barnstable	South Harwich .	–	Church	1853–1885	Good
HAVERHILL, .	Essex .	Grace . . .	–	Church	1870–1885	Good
Heath, . .	Franklin .	–	1859	Church	–	–
Hingham, . .	Plymouth	–	–	Church	1818–1885	Good
Holbrook, . .	Norfolk .	–	1879	Church	1879–1885	Good
Holliston, . .	Middlesex	–	–	Church	1833–1885	Good
HOLYOKE, .	Hampden.	–	–	Church	1853–1885	Good
Hopkinton, .	Middlesex	–	–	Church	1835–1885	–
Hubbardston, .	Worcester	–	–	Church	1840–1885	7–
Hudson, . .	Middlesex	–	–	Church	1865–1885	Good
Hull, . . .	Plymouth	–	–	Church	1816–1885	Good⁸
Hyde Park, .	Norfolk .	–	–	Church	1870–1885	Good
Ipswich, . .	Essex .	–	–	Church	1822–1885	Good
Lanesborough, .	Berkshire	–	–	Church	1864–1885⁹	Good
LAWRENCE, .	Essex .	Bodwell Street .	–	Church	1879–1885	Good
		Gardner Street .	–	Church	1853–1885	Good
		Haverhill Street .	–	Church	1847–1885	Good
		Parker Street .	–	Church	1870–1885	Good

¹ There are no formal records.
² The church records prior to 1861 were carried away.
³ The records from 1830 to 1849 are imperfect.
⁴ Imperfect to 1877; in much better condition since that year.
⁵ Records have been regularly kept by pastors.
⁶ The records from 1841 to 1849 are in existence, but are missing.
⁷ The records prior to 1884 are incomplete.
⁸ The records prior to 1860 were imperfectly kept.
⁹ The record from 1873 to 1881 is a partial record only.

Existing Churches : By Denominations — Continued.

Methodist Episcopal — Continued.

Cities and Towns.	Counties	Distinguishing Name	Year in which Organized	Records		
				Kind	Years covered	Condition
Lee, . . .	Berkshire	–	–	Church	1839–1885	Good
Leicester, . .	Worcester	Cherry Valley .	–	Church	1851–1885	Good
Lenox, . .	Berkshire	–	–	Church	1834–1885	Good[1]
Leominster,	Worcester	–	–	Church	1823–1885	Good
Leyden, . .	Franklin .	–	–	Church	1860–1885	Good
Longmeadow, .	Hampden .	East Longmeadow	–	Church	1853–1885	Good
Lowell, . .	Middlesex	Central . . .	–	Church	1854–1885	Good
		Highland . .	–	Church	1879–1885	–
		Saint Paul's . .	–	Church	1835–1885	Incomplete
		Worthen Street	–	Church	1841–1885	2–
Ludlow, . .	Hampden .	Ludlow Centre .	–	Church	1793–1885	Good
Lunenburg, .	Worcester	–	–	Church	1805–1885	Good
Lynn, . .	Essex .	Boston Street .	–	Church	1850–1885	Good
		Common Street .	–	Church[3]	1794–1885	Good
		Maple Street	–	Church	1850–1885	Good
		Saint Paul's . .	–	Church[4]	1811–1885	–
		South Street . .	–	Church	1830–1885	Good
		Trinity . . .	–	Church	1873–1885	Good
Malden, . .	Middlesex	Malden . . .	–	Church	1819–1885	Good
		Maplewood . .	–	Church	1859–1885	Good
Mansfield, . .	Bristol .	Emmanuel . .	–	Church	1860–1885	Good
		First . . .	–	Church	1811–1885	Good
Marblehead, .	Essex .	–	–	Church	1794–1885	Incomplete[5]
Marion, . .	Plymouth	–	1866	Church	1866–1885	Good
Marlborough, .	Middlesex	–	–	Church	1854–1885	Good
Marshfield, .	Plymouth	–	1813	Church	1825–1885	Incomplete
Maynard, . .	Middlesex	–	–	Church	1868–1885	Incomplete
Medford, . .	Middlesex	Medford . .	–	Church	1872–1885	Good
		West Medford .	–	Church	1872–1885	Good
Medway, . .	Norfolk .	West Medway .	–	Church	1857–1885	Good
Melrose, . .	Middlesex	–	–	Church	1813–1885	–
Mendon, . .	Worcester	–	–	Church	1741–1885	Good
Merrimac, . .	Essex .	Merrimac Port .	–	Church	1883–1885	–
Methuen, . .	Essex .	–	–	Church	1853–1885	Good
Middleborough,	Plymouth	Middleborough .	–	Church	1865–1885	Good
		So. Middleborough	–	Church	1858–1885	Good
Middleton, .	Essex .	–	–	Church	1879–1885	–
Milford, . .	Worcester	–	–	{ Church	1848–1885	Good
				{ Parish	1870–1885	Good
Millbury, . .	Worcester	–	–	Church	1877–1885	Good
Monson, . .	Hampden .	–	–	Church	1850–1885	Good
Montgomery, .	Hampden .	–	–	Church	1847–1885	Good
Nantucket, .	Nantucket	–	–	Church	1815–1885	Good
Natick, . .	Middlesex	–	–	Church	1865–1885[6]	–
Needham, . .	Norfolk .	Highlandville .	–	Church	1865–1885	Incomplete
New Ashford, .	Berkshire	7–	–	Church	1825–1885	Incomplete
New Bedford,	Bristol .	Allen Street . .	–	Church	1852–1885	Good
		County Street .	–	Church	1820–1885	Good
		Fourth Street .	–	Church	1835–1885	Good
		Pleasant Street .	–	Church	1844–1885	Good
Newbury, . .	Essex .	Byfield . . .	–	Church	1827–1885	Good
Newburyport,	Essex .	Purchase Street .	–	Church	1835–1885	Good
		Washington Street	–	Church	1865–1885	–
New Marlboro',	Berkshire	Hartsville . .	1844	Church	1858–1885[8]	Good
Newton, . .	Middlesex	Newton . . .	1863	Church	1863–1885	Good
		Newton Centre .	–	Church	1880–1885	Good
		Newton Lower Falls . . .	–	Church	1861–1885	–
		Newton Upper Falls . . .	–	Church	1828–1885	Good
		Newtonville . .	–	Church	1870–1885	Good

[1] The records prior to 1834 are incomplete.   [2] The earlier records are in very poor condition.
[3] Church records are known to exist but are missing at present from their proper custody.
[4] There are other records extant but they are missing.
[5] The records for the first fifty years are very imperfect, and the later records are defective.
[6] The records from 1836 to 1865 are lost.
[7] The church edifice was never dedicated to any denomination.
[8] The records from 1844 to 1858 are missing.

EXISTING CHURCHES: BY DENOMINATIONS — Continued.

METHODIST EPISCOPAL — Continued.

Cities and Towns.	Counties	Distinguishing Name	Year in which Organized	Records		
				Kind	Years covered	Condition
North Adams, .	Berkshire	–	–	Church	1792-1885	1-
NORTHAMPTON,	Hampshire	Florence	–	Church	1871-1885	Good
		Northampton	–	Church	1842-1885	Good
North Andover,	Essex	–	–	Church	1848-1885	Good
Northbridge, .	Worcester	Whitinsville .	1850	Church	1850-1885	Good
No. Brookfield,.	Worcester	–	–	Church	1830-1885	Good
North Reading,	Middlesex	–	–	Church	1880-1885	Good
Norton, . .	Bristol .	Chartley	–	Church	1876-1885	Good
Orange, . .	Franklin .	–	–	Church	1875-1885	Good
Orleans, . .	Barnstable	–	–	Church	1837-1885	Good
Oxford, . .	Worcester	–	–	Church	1836-1885	Good
Palmer, . .	Hampden .	Bondsville	–	Church	1866-1885	Good
		Palmer .	–	Church	1840-1885	Good
Peabody, . .	Essex .	–	–	Church	1840-1885	–
Pelham , . .	Hampshire	–	–	Church	1831-1885	–
Pembroke, .	Plymouth	Bryantville .	–	Church	1825-1885	Fair
Pepperell, . .	Middlesex	East Pepperell .	–	Church	1866-1885	–
Phillipston, .	Worcester	–	– {	Church	1829-1868	Poor
			{	Church	1879-1885	Poor
Pittsfield, . .	Berkshire	–	–	Church	1831-1885[2]	Good
Plymouth, .	Plymouth	–	1843	Church	1843-1885	–
Prescott, . .	Hampshire	North Prescott .	–	Church	1868-1885	Fair
Princeton, . .	Worcester	–	–	Church	1840-1885	Good
Provincetown, .	Barnstable	Centenary	–	Parish	1860-1885	Good
		Centre . .	1795	Church	1839-1885[3]	Complete
Quincy, . .	Norfolk .	West Quincy .	– {	Church and Parish }	1872-1885	Good
		Wollaston .	–	Church	1874-1885	Good
Reading, . .	Middlesex	–	–	Church	1869-1885	–
Rehoboth, . .	Bristol .	North Rehoboth .	–	Church	1849-1885	Good
Rockland, . .	Plymouth	–	–	Church	1832-1885	Good
Rockport, . .	Essex .	–	– {	Church and Parish }	1808-1885	–
Rowe, . .	Franklin .	–	–	Church	1840-1885	Fair
Royalston, .	Worcester	South Royalston .	–	Church	1845-1885	Good
Russel, . .	Hampden .	–	–	Church	1868-1885	Good
SALEM, .	Essex .	Lafayette Street .	–	Church	1847-1885	–
		Wesley Chapel .	–	Church	1871-1885	Good
Salisbury, . .	Essex .	East Parish .	–	Parish	1793-1885	Good
		Pond Street .	–	Church	1847-1885	Good
Sandwich, . .	Barnstable	–	1796	Church	1796-1885	Good
Saugus, . .	Essex .	Cliftondale .	–	Church	1854-1885	Good
		East Saugus .	– {	Church	1863-1885	Good
			{	Parish	1822-1885	Good
		Saugus .	–	Church	1877-1885	Good
Savoy, . .	Berkshire	Savoy Circuit	–	Church	1880-1885	Good
Scituate, . .	Plymouth	–	–	Church	1821-1885	Fair
Sheffield, . .	Berkshire	Ashley Falls .	–	Church	1857-1885	Good
		Sheffield .	–	Church	1848-1885	Good
Shelburne, .	Franklin .	Shelburne Falls	–	Church	1870-1885	4-
Shrewsbury, .	Worcester	–	–	Church	1846-1885	Fair
Somerset, . .	Bristol .	Somerset .	1842	Church	1842-1885	Good
		South Somerset .	–	Church	1802-1885	Good
SOMERVILLE, .	Middlesex	Broadway .	–	Church	1873-1885	Good
		Flint Street .	–	Church	1868-1885	Good
		Park Avenue .	–	Church	1872-1885	Good
		Union Square .	–	Church	1857-1885	Good
South Abington,	Plymouth	–	–	Church	1874-1885	Good
Southampton, .	Hampshire	–	–	Church	1840-1885	Good
Southbridge, .	Worcester	–	–	Church	1836-1885	Good
South Hadley, .	Hampshire	So. Hadley Falls .	–	Church	1833-1885	Fair
South Scituate, .	Plymouth	–	–	Parish	1852-1885	Good
Southwick, .	Hampden .	–	–	Church	1816-1885	5-
Spencer, . .	Worcester	–	–	Church	1843-1885	Good

1 The records prior to 1802 are meagre.

2 The records from about 1791 are lost. William Renne of Pittsfield has valuable private memoranda relating to the early history of this church.

3 The records from 1795 to 1839 are lost.   4 The earlier records are incomplete

5 The records from 1844 to 1858 are incomplete.

EXISTING CHURCHES: BY DENOMINATIONS — Continued.

METHODIST EPISCOPAL — Continued.

CITIES AND TOWNS.	Counties	Distinguishing Name	Year in which Organized	RECORDS		
				Kind	Years covered	Condition
SPRINGFIELD, .	Hampden .	Florence Street	–	Church	1815–1885	Fair
		Grace . . .	–	Church	1867–1885	Good
		State Street .	–	Church	1823–1885	Fair
		Trinity . . .	–	Church	1844–1885	Good
		Union American .	–	Church	1865–1885	Good
Stockbridge, .	Berkshire	–	–	Church	1835–1885	Incomplete
Stoneham, .	Middlesex	–	–	Church	1857–1885	Good
Stoughton, .	Norfolk .	North Stoughton .	–	Church	1817–1885	Good
		Stoughton .	–	Church	1813–1885	Good
Stow, . . .	Middlesex	Rock Bottom[1]	–	Church	1823–1885	Good
Sudbury, . .	Middlesex	–	–	Church	1830–1885	–
Swampscott, .	Essex .	–	–	Church	1854–1885	Fair
TAUNTON, .	Bristol .	Central . . .	–	Church	1852–1885	Good
		First . . .	–	Church	1835–1885	Fair
		Grace . . .	–	Church	1874–1885	Good
Templeton, .	Worcester	East Templeton .	–	Church	1843–1885	Good
Tisbury, . .	Dukes Co.	North Tisbury .	–	Church	1857–1885	–
		Vineyard Haven .	–	Church	1857–1885	–
Topsfield, . .	Essex .	–	–	Church	1824–1885	Good
Townsend, .	Middlesex	–	–	2 .	–	–
Truro, . .	Barnstable	South Truro . .	–	Church	1794–1885	–
		Truro . . .	1826	Parish	1826–1885	Good
Tyringham, .	Berkshire	–	–	Church	1852–1885	Good
Upton, . .	Worcester	–	–	Church	1874–1885	Good
Uxbridge, . .	Worcester	–	–	Church	1875–1885	Good
Wakefield, .	Middlesex	–	–	Church	1864–1885	–
Wales, . .	Hampden .	–	–	Church	1830–1885	–
Walpole, . .	Norfolk .	First (So. Walpole)	–	Church	1850–1885	–
		Walpole . .	–	Society	1835–1885	Good
WALTHAM, .	Middlesex	–	1837	Church	1837–1885	Good
Ware, . .	Hampshire	–	–	Church	1843–1885	Incomplete
Wareham, .	Plymouth	–	–	Church	1843–1885[3]	Good
Warren, . .	Worcester	Warren . . .	–	Church	1854–1885	Good
		West Warren .	–	Church	1876–1885	–
Washington, .	Berkshire	–	–	Church	1843–1885	Good
Watertown, .	Middlesex	–	–	Church	1837–1885	Good
Wayland, . .	Middlesex	Cochituate . .	–	Church	1880–1885[4]	Fair
Webster, . .	Worcester	–	–	Church	1834–1885	–
Wellfleet, . .	Barnstable	–	–	Church	1818–1885	Good
Westborough, .	Worcester	–	–	Church	1858–1885	Good
West Boylston, .	Worcester	Oakdale . . .	–	Church	1860–1885	Good
		West Boylston .	–	Church	1858–1885	Good
W. Bridgewater, .	Plymouth	Cochesett . .	–	Church	1841–1885	–
W. Brookfield, .	Worcester	–	–	Church	1852–1885	Good
Westfield, . .	Hampden .	Westfield . .	–	Church	1835–1885	Good
		West Parish .	–	Church	1795–1885	Good
Westford, . .	Middlesex	Graniteville .	–	Church	1869–1885	–
Weston, . .	Middlesex	–	–	Church	1811–1885	Fair
Westport, . .	Bristol .	Westport Point .	–	Church	1840–1885	Fair
W. Springfield, .	Hampden .	–	–	Church	1870–1885	–
W. Stockbridge,	Berkshire	–	–	Church and Parish	1838–1885	–
Weymouth, .	Norfolk .	East Weymouth .	–	Church	1822–1885	Good
		Porter (East Weymouth) . .	–	Church	1878–1885	Good
Wilbraham, .	Hampden .	Glendale . .	–	Church	1875–1879[5]	–
				Church	1882–1885	–
		Wilbraham . .	–	Church	1791–1885	–
Williamsburg, .	Hampshire	–	–	Church	1851–1885	–
Williamstown, .	Berkshire	–	–	Church	1855–1885	Good
Wilmington, .	Middlesex	–	–	Church	1882–1885	–
Winchendon, .	Worcester	–	1796	Church	1796–1885	–
Winchester, .	Middlesex	–	1872	Church	1872–1885	Complete
Winthrop, . .	Suffolk .	–	–	Church	1835–1885	Good

[1] Originally the Methodist Religious Society of Marlborough.

[2] The only record extant is to be found in a history of Townsend.

[3] The records from 1826 to 1842 are lost.

[4] No records prior to 1880 have been preserved.

[5] The records from 1869 to 1874 are in possession of the Town Clerk.

EXISTING CHURCHES: BY DENOMINATIONS — Continued.

METHODIST EPISCOPAL — Concluded.

CITIES AND TOWNS.	Counties	Distinguishing Name	Year in which Organized	RECORDS		
				Kind	Years covered	Condition
Woburn, . .	Middlesex	–	–	Church	1850–1885	Fair
WORCESTER, .	Worcester	Coral Street . .	–	Church	1872–1885	Good
		First Swedish Society . . .	–	Church	1883–1885	Good
		Grace . . .	–	Church	1867–1885	Good
		Laurel Street .	–	Church	1845–1885	Good
		Trinity . . .	–	Church	1834–1885	Fair
		Webster Square .	–	Church	1860–1885	Good
Worthington, .	Hampshire	So. Worthington .	–	Church	1863–1885	Good
		W. Worthington .	–	Church	1877–1885	Good
Yarmouth, .	Barnstable	South Yarmouth .	–	Church	1853–1885	Good
		Yarmouth Port .	–	Parish	1840–1885	–

NEW JERUSALEM.

Abington, . .	Plymouth	–	1835	Society	1833–1885	Good
BOSTON, . .	Suffolk .	Boston . . .	1818	Church	1817–1885	1–
		Roxbury . .	1870	Church	1870–1885	–
Bridgewater, .	Plymouth	–	1833	Church	1833–1885	Good
BROCKTON, .	Plymouth	–	1838	Church	1832–1885	Good
Brookline, .	Norfolk	–	1857	Society	1857–1885	Incomplete
E. Bridgewater,	Plymouth	–	1838	Church and Parish	1838–1885	Good
FALL RIVER, .	Bristol .	–	1854	Society	1854–1885	Good
Lancaster, .	Worcester	–	1875	Church	1875–1885	Good
Mansfield, .	Bristol .	2–	1846	Church	1846–1885	Good
NEWTON, .	Middlesex	–	1869	Church	1857–1885	Good
SALEM, . .	Essex .	–	–	Church and Parish	1869–1885	Good
SPRINGFIELD, .	Hampden .	–	–	Church	1853–1885	Good
WALTHAM, .	Middlesex	–	1869	Society	1860–1885	Good
Yarmouth, .	Barnstable	–	1843	Society	1838–1885	Good

PRESBYTERIAN.

BOSTON, . .	Suffolk .	East Boston . .	–	Church	1859–1885[3]	Good
		First . . .	–	Church	1862–1885	Good
		Saint Andrew's[4]	1880	Church	1882–1885	Good
		South Boston .	–	Church	1870–1885	Good
FALL RIVER, .	Bristol .	–	–	Church	1849–1885	–
LAWRENCE, .	Essex .	–	–	Church	1868–1885	Good
LOWELL, . .	Middlesex	First . . .	1869	Church	1869–1885	Good
NEWBURYPORT,	Essex .	Newburyport .	–	Parish	1764–1885	Good
		Second . .	1796	Parish	1796–1885	Good
Reading, . .	Middlesex	–	–	Church	1873–1885	Good
TAUNTON, .	Bristol .	First . . .	–	Church	1883–1885	Good

PRIMITIVE METHODIST.

FALL RIVER, .	Bristol .	–	–	Church	1872–1885	Good
LOWELL, . .	Middlesex	–	–	Church and Parish	1879–1885	Good

1 The records have been irregularly kept at times.

2 Originally instituted as the Foxborough and Mansfield Society.

3 The earlier records are lost.

4 Prior to 1869 the Springfield Street Congregational. .

EXISTING CHURCHES: BY DENOMINATIONS — Continued.

PROTESTANT EPISCOPAL.

CITIES AND TOWNS.	Counties	Distinguishing Name	Year in which Organized	RECORDS		
				Kind	Years covered	Condition
Adams, . .	Berkshire	Saint Mark's . .	–	Church	1869–1885	Good
Amesbury, .	Essex .	Saint James's .	–	Church	1833–1885	Good
Amherst, .	Hampshire	Grace . . .	–	Church	1864–1885	Good
Andover, .	Essex .	Christ . . .	–	Church	1835–1885	Good
Arlington, .	Middlesex	Saint John's .	1875	Church	1875–1885	–
Ashfield, .	Franklin .	Saint John's .	–	Church	1830–1885	–
Attleborough, .	Bristol .	Grace (North Attleborough)	1858	Parish	1858–1885	Good
Beverly, .	Essex .	Saint Peter's . .	–	Church	1864–1885	Good
Blackstone, .	Worcester	Saint John's (Millville) . . .	–	Parish	1851–1885	Good
BOSTON, . .	Suffolk .	Advent . . .	–	Church	1844–1885	Good
		All Saints' (Dorchester) . .	–	Church	1874–1885	Good
		Christ . . .	–	Society	1806–1885[1]	Good
		Emmanuel . .	–	Church	1860–1885	–
		Good Shepherd .	–	Church	1877–1885	Good
		Grace (So. Boston)	–	Church	1877–1885	Good
		Messiah . . .	1843 {	Parish	1871–1885	Good
				Treasurer's	1843–1885	Good
		Saint Andrew's	–	Church	1876–1885	Good
		Saint Ann's (Dorchester) . .	–	Church	1877–1885	Good
		Saint James's (Roxbury) . .	–˙	Church	1833–1885	Good
		Saint John's (Charlestown) .	–	Church	1841–1885	–
		Saint John's (East Boston) . .	–	Church	1845–1885	–
		Saint John's (Roxbury) . . .	–	Church	1871–1885	Good
		Saint John's (West Roxbury) . .	–	Church	1841–1885	Good
		Saint John the Evangelist's .	–	Church	1883–1885	Good
		Saint Margaret's (Brighton) . .	–	Church	1872–1885	Good
		Saint Mark's . .	–	Church	1851–1885	Good
		Saint Mary's (Dorchester) . .	–	Church	1847–1885	Good
		Saint Matthew's (South Boston) .	–	Church	1816–1885	Fair
		Saint Paul's . .	–	Church	1820–1885	Good
		Trinity . . .	–	Church[2]	1733–1885	Good
Bridgewater, .	Plymouth	Trinity . . .	1747	Church	1747–1885	Good
BROCKTON, .	Plymouth	Saint Paul's . .	–	Church	1875–1885	Good
Brookline, .	Norfolk .	Church of our Saviour (Longwood)	–	Church	1868–1885	Good
		Saint Paul's . .	–	Church	1861–1885	Good
CAMBRIDGE, .	Middlesex	Ascension . .	–	Church	1875–1885	3–
		Christ . . .	– {	Church	1862–1885	Good
				Parish	1870–1885	Good
		Saint James's .	–	Parish	1865–1885	Good
		Saint John's Memorial . .	–	Church	1868–1885	Good
		St. Peter's (Cambridgeport) }	– {	Church	1863–1885	Good
				Parish	1842–1885	Good
Chelmsford, .	Middlesex	Saint Ann's . .	–	Parish	1875–1885	–
CHELSEA, .	Suffolk .	Saint Luke's . .	–	Church	1842–1885	Good
Chicopee, .	Hampden .	Grace . . .	–	Church	4–	
Clinton, .	Worcester	Good Shepherd .	1879	Church	1879–1885	Good
Concord, .	Middlesex	Trinity . . .	–	Church	1884–1885	Good
Danvers, .	Essex .	Calvary . .	–	Church	1858–1885	Complete
Dedham, .	Norfolk .	Good Shepherd .	–	Church	1873–1885	Good
		Saint Paul's . .	–	Church	1874–1885	Good

[1] Formed in 1722; the records prior to 1806 are lost.

[2] There are copies in possession of the City Registrar.

[3] The records prior to 1882 are very meagre.

[4] The records cover occasional years from 1846 to 1877.

EXISTING CHURCHES: BY DENOMINATIONS — Continued.

PROTESTANT EPISCOPAL — Continued.

CITIES AND TOWNS.	Counties	Distinguishing Name	Year in which Organized	RECORDS		
				Kind	Years covered	Cond tion
Easthampton, .	Hampshire	Saint Philip's .	–	Church	1871–1885	Good
FALL RIVER, .	Bristol .	Ascension . .	–	Church	1837–1885	Good
		Saint James's .	– {	Church and Parish }	1884–1885	Good
		Saint John's . .	–	Church	1878–1885	Good
Falmouth, .	Barnstable	Church of Messiah (Wood's Holl) .	–	Church	1851–1885	–
FITCHBURG, .	Worcester	Christ . . .	–	Church	1883–1885	Good
Framingham, .	Middlesex	Saint John's . .	–	Parish	1860–1885	Good
GLOUCESTER, .	Essex .	Saint John's . .	–	Church	1862–1885	Good
Gt. Barrington,	Berkshire	Saint James's .	–	Church	1821–1885	Incomplete
		Trinity (Van Deu-senville) .	–	Church	1873–1885[1]	Good
Greenfield, .	Franklin .	Saint James's .	–	Church	1812–1885	Good
Groton, .	Middlesex	Saint John's Chapel	–	Church	1884–1885	–
Groveland, .	Essex .	Saint James's (So. Groveland) .	–	Parish	1873–1885	Good
Hanover, .	Plymouth	Saint Andrew's[2] .	– {	Church Church Parish	1782–1809 1819–1885 1780–1885	– – –
HAVERHILL, .	Essex .	Saint John's . .	–	Church	1875–1885	Good
		Trinity . . .	–	Parish	1855–1885	[3]–
Hingham, .	Plymouth	Saint John's . .	–	[4]–	–	–
HOLYOKE, .	Hampden .	Saint Paul's .	–	Church	1863–1885	Good
Hopkinton, .	Middlesex	Saint Paul's[5] .	–	Church	1817–1885	–
Hyde Park, .	Norfolk .	Christ . . .	–	Church	1860–1885	Good
Ipswich, .	Essex .	Ascension . .	–	Parish	1873–1885	Good
Lanesborough, .	Berkshire	Saint Luke's . .	– {	Church Parish	1823–1885 1767–1885	Good Good
LAWRENCE, .	Essex .	Grace . . .	–	Church	1846–1885	Good
		Saint John's . .	–	Church	1866–1885	Good[6]
		Saint Thomas's .	–	Church	1878–1885	Good
Lee, . .	Berkshire	Saint George's .	–	Church	1856–1885	Good
Lenox, .	Berkshire	Trinity . . .	–	Church	1794–1885	–
Lexington, .	Middlesex	Church of Our Re-deemer .	–	Church	1884–1885	Good
Lincoln, .	Middlesex	Saint Ann's (South Lincoln) .	–	Parish	1874–1885	Good
LOWELL, .	Middlesex	House of Prayer .	1877	Church	1877–1885	Good
		Saint Anne's . .	– {	Church and Parish }	1824–1885	Good
		Saint John's . .	– {	Church and Parish }	1860–1885	Good
LYNN, .	Essex .	Saint Stephen's .	–	Church	1844–1885	Good
MALDEN, .	Middlesex	Saint Luke's (Lin-den) . . .	–	Church	1883–1885	Good
		Saint Paul's . .	–	Church	1864–1885	Good
Marblehead, .	Essex .	Saint Michael's .	– {	Church Church	1714–1775 1802–1885	– –
Medford, .	Middlesex	Grace . . .	–	Church	1848–1885	Fair
Melrose, .	Middlesex	Trinity . . .	1857	Church	1857–1885	–
Methuen, .	Essex .	Saint Thomas's .	–	Church	1885 –	Good
Milford, .	Worcester	Trinity . . .	–	Church	1863–1885	Good
Nantucket, .	Nantucket	Saint Paul's . .	–	Parish	1846–1885	Fair
Natick, .	Middlesex	Saint Paul's . .	–	Parish	1871–1885	Good
NEW BEDFORD,	Bristol .	Grace . . .	–	Church	1833–1885	Good
		Saint James's .	–	Parish	1878–1885	Good
NEWBURYPORT,	Essex .	Saint Paul's . .	–	Church	1714–1885	Good
NEWTON, .	Middlesex	Grace . . .	– {	Church and Parish }	1855–1885	Good
		Messiah (Auburn-dale) . .	–	Church	1871–1885	Good
		Saint Mary's (New-ton Lower Falls)	–	Church	1872–1885	Good

1 The records from 1845 to 1873 are lost.
2 From 1731 to 1811, Saint Andrew's Church of Scituate.
3 Portions of the records prior to 1873 are lost; since 1873 the records are complete.
4 There has been no parish organization and there are no records.
5 The church edifice was destroyed by fire in 1865, but the society retains its organization.
6 The records from 1874 to 1878 are partial records only.

EXISTING CHURCHES: BY DENOMINATIONS — Continued.

PROTESTANT EPISCOPAL — Concluded.

CITIES AND TOWNS.	Counties	Distinguishing Name	Year in which Organized	RECORDS		
				Kind	Years covered	Condition
North Adams, .	Berkshire	Saint John's .	–	Church	1855–1885	Complete
NORTHAMPTON,	Hampshire	Saint John's .	–	Church	1826–1885	–
North Andover,	Essex	Saint Paul's .	–	Church	1881–1885	Good
Otis, . . .	Berkshire	Saint Paul's .	–	Church	1828–1885	Good
Oxford, . .	Worcester	Grace . . .	–	Church	1863–1885	Good
Peabody, . .	Essex	Saint Paul's .	–	Church	1874–1885	–
Pittsfield, . .	Berkshire	Saint Stephen's	–	Church	1832–1885	–
Plymouth, . .	Plymouth	Christ . . .	–	Church	1844–1885	Good
Quincy, . .	Norfolk .	Christ . . .	–	Church	1728–1885	Good
SALEM, . .	Essex .	Grace . . .	–	Church	1859–1885	Good
		Saint Peter's .	–	Parish	1735–1885	1–
Sandwich, . .	Barnstable	Saint John's .	1853	Church	1884–1885[2]	–
Sheffield, . .	Berkshire	Christ . . .	–	Church	1866–1885	Good
Shelburne, .	Franklin .	Emmanuel Memorial (Shelburne Falls) . . .	–	Parish	1882–1885	Good
SOMERVILLE, .	Middlesex	Emmanuel .	–	Church	1866–1885	Good
		Saint Thomas's	–	Church	1866–1885	Good
Southborough, .	Worcester	Saint Mark's .	–	Church	1860–1885	–
SPRINGFIELD, .	Hampden .	Christ . . .	–	Church	1821–1885	Good
Stockbridge, .	Berkshire	Saint Paul's .	–	Church	1839–1885	Good
Sutton, .	Worcester	Saint John's (Wilkinsonville)	–	Parish / Parish Register	1827–1885[3] / 1825–1861	Good / Good
Swansea, . .	Bristol .	Christ . . .	–	Church	1846–1885	Good
TAUNTON, . .	Bristol .	Saint John's .	–	Church	1867–1885	Good
		Saint Thomas's .	–	Parish / Parish	1750–1790 / 1825–1885	Mutilated / Good
Tisbury, . .	Dukes Co.	Grace (Vineyard Haven) . .	–	Parish	1862–1885	Good
Wakefield, .	Middlesex	Emmanuel .	–	Church	1870–1885	–
WALTHAM, .	Middlesex	Christ . . .	–	Parish	1848–1885	Good
Wareham, . .	Plymouth	Good Shepherd .	–	Church	1883–1885	–
Watertown, .	Middlesex	Mission . .	–	Parish	1883–1885	Good
Webster, . .	Worcester	Reconciliation .	–	Church	1868–1885	–
Westfield, . .	Hampden .	Atonement .	–	Church	1873–1885	Good
Weymouth, .	Norfolk .	Trinity . .	–	Parish	1870–1885	Good
Williamstown, .	Berkshire	Saint John's .	–	Church	1870–1885	Fair
Winchester, .	Middlesex	Epiphany .	1884	Church	1884–1885	Complete
Woburn, . .	Middlesex	Trinity . .	–	Church	1867–1885	Good
WORCESTER, .	Worcester	All Saints' .	–	Church	1835–1885	Fair
		Saint John's .	–	Church	1884–1885	Good.
		Saint Matthew's .	–	Church	1871–1885	Fair
Wrentham, .	Norfolk .	Trinity . .	–	Church	1864–1885	Good

REFORMED EPISCOPAL.

BOSTON, . .	Suffolk .	–	–	Church	1882–1885	Good

REFORMED PRESBYTERIAN.

BOSTON, . .	Suffolk .	First . . .	–	Church	1854–1885	Good
		Second . . .	–	Church	1871–1885	Good

[1] The records from 1735 to 1835 are incomplete; from 1835 to 1885 they are good.

[2] No services were held between 1865 and 1884; there are no records prior to 1884.

[3] Prior to 1861 these are copies only, the original records having been destroyed by the copyist.

EXISTING CHURCHES : BY DENOMINATIONS — Continued.

ROMAN CATHOLIC.

CITIES AND TOWNS.	Counties	Distinguishing Name	Year in which Organized	RECORDS		
				Kind	Years covered	Condition
Abington, . .	Plymouth	Saint Bridget's .	–	Church	1864–1885	–
Adams, . .	Berkshire	Church of the Seven Dolors (South Adams) .	–	Church	1882–1885	Good
		Saint Charles's (South Adams) .	–	Church	1875–1885	Good
Amesbury, .	Essex	Saint Joseph's .	–	Church	1867–1885	Good
Amherst, .	Hampshire	Saint Patrick's . .	–	Church	1869–1885	1–
Andover, .	Essex	Saint Augustine's .	–	Church	1851–1885	–
		Saint Joseph's (Ballardvale)[2] .	–	–	–	–
Arlington, .	Middlesex	Saint Malachi's .	–	Church	1873–1885	–
Ashburnham, .	Worcester	Saint Dennis's[3] .	–	–	–	–
Ashland, .	Middlesex	Saint Cecilia's .	–	Church	1884–1885	–
Athol, .	Worcester	Saint Catherine's .	–	Church	1882–1885	Good
Attleborough, .	Bristol .	Saint John's (East Attleborough) .	1883	Church	1883–1885	–
		Saint Mary's (No. Attleborough) .	–	Church	1850–1885	Good
Auburn, .	Worcester	Saint Joseph's (Stoneville)[4] .	–	–	–	–
Ayer, . .	Middlesex	Saint Mary's . .	–	Church	1867–1885	Fair
Barnstable, .	Barnstable	Hyannis[5] . .	–	–	–	–
Barre, .	Worcester	Saint Joseph's[6] .	–	–	–	–
Becket, .	Berkshire	[7]–	–	–	–	–
Bedford, .	Middlesex	Saint Michael's[8] .	–	–	–	–
Belmont, .	Middlesex	Patronage of Saint Joseph[9] . .	–	–	–	–
Beverly, .	Essex .	Star of the Sea .	–	Church	1865–1885	Good
Billerica, .	Middlesex	Saint Andrew's[10] .	–	–	–	–
Blackstone, .	Worcester	Saint Augustine's (Millville) . .	–	Church	1884–1885	–
		Saint Paul's . .	–	Church	1850–1885	Good
BOSTON, . .	Suffolk .	Cathedral of the Holy Cross .	–	Church	1803–1885	–
		Church of our Lady of the Assumption (East Boston) . .	–	Church	1869–1885	Good
		Church of the Sacred Heart (East Boston) . .	–	Church	1874–1885	Good
		Gate of Heaven (South Boston) .	–	Church	1863–1885	Good
		Holy Trinity . .	–	Church	1846–1885	Good
		Immaculate Conception . .	–	Church	1858–1885	Well kept
		Most Holy Redeemer (East Boston) . .	–	Church	1844–1885	Good
		Notre Dame des Victoires . .	–	Church	1880–1885	Good
		Our Lady of Perpetual Help (Roxbury) . . .	–	Church	1883–1885	Good
		Our Lady of the Rosary (South Boston) . .	–	Church	1884–1885	Good
		Saint Augustine's (South Boston) .	–	Church	1868–1885	Good
		Saint Columbkille's (Brighton) .	–	Church	1870–1885	Good
		Saint Francis de Sales's (Roxbury)	–	Church	1855–1885	Good

[1] The records are incomplete and are being reviewed.
[2] Attended from Andover.
[3] Attended from Winchendon.
[4] Attended from Oxford.
[5] Attended from Wood's Holl.
[6] Attended from Templeton.
[7] Attended from Hinsdale.
[8] Attended from Lexington.
[9] Attended from Arlington.
[10] Attended from Lowell.

EXISTING CHURCHES: BY DENOMINATIONS — Continued.

ROMAN CATHOLIC — Continued.

CITIES AND TOWNS.	Counties	Distinguishing Name	Year in which Organized	RECORDS		
				Kind	Years covered	Condition
BOSTON — Con.	Suffolk	Saint Francis de Sales's (Charlestown)	–	Church	1859–1885	Good
		Saint Gregory's (Dorchester)	–	Church	1864–1885	Good
		Saint James's	–	Church	1853–1885	Well kept
		Saint John the Baptist's	–	Church	1873–1885	Well kept
		Saint Joseph's	–	Church	1862–1885	Good
		Saint Joseph's (Roxbury)	–	Church	1846–1885	Good
		Saint Leonard of Port Maurice's	–	Church	1873–1885	Good
		Saint Mary's	–	Church	1836–1885	Good
		Saint Mary's (Charlestown)	–	Church	1829–1885	Good
		Saint Mary's, Star of the Sea (East Boston)	–	Church	1868–1885	Good
		Saint Patrick's (Roxbury)	–	Church	1836–1885	Good
		Saint Peter's (Dorchester)	–	Church	1873–1885	–
		Saints Peter and Paul's (South Boston)	–	Church	1847–1885	Good
		Saint Stephen's	–	Church	1862–1885	–
		Saint Thomas Aquinas's	–	Church	1869–1885	–
		Saint Vincent de Paul's (South Boston)	–	Church	1872–1885	Good
Braintree,	Norfolk	Saint Francis's (South Braintree)[1]	–	–	–	–
Bridgewater,	Plymouth	Saint Thomas Aquinas's	1855	Church	1855–1885	Good
BROCKTON,	Plymouth	Saint Paul's	–	Church	1856–1885	Good
Brookfield,	Worcester	Saint Mary's	–	Church	1885 –	–
Brookline,	Norfolk	Assumption	–	Church	1852–1885	Good
CAMBRIDGE,	Middlesex	Sacred Heart of Jesus (East Cambridge)	–	Church	1842–1885	Good
		Saint Mary's	–	Church	1867–1885	Good
		Saint Peter's	–	Church	1842–1885	Good
Canton,	Norfolk	Saint John's	–	Church	1861–1885	Good
Chelmsford,	Middlesex	Saint John the Evangelist's[2]	–	–	–	–
CHELSEA,	Suffolk	Saint Rose's	–	Church	1862–1885	Good
Cheshire,	Berkshire	Assumption[3]	–	–	–	–
Chester,	Hampden	4_	–	–	–	–
Chicopee,	Hampden	French	–	Church	1876–1885	Good
		Holy Name of Jesus	–	Church	1842–1885	Good
		Saint Patrick's (Chicopee Falls)	–	Church	1873–1885	Good
Clinton,	Worcester	Saint John's	–	Church	1845–1885	Good
Concord,	Middlesex	Saint Bernard's	–	Church	1868–1885	–
Conway,	Franklin	–	–	Church	1883–1885	Good
Danvers,	Essex	Church of Annunciation	–	Church	1862–1885	Good
Dartmouth,	Bristol	5_	–	–	–	–
Dedham,	Norfolk	Saint Mary's	–	Church	1870–1885	Fair
Deerfield,	Franklin	6_	–	–	–	–
Dighton,	Bristol	7_	–	–	–	–
Douglas,	Worcester	Saint Patrick's (East Douglas)	–	Church	1865–1885	–

[1] Attended from Quincy.
[2] Attended from Saint Patrick's at Lowell.
[3] Attended from South Adams.
[4] Attended from Westfield.

[5] Attended from New Bedford.
[6] Attended from Greenfield.
[7] Attended from Taunton.

Existing Churches: By Denominations — Continued.

Roman Catholic — Continued.

Cities and Towns.	Counties	Distinguishing Name	Year in which Organized	Kind	Years covered	Condition
E. Bridgewater,	Plymouth	Saint John's[1]	–	–	–	–
Easthampton, .	Hampshire	Immaculate Conception . .	–	Church	1871–1885	Good
Easton, . .	Bristol .	Immaculate Conception (North Easton) . .	1840	Church	1840–1885	Good
Enfield, . .	Hampshire	2_	–	–	–	–
Fairhaven, .	Bristol .	3_	–	–	–	–
FALL RIVER, .	Bristol .	Immaculate Conception . .	–	Church	1883–1885	Good
		Notre Dame de Lourdes . .	–	Church	1872–1885	Good
		Sacred Heart .	–	Church	1873–1885	Good
		Saint Ann's . .	–	Church	1869–1885[4]	Good
		Saint Joseph's .	–	Church	1873–1885	Good
		Saint Louis's . .	–	Church	1885 –	Good
		Saint Mary's . .	–	Church	1840–1885	Good
		Saint Patrick's .	–	Church	1872–1885	Good
		Saints Peter and Paul's . . .	–	Church	1882–1885	Good
Falmouth, . .	Barnstable	Falmouth[5] . .	–	–	–	–
		Wood's Holl . .	–	Church	1880–1885	–
FITCHBURG, .	Worcester	Sacred Heart (W. Fitchburg) .	–	Church	1880–1885	Good
		Saint Bernard's .	–	Church	1848–1885	Good
		Saint Mary's . .	–	Church	1878–1885	Good
Foxborough, .	Norfolk .	Saint Bridget's[6] .	–	–	–	–
Framingham, .	Middlesex	Saint George's (Saxonville) .	–	Church	1840–1885	–
		Saint Stephen's(So. Framingham) .	–	Church	1878–1885	Good
Franklin, . .	Norfolk .	Saint Mary's . .	–	Church	1877–1885	Good
Gardner, . .	Worcester	Sacred Heart of Jesus . .	–	Church	1879–1885	Good
Georgetown, .	Essex .	Saint Mary's . .	–	Church	1874–1885	–
GLOUCESTER, .	Essex .	Sacred Heart (Lanesville)[7] .	–	–	–	–
		Saint Ann's . .	–	Church	1852–1885	Good
Grafton, . .	Worcester	Saint Philip's .	–	Church	1869–1885	Good
Gt. Barrington,	Berkshire	Saint Bridget's (Housatonic)[8] .	–	–	–	–
		Saint Peter's . .	–	Church	1855–1885	Good
Greenfield, .	Franklin .	Holy Trinity . .	–	Church	1868–1885	Good
Groveland, .	Essex .	Saint Patrick's (So. Groveland)[9] .	–	–	–	–
Hanover, . .	Plymouth	Our Lady of the Sacred Heart[10] .	–	–	–	–
Hardwick, .	Worcester	Saint Aloysius's (Gilbertville)[2] .	–	–	–	–
Harwich, . .	Barnstable	5_	–	–	–	–
HAVERHILL, .	Essex .	Saint James's .	–	Church	1851–1885	Good
		Saint Joseph's .	–	Church	1876–1885	Good
Hingham, . .	Plymouth	Saint Paul's . .	–	Church	1872–1885	Good
Hinsdale, . .	Berkshire	Saint Patrick's .	1868	Church	1868–1885	Good
Holden, . .	Worcester	Saint Mary's .	–	Church	1884–1885	Good
Holliston, . .	Middlesex	Saint Mary's . .	–	Church	1870–1885	–
HOLYOKE, . .	Hampden .	Precious Blood .	–	Church	1869–1885	Good
		Sacred Heart .	–	Church	1878–1885	Good
		Saint Jerome's . .	–	Church	1854–1885	Good
Hopkinton, .	Middlesex	Saint John the Evangelist's .	–	Church	1855–1885	Good
Hudson, . .	Middlesex	Saint Michael's .	–	Church	1871–1885	Good

[1] Attended from Bridgewater.
[2] Attended from Ware.
[3] Attended from New Bedford.
[4] The records of burials are not continued after 1878.
[5] Attended from Wood's Holl.
[6] Attended from South Framingham.
[7] Attended from Rockport.
[8] Attended from Great Barrington.
[9] Attended from Georgetown.
[10] Attended from Rockland.

EXISTING CHURCHES: BY DENOMINATIONS — Continued.

ROMAN CATHOLIC — Continued.

CITIES AND TOWNS.	Counties	Distinguishing Name	Year in which Organized	RECORDS		
				Kind	Years covered	Condition
Hyde Park, .	Norfolk .	Most Precious Blood . . .	–	Church	1863–1885	Good
Ipswich, . .	Essex .	Saint Joseph's[1] . .	–	–	–	–
Kingston, . .	Plymouth	Saint Joseph's[2] . .	–	–	–	–
LAWRENCE, .	Essex .	Saint Ann's . . .	–	Church	1871–1885	Good
		Saint Augustine's Chapel[3] . . .	–	–	–	–
		Saint Lawrence O'Toole's[3] . .	–	–	–	–
		Saint Mary's . .	–	Church	1849–1885	Good
		Saint Patrick's (South Lawrence)	–	Church	1872–1885	Good
Lee, . . .	Berkshire	Saint Mary's . .	–	Church	1857–1885	Fair
Leicester, .	Worcester	Saint Aloysius's (Rochdale) .	–	Church	1855–1885	Good
		Saint Joseph's .	–	Church	1855–1885	Good
Lenox, . .	Berkshire	Saint Anne's[4] .	–	–	–	–
Leominster, .	Worcester	Saint Leo's . .	–	Church	1871–1885	Fair
Lexington, .	Middlesex	Saint Bridget's .	–	Church	1874–1885	Good
Longmeadow, .	Hampden .	Saint Mary's[5] .	–	–	–	–
LOWELL, . .	Middlesex	Immaculate Conception . .	–	Church	1868–1885	–
		Saint Joseph's .	–	Church	1868–1885	Good
		Saint Patrick's .	–	Church	1836–1885	–
		Saint Peter's . .	–	Church	1842–1885	–
LYNN, . .	Essex .	Saint Joseph's .	–	Church	1874–1885	Good
		Saint Mary's . .	–	Church	1849–1885	Good
MALDEN, .	Middlesex	Immaculate Conception . .	–	Church	6–	–
Manchester, .	Essex .	Sacred Heart[1]	–	–	–	–
Mansfield, . .	Bristol .	7–	–	–	–	–
Marblehead, .	Essex .	Our Lady, Star of the Sea . .	–	Church	1870–1885	Good
Marlborough, .	Middlesex	Immaculate Conception . .	1851	Church	1858–1885	Good
		Saint Mary's . .	–	Church	1870–1885	–
Maynard, . .	Middlesex	Saint Bridget's[8] .	–	–	–	–
Medfield, . .	Norfolk .	9–	–	–	–	–
Medford, . .	Middlesex	Saint Joseph's .	–	Church	1883–1885	–
Medway, . .	Norfolk .	Saint Joseph's .	–	Church	1863–1885	Good
Melrose, . .	Middlesex	Saint Bridget's[10] .	–	–	–	–
Merrimac, . .	Essex .	Church of the Nativity[11] . .	–	–	–	–
Methuen, . .	Essex .	3–	–	–	–	–
Milford, . .	Worcester	Saint Mary's . .	–	Church	1848–1885	Good
Millbury, . .	Worcester	French . . .	–	Church	1884–1885	Good
		Saint Bridget's .	–	Church	1869–1885	Good
Monson, . .	Hampden .	Saint Patrick's .	–	Church	1878–1885	Good
Montague, . .	Franklin .	French . . .	–	Church	1884–1885	Good
		Saint Mary's (Turner's Falls) .	1872	Church	1872–1885	Good
Nahant, . .	Essex .	Saint Thomas Apostle[12] . .	–	–	–	–
Nantucket, .	Nantucket	Our Lady of the Isle[13] . . .	–	–	–	–
Natick, . .	Middlesex	Sacred Heart (South Natick)[14] .	–		•	–
		Saint Patrick's .	–	Church	1861–1885	Good

[1] Attended from Beverly.
[2] Attended from Plymouth.
[5] Attended from West Springfield.
[6] Records of marriages from 1861 to 1885, and of baptisms from 1868 to 1885.
[7] Attended from Attleborough.
[8] Attended from Concord.
[9] Attended from Foxborough.
[10] Attended from Stoneham.

[3] Attended from Saint Mary's at Lawrence.
[4] Attended from Lee.
[11] Attended from Amesbury.
[12] Attended from Saint Mary's at Lynn.
[13] Attended from Wood's Holl.
[14] Attended from Natick.

EXISTING CHURCHES: BY DENOMINATIONS — Continued.

ROMAN CATHOLIC — Continued.

CITIES AND TOWNS.	Counties	Distinguishing Name	Year in which Organized	RECORDS		
				Kind	Years covered	Condition
NEW BEDFORD,	Bristol .	Sacred Heart .	–	Church	1877–1885	Good
		Saint John the Baptist's . . .	–	Church	1875–1885	Good
		Saint Lawrence's .	–	Church	1870–1885	Good
		Saint Mary's[1]	–	–	–	–
NEWBURYPORT,	Essex .	Immaculate Conception .	–	Church	1850–1885	–
New Marlboro',	Berkshire	Immaculate Conception (Mill River)[2] . .	–	–	–	–
		Saint Mary's . .	–	Church	1866–1885	–
NEWTON, . .	Middlesex	Our Lady, Help of Christians .	–	Church	1868–1885	Good
		Saint Bernard's (West Newton) .	–	Church	1876–1885	Good
		Saint Mary's (Newton Upper Falls) . . .	–	Church	1870–1885	Good
North Adams, .	Berkshire	Notre Dame .	–	Church	1871–1885	Good
		Saint Francis's .	–	Church	1865–1885	Good
NORTHAMPTON,	Hampshire	Church of the Annunciation (Florence) . . .	–	Church	1878–1885	Good
		Saint Mary's . .	–	Church	1846–1885	Good
North Andover,	Essex .	Saint Michael's[3] .	–	–	–	–
Northbridge, .	Worcester	Saint Patrick's (Whitinsville)[4] .	–	–	–	–
No. Brookfield,	Worcester	Saint Joseph's .	–	[5]–	–	–
Norton, . .	Bristol .	Saint Mary's[6] .	–	–	–	–
Norwood, . .	Norfolk .	Saint Catherine's[7] .	–	–	–	–
Orange, . .	Franklin .		–	Church	1882–1885	Good
Orleans, . .	Barnstable	[8]–	–	–	–	–
Oxford, . .	Worcester	Saint Roch's .	–	Church	1858–1885	Good
Palmer, . .	Hampden .	Saint Bartholomew's (Bondsville) . .	–	Church	1876–1885	Good
		Saint Mary's (Thorndike) .	–	Church	1874–1885	Good
		Saint Thomas's .	–	Church	1879–1885	Good
Peabody, . .	Essex .	Saint John's . .	–	Church	1874–1885	–
Pepperell, . .	Middlesex	Saint Joseph's .	–	Church	1885 –	Good
Pittsfield, . .	Berkshire	Notre Dame . .	–	Church	1869–1885	Good
		Saint Joseph's .	–	Church	1844–1885	Good
Plymouth, . .	Plymouth	Saint Peter's . .	–	Church	1876–1885	–
Provincetown, .	Barnstable	Saint Peter's . .	–	Church	1868–1885	Good
Quincy, . .	Norfolk .	Sacred Heart (No. Quincy)[9] . .	–	–	–	–
		Saint John's . .	–	Church	1843–1885	Good
		Saint Mary's (W. Quincy)[9] . .	–	–	–	–
Randolph, . .	Norfolk .	Saint Mary's . .	–	Church	1850–1885	Good
Reading, . .	Middlesex	Saint Agnes's[10] .	–	–	–	–
Rockland, . .	Plymouth	Holy Family . .	1883	Church	1883–1885	Good
Rockport, . .	Essex .	Saint Joachim's .	–	Church	1856–1885	Good
SALEM, . .	Essex .	Immaculate Conception .	–	Church	1831–1885	Fair
		Saint James's .	–	Church	1848–1885	–
		Saint Joseph's .	–	Church	1873–1885	–
Sandwich, . .	Barnstable	Saint Peter's . .	1843	Church	1843–1885	Good
Scituate, . .	Plymouth	Church of the Nativity[11] . .	–	–	–	–
Sharon, . .	Norfolk .	Saint Aloysius's Chapel[12] . .	–	–	–	–

[1] Attended from Saint Lawrence's.
[2] Attended from Great Barrington.
[3] Attended from Saint Patrick's at South Lawrence.
[4] Attended from Uxbridge.
[5] There are no records.
[6] Attended from East Attleborough.
[7] Attended from Dedham.
[8] Attended from Sandwich.
[9] Attended from Quincy.
[10] Attended from Wakefield.
[11] Attended from Cohasset.
[12] Attended from Stoughton.

EXISTING CHURCHES: BY DENOMINATIONS — Continued.

ROMAN CATHOLIC — Continued.

CITIES AND TOWNS.	Counties	Distinguishing Name	Year in which Organized	RECORDS		
				Kind	Years covered	Condition
Sheffield, . .	Berkshire	1_	–	–	–	–
Shelburne, .	Franklin .	Shelburne Falls .	–	Church	1884–1885	–
Shrewsbury, .	Worcester	Saint Theresa's[2] .	–	–	–	–
Somerset, . .	Bristol .	Saint Patrick's .	–	Church	1874–1885	Good
SOMERVILLE, .	Middlesex	Patronage of Saint Joseph . .	–	Church	1869–1885	Good
		Saint Ann's . .	–	Church	1881–1885	–
South Abington,	Plymouth	Church of the Holy Ghost[3] . .	–	–	–	–
Southbridge, .	Worcester	Notre Dame . .	–	Church	1869–1885	–
		Saint Mary's .	–	Church	1853–1885	Good
South Hadley, .	Hampshire	Saint Patrick's .	–	Church	1877–1885	Well kept
Spencer, . .	Worcester	Saint Mary's .	–	Church	1852–1885	Good
SPRINGFIELD, .	Hampden	Sacred Heart .	–	Church	1874–1885	Good
		Saint Aloysius's (Indian Orchard)	–	Church	1874–1885	Good
		Saint Joseph's .	–	Church	1876–1885	Good
		Saint Matthew's . (Indian Orchard)	–	Church	1868–1885	Good
		Saint Michael's .	–	Church	1861–1885	Good
Stockbridge, .	Berkshire	Saint Joseph's[4] .	–	–	–	–
Stoneham, . .	Middlesex	Saint Patrick's .	–	Church	1868–1885	Good
Stoughton, .	Norfolk .	Immaculate Conception .	–	Church	1858–1885	Good
		Saint Michael's (East Stoughton)[5]	–	–	–	–
Swampscott, .	Essex .	6_	–	–	–	–
TAUNTON, .	Bristol .	Sacred Heart .	–	Church	1873–1885	Good
		Saint James's[7] .	–	Church	1883–1885	Good
		Saint Mary's .	–	Church	1832–1885	–
Templeton, .	Worcester	Saint Martin's (Otter River) . .	–	Church	1850–1885	–
Tewksbury, .	Middlesex	8_	–	–	–	–
Townsend, .	Middlesex	Saint John's[9] .	–	–	–	–
Truro, . .	Barnstable	10_	–	–	–	–
Upton, . .	Worcester	Holy Angels'[11] .	–	–	–	–
Uxbridge, . .	Worcester	Saint Mary's .	–	Church	1867–1885	–
Wakefield, .	Middlesex	Saint Joseph's .	–	Church	1873–1885	Good
Walpole, . .	Norfolk .	Saint Francis's .	–	Church	1873–1885	Good
WALTHAM, .	Middlesex	Saint Mary's .	–	Church	1864–1885	Good
Ware, . .	Hampshire	Our Lady of Mount Carmel .	–	Church	1871–1885	Good
		Saint William's .	–	Church	1860–1885	Good
Wareham, . .	Plymouth	Saint Patrick's[12] .	–	–	–	–
Warren, . .	Worcester	Saint Athanasius's .	–	Church	1873–1885	–
		Saint Thomas's (West Warren)[13]	–	–	–	–
Watertown, .	Middlesex	Saint Patrick's .	–	Church	1855–1885	Good
Webster, . .	Worcester	Sacred Heart .	–	Church	1870–1885	Good
		Saint Louis's .	–	Church	1853–1885	Good
Wellfleet, . .	Barnstable	10_	–	–	–	–
Westborough, .	Worcester	Saint Luke's .	–	Church	1870–1885	Good
West Boylston,	Worcester	Saint Luke's .	–	Church	1870–1885[14]	Good
Westfield, . .	Hampden .	Saint Mary's .	–	Church	1862–1885	Good
West Newbury,	Essex .	Saint Ann's[15] .	–	–	–	–
Westport, . .	Bristol .	16_	–	–	–	–
W. Springfield, .	Hampden .	Immaculate Conception . .	–	Church	1875–1885	–

[1] Attended from Great Barrington.
[2] Attended from West Boylston.
[3] Attended from Abington.
[4] Attended from West Stockbridge.
[5] Attended from Holbrook.
[6] Attended from Saint Joseph's at Lynn.
[7] Called also Immaculate Conception.
[8] Attended by the Oblate Fathers.
[9] Attended from East Pepperell.
[10] Attended from Provincetown.
[11] Attended from Grafton.
[12] Attended from Sandwich.
[13] Attended from Warren.
[14] There were earlier records which were burned.
[15] Attended from Georgetown.
[16] Attended from Fall River.

EXISTING CHURCHES: BY DENOMINATIONS — Continued.

ROMAN CATHOLIC — Concluded.

CITIES AND TOWNS.	Counties	Distinguishing Name	Year in which Organized	RECORDS		
				Kind	Years covered	Condition
W. Springfield — Cen.	Hampden	Saint Thomas's (Mittineague)[1]	—	—	—	—
W. Stockbridge,	Berkshire	Saint Patrick's	—	Church	1871–1885	Good
Weymouth,	Norfolk	Immaculate Conception (East Weymouth)	—	Church	1882–1885	Good
		Sacred Heart	—	Church	1866–1885	—
		Saint Francis Xavier's (South Weymouth)[2]	—	—	—	—
		Saint Jerome's (N. Weymouth)[3]	—	—	—	—
Wilbraham,	Hampden	North Wilbraham[4]	—	—	—	—
Williamsburg,	Hampshire	Saint Mary's (Haydenville)[5]	—	—	—	—
Winchendon,	Worcester	Immaculate Heart of Mary	—	Church	1871–1885	—
Winchester,	Middlesex	Saint Mary's	1873	Church	1873–1885	Complete
Winthrop,	Suffolk	Point Shirley[5]	—	—	—	—
		Saint John the Evangelist's[6]	—	—	—	—
Woburn,	Middlesex	Saint Charles's	—	Church	1854–1885	Fair
		Saint Joseph's (East Woburn)[7]	—	—	—	—
WORCESTER,	Worcester	Immaculate Conception	—	Church	1874–1885	Good
		Notre Dame	—	Church	1869–1885	Good
		Sacred Heart	—	Church	1880–1885	Good
		Saint Ann's	—	Church	1853–1885	Good
		Saint John the Apostle and Evangelist's	—	Church	1846–1885	Good
		Saint Paul's	—	Church	1856–1885	Good
Wrentham,	Norfolk	[8]—	—	—	—	—
Yarmouth,	Barnstable	[9]—	—	—	—	—

SECOND ADVENT.

Athol,	Worcester	—	—	Church	1864–1885	Good
BOSTON,	Suffolk	Church of Christ	—	Church	1866–1885	Good
Carver,	Plymouth	Advent Christian	—	Church	1820–1885	—
CHELSEA,	Suffolk	—	—	Church	1867–1885	Good
Clinton,	Worcester	—	—	Church	1879–1885	Good
HAVERHILL,	Essex	—	—	Church	1875–1885	Incomplete
LAWRENCE,	Essex	—	—	Church and Parish	1867–1885	Good
NEW BEDFORD,	Bristol	—	—	Church	1854–1885	Good
NEWBURYPORT,	Essex	—	1846	Parish	1856–1885	Good
SALEM,	Essex	—	—	Church	1850–1885	Good
Savoy,	Berkshire	[10]—	—	—	—	—
SPRINGFIELD,	Hampden	—	—	Church	1860–1885	Good
Webster,	Worcester	—	1885	Church	1885 –	—
Westfield,	Hampden	—	—	Church	1869–1885	Good

[1] Attended from Immaculate Conception at West Springfield.
[2] Attended from Weymouth.
[3] Attended from East Weymouth.
[4] Attended from Palmer.
[5] Attended from Annunciation at Florence.
[6] Attended from Saint Mary's, Star of the Sea, at East Boston.
[7] Attended from Winchester.
[8] Attended from Franklin.
[9] Attended from Wood's Holl.
[10] This church is said to be nearly extinct; no information has been obtained.

EXISTING CHURCHES: BY DENOMINATIONS — Continued.

SEVENTH DAY ADVENT.

CITIES AND TOWNS.	Counties	Distinguishing Name	Year in which Organized	RECORDS		
				Kind	Years covered	Condition
Lancaster, . .	Worcester	–	–	Church	1864–1885	Good

UNDENOMINATIONAL.

Attleborough, .	Bristol .	Union (Hebron-ville) . . .	–	Church	1828–1885	Good
Brookfield,	Worcester	Union (East Brook-field) . . .	–	Church	1878–1885	Good
		Union (Podunk) .	–	Church	1885 –	–
Hardwick, . .	Worcester	Union . . .	1842	Church	1842–1885	Good
Lee, . . .	Berkshire	Union (South Lee)	–	Church	1827–1885	Good
NEW BEDFORD,	Bristol .	Christian Union .	–	Church	1874–1885	Good
West Boylston,.	Worcester	First Liberal . .	–	Parish	1830–1885	Good
Wilbraham, .	Hampden .	Christian Union Society . .	–	Society	1868–1885	–
		Grace Chapel Society . . .	–	Parish	1876–1885	–
Williamstown, .	Berkshire	Church of Christ in the White Oaks	–	–	–	–
WORCESTER, .	Worcester	Church of the Covenant . . .	1885	Church	1885 –	Good

UNION EVANGELICAL.

SPRINGFIELD, .	Hampden .	Memorial . .	–	Church	1865–1885	Good

UNITARIAN.

Arlington, . .	Middlesex	First Congregational Parish	1733	Church Parish	1739–1885 1732–1885	Good Good
Ashby, . .	Middlesex	First Parish . .	1767	Parish[1]	1841–1885	– Good
Athol, . .	Worcester	First Congregational Church[2] .	1750	Church	1750–1885	Good[3]
		Second Unitarian Society . .	1877	Church	1877–1885	Good
Ayer, . . .	Middlesex	First Unitarian Parish[4] . .	1864	Church and Parish	1855–1885	Good
Barnstable, .	Barnstable	Congregational Church and Society in the East Precinct . .	1639[5]	Parish	1725–1885	Good
Barre, . .	Worcester	First Parish . .	1756	Church	1818–1885	Good
Bedford, . .	Middlesex	First Parish . .	1730	Church Parish	1730–1885 1730–1885	6– 6–
Belmont, . .	Middlesex	Christian Union Society . .	1882	Society	1882–1885	Good
		Congregational Society .	1856	Church Parish	1859–1885 1856–1885	Good Good

¹ The pastor has private records from 1868 to 1885.
² Originally the Church of Christ of Pergauge.
³ Sixty leaves have been cut out.
⁴ Name changed from South Groton Christian Union in 1864.
⁵ Originally gathered in England in 1639 by Rev. John Lothrop. Accepting his diary, in possession of the Congregational church at West Barnstable, as a record, together with the records of that church, the records are nearly continuous from 1639 to 1885.
⁶ The records from 1730 to 1796 are incomplete.

CITIES AND TOWNS.	Counties	Distinguishing Name	Year in which Organized	RECORDS		
				Kind	Years covered	Condition
Berlin, . .	Worcester	First Unitarian Society . . .	1872	Church	1871–1885	Good
Bernardston, .	Franklin .	First Congregational . . .	1741	Parish	1817–1885	Good
Beverly, . .	Essex .	First Parish . .	1667	Church[1]	1668–1885	Good
Billerica, . .	Middlesex	First Congregational Society .	1663	Society	1663–1885	Fair
Bolton, . .	Worcester	{ First Congregational Church {	1740	Church Parish	– 1834–1885	– –
BOSTON, . .	Suffolk .	Appleton Street Free Chapel	1883	Church	1883–1885	Good
		Arlington Street[2] .	1730	Church	1786–1885	Good
		Church in Brattle Square[3] . . .	1699	Church[4]	1699–1840	–
		Church of the Disciples . . .	1841	Parish	1841–1885	Good
		Church of our Father (East Boston) . . .	1846	Parish	1846–1885	Fair
		Church of the Unity . . .	1857	Church	1857–1885	Good
		Church of the Unity (Neponset) . . .	1859	Church	1859–1885	Good
		First Congregational Society of Jamaica Plain[5] .	1770	Church	1760–1885	Good
		First Parish of Dorchester[6]	{ 1630 {	Church Parish	1636–1885 1808–1885	Good Good
		First Religious Society in Roxbury[7]	1631	Church	1641–1885	Good
		Harrison Square Society (Dorchester) . .	} 1848	Church	1848–1885	Good
		Harvard (Charlestown)[8] . .	{ 1815 {	Church Parish	1817–1885 1815–1885	Good Good
		Hawes Place Congregational Society (So. Boston)	} 1822	Church	1819–1885	Good
		Hollis Street[9] .	1732	Church	1730–1885	Good
		King's Chapel[10] .	1686	Church	1686–1885	Good
		Mount Pleasant Congregational (Roxbury) .	} 1846	Church	1845–1885	Good
		New South[11] . .	1867	Parish	1867–1885	Good
		Second[12] . .	1649	Church	1662–1885	Fair

[1] There are copies of parish records from 1667 to 1830 in possession of the Town Clerk.

[2] Formed in 1727 as the Presbyterian Church in Long Lane; later the Federal Street Unitarian.

[3] Originally Congregational; the church edifice was sold in 1876.

[4] The parish records were burned in the Boston fire in 1872.

[5] Originally Congregational.

[6] Originally Congregational. The earliest records since 1636 have been copied; the records prior to 1636 are missing and are supposed to have been carried to Windsor, Conn.

[7] Originally Congregational.

[8] Prior to 1818 the Second Congregational Society in Charlestown, and from 1818 to 1837 the New Church in Charlestown.

[9] Originally Congregational. The records of meetings prior to 1730 were written in 1730.

[10] Protestant Episcopal prior to 1786.

[11] Originally organized in 1719 as Congregational; reorganized in 1867. The records from 1815 to 1867, with the exception of a few in possession of the parish clerk, are in possession of the Massachusetts Historical Society.

[12] Organized as the Old North Church, originally Congregational.

EXISTING CHURCHES: BY DENOMINATIONS — Continued.

UNITARIAN — Continued.

CITIES AND TOWNS.	Counties	Distinguishing Name	Year in which Organized	RECORDS		
				Kind	Years covered	Condition
BOSTON — Con.	Suffolk .	Second Hawes Congregational Unitarian Society (South Boston)	1845	Church	1845–1885	Good
		South Congregational . . .	1828	Church	1827–1885	Good
		The First Church in Boston[1] . .	1630	Parish	1630–1885	Good
		The First Congregational Parish of West Roxbury[2]	1712	Church / Parish	1712–1885 / 1733–1885	Good / Good
		The First Parish of Brighton[2] .	1730	Church	1772–1885	Good
		Third Religious Society in Dorchester .	1813	Church	1815–1885	Good
		Unity Chapel (South Boston) .	1856	Church	1855–1885	Good
		Warren St. Chapel	1835	Church	1836–1885	Good[3]
		West Boston Society (Independent Congregational) .	1737	Church	1806–1885[4]	Good
Brewster, . .	Barnstable	First Parish . .	1700	Parish	1747–1885	Fair
Bridgewater, .	Plymouth	First Congregational Society .	1716	Society	1716–1885[5]	Good
BROCKTON, .	Plymouth	Unity . . .	1881	Parish	1881–1885	Good
Brookfield, .	Worcester	First Congregational . . .	1754	Church	1755–1885	Good
Brookline, . .	Norfolk .	First Parish . .	1717	Parish	1834–1885	Good
CAMBRIDGE, .	Middlesex	Cambridgeport Parish . .	1809	Church and Parish	1808–1885	–
		First Parish . .	1636	Church / Parish / Parish	1696–1885[6] / 1733–1771 / 1782–1885	Good / Poor . / Good
		Lee Street . .	1846	Church and Parish	–	–
		Third Congregational Society .	1827	Parish	1827–1885	Good
Canton, . .	Norfolk .	First Congregational Parish .	1717	Church[7] / Church / Church / Church / Parish[8]	1717–1799 / 1808–1819 / 1823–1848 / 1853–1885 / 1820–1885	Good / Good / Good / Good / Good
Carlisle, . .	Middlesex	First Religious Society . .	1780	Church	1842–1885	Good
Charlemont, .	Franklin .	Unitarian Congregational Society	–	Society	1826–1885	Incomplete[9]
Chelmsford, .	Middlesex	First Congregational . .	1655	Society[10]	1741–1885	Good
CHELSEA, . .	Suffolk .	First Unitarian Society .	1837	Church	1838–1885	Good
Chicopee, . .	Hampden .	First Unitarian Society .	1841	Church	1842–1885	Good

[1] Originally Congregational. The earlier records have been copied.

[2] Originally Congregational.   [3] There are occasional intervals in the records.

[4] During the Revolution the earlier records were carried to the British Provinces, and the church was disorganized; reorganized in 1806.

[5] There is an interval in the records for about twenty years, the years not being specified.

[6] The earlier church records are lost.

[7] The church has copies only of the records from 1717 to 1783. The original records from 1727 to 1783 are in possession of Charles F. Dunbar, Buffalo, N. Y.

[8] The first volume covering the years from 1726 to 1797 is lost.

[9] Some of the records were burned.

[10] There are private records kept by Rev. John Fiske, in possession of David Pulsifer of Boston.

EXISTING CHURCHES: BY DENOMINATIONS — Continued.

UNITARIAN — Continued.

CITIES AND TOWNS.	Counties	Distinguishing Name	Year in which Organized	RECORDS		
				Kind	Years covered	Condition
Clinton, . .	Worcester	First Unitarian Society .	1850	Church	1852–1885	Good
Cohasset, .	Norfolk .	First Parish . .	1721	Church and Parish	1721–1885	Good
Concord, . .	Middlesex	First Parish . .	1636	Parish	1738–1885	Good
Danvers, . .	Essex	Unitarian Congregational Society	1865	Church and Parish	1865–1885	Good
Dedham, . .	Norfolk .	First Parish . .	1638	Church	1638–1670[1]	Good
				Church	1724–1885	Good
		Third Parish (West Dedham) .	1735	Parish	1737–1885	Fair
Deerfield, . .	Franklin	First Congregational .	1688	Church and Parish	1820–1885	Good
Dighton, . .	Bristol .	Pedobaptist Congregational Society . . .	1797	Parish	1797–1885	Fair
Dover, . .	Norfolk .	First Parish . .	1749	Parish	1832–1885	–
Duxbury, . .	Plymouth	First . . .	1632	Church	1739–1885	Incomplete
				Parish	1828–1885	Good
E. Bridgewater,	Plymouth	First Parish . .	1724	Church and Parish	1724–1885	Good
Easton, . .	Bristol .	First Parish of Easton .	1720	Parish	1792–1885	Good
		Unity Church (North Easton) .	1855	Parish	1868–1885	Good
Fairhaven, .	Bristol .	Washington Street Christian Church	1832	Church	1819–1885	Good
FALL RIVER, .	Bristol .	Unitarian Society .	1832	Church[2]	1839–1885	–
FITCHBURG,	Worcester	First Parish . .	1768	Church	1805–1885	Good
Framingham, .	Middlesex	First . . .	1701	Parish	1840–1885	Good
Gardner, . .	Worcester	First Unitarian Society . . .	1884	Church	1884–1885	Good
GLOUCESTER, .	Essex .	First Parish . .	1642	Church	1702–1849	Meagre
				Parish	1728–1885	Good
Grafton, . .	Worcester	Congregational Society . .	1731	Church	1861–1885	Good
Greenfield, .	Franklin .	Third Congregational . .	1825	Church	1825–1885	Good
Groton . .	Middlesex	First Parish . .	1655	Parish	1815–1885	–
Harvard, . .	Worcester	First Congregational Parish .	1733	Church	1733–1885	–
HAVERHILL, .	Essex .	First Parish . .	1645	Church and Parish	1790–1885	Good
Hingham, . .	Plymouth	First Parish . .	1635	Church and Parish	1720–1885[3]	Good
		Second Parish (South Hingham)	1745	Parish	1745–1885	Good
		Third Congregational Society .	1807	Parish	1807–1885	Good
HOLYOKE, .	Hampden .	Liberal Christian Congregational Society . .	1874	Church	1874–1885	Good
Hubbardston, .	Worcester	First Congregational Society	1770	Church	1770–1885	Good
				Parish	1835–1885	Good
Hudson, . .	Middlesex	Union Society .	1860	Society	1865–1885	Good
Hyde Park, .	Norfolk .	First Unitarian Society . . .	1868	Church	1868–1885	Good
Kingston, . .	Plymouth	First Congregational Parish .	1717	Parish	1720–1885	4–
Lancaster, . .	Worcester	First Congregational Society .	1653	Parish	1836–1885	Good
LAWRENCE, .	Essex .	First Unitarian Society . . .	1847	Society	1847–1885	Good
Leicester, . .	Worcester	Second Congregational Society .	1833	Church	1833–1885	–

[1] A volume covering the years from 1670 to 1724 is lost.

[2] A private record is in possession of J. M. Aldrich.

[3] The record kept by Rev. Ebenezer Gay, from 1718 to 1787, and by Rev. Henry Ware, from 1787 to 1805, is in possession of the church.   [4] The records prior to 1784 are imperfect.

EXISTING CHURCHES: BY DENOMINATIONS — Continued.

UNITARIAN — Continued.

CITIES AND TOWNS.	Counties	Distinguishing Name	Year in which Organized	RECORDS		
				Kind	Years covered	Condition
Leominster, .	Worcester	First Congregational Society .	1835	Church	1743–1885	Good
Lexington, .	Middlesex	First Congregational Society .	1696	Society	1696–1885[1]	Good
		The Church of the Redeemer (East Lexington) .	1865	Church	1840–1885	Good
Lincoln, . .	Middlesex	Unitarian Congregational Society	1841	Parish	1841–1885[2]	–
Littleton, . .	Middlesex	First Congregational Society .	1717	Society	1830–1885	–
LOWELL, . .	Middlesex	First Unitarian Society . . .	1830	Church	1829–1885	Good
LYNN, .	Essex .	{ Second Congregational }	1822 {	Church	1822–1848	Incomplete
				Society	1822–1885	Complete
Lynnfield, .	Essex .	First Congregational Society .	1715	Church	1720–1885	–
MALDEN, .	Middlesex	First Congregational Unitarian Society . .	1875	Church	1875–1885	Good
Mansfield, .	Bristol .	First Congregational Parish .	1731	Church	1734–1885	Fair
Marblehead, .	Essex .	Second Congregational Society .	1716 {	Church and Parish }	1716–1885	Good
Marlborough, .	Middlesex	West Parish . .	1806	Parish	1804–1885	Good
Marshfield, .	Plymouth	Grace Chapel .	1882	Society	1882–1885	Good
		Second Congregational Society .	1738	Parish	1738–1885	Good
Medfield, . .	Norfolk .	First Congregational Parish .	1650	Parish	1652–1885	–
Medford, . .	Middlesex	First Parish . .	1713	Church	1712–1885	Fair
Melrose, . .	Middlesex	Congregational Unitarian Society	1867	Parish	1867–1885	Good
Mendon, . .	Worcester	First Parish . .	1669 {	Church	1728–1885	Good
				Parish	1769–1885	Good
Milford, . .	Worcester	The Hopedale Parish .	1867	Parish	1867–1885	Good
Millbury, . .	Worcester	First Unitarian Society . .	1884	Church	1885 –	Good
Milton, . .	Norfolk .	First Congregational Society .	1662 {	Church	1678–1885	Incomplete
				Parish	1818–1885	Good
Montague, . .	Franklin .	Second Congregational Society .	1825	Church	1825–1885	Good
		Unitarian Society of Turner's Falls	1873	Church	1873–1885	Good
Nantucket, .	Nantucket	Parish of the Second Congregational Meeting House .	1808	Parish	1846–1885[3]	–
Natick, . .	Middlesex	First Unitarian Parish (South Natick) .	1828	Church	1830–1885	Good
Needham, . .	Norfolk .	First Congregational Society .	1711 {	Church	–	–
				Parish	1778–1885	–
NEW BEDFORD,	Bristol .	Congregational Parish .	1714	Church	1731–1885	Good
		First Congregational Society[4] .	1795 {	Church and Parish }	1811–1885	Good .
NEWBURYPORT,	Essex .	First Religious Society .	1725	Church	1800–1885	Good
New Salem, .	Franklin .	Congregational Society . .	1742	Parish[5]	1742–1885	Fair

[1] There are omissions in the records at times when the society was without a pastor.

[2] The records for 1878, 1879, and 1880 are omitted.

[3] The records from 1809 to 1846 were destroyed in the fire of 1846.

[4] Papers of the late Rev. Samuel West, relating to the original First Congregational Parish, are in possession of Rev. William J. Potter.

[5] There are also records kept by pastors which commence earlier than the parish records.

EXISTING CHURCHES: BY DENOMINATIONS — Continued.

UNITARIAN — Continued.

CITIES AND TOWNS.	Counties	Distinguishing Name	Year in which Organized	RECORDS		
				Kind	Years covered	Condition
NEWTON, . .	Middlesex	Channing Religious Society .	1851	Church	1851–1885	Good
		First Unitarian Society . .	1848	Society	1854–1885	Good
		Unitarian Society (Newton Centre)	1877	Society	–	
NORTHAMPTON,	Hampshire	Second Congregational . . .	1825	Church	1825–1885	Good
North Andover,	Essex .	North Parish Church and Society	1645 {	Church and Society	1686–1885	Wel preserved
Northfield, .	Franklin .	First Congregational Society .	1718	Parish	1826–1885	Good
Northborough, .	Worcester	First Congregational Church and Society .	1746	Parish	1830–1885	Good
Peabody, . .	Essex .	First . . .	1825	Church	1826–1885	–
Pembroke, .	Plymouth	First . . .	1712	Parish	1764–1885	Good
Pepperell, . .	Middlesex	First Parish . .	1747 {	Church Parish	– 1833–1885	– –
Petersham, .	Worcester	First Congregational Parish . .	1738	Parish -	1738–1885	–
Plymouth, . .	Plymouth	First Parish . .	1620	Church	1620–1885	Incomplete
Quincy, . .	Norfolk .	First Congregational Society .	1639	Church[1]	1865–1885	Good
Raynham, . .	Bristol .	Second Congregational Society .	1828	Church	2_	–
Reading, . .	Middlesex	Christian Union Society[3] . .	1869	Church	1869–1885	Good
Revere, . .	Suffolk .	First Congregational Society .	1715 {	Church Church	1715–1776 1783–1885	Good Good
Rockland, . .	Plymouth	The Unitarian Society of Rockland . . .	1884	Parish	1884–1885	Good
Rowe, . .	Franklin .	First Congregational . .	1780	Parish	1804–1885	Good
SALEM, . .	Essex .	First Congregational Society .	1629 {	Church and Society	1829–1885	Good
		Independent Congregational in Barton Square .	1824	Parish	1824–1885	Good
		Second . . .	1717	Parish	1846–1885	Good
		The North Society[4]	1772 {	Church and Parish	1772–1885	Good
Sandwich, . .	Barnstable	First Church of Christ . {	1638 {	Church Parish	1695–1885 1780–1885	Good Good
Scituate, . .	Plymouth	First Parish . .	1634	Parish	1695–1885	Good
Sharon, . .	Norfolk .	First Congregational Society {	1740 {	Church Parish	1741–1885 1740–1885	– Incomplete
Sherborn, . .	Middlesex	First Congregational {	1685 {	Church Parish	1734–1885 1685–1885	– –
Shirley, . .	Middlesex	First Congregational Society .	1753	Church	1822–1885	–
SOMERVILLE, .	Middlesex	First Congregational Society {	1846 {	Church and Parish	1844–1885	Good
South Scituate, .	Plymouth	First Parish . .	1644 {	Church and Parish	1797–1885	Good

[1] Edward W. Marsh has a copy of an incomplete record from 1688 to 1832 of the First Church of Braintree (now Quincy).

[2] Twenty or more years. Services were discontinued in 1840, although the society still holds its organization.

[3] This society was originally organized as Unitarian, April 2, 1827; in 1838 united with the Second Universalist Society of Reading, which had been organized a few years previously; in 1856 the Second Universalist Society was reorganized as the First Universalist Society of Reading, and in 1869 was again reorganized as Unitarian under its present name. Very meagre records prior to 1869 are in possession of the clerk of the present society.

[4] The records of the First Church, from which the North Church was formed, are included in these records.

EXISTING CHURCHES: BY DENOMINATIONS — Continued.

UNITARIAN — Concluded.

CITIES AND TOWNS.	Counties	Distinguishing Name	Year in which Organized	RECORDS		
				Kind	Years covered	Condition
SPRINGFIELD, .	Hampden .	Third Congregational Society .	1819	Church	1819–1885	Fair
Sterling, . .	Worcester	{ First Congregational Society	1742 {	Church	1745–1885	Good
				Parish	1836–1885	Good
Stoneham, .	Middlesex	Christian Union .	1866	Church	1867–1885	Good
Stow, . .	Middlesex	First Parish . .	1700	Parish	1833–1885	Good
Sturbridge, .	Worcester	Unitarian Congregational Society	1864	Church	1864–1885	Good
Sudbury, . .	Middlesex	First Congregational Society .	1636	Church	1785–1885	–
TAUNTON, .	Bristol .	{ First Congregational Society[1]	1637 {	Church and Parish	1637–1885	Good
Templeton, .	Worcester	First Parish . .	1733	Church	1806–1885	Good
Tyngsborough, .	Middlesex	First Parish . .	1755	Church	1834–1885	Good
Upton, . .	Worcester	First Unitarian Society . . .	1848	Church	1848–1885	–
Uxbridge, . .	Worcester	{ First Congregational Society	1731 {	Church	1833–1885	Good
				Parish	1797–1885	Good
Walpole, . .	Norfolk .	{ First Congregational Society	1730 {	Church	1724–1885	Good
				Parish	1826–1885	Good
WALTHAM, .	Middlesex	First Parish . .	1696 {	Church and Parish	1837–1885[2]	Fair
Ware, .	Hampshire	First Unitarian Society . .	1846	Society	1846–1885	Good
Warwick, . .	Franklin .	First Congregational Parish .	1763	Church	1760–1885	Good
Watertown, .	Middlesex	{ First Congregational Society	1630 {	Church	1686–1885	–
				Parish	1835–1885	–
Wayland, . .	Middlesex	First . . .	1722 {	Church[3]	1803–1885	–
				Parish	1834–1885	–
Wellesley, . .	Norfolk .	Wellesley Hills[4] .	1871	Church	1871–1885	Good
Westborough, .	Worcester	First Congregational Society .	1717	Parish	1825–1885	–
W. Bridgewater,	Plymouth	{ First Congregational Society	1651 {	Church	1721–1808	–
				Church	1836–1885	–
				Society	1726–1806	–
				Society	1821–1885	–
Westford, . .	Middlesex	{ First Congregational Parish	1727 {	Church	1727–1885	–
				Parish	1826–1885	–
Weston, . .	Middlesex	First . . .	1698	Church and Parish	1709–1885	Good
Weymouth, .	Norfolk .	First Unitarian Society . . .	1873	Society	1873–1885	Incomplete
Winchendon, .	Worcester	Church of the Unity . .	1865	Church	1865–1885	Good
Winchester, .	Middlesex	The Winchester Unitarian Society . .	1865	Church	1865–1885	Complete
Woburn, . .	Middlesex	First Unitarian Parish . .	1847	Parish	1852–1885	Good
WORCESTER, .	Worcester	Second Congregational Church .	1785	Church	1785–1885	Good
		The Church of the Unity . . .	1846	Church	1846–1885	Good

UNITED PRESBYTERIAN.

BOSTON, .	Suffolk .	–	–	Church	1846–1885	Good
Grafton, .	Worcester	Sutton United Presbyterian .	–	Church	1856–1885	Good
Northbridge, .	Worcester	Whitinsville .	1871	Church	1871–1885	–

[1] Called the "Pilgrim Church" until about 1821, when it became Unitarian.
[2] The records prior to 1837 are in possession of the City Clerk.
[3] There are private records in possession of Horace Heard.
[4] Called also the Grantville Unitarian.

EXISTING CHURCHES: BY DENOMINATIONS — Continued.

UNITED SOCIETY (SHAKERS).

CITIES AND TOWNS.	Counties	Distinguishing Name	Year in which Organized	Kind	Years covered	Condition
Hancock, . .	Berkshire	–	1790	Society	1790–1885	–
Harvard, . .	Worcester	–	–	Society	1791–1885	–
Shirley, . .	Middlesex	–	–	Society	1792–1885	Good

UNIVERSALIST.

CITIES AND TOWNS.	Counties	Distinguishing Name	Year in which Organized	Kind	Years covered	Condition
Abington, . .	Plymouth	First . . .	1863	Church	1836–1885	Good
Acton, . .	Middlesex	South Acton . .	–	Parish	1866–1885	Good
		West Acton . .	1876	Church	1859–1885	Good
Adams, . .	Berkshire	–	1872	Church	1872–1885	Good
Amesbury, .	Essex	–	– {	Church	1833–1871	Incomplete
				Church	1871–1885	Good
Arlington, .	Middlesex	–	1842	Church	1840–1885	Good
Attleborough, .	Bristol .	–	1874	Church	1874–1885	Good
		No. Attleborough	–	Church	1816–1885	Good
Barnstable, .	Barnstable	Hyannis . .	1880	Society	1875–1885	Good
Bernardston, .	Franklin .	[1]–	1872 {	Society	1820–1839	Good
				Society	1845–1885	Good
Beverly, . .	Essex .	–	1856 {	Parish	1840–1861[2]	Good
				Parish	1867–1885	Good
BOSTON, . .	Suffolk .	Brighton . .	1872	Church	1860–1885	Good
		Charlestown . .	1812	Church	1810–1885	Good
		East Boston . .	1865[3]	Church	1865–1885	Good
		Grove Hall (Dorchester) . .	1878	Church	1877–1885	Good
		Jamaica Plain (West Roxbury)	–	Church	1871–1885	–
		Roxbury . .	1822	Church	1820–1885	Good
		Saint John's (Dorchester)[4] . .	1874 {	Church	1859–1862	Complete
				Church	1876–1885[5]	Complete
		Second Society .	1837	Church	1817–1885	Good
		Shawmut[6] . .	1837	Church	1836–1885	–
		South Boston[7] . .	1870	Church	1830–1885	–
Brewster, . .	Barnstable	–	1824	Society	1824–1885	Good
BROCKTON, .	Plymouth	–	–	Parish	1884–1885	Good
CAMBRIDGE, .	Middlesex	First Universalist Society	1827	Society	1822–1885	Good
		Second . . .	–	Church	1827–1885	Good
		Third . . .	1872	Church	1872–1885	Fair
Canton, . .	Norfolk .	–	1853 {	Parish	1819–1830	Good
				Parish	1849–1885	Good
Charlton, . .	Worcester	–	1864	Church	1851–1885	Well preserved
Chatham, . .	Barnstable	–	1835 {	Church	1820–1885	Fair
				Society	1822–1885	Fair
CHELSEA, . .	Suffolk .	–	1842	Church	1845–1885	Good
Cheshire, . .	Berkshire	–	1849	Church	1849–1885	Good
Chicopee, . .	Hampden .	–	1840	Church	1845–1885	Good
Cummington, .	Hampshire	West Cummington	–	Church	1840–1885	Good
Danvers, . .	Essex .	–	1877	Parish	1815–1885	Good
Dunstable, .	Middlesex ·	–	– {	Parish	1818–1843	Good
				Parish	1876–1885[8]	Good
Essex, . .	Essex .	–	1876	Church	1829–1885	Complete
Everett, . .	Middlesex	–	–	Church	1872–1885	Good
FITCHBURG, .	Worcester	–	1858	Church	1844–1885	Good
Foxborough, .	Norfolk .	–	1865	Church	1809–1885[9]	–

[1] Originally organized in 1820 as The First Restoration Society.

[2] The records from 1862 to 1866 are lost.

[3] Originally organized in 1840, but no records prior to 1865 are in existence.

[4] Organized in 1859 as the Dorchester Universalist Society.

[5] There is a record also of one meeting in 1870, and one in 1874.

[6] Originally the Fifth Universalist Church.   [8] Reorganized in 1876.

[7] Organized as the Fourth Universalist.   [9] The records prior to 1809 were burned.

Existing Churches: By Denominations — Continued.

Universalist — Continued.

Cities and Towns.	Counties	Distinguishing Name	Year in which Organized	Records		
				Kind	Years covered	Condition
Framingham, .	Middlesex	South Framingham	1878	Parish	1878–1885	–
Franklin, .	Norfolk .	–	1859 {	Church	1859–1885	Good
				Parish	1856–1885	Good
Gardner, .	Worcester	–	1868	Church	1868–1885	Good
GLOUCESTER, .	Essex .	East Gloucester .	–	Church	1884–1885	Good
		Gloucester . .	1799 {	Church and Parish }	1779–1885	Fair
		Lanesville . .	–	Parish	1876–1885	Good
		West Gloucester .	1716[1]	Parish	1716–1885	Incomplete
HAVERHILL, .	Essex .	Haverhill . .	–	Church	1853–1885	Good
		West Haverhill .	–	Church	1844–1885	Good
Hingham, .	Plymouth	–	1823	Parish	1861–1885	–
LAWRENCE, .	Essex .	–	1859 {	Church and Society }	1847–1885	Good
Leyden, .	Franklin .	–	–	Church	1867–1885	Good
LOWELL, .	Middlesex	First . . .	1827 {	Church and Parish }	1827–1885	Good
		Second . . .	–	Church	1838–1885	Good
LYNN, .	Essex .	First . . .	–	{ Church and Parish }	1833–1885	Good
		Second . . .	–	Church	1837–1885	Good
MALDEN, .	Middlesex	–	1826	Church	1828–1885	Good .
Marblehead, .	Essex .	–	– {	Church and Parish }	1836–1885	Good
Marion, .	Plymouth	–	1828	Church	1844–1885[2]	Good
Marlborough, .	Middlesex	–	1866	Church	1863–1885	Good
Mattapoisett, .	Plymouth	–	1831	Church	1828–1885	Good
Medford, .	Middlesex	–	1834	Church	1831–1885	Good
Melrose, .	Middlesex	–	1882 {	Church and Parish }	1867–1885	Good
Merrimac, .	Essex .	–	1865 {	Church and Parish }	1840–1885	–
Methuen, .	Essex .	–	1840	Church	1832–1885	3_
Middleton, .	Essex .	–	–	Church	1829–1885	–
Milford, .	Worcester	–	1851	Church	1785–1885	Good
Monson, .	Hampden .	–	–	Church	1883–1885	Good
Natick, .	Middlesex	–	1882	Parish	1876–1885	Good
NEW BEDFORD, .	Bristol .	–	–	Church	1835–1885	Good
NEWTON, .	Middlesex	–	1873	Church	1872–1885	Good
North Adams, .	Berkshire	–	1861	Parish	1859–1885	Good
North Reading, .	Middlesex	–	–	Parish	1713–1885	Fair
Norwood, .	Norfolk .	–	1857	Church	1827–1885	Fair
Orange, .	Franklin .	North Orange .	1878 {	Church and Parish }	1878–1885	Complete
		Orange . . .	1858 {	Church and Parish }	1851–1885	Good
Orleans, .	Barnstable	–	1876	Society	1835–1885	Good
Oxford, .	Worcester	–	–	Church	1785–1885	Good
Palmer, .	Hampden .	–	1876	Church	1875–1885	Good
Peabody, .	Essex .	–	1877	Church	1832–1885	Good
Plymouth, .	Plymouth	–	1827	Church	1826–1885	Fair
Provincetown, .	Barnstable	–	1843	Parish	1829–1885	–
Quincy, .	Norfolk .	–	1833	Church	1831–1885	Good
Rockport, .	Essex .	First . . .	1842	Church	1821–1885	Good
		Pigeon Cove . .	–	Church	1869–1885	Good
Rowley, .	Essex .	–	– {	Church	1877–1885	Good
				Society }	1858–1869	Good
SALEM, .	Essex .	–	1810	Church	1805–1885	–
Salisbury, .	Essex .	–	–	Church	1826–1885	Good
Saugus, .	Essex .	4_	1876	Parish	1738–1885	Good
Scituate, .	Plymouth	West Scituate .	– {	Society	1812–1885	Good
				5_ }	1772–1885	Good
Shelburne, .	Franklin .	Shelburne Falls .	1864	Church	1867–1885	Good

[1] Reorganized in 1867 as the Third Universalist.

[2] The records prior to 1844 are lost.

[3] The records prior to 1874 are meagre; since 1874 they are complete.

[4] From 1738 to 1832 this church was Congregational, since which time it has been Universalist. It was reorganized in 1876.

[5] Records of the proprietors of the meeting-house.

EXISTING CHURCHES : BY DENOMINATIONS — Concluded.

UNIVERSALIST — Concluded.

CITIES AND TOWNS.	Counties	Distinguishing Name	Year in which Organized	RECORDS		
				Kind	Years covered	Condition
Shirley, . .	Middlesex	Shirley Village .	–	Church and Parish	1812–1885	Good
SOMERVILLE, .	Middlesex	Somerville .	1861	Church	1864–1885	Fair
		Third (West Somerville) .	–	Church and Parish	1880–1885	Good
Southbridge, .	Worcester	–	1850	Church	1840–1885	Fair
South Scituate, .	Plymouth	–	–	Church and Parish	1863–1885	Good
Spencer, . .	Worcester	–	1878	Church	1876–1885	Good
SPRINGFIELD, .	Hampden .	Saint Paul's . .	1825	Church	1827–1885	Fair
Stoughton, .	Norfolk .	–	1831	Church	1743–1885	Incomplete
				Parish	1743–1885	Good
Swansea, . .	Bristol .	North Swansea .	–	Church	1876–1885	Good
TAUNTON, . .	Bristol .	–	–	Church and Parish	1841–1885	Good
Tyngsborough, .	Middlesex	–	1874	Church	1841–1885	Fair
Wakefield, .	Middlesex	–	1843	Church	1843–1885	Good
WALTHAM, .	Middlesex	–	1874	Church	1874–1885	Good
				Society	1865–1885	Good
Warren, . .	Worcester	1_	1864	Church	1830–1885	Fair
Webster, . .	Worcester	–	1860	Church	1866–1885	Good
Wellfleet, . .	Barnstable	–	1874	Parish	1840–1885	Good
Westfield, . .	Hampden .	–	–	Church	1853–1885	Good
Westminster, .	Worcester	–	–	Church	1820–1885	Good
Weymouth, .	Norfolk .	First . . .	1840	Church	1836–1885	Good
		Second (South Weymouth) .	–	Society	1864–1885	Good
		Third (North Weymouth) .	–	Church	1858–1885	Good
WORCESTER, .	Worcester	All Souls . . .	–	Church	1884–1885	Good
		First . . .	1843	Church	1841–1885	Good
Wrentham, .	Norfolk .	West Wrentham .	–	Society	1845–1885	Good
Yarmouth, .	Barnstable	–	1867	Society	1836–1885	–

WESLEYAN METHODIST.

HAVERHILL, .	Essex .	–	–	Church	1852–1885	Good

1 Organized in 1830 as the Independent Believers; afterward the Second Universalist of Western.

CHURCH RECORDS.

EXTINCT CHURCHES: BY TOWNS.

[The denominations considered in this table, and the abbreviations used to denote them, are as follows: — African Methodist Episcopal (A. M. E.); African Methodist Episcopal Zion (A. M. E. Z.); Baptist (Bapt.); Christian (Chris.); Congregational (Cong.); Dissenting Congregational (Dis. Cong.); Evangelical (Evang.); Free Baptist (Free Bapt.); Friends; Independent Congregational (Ind. Cong.); Jewish; Methodist (Meth); Methodist Episcopal (M. E.); Methodist Protestant (Meth. Prot.); Presbyterian (Presb.); Protestant Episcopal (Prot. Epis.); Reformed Methodist (Ref. Meth.); Roman Catholic (Rom. Cath.); Second Advent (Sec. Adv.); Six Principles Baptist (S. P. Bapt.); Undenominational (Undenom.); United Brethren (Un. Breth.); Unitarian (Unit.); United Society, or Shakers (Un. Soc.); Universalist (Univ.); Wesleyan (Wes.); Wesleyan Methodist (Wes. Meth.).

The following abbreviations are also used: — Ch., for Church; M't'g, for Meeting; M. M't'g, for Monthly Meeting; Par., for Parish; Soc., for Society, and St., for Saint or Street, as the context requires. Cong., for Congregational, is used in the column headed "Distinguishing Name," when Congregational is part of the name, although the denomination is not the present Congregational.

The use of the dash signifies in the column headed "Denomination," that the particular denomination could not be ascertained; in the column headed "Distinguishing Name," that no name other than that of the town was given, and in the other columns that the information is wanting.

The asterisk preceding a date signifies that it is the nearest date obtainable.

When the residence of the person having the possession of the records is other than in the town where the church was located the residence is given in a foot-note, and if the residence specified is not in Massachusetts the state is also given.

In some cases the records commenced at an earlier date than the year in which the church was organized, services having been held by the congregation and records kept before the formal organization as a church or society.]

County of Barnstable.

Cities and Towns.	Denomination	Distinguishing Name	Year in which Organized	Year in which Terminated	Records	
					Years covered	In Possession of—
Barnstable,	M. E.	Hyannis	–	–	–	–
	Wes.	Hyannis	–	–	–	–
Bourne,	Cong.[1]	Monument Beach	–	1852	1800–1852	Ebenezer Nye
	Meth Prot.	Pocasset	1852	1866	1852–1866	–
Chatham,	Cong.	–	1720	1869	1824–1869	Town Clerk
Dennis,	Cong.	First Cong.	1829	–	1727–1845	Isaiah B. Hall
	Univ.	South Dennis	[2]–	[2]–	–	Burned
	Wes.	–	–	1866	–	Nathan A. Howes
Harwich,	Ref. Meth.[3]	–	1820	1845	1820–1845	–
	Wes. Meth.[4]	–	1845	1853	1845–1853	–
Orleans,	Bapt.	–	–	–	–	–
Sandwich,	Prot. Epis.	Puritan	–	*1860	–	–
Wellfleet,	M. E.	–	–	–	–	John R. Higgins[5]
	M. E.	South Wellfleet	–	–	–	Rev. M. L. Bealey[6]
Yarmouth,	–	Yarmouth Port	–	–	–	Rev. Philo Hawks[7]

[1] United with the Methodist.
[2] Church edifice built in 1839; sold and removed in 1873.
[3] Succeeded by the Wesleyan Methodist, also extinct.
[4] Succeeded by the Methodist Episcopal.

[5] Providence, R. I.
[6] Easton.
[7] Barnstable.

EXTINCT CHURCHES: BY TOWNS — Continued.

COUNTY OF BERKSHIRE.

CITIES AND TOWNS.	Denomination	Distinguishing Name	Year in which Organized	Year in which Terminated	Records Years covered	Records In Possession of—
Alford, . .	M. E.	–	1_	–	1807–1812	–
Cheshire, . .	Bapt.[2]	First Bapt.. .	1799	1834	1799–1834	F. A. Martin
	Bapt.	Lanesborough .	1789	1799	1789–1799	F. A. Martin
	Bapt.	Stafford's Hill .	–	–	–	Shuball W. Lincoln
Egremont,. .	Cong.	–	–	–	–	–
Hancock, . .	Bapt.	Second Bapt. .	–	–	1843–1845	Caleb Eldridge
Hinsdale, . .	M. E.	–	–	–	–	–
Lee, . . .	A. M. E. .	–	–	–	–	–
	A. M. E. Z.	–	–	–	–	–
Mt. Washington,	Cong.	–	1831	–	–	H. F. Keith[3]
	M. E.	–	4_	–	–	Rev. Mervin B. Lent[5]
North Adams, .	Bapt.	–	*1776	–	–	6_
	Cong.	–	1776	1777	1776–1777	Lost
Otis, . . .	Bapt.	West Otis . .	–	–	–	–
	M. E.	East Otis . .	–	–	–	–
Pittsfield, .	Cong.[7]	Union Par.. .	–	–	1809–1817	Henry A. Brewster
Sandisfield, .	Bapt.	First Bapt.. .	–	–	–	A. W. Merrill
	Bapt.	Second Bapt. .	–	–	–	A. W. Merrill
Savoy, . .	Bapt.	Second Bapt. .	–	–	–	8_
	M. E.	–	–	–	–	Ebenezer Codding
Tyringham, .	Un. Soc.[9] .	–	1791	1875	–	Soc. at Hancock
Washington, .	Cong.	–	–	–	–	A. S. Pomeroy
W. Stockbridge,	Bapt.	–	–	*1825	–	Disappeared
Windsor, . .	Bapt.	–	1821	1851	1821–1851	H. C. Estes[10]

COUNTY OF BRISTOL.

Attleborough, .	–	Trinity . .	–	–	–	Rev. G. E. Osgood
Berkley, . .	Cong.[11]	Second Cong. .	–	–	–	–
Dartmouth, .	Bapt.	South Dartmouth	–	–	–	–
	Friends	Newtown M't'g .	1745	–	–	–
Fairhaven, .	Cong.	–	1840	1849	1840–1849	Eben. Akin, Jr.
FALL RIVER, .	Friends	Independent .	1845	*1865	13_	–
	Univ.	–	· –	121850	–	–
	–	Bible Union .	–	–	14_	–
NEW BEDFORD,	Cong.	Pacific Cong. .	–	–	–	George F. Bartlett
	M. E.	Mount Pleasant .	–	–	–	Pastor of M. E. Ch.[15]
Norton, . .	Dis. Cong.	–	1748	–	1748–1761	16_
Rehoboth, .	Ref. Meth.	North Rehoboth	1826	–	–	Francis W. Stevens[17]
Swansea, . .	S. P. Bapt.	–	–	–	–	Samuel Arnold[18]
	–	Swansea Village M't'g House .	–	–	–	19_
TAUNTON, .	Free Bapt.	Weir Street .	–	–	–	D. J. Lawrence
	Univ.	–	1825	1835	1825–1835	Charles Foster
Westport, .	Cong.[20]	–	–	–	–	–
	Friends	Centre M't'g .	*1780	1880	1780–1880	Westport M. M't'g
	–	First Chris. .	–	–	–	John Smith[21]

1 Reference is made to reorganization about 1855; no other information can be obtained.
2 Succeeded by the present Baptist.   4 Meetings were held in 1789.
3 Great Barrington.   5 Millerton, N. Y.
6 Supposed to be in possession of Rev. C. W. Anable, Adams.
7 Reunited with the First Church.   8 Supposed to be in possession of Mark Deming.
9 Succeeded by the Societies at Hancock, Mass., and Enfield, Conn.
10 Pastor of Greenville Baptist Church in Leicester, for the purpose of depositing them in the archives of the Backus Historical Society of Newton Centre.
11 Succeeded by the Methodist Episcopal.   12 About 1850 or prior to that year.
13 Records covering a few years are known to have been kept.
14 Records cover about three years.   15 Long Plain.
16 In possession of the Baptist Church which succeeded the Dissenting Congregational.
17 North Rehoboth.   18 Providence, R. I.
19 Certain records relating to this church are in a volume with other records, in the office of the Town Clerk.   20 A few persons are living who know something about this church.
21 Clerk of the church.

EXTINCT CHURCHES: BY TOWNS — Continued.

COUNTY OF DUKES COUNTY.

CITIES AND TOWNS.	Denomination	Distinguishing Name	Year in which Organized	Year in which Terminated	RECORDS	
					Years covered	In Possession of—
Tisbury, . .	Bapt. .	South Bapt.[1] .	–	–	[2]–	–

COUNTY OF ESSEX.

CITIES AND TOWNS.	Denomination	Distinguishing Name	Year in which Organized	Year in which Terminated	Years covered	In Possession of—
Andover, . .	Bapt. .	–	–	1857	1831–1857	–
Boxford, . .	Cong. .	Third Cong. Soc.	–	–	1824–1834	Benj. S. Barnes
Essex, . .	–	Chris. Soc. .	1808	1827	1808–1827	[3]–
Georgetown, .	Free Bapt. .	–	–	–	*1820 –	–
	Undenom. .	Union Soc. . .	–	–	1843 –	–
	Univ. .	–	1829	1853	1829–1853	–
GLOUCESTER, .	Univ. .	Second Univ. Soc.	–	–	– 1860	–
Groveland, .	Bapt. .	–	–	[4]–	–	–
HAVERHILL, .	Cong. .	Winter Street .	–	1860	–	–
	Cong.[5] .	Central Cong. .	–	1883	1849–1883	[6]–
LAWRENCE, {	Cong.[5] .	Central Cong.Soc.	–	1883	1850–1883	Charles U. Bell
	Cong.[5] .	Eliot Cong. .	–	–	[7]–	Trinity Cong. Ch.
	Cong. .	Lowell St. Cong.	–	1869	–	John Jowett[8]
	Meth. .	Trinity Meth. .	–	–	–	–
Lynnfield, .	M. E. .	–	1816	1862	1816–1862	Henry E. Smith
Marblehead, .	Cong.[9] .	Third Cong. .	–	1877	1858–1877	Benjamin Savoy
Methuen, . .	Cong.[10] .	Second Par. .	1766	1816	1780–1790	Clerk of First Par.
Newbury, . .	Bapt.[11] .	First Bapt. .	1811	1869	1811–1869	[11]–
	Cong. .	Fourth Cong. .	1832	1846	1832–1846	Town Clerk
NEWBURYPORT,	Chris. .	Court St. Chris.	–	1875	–	Rev. D. P. Pike
Rockport, . .	Cong. .	Second Cong. .	–	–	1855–1868	John W. Marshall
SALEM, . .	Meth. .	First Meth. .	–	–	1820 –	Mathew Robson
	–	Howard St.[12] .	–	–	1828–1832	Henry J. Pratt
Salisbury, . .	Cong. .	East Par. . .	1687	–	1687–1754	John M. Cushing[13]
West Newbury,	Friends, .	–	1841	1881	1841–1881	Amesbury M. M't'g

COUNTY OF FRANKLIN.

CITIES AND TOWNS.	Denomination	Distinguishing Name	Year in which Organized	Year in which Terminated	Years covered	In Possession of—
Ashfield, . .	Bapt. .	First Bapt. .	1761	*1846	1761–1846	Arnold Smith
	Univ. .	–	–	–	–	Frederick Guilford
Bernardston, .	Bapt. .	–	–	[14]–	–	[15]–
Buckland, . .	Bapt. .	–	–	–	–	Mrs. Wm. Stetson
Charlemont, .	–	–	–	–	–	Thomas A. Taylor

---

[1] West Tisbury.

[2] There are records covering thirty-five years, the years not being specified.

[3] Reorganized in 1849, and erected the same year a church edifice, which is now used by the Methodist Episcopal. There is a church record since 1849 and a volume of records previous to that year is supposed to be in existence.

[4] A few years ago.

[5] United and formed Trinity Congregational.

[6] From 1849 to 1858 in possession of Charles U. Bell; from 1859 to 1883 in possession of Trinity Congregational.

[7] Church records from 1865 to 1883; parish records from 1871 to 1883.

[8] Address unknown.

[9] Church edifice was destroyed by fire, and the parish united with the First Congregational.

[10] Reorganized in 1830 and reunited soon after with the First Parish.

[11] Merged in the Baptist Church of Newburyport; records in possession of the Historical Society of Newburyport and Newbury.   [12] Called also First Presbyterian.

[13] Mrs. Mary P. Graves of Newburyport has records from 1752 to 1805.

[14] Prior to 1808.

[15] Records were loaned and not returned.

EXTINCT CHURCHES: BY TOWNS — Continued.

COUNTY OF FRANKLIN — Concluded.

CITIES AND TOWNS.	Denomination	Distinguishing Name	Year in which Organized	Year in which Terminated	RECORDS	
					Years covered	In Possession of —
Erving, . .	M. E. .	–	1859	1864	–	1_
	Univ. .	–	1836	–	–	–
Heath, . .	Bapt. .	–	1805	1875	1805–1875	Henry Fairbanks
	Cong.[2] .	Second Cong. .	1842	1846	1842–1846	3_
	Unit. .	–	1825	–	–	–
Leverett, .	Unit. .	–	*1848	–	–	–
Leyden, .	Bapt. .	–	–	–	–	–
Montague, .	Unit. .	–	–	–	–	C. P. Wright[4]
New Salem, .	M. E. .	No. New Salem .	–	–	1869–1875	Pastor M. E. Ch.[5]
	Univ. .	Cooleyville	–	–	1878–1883	Willard Putnam
Northfield, .	Bapt. .	–	–	–	–	Joseph Callencer
	M. E. .	–	–	–	–	Joseph Callencer
Orange, . .	Meth. .	–	–	–	–	6_
	Unit.[7] .	North Orange .	1843	–	–	8_
	Un. Breth. .	–	–	1856	–	Rev. J H. Garmon
Whately, .	Bapt. .	First Bapt. Ch. of Christ	1789	1850	1789–1850	{ Pastor First Cong. Ch.[9]
	Cong.[10] .	Second Cong. .	1842	1864	1842–1864	First Cong. Ch.
	Meth. .	–	–	11_	–	11_
	Unit. .	Unit. Cong. Soc.	1866	–	1866–1877	Cannot be found
	Univ.[12] .	First Univ.. .	1839	1865	1839–1865	James M. Crafts

COUNTY OF HAMPDEN.

Blandford, .	Bapt.[13] .	–	–	–	–	–
	M. E.[14] .	Beech Hill .	–	–	–	–
	Presb. .	–	–	1800	–	–
Brimfield, .	Un. Breth. .	West Brimfield .	*1856	–	–	–
	–	East Brimfield .	–	–	–	–
Chicopee, .	Sec. Adv..	–	–	–	–	Ansel B. Howard
Granville, .	M. E. .	–	15_	–	–	15_
Holland, .	Bapt. .	–	–	–	–	–
	Meth. .	–	–	–	–	–
Palmer, .	Prot. Epis. .	–	–	–	1873–1876	–
	M. E.[16] .	Thorndike .	–	–	–	Pastor of M. E Ch.[17]
Russell, .	18_ .	Union . . .	–	–	–	–
Westfield, .	Bapt. .	Second Bapt. .	–	–	1806–1836	Present Bapt. Ch.
	Bapt. .	West Farms .	–	–	1819–1872	R. S. Merriman
West Springfield,	Meth.[19] .	–	–	–	*1845 –	–
	Prot Epis.[20] .	–	–	–	1871 –	–

[1] Records are known to be somewhere in the town.

[2] United with the First Church.

[3] The records of the treasurer are the only ones known to be in existence.

[4] Greenfield.   [5] Orange.

[6] No trace of any records since 1865.

[7] Formerly Congregational.

[8] Parish records in possession of the present Universalist; church records in possession of the present Congregational.

[9] Private records in possession of James M. Crafts.

[10] Reunited with the First Congregational.

[11] Town records refer to a Methodist church formed in 1818; no records are known to be in existence.

[12] Succeeded by the First Unitarian Society.   [13] United with the Russell Baptist.

[14] United with the Blandford Methodist Episcopal.

[15] Supposed to have organized about one hundred years ago, and to have been the first Methodist Episcopal church west of the Connecticut River. All records have been destroyed.

[16] United with the Bondsville Methodist Episcopal.

[17] Bondsville.

[18] The church edifice was built by Methodists and Congregationalists.

[19] Church edifice was sold to the Congregationalists.   [20] Removed to Springfield.

EXTINCT CHURCHES: BY TOWNS — Continued.

COUNTY OF HAMPSHIRE.

CITIES AND TOWNS.	Denomination	Distinguishing Name	Year in which Organized	Year in which Terminated	RECORDS	
					Years covered	In Possession of —
Belchertown, .	M. E. .	So. Belchertown	–	–	1816–1869	Jesse Morse[1]
Chesterfield, .	Free Bapt.	–	–	–	1847–1865	Town Clerk
Cummington, .	Cong. .	First Cong. Soc.	–	–	1834–1841[2]	L. F. Stevens[3]
	Cong.[4] .	Windsor Bush .	–	1840	–	Cong. Ch.[5]
	Meth. .	–	–	–	1833–1845	Town Clerk
Goshen, .	Bapt. .	Bapt. Soc. . .	–	–	–	Hinckley Williams
Granby, . .	Cong. .	West Par.and Ch.	–	–	1795–1820	Charles Gridley[6]
Hadley, . .	Meth. .	Meth. Soc. . .	–	–	–	Mrs. E. S. Keith
Pelham, . .	Bapt.[7] .	Packardville .	–	–	–	Albert Firman
Prescott, . .	Bapt. .	North Prescott .	–	–	–	Hosea Hunt[8]
South Hadley, .	Cong.[9] .	[10]–	–	1878	1861–1878	Cong. Ch.[11]
	Cong.[9] .	[12]–	1824	1878	1824–1878	Cong. Ch.[11]

COUNTY OF MIDDLESEX.

CITIES AND TOWNS.	Denomination	Distinguishing Name	Year in which Organized	Year in which Terminated	Years covered	In Possession of —
Acton, . .	Cong. .	First	–	–	1738–1838	Samuel Hosmer
Boxborough, .	–	Unit. or Univ.[13] .	–	–	–	[13]–
CAMBRIDGE, .	Cong. .	Second . .	1842	1865	1842–1865	Edward Kendall
	Unit. .	Allen St. Cong..				
Concord, . .	Univ. .	–	1838	1852	1838–1852	Rev. G. Reynolds
Groton, . .	Presb. .	–	–	–	1776–1799	–
Hopkinton, .	Presb.[14] .	–	1734	–	–	–
LOWELL, . .	Bapt. .	Central Bapt. .	*1850	–	1849 –[15]	–
	Bapt. .	Third Bapt. .	–	–	1840–1862	–
	Presb. .	–	–	[16]1869	–	Probably lost
	Prot. Epis. .	St. Luke's . .	1841	–	–	St. Anne's Ch.
	Rom.Cath. .	St. Mary's . .	–	1861	1847–1861	St. Patrick's Ch.
	Unit. .	Church of the Pilgrims[17] .	1846	1861	1846–1861	First Unit. Ch.
	Unit. .	North Cong. of Chelmsford[18] .	–	–	1830–1836	First Unit. Ch.
Marlborough, .	Univ. .	–	–	–	1818–1855	[19]–
Natick, . .	Univ. .	–	–	[20]–	–	–
NEWTON, . .	Univ. .	Old Watertown Univ. .	–	–	–	[21]–
Reading, . .	Evang.[22] .	Evang. Soc. .	1871	1873	1871–1873	First Presb. Ch.
Stoneham,. .	Univ. .	–	–	–	–	–
Stow, . . .	Evang. .	–	–	–	–	Francis W. Warren
WALTHAM, .	Univ. .	First Univ. Soc.	1839	1861	1839–1861	Present Univ. Ch.
Woburn, . .	Univ.[23] .	–	–	–	–	–

[1] Barrett.   [2] Society records; church records are missing.

[3] Worthington.

[4] United with the West Cummington Congregational.

[5] West Cummington.   [7] Church edifice burned.

[6] South Hadley.   [8] North Prescott.

[9] Succeeded by the Congregational Church and Society of South Hadley Falls.

[10] The First Congregational Church of South Hadley Falls, and the Ecclesiastical Society.

[11] South Hadley Falls.

[12] The Religious Society of South Hadley Falls, and Congregational Church of South Hadley Falls.

[13] Included in town records about one hundred years ago; no other information can be obtained.

[14] Removed to Blandford.   [16] Prior to 1869.

[15] Existed a few years.   [17] Commonly called Lee Street Unitarian.

[18] The church site was formerly included within the limits of Chelmsford.

[19] Heirs of the late Silas Felton of Hudson.

[20] In existence about ten years; property sold in 1861.

[21] Tufts College Library, College Hill.

[22] Succeeded by the First Presbyterian.

[23] Two Universalist churches have become extinct, but nothing is known of any records. Rev. William S. Barnes, Montreal, Canada, has private records of facts gathered in relation to these two churches.

EXTINCT CHURCHES : BY TOWNS — Continued.

COUNTY OF NANTUCKET.

CITIES AND TOWNS.	Denomination	Distinguishing Name	Year in which Organized	Year in which Terminated	Years covered	In Possession of —
Nantucket, .	Bapt. .	Pleasant St.[1]	–	–	–	
	Prot. Epis.[2]	Trinity . .	–	–	–	Burned in 1846

COUNTY OF NORFOLK.

Bellingham, .	Cong. .	–	–	–	1821–1827	Town Clerk
Braintree, .	Bapt. .	First Bapt..	–	–	–	–
	Bapt. .	Second Bapt. .	–	–	–	–
Holbrook, .	M. E.[3] .	–	1832	1836	1832–1836	Present M. E. Ch.
Medway, .	Univ. .	Second Cong. .	–	–	1835–1865	Marcellus A. Ware

COUNTY OF PLYMOUTH.

Abington, . .	Sec. Adv..	–	–	–	–	–
BROCKTON,	Bapt. .	–	1850	1855	1850–1855	–
	Unit. .	Second Cong. Soc. No. Bridgewater	1825	1831	1825–1831	–
	Univ. .	Church of the Disciples .	1858	1875	1858–1875	Unit. Ch.
Carver, . .	Ref. Meth.	South Carver .	–	1867	1831–1867	Thomas M. Ryder[4]
E. Bridgewater,	Cong. .	Trinitarian .	1849	1861	1849–1861	Miss Eudora Sanford
	M. E.[5] .	–	–	–	1850–1860	William B. Hall
	Meth. Prot.	Satucket . .	1842	1850	–	–
	Univ. .	–	–	–	–	[6]–
Halifax, . .	Bapt. .	–	–	–	–	–
Hanson, . .	Univ. .	–	–	–	*1825–1850	–
Hull, . . .	Cong. .	–	–	1789	–	Miss Sarah Jones[7]
Lakeville, . .	Bapt.[8] .	–	–	–	–	[8]–
Marion, . .	Meth. Prot.	–	–	–	–	–
Marshfield, .	Prot. Epis. .	–	–	–	[9]–	St. Andrew's Ch.
Middleborough,	Bapt.[10] .	Central Bapt. Soc. of Lakeville .	–	–	1795–1867	Joseph T. Wood
Plymouth, . .	Chris.[11] .	Russell's Mills .	1857	1865	1857-1865[12]	M. E. Ch.
	M. E. .	–	1866	1875	1866–1875	Present M. E. Ch.
South Scituate, .	Friends .	Scituate M't'g .	1679	–	–	New Bedford M. M't'g
W. Bridgewater,	Bapt. .	–	1783	1833	1783–1833	Present Bapt. Ch.

COUNTY OF SUFFOLK.

BOSTON, . .	Bapt. .	High St.[13] . .	1844	1863	1844–1863	–
	Bapt.[14] .	Merrimack St. . .	–	1863	–	Bapt. Missionary Union
	Bapt. .	North Bapt. .	1835	1840	1835–1840	–

[1] Originally called the York Street.
[2] The church edifice was destroyed by fire in 1846, and the parish soon after dissolved.
[3] Changed to Baptist.   [4] Middleborough.
[5] Originally organized in South Abington.
[6] Certain deeds and papers are in possession of the Town Clerk, Middleborough.
[7] There are pastors' records of marriages, baptisms, and deaths from 1726 to 1768 in possession of Miss Sarah Jones, Hingham. Copies of these records and of the diary of Rev. Zachariah Whitman from 1670 to 1726 are in possession of the Town Clerk.
[8] There are several extinct Baptist churches; nothing is known concerning the records.
[9] Church records from 1775 to 1834; parish records from 1791 to 1867.
[10] Originally United Brethren; afterward Second Baptist Church of Middleborough, and Fourth Baptist Church of Middleborough.
[11] Succeeded by the Methodist Episcopal.   [13] Charlestown.
[12] Miscellaneous records.   [14] Succeeded by the Union Temple Church.

EXTINCT CHURCHES : BY TOWNS — Continued.

COUNTY OF SUFFOLK — Concluded.

CITIES AND TOWNS.	Denomination	Distinguishing Name	Year in which Organized	Year in which Terminated	RECORDS	
					Years covered	In Possession of —
BOSTON — Con.,	Bapt.	Tabernacle[1]	1873	1877	1873–1877	–
	Bapt.[2]	Tremont	1845	1866	–	–
	Bapt.[3]	Tremont St.	1839	–	–	Bapt. Missionary Union
	Cong [4]	Bethesda[5]	1847	1849	–	–
	Cong.	Bowdoin St.	1825	1861	1825–1861	[6]–
	Cong.[7]	Chambers St.	1861	1879	–	–
	Cong.	Church of the Pilgrims[5]	1844	1852	–	–
	Cong.[8]	Church of the Unity[9]	1857	1860	–	–
	Cong.	Edwards	1849	1853	–	–
	Cong.	Free Ch. Marlborough Chapel	1836	1842	–	–
	Cong.[10]	Garden St.	1841	1844	–	–
	Cong.[10]	Green St.	1823	1844	–	–
	Cong.	Leyden	1844	1847	–	–
	Cong.[11]	Mariners	1830	1866	–	–
	Cong.	Messiah	1844	1846	–	–
	Cong.[12]	Oak Place	1860	1864	–	–
	Cong.[8]	Payson[9]	1845	1860	–	–
	Cong [13]	Salem St.	1827	1866	–	–
	Cong.	Salem and Mariners	1866	1879	–	–
	Cong.	Samuel Mather	1742	1785	–	–
	Cong.	School St.	1748	1785	–	–
	Friends	Boston M't'g	[14]1664	1808	–	Salem M. M't'g
	Ind. Cong.	New England	1875	1878	1875–1878	William H. Merrill
	Jewish[15]	Beth Abraham	–	1868	–	–
	Jewish[16]	Shomrai Shaboth	–	1863	–	–
	M. E.[17]	No. Russell St.	1837	1873	–	–
	M. E.[17]	Richmond St.	1841	1849	–	–
	M. E.	Ruggles St.	1869	–	–	–
	Prot. Epis.	Grace	1830	1865	1830–1865	[18]–
	Rom.Cath.[19]	St. Vincent de Paul's,	–	1871	1862–1871	[19]–
	Unit.[20]	Bulfinch St.	1822	1863	1822–1863	City Clerk
	Unit.[21]	Church of the Saviour,	1845	1854	–	–
	Unit.[22]	Indiana St.	1845	1855	1845–1855	–
	Unit.	New North	1714	[23]–	1714–1862	City Clerk
	Unit.	Thirteenth Cong.	1826	1858	–	–
	Unit.	Twelfth Cong.	1825	1865	1823–1865	City Clerk
	Univ.[24]	Church of the Paternity	1859	1863	–	Shawmut Ch.
	Univ.	First Univ.	1785	1864	1785–1864	[25]–
CHELSEA, . .	M. E.	Broadway	–	–	[26]–	–
	–	St. Andrew's	–	–	–	–

[1] Roxbury.   [4] Merged in the Winthrop Church.

[2] Succeeded by the Ruggles Street Baptist.   [5] Charlestown.

[3] Succeeded by the Union Temple Church.   [6] Records burned in the fire of 1872.

[7] Merged in the Mount Vernon Congregational.

[8] Merged in the E Street Congregational, South Boston.   [extinct.

[9] South Boston.   [10] United and formed the Messiah Church, also

[11] United with the Salem St. and formed the Salem and Mariners, also extinct.

[12] Merged in the First Presbyterian.

[13] United with the Mariners and formed the Salem and Mariners, also extinct.

[14] Boston Meeting was again set up in 1870.

[15] United with Shomrai Shaboth and formed Shomrai Beth Abraham.

[16] United with Beth Abraham and formed Shomrai Beth Abraham.

[17] United with the First Methodist Episcopal.   [18] Registrar of the Diocese.

[19] Merged in St. James. Records in possession of the present St. Vincent de Paul's, So. Boston.

[20] Originally Universalist.   [23] Soon after 1863.

[21] United with the Second Church.   [24] United with the Fifth Universalist.

[22] Merged in the Church of the Disciples.   [25] Tufts College Library, College Hill.

[26] There are records covering about twelve years, the years not being specified.

EXTINCT CHURCHES: BY TOWNS — Concluded.

COUNTY OF WORCESTER.

CITIES AND TOWNS.	Denomination	Distinguishing Name	Year in which Organized	Year in which Terminated	RECORDS	
					Years covered	In Possession of—
Auburn, . .	Bapt. .	–	–	1838	–	North Oxford Bapt.
Barre, . .	Univ .	–	–	1_	–	–
Berlin, . .	2_	–	–	–	–	–
Blackstone, .	Friends .	Blackstone M't'g	1812	1883	1812–1883	Smithfield (R. I.) M. M't'g
Bolton, . .	Cong. .	Hillside . .	–	–	1826 –	s_
Brookfield, .	M. E. .	East Brookfield .	1865	1878	–	–
	Univ. .	Podunk . .	–	1876	1819–1876	Moses Hobbs
Charlton, . .	Univ. .	Union Soc. . .	–	1859	1838–1859	Present Univ. Ch.
	–	Leland's Village	–	–	–	–
Douglas, . .	–	–	–	–	–	Lovell Parker
Dudley. . .	Univ. .	–	–	1861	1835–1861	Waldo Healy
Gardner, . .	Cong. .	–	–	–	–	–
Grafton, . .	Bapt. .	–	–	–	–	Jona. D. Wheeler
Hardwick, .	Meth. .	–	4_	–	–	–
	Unit.5 .	First Cong. .	1736	1842	1736–1842	Union Ch.
	Univ.5 .	–	1824	1842	1824–1842	Union Ch.
Lancaster, .	Univ. .	–	–	–	–	Mrs. C. Bennett
Leicester, . .	Wes. Meth.6	–	1845	1866	–	Francis Washburn
Lunenburg, .	Unit. .	–	–	*1860	–	Benj. G. Whiting
Mendon, . .	Cong. .	Evang. .	–	–	–	–
	Friends .	Mendon M't'g .	1727	1841	1727–1841	Smithfield (R. I.) M. M't'g
Milford, . .	Bapt. .	South Milford .	1846	–	1846–1853	Mrs. J. L. Townsend
	–	Hopedale Community and Ch.	–	–	1841–1867	Rev. Adin Ballou
Millbury, . .	Cong. .	–	–	–	–	First Cong. Ch.
Paxton. . .	Cong.7 .	–	1785	1793	–	–
Princeton, .	Bapt. .	–	1817	1847	1817–1847	8_
Royalston, .	Bapt. .	–	1836	1855	1836–1855	Eri Shepardson
Rutland, . .	M. E. .	–	–	–	1845–1865	Cyrus H. Weston
Shrewsbury, .	Bapt. .	–	–	–	–	–
	Univ. .	–	–	9_	–	–
Southborough, .	Unit. .	–	–	–	–	10_
Spencer, . .	Bapt. .	First Bapt. .	1819	1877	1819–1877	Joshua Cole11
	Univ. .	–	[11]1830	–	–	12_
Sterling, . .	Univ. .	–	–	–	–	Levi Reed
Templeton, .	Univ. .	–	*1850	–	–	LateRev.G.Bushnell
Warren, . .	Univ. .	First Univ. of Western . .	–	–	–	–
	Univ. .	–	–	*1820	13_	–

1 Church edifice sold in 1851.

2 Became extinct during the War of the Rebellion.

3 The church records were carried out of the state by the clerk; the parish records are in possession of S. R. Merrick, Lancaster.

4 Church edifice built about 1845.

5 United and formed the Union Church.

6 Succeeded by the Methodist Episcopal.

7 Reunited with the Congregational.

8 Deposited in the Town Library building.

9 No services have been held since about 1845; the church edifice was sold about 1865.

10 Henry S. Wheeler and Mrs. Trowbridge Brigham.

11 East Brookfield.

12 Existed fifteen or twenty years; records searched for but not found.

13 Existed about fifteen years.

EXTINCT CHURCHES: BY DENOMINATIONS.

[In this table, the names of cities and towns are presented alphabetically under the name of each denomination, and are followed respectively by the names of the counties in which they are located.

In the column headed " Distinguishing Name " and in the column under " RECORDS " headed "In Possession of—," the following abbreviations are used: — Bapt., for Baptist; Chris., for Christian; Cong., for Congregational; Evang., for Evangelical; Meth., for Methodist; M. E., for Methodist Episcopal; Presb., for Presbyterian; Un. Breth., for United Brethren; Unit., for Unitarian; and Univ., for Universalist; also, Ch., for Church; M't'g, for Meeting; M. M't'g, for Monthly Meeting; Par., for Parish; Soc., for Society, and St., for Saint or Street, as the context requires.

The use of the dash signifies in the column headed " Distinguishing Name," that no other name than that of the town was given, and in the other columns that the information is wanting.

The asterisk preceding a date signifies that it is the nearest date obtainable.

When the residence of the person having the possession of the records is other than in the town where the church was located the residence is given in a foot-note, and if the residence specified is not in Massachusetts the state is also given.

In some cases the records commenced at an earlier date than the year in which the church was organized, services having been held by the congregation and records kept before the formal organization as a church or society.]

AFRICAN METHODIST EPISCOPAL.

CITIES AND TOWNS.	Counties	Distinguishing Name	Year in which Organized	Year in which Terminated	RECORDS	
					Years covered	In Possession of—
Lee, . . .	Berkshire	–	–	–	–	–

AFRICAN METHODIST EPISCOPAL ZION.

Lee, . . .	Berkshire	–	–	–	–	–

BAPTIST.

Andover, .	Essex .	–	–	1857	1831–1857	–
Ashfield, .	Franklin .	First Bapt.. .	1761	*1846	1761–1846	Arnold Smith
Auburn, .	Worcester	–	–	1838	–	North Oxford Bapt.
Bernardston,	Franklin .	–	.	1_	–	2_
Blandford,	Hampden.	3_	–	–	–	. –
BOSTON, .	Suffolk .	High St.4 . .	1844	1863	1844–1863	–
		Merrimack St.5 .	–	1863	–	Bapt. Missionary Union
		North Bapt. .	1835	1840	1835–1840	–
		Tabernacle6 .	1873	1877	1873–1877	–
		Tremont7 .	1845	1866	–	–
		Tremont St.8 .	1839	–	–	Bapt. Missionary Union

1 Prior to 1808.
2 Records were loaned and not returned.
3 United with the Russell Baptist.
4 Charlestown.

5 Succeeded by the Union Temple Church.
6 Roxbury.
7 Succeeded by the Ruggles Street Baptist.
8 Succeeded by the Union Temple Church.

EXTINCT CHURCHES: BY DENOMINATIONS — Continued.

BAPTIST — Concluded.

CITIES AND TOWNS.	Counties	Distinguishing Name	Year in which Organized	Year in which Terminated	RECORDS	
					Years covered	In Possession of—
Braintree, . .	Norfolk .	First Bapt.. .	–	–	–	–
		Second Bapt. .	–	–	–	–
BROCKTON, .	Plymouth .	–	1850	1855	1850–1855	–
Buckland, . .	Franklin .	–	–	–	–	Mrs. Wm. Stetson
Cheshire, . .	Berkshire	First Bapt.[1] .	1799	1834	1799–1834	F. A. Martin
		Lanesborough	1789	1799	1789–1799	F. A. Martin
		Stafford's Hill .	–	–	–	Shuball W. Lincoln
Dartmouth, .	Bristol .	South Dartmouth	–	–	–	–
Goshen, . .	Hampshire	Bapt. Soc. . .	–	–	–	Hinckley Williams
Grafton, . .	Worcester	–	–	–	–	Jona. D. Wheeler
Groveland, .	Essex .	–	–	2–	–	–
Halifax, . .	Plymouth .	–	–	–	–	3–
Hancock, . .	Berkshire	Second Bapt. .	–	–	1843–1845	Caleb Eldridge
Heath, . .	Franklin .	–	1805	1875	1805–1875	Henry Fairbanks
Holland, . .	Hampden .	–	–	–	–	–
Lakeville, . .	Plymouth .	4–	–	–	–	4–
Leyden, . .	Franklin .	–	–	–	–	–
LOWELL, . .	Middlesex	Central Bapt. .	*1850	–	1849 –5	–
		Third Bapt. .	–	–	1840–1862	–
Middleborough,	Plymouth	Central Bapt. Soc. of Lakeville[6] .	–	–	1795–1867	Joseph T. Wood
Milford, . .	Worcester	South Milford .	1846	–	1846–1853	Mrs. J. L. Townsend
Nantucket, .	Nantucket	Pleasant St.[7] .	–	–	–	–
Newbury, . .	Essex .	First Bapt.[8] .	1811	1869	1811–1869	8–
North Adams, .	Berkshire	–	*1776	–	–	9–
Northfield, .	Franklin .	–	–	–	–	Joseph Callender
Orleans, . .	Barnstable	–	–	–	–	–
Otis, . . .	Berkshire	West Otis . .	–	–	–	–
Pelham, . .	Hampshire	Packardville[10] .	–	–	–	Albert Firman
Prescott, . .	Hampshire	North Prescott .	–	–	–	Hosea Hunt[11]
Princeton, . .	Worcester	–	1817	1847	1817–1847	12–
Royalston, .	Worcester	–	1836	1855	1836–1855	Eri Shepardson
Sandisfield, .	Berkshire	First Bapt.. .	–	–	–	A. W. Merrill
		Second Bapt. .	–	–	–	A. W. Merrill
Savoy, . .	Berkshire	Second Bapt. .	–	–	–	13–
Shrewsbury, .	Worcester	–	–	–	–	–
Spencer, . .	Worcester	First Bapt. .	1819	1877	1819–1877	Joshua Cole[14]
Tisbury, . .	Dukes Co.	South Tisbury.[15] .	–	–	16–	–
W. Bridgewater,	Plymouth	–	1783	1833	1783–1833	Present Bapt. Ch.
Westfield, . .	Hampden .	Second Bapt. .	–	–	1806–1836	Present Bapt. Ch.
		West Farms .	–	–	1819–1872	R. S. Merriman
W. Stockbridge,	Berkshire	–	–	*1825	–	Disappeared
Whately, . .	Franklin .	First Bapt. Ch. of Christ	} 1789	1850	1789–1850	{ Pastor First Cong. Ch.[17]
Windsor, . .	Berkshire	–	1821	1851	1821–1851	H. C. Estes[18]

[1] Succeeded by the present Baptist.

[2] A few years ago.

[3] Certain deeds and papers are in possession of the Town Clerk, Middleborough.

[4] There are several extinct Baptist churches; nothing is known concerning the records.

[5] Existed a few years.

[6] Originally United Brethren; afterward Second Baptist Church of Middleborough, and Fourth Baptist Church of Middleborough.

[7] Originally called the York Street.

[8] Merged in the Baptist Church of Newburyport; records in possession of the Historical Society of Newburyport and Newbury.

[9] Supposed to be in possession of Rev. C. W. Anable, Adams.

[10] Church edifice burned.   [11] North Prescott.

[12] Deposited in the Town Library building.

[13] Supposed to be in possession of Mark Deming.

[14] East Brookfield.   [15] West Tisbury.

[16] There are records covering thirty-five years, the years not being specified.

[17] Private records in possession of James M. Crafts.

[18] Pastor of Greenville Baptist Church in Leicester, for the purpose of depositing them in the archives of the Backus Historical Society of Newton Centre.

EXTINCT CHURCHES: BY DENOMINATIONS — Continued.

CHRISTIAN.

CITIES AND TOWNS.	Counties	Distinguishing Name	Year in which Organized	Year in which Terminated	RECORDS	
					Years covered	In Possession of —
NEWBURYPORT,	Essex .	Court St. Chris.	–	1875	–	Rev. D. P. Pike
Plymouth, . .	Plymouth	Russell's Mills[1] .	1857	1865	1857–1865[2]	M. E. Ch.

CONGREGATIONAL.

Acton, . .	Middlesex	First . . .	–	–	1738–1838	Samuel Hosmer
Bellingham, .	Norfolk .	–	–	–	1821–1827	Town Clerk
Berkley, . .	Bristol .	Second Cong.[1] .	–	–	–	–
Bolton, . .	Worcester	Hillside . .	–	–	1826–	3_
BOSTON, . .	Suffolk .	Bethesda[4] . .	1847	1849	–	–
		Bowdoin St. .	1825	1861	1825–1861	5_
		Chambers St.[6] .	1861	1879	–	–
		Church of the Pilgrims[7] .	1844	1852	–	–
		Church of the Unity[8] . .	1857	1860	–	–
		Edwards . .	1849	1853	–	–
		Free Ch. Marlborough Chapel	1836	1842	–	–
		Garden St.[9] .	1841	1844	–	–
		Green St.[9] . .	1823	1844	–	–
		Leyden . .	1844	1847	–	–
		Mariners[10] . .	1830	1866	–	–
		Messiah . .	1844	1846	–	–
		Oak Place[11] .	1860	1864	–	–
		Payson[12] . .	1845	1860	–	–
		Salem St.[13] . .	1827	1866	–	–
		Salem and Mariners . .	1866	1879	–	–
		Samuel Mather .	1742	1785	–	–
		School St. . .	1748	1785	–	–
Bourne, . .	Barnstable	Monument Beach[14] . .	–	1852	1800–1852	Ebenezer Nye
Boxford, . .	Essex .	Third Cong. Soc.	–	–	1824–1834	Benj. S. Barnes
CAMBRIDGE, .	Middlesex	Second . .	1842	1865	1842–1865	Edward Kendall
Chatham, . .	Barnstable	–	1720	1869	1824–1869	Town Clerk
Cummington, .	Hampshire	First Cong. Soc.	–	–	1834–1841[15]	L. F. Stevens[16]
		Windsor Bush[17]	–	1840	–	Cong. Ch.[18]
Dennis, . .	Barnstable	First Cong. .	1829	–	1727–1845	Isaiah B. Hall
E. Bridgewater, .	Plymouth	Trinitarian .	1849	1861	1849–1861	Miss Eudora Sanford
Egremont, . .	Berkshire	–	–	–	–	–
Fairhaven, . .	Bristol .	–	1840	1849	1840–1849	Eben. Akin, Jr.
Gardner, . .	Worcester	–	–	–	–	–
Granby, . .	Hampshire	West Par. and Ch.	–	–	1795–1820	Charles Gridley[19]
HAVERHILL, .	Essex .	Winter Street .	–	1860	–	–

[1] Succeeded by the Methodist Episcopal.   [2] Miscellaneous records.

[3] The church records were carried out of the state by the clerk; the parish records are in possession of S. R. Merrick, Lancaster.

[4] Charlestown. Merged in the Winthrop Church.

[5] Records burned in the fire of 1872.

[6] Merged in the Mount Vernon Congregational.   [7] Charlestown.

[8] South Boston. Merged in the E Street Congregational, South Boston.

[9] United and formed the Messiah Church, also extinct.

[10] United with the Salem St. and formed the Salem and Mariners, also extinct.

[11] Merged in the First Presbyterian.

[12] South Boston. Merged in the E Street Congregational, South Boston.

[13] United with the Mariners and formed the Salem and Mariners, also extinct.

[14] United with the Methodist.   [15] Society records; church records are missing.

[16] Worthington.

[17] United with the West Cummington Congregational.

[18] West Cummington.   [19] South Hadley.

EXTINCT CHURCHES: BY DENOMINATIONS — Continued.

CONGREGATIONAL — Concluded.

CITIES AND TOWNS.	Counties	Distinguishing Name	Year in which Organized	Year in which Terminated	RECORDS	
					Years covered	In Possession of—
Heath,	Franklin	Second Cong.[1]	1842	1846	1842–1846	[2]
Hull,	Plymouth	–		1789	–	Miss Sarah Jones[3]
LAWRENCE,	Essex	Central Cong.[4]	–	1883	1849–1883	[5]
		Central Cong. Soc.[4]	–	1883	1850–1883	Charles U. Bell
		Eliot Cong.[4]	–		[6]	Trinity Cong. Ch.
		Lowell St. Cong.	–	1869	–	John Jowett[7]
Marblehead,	Essex	Third Cong.[8]	–	1877	1858–1877	Benjamin Savoy
Mendor,	Worcester	Evang.	–		–	–
Methuen,	Essex	Second Par.[9]	1766	1816	1780–1790	Clerk of First Par.
Millbury,	Worcester	–			–	First Cong. Ch.
Mt. Washington,	Berkshire	–	1831		–	H. F. Keith[10]
NEW BEDFORD,	Bristol	Pacific Cong.	–		–	George F. Bartlett
Newbury,	Essex	Fourth Cong.	1832	1846	1832–1846	Town Clerk
North Adams,	Berkshire	–	1776	1777	1776–1777	Lost
Paxton,	Worcester	[11]	1785	1793	–	–
Pittsfield,	Berkshire	Union Par.[12]	–		1809–1817	Henry A. Brewster
Rockport,	Essex	Second Cong.	–		1855–1868	John W. Marshall
Salisbury,	Essex	East Par.	1687		1687–1754	John M. Cushing[13]
South Hadley,	Hampshire	[14]	–	1878	1861–1878	Cong. Ch.[15]
		[16]	1824	1878	1824–1878	Cong. Ch.[15]
Washington,	Berkshire	–	–		–	A. S. Pomeroy
Westport,	Bristol	[17]	–		–	–
Whately,	Franklin	Second Cong.[18]	1842	1864	1842–1864	First Cong. Ch.

DISSENTING CONGREGATIONAL.

Norton,	Bristol	–	1748	–	1748–1761	[19]

EVANGELICAL.

Reading,	Middlesex	Evang. Soc.[20]	1871	1873	1871–1873	First Presb. Ch.
Stow,	Middlesex	–			–	Francis W. Warren

[1] United with the First Church.

[2] The records of the treasurer are the only ones known to be in existence.

[3] There are pastors' records of marriages, baptisms, and deaths from 1726 to 1768 in possession of Miss Sarah Jones, Hingham. Copies of these records and of the diary of Rev. Zacariah Whitman from 1670 to 1726 are in possession of the Town Clerk.

[4] United and formed Trinity Congregational.

[5] From 1849 to 1858 in possession of Charles U. Bell; from 1859 to 1883 in possession of Trinity Congregational.

[6] Church records from 1865 to 1883; parish records from 1871 to 1883.

[7] Address unknown.

[8] Church edifice was destroyed by fire, and the parish united with the First Congregational.

[9] Reorganized in 1830 and reunited soon after with the First Parish.

[10] Great Barrington.   [11] Reunited with the Congregational.

[12] Reunited with the First Church.

[13] Mrs. Mary P. Graves of Newburyport has records from 1752 to 1805.

[14] The First Congregational Church of South Hadley Falls, and the Ecclesiastical Society. Succeeded by the Congregational Church and Society of South Hadley Falls.

[15] South Hadley Falls.

[16] The Religious Society of South Hadley Falls, and Congregational Church of South Hadley Falls. Succeeded by the Congregational Church and Society of South Hadley Falls.

[17] A few persons are living who know something about this church.

[18] Reunited with the First Congregational.

[19] In possession of the Baptist Church which succeeded the Dissenting Congregational.

[20] Succeeded by the First Presbyterian.

EXTINCT CHURCHES: BY DENOMINATIONS — Continued.

FREE BAPTIST.

CITIES AND TOWNS.	Counties	Distinguishing Name	Year in which Organized	Year in which Terminated	RECORDS Years covered	In Possession of —
Chesterfield, .	Hampshire	–	–	–	1847–1865	Town Clerk
Georgetown, .	Essex .	–	–	–	*1820 –	–
TAUNTON, . .	Bristol .	Weir Street .	–	–	–	D. J. Lawrence

FRIENDS.

Cities and Towns	Counties	Distinguishing Name	Year organized	Year terminated	Years covered	In Possession of —
Blackstone, .	Worcester	Blackstone M't'g	1812	1883	1812–1883	Smithfield (R. I.) M. M't'g
BOSTON, . .	Suffolk .	Boston M't'g .	[1]1664	1808	–	Salem M. M't'g
Dartmouth, .	Bristol .	Newtown M't'g .	1745	–	–	–
FALL RIVER, .	Bristol .	Independent M't'g .	1845	*1865	–	–
Mendon, . .	Worcester	Mendon M't'g .	1727	1841	1727–1841	Smithfield (R. I.) M. M't'g
South Scituate,.	Plymouth	Scituate M't'g .	1679	–	–	New Bedford M. M't'g
West Newbury,	Essex .	–	1841	1881	1841–1881	Amesbury M. M't'g
Westport, . .	Bristol .	Centre M't'g .	*1780	1880	1780–1880	Westport M. M't'g

INDEPENDENT CONGREGATIONAL.

Cities and Towns	Counties	Distinguishing Name	Year organized	Year terminated	Years covered	In Possession of —
BOSTON, . .	Suffolk .	New England .	1875	1878	1875–1878	William H. Merrill

JEWISH.

Cities and Towns	Counties	Distinguishing Name	Year organized	Year terminated	Years covered	In Possession of —
BOSTON, . .	Suffolk .	Beth Abraham[2]	–	1868	–	–
		Shomrai Shaboth[3]	–	1868	–	–

METHODIST.

Cities and Towns	Counties	Distinguishing Name	Year organized	Year terminated	Years covered	In Possession of —
Cummington, .	Hampshire	–	–	–	1833–1845	Town Clerk
Hadley, . .	Hampshire	Meth. Soc. . .	–	–	–	Mrs. E. S. Keith
Hardwick,. .	Worcester	–	4_	–	–	–
Holland, . .	Hampden .	–	–	–	–	–
LAWRENCE, .	Essex .	Trinity Meth. .	–	–	–	5_
Orange, . .	Franklin .	–	–	–	–	6_
SALEM, . .	Essex .	First Meth. .	–	–	1820 –	Mathew Robson
W. Springfield,.	Hampden .	6_	–	–	*1845 –	–
Whately, . .	Franklin .	–	7_	–	–	_7

METHODIST EPISCOPAL.

Cities and Towns	Counties	Distinguishing Name	Year organized	Year terminated	Years covered	In Possession of —
Alford, . .	Berkshire	–	8_	–	1807–1812	–
Barnstable, .	Barnstable	Hyannis . .	–	–	–	–
Belchertown, .	Hampshire	So. Belchertown	–	–	1816–1869	Jesse Morse[9]

[1] Boston Meeting was again set up in 1870.

[2] United with Shomrai Shaboth and formed Shomrai Beth Abraham.

[3] United with Beth Abraham and formed Shomrai Beth Abraham.

[4] Church edifice built about 1845. [5] No trace of any records since 1865.

[6] Church edifice was sold to the Congregationalists.

[7] Town records refer to a Methodist church formed in 1818; no records are known to be in existence.

[8] Reference is made to reorganization about 1855; no other information can be obtained.

[9] Barrett.

EXTINCT CHURCHES : BY DENOMINATIONS — Continued.

METHODIST EPISCOPAL — Concluded.

CITIES AND TOWNS.	Counties	Distinguishing Name	Year in which Organized	Year in which Terminated	RECORDS	
					Years covered	In Possession of —
Blandford, .	Hampden .	Beech Hill[1]	–	–	–	–
BOSTON, .	Suffolk .	No. Russell St.[2]	1837	1873	–	–
		Richmond St.[2]	1841	1849	–	–
		Ruggles St.	1869	–	–	–
Brookfield, .	Worcester	East Brookfield .	1865	1878	–	–
CHELSEA, . .	Suffolk .	Broadway . .	–	–	[3]–	–
E. Bridgewater,	Plymouth	[4]–	–	–	1850–1860	William B. Hall
Erving, . .	Franklin .	–	1859	1864	–	[5]–
Granville, . .	Hampden .	–	[6]–	–	–	[6]–
Hinsdale, . .	Berkshire	–	–	–	–	–
Holbrook, . .	Norfolk .	[7]–	1832	1836	1832–1836	Present M. E. Ch.
Lynnfield, . .	Essex .	–	1816	1862	1816–1862	Henry E. Smith
Mt Washington,	Berkshire	–	[8]–	–	–	Rev.MervinB.Lent[9]
NEW BEDFORD,	Bristol .	Mount Pleasant .	–	–	–	Pastor of M.E.Ch.[10]
New Salem, .	Franklin .	No. New Salem .	–	–	1869–1875	Pastor M. E. Ch.[11]
Northfield, .	Franklin .	–	–	–	–	Joseph Callender
Otis, . . .	Berkshire	East Otis .	–	–	–	–
Palmer, . .	Hampden .	Thorndike[12] .	–	–	–	Pastor M. E. Ch.[13]
Plymouth, .	Plymouth	–	1866	1875	1866–1875	Present M. E. Ch.
Rutland, . .	Worcester	–	–	–	1845–1865	Cyrus H. Weston
Savoy, . .	Berkshire	–	–	–	–	Ebenezer Codding
Wellfleet, . .	Barnstable	–	–	–	–	John R. Higgins[14]
		South Wellfleet .	–	–	–	Rev. M. L. Besley[15]

METHODIST PROTESTANT.

CITIES AND TOWNS.	Counties	Distinguishing Name	Year in which Organized	Year in which Terminated	Years covered	In Possession of —
Bourne, . .	Barnstable	Pocasset . .	1852	1866	1852–1866	–
E. Bridgewater,	Plymouth	Satucket . .	1842	1850	–	–
Marion, . .	Plymouth	–	–	–	–	–

PRESBYTERIAN.

CITIES AND TOWNS.	Counties	Distinguishing Name	Year in which Organized	Year in which Terminated	Years covered	In Possession of —
Blandford, .	Hampden .	–	–	1800	–	–
Groton, . .	Middlesex	–	–	–	1776–1799	–
Hopkinton, .	Middlesex	[16]–	1734	–	–	–
LOWELL, . .	Middlesex	–	–	[17]1869	–	Probably lost

PROTESTANT EPISCOPAL.

CITIES AND TOWNS.	Counties	Distinguishing Name	Year in which Organized	Year in which Terminated	Years covered	In Possession of —
BOSTON, . .	Suffolk .	Grace . . .	1830	1865	1830–1865	[18]–
LOWELL, . .	Middlesex	St. Luke's . .	1841	–	–	St. Anne's Ch.
Marshfield, .	Plymouth	–	–	–	[19]–	St. Andrew's Ch.

[1] United with the Blandford Methodist Episcopal.
[2] United with the First Methodist Episcopal.
[3] There are records covering about twelve years, the years not being specified.
[4] Originally organized in South Abington.
[5] Records are known to be somewhere in the town.
[6] Supposed to have been organized about one hundred years ago, and to have been the first Methodist Episcopal church west of the Connecticut River. All records have been destroyed.
[7] Changed to Baptist.
[8] Meetings were held in 1789.
[9] Millerton, N. Y.
[10] Long Plain.
[11] Orange.
[12] United with the Bondsville Methodist Episcopal.
[13] Bondsville.
[14] Providence, R. I.
[15] Easton.
[16] Removed to Blandford.
[17] Prior to 1869.
[18] Registrar of the Diocese.
[19] Church records from 1775 to 1834; parish records from 1791 to 1867.

EXTINCT CHURCHES: BY DENOMINATIONS — Continued.

PROTESTANT EPISCOPAL — Concluded.

CITIES AND TOWNS.	Counties	Distinguishing Name	Year in which Organized	Year in which Terminated	RECORDS	
					Years covered	In Possession of —
Nantucket,	Nantucket	Trinity[1]	–	–	–	Burned in 1846
Palmer,	Hampden	–	–	–	1873–1876	–
Sandwich,	Barnstable	Puritan	–	*1860	–	–
W. Springfield,	Hampden	[2]	–	–	1871 –	–

REFORMED METHODIST.

Carver,	Plymouth	South Carver	–	1867	1831–1867	Thomas M. Ryder[3]
Harwich,	Barnstable	[4]	1820	1845	1820–1845	–
Rehoboth,	Bristol	North Rehoboth	1826	–	–	Francis W. Stevens[5]

ROMAN CATHOLIC.

| BOSTON, | Suffolk | St. Vincent de Paul's[6] | – | 1871 | 1862–1871 | [6] |
| LOWELL, | Middlesex | St. Mary's | – | 1861 | 1847–1861 | St. Patrick's Ch. |

SECOND ADVENT.

| Abington, | Plymouth | – | – | – | – | – |
| Chicopee, | Hampden | – | – | – | – | Ansel B. Howard |

SIX PRINCIPLES BAPTIST.

| Swansea, | Bristol | – | – | – | – | Samuel Arnold[7] |

UNDENOMINATIONAL.

| Georgetown, | Essex | Union Soc. | – | – | 1843 – | – |

UNITED BRETHREN.

| Brimfield, | Hampden | West Brimfield | *1856 | – | – | – |
| Orange, | Franklin | – | – | 1856 | – | Rev. J. H. Garmon |

UNITARIAN.

Boston,	Suffolk	Bulfinch St.[8]	1822	1863	1822–1863	City Clerk
		Church of the Saviour[9]	1845	1854	–	–
		Indiana St.[10]	1845	1855	1845–1855	–
		New North	1714	[11]	1714–1862	City Clerk
		Thirteenth Cong.	1826	1858	–	–
		Twelfth Cong.	1825	1865	1823–1865	City Clerk

[1] The church edifice was destroyed by fire in 1846, and the parish soon after dissolved.
[2] Removed to Springfield.   [4] Succeeded by the Wesleyan Methodist, also extinct.
[3] Middleborough.   [5] North Rehoboth.
[6] Merged in St. James. Records in possession of the present St. Vincent de Paul's, So. Boston.
[7] Providence, R. I.
[8] Originally Universalist.   [10] Merged in the Church of the Disciples.
[9] United with the Second Church.   [11] Soon after 1863.

EXTINCT CHURCHES : BY DENOMINATIONS — Continued.

UNITARIAN — Concluded.

CITIES AND TOWNS.	Counties	Distinguishing Name	Year in which Organized	Year in which Terminated	RECORDS	
					Years covered	In Possession of —
BROCKTON, .	Plymouth	Second Cong. Soc. No. Bridgewater	1825	1831	1825–1831	–
CAMBRIDGE, .	Middlesex	Allen St. Cong. .	–	–	–	–
Hardwick, .	Worcester	First Cong.[1] .	1736	1842	1736–1842	Union Ch.
Heath, .	Franklin .	–	1825	–	–	–
Leverett, .	Franklin .	–	*1848	–	–	–
LOWELL, .	Middlesex	Church of the Pilgrims[2] .	1846	1861	1846–1861	First Unit. Ch.
		North Cong. of Chelmsford[3] .	–	–	1830–1836	First Unit. Ch.
Lunenburg, .	Worcester	–	–	*1860	–	Benj. G. Whiting
Montague, .	Franklin .	–	–	–	–	C. P. Wright[4]
Orange, . .	Franklin .	North Orange[5] .	1843	–	–	6–
Southborough, .	Worcester	–	–	–	–	7–
Whately, .	Franklin .	Unit. Cong. Soc.	1866	–	1866–1877	Cannot be found

UNITED SOCIETY (OR SHAKERS).

Tyringham, .	Berkshire	8–	1791	1875	–	Soc. at Hancock

UNIVERSALIST.

Ashfield, . .	Franklin .	–	–	–	–	Frederick Guilford
Barre, .	Worcester	–	–	9–	–	–
BOSTON, .	Suffolk .	Church of the Paternity[10]	1859	1863	–	Shawmut Ch.
		First Univ. .	1785	1864	1785–1864	11–
BROCKTON, .	Plymouth	Church of the Disciples	1858	1875	1858–1875	Unit. Ch.
Brookfield, .	Worcester	Podunk . .	–	1876	1819–1876	Moses Hobbs
Charlton, . .	Worcester	Union Soc. .	–	1859	1838–1859	Present Univ. Ch.
Concord, . .	Middlesex	–	1838	1852	1838–1852	Rev. G. Reynolds
Dennis, . .	Barnstable	South Dennis .	12–	12 –	–	Burned
Dudley, . .	Worcester	–	–	1861	1835–1861	Waldo Healy
E. Bridgewater,	Plymouth	–	–	–	–	–
Erving, . .	Franklin .	–	1836	–	–	–
FALL RIVER, .	Bristol .	–	–	131850	14–	–
Georgetown, .	Essex .	–	1829	1853	1829–1853	–
GLOUCESTER, .	Essex .	Second Univ. Soc.	–	–	– 1860	–
Hanson, . .	Plymouth	–	–	–	*1825–1850	–
Hardwick, .	Worcester	15–	1824	1842	1824–1842	Union Ch.
Lancaster, .	Worcester	–	–	–	–	Mrs. C. Bennett
Marlborough, .	Middlesex	–	–	–	1818–1855	16–
Medway, . .	Norfolk .	Second Cong. .	–	–	1835–1865	Marcellus A. Ware
Natick, . .	Middlesex	–	–	17–	–	–
New Salem, .	Franklin .	Cooleyville .	–	–	1878–1883	Willard Putnam

[1] United with the Universalist and formed the Union Church.

[2] Commonly called Lee Street Unitarian.

[3] The church site was formerly included within the limits of Chelmsford.

[4] Greenfield.   [5] Formerly Congregational.

[6] Parish records in possession of the present Universalist; church records in possession of the present Congregational.   [7] Henry S. Wheeler and Mrs. Trowbridge Brigham.

[8] Succeeded by the Societies at Hancock, Mass., and Enfield, Conn.

[9] Church edifice sold in 1851.   [10] United with the Fifth Universalist.

[11] Tufts College Library, College Hill.

[12] Church edifice built in 1839; sold and removed in 1873.

[13] About 1850 or prior to that year.

[14] Records covering a few years are known to have been kept.

[15] United with the Unitarian and formed the Union Church.

[16] Heirs of the late Silas Felton of Hudson.

[17] In existence about ten years; property sold in 1861.

EXTINCT CHURCHES: BY DENOMINATIONS — Concluded.

UNIVERSALIST — Concluded.

CITIES AND TOWNS.	Counties	Distinguishing Name	Year in which Organized	Year in which Terminated	Years covered	RECORDS In Possession of —
NEWTON, . .	Middlesex	Old Watertown Univ. . . .	–	–	–	1_
Shrewsbury, .	Worcester	–		2_	–	
Spencer, . .	Worcester	–	31830	–	–	3_
Sterling, . .	Worcester	–	–	–	–	Levi Reed
Stoneham, .	Middlesex	–	–	–	–	
TAUNTON, .	Bristol .	–	1825	1835	1825–1835	Charles Foster
Templeton, .	Worcester	–	*1850	–	–	Late Rev. G. Bushnell
WALTHAM, .	Middlesex	First Univ. Soc.	1839	1861	1839–1861	Present Univ. Ch.
Warren, . .	Worcester	First Univ. of Western . .	–	4_	–	–
		–	–	*1820	–	
Whately, . .	Franklin .	First Univ.5 .	1839	1865	1839–1865	James M. Crafts
Woburn, . .	Middlesex	6_	–	–	–	

WESLEYAN.

| Barnstable, . | Barnstable | Hyannis . . . | – | – | – | – |
| Dennis, . . | Barnstable | – | – | 1866 | – | Nathan A. Howes |

WESLEYAN METHODIST.

| Harwich, . . | Barnstable | 7_ | 1845 | 1853 | 1845–1853 | – |
| Leicester, . . | Worcester | 7_ | 1845 | 1866 | – | Francis Washburn |

DENOMINATION NOT GIVEN.

Attleborough, .	Bristol .	Trinity . .	–	–	–	Rev. G. E. Osgood
Berlin, . .	Worcester	8_	–	–	–	–
Boxborough, .	Middlesex	Unit. or Univ.9 .	–	–	–	9_
Brimfield, .	Hampden .	East Brimfield .	–	–	–	–
Charlemont, .	Franklin .	–	–	–	–	Thomas A. Taylor
Charlton, . .	Worcester	Leland's Village	–	–	–	–
CHELSEA, .	Suffolk .	St. Andrew's .	–	–	–	–
Douglas, . .	Worcester	–	–	–	–	Lovell Parker
Essex, . .	Essex .	Chris. Soc.. .	1808	1827	1808–1827	10_
FALL RIVER, .	Bristol .	Bible Union .	–	–	11_	–
Milford, . .	Worcester	Hopedale Community and Ch.	–	–	1841–1867	Rev. Adin Ballou
Russell, . .	Hampden .	Union12 .	–	–	–	–
SALEM, . .	Essex .	Howard St.13 .	–	–	1828–1832	Henry J. Pratt
Swansea, . .	Bristol .	Swansea Village M't'g House .	–	–	–	14_
Westport, . .	Bristol .	First Chris. .	–	–	–	John Smith15
Yarmouth, .	Barnstable	Yarmouth Port .	–	–	–	Rev. Philo Hawks16

---

1 Tufts College Library, College Hill.

2 No services have been held since about 1845; the church edifice was sold about 1865.

3 Existed fifteen or twenty years; records searched for but not found.

4 Existed about fifteen years.　　　　5 Succeeded by the First Unitarian Society.

6 Two Universalist churches have become extinct, but nothing is known of any records. Rev. William S. Barnes, Montreal, Canada, has private records of facts gathered in relation to these two churches.　　　　7 Succeeded by the Methodist Episcopal.

8 Became extinct during the War of the Rebellion.

9 Included in town records about one hundred years ago; no other information can be obtained.

10 Reorganized in 1849, and erected the same year a church edifice, which is now used by the Methodist Episcopal. There is a church record since 1849 and a volume of records previous to that year is supposed to be in existence.　　　　11 Records cover about three years.

12 The church edifice was built by Methodists and Congregationalists.

13 Called also First Presbyterian.

14 Certain records relating to this church are in a volume with other records, in the office of the Town Clerk.　　　　15 Clerk of the church.　　　　16 Barnstable.

TOWN RECORDS.

[The laws relating to Town and City Records are given on pages 2 and 3.

The following table gives, by towns, the information received concerning the records of the several towns and cities in the Commonwealth as they existed in 1885. The presentation for each town and city is followed by notes giving the first mention found in the Colonial, Provincial, or State records of the present town name, this being succeeded chronologically by a summary of subsequent legislation, so far as ascertained, in regard to changes in its territorial limits, change of name, or subsequent incorporation as a city. The original spelling of the town name is given in the first mention, the present accepted spelling being subsequently used. The word "established" has been uniformly used to denote incorporation; there is no uniformity of language in the earlier records, and the term "shalbe a towne" is often used. Reference to volume and page is given in each instance, except for the Resolves, until January 6, 1779, since which time the date of the act is deemed sufficient reference. The resolves passed between May 20, 1686, and May 10, 1776, are not yet printed, and the various volumes of written copies being differently arranged no reference to volumes is practicable.

The information relating to the records extends to the summer of 1885, while the notes cover legislation to the close of the session of 1888.

The records classified under the name of "Town proceedings" include the records of the proceedings of the town in town meeting, and such general records as have not been recorded in volumes intended for records of special matters. In the earlier years of the older towns all matters were recorded in the volumes of "Town proceedings." The records classified under the name of "Proprietors" are the records of the Common and Undivided Lands, further information in regard to which is presented on page 5. The records classified under the name "Miscellaneous" include the records not presented under any of the other names, but which were too numerous in kind to present in detail.

Unless otherwise stated, the copies of records referred to in foot-notes are in the possession of the Town Clerk.

When the residence of the person having the possession of the records is other than in the town to which the records relate the residence is given in a foot-note, and if the residence specified is not in Massachusetts the name of the state is also given.

In many cases the records called "Town proceedings" commenced at an earlier date than the year in which the town was established, the records of the Proprietors in such cases having been the first records in the volumes.

The use of the dash signifies that the information is wanting.

Reference to legislation concerning towns and districts which have become extinct will be found under "Extinct Cities, Towns, and Districts."

County of Barnstable. Town of Barnstable.

KIND OF RECORDS.	Number of Volumes	In Keeping of —	Years Covered	Whether Indexed	Condition
Town proceedings, . . .	[1]12	Town Clerk	1640–1885	No	Good
Births, marriages, and deaths,	10	Town Clerk	1640–1885	No	Good
Assessors, ... }	–	Town Clerk	1831–1860	–	–
		Assessors	1860–1885	–	–
Proprietors, ...	[2]1	Town Clerk	1703–1795	No	Good
Soldiers in the Rebellion, .	1	Town Clerk	–	No	Good
Miscellaneous, ...	7	Town Clerk	–	No	Good

1638. Mar. 5. Ply. Col. Rec., Vol. XI., p. 31. "For Barnstable, Mr. Thom. Dimmack."
1641. June 17. Ply. Col. Rec., Vol. II., pp. 19 and 21. Bounds between Barnstable and Yarmouth established.

[1] There is a copy also of the first volume.

[2] There is a copy also in possession of Allen H. Bearse, Hyannis, and one in the Registry of Probate at Barnstable.

TOWN RECORDS — Continued.

COUNTY OF BARNSTABLE.   TOWN OF BARNSTABLE — Con.

1652.   **Mar.**   **2.**   Ply. Col. Rec., Vol. III., p. 4.   Bounds between Barnstable and Sandwich to be established.

1658.   **Mar.**   **11.**   Ply. Col. Rec., Vol. III., p. 175.   Barnstable and Yarmouth agreed upon bounds.

1662.   **June**   **3.**   Ply. Col. Rec., Vol. IV., p. 20.   Additional lands granted to Barnstable.

1662.   **June**   **10.**   Ply. Col. Rec., Vol. IV., p. 21.   Bounds between Barnstable and Sandwich to be established.

COUNTY OF BARNSTABLE.   TOWN OF BOURNE.

KIND OF RECORDS.	Number of Volumes	In Keeping of —	Years Covered	Whether Indexed	Condition
Town proceedings, . . .	1	Town Clerk	1884–1885	No	Good
Births, marriages, and deaths,	1	Town Clerk	1884–1885	Yes	Good
Selectmen and Assessors, .	1	Selectmen	1884–1885	–	–

1884.   **April**   **2.**   Part of Sandwich established as Bourne.

COUNTY OF BARNSTABLE.   TOWN OF BREWSTER.

KIND OF RECORDS.	Number of Volumes	In Keeping of —	Years Covered	Whether Indexed	Condition
Town proceedings, . . .	4	Town Clerk	1803–1885	No	Good
Births, marriages, and deaths,	4	Town Clerk	1803–1885	–	Good
Assessors, ...	–	–	–	–	–

1803.   **Feb.**   **19.**   Part of Harwich established as Brewster.

1811.   **June**   **21.**   Part of Harwich annexed to Brewster.

1848.   **April**   **25.**   Part of Brewster annexed to Harwich.

1861.   **Feb.**   **20.**   Bounds between Brewster and Orleans established.

COUNTY OF BARNSTABLE.   TOWN OF CHATHAM.

KIND OF RECORDS.	Number of Volumes	In Keeping of —	Years Covered	Whether Indexed	Condition
Town proceedings, . . .	[1]5	Town Clerk	1712–1885	No	Fair
Births, marriages, and deaths,	3	Town Clerk	1712–1885	No	Fair
Assessors, ...	–	–	–	–	–
Parish, ...	2	Town Clerk	1824–1869	No	Fair

1712.   **June**   **11.**   Resolve. Village or district of Manamoit established as Chatham.

1862.   **April**   **14.**   Bounds between Chatham and Orleans, and Chatham and Harwich established.

[1] There is a copy also of the first and second volumes.

TOWN RECORDS — Continued.
COUNTY OF BARNSTABLE. TOWN OF DENNIS.

KIND OF RECORDS.	Number of Volumes	In Keeping of —	Years Covered	Whether Indexed	Condition
Town proceedings, . . .	4	Town Clerk	1794–1885	No	Good
Births, marriages, and deaths,	8	Town Clerk	1794–1885[1]	Yes	Good
Assessors, ...	–	Assessors	–	–	–
Miscellaneous, ...	1	Town Clerk	–	No	Good

1793. June 19. Part of Yarmouth established as Dennis.

COUNTY OF BARNSTABLE. TOWN OF EASTHAM.

KIND OF RECORDS.	Number of Volumes	In Keeping of —	Years Covered	Whether Indexed	Condition
Town proceedings, . . .	11	Town Clerk	1654–1885	No	Fair
Births, marriages, and deaths,	5	Town Clerk	1654–1885	No	Fair
Assessors, ...	51	Town Clerk	–	–	–
Selectmen, ...	5	Selectmen	–	–	–
Proprietors, ...	1	Peter Higgins	1743–1885	–	–
Miscellaneous, ...	3	Town Clerk	1654–1885	No	Fair

1651. June 7. Ply. Col. Rec., Vol. XI., p. 59. Town of Nawsett[2] to be called Eastham.
1678. Mar. 5. Ply. Col. Rec., Vol. V., p. 255. Eastham and purchasers on both sides to settle the bounds.
1772. July 14. Prov. Laws, Vol. V., p. 202. Part of Harwich annexed to Eastham.
1797. Mar. 3. Part of Eastham established as Orleans.
1839. Mar. 9. Part of Eastham annexed to Orleans.
1867. Mar. 23. Bounds between Eastham and Orleans established and part of each town annexed to the other town.
1887. May 6. Bounds between tidewaters of Eastham and Wellfleet established.

COUNTY OF BARNSTABLE. TOWN OF FALMOUTH.

KIND OF RECORDS.	Number of Volumes	In Keeping of—	Years Covered	Whether Indexed	Condition
Town proceedings, . . .	6	Town Clerk	1681–1751[3] 1765–1885	No	Good
Births, marriages, and deaths,	10	Town Clerk	1681–1751 1765–1885	5 volumes	Good
Assessors, ...	59	Town Clerk	–	–	–
Proprietors, ...	41	Town Clerk	1661–1805	No	Good

1694. Sept. 14. Prov. Laws, Vol. I., p. 178. Falmouth is mentioned in the Tax Act.
1841. Mar. 17. A tract of land formerly in the plantation of Marshpee annexed to Falmouth.
1880. Mar. 19. Bounds between Falmouth and Sandwich established.
1885. June 18. Bounds between Falmouth and Mashpee established.

---

[1] The record of marriages from 1847 to 1885 is omitted.
[2] For legislation concerning the town of Nawsett, see "Extinct Cities, Towns, and Districts."
[3] The omissions from 1751 to 1765 are partially covered by proprietors records.
[4] There is also a copy.

TOWN RECORDS — Continued.

COUNTY OF BARNSTABLE.   TOWN OF HARWICH.[1]

KIND OF RECORDS.	Number of Volumes	In Keeping of—	Years Covered	Whether Indexed	Condition
Town proceedings, . . .	25	Town Clerk	1703–1885[3]	First 3 vols.	Good[4]
Births, marriages, and deaths,	5	Town Clerk	1703–1885	No	Good
Selectmen and Assessors, .	3	Selectmen	1815–1885	–	–
Proprietors, ...	1	Sidney Brooks	–	No	–

1694. Sept. 14. Prov. Laws, Vol. I., p. 181. Tract of land known as Satuckett established as Harwich.
1772. July 14. Prov. Laws, Vol. V., p. 202. Part of Harwich annexed to Eastham.
1803. Feb. 19. Part of Harwich established as Brewster.
1811. June 21. Part of Harwich annexed to Brewster.
1848. April 25. Part of Brewster annexed to Harwich.
1862. April 4. Bounds between Harwich and Orleans established.
1862. April 14. Bounds between Harwich and Chatham established.

COUNTY OF BARNSTABLE.   TOWN OF MASHPEE.

KIND OF RECORDS.	Number of Volumes	In Keeping of—	Years Covered	Whether Indexed	Condition
Town proceedings, . . .	2	Town Clerk	1834–1885	No	Good
Births, marriages, and deaths,	4	Town Clerk	1834–1885	3 volumes	Good
Assessors, ...	10	Town Clerk	1834–1871 / 1876–1885	–	–
Proprietors, ...	1	William H. Simon	1834 –	No	Good
Miscellaneous, ...	4	Town Clerk	1834–1885	Partially	Good

1763. June 14. Prov. Laws, Vol. IV., p. 639. Mashpee established as the district of Mashpee for three years.
1767. Mar. 20. Prov. Laws, Vol. IV., p. 920. The above act revived, to be in force until July 1, 1770.
1770. Nov. 15. Prov. Laws, Vol. V., p. 88. The act again revived, to be in force until the end of the session of the General Court next after Nov. 1, 1775.
1776. Feb. 9. Prov. Laws, Vol. V., p. 460. The act to continue in force until the end of the session next after Nov. 1, 1779.
1779. Nov. 25. The act again continued until Nov. 1, 1785.
1788. June 13. The above act repealed and three "Guardians to the Proprietors" appointed, the act now passed to be in force for ten years.
1797. Mar. 7. The act of June 13, 1788, made perpetual until repealed by the Legislature.
1834. Mar. 31. The Plantation of Marshpee established as the District of Marshpee, to be under the guardianship of a commissioner appointed by the Governor.
1870. May 28. District of Marshpee abolished and the town of Mashpee established.
1872. Mar. 19. Part of Sandwich re-annexed to Mashpee.
1885. June 18. Bounds between Mashpee and Falmouth established.

[1] Private town and parish records are in possession of Josiah Paine.
[2] There are copies also of the first two volumes.
[3] The records from 1694 to 1703 are lost.
[4] With the exception of the first two volumes. The first twenty-two pages of the first volume are missing.

TOWN RECORDS — Continued.
COUNTY OF BARNSTABLE.   TOWN OF ORLEANS.

KIND OF RECORDS.	Number of Volumes	In Keeping of—	Years Covered	Whether Indexed	Condition
Town proceedings, . . .	4	Town Clerk	1797–1885	No	Fair
Births, marriages, and deaths,	6	Town Clerk	1797–1885	Yes	Fair
Assessors, ...	–	–	– .	–	–
Selectmen, ...	3	Selectmen	–	–	–
Miscellaneous, ...	5	Town Clerk	1797–1885	No	Fair

1797. **Mar. 3.** Part of Eastham established as Orleans.
1839. **Mar. 9.** Part of Eastham annexed to Orleans.
1861. **Feb. 20.** Bounds between Orleans and Brewster established.
1862. **April 4.** Bounds between Orleans and Harwich established.
1862. **April 14.** Bounds between Orleans and Chatham established.
1867. **Mar. 23.** Bounds between Orleans and Eastham established and part of each town annexed to the other town.

COUNTY OF BARNSTABLE.   TOWN OF PROVINCETOWN.

KIND OF RECORDS.	Number of Volumes	In Keeping of—	Years Covered	Whether Indexed	Condition
Town proceedings, . . .	17	Town Clerk	1724–1775[2] 1789–1885	3 volumes	Good[3]
Births, ...	5	Town Clerk	1724–1885	No	Good
Marriages, ...	5	Town Clerk	1724–1885	No	Good
Deaths, ...	5	Town Clerk	1724–1885	No	Good
Selectmen and Assessors, .	61	Selectmen	–	–	–
Miscellaneous, . . .	12	Town Clerk	1853–1885	No	Good

1727. **June 14.** Prov. Laws, Vol. I., p. 742. Precinct of Cape Cod established as Provincetown.
1813. **June 12.** Part of Truro annexed to Provincetown and bounds between the towns established.
1829. **Mar. 2.** Part of Truro annexed to Provincetown and bounds again established.
1836. **Mar. 30.** Part of Truro annexed to Provincetown.

COUNTY OF BARNSTABLE.   TOWN OF SANDWICH.

KIND OF RECORDS.	Number of Volumes	In Keeping of—	Years Covered	Whether Indexed	Condition
Town proceedings, . . .	46	Town Clerk	1650–1885	No	Good[5]
Births, marriages, and deaths,	8	Town Clerk	1650–1885	Yes	Good
Selectmen and Assessors, .	147	Town Clerk	–	–	–
Proprietors, . . .	2	Town Clerk	1685–1722	No	Good
Soldiers in the Rebellion, .	1	Town Clerk	–	No	Good
Miscellaneous, . . .	10	Town Clerk	1650–1885	No	Good

1638. **Mar. 6.** Ply. Col. Rec., Vol. I., p. 80. Certain persons were ordered to go to "Sanditch" to set forth the bounds.
1652. **Mar. 2.** Ply. Col. Rec., Vol. III., p. 4. Bounds between Sandwich and Barnstable established.

---

[1] The old records are being copied.   [2] The records from 1776 to 1788 are missing.
[3] With the exception of the first volume, nineteen pages of which are missing.
[4] There is a copy also of the first two volumes.   [5] With the exception of the first two volumes.

Town Records — Continued.

County of Barnstable. Town of Sandwich — Con.

1662. June 10. Ply. Col. Rec., Vol. IV., p. 21. Bounds between Sandwich and Barnstable established.
1670. June 7. Ply. Col. Rec., Vol. V., p. 41. The bounds established January 19,
1663, ordered to be entered on the records of the court.
1684. Oct. 28. Ply. Col. Rec., Vol. VI., p. 147. Bounds established.
1811. Feb. 26. Part of the plantation of Marshpee annexed to Sandwich.
1859. April 1. Part of the district of Marshpee annexed to Sandwich.
1860. Mar. 13. Part of the district of Marshpee annexed to Sandwich.
1872. Mar. 19. Part of Sandwich annexed to Mashpee.
1880. Mar. 19. Bounds between Sandwich and Falmouth established.
1884. April 2. Part of Sandwich established as Bourne.

County of Barnstable. Town of Truro.

KIND OF RECORDS.	Number of Volumes	In Keeping of —	Years Covered	Whether Indexed	Condition
Town proceedings, . . .	[1]6	Town Clerk	1710–1885	No	Good
Births, marriages, and deaths,	1	Town Clerk	1844–1885	Yes	Good
Births, ...	1	Town Clerk	1853–1885	Yes	Good
Marriages, ...	1	Town Clerk	1851–1885	Yes	Good
Deaths, ...	1	Town Clerk	1854–1885	Yes	Good
Marriage intentions, . .	1	Town Clerk	1871–1885	No	Good
Selectmen and Assessors, .	[2]1	Selectmen	–	–	–
Proprietors, ...	[3]1	Town Clerk	1699–1800	Yes	Fair
Miscellaneous, ...	1	Town Clerk	1871–1885	No	Good

1709. July 16. Prov. Laws, Vol. I., p. 642. A tract of land called Pawmett established
as "Truroe."
1813. June 12. Part of Truro annexed to Provincetown and bounds established.
1829. Mar. 2. Part of Truro annexed to Provincetown and bounds established.
1836. Mar. 30. Part of Truro annexed to Provincetown.
1837. Feb. 22. Bounds between Truro and Wellfleet established.

County of Barnstable. Town of Wellfleet.

KIND OF RECORDS.	Number of Volumes	In Keeping of —	Years Covered	Whether Indexed	Condition
Town proceedings, . . .	5	Town Clerk	1723–1885	No	Good
Births, ...	[4]3	Town Clerk	1723–1885	Yes	Good
Marriages, ...	[4]3	Town Clerk	1723–1885	Yes	Good
Deaths, ...	[4]3	Town Clerk	1723–1885	Yes	Good
Selectmen and Assessors, .	85	Selectmen	–	–	–
Soldiers in the Rebellion, .	1	Town Clerk	–	No	Good
Miscellaneous, ...	3	Town Clerk	–	No	Good

1763. June 16. Prov. Laws, Vol. IV., p. 664. Part of Eastham established as the district of Wellfleet.
1775. Aug. 23. Prov. Laws, Vol. V., p. 419. District of Wellfleet made the town of
Wellfleet by this general act.
1837. Feb. 22. Bounds between Wellfleet and Truro established.
1847. April 26. Part of Eastham annexed to Wellfleet.
1887. May 6. Bounds between the tidewaters of Wellfleet and Eastham established.

[1] The records of births, marriages, and deaths are included in the town records from 1710 to
1844.
[2] There are valuation books also, the number of volumes not being given.
[3] Part of the proprietors records has been copied.
[4] There are copies also of each volume.

Town Records — Continued.

County of Barnstable.   Town of Yarmouth.

Kind of Records.	Number of Volumes	In Keeping of—	Years Covered	Whether Indexed	Condition
Town proceedings, . . .	6	Town Clerk	1677–1885[1]	No	–
Births, ...	[2]6	Town Clerk	1690–1885	Yes	[3]–
Marriages and deaths, . .	6	Town Clerk	1690–1885[4]	No	–
Assessors, ...	–	–	–	–	–
Proprietors, ...	[5]2	Town Clerk	{ 1669–1706 1710–1733 }	} No	–

1639. Jan. 7. Ply. Col. Laws, Vol. I., p. 108. "The land at Mattacheeset, now called Yarmouth."

1641. June 17. Ply. Col. Rec., Vol. II., p. 21. Bounds between Yarmouth and Barnstable established.

1658. Mar. 11. Ply. Col. Rec., Vol. III., p 175. Yarmouth and Barnstable agree upon bounds.

1793. June 19. Part of Yarmouth established as Dennis.

County of Berkshire.   Town of Adams.[6]

Kind of Records.	Number of Volumes	In Keeping of—	Years Covered	Whether Indexed	Condition
Town proceedings, . . .	1	Town Clerk	1878–1885	Yes	Good
Births, marriages, and deaths,	3	Town Clerk	1878–1885	Yes	Good
Assessors, ...	13	Town Clerk	–	–	–
Selectmen, ...	3	Town Clerk	1878–1885	–	–
Proprietors, ...	[7]1	Unknown	–	–	–
Miscellaneous, . . .	8	Town Clerk	1878–1885	Yes	Good

1778. Oct. 15. The plantation called East Hoosuck established as Adams.

1780. April 10. The plantation called New Providence annexed to Adams.

1793. Mar. 14. Parts of Adams, Lanesborough, Windsor, and the district of New Ashford annexed to Cheshire.

1878. April 16. Part of Adams established as North Adams.

County of Berkshire.   Town of Alford.

Kind of Records.	Number of Volumes	In Keeping of—	Years Covered	Whether Indexed	Condition
Town proceedings, . . .	3	Town Clerk	1774–1885	No	Good
Births, marriages, and deaths,	4	Town Clerk	1774–1885	No	Good
Assessors, ...	25	Town Library	1861–1885[8]	–	–
Selectmen, ...	2	Selectmen	1822–1885	–	–

[1] The records prior to 1677 were destroyed by the burning of the town clerk's house.

[2] There is a copy also of each volume.

[3] The first twenty-six pages of the first volume are missing.

[4] The records of marriages and deaths from November, 1783, to February, 1786, are omitted.

[5] There is a copy also of the second volume.

[6] Some of the old records were destroyed; those prior to 1878 are in North Adams.

[7] There is a copy in the possession of C. F. Sayles.

[8] The records prior to 1861 have not been preserved.

Town Records — Continued.

County of Berkshire.   Town of Alford — Con.

1773.   Feb.   16.   Prov. Laws, Vol. V., p. 236.   Part of Great Barrington and certain common lands established as the district of Alford.
1775.   Aug.   23.   Prov. Laws, Vol. V., p. 419.   District of Alford made the town of Alford by this general act.
1779.   Feb.   11.   Part of Great Barrington annexed to Alford.
1790.   Feb.   6.   Bounds between Alford and Egremont established.
1819.   Feb.   18.   Part of Great Barrington annexed to Alford.
1847.   Mar.   17.   Part of West Stockbridge annexed to Alford.

County of Berkshire.   Town of Becket.

KIND OF RECORDS.	Number of Volumes	In Keeping of —	Years Covered	Whether Indexed	Condition
Town proceedings, . . .	4	Town Clerk	1765–1885	No	Good
Births, ...	2	Town Clerk	1765–1885	No	Good
Marriages, ...	2	Town Clerk	1765–1885	No	Good
Deaths, ...	2	Town Clerk	1765–1885	No	Good
Selectmen and Assessors, .	2	Selectmen	1765–1885	–	–
Proprietors, ...	1	Town Clerk	1737–1765	No	Good

1765.   June   21.   Prov. Laws, Vol. IV., p. 817.   The new plantation called Number Four established as Becket.
1783.   Mar.   12.   Parts of Becket, Chester, Partridgefield, Washington, and Worthington, and certain common lands, established as Middlefield.
1798.   Feb.   3.   Certain common lands lying between Becket, Blandford, Chester, and Loudon annexed to Becket.
1810.   Mar.   1.   Part of Loudon annexed to Becket.

County of Berkshire.   Town of Cheshire.

KIND OF RECORDS.	Number of Volumes	In Keeping of —	Years Covered	Whether Indexed	Condition
Town proceedings, . . .	5	Town Clerk	1793–1885	Partially	Good
Births and deaths, . . .	2	Town Clerk	1858–1885	No	Good
Marriages, ...	2	Town Clerk	1793–1885	No	Good
Assessors, ...	51	Town Clerk	—[1]	–	–
Soldiers in the Rebellion, .	1	Town Clerk	–	No	Good

1793.   Mar.   14.   Parts of Adams, Lanesborough, Windsor, and the district of New Ashford established as Cheshire.
1798.   Feb.   6.   Part of the district of New Ashford annexed to Cheshire.

[1] The records for nineteen years between 1793 and 1856 are missing.

Town Records — Continued.

County of Berkshire. Town of Clarksburg.

KIND OF RECORDS.	Number of Volumes	In Keeping of—	Years Covered	Whether Indexed	Condition
Town proceedings, . . .	2[1]	Town Clerk	1855–1885	Yes	Good
Births, marriages, and deaths,	3	Town Clerk	1846–1885	No	Good
Assessors, ...	25	Town Clerk	1860–1885	–	–
Selectmen, ...	2	Town Clerk	1836–1860	–	–

1798. Mar. 2. A gore of common land lying north of Adams established as Clarksburg.
1848. May 2. Part of Clarksburg annexed to Florida.
1852. May 20. Part of Florida annexed to Clarksburg.

County of Berkshire. Town of Dalton.

KIND OF RECORDS.	Number of Volumes	In Keeping of—	Years Covered	Whether Indexed	Condition
Town proceedings, . . .	1	Town Clerk	1784–1885	No	Good
Births, marriages, and deaths,	6	Town Clerk	1784–1885	No	Good
Selectmen and Assessors, .	1	Town Clerk	1784–1885	–	–

1784. Mar. 20. The new plantation of Ashuelot Equivalent established as Dalton.
1795. Feb. 28. Part of Windsor annexed to Dalton.

County of Berkshire. Town of Egremont.

KIND OF RECORDS.	Number of Volumes	In Keeping of—	Years Covered	Whether Indexed	Condition
Town proceedings, . . .	2	Town Clerk	1840–1885	No	Good
Births, marriages, and deaths,	5	Town Clerk	1840–1885	No	Good
Assessors, ...	25	Selectmen	–	–	–
Selectmen, ...	4	Selectmen	–	–	–
Proprietors, ...	1	Town Clerk	1756–1862	No	Good
Miscellaneous, ...	3	Town Clerk	1845–1885	No	Good

1760. Feb. 13. Prov. Laws, Vol. IV., p. 286. Certain common lands lying west of Sheffield established as the district of Egremont.
1775. Aug. 23. Prov. Laws, Vol. V., p. 419. District of Egremont made the town of Egremont by this general act.
1790. Feb. 6. Boundary line between Alford and Egremont established.
1790. Feb. 22. Part of Sheffield annexed to Egremont.
1817. June 17. Part of Egremont annexed to Mount Washington.
1824. Feb. 16. Part of Sheffield annexed to Egremont.
1869. June 4. Bounds between Egremont and Sheffield established.

---

[1] A volume covering the years from 1798 to 1855 is missing.

Town Records — Continued.

County of Berkshire. Town of Florida.

KIND OF RECORDS.	Number of Volumes	In Keeping of —	Years Covered	Whether Indexed	Condition
Town proceedings, . . .	6	Town Clerk	1805–1885	No	Good
Births, marriages, and deaths,	4	Town Clerk	1805–1885	Yes	Good
Selectmen and Assessors, .	2	Town Clerk	1805–1885	–	–
Miscellaneous, ...	2	Town Clerk	1805–1885	–	Good

1805. June 15. Barnardstone's Grant and part of Bullock's Grant established as Florida.

1848. May 2. Part of Clarksburg annexed to Florida.

1852. May 20. Part of Florida annexed to Clarksburg.

County of Berkshire. Town of Great Barrington.

KIND OF RECORDS.	Number of Volumes	In Keeping of —	Years Covered	Whether Indexed	Condition
Town proceedings, . . .	6	Town Clerk	1742–1812 1817–1885[1]	No	Good
Births, marriages, and deaths,	5	Town Clerk	1742–1885	Yes	Good
Assessors, ...	32	Town Clerk	–	–	–
Miscellaneous, ...	2	Town Clerk	1878–1885	No	Good

1761. June 30. Prov. Laws, Vol. IV., p. 465. Part of Sheffield established as Great Barrington.

1773. Feb. 16. Prov. Laws, Vol. V., p. 236. Part of Great Barrington and lands adjoining established as Alford.

1773. Feb. 16. Prov. Laws, Vol. V., p. 239. Lands adjoining annexed to Great Barrington.

1777. Oct. 21. Parts of Great Barrington and Washington, the Glassworks Grant, and part of Williams's Grant established as Lee.

1779. Feb. 11. Part of Great Barrington annexed to Alford.

1819. Feb. 18. Part of Great Barrington annexed to Alford.

County of Berkshire. Town of Hancock.

KIND OF RECORDS.	Number of Volumes	In Keeping of —	Years Covered	Whether Indexed	Condition
Town proceedings, . . .	4	Town Clerk	1776–1885	Vol. II.	Good
Births, ...	4	Town Clerk	1776–1885	No	Good
Marriages, ...	4	Town Clerk	1776–1885	No	Good
Deaths, ...	4	Town Clerk	1776–1885	No	Good
Assessors, ...	25	Town Clerk	–	–	–
Miscellaneous, ...	3	Town Clerk	1833–1885	No	Good

1776. July 2. Prov. Laws, Vol. V., p. 550. The plantation called Jericho established as Hancock.

1798. June 26. Part of Hancock annexed to New Ashford.

1851. May 20. Bounds between Hancock and New Ashford established.

· [1] The records from 1812 to 1817 were burned.

TOWN RECORDS — Continued.

COUNTY OF BERKSHIRE. TOWN OF HINSDALE.

KIND OF RECORDS.	Number of Volumes	In Keeping of—	Years Covered	Whether Indexed	Condition
Town proceedings, . . .	5	Town Clerk	1795–1885	Vols. IV. and V.	Good
Births, marriages, and deaths,	4	Town Clerk	1795–1885	No	Good
Selectmen and Assessors, .	32	Selectmen	–	–	–

1804. June 21. Part of Partridgefield established as Hinsdale.

COUNTY OF BERKSHIRE. TOWN OF LANESBOROUGH.

KIND OF RECORDS.	Number of Volumes	In Keeping of—	Years Covered	Whether Indexed	Condition
Town proceedings, . . .	2	Town Clerk	1765–1885	Yes	Fair
Births, ...	2	Town Clerk	1765–1885	Yes	Fair
Marriages, ...	1	Town Clerk	1765–1885	Yes	Fair
Deaths	1	Town Clerk	1765–1885	Yes	Fair
Assessors, ...	82	Selectmen	–	–	–
Selectmen, ...	2	Selectmen	–	–	–
Proprietors, ...	2	Town Clerk	1742–1766	–	–

1765. June 21. Prov. Laws, Vol. IV., p. 815. The Plantation of New Framingham established as Lanesborough.
1793. Mar. 14. Parts of Lanesborough, Adams, New Ashford, and Windsor established as Cheshire.

COUNTY OF BERKSHIRE. TOWN OF LEE.

KIND OF RECORDS.	Number of Volumes	In Keeping of—	Years Covered	Whether Indexed	Condition
Town proceedings, . . .	3[1]	Town Clerk	1777–1885[2]	Vol. I.	Good
Births, marriages, and deaths,	7	Town Clerk	1777–1885	No	Good
Assessors, ...	55	Assessors	–	–	–
Selectmen, ...	3	Town Clerk	1777–1885	–	–

1777. Oct. 21. Prov. Laws, Vol. V., p. 739. Parts of Great Barrington and Washington, the Glass Works Grant, and part of Williams's Grant established as Lee.
1806. Mar. 7. Bounds between Lee and Lenox established.
1820. Feb. 7. Bounds between Lee and Lenox established.

[1] There is a copy also of the first volume.
[2] The records for the year 1867 are omitted from the second volume.

TOWN RECORDS — Continued.

COUNTY OF BERKSHIRE.   TOWN OF LENOX.

KIND OF RECORDS.	Number of Volumes	In Keeping of—	Years Covered	Whether Indexed	Condition
Town proceedings, . . .	6[1]	Town Clerk	–	Partially	Good[2]
Births, marriages, and deaths,	4	Town Clerk	–	Partially	Good
Assessors, ...	40	Town Clerk	–	–	–
Proprietors, ...	1	Town Clerk	1764–1769	No	Good
Miscellaneous, ...	7	Town Clerk	1800–1885	Partially	Good

1767. Feb. 26. Prov. Laws, Vol. IV., p. 905. Part of Richmont established as the district of Lenox.

1770. Nov. 20. Prov. Laws, Vol. V., p. 115. Lands adjoining annexed to Lenox.

1775. Aug. 23. Prov. Laws, Vol. V., p. 419. District of Lenox made the town of Lenox by this general act.

1795. Jan. 31. Part of Washington annexed to Lenox.

1802. Feb. 18. Part of Washington annexed to Lenox.

1806. Mar. 7. Bounds between Lenox and Lee established.

1820. Feb. 7. Bounds between Lenox and Lee established.

COUNTY OF BERKSHIRE.   TOWN OF MONTEREY.

KIND OF RECORDS.	Number of Volumes	In Keeping of—	Years Covered	Whether Indexed	Condition
Town proceedings, . . .	5[3]	Town Clerk	1847–1885	No	Good
Births, marriages, and deaths,	4[4]	Town Clerk	1847–1885	Yes	Good
Assessors, ...	–	Assessors	–	–	–
Selectmen, ...	1	Selectmen	1847–1885	–	–
Proprietors, ...	1	Town Clerk	1737–1762	No	Good

1847. April 12. Part of Tyringham established as Monterey.

1851. May 24. Part of New Marlborough annexed to Monterey.

COUNTY OF BERKSHIRE.   TOWN OF MOUNT WASHINGTON.

KIND OF RECORDS.	Number of Volumes	In Keeping of—	Years Covered	Whether Indexed	Condition
Town proceedings, . . .	2	Town Clerk	1796–1885[5]	Vol. II.	Good
Births, ...	1	Town Clerk	1860–1885	No	Good
Marriages, ...	1	Town Clerk	1860–1885	No	Good
Deaths, ...	1	Town Clerk	1860–1885	No	Good
Assessors, ...	–	–	–	–	–
Selectmen, ...	1	Town Clerk	1863–1885[6]	–	–
Proprietors, ...	1[7]	Unknown	1750 –	–	–
Soldiers in the Rebellion, .	1	Town Clerk	1861–1865	No	Good
Miscellaneous, . . .	2	Town Clerk	1835–1885	Vol. II.	Good

[1] There is a copy also of the first volume.

[2] With the exception of the first volume, which is badly worn.

[3] Three volumes contain records of the town of Tyringham from 1762 to 1834.

[4] One volume contains records of births, marriages, and deaths in Tyringham from 1803 to 1845. Copies of records of births, marriages, and deaths kept by Rev. A. Bidwell from 1750 to 1784 and by Rev. Joseph Avery from 1789 to 1795 are in the office of the Town Clerk.

[5] The records prior to 1796 were burned.   [6] The records prior to 1863 were burned.

[7] There is a copy also which is supposed to be with the original records.

TOWN RECORDS — Continued.

COUNTY OF BERKSHIRE. TOWN OF MOUNT WASHINGTON — Col.

1779. June 21. The plantation called Tauconnuck Mountain established as Mount Washington.
1817. June 17. Part of Egremont annexed to Mount Washington.
1847. Mar. 12. Bounds between Mount Washington and the district of Boston Corner established.

COUNTY OF BERKSHIRE. TOWN OF NEW ASHFORD.

KIND OF RECORDS.	Number of Volumes	In Keeping of —	Years Covered	Whether Indexed	Condition
Town proceedings, . . .	3	Town Clerk	1775–1885	No	Good[1]
Births, marriages, and deaths,	2	Town Clerk	1775–1885	No	Good
Assessors, ...	40	Town Clerk	–	–	–

1781. Feb. 26. Land called New Ashford, lying between Adams, Hancock, Lanesborough, and Williamstown, established as the district of New Ashford.
1793. Mar. 14. Parts of New Ashford, Adams, Lanesborough, and Windsor established as Cheshire.
1798. Feb. 6. Part of New Ashford annexed to Cheshire.
1798. June 26. Part of Hancock annexed to New Ashford.
1836. May 1. District of New Ashford made the town of New Ashford by chapter 15 of the Revised Statutes.
1851. May 20. Bounds established between New Ashford and Hancock.

COUNTY OF BERKSHIRE. TOWN OF NEW MARLBOROUGH.

KIND OF RECORDS.	Number of Volumes	In Keeping of —	Years Covered	Whether Indexed	Condition
Town proceedings, . . .	4	Town Clerk	1797–1885	No	Good[2]
Births, marriages, and deaths,	4[3]	Town Clerk	1734–1852	No	Good
Births, ...	1	Town Clerk	1853–1885	No	Good
Marriages, . . .	1	Town Clerk	1853–1885	No	Good
Deaths, ...	1	Town Clerk	1853–1885	No	Good
Selectmen and Assessors, .	2	Town Clerk	1840–1860	–	–
Proprietors, . . .	2	Town Clerk	1737–1801	No	Good

1759. June 15. Prov. Laws, Vol. IV., p. 263. The plantation called New Marlborough established as the district of New Marlborough.
1775. Aug. 23. Prov. Laws, Vol. V., p. 419. District of New Marlborough made the town of New Marlborough by this general act.
1795. June 19. Part of Sheffield annexed to New Marlborough.
1798. Feb. 7. Part of Sheffield annexed to New Marlborough.
1811. Feb. 27. Part of Tyringham annexed to New Marlborough.
1812. Feb. 11. Part of New Marlborough annexed to Tyringham.
1851. May 24. Part of New Marlborough annexed to Monterey.
1871. April 19. Part of Sheffield annexed to New Marlborough and bounds established.

[1] With the exception of the first volume, which is mutilated.
[2] With the exception of the first volume.
[3] There are copies also of the first three volumes.

TOWN RECORDS — Continued.

COUNTY OF BERKSHIRE.   TOWN OF NORTH ADAMS.

KIND OF RECORDS.	Number of Volumes	In Keeping of —	Years Covered	Whether Indexed	Condition
Town proceedings, . . .	6[1]	Town Clerk	1778–1885	First 3 vols.	Good
Births, ...	4	Town Clerk	1778–1885	No	Good
Marriages, ...	4	Town Clerk	1778–1885	No	Good
Deaths, ...	3	Town Clerk	1778–1885	No	Good
Assessors, ...	10	Town Clerk	1876–1885[2]	–	–

1878.   April 16.   Part of Adams established as North Adams.

COUNTY OF BERKSHIRE.   TOWN OF OTIS.

KIND OF RECORDS	Number of Volumes	In Keeping of —	Years Covered	Whether Indexed	Condition
Town proceedings, . . .	5[3]	Town Clerk	1776–1885	No	Good
Births, marriages, and deaths,	7	Town Clerk	1776–1885	No	Good
Selectmen and Assessors, .	10	Town Clerk	–	–	–
Soldiers in the Rebellion, .	1	Town Clerk	–	No	Good

1810.   June 13.   The name of the town of Loudon[4] changed to Otis.
1838.   April 9.   Part of the common lands called East Eleven Thousand Acres annexed to Otis.

COUNTY OF BERKSHIRE.   TOWN OF PERU.

KIND OF RECORDS.	Number of Volumes	In Keeping of —	Years Covered	Whether Indexed	Condition
Town proceedings, . . .	5	Town Clerk	1775–1885	No	Good
Births, marriages, and deaths,	4[5]	Town Clerk	1775–1885	No	Good
Assessors, ...	40	Selectmen	1775–1885	–	–
Miscellaneous, ...	4	Town Clerk	1775–1885	No	Good

1806.   June 19.   The name of the town of Partridgefield[6] changed to Peru.

---

[1] The first five volumes contain the records of the town of Adams from 1778 to 1877.

[2] The records prior to 1876 were burned.

[3] The first volume contains records of the district of Bethlehem from 1789 to 1810; the second and third volumes contain records of the town of Loudon from 1776 to 1810.

[4] For legislation concerning the town of Loudon, see " Extinct Cities, Towns, and Districts."

[5] There are private records of births, marriages, and deaths in possession of S. S. Bowen.

[6] For legislation concerning the town of Partridgefield, see " Extinct Cities, Towns, and Districts."

TOWN RECORDS — Continued.

COUNTY OF BERKSHIRE. TOWN OF PITTSFIELD.

KIND OF RECORDS.	Number of Volumes	In Keeping of—	Years Covered	Whether Indexed	Condition
Town proceedings, . . .	9[1]	Town Clerk	1753–1885	First vol.	Good
Births, marriages, and deaths,	8	Town Clerk	1753–1885	No	Good
Assessors, ...	27	Town Clerk	–	–	–
Parish, ...	1[2]	Town Clerk	1753–1845	No	Good

1761. April 21. Prov. Laws, Vol. IV., p. 434. The plantation called Pontoosuck established as Pittsfield.

COUNTY OF BERKSHIRE. TOWN OF RICHMOND.

KIND OF RECORDS.	Number of Volumes	In Keeping of—	Years Covered	Whether Indexed	Condition
Town proceedings, . . .	5	Town Clerk	1776–1885[3]	No	Fair
Births, ...	5	Town Clerk	1776–1885	No	Fair
Marriages, ...	4	Town Clerk	1776–1885	No	Fair
Deaths, ...	3	Town Clerk	1776–1885	No	Fair
Selectmen and Assessors, .	–	Selectmen	–	–	–
Proprietors, ...	1	Town Clerk	1764–1769	No	Fair
Soldiers in the Rebellion, .	1	Town Clerk	1862–1864	No	Fair
Miscellaneous, ...	1	Town Clerk	1827–1867	No	Fair

1785. Mar. 3. The name Richmont[4] having been given to this town by a mistake the name Richmond, originally petitioned for, was substituted.

1834. Mar. 27. Bounds between Richmond and West Stockbridge established.

COUNTY OF BERKSHIRE. TOWN OF SANDISFIELD.

KIND OF RECORDS.	Number of Volumes	In Keeping of—	Years Covered	Whether Indexed	Condition
Town proceedings, . . .	5	Town Clerk	1762–1885	Yes	Good[5]
Births, ...	3[6]	Town Clerk	1756–1885	Yes	Good
Marriages, ...	3[6]	Town Clerk	1759–1885	Yes	Good
Deaths, ...	3[6]	Town Clerk	1756–1885	Yes	Good
Assessors, ...	–	–	–	–	–
Selectmen, ...	2	Selectmen	–	–	–
Proprietors, ...	1	Town Clerk	1735–1862	No	Fair
Miscellaneous, ...	3	Town Clerk	1708–1885	Yes	Poor

1762. Mar. 6. Prov. Laws, Vol. IV., p. 531. The new plantation called Number Three established as Sandisfield.

1819. Feb. 10. District of Southfield[7] and the town of Sandisfield united as the town of Sandisfield.

---

[1] There is a copy also of the first volume.　　[2] This volume is a copy only.

[3] The town and parish records prior to 1776 were burned.

[4] For legislation concerning the town of Richmont, see "Extinct Cities, Towns, and Districts."

[5] The first volume is mutilated.

[6] The records of births, marriages, and deaths from 1762 to 1844 have been copied and indexed.

[7] For legislation concerning the district of Southfield, see "Extinct Cities, Towns, and Districts."

TOWN RECORDS — Continued.

COUNTY OF BERKSHIRE. TOWN OF SANDISFIELD — Con.

1838.	April	9.	Part of the common lands called East Eleven Thousand Acres annexed to Sandisfield.
1853.	May	4.	Bounds between Sandisfield and Tolland established.
1855.	May	15.	Bounds between Sandisfield and Tolland established.
1875.	April	24.	Part of Sandisfield annexed to Monterey.
1875.	May	19.	Act of April 24, 1875, accepted by Monterey.
1875.	June	1.	Act of April 24, 1875, took effect.

COUNTY OF BERKSHIRE. TOWN OF SAVOY.

KIND OF RECORDS.	Number of Volumes	In Keeping of—	Years Covered	Whether Indexed	Condition
Town proceedings, . . .	5[1]	Town Clerk	1797–1885	No	Poor
Births, marriages, and deaths,	4	Town Clerk	1797–1885	No	Poor
Assessors, ...	–	–	–	–	–
Proprietors, ...	1[2]	Town Clerk	1771–1801[3]	No	Good

1797.   Feb.   20.   Certain lands established as Savoy.

COUNTY OF BERKSHIRE. TOWN OF SHEFFIELD.

KIND OF RECORDS.	Number of Volumes	In Keeping of—	Years Covered	Whether Indexed	Condition
Town proceedings, . . .	6	Town Clerk	1733–1792 1794–1885	No	Good
Births, marriages, and deaths,	4	Town Clerk	1776–1885	Yes	Good
Assessors, ...	94	Town Clerk	1769–1885[4]	–	–
Proprietors, ...	2	5—	–	–	–
Miscellaneous, ...	8	Town Clerk	1772–1885	No	Good

1733.	June	22.	Prov. Laws, Vol. II., p. 673. Part of the lower plantation called "Houssatannick" established as Sheffield.
1761.	June	30.	Prov. Laws, Vol. IV., p. 465. Part of Sheffield established as Great Barrington.
1790.	Feb.	22.	Part of Sheffield annexed to Egremont.
1795.	June	19.	Part of Sheffield annexed to New Marlborough.
1798.	Feb.	7.	Part of Sheffield annexed to New Marlborough.
1824.	Feb.	16.	Part of Sheffield annexed to Egremont.
1869.	June	4.	Bounds between Sheffield and Egremont established.
1871.	April	19.	Part of Sheffield annexed to New Marlborough and bounds established.

[1] There is a copy also of the first volume.

[2] There is also a copy.

[3] Dated at Rehoboth.

[4] The records for twenty-three years between 1772 and 1850 are missing, the years not being specified.

[5] There were two volumes in the Registry of Deeds at Great Barrington, one of which is now missing.

Town Records — Continued.

County of Berkshire. Town of Stockbridge.

Kind of Records.	Number of Volumes	In Keeping of—	Years Covered	Whether Indexed	Condition
Town proceedings, . . .	5	Town Clerk	1739–1885	No	Good
Births, marriages, and deaths,	6	Town Clerk	1739–1885	No	Good
Assessors, ...	–	–	–	–	–
Selectmen, ...	–	–	–	–	–
Proprietors, ...	3	Town Clerk	1739–1825	No	Good

1739. June 22. Prov. Laws, Vol. II., p. 991. The plantation called the Indian town established as Stockbridge.

County of Berkshire. Town of Tyringham.[2]

Kind of Records.	Number of Volumes	In Keeping of—	Years Covered	Whether Indexed	Condition
Town proceedings, . . .	3	Town Clerk	1834–1885	No	–
Births, marriages, and deaths,	1	Town Clerk	–	No	–
Births, ...	1	Town Clerk	1847–1885	Yes	–
Marriages, . . .	1	Town Clerk	1847–1885	Yes	–
Deaths, ...	1	Town Clerk	1847–1885	Yes	–
Marriage intentions, . .	1	Town Clerk	1847–1885	No	–
Assessors, ...	–	–	–	–	–
Selectmen, ...	1	Selectmen	1834–1885	–	–
Soldiers in the Rebellion, .	1	Town Clerk	–	No	–
Miscellaneous, . . .	2	Town Clerk	1834–1885	Yes	–

1762. Mar. 6. Prov. Laws, Vol. IV., p. 534. The new plantation called Number One established as Tyringham.

1811. Feb. 27. Part of Tyringham annexed to New Marlborough.

1812. Feb. 11. Part of New Marlborough annexed to Tyringham.

1847. April 12. Part of Tyringham established as Monterey.

County of Berkshire. Town of Washington.

Kind of Records.	Number of Volumes	In Keeping of—	Years Covered	Whether Indexed	Condition
Town proceedings, . . .	3	Town Clerk	–	No	Good
Births, marriages, and deaths,	5	Town Clerk	–	No	Good
Assessors, ...	–	Selectmen	–	–	–
Miscellaneous, . . .	1	Town Clerk	–	No	Poor

1777. April 12. Prov. Laws, Vol. V., p. 635. The plantation called Hartwood, with several contiguous grants, established as Washington.

1777. Oct. 21. Prov. Laws, Vol. V., p. 739. Parts of Washington and Great Barrington, the Glass Works Grant, and part of Williams's Grant established as Lee.

1783. Mar. 12. Parts of Washington, Becket, Chester, Partridgefield, and Worthington, and certain common lands, established as Middlefield.

1795. Jan. 31. Part of Washington annexed to Lenox.

1802. Feb. 18. Part of Washington annexed to Lenox.

---

[1] There is a copy also of the records from 1730 to 1760.

[2] The records prior to 1847, the time of the division of the town, are in the keeping of the Town Clerk of Monterey.

Town Records — Continued.

County of Berkshire.   Town of West Stockbridge.

Kind of Records.	Number of Volumes	In Keeping of—	Years Covered	Whether Indexed	Condition
Town proceedings, . . .	4[1]	Town Clerk	–	Vol. II.	Good[2]
Births, marriages, and deaths,	1	Town Clerk	–	Yes	Fair
Births, ...	1	Town Clerk	–	Yes	Fair
Marriages, ...	1	Town Clerk	–	Yes	Fair
Deaths, ...	1	Town Clerk	–	Yes	Fair
Assessors, ...	26	Town Clerk	1861–1885	–	–
Soldiers in the Rebellion, .	1	Town Clerk	1861–1885	No	Fair
Miscellaneous, ...	12	Town Clerk	–	No	Fair

1774. Mar. 9. Prov. Laws, Vol. V., p. 325. Part of Stockbridge established as the district of West Stockbridge.
1775. Aug. 23. Prov. Laws, Vol. V., p. 419. District of West Stockbridge made the town of West Stockbridge by this general act.
1793. Mar. 2. A gore of common land annexed to West Stockbridge.
1829. Mar. 2. Part of Stockbridge annexed to West Stockbridge.
1830. Feb. 6. The act of March 2, 1829, perfected.
1834. Mar. 27. Bounds between West Stockbridge and Richmond established.
1847. Mar. 17. Part of West Stockbridge annexed to Alford.

County of Berkshire.   Town of Williamstown.

Kind of Records.	Number of Volumes	In Keeping of—	Years Covered	Whether Indexed	Condition
Town proceedings, . . .	4	Town Clerk	1804–1885	No	Good
Births, marriages, and deaths,	4	Town Clerk	1861–1885[3]	No	Good
Assessors, ...	15	Selectmen	–	–	–
Proprietors, ...	1	[4]	–	No	Good

1765. June 21. Prov. Laws, Vol. IV., p. 809. The plantation called West Hoosuck established as Williamstown.
1838. April 9. Certain unincorporated lands annexed to Williamstown.

County of Berkshire.   Town of Windsor.

Kind of Records.	Number of Volumes	In Keeping of—	Years Covered	Whether Indexed	Condition
Town proceedings, . . .	3	Town Clerk	1772–1885	No	Good
Births, marriages, and deaths,	4	Town Clerk	1772–1885	Yes	Good
Assessors, ...	–	–	–	–	–
Selectmen, ...	4	Selectmen	–	–	–

1778. Oct. 16. Prov. Laws, Vol. V., p. 911. The name of the town of Gageborough[5] changed to Windsor.

[1] There is a copy also of the first volume.
[2] The records for the years 1831 and 1832 are imperfect and incomplete. The second volume needs rebinding.   [3] The records from 1843 to 1860 were burned.
[4] The Chairman of the Selectmen, temporarily.
[5] For legislation concerning the town of Gageborough, see "Extinct Cities, Towns, and Districts."

TOWN RECORDS — Continued.

COUNTY OF BERKSHIRE. TOWN OF WINDSOR — Con.

1793. Mar. 14. Parts of Windsor, Adams, Lanesborough, and the district of New Ashford established as Cheshire.

1794. Feb. 26. Part of Cheshire re-annexed to Windsor.

1795. Feb. 28. Part of Windsor annexed to Dalton.

COUNTY OF BRISTOL. TOWN OF ACUSHNET.

KIND OF RECORDS.	Number of Volumes	In Keeping of—	Years Covered	Whether Indexed	Condition
Town proceedings, . . .	2	Town Clerk	1860–1885	No	Gcod
Births, ...	1	Town Clerk	1860–1885	Yes	Gcod
Marriages, ...	1	Town Clerk	1860–1885	Yes	Gcod
Deaths, ...	1	Town Clerk	1860–1885	Yes	Good
Assessors, ...	–	–	–	–	–
Selectmen, ...	3	Selectmen	–	–	–

1860. Feb. 13. Part of Fairhaven established as Acushnet.

1875. April 9. Part of Acushnet annexed to New Bedford.

COUNTY OF BRISTOL. TOWN OF ATTLEBOROUGH.

KIND OF RECORDS.	Number of Volumes	In Keeping of—	Years Covered	Whether Indexed	Condition
Town proceedings, . . .	9[1]	Town Clerk	1697–1885	No	Good
Births, marriages, and deaths,	14	Town Clerk	1697–1885	Yes	Fair[2]
Assessors, ...	52	Town Clerk	–	–	–
Proprietors, ...	5	Town Clerk	1666–1839	–	–
Miscellaneous, ...	41	Town Clerk	1750–1885	No	Good

1694. Oct. 19. Prov. Laws, Vol I., p. 184. Part of the land called the North Purchase established as Attleborough.

1830. Feb. 18. Bounds between Attleborough and Wrentham established.

1887. June 14. Part of Attleborough established as North Attleborough.

1887. July 30. Act of June 14, 1887, accepted by the town of Attleborough.

1888. Mar. 6. The acceptance of the act by the town confirmed.

COUNTY OF BRISTOL. TOWN OF BERKLEY.

KIND OF RECORDS.	Number of Volumes	In Keeping of—	Years Covered	Whether Indexed	Condition
Town proceedings, . . .	5	Town Clerk	1735–1885	No	Fair
Births, marriages, and deaths,	8	Town Clerk	1735–1885	No	Fair
Assessors, ...	16	Town Clerk	–	–	–
Selectmen, ...	1	Selectmen	–	–	–
Miscellaneous, ...	5	Town Clerk	1735–1885	No	Fair

[1] The first volume is being copied.

[2] The first four volumes are mutilated.

TOWN RECORDS — Continued.

COUNTY OF BRISTOL. TOWN OF BERKLEY — Con.

1735. April 18. Prov. Laws, Vol. II., p. 742. Parts of Dighton and Taunton established as Berkley.

1799. Feb. 26. Part of Dighton annexed to Berkley.

1810. Feb. 6. Certain lands in Berkley belonging to Taunton annexed to Berkley.

1842. Mar. 3. Certain lands in Berkley belonging to Taunton annexed to Berkley.

1879. April 1. Part of Taunton annexed to Berkley.

1879. April 12. Act of April 1, 1879, accepted by the town of Berkley.

COUNTY OF BRISTOL. TOWN OF DARTMOUTH.

KIND OF RECORDS.	Number of Volumes	In Keeping of —	Years Covered	Whether Indexed	Condition
Town proceedings, . . .	5[1]	Town Clerk	–	First 2 vols.	–
Births, marriages, and deaths,	6	Town Clerk	–	No	–
Assessors, ...	–	–	–	–	–
Proprietors, ...	2	_[2]	–	–	–
Miscellaneous, ...	6	Town Clerk	1670–1885	No	–

1652. Oct. 5. Ply. Col. Rec., Vol. III., p. 19. "Dartmouth is to pay £2."

1664. June 8. Ply. Col. Rec., Vol. IV., p. 65. The tract of land called Acushena, Ponagansett, and Coaksett established as Dartmouth.

1668. June 3. Ply. Col. Rec., Vol. IV., p. 185. Bounds of Dartmouth established.

1787. Feb. 23. Part of Dartmouth established as New Bedford.

1787. July 2. Part of Dartmouth established as Westport.

1793. Feb. 25. Part of Dartmouth annexed to Westport.

1795. Feb. 28. Part of Dartmouth annexed to Westport.

1805. Mar. 4. Part of Dartmouth annexed to Westport.

1828. Feb. 20. Bounds between Dartmouth and Westport established.

1831. Feb. 19. Bounds between Dartmouth and New Bedford established.

1845. Mar. 20. Part of Dartmouth annexed to New Bedford.

COUNTY OF BRISTOL. TOWN OF DIGHTON.

KIND OF RECORDS.	Number of Volumes	In Keeping of —	Years Covered	Whether Indexed	Condition
Town proceedings, . . .	5	Town Clerk	1712–1885	No	Good
Births, marriages, and deaths,	7	Town Clerk	1710–1885	Yes	Good
Assessors, ...	25	Assessors	–	–	–
Selectmen, ...	4	Selectmen	–	–	–
Proprietors, . . .	1[3]	Town Clerk	1674–1740	Yes	Good

1712. May 30. Prov. Laws, Vol. III., p. 220. Part of Taunton established as Dighton.

1735. April 12. Prov. Laws, Vol. II., p. 742. Parts of Dighton and Taunton established as Berkley

1743. Mar. 2. Mass. Archives, Plan Book, Vol. XVI., p. 5. Bounds of Dighton established.

1745. Jan. 8. Prov. Laws, Vol. III., p. 215 Bounds of Dighton established.

1799. Feb. 26. Part of Dighton annexed to Berkley.

1814. June 9. Part of Dighton established as Wellington.[4]

---

[1] The first volume is partly copied.   [2] Registry of Deeds at New Bedford.

[3] There is also a copy.

[4] For legislation concerning the town of Wellington, see "Extinct Cities, Towns, and Districts"

TOWN RECORDS — Continued.

COUNTY OF BRISTOL. TOWN OF DIGHTON — Con.

1824. Feb. 12. Bounds between Dighton and Wellington established and part of Dighton annexed to Wellington.
1826. Feb. 28. Dighton and Wellington united as the town of Dighton.
1854. April 4. Part of Dighton annexed to Somerset.

COUNTY OF BRISTOL. TOWN OF EASTON.

KIND OF RECORDS.	Number of Volumes	In Keeping of—	Years Covered	Whether Indexed	Condition
Town proceedings, . . .	5[1]	Town Clerk	1726–1885	Partially	Good
Births, marriages, and deaths,	7[2]	Town Clerk	1726–1885	Partially	Good
Assessors, ...	–[3]	Selectmen	1767–1885	–	
Proprietors, ...	–[4]	[4]	1668–1885	–	Good
Miscellaneous, ...	5	Town Clerk	1735–1885	Partially	Good

1725. Dec. 21. Prov. Laws, Vol. II., p. 368. Part of the land in Norton called the Taunton North Purchase established as Easton.

COUNTY OF BRISTOL. TOWN OF FAIRHAVEN.[5]

KIND OF RECORDS.	Number of Volumes	In Keeping of—	Years Covered	Whether Indexed	Condition
Town proceedings, . . .	5	Town Clerk	1815–1885	No	Good
Births, marriages, and deaths,	5	Town Clerk	1815–1885	Yes	Good
Marriage intentions, . .	1	Town Clerk	1815–1885	Yes	Good
Assessors, ...	–	–		–	–
Miscellaneous, ...	2	Town Clerk	1815–1885	No	Good

1812. Feb. 22. Part of New Bedford established as Fairhaven.
1815. June 15. Part of Freetown annexed to Fairhaven.
1836. April 9. Bounds between Fairhaven and Rochester established.
1860. Feb. 13. Part of Fairhaven established as Acushnet.

COUNTY OF BRISTOL. CITY OF FALL RIVER.

KIND OF RECORDS.	Number of Volumes	In Keeping of—	Years Covered	Whether Indexed	Condition
Town proceedings,[6] . . .	3	City Clerk	1803–1853	Yes	Good
City proceedings, . . .	13	City Clerk	1854–1885	Yes	Good
Births, marriages, and deaths,	22	City Clerk	1803–1885	Yes	Good
Assessors, ...	–	Assessors		–	–

[1] There are copies of the first two volumes.

[2] There are several private records and also a copy of the first volume.

[3] The later records only are bound.

[4] The proprietors records are embraced in the records of the Taunton North Purchase Company, in keeping of the clerk of that company.

[5] All records from 1812 to 1815 are lost.

[6] The miscellaneous records are lost or destroyed.

Town Records — Continued.

County of Bristol.   City of Fall River — Con.

1803.   Feb. 26. Part of Freetown established as Fall River.
1804.   June 18. The name of the town of Fall River changed to Troy.[1]
1834.   Feb. 12. The name of the town of Troy changed to Fall River.
1854.   April 12. Fall River incorporated as a city.
1854.   April 22. Act of incorporation accepted by the town.
1861.   April 10. Certain lands on the east side of Mount Hope Bay annexed to Fall
                   River by the change of the bounds of Massachusetts and Rhode
                   Island.

County of Bristol.   Town of Freetown.

KIND OF RECORDS.	Number of Volumes	In Keeping of –	Years Covered	Whether Indexed	Condition
Town proceedings, . . .	6	Town Clerk	1688–1885	Yes	–[3]
Births, marriages, and deaths,	1[2]	Town Clerk	1686–1844	Yes	Fair
Births, ...	1	Town Clerk	1844–1885	Yes	Good
Marriages, ...	1	Town Clerk	1844–1885	Yes	Good
Deaths, ...	1	Town Clerk	1844–1885	Yes	Good
Assessors, ...	33	Town Clerk	–	–	–
Proprietors, ...	1[4]	James Winslow	–	–	–
Miscellaneous, ...	5	Town Clerk	–	No	–

1683.   July   —. Ply. Col. Rec., Vol. VI., p. 113. "The inhabitants of the freemen's
                   land at the Fall River shall be a township and be henceforth called
                   by the name of Freetowne."
1803.   Feb. 26. Part of Freetown established as Fall River.
1815.   June 15. Part of Freetown annexed to Fairhaven.

County of Bristol.   Town of Mansfield.

KIND OF RECORDS.	Number of Volumes	In Keeping of—	Years Covered	Whether Indexed	Condition
Town proceedings, . . .	5	Town Clerk	1772–1885	No	Good
Births, marriages, and deaths,	5	Town Clerk	1772–1885	Yes	Fair
Assessors, ...	113	Selectmen	–	–	–
Miscellaneous, ...	5	Town Clerk	1772–1885	No	Good

1770.   April 26. Prov. Laws, Vol. V., p. 48. Part of Norton established as the district
                   of Mansfield.
1775.   Aug. 23. Prov. Laws, Vol. V., p. 419. District of Mansfield made the town of
                   Mansfield by this general act.

---

[1] For legislation concerning the town of Troy, see "Extinct Cities, Towns, and Districts."

[2] This volume contains the record of births, marriages, and deaths copied from the general town records.

[3] The records from 1686 to 1800 are fast becoming illegible.

[4] The first volume of proprietors records is lost. The town records from 1683 to 1688 were probably kept in that volume.

TOWN RECORDS — Continued.

COUNTY OF BRISTOL. CITY OF NEW BEDFORD.

KIND OF RECORDS.	Number of Volumes	In Keeping of—	Years Covered	Whether Indexed	Condition
Town proceedings, . . .	4	City Clerk	1787–1847	Yes[1]	Fair
City proceedings, . . .	18	City Clerk	1847–1885	Yes	Fair
Births, marriages, and deaths (town), ...	4	City Clerk	1787–1847	Yes	Fair
Births, marriages, and deaths (city), ...	18	City Clerk	1847–1885	Yes	Fair
Assessors, ...	280	Assessors	1826–1885	–	–
Assessors, ...	22	Overseers of Poor	1787–1826	–	–
Assessors, ...	1[2]	Overseers of Poor	1778–1786	–	–
Selectmen, ...	8	City Clerk	1815–1847	–	–
Proprietors, ...	2[3]	Registry of Deeds[4]	–	–	–
Miscellaneous, . . .	8	City Clerk	1787–1847	Yes	Fair

1787. **Feb. 23.** Part of Dartmouth established as New Bedford.
1831. **Feb. 19.** Bounds between Dartmouth and New Bedford established.
1845. **Mar. 20.** Part of Dartmouth annexed to New Bedford.
1847. **Mar. 9.** New Bedford incorporated as a city.
1847. **Mar. 18.** Act of incorporation accepted by the town.
1812. **Feb. 22.** Part of New Bedford established as Fairhaven.
1875. **April 9.** Part of Acushnet annexed to New Bedford.

COUNTY OF BRISTOL TOWN OF NORTON.

KIND OF RECORDS.	Number of Volumes	In Keeping of—	Years Covered	Whether Indexed	Condition
Town proceedings, . . .	3	Town Clerk	1715–1760[5] 1769–1885	No	Good
Births, marriages, and deaths,	6	Town Clerk	1796–1885	Yes	Fair
Selectmen and Assessors, .	3	Town Clerk	–	–	Good[6]

1710. **Mar. 17.** Resolve. The North Precinct of Taunton granted to be a town by the name of Norton, a bill to perfect the grant to be brought in to the next session of the General Court.
1711. **June 12.** Prov. Laws, Vol. I., p. 676. The land called the North Purchase established as Norton.
1725. **Dec. 21.** Prov. Laws, Vol. II., p. 368. Part of the land in Norton called Taunton North Purchase established as Easton.
1770. **April 26.** Prov. Laws, Vol. V., p. 48. Part of Norton established as the district of Mansfield.

---

[1] Part of the indexes are imperfect, but they are being revised.
[2] This volume is a record for Acushnet village in the town of Dartmouth.
[3] There are also copies.
[4] At New Bedford.
[5] The records from 1760 to 1769 are missing.
[6] The records prior to 1831 are imperfect.

TOWN RECORDS — Continued.

COUNTY OF BRISTOL. TOWN OF RAYNHAM.

KIND OF RECORDS.	Number of Volumes	In Keeping of —	Years Covered	Whether Indexed	Condition
Town proceedings, . . .	4	Town Clerk	1731–1885	No	Good
Births, marriages, and deaths,	2	Town Clerk	1731–1843	Yes	Good[1]
Births, ...	2	Town Clerk	1843–1885	Yes	Good[1]
Marriages, ...	1	Town Clerk	1843–1885	Yes	Good[1]
Deaths, ...	1[2]	Town Clerk	1843–1885	Yes	Good[1]
Marriage intentions, . .	1	Town Clerk	1843–1885	Yes	Good
Assessors, ...	–	Assessors	–	–	–

1731. April 2. Prov. Laws, Vol. II., p. 590. Part of Taunton established as Raynham.
1866. Feb. 27. Bounds between Raynham and Taunton established.

COUNTY OF BRISTOL. TOWN OF REHOBOTH.

KIND OF RECORDS.	Number of Volumes	In Keeping of —	Years Covered	Whether Indexed	Condition
Town proceedings, . . .	9[3]	Town Clerk	1645–1885	No	Fair
Births, marriages, and deaths,	11[4]	Town Clerk	–	First 2 vols.	Bad
Assessors, ...	61	Assessors	–	–	–
Selectmen, ...	6	Selectmen	–	–	–
Proprietors, ...	1	Soion Carpenter[5]	–	–	–
Miscellaneous, . .	6	Town Clerk	1700–1885	No	–

1645. June 4. Ply. Col. Rec., Vol. XI., p. 46. "That Seacunck be called Rehoboth."
1649. June 6. Ply. Col. Rec., Vol. II., p. 141. Bounds of Rehoboth to be established.
1668. June 3. Ply. Col. Rec., Vol. IV., p. 185. Certain common lands annexed to Rehoboth.
1670. Aug. 11. Ply. Col. Rec., Vol. V., p. 49. Bounds between Rehoboth and Swansea established
1671. July 5. Ply. Col. Rec., Vol. V., p. 68. The land called the North Purchase granted to Rehoboth.
1682. July 7. Ply. Col. Rec., Vol. VI., p. 94. Bounds of Rehoboth established.
1812. Feb. 26. Part of Rehoboth established as Seekonk.

COUNTY OF BRISTOL. TOWN OF SEEKONK.

KIND OF RECORDS	Number of Volumes	In Keeping of —	Years Covered	Whether Indexed	Condition
Town proceedings, . . .	4	Town Clerk	1812–1885	No	Good
Births, marriages, and deaths,	7	Town Clerk	1812–1885	Yes	Good
Assessors, ...	–	Assessors	–	–	–
Selectmen, ...	3	Selectmen	–	–	–
Miscellaneous, . .	1	Town Clerk	1812–1885	Yes	Good

[1] Very imperfectly kept prior to 1843.

[2] The Town Clerk has private records of deaths prior to 1749, and Otis Holmes has a record since 1842.

[5] There are copies also of four volumes.

[4] There are copies also of the first two volumes.

[5] Seekonk.

Town Records — Continued.

County of Bristol. Town of Seekonk — Con.

1812. **Feb. 26.** Part of Rehoboth established as Seekonk.

1861. **April 10.** Part of the town of Pawtucket, R. I., and certain lands over which See-konk may have claimed jurisdiction lying east of a conventional line to be determined by the U. S. Supreme Court, after the entry of the decree of said court, to be part of Seekonk.

1862. **Jan. 29.** A municipal district by the name of East Seekonk, to consist of the territory named in the act of April 10, 1861, established. Said district to cease " so soon as the proper officers of the future town of Seekonk shall have been elected and qualified."

County of Bristol. Town of Somerset.

Kind of Records.	Number of Volumes	In Keeping of—	Years Covered	Whether Indexed	Condition
Town proceedings, . . .	6	Town Clerk	1790–1885	No	Good
Births, marriages, and deaths,	3	Town Clerk	1790–1885	Vol. I.	Good
Selectmen and Assessors, .	21	Town Clerk	–	–	–
Proprietors, ...	1	Town Clerk	1680–1830	No	Good

1790. **Feb. 20.** Part of Swansea called Shewamet Purchase established as Somerset.

1854. **April 4.** Part of Dighton annexed to Somerset.

County of Bristol. Town of Swansea.

Kind of Records.	Number of Volumes	In Keeping of—	Years Covered	Whether Indexed	Condition
Town proceedings, . . .	8	Town Clerk	1667–1885	No	–
Births, marriages, and deaths,	5[1]	Town Clerk	1666–1854[2]	No	–
Births, ...	1	Town Clerk	1855–1885	Yes	–
Marriages, ...	1	Town Clerk	1855–1885	Yes	–
Deaths, ...	1	Town Clerk	1855–1885	Yes	–
Marriage intentions, . .	2	Town Clerk	1850–1885	Yes	–
Assessors, ...	–	–	–	–	–
Proprietors, ...	4	Town Clerk	1668–1769	No	–
Soldiers in the Rebellion, .	1	Town Clerk	1861–1865	Yes	–
Miscellaneous, . . .	4	Town Clerk	1681–1885	No	–

1668. **Mar. 5.** Ply. Col. Rec., Vol. IV., p. 175. The township at Wannamoisett and places adjacent established as " Swansey."

1669. **July 5.** Ply. Col. Rec., Vol. V., p. 24. A neck of land called Papasquash Neck, excepting one hundred acres, annexed to Swansea.

1670. **Aug. 11.** Ply. Col. Rec., Vol. V., p. 49. Bounds between Swansea and Rehoboth established.

1679. **July 5.** Ply. Col. Rec., Vol. VI., p. 16. Bounds established.

1679. **Nov. 1.** Ply. Col. Rec., Vol. VI., p. 28. Bounds between Swansea and Mount Hope to be established.

1790. **Feb. 20.** Part of Swansea established as Somerset.

[1] There is a copy also of each volume.

[2] The records of deaths from 1800 to 1843 are missing.

TOWN RECORDS — Continued.

COUNTY OF BRISTOL. CITY OF TAUNTON.

KIND OF RECORDS.	Number of Volumes	In Keeping of—	Years Covered	Whether Indexed	Condition
Town proceedings, . . .	5	City Clerk	1804–1865[1]	Yes	Good
City proceedings, . . .	6	City Clerk	1865–1885	Yes	Good
Births, marriages, and deaths,	16	City Clerk	1800–1885[2]	Yes	Good
Assessors, ...	–	Assessors	1787–1885	–	–
Selectmen, ...	1	City Clerk	–	–	–
Proprietors, ...	{ 6[3]	City Clerk	1661–1804	Yes	Good
	{ 1	W. K. Watkins[4]	1638–1656	Yes	Good

1639.	Mar. 3.	Ply. Col. Rec., Vol. XI., p. 34. "That Cohannett shall be called Taunton."
1640.	Mar. 3.	Ply. Col. Rec., Vol. I., p. 142. Land at Assonet granted to Taunton.
1640.	June 19.	Ply. Col. Rec., Vol. II., p. 99. Bounds of Taunton established.
1672.	Oct. 29.	Ply. Col. Rec., Vol. V., p. 106. Certain lands granted to Taunton.
1682.	July —.	Ply. Col. Rec., Vol. VI., p. 94. Land called Assonet Neck annexed to Taunton.
1710.	Mar. 17.	Resolve. The North Precinct of Taunton granted to be a town by the name of Norton, a bill to perfect the grant to be brought in to the next session of the General Court.
1711.	June 12.	Prov. Laws, Vol. I., p. 676. The land called the North Purchase established as Norton.
1712.	May 30.	Prov. Laws, Vol. III., p. 220. South Precinct of Taunton established as Dighton.
1731.	April 2.	Prov. Laws, Vol. II., p. 590. Part of Taunton established as Raynham.
1735.	April 18.	Prov. Laws, Vol. II., p. 741. Parts of Taunton and Dighton established as Berkley.
1810.	Feb. 6.	Certain lands in Berkley belonging to Taunton annexed to Berkley.
1842.	Mar. 3.	Certain lands in Berkley belonging to Taunton annexed to Berkley.
1864.	May 11.	Taunton incorporated as a city.
1864.	June 6.	Act of incorporation accepted by the town.
1866.	Feb. 27.	Bounds between Taunton and Raynham established.
1867.	June 1.	Bounds between Taunton and Lakeville established.
1879.	April 1.	Part of Taunton annexed to Berkley.
1879.	April 12.	Act of April 1, 1879, accepted by Berkley.

COUNTY OF BRISTOL. TOWN OF WESTPORT.

KIND OF RECORDS.	Number of Volumes	In Keeping of —	Years Covered	Whether Indexed	Condition
Town proceedings, . . .	4	Town Clerk	1787–1885	No	Good[5]
Births, marriages, and deaths,	5	Town Clerk	–	–	Good
Selectmen and Assessors, .	–		–	–	–
Miscellaneous, . . .	6	Town Clerk	1788–1885	Yes	Good[5]

1787.	July 2.	Part of Dartmouth established as Westport.
1793.	Feb. 25.	Part of Dartmouth annexed to Westport.
1795.	Feb. 28.	Part of Dartmouth annexed to Westport.
1805.	Mar. 4.	Part of Dartmouth annexed to Westport.

---

[1] The records prior to 1804 were burned in 1838.
[2] The records from 1660 to 1700 are included in the proprietors records.
[3] There are also copies deposited in the Registry of Deeds at Taunton.
[4] Boston.　　　[5] With the exception of the first volume.

TOWN RECORDS — Continued.

COUNTY OF BRISTOL. TOWN OF WESTPORT — Con.

1828. **Feb. 20.** Bounds between Westport and Dartmouth established.
1861. **April 10.** Certain lands lying east and south of a line described, after the entry of the decree of the U. S. Supreme Court concerning the Rhode Island boundary, to be a part of Westport.

COUNTY OF DUKES COUNTY. TOWN OF CHILMARK.

KIND OF RECORDS.	Number of Volumes	In Keeping of —	Years Covered	Whether Indexed	Condition
Town proceedings, . . .	3	Town Clerk	1704–1885	No	–
Births, ...	1[1]	Town Clerk	1704–1885	No	–
Marriages, ...	1	Town Clerk	1704–1885	No	–
Deaths, ...	1	Town Clerk	1704–1885	No	–
Assessors, ...	–	Assessors	–	–	–
Selectmen, ...	1	Selectmen	–	–	–
Miscellaneous, ...	3	Town Clerk	1704–1885	No	–

1694. **Sept. 14.** Prov. Laws, Vol. I., p. 179. Chilmark is mentioned in the Tax Act. [Tisbury is also named.]
1696. **June 17.** Resolve. The constable of Chilmark empowered to collect the tax levied in 1694.
1714. **Oct. 30.** Resolve. "The Mannour of Tisbury, commonly called Chilmark," to have all the powers of a town. [Whether under the name of Chilmark or Tisbury is not stated.]
1856. **May 28.** Bounds between Chilmark and Gay Head, as established May 9, 1855, confirmed.
1864. **Mar. 17.** Part of Chilmark known as the Elizabeth Islands established as Gosnold.
1882. **Feb. 27.** Bounds between Chilmark and Tisbury established.

COUNTY OF DUKES COUNTY. TOWN OF COTTAGE CITY.

KIND OF RECORDS.	Number of Volumes	In Keeping of —	Years Covered	Whether Indexed	Condition
Town proceedings, . . .	1	Town Clerk	1880–1885	Yes	Good
Births, ...	1	Town Clerk	1880–1885	Yes	Good
Marriages, ...	1	Town Clerk	1880–1885	Yes	Good
Deaths, ...	1	Town Clerk	1880–1885	Yes	Good
Assessors, ...	–	–	–	–	–

1880. **Feb. 17.** Part of Edgartown established as Cottage City.

COUNTY OF DUKES COUNTY. TOWN OF EDGARTOWN.

KIND OF RECORDS.	Number of Volumes	In Keeping of —	Years Covered	Whether Indexed	Cond tion
Town proceedings, . . .	8	Town Clerk	–	Yes	Good
Births, marriages, and deaths,	6	Town Clerk	–	Yes	Good
Selectmen and Assessors, .	104	Selectmen	–	–	–
Proprietors, ...	1	Town Clerk	1676–1827	No	Good

·[1] Jonathan Allen has private records of births, marriages, and deaths.

Town Records — Continued.

COUNTY OF DUKES COUNTY. TOWN OF EDGARTOWN — Con.

1671. July   8. N. Y. Land Grants, Lib. IV., p. 75. "Edgar-Towne" is mentioned.
1830. Feb.   5. Bounds between Edgartown and Tisbury established.
1862. April 23. Bounds between Edgartown and Tisbury established.
1880. Feb. 17. Part of Edgartown incorporated as Cottage City.

COUNTY OF DUKES COUNTY. TOWN OF GAY HEAD.

KIND OF RECORDS.	Number of Volumes	In Keeping of—	Years Covered	Whether Indexed	Condition
General,	1	Town Clerk	1862–1885	No	Good
Town proceedings,	3[1]	Town Clerk	1862–1885	No	Good
Births, marriages, and deaths,	3	Town Clerk	1862–1885	Yes	Good
Assessors,	–		–	–	–
Selectmen,	1	Selectmen	–	–	–

1856. May 28. Bounds between the land of the Indians of Gay Head and the town of Chilmark, as established March 9, 1855, confirmed.
1870. April 30. District of Gay Head made the town of Gay Head.

COUNTY OF DUKES COUNTY. TOWN OF GOSNOLD.

KIND OF RECORDS.	Number of Volumes	In Keeping of—	Years Covered	Whether Indexed	Condition
General,	1	Town Clerk	1865–1885	No	Good
Births,	1	Town Clerk	1865–1885	No	Good
Marriages,	1	Town Clerk	1865–1885	No	Good
Deaths,	1	Town Clerk	1865–1885	No	Good
Selectmen and Assessors,	1	Town Clerk	1865–1885	–	–

1864. Mar. 17. Part of Chilmark known as the Elizabeth Islands established as Gosnold.

COUNTY OF DUKES COUNTY. TOWN OF TISBURY.

KIND OF RECORDS	Number of Volumes	In Keeping of—	Years Covered	Whether Indexed	Condition
General,	4	Town Clerk	1690–1800[2]	No	Good
Town proceedings,	5	Town Clerk	1838–1885	No	Good
Births, marriages, and deaths,	2	Town Clerk	1700–1838	No	Good
Births,	2	Town Clerk	1845–1885	No	Good
Marriages,	1	Town Clerk	1853–1885	No	Good
Deaths,	1	Town Clerk	1855–1885	No	Good
Assessors,	–	–	–	–	–
Proprietors,	1	Town Clerk	1750–1885	No	Good

[1] One volume covering the years from 1876 to 1880 is lost.
[2] The records are very confused and these are approximate dates only.

TOWN RECORDS — Continued.

COUNTY OF DUKES COUNTY, TOWN OF TISBURY — Con.

1671.	July	8.	N. Y. Land Grants, Lib. IV., p. 77. "Tisbury-Towne" is mentioned.
1714.	Oct.	30.	Resolve. "The Mannour of Tisbury, commonly called Chilmark," to have all the powers of a town. [Whether under the name of Tisbury or Chilmark is not stated.]
1830.	Feb.	5.	Bounds between Tisbury and Edgartown established.
1862.	April	23.	Bounds between Tisbury and Edgartown established.
1882.	Feb.	27.	Bounds between Tisbury and Chilmark established.

COUNTY OF ESSEX. TOWN OF AMESBURY.

KIND OF RECORDS	Number of Volumes	In Keeping of —	Years Covered	Whether Indexed	Condition
General, ...	19	Town Clerk	1642–1885	No	Good
Town proceedings, . . .	4	Town Clerk	1642–1885	No	Good
Births, marriages, and deaths,	12[2]	Town Clerk	1642–1665[1] 1687–1885	Yes	Good
Selectmen and Assessors, .	58	Selectmen	–	–	–

1668.	May	27.	Mass. Rec., Vol. IV., Part 1, p. 376. "Salisbury new town * * * may be named Emesbury." [The spelling in the margin of the records is "Amsbury."]
1675.	May	12.	Mass. Rec., Vol. V., p. 40. Just and full bounds allowed to Amesbury.
1844.	Mar.	15.	Part of Salisbury called "Little Salisbury" annexed to Amesbury.
1876.	April	11.	Part of Amesbury established as Merrimac.
1886.	June	16.	Part of Salisbury annexed to Amesbury.
1886.	July	1.	Act of June 16, 1886, took effect.

COUNTY OF ESSEX. TOWN OF ANDOVER.

KIND OF RECORDS.	Number of Volumes	In Keeping of –	Years Covered	Whether Indexed	Condition
General, ...	43	Town Clerk	1643–1885	No	Good
Town proceedings, . . .	9	Town Clerk	1643–1885	No	Good
Births, marriages, and deaths,	13[3]	Town Clerk	1649–1885	No[3]	Poor
Assessors, ...	68	Assessors	–	–	–
Selectmen, ...	5	Selectmen	–	–	–
Proprietors, ...	2[4]	Town Clerk	1643–1851	No	Good
Miscellaneous, ...	5	Town Clerk	1704–1885	No	Good

1646.	May	22.	Mass. Rec., Vol. II., p. 159. "Cochicawick now called Andiver."
1658.	May	26.	Mass. Rec., Vol. IV., Part 1, p. 333. Bounds between Andover and "Billirikey" established.
1678.	May	9.	Mass. Rec., Vol. V., p. 190. Bounds between Andover and Wills Hill established.

[1] One volume covering the years from 1666 to 1686 is lost.

[2] There are copies also of the earlier records of births, marriages, and deaths.

[3] The records of births, marriages, and deaths from 1649 to 1844 have been copied separately and indexed.

[4] It is believed that some of the earliest proprietors records, and miscellaneous records from 1643 to 1703, were destroyed.

TOWN RECORDS — Continued.

COUNTY OF ESSEX.   TOWN OF ANDOVER — Con.

1728.   June 20.   Prov. Laws, Vol. II., p. 502. Parts of Andover, Boxford, Salem, and
                          Topsfield established as Middleton.
1847.   April 17.   Parts of Andover and Methuen established as Lawrence.
1855.   April   7.   Part of Andover established as North Andover.
1879.   Feb.   4.   Part of Andover annexed to Lawrence.

COUNTY OF ESSEX.   TOWN OF BEVERLY.

KIND OF RECORDS.	Number of Volumes	In Keeping of –	Years Covered	Whether Indexed	Condition
General, ...	13[1]	Town Clerk	1665–1885	3 volumes	Fair
Births, marriages, and deaths,	12[2]	Town Clerk	1665–1885	No	Fair
Assessors, ...	–	–	–	–	–
Parish, ...	3[3]	Town Clerk	1667–1830	No	Fair
Proprietors, ...	2	Town Clerk	1698–1817	No	Fair

1668.   Oct. 14.   Mass. Archives, Vol. CXII., pp. 182, 183. Part of Salem called Bass
                          River established as Beverly.
1753.   Sept. 11.   Prov. Laws, Vol. III., p. 704. Part of Salem annexed to Beverly.
1857.   April 27.   Part of Beverly annexed to Danvers.

COUNTY OF ESSEX.   TOWN OF BOXFORD.

KIND OF RECORDS.	Number of Volumes	In Keeping of –	Years Covered	Whether Indexed	Condition
Town proceedings, . . .	5[4]	Town Clerk	1685–1885	No	Good[5]
Births, marriages, and deaths,	7[6]	Town Clerk	1742–1885	Since 1842	Good
Assessors, ...	–	Selectmen	1711 –	–	–
Selectmen, ...	1	Selectmen	–	–	–
Miscellaneous, ...	12	Town Clerk	1825–1885	No	Good

1694.   Sept. 14.   Prov. Laws, Vol. I., p. 178. Boxford is named in the Tax Act.
1701.   Feb. 25.   Resolve. Bounds fixed between Boxford and Topsfield.
1728.   June 20.   Prov. Laws, Vol. II., p. 502. Parts of Boxford, Andover, Salem, and
                          Topsfield established as Middleton.
1825.   June 18.   Bounds between Boxford and Rowley established.
1846.   Mar.   7.   Part of Ipswich annexed to Boxford.
1856.   Mar. 21.   Part of Boxford annexed to Groveland.

---

[1] There are copies also of the first, third, and sixth volumes.
[2] There is a record also of marriages in other towns of residents of Beverly from 1683 to 1799.
[3] These are copies only.
[4] There is a copy also of the first volume.
[5] With the exception of the first volume.
[6] There are copies also of the first two volumes.

Town Records — Continued.

County of Essex. Town of Bradford.

Kind of Records.	Number of Volumes	In Keeping of —	Years Covered	Whether Indexed	Condition
Town proceedings, . . .	6[1]	Town Clerk	1668–1885	No	Good
Births, marriages, and deaths,	12[1]	Town Clerk	1669–1885	Yes	Good
Assessors, ...	23	Assessors	1861–1885	–	–
Selectmen, ...	3	Town Clerk	1796–1861	–	–
Soldiers in the Rebellion, .	1	Town Clerk	1862 –	No	Good
Miscellaneous, ...	131	Town Clerk	1858–1868	No	Good

1675. Oct. 13. Mass. Rec., Vol. V., p. 56. Bradford is mentioned in the Tax Act.
1701. Feb. 24. Resolve. The line agreed to by Rowley at the time of the setting off of " their township now Bradford " confirmed.
1850. Mar. 8. Part of Bradford established as Groveland.

County of Essex. Town of Danvers.

Kind of Records.	Number of Volumes	In Keeping of —	Years Covered	Whether Indexed	Condition
Town proceedings, . . .	13	Town Clerk	1752–1885	Yes	Good[2]
Births, marriages, and deaths,	19[3]	Town Clerk	1752–1885	No	Good[4]
Selectmen and Assessors, .	133	Town Clerk	–	No	–
Proprietors, ...	2	Town Clerk	1772–1841	No	Good
Miscellaneous, ...	100	Town Clerk	1752–1885	No	Good

1752. Jan. 28. Prov. Laws, Vol. III., p. 598. The Village and Middle Parishes in Salem established as the district of Danvers.
1757. June 16. Prov. Laws, Vol. IV., p. 5. District of Danvers made the town of Danvers. [Act disallowed by the Privy Council, August 10, 1759.]
1775. Aug. 23. Prov. Laws, Vol. V., p. 419. District of Danvers made the town of Danvers by this general act.
1840. Mar. 17. Bounds between Danvers and Salem established.
1855. May 18. Part of Danvers established as South Danvers.
1856. May 31. Bounds between Danvers and South Danvers established.
1857. April 27. Part of Beverly annexed to Danvers.

County of Essex. Town of Essex.

Kind of Records.	Number of Volumes	In Keeping of –	Years Covered	Whether Indexed	Condition
Town proceedings, . . .	3	Town Clerk	1818–1885	No	Good
Births, marriages, and deaths,	6	Town Clerk	1818–1885[5]	No	Good
Selectmen and Assessors, .	67	Selectmen	1818–1885	–	–
Proprietors, ...	1	Town Clerk	1722–1747	No	Good
Miscellaneous, ...	3	Town Clerk	1818–1885	No	Good

1819. Feb. 15. Part of Ipswich established as Essex.

[1] There is a copy also of the first volume.
[2] A few pages lost from the first volume have been replaced by copies.
[3] The records of births, marriages, and deaths, from 1752 to the time of the setting off of South Danvers in 1856, have been copied.
[4] A few pages of the earliest book of marriages are missing.
[5] The records prior to 1840 are incomplete.

TOWN RECORDS — Continued.

COUNTY OF ESSEX. TOWN OF GEORGETOWN.

KIND OF RECORDS.	Number of Volumes	In Keeping of —	Years Covered	Whether Indexed	Condition
Town proceedings, . . .	3	Town Clerk	1838–1885	No	Good
Births, marriages, and deaths,	3	Town Clerk	1838–1885	No	Good
Selectmen and Assessors, .	47	Selectmen	1838–1885	–	–

1838. April 21. Part of Rowley established as Georgetown.

COUNTY OF ESSEX. CITY OF GLOUCESTER.

KIND OF RECORDS.	Number of Volumes	In Keeping of —	Years Covered	Whether Indexed	Condition
Town proceedings, . . .	10[1]	City Clerk	1642–1715 1728–1873	1_	–
Board of Aldermen, . .	7	City Clerk	1874–1885	Yes	–
Common Council, . . .	4	City Clerk	1874–1885	Yes	–
Births, marriages, and deaths,	6[2]	City Clerk	1716–1828 1839–1851	Yes	–
Births, ...	4	City Clerk	1851–1885	Yes	–
Marriages, ...	2[2]	City Clerk	1851–1885	Yes	–
Deaths, ...	4	City Clerk	1851–1885	Yes	–
Marriage intentions, . .	1	City Clerk	1874–1883	Yes	–
Assessors, ...	200	Assessors	–	–	–
Selectmen, ...	9	City Clerk	1699–1781 1800–1873	–	–
Parish, ...	–[3]	City Clerk	–	–	–
Proprietors, ...	2[4]	City Clerk	1707–1820	No[4]	–
Miscellaneous, ...	55	City Clerk	–	No	–

1642. June 14. Mass. Rec., Vol. II., p. 14. "Glocester" is mentioned in the Tax Act.
1672. May 15. Mass. Rec., Vol. IV., Part 2, p. 520. Bounds between Gloucester and Manchester established.
1840. Feb. 27. Part of Gloucester established as Rockport.
1873. April 28. Gloucester incorporated as a city.
1873. May 15. Act of incorporation accepted by the town.

COUNTY OF ESSEX. TOWN OF GROVELAND.

KIND OF RECORDS.	Number of Volumes	In Keeping of —	Years Covered	Whether Indexed	Condition
Town proceedings, . . .	2	Town Clerk	1850–1885	No	Good
Births, ...	1[5]	Town Clerk	1850–1885	Yes	Good
Marriages, ...	1	Town Clerk	1850–1885	Yes	Good
Deaths, ...	1	Town Clerk	1850–1885	Yes	Good
Marriage intentions, . .	1	Town Clerk	1850–1885	Yes	Good
Selectmen and Assessors, .	–	Selectmen	–	–	–
Miscellaneous, ...	6	Town Clerk	1850–1885	No	Good

[1] The first two volumes have been copied and indexed.

[2] The first four volumes of records of births, marriages, and deaths, one volume of marriages, and two of births and deaths have been copied and indexed.

[3] A copy of the records of baptisms, births, marriages, and deaths recorded in the records of various churches is in the keeping of the City Clerk.

[4] Both volumes have been copied and indexed.

[5] M. P. Atwood has private records of births, marriages, and deaths.

Town Records — Continued.

County of Essex. Town of Groveland — Con.

1850. Mar. 8. Part of Bradford established as Groveland.
1856. Mar. 21. Part of Boxford annexed to Groveland.

County of Essex. Town of Hamilton.

Kind of Records	Number of Volumes	In Keeping of —	Years Covered	Whether Indexed	Condition
Town proceedings, . . .	2	Town Clerk	1793–1885	Yes	Good
Births, marriages, and deaths,	3	Town Clerk	1793–1885	Yes	Good
Selectmen and Assessors, .	–	Selectmen	1793–1885	–	–
Soldiers in the Rebellion, .	1	Town Clerk	–	Yes	Good

1793. June 21. Part of Ipswich called the Parish of Ipswich-Hamlet established as Hamilton.

County of Essex. City of Haverhill.

Kind of Records.	Number of Volumes	In Keeping of —	Years Covered	Whether Indexed	Condition
General, ...	8[1]	City Clerk	1643–1869	No	–
City proceedings, . . .	5	City Clerk	1870–1885	Yes	–
Births, marriages, and deaths,	6[2]	City Clerk	1658–1872	Yes[3]	–
Births, ...	3	City Clerk	1858–1885	Yes	–
Marriages, ...	3	City Clerk	1858–1885	Yes	–
Deaths.	3	City Clerk	1858–1885	Yes	–
Marriage intentions, . .	7	City Clerk	1782–1885	No	–
Assessors, ...	75	Assessors	–	–	–
Proprietors, ...	4	City Clerk	1713–1763	–	–
Miscellaneous, ...	54	City Clerk	1828–1885	No	–

1641. June 2. Mass. Rec., Vol. I., p. 319. Bounds to be set out " between Salsberry and Pautucket, alis Haverell."

1643. May 10. Mass. Rec., Vol. II., p. 38. Haverhill is named as in one of the four shires established.

1650. May 23. Mass. Rec., Vol. III., p. 189. An island in the Merrimack river granted to Haverhill unless some person prove a clear title to it within three years.

1651. Oct. 30. Mass. Rec., Vol. IV., Part 1, p. 76. Bounds established.

1654. Nov. 1. Mass. Rec., Vol. IV., Part 1, p. 209. Bounds between Haverhill and Salisbury established.

1664. May 18. Mass. Rec., Vol. IV., Part 2, p. 105. Bounds established between Haverhill and " lands of Maj. Gen'l Dennison."

1667. May 15. Mass. Rec., Vol. IV., Part 2, p. 335. Bounds established.

1675. May 12. Mass. Rec., Vol. V., p. 40. Bounds established.

1725. Dec. 8. Prov. Laws, Vol. II , p. 367. Part of Haverhill, and certain common lands, established as Methuen.

1869. Mar. 10. Haverhill incorporated as a city.

1869. May 15. Act of incorporation accepted by the town.

[1] There are copies also, which are indexed, of the records from 1643 to 1776.

[2] Prior to 1871 the records of births, marriages, and deaths were kept in the general town records.

[3] From 1781 to 1872.

Town Records — Continued.

County of Essex. Town of Ipswich.

Kind of Records.	Number of Volumes	In Keeping of —	Years Covered	Whether Indexed	Condition
Town proceedings, . . .	11[1]	Town Clerk	1634–1885	No	2_
Births, marriages, and deaths,	4[3]	Town Clerk	1664–1885	Yes	–
Assessors, ...	–	–	–	–	–
Proprietors, ...	1	Town Clerk	1638–1680	No	–

1634. **Aug.** 5. Mass. Rec., Vol I., p. 123. " Aggawam shall be called Ipswich."
1648. **Oct.** 18. Mass. Rec., Vol. II., p. 258. Part of Ipswich called the Village at the New Meadows named "Toppesfield." [October 18, 1650, Topsfield was made a town.]
1785. **Nov.** 29. Part of Ipswich annexed to Rowley.
1793. **June** 21. Part of Ipswich established as Hamilton.
1819. **Feb.** 15. Part of Ipswich established as Essex.
1846. **Mar.** 7. Part of Ipswich annexed to Boxford.

County of Essex. City of Lawrence.

Kind of Records.	Number of Volumes	In Keeping of —	Years Covered	Whether Indexed	Condition
Town proceedings, . . .	2	City Clerk	1847–1852	Yes	Good
City proceedings, . . .	11	City Clerk	1853–1885	Yes	Good
Births, ...	5	City Clerk	1847–1885	Yes	Good
Marriages, ...	6	City Clerk	1847–1885[4]	Yes	Good
Deaths, ...	4	City Clerk	1847–1885[4]	Yes	Good
Assessors, ...	38	Assessors	1847–1885	–	–
Selectmen, ...	2	City Clerk	–	–	–
Miscellaneous, . . .	98	City Clerk	1847–1885	Yes	Good

1847. **April** 17. Parts of Andover and Methuen established as Lawrence.
1853. **Mar.** 21. Lawrence incorporated as a city.
1853. **Mar.** 29. Act of incorporation accepted by the town.
1854. **April** 4. Part of Methuen annexed to Lawrence.
1879. **Feb.** 4. Parts of Andover and North Andover annexed to Lawrence.

County of Essex. City of Lynn.[5]

Kind of Records.	Number of Volumes	In Keeping of —	Years Covered	Whether Indexed	Condition
Town proceedings, . . .	7	City Clerk	1691–1817	No	6_
City proceedings, . . .	14	City Clerk	1850–1885	No	–
Births, marriages, and deaths,	26[7]	City Clerk	1675–1885	Partially	–
Assessors, ...	35	Assessors	1850–1885	–	–
Proprietors, ...	1[8]	City Clerk	1706 –	No	–
Miscellaneous, . . .	75	City Clerk	1800–1885	No	–

[1] There are copies also of three volumes.   [2] The earlier records are in poor condition.

[3] There are copies also covering the years from 1664 to 1844.

[4] There are a few omissions during the year 1853.

[5] The greater part of the old records were burned in 1863.

[6] All the old records are in an imperfect condition, being small books containing evidently fragments of records.

[7] One volume of records of births, marriages, and deaths from 1645 to 1700 is lost. One volume contains a copy of the first five original volumes.

[8] This is made up of copies of original records.

TOWN RECORDS — Continued.

COUNTY OF ESSEX. CITY OF LYNN — Con.

1637. Nov. 20. Mass. Rec., Vol. I., p. 211. "Saugust is called Lin."
1782. July 3. Part of Lynn established as the district of Lynnfield.
1815. Feb. 17. Part of Lynn established as Saugus.
1850. April 10. Lynn incorporated as a city.
1850. April 19. Act of incorporation accepted by the town.
1852. May 21. Part of Lynn established as Swampscott.
1853. Mar. 29. Part of Lynn established as Nahant.

COUNTY OF ESSEX. TOWN OF LYNNFIELD.

KIND OF RECORDS.	Number of Volumes	In Keeping of —	Years Covered	Whether Indexed	Condition
Town proceedings, . . .	7	Town Clerk	1757–1885	No	[1]_
Births, marriages, and deaths,	5	Town Clerk	1757–1885	No	–
Assessors, ...	12	Town Clerk	–	–	–
Soldiers in the Rebellion,	2	Town Clerk	–	No	–

1782. July 3. Part of Lynn established as the district of Lynnfield.
1814. Feb. 28. District of Lynnfield made the town of Lynnfield.
1854. April 10. Bounds between Lynnfield and Reading established.
1857. May 27. Bounds between Lynnfield and North Reading established and part of each town annexed to the other town, provided the act is accepted by both towns.
1857. Nov. 3. Act of May 27, 1857, accepted by Lynnfield. [Accepted by North Reading, January 7, 1858.]

COUNTY OF ESSEX. TOWN OF MANCHESTER.

KIND OF RECORDS.	Number of Volumes	In Keeping of —	Years Covered	Whether Indexed	Condition
Town proceedings, . . .	6[2]	Town Clerk	1654–1885	No	Pcor[3]
Births, marriages, and deaths,	13[4]	Town Clerk	1654–1885	1 volume	–
Selectmen and Assessors,	171	Selectmen	–	–	–
Proprietors, ...	2[5]	Town Clerk	1718–1769	–	–
Miscellaneous, . . .	46	Town Clerk	1645–1885	No	–

1645. May 14. Mass. Rec., Vol. II., p. 109. "Jeffryes Creeke shall be called Manchester."
1672. May 15. Mass. Rec., Vol. IV., Part 1, p. 520. Bounds between Manchester and Gloucester established.

---

[1] The earlier volumes are in poor condition.

[2] The first volume of town proceedings is missing.

[3] The earlier records were badly kept and show many omissions of years. The second volume is so illegible and mutilated as to be useless as a record.

[4] The records of births, marriages, and deaths prior to 1840 have been copied.

[5] There is a copy also in possession of the Town Clerk.

Town Records — Continued.

County of Essex.   Town of Marblehead.

Kind of Records.	Number of Volumes	In Keeping of —	Years Covered	Whether Indexed	Condition
Town proceedings, . . .	10[1]	Town Clerk	1648–1709 1722–1885	No	2_
Births, marriages, and deaths,	11	Town Clerk	1653–1885	No	–
Assessors, ...	–	Assessors	1770–1885	–	–
Selectmen, ...	4	Selectmen	1770–1885	–	–

1635.   May   6.   Mass. Rec., Vol. I., p. 147.   "There shall be a plantation at Marble Head."
1649.   May   2.   Mass. Rec., Vol. II., p. 266.   Marblehead established as a town.

County of Essex.   Town of Merrimac.

Kind of Records.	Number of Volumes	In Keeping of —	Years Covered	Whether Indexed	Condition
Town proceedings, . . .	1	Town Clerk	1876–1885	No	Good
Births, ...	1	Town Clerk	1876–1885	Yes	Good
Marriages, ...	1	Town Clerk	1876–1885	Yes	Good
Deaths, ...	1	Town Clerk	1876–1885	Yes	Good
Selectmen and Assessors, .	1	Town Clerk	1876–1885	–	–
Miscellaneous, . . .	3	Town Clerk	1876–1885	No	Good

1876.   April   11.   Part of Amesbury established as Merrimac.

County of Essex.   Town of Methuen.

Kind of Records	Number of Volumes	In Keeping of —	Years Covered	Whether Indexed	Condition
General, ...	21	Town Clerk	1725–1885	No	Fair
Town proceedings, . . .	5[3]	Town Clerk	1725–1885	No	Fair
Births, marriages, and deaths,	6[4]	Town Clerk	1725–1885	No	Fair
Assessors, ...	75	Selectmen	–	–	–
Selectmen, ...	18	Selectmen	–	–	–
Miscellaneous, . . .	6	Town Clerk	1725–1885	No	Fair

1725.   Dec.   8.   Prov. Laws, Vol. II., p. 367.   Part of Haverhill, and certain common lands, established as Methuen.
1847.   April   17.   Parts of Methuen and Andover established as Lawrence.
1854.   April   4.   Part of Methuen annexed to Lawrence.

---

[1] There is a copy also of the first volume.   The second volume covering the years from 1710 to 1721 is lost.

[2] The first volume is in very poor condition.

[3] There is a copy also of the first volume.

[4] There are copies also of the first three volumes covering the years from 1725 to 1844.

Town Records — Continued.
County of Essex. Town of Middleton.

KIND OF RECORDS.	Number of Volumes	In Keeping of—	Years Covered	Whether Indexed	Condition
Town proceedings, . . .	6	Town Clerk	1728–1885	No	Good
Births, marriages, and deaths,)	1[1]	Town Clerk	1728–1843	No)	Good
)	1	Town Clerk	1843–1875	Yes)	
Births, ...	1	Town Clerk	1875–1885	Yes	Good
Marriages, ...	1	Town Clerk	1871–1885	Yes	Good
Deaths, ...	1	Town Clerk	1875–1885	Yes	Good
Marriage intentions, . .	2	Town Clerk	1801–1885	Yes	Good
Selectmen and Assessors, .	–	Selectmen	–	–	–
Soldiers in the Rebellion, .	1	Town Clerk	1861–1865	No	Good
Miscellaneous, . . .	18	Town Clerk	1729–1885	No	Fair

1728. June 20. Prov. Laws, Vol. II., p. 502. Parts of Andover, Boxford, Salem, and Topsfield established as Middleton.

County of Essex. Town of Nahant.

KIND OF RECORDS.	Number of Volumes	In Keeping of—	Years Covered	Whether Indexed	Condition
Town proceedings, . . .	1	Town Clerk	1853–1885	No	Good
Births, ...	1[2]	Town Clerk	1853–1885	No	Good
Marriages, ...	1	Town Clerk	1853–1885	No	Good
Deaths, ...	1	Town Clerk	1853–1885	No	Good
Assessors, ...	–	–	–	–	–
Selectmen, ...	2	Selectmen	–	–	–
Miscellaneous, . . .	1	Town Clerk	1853–1885	Yes	Good

1853. Mar. 29. Part of Lynn established as Nahant.

County of Essex. Town of Newbury.

KIND OF RECORDS.	Number of Volumes	In Keeping of—	Years Covered	Whether Indexed	Condition
Town proceedings, . . .	14 .	Town Clerk	1635–1885	No	Good
Births, marriages, and deaths,	13[3]	Town Clerk	1635–1885	Yes	Good
Assessors, ...	–	–	–	–	–
Selectmen, ...	4	Selectmen	1635–1885	–	–
Proprietors, ...	4	Town Clerk	1635–1828	No	Good
Miscellaneous, . . .	4	Town Clerk	1635–1885	No	Good

1635. May 6. Mass. Rec., Vol. I., p. 146. Plantation called Wessacucon established as "Neweberry."

1764. Jan. 28. Prov. Laws, Vol. IV., p. 676. Part of Newbury established as Newburyport.

1819. Feb. 18. Part of Newbury established as Parsons.

1851. April 17. Part of Newbury annexed to Newburyport.

---

[1] There is also one volume containing a copy of the records of the births, marriages, and deaths recorded in the volumes of town proceedings.

[2] E. J. Johnson has private records of births, marriages, and deaths.

[3] Two volumes are copies only.

Town Records — Continued.

County of Essex.   City of Newburyport.

Kind of Records.	Number of Volumes	In Keeping of —	Years Covered	Whether Indexed	Condition
General, ...	4	City Clerk	1764–1851	No	–
City proceedings, . . .	12	City Clerk	1851–1885	No	–
Births, ...	6	City Clerk	1764–1885	No	–
Marriages, ...	5	City Clerk	1764–1885	No	–
Deaths, ...	4	City Clerk	1763–1885	No	–
Marriage intentions, . .	3	City Clerk	1764–1885	No	–
Assessors, ...	200	City Clerk	1764–1885	–	–
Selectmen, ...	35	City Clerk	1764–1885	–	–
Miscellaneous, ...	41	City Clerk	1764–1885	No	–

1764.   Jan.   28.   Prov. Laws, Vol. IV., p. 676.   Part of Newbury established as Newburyport.
1851.   April 17.   Part of Newbury annexed to Newburyport.
1851.   May   24.   Newburyport incorporated as a city.
1851.   June   3.   Act of incorporation accepted by the town.

County of Essex.   Town of North Andover.

Kind of Records.	Number of Volumes	In Keeping of —	Years Covered	Whether Indexed	Condition
Town proceedings, . . .	2	Town Clerk	1854–1885	No	–
Births, ...	2	Town Clerk	1854–1885	No	–
Marriages, ...	1	Town Clerk	1854–1885	No	–
Deaths, ...	2	Town Clerk	1854–1885	No	–
Assessors, ...	–	–	–	–	–

1855.   April   7.   Part of Andover established as North Andover.
1879.   Feb.   4.   Part of North Andover annexed to Lawrence.

County of Essex.   Town of Peabody.

Kind of Records.	Number of Volumes	In Keeping of —	Years Covered	Whether Indexed	Condition
Town proceedings, . . .	3	Town Clerk	1855–1885	Yes	Good
Births, ...	2	Town Clerk	1855–1885	Yes	Good
Marriages, ...	1	Town Clerk	1855–1885	Yes	Good
Deaths, ...	2	Town Clerk	1855–1885	Yes	Good
Assessors, ...	2	Town Clerk	1855–1885	–	–
Selectmen, ...	2	Town Clerk	1855–1885	–	–
Miscellaneous, ...	41	Town Clerk	1855–1885	Yes	Good

1868.   April 13.   Name of the town of South Danvers[1] changed to Peabody.
1868.   April 30.   Act of April 13, 1868, accepted by the town.
1882.   Mar. 27.   Part of Peabody annexed to Salem.

[1] For legislation concerning the town of South Danvers, see "Extinct Cities, Towns, and
Districts."

Town Records — Continued.

County of Essex. Town of Rockport.

Kind of Records.	Number of Volumes	In Keeping of —	Years Covered	Whether Indexed	Condition
Town proceedings, . . .	2	Town Clerk	1840–1885	Partially	Good
Births, marriages, and deaths,	1[1]	Town Clerk	1840–1868	Partially	Good
Births, ...	1	Town Clerk	1869–1885	Partially	Good
Marriages, ...	1	Town Clerk	1869–1885	Partially	Good
Deaths, ...	1	Town Clerk	1869–1885	Partially	Good
Selectmen and Assessors, .	45	Selectmen	1840–1885	–	–

1840. Feb. 27. Part of Gloucester established as Rockport.

County of Essex. Town of Rowley.

Kind of Records.	Number of Volumes	In Keeping of —	Years Covered	Whether Indexed	Condition
Town proceedings, . . .	9	Town Clerk	1639–1885	Yes	–[2]
Births, marriages, and deaths,	5	Town Clerk	1639–1885	Yes	–[2]
Births, marriages, and deaths,	1	Town Clerk	–[3]	Yes	Good
Births, ...	1	Town Clerk	1843–1885	Yes	Good
Marriages, ...	1	Town Clerk	1843–1885	Yes	Good
Deaths, ...	1	Town Clerk	1843–1885	Yes	Good
Marriage intentions, . .	–[4]	Town Clerk	1697–1885	Yes	Good
Assessors, ...	31	Town Clerk	1788–1860[5]	–	–
Selectmen, ...	2	Town Clerk	1758–1864	–	–
Selectmen and Assessors, .	–	Selectmen	1860–1885	–	–
Proprietors, ...	4[6]	Town Clerk	1643–1844	No	Good
Soldiers in the Rebellion, .	2	Town Clerk	1861–1865	No	{ Incom- plete
Miscellaneous, ...	381	Town Clerk	1731–1885	No	Good

1639. Sept. 4. Mass. Rec., Vol. I., p. 271. "Mr. Ezechi Rogers plantation shall be called Rowley."

1701. Feb. 24. Resolve. Bounds between Rowley and Bradford established.

1785. Nov. 29. Part of Ipswich annexed to Rowley.

1825. June 18. Bounds between Rowley and Boxford established.

1838. April 21. Part of Rowley established as Georgetown.

---

[1] Valuable genealogical notes by the late Ebenezer Pool are in the hands of a historical committee.

[2] The first two volumes are fast becoming illegible and should be copied; the other volumes are in good condition.

[3] A record of births from 1843 to 1860, of marriages from 1843 to 1854, and of deaths from 1843 to 1858. This volume has been copied into the three current volumes of births, marriages, and deaths.

[4] Marriage intentions are contained in the first five volumes of births, marriages, and deaths.

[5] The record for the year 1824 is omitted.

[6] One volume is in the Massachusetts State Library.

Town Records — Continued.

County of Essex. City of Salem.

Kind of Records.	Number of Volumes	In Keeping of —	Years Covered	Whether Indexed	Condition
Town proceedings, . . .	14[1]	City Clerk	1636–1885	Partially	Good
City proceedings, . . .	10	City Clerk	1836–1885	Partially	Good
Births, marriages, and deaths,	21	City Clerk	1658–1885	Partially	Good
Marriage intentions, . .	7	City Clerk	1707–1885	Partially	Good
Assessors, ...	73	Assessors	1837–1885	–	–
Selectmen, ...	30	City Clerk		–	–
Proprietors, ...	1[2]	City Clerk	1713–1739	Yes	Poor
Soldiers in the Rebellion, .	3	City Clerk	1861–1864	–	Good
Miscellaneous, . . .	123	City Clerk	1636–1885	Partially	Good

1630.	Aug.	23.	Mass. Rec., Vol. I., p. 73. "Mattapan and Salem only exempted."
1634.	Mar.	4.	Mass. Rec., Vol. I., p. 141. Bounds between Salem and Saugus (now Lynn), and Salem and Marble Harbor, to be established.
1658.	Oct.	19.	Mass Rec., Vol. IV., Part 1, p. 352. Bounds between Salem and Topsfield established.
1664.	May	29.	Mass. Rec., Vol. IV., Part 2, p. 113. Bounds between Salem and Topsfield established.
1668.	Oct.	14.	Mass. Archives, Vol. CXII., pp. 182, 183. Part of Salem called Bass River established as Beverly.
1728.	June	20.	Prov. Laws, Vol. II., p. 502. Parts of Salem, Andover, Boxford, and Topsfield established as Middleton.
1752.	Jan.	28.	Prov. Laws, Vol. III., p. 598. Part of Salem established as the district of Danvers.
1753.	Sept.	11.	Prov. Laws, Vol. III., p. 704. Part of Salem annexed to Beverly.
1836.	Mar.	23.	Salem incorporated as a city.
1836.	April	4.	Act of incorporation accepted by the town.
1840.	Mar.	17.	Bounds between Salem and Danvers established.
1856.	April	30.	Bounds between Salem and South Danvers established and part of each place annexed to the other place.
1867.	April	3.	Part of Salem annexed to Swampscott.
1882.	Mar.	27.	Part of Peabody annexed to Salem.

County of Essex. Town of Salisbury.

Kind of Records.	Number of Volumes	In Keeping of —	Years Covered	Whether Indexed	Condition
Town proceedings, . . .	3[3]	Town Clerk	1638–1885	No	Good
Births, marriages, and deaths,	12[4]	Town Clerk	1637–1885	Yes	–[5]
Assessors, ...	–	Selectmen	1775–1885	–	–
Proprietors, ...	–[6]	–		–	–
Soldiers in the Rebellion, .	1	Town Clerk		No	Good
Miscellaneous, . . .	4	Town Clerk	1638–1885	No	Good

[1] There are copies also of the first three volumes.

[2] There is also a copy.

[3] There is a copy also of the first volume covering the years from 1638 to 1733.

[4] The records of births, marriages, and deaths contained in the town records from 1637 to 1821 have been copied into separate volumes.

[5] The volumes since 1866 need rebinding.

[6] The town records were called proprietors records until 1738.

TOWN RECORDS — Continued.

COUNTY OF ESSEX. TOWN OF SALISBURY — Con.

1640. **Oct.** 7. Mass. Rec., Vol. I., p. 305. "Colechester is henceforward to be called Salsbury."

1641. **June** 2. Mass. Rec., Vol. I., p. 319. Bounds between Salisbury and "Pautackct, ali : Haverell " established.

1654. **Nov.** 1. Mass. Rec., Vol. IV., Part 1, p. 209. Bounds between Salisbury and Haverhill established.

1668. **May** 27. Mass. Rec., Vol. IV., Part 1, p. 376. Part of Salisbury established as Amesbury.

1844. **Mar.** 15. Part of Salisbury annexed to Amesbury.

1886. **June** 16. Part of Salisbury annexed to Amesbury.

1886. **July** 1. Act of June 16, 1886, took effect.

COUNTY OF ESSEX. TOWN OF SAUGUS.[1]

KIND OF RECORDS	Number of Volumes	In Keeping of —	Years Covered	Whether Indexed	Condition
Town proceedings, . . .	4	Town Clerk	1815–1885	2 volumes	Good
Births, marriages, and deaths,	6	Town Clerk	1815–1885	No	Good
Assessors, ...	38	Assessors	–	–	–

1815. **Feb.** 17. Part of Lynn established as Saugus.

1841. **Feb.** 22. Part of Chelsea annexed to Saugus.

COUNTY OF ESSEX. TOWN OF SWAMPSCOTT.

KIND OF RECORDS.	Number of Volumes	In Keeping of —	Years Covered	Whether Indexed	Condition
Town proceedings, . . .	2	Town Clerk	1852–1885	Yes	Good
Births, ...	1	Town Clerk	1852–1885	No	Good
Marriages, ...	1	Town Clerk	1852–1885	No	Good
Deaths, ...	1	Town Clerk	1852–1885	No	Good
Assessors, ...	1	Assessors	1852–1885	–	–
Selectmen, ...	1	Selectmen	1852–1885	–	–
Miscellaneous, . . .	5	Town Clerk	1852–1885	No	Good

1852. **May** 21. Part of Lynn established as Swampscott.

1867. **April** 3. Part of Salem annexed to Swampscott.

[1] For legislation concerning the original town of Saugus, see " Extinct Cities, Towns, and Districts."

Town Records — Continued.

County of Essex. Town of Topsfield.

KIND OF RECORDS.	Number of Volumes	In Keeping of —	Years Covered	Whether Indexed	Condition
Town proceedings, . . .	6	Town Clerk	1675–1885[1]	No	Good
Births, marriages, and deaths,	7[2]	Town Clerk	1645–1885	No	Good
Marriage intentions, . .	–	Town Clerk		No	Good
Assessors, ...	–	Town Clerk	1744–1885	–	–
Selectmen, ...	5	Town Clerk	–	–	–
Parish, ...	2	Town Clerk	1684–1725 / 1728–1867	No	Good
Proprietors, ...	4	Town Clerk	1711–1779 / 1792–1804 / 1816–1850	No	Good
Soldiers in the Rebellion, .	1	Town Clerk	1861–1865	No	Good
Miscellaneous, ...	6	Town Clerk	1811–1885	No	Good

1648. Oct. 18. Mass. Rec., Vol. II., p. 258. Part of Ipswich called the Village at the New Meadows was named "Toppesfield."

1650. Oct. 18. Mass. Rec., Vol. IV., Part 1, p. 33. Topsfield established as a town.

1658. Oct. 19. Mass. Rec., Vol. IV., Part 1, p. 352. Bounds between Topsfield and Salem established.

1664. May 29. Mass. Rec., Vol. IV., Part 2, p. 113. Bounds between Topsfield and Salem established.

1701. Feb. 25. Resolve. Bounds between Topsfield and Boxford established.

1728. June 20. Prov. Laws, Vol. II., p. 502. Parts of Topsfield, Andover, Boxford, and Salem established as Middleton.

County of Essex. Town of Wenham.

KIND OF RECORDS.	Number of Volumes	In Keeping of—	Years Covered	Whether Indexed	Condition
Town proceedings, . . .	6[3]	Town Clerk	1642–1885	No[4]	Good
Births, marriages, and deaths,	4[5]	Town Clerk	1695–1850	No	Good
Births, ...	1	Town Clerk	1851–1885	Yes	Good
Marriages, ...	1	Town Clerk	1851–1885	Yes	Good
Deaths, ...	1	Town Clerk	1851–1885	Yes	Good
Marriage intentions, . .	1	Town Clerk	1851–1885	Yes	Good
Selectmen, ...	6	Town Clerk	–	–	–
Assessors, ...	7	Town Clerk	–[6]	–	–
Miscellaneous, ...	20	Town Clerk	1841–1885	No	Good

1643. Sept. 7. Mass. Rec., Vol. II., p. 44. "Enon shall be called Wennam."

[1] The records from 1650 to 1675 are lost.

[2] The original records of births, marriages, and deaths from 1645 to 1695 are lost, but the omissions have been supplied by copies made from the records of the County Court.

[3] There are copies also of the first two volumes.

[4] The first volume has been indexed. The records from 1646 to 1652 are missing from the first volume.

[5] There are copies also of the first two volumes which are indexed. The records prior to 1695 are lost.

[6] The records from 1778 to 1782 are missing.

Town Records — Continued.

County of Essex. Town of West Newbury.

Kind of Records.	Number of Volumes	In Keeping of —	Years Covered	Whether Indexed	Condition
Town proceedings, . . .	4	Town Clerk	1819–1885	No	Good
Births, marriages, and deaths,	2	Town Clerk	1819–1885	No	Good
Selectmen and Assessors, .	–	Selectmen	–	–	–

1820. June 14. The name of the town of Parsons[1] changed to West Newbury.

County of Franklin. Town of Ashfield.

Kind of Records.	Number of Volumes	In Keeping of —	Years Covered	Whether Indexed	Condition
Town proceedings, . . .	4[2]	Town Clerk	1776–1885	Partially	Good
Births, marriages, and deaths,	5	Town Clerk	1765–1885	–	Good
Selectmen and Assessors, .	80	Selectmen	–	–	–
Proprietors, ...	2	Town Clerk	1738–1802	–	Good
Miscellaneous, . . .	3	Town Clerk	1762–1885	–	Good

1765. June 21. Prov. Laws, Vol. IV., p. 815. The new plantation called Huntstown established as Ashfield.

County of Franklin. Town of Bernardston.

Kind of Records.	Number of Volumes	In Keeping of —	Years Covered	Whether Indexed	Condition
Town proceedings, . . .	5	Town Clerk	1762–1885	No	–
Births, marriages, and deaths,	5[3]	Town Clerk	1762–1885	No	–
Selectmen and Assessors, .	73	Selectmen	–	–	–
Proprietors, ...	2[4]	Town Clerk	1735–1819	No	–

1762. Mar. 6. Prov. Laws, Vol. IV., p. 530. The new plantation called Falltown established as Bernardston.
1779. Dec. 2. Part of Bernardston annexed to Colrain.
1784. Mar. 12. Part of Bernardston established as the district of Leyden.
1838. April 14. Part of Greenfield annexed to Bernardston.
1886. May 7. Part of Leyden annexed to Bernardston, if this act is accepted by Bernardston.
1886. June 7. Act of May 7, 1886, accepted by Bernardston.

[1] For legislation concerning the town of Parsons, see " Extinct Cities, Towns, and Districts."

[2] No records were kept prior to 1776.

[3] There is a copy also of the records of births, marriages, and deaths from 1762 to 1843.

[4] A copy of the proprietors records is in possession of the Pocomtuck Memorial Association at Deerfield.

TOWN RECORDS — Continued.

COUNTY OF FRANKLIN. TOWN OF BUCKLAND.[1]

KIND OF RECORDS.	Number of Volumes	In Keeping of —	Years Covered	Whether Indexed	Condition
Town proceedings, . . .	1	Town Clerk	1876–1885	No	Good
Births, ...	1	Town Clerk	1876–1885	Yes	Good
Marriages, ...	1	Town Clerk	1876–1885	Yes	Good
Deaths, ...	1	Town Clerk	1876–1885	Yes	Good
Selectmen and Assessors, .	8	Town Clerk	1876–1885	–	–
Miscellaneous, ...	9	Town Clerk	1876–1885	Partially	Good

1779.   April 14.   The plantation called No-town and part of Charlemont established as Buckland.

1838.   April 14.   Part of Conway annexed to Buckland.

COUNTY OF FRANKLIN. TOWN OF CHARLEMONT.

KIND OF RECORDS.	Number of Volumes	In Keeping of —	Years Covered	Whether Indexed	Condition
Town proceedings, . . .	3	Town Clerk	1765–1885	No	Good
Births, marriages, and deaths,	6	Town Clerk	1765–1885	1 volume[2]	Good
Assessors, ...	–	–	–	–	–

1765.   June 21.   Prov. Laws, Vol. IV., p. 816. The new plantation called Charlemont established as the town of Charlemont.

1779.   April 14.   The plantation called No-town and part of Charlemont established as Buckland.

1785.   Feb. 14.   Part of Charlemont and part of the common lands known as Green and Walker's land established as Heath.

1793.   Mar. 19.   Certain common lands between Charlemont and North River, so called, annexed to Charlemont.

1838.   April 2.   Part of the common lands called Zoar annexed to Charlemont.

COUNTY OF FRANKLIN. TOWN OF COLRAIN.

KIND OF RECORDS.	Number of Volumes	In Keeping of —	Years Covered	Whether Indexed	Condition
Town proceedings, . . .	3	Town Clerk	1741–1798 1803–1885	No	Good
Births, marriages, and deaths,	4	Town Clerk	1741–1885	Yes	Good
Assessors, ...	–	Selectmen	1824–1885	–	–

1761.   June 30.   Prov. Laws, Vol. IV., p. 466. The new plantation of Colrain established as the town of Colrain.

1779.   Dec. 2.   Part of Bernardston annexed to Colrain.

[1] All records were burned July 22, 1876.

[2] Covering the years from 1805 to 1864.

TOWN RECORDS — Continued.

COUNTY OF FRANKLIN. TOWN OF CONWAY.

KIND OF RECORDS.	Number of Volumes	In Keeping of—	Years Covered	Whether Indexed	Condition
Town proceedings, . . .	7[1]	Town Clerk	1767–1885	–[2]	Fair
Births, marriages, and deaths,	8	Town Clerk	1767–1885	–[3]	Fair
Assessors, ...	50	Town Clerk	–	–	–
Miscellaneous, ...	7	Town Clerk	1767–1885	–	Fair

1767. June 17. Prov. Laws, Vol. IV., p. 955. Part of Deerfield established as the district of Conway.

1775. Aug. 23. Prov. Laws, Vol. V., p. 419. District of Conway made the town of Conway by this general act.

1781. Feb. 19. Part of Shelburne annexed to Conway.

1791. June 17. Part of Deerfield annexed to Conway.

1811. June 21. Part of Deerfield annexed to Conway and bounds between Conway and Whately established.

1838. April 14. Part of Conway annexed to Buckland.

COUNTY OF FRANKLIN. TOWN OF DEERFIELD.

KIND OF RECORDS.	Number of Volumes	In Keeping of—	Years Covered	Whether Indexed	Condition
Town proceedings, . . .	6[4]	Town Clerk	1683–1885	No	Good
Births, marriages, and deaths,	5[5]	Town Clerk	1683–1885	3 volumes	Good
Assessors, ...	45	Assessors	–	–	–
Selectmen, ...	2	Selectmen	–	–	–
Proprietors, ...	2	–[6]	1699–1801 / 1734–1858	No	Good
Miscellaneous, ...	9	Town Clerk	–	No	Good

1677. Oct. 22. Mass. Rec., Vol. V., p. 167. "Deerefeild" is mentioned.

1678. Oct. —. Mass Rec., Vol. V., p. 209. The encouraging of the rebuilding of the plantation of Deerfield provided for.

1753. June 9. Prov. Laws, Vol. III., p. 671. Part of Deerfield established as the district of Greenfield.

1767. June 17. Prov. Laws, Vol. IV., p. 955. Part of Deerfield established as the district of Conway.

1768. June 21. Prov. Laws, Vol. IV., p. 1013. Part of Deerfield established as the district of Shelburne.

1791. June 17. Part of Deerfield annexed to Conway.

1810. Mar. 5. Part of Deerfield annexed to Whately.

1811. June 21. Part of Deerfield annexed to Conway and bounds established.

1 The earlier town records have been copied.

2 The records since 1861 are indexed.

3 The records since 1843 are indexed.

4 There is a copy also of the first volume.

5 The records of births and deaths from 1683 to 1840, and of marriages from 1695 to 1833, have been copied into one volume.

6 Pocomtuck Valley Memorial Association.

TOWN RECORDS — Continued.

COUNTY OF FRANKLIN. TOWN OF ERVING.

KIND OF RECORDS.	Number of Volumes	In Keeping of —	Years Covered	Whether Indexed	Condition
Town proceedings, . . .	3	Town Clerk	1816–1885	No	Good
Births, ...	2	Town Clerk	1816–1885	No	Good
Marriages, ...	2	Town Clerk	1816–1885	No	Good
Deaths, ...	2	Town Clerk	1816–1885	No	Good
Assessors, ...	–	–	–	–	–
Miscellaneous, ...	1	Town Clerk	–	No	Good

1838. April 17. The common lands called Erving's Grant established as Erving.
1841. Feb.   27. Bounds between Erving and Orange established.
1860. Feb.   10. Part of Northfield called Hack's Grant, entirely detached from North-field and bounded on all sides by Erving, annexed to Erving.

COUNTY OF FRANKLIN. TOWN OF GILL.

KIND OF RECORDS.	Number of Volumes	In Keeping of —	Years Covered	Whether Indexed	Condition
Town proceedings, . . .	4	Town Clerk	1793–1885	–[1]	Good
Births, marriages, and deaths,	6[2]	Town Clerk	1793–1885	No	Good
Assessors, ...	63	Assessors	–	–	–
Miscellaneous, . . .	4	Town Clerk	1793–1885	No	Good

1793. Sept. 28. Part of Greenfield established as Gill.
1795. Feb.   28. Part of Northfield annexed to Gill.
1805. Mar.   14. The island called Great Island annexed to Gill after April 1, 1805.

COUNTY OF FRANKLIN. TOWN OF GREENFIELD.

KIND OF RECORDS.	Number of Volumes	In Keeping of —	Years Covered	Whether Indexed	Condition
General, ...	6	Town Clerk	1756–1885	No	–
Births, marriages, and deaths,	4	Town Clerk	1755–1885[3]	Yes	–
Marriage intentions, . .	1	Town Clerk	–	Yes	–
Assessors, ...	65	Town Clerk	–	–	–
Miscellaneous, ...	11	Town Clerk	–	No	–

1753. June   9. Prov. Laws, Vol. III., p. 671. Part of Deerfield established as the district of Greenfield.
1775. Aug.   23. Prov. Laws, Vol. V., p. 419. District of Greenfield made the town of Greenfield by this general act.
1793. Sept. 28. Part of Greenfield established as Gill.
1838. April 14. Part of Greenfield annexed to Bernardston.

[1] The third volume is partially indexed.
[2] Josiah D. Canning has private records of births, marriages, and deaths.
[3] The records of births, marriages, and deaths prior to 1855 are incomplete.

TOWN RECORDS — Continued.
COUNTY OF FRANKLIN. TOWN OF HAWLEY.

KIND OF RECORDS.	Number of Volumes	In Keeping of —	Years Covered	Whether Indexed	Condition
Town proceedings, . . .	3	Town Clerk	1797–1885	No	–
Births and deaths, . .	1[1]	Town Clerk	1825–1885	–	–
Marriages, ...	1	Town Clerk	1795–1885	–	–
Assessors, ...	–	Town Clerk	1861–1885	–	–
Miscellaneous, . . .	7	Town Clerk	1797–1885	No	–

1792. Feb. 6. The plantation called Number Seven established as Hawley.
1793. Mar. 9. Part of plantation Number Seven, accidentally omitted in the bounds described " in the act of February 5, 1792 " (probably February 6), annexed to Hawley.
1803. June 21. Part of Hawley annexed to the district of Plainfield.

COUNTY OF FRANKLIN. TOWN OF HEATH.

KIND OF RECORDS.	Number of Volumes	In Keeping of —	Years Covered	Whether Indexed	Condition
Town proceedings, . . .	3	Town Clerk	1785–1885	No	Good
Births, marriages, and deaths,	4	Town Clerk	1785–1885	No	Good
Assessors, ...	100	Assessors	1785–1885	–	–
Selectmen, ...	1	Selectmen	1785–1885	–	–

1785. Feb. 14. Part of Charlemont and part of the common lands called Green and Walker's land established as Heath.

COUNTY OF FRANKLIN. TOWN OF LEVERETT.

KIND OF RECORDS.	Number of Volumes	In Keeping of —	Years Covered	Whether Indexed	Condition
Town proceedings, . . .	3	Town Clerk	1774–1885	No	Good
Births, marriages, and deaths,	5	Town Clerk	1774–1885	No	Good
Assessors, ...	–	–	–	–	–
Selectmen, ...	2	Town Clerk	–	–	–

1774. Mar. 5. Prov. Laws, Vol. V., p. 327. Part of Sunderland established as Leverett.

COUNTY OF FRANKLIN. TOWN OF LEYDEN.

KIND OF RECORDS.	Number of Volumes	In Keeping of —	Years Covered	Whether Indexed	Condition
Town proceedings, . . .	7	Town Clerk	1808–1885[2]	No	–
Births, marriages, and deaths,	5	Town Clerk	1808–1885	No	–
Assessors, ...	20	Assessors	–	–	–
Miscellaneous, . . .	5	Town Clerk	–	No	–

[1] There is also a copy.   [2] There are omissions in the records prior to 1842.

Town Records — Continued.

County of Franklin. Town of Leyden — Con.

1784. Mar. 12. Part of Bernardston established as the district of Leyden.
1809. Feb. 22. District of Leyden established as the town of Leyden.
1886. May 7. Part of Leyden annexed to Bernardston, if this act is accepted by Bernardston.
1886. June 7. Act of May 7, 1886, accepted by Bernardston.

County of Franklin. Town of Monroe.

Kind of Records.	Number of Volumes	In Keeping of —	Years Covered	Whether Indexed	Condition
Town proceedings, .	2	Town Clerk	1822–1885	No	Good
Births, marriages, and deaths,	1	Town Clerk	1822–1850	No	Good
Births, .	1	Town Clerk	1850–1885	Yes	Good
Marriages, .	1	Town Clerk	1850–1885	No	Good
Deaths, .	1	Town Clerk	1850–1885	Yes	Good
Assessors, .	23	Assessors	–	–	–
Miscellaneous, .	6	Town Clerk	–	No	Good

1822. Feb. 21. Part of Rowe and a gore of common lands lying north of Florida established as Monroe.

County of Franklin. Town of Montague.[1]

Kind of Records.	Number of Volumes	In Keeping of —	Years Covered	Whether Indexed	Condition
General, .	2	Town Clerk	1754–1885	Partially	–
Births, marriages, and deaths,	8	Town Clerk	1754–1885	Partially	–
Assessors, .	–	Assessors	–	–	–
Proprietors, .	1	County Commissioners	–	–	–
Miscellaneous, .	6	Town Clerk	1865–1885	Partially	–

1754. Jan. 25. Prov. Laws, Vol. III., p. 713. Part of Sunderland established as the district of Montague.
1775. Aug. 23. Prov. Laws, Vol. V., p. 419. District of Montague made the town of Montague by this general act.
1803. Feb. 28. Part of Montague annexed to Wendell.

County of Franklin. Town of New Salem.[2]

Kind of Records.	Number of Volumes	In Keeping of —	Years Covered	Whether Indexed	Condition
Town proceedings, .	2	Town Clerk	1855–1885	No	Good
Births, .	1	Town Clerk	1855–1885	No	Good
Marriages, .	1	Town Clerk	1855–1885	No	Good
Deaths, .	1	Town Clerk	1855–1885	No	Good
Assessors, .	24	Selectmen	1861–1885	–	–

[1] The records of Montague are scattered, a part being at Turner's Falls, in possession of the Town Clerk, a part at Montague Centre, and parts in other places.
[2] All the records prior to 1855 were burned in that year.

TOWN RECORDS — Continued.

COUNTY OF FRANKLIN. TOWN OF NEW SALEM — Con.

1753. June 15. Prov. Laws, Vol. III., p. 670. The "township" of New Salem with the additional grant made to said "township" established as the district of New Salem.

1775. Aug. 23. Prov. Laws, Vol. V., p. 419. District of New Salem made the town of New Salem by this general act.

1822. Jan. 28. Parts of New Salem and Pelham established as Prescott.

1824. Feb. 20. Part of Shutesbury annexed to New Salem.

1830. Feb. 5. Part of New Salem annexed to Athol.

1837. Mar. 16. Part of New Salem annexed to Orange and part to Athol.

COUNTY OF FRANKLIN. TOWN OF NORTHFIELD.

KIND OF RECORDS.	Number of Volumes	In Keeping of —	Years Covered	Whether Indexed	Condition
Town proceedings, . . .	3[1]	Town Clerk	1766–1885	No	Good
Births, marriages, and deaths,	5	Town Clerk	1717–1885	3 volumes	Good
Assessors, ...	–	–	–	–	–
Selectmen, . . .	5	Selectmen	–	–	–
Proprietors, ...	1	Town Clerk	1685–1723	No	Good
Soldiers in the Rebellion, .	1	Town Clerk	–	No	Good

1713. Feb. 22. Resolve. Upon the petition of inhabitants of the "plantation at Squakead formerly called Northfield" the grant for a plantation was "revived," the "town to be named Northfield."

1795. Feb. 28. Part of Northfield annexed to Gill.

1860. Feb. 10. Part of Northfield called Hack's Grant, entirely detached from Northfield and bounded on all sides by Erving, annexed to Erving.

COUNTY OF FRANKLIN. TOWN OF ORANGE.

KIND OF RECORDS.	Number of Volumes	In Keeping of —	Years Covered	Whether Indexed	Condition
Town proceedings, . . .	4	Town Clerk	1783–1885	–	–[2]
Births, marriages, and deaths,	7	Town Clerk	1783–1885	Partially	–
Assessors, ...	56	Selectmen	–	–	–
Selectmen, ...	8	Selectmen	–	–	–
Miscellaneous, . . .	27	Town Clerk	1783–1885	Partially	–

1783. Oct. 15. Parts of Athol, Royalston, Warwick, and certain common lands called Ervingshire established as the district of Orange.

1810. Feb. 24. District of Orange established as the town of Orange.

1816. Feb. 7. Part of Orange annexed to Athol.

1837. Mar. 16. Part of the common lands called Erving's Grant annexed to Orange.

1837. Mar. 16. Part of New Salem called Little Grant annexed to Orange.

1841. Feb. 27. Bounds between Orange and Erving established.

[1] The first volume covering the years from 1723 to 1766 is lost.

[2] The first volume is somewhat mutilated and some of the pages are missing.

TOWN RECORDS — Continued.

COUNTY OF FRANKLIN.   TOWN OF ROWE.

KIND OF RECORDS.	Number of Volumes	In Keeping of —	Years Covered	Whether Indexed	Condition
Town proceedings, . . .	3	Town Clerk	1785–1885	No	Good
Births, marriages, and deaths,	5	Town Clerk	1785–1885	No	Good
Assessors, ...	–	–	–	–	–
Miscellaneous, ...	4	Town Clerk	1785–1885	No	Good

1785.   Feb.   9.   The common lands called Myrifield with lands adjoining established as Rowe.
1822.   Feb.   21.   Part of Rowe and certain common lands established as Monroe.
1838.   April   2.   Part of the common lands called Zoar annexed to Rowe.

COUNTY OF FRANKLIN.   TOWN OF SHELBURNE.

KIND OF RECORDS.	Number of Volumes	In Keeping of —	Years Covered	Whether Indexed	Condition
Town proceedings, . . .	3	Town Clerk	1768–1885	–	–
Births, marriages, and deaths,	2	Town Clerk	1768–1885	–	–
Marriages, ...	2	Town Clerk	1868–1885	–	–
Deaths, ...	2	Town Clerk	1868–1885	–	–
Assessors, ...	–	–	–	–	–
Selectmen, ...	–	Selectmen	–	–	–
Miscellaneous, ...	2	Town Clerk	–	–	–

1768.   June   21.   Prov. Laws, Vol. IV., p. 1013.   Part of Deerfield established as the district of Shelburne.
1775.   Aug.   23.   Prov. Laws, Vol. V., p. 419.   District of Shelburne made the town of Shelburne by this general act.
1781.   Feb.   19.   Part of Shelburne annexed to Conway.
1793.   Mar.   19.   Certain common lands lying between Shelburne and North River, so called, annexed to Shelburne.

COUNTY OF FRANKLIN.   TOWN OF SHUTESBURY.

KIND OF RECORDS.	Number of Volumes	In Keeping of —	Years Covered	Whether Indexed	Condition
Town proceedings, . . .	5	Town Clerk	1761–1885	No	–
Births, marriages, and deaths,	4	Town Clerk	1761–1885	Partially	–
Assessors, ...	50	Town Clerk	–	–	–
Proprietors, ...	2	Town Clerk	1760–1805	No	–
Miscellaneous, ...	11	Town Clerk	1798–1885	No	–

1761.   June   30.   Prov. Laws, Vol. IV., p. 464.   The plantation called Roadtown established as Shutesbury.
1781.   May   8.   Part of Shutesbury and part of the common lands called Ervingshire established as Wendell.
1824.   Feb.   20.   Part of Shutesbury annexed to New Salem.

TOWN RECORDS — Continued.

COUNTY OF FRANKLIN. TOWN OF SUNDERLAND.

KIND OF RECORDS.	Number of Volumes	In Keeping of —	Years Covered	Whether Indexed	Condition
Town proceedings, . . .	6[1]	Town Clerk	1713–1885[2]	3 volumes[3]	Good
Births, marriages, and deaths,	5[4]	Town Clerk	1713–1885	No	Good
Assessors, ...	51	Town Clerk	–	–	–
Proprietors, ...	–[5]	Town Clerk	1673–1718	No	Good
Miscellaneous, ...	6[6]	Town Clerk	1730–1885	No	Good

1718. Nov. 12. Resolve. "The place" made a township and ordered that "the name of the township be henceforward called Sunderland."
1740. Jan. 2. Resolve. Bounds fixed between Hadley and Sunderland.
1754. Jan. 25. Prov. Laws, Vol. III., p. 713. Part of Sunderland established as the district of Montague.
1774. Mar. 5. Prov. Laws, Vol. V., p. 327. Part of Sunderland established as Leverett.

COUNTY OF FRANKLIN. TOWN OF WARWICK.

KIND OF RECORDS.	Number of Volumes	In Keeping of —	Years Covered	Whether Indexed	Condition
Town proceedings, . . .	5	Town Clerk	1763–1885	Partially	Good
Births, marriages, and deaths,	4	Town Clerk	1763–1885	Partially	Good
Assessors, ...	–	Town Clerk	1802–1885	–	–
Proprietors, ...	1	Town Clerk	1735–1772	No	Good

1763. Feb. 17. Prov. Laws, Vol. IV., p. 604. The new plantation called Roxbury-Canada, "with sundry farms lying therein" and certain common lands, established as Warwick.
1783. Oct. 15. Parts of Warwick, Athol, Royalston, and certain common lands called Ervingshire established as Orange.

COUNTY OF FRANKLIN. TOWN OF WENDELL.

KIND OF RECORDS.	Number of Volumes	In Keeping of —	Years Covered	Whether Indexed	Condition
Town proceedings, . . .	4	Town Clerk	1781–1885	No	Good
Births, marriages, and deaths,	4	Town Clerk	1781–1885	Yes	Good
Assessors, ...	29	Assessors	–	–	–
Selectmen, ...	3	Selectmen	–	–	–
Miscellaneous, ...	4	Town Clerk	–	No	Good

1781. May 8. Part of Shutesbury and part of the common lands called Ervingshire established as Wendell.
1803. Feb. 28. Part of Montague and a gore of common lands lying between Wendell and Montague annexed to Wendell.

[1] There is a partial copy of the first volume.   [2] The records from 1673 to 1713 are lost.
[3] Covering the years from 1833 to 1885.
[4] There is a copy also of the first volume.   [5] There is also a copy.
[6] There is a copy of the records of grants of land.

TOWN RECORDS — Continued.

COUNTY OF FRANKLIN.   TOWN OF WHATELY.

KIND OF RECORDS.	Number of Volumes	In Keeping of—	Years Covered	Whether Indexed	Condition
Town proceedings, . . .	3	Town Clerk	1771–1885	No	–
Births, marriages, and deaths,	4[1]	Town Clerk	1771–1885[1]	Since 1844	–
Assessors, ...	–	Assessors	1800–1885	–	–
Miscellaneous, ...	9	Town Clerk	1771–1885	No	–

1771.   April 24. Prov. Laws, Vol. V., p. 122. Part of Hatfield established as Whately.
1810.   Mar.   5. Part of Deerfield annexed to Whately.
1811.   June 21. Bounds between Whately and Conway established.
1849.   Feb.   2. Resolve. Bounds between Whately and Williamsburg established.

COUNTY OF HAMPDEN.   TOWN OF AGAWAM.

KIND OF RECORDS.	Number of Volumes	In Keeping of—	Years Covered	Whether Indexed	Condition
Town proceedings, . . .	2	Town Clerk	1855–1885	No	Good
Births, ...	1[2]	Town Clerk	1855–1885	No	Good
Marriages, ...	1[2]	Town Clerk	1855–1885	No	Good
Deaths, ...	1[2]	Town Clerk	1855–1885	No	Good
Assessors, ...	30	Selectmen	–	–	–
Parish, ...	1	Town Clerk	1758–1836	No	Good
Proprietors, ...	1	Unknown	–	–	–
Miscellaneous, . . .	3	Town Clerk	1855–1885	No	Good

1855.   May   17. Part of West Springfield established as Agawam.

COUNTY OF HAMPDEN.   TOWN OF BLANDFORD.

KIND OF RECORDS.	Number of Volumes	In Keeping of—	Years Covered	Whether Indexed	Condition
Town proceedings, . . .	6	Town Clerk	1742–1885[3]	No	Fair
Births, marriages, and deaths,	4	Town Clerk	1844–1885	Yes	Fair
Assessors, ...	14	Town Clerk	1816–1885	–	–[4]
Miscellaneous, ...	3	Town Clerk	1834–1885	–	Fair

1741.   April 10. Prov. Laws, Vol. II., p. 1058. Suffield Equivalent lands, commonly
                     called Glasgow, established as Blandford.
1809.   Feb. 22. Bounds between Blandford and Russell, and Blandford and Chester,
                     established.
1810.   June 13. Bounds between Blandford and Chester established.
1853.   May   25. Part of Blandford annexed to Norwich.

[1] The records of births, marriages, and deaths prior to 1850 were made from private records.
[2] There are private records of births, marriages, and deaths in possession of Rev. Ralph Perry.
[3] The records prior to 1742 were burned.   [4] Incomplete prior to 1861.

Town Records — Continued.

County of Hampden. Town of Brimfield.

Kind of Records.	Number of Volumes	In Keeping of—	Years Covered	Whether Indexed	Condition
Town proceedings, . . .	5	Town Clerk	1730–1885	No	Good
Births, marriages, and deaths,	6[1]	Town Clerk	1730–1885	Yes	Good
Marriage intentions, . .	1	Town Clerk	1826–1885	No	Good
Assessors, ...	26	Assessors	–	–	–
Selectmen, ...	5	Selectmen	–	–	–
Proprietors, ...	1	Town Clerk	1731–1824[2]	No	Good
Soldiers in the Rebellion, .	1	Town Clerk	–	Yes	Good
Miscellaneous, ...	28	Town Clerk	1808–1885	Partially	Good

1722.   Aug. 16.   Prov. Laws, Vol. II., p. 260. Brimfield is mentioned in a list of frontier towns.

1731.   Dec. 24.   Resolve. The town of Brimfield "incorporated."

1742.   Jan. 16.   Prov. Laws, Vol. II., p. 1088. Parts of Brimfield, Brookfield and Kingsfield established as Western.

1760.   April 28.   Prov. Laws, Vol. IV., p. 334. Part of Brimfield established as the district of Monson.

1763.   Feb. 7.   Prov. Laws, Vol. IV., p. 362. Bounds definitely established.

1763.   Sept. 18.   Prov. Laws, Vol. IV., p. 601. Part of Brimfield established as the district of South Brimfield.

County of Hampden. Town of Chester.

Kind of Records.	Number of Volumes	In Keeping of—	Years Covered	Whether Indexed	Condition
Town proceedings, . . .	5	Town Clerk	1790–1885	No	Good[3]
Births, marriages, and deaths,	3	Town Clerk	1790–1885	No	Good
Selectmen and Assessors, .	20	Selectmen	–	–	–
Proprietors, ...	–	J. Merrick Bell	–	–	–
Miscellaneous, . . .	2	Town Clerk	1790–1885	No	Good

1783.   Feb. 21.   The name of the town of Murrayfield[4] changed to Chester.

1783.   Mar. 12.   Parts of Chester, Becket, Partridgefield, Washington, and Worthington, and certain common lands called Prescott's Grant, established as Middlefield.

1799.   June 21.   Part of Chester annexed to Worthington.

1809.   Feb. 22.   Bounds between Chester and Blandford established.

1810.   June 13.   Bounds between Chester and Blandford established.

1853.   May 25.   Part of Chester annexed to Norwich.

[1] There are copies also of the first two volumes.

[2] The proprietors records prior to 1731 were burned.

[3] A few leaves are missing from the first volume.

[4] For legislation concerning the town of Murrayfield, see "Extinct Cities, Towns, and Districts."

TOWN RECORDS — Continued.

COUNTY OF HAMPDEN. TOWN OF CHICOPEE.

KIND OF RECORDS.	Number of Volumes	In Keeping of —	Years Covered	Whether Indexed	Condition
Town proceedings, . . .	2	Town Clerk	1848–1885	No	Good
Births, ...	2	Town Clerk	1848–1885	No	Good
Marriages, ...	3	Town Clerk	1848–1885	No	Good
Deaths, ...	2	Town Clerk	1848–1885	No	Good
Assessors, ...	37	Town Clerk	1848–1885	–	–
Selectmen, ...	2	Town Clerk	1848–1885	–	–
Soldiers in the Rebellion, .	1	Town Clerk	1861–1865	No	Good
Miscellaneous, ...	25	Town Clerk	1848–1885	No	Good

1848. April 29. Part of Springfield established as Chicopee.

COUNTY OF HAMPDEN. TOWN OF GRANVILLE.

KIND OF RECORDS.	Number of Volumes	In Keeping of —	Years Covered	Whether Indexed	Condition
Town proceedings, . . .	5	Town Clerk	1737–1885	No	–[1]
Births, marriages, and deaths,	4	Town Clerk	1737–1885	–	–
Selectmen and Assessors, .	25	Selectmen	–	–	–

1754. Jan. 25. Prov. Laws, Vol. III., p. 712. The plantation of Bedford established as the district of Granville.

1775. Aug. 23. Prov. Laws, Vol. V., p. 419. District of Granville made the town of Granville by this general act.

1810. June 14. Part of Granville established as Tolland.

COUNTY OF HAMPDEN. TOWN OF HAMPDEN.

KIND OF RECORDS.	Number of Volumes	In Keeping of —	Years Covered	Whether Indexed	Condition
Town proceedings, . . .	1	Town Clerk	1878–1885	No	Good
Births, ...	1	Town Clerk	1878–1885	Yes	Good
Marriages, ...	1	Town Clerk	1878–1885	Yes	Good
Deaths, ...	1	Town Clerk	1878–1885	Yes	Good
Assessors, ...	15	Assessors	1878–1885	–	–
Selectmen, ...	6	Selectmen	1878–1885	–	–
Miscellaneous, ...	7	Town Clerk	1878–1885	No	Good

1878. Mar. 28. Part of Wilbraham established as Hampden.

[1] The earlier records were poorly kept.

Town Records — Continued.

County of Hampden. Town of Holland.

KIND OF RECORDS.	Number of Volumes	In Keeping of—	Years Covered	Whether Indexed	Condition
Town proceedings, . . .	3	Town Clerk	1775–1885	No	Good
Births, marriages, and deaths,	8	Town Clerk	1775–1885	Yes	Good
Selectmen and Assessors, .	–	Selectmen	–	–	–
Miscellaneous, ...	4	Town Clerk	1825–1885	–	–

1783. July 5. Part of South Brimfield established as the district of Holland.
1796. Feb. 8. Bounds between the district of Holland and South Brimfield established.
1836. May 1. District of Holland made the town of Holland by the provisions of chapter 15 of the Revised Statutes.

County of Hampden. City of Holyoke.

KIND OF RECORDS.	Number of Volumes	In Keeping of—	Years Covered	Whether Indexed	Condition
Town proceedings, . . .	2	City Clerk	1850–1873	No	Good
City proceedings, . . .	2	City Clerk	1874–1885	Yes	Good
Births, ...	3	City Clerk	1850–1885	–	Good
Marriages, ...	3	City Clerk	1850–1885	–	Good
Deaths, ...	3	City Clerk	1850–1885	–	Good
Marriage intentions, . .	1	City Clerk	1850–1869	No	Good
Assessors, ...	32	Assessors	–	–	–
Miscellaneous, ...	3	City Clerk	1850–1885	No	Good

1850. Mar. 14. Part of West Springfield established as Holyoke.
1873. April 7. Holyoke incorporated as a city.
1873. May 29. Act of incorporation accepted by the town.

County of Hampden. Town of Longmeadow.

KIND OF RECORDS.	Number of Volumes	In Keeping of—	Years Covered	Whether Indexed	Condition
Town proceedings, . . .	3	Town Clerk	1783–1885	No	Good
Births, marriages, and deaths,	7	Town Clerk	1783–1885	Yes	Good
Selectmen and Assessors, .	–	Selectmen	–	–	–
Proprietors, ...	–	Proprietors Clerk	–	–	–
Genealogy of families, . .	1[1]	Town Clerk	1700–1813	No	Good
Miscellaneous, ...	9	Town Clerk	–	Partially	Good

1783. Oct. 13. Part of Springfield called Longmeadow established as Longmeadow.
1787. Nov. 16. Certain common lands called the Gore annexed to Longmeadow.

[1] There is a copy in possession of S. T. Colton.

TOWN RECORDS — Continued.

COUNTY OF HAMPDEN. TOWN OF LUDLOW.

KIND OF RECORDS.	Number of Volumes	In Keeping of—	Years Covered	Whether Indexed	Condition
General, ...	3[1]	Town Clerk	1774–1885	No	Fair
Births, marriages, and deaths,	4	Town Clerk	1774–1869	Partially	Fair
Births, ...	1	Town Clerk	1869–1885	Yes	Fair
Marriages, ...	1	Town Clerk	1869–1885	Yes	Fair
Deaths, ...	1	Town Clerk	1869–1885	Yes	Fair
Selectmen and Assessors, .	–	–	–	–	–

1774. Feb.. 28. Prov. Laws, Vol. V., p. 337. Part of Springfield called Stony Hill established as the district of Ludlow.

1775. Aug. 23. Prov. Laws, Vol. V., p. 419. District of Ludlow made the town of Ludlow by this general act.

1830. June 5. Bounds between Ludlow and Springfield established.

COUNTY OF HAMPDEN. TOWN OF MONSON.

KIND OF RECORDS.	Number of Volumes	In Keeping of—	Years Covered	Whether Indexed	Condition
Town proceedings, . . .	5	Town Clerk	1762–1885	No	Good
Births, marriages, and deaths,	9[2]	Town Clerk	1760–1885[3]	Yes[4]	Good[5]
Assessors, ...	79	Assessors	1803–1885[6]	–	–
Miscellaneous, . . .	8	Town Clerk	1830–1885	No	Good

1760. April 28. Prov. Laws, Vol. IV., p. 334. Part of Brimfield established as the district of Monson.

1763. Feb. 7. Prov. Laws, Vol. IV., p. 362. Bounds of Monson definitely established.

1775. Aug. 23. Prov. Laws, Vol. V., p. 419. District of Monson made the town of Monson by this general act.

1828. Feb. 8. Bounds between Monson and Palmer established.

COUNTY OF HAMPDEN. TOWN OF MONTGOMERY.

KIND OF RECORDS.	Number of Volumes	In Keeping of—	Years Covered	Whether Indexed	Condition
Town proceedings, . . .	3	Town Clerk	1780–1885	Yes	Good
Births, marriages, and deaths,	4	Town Clerk	1780–1885	No	Good
Assessors, ...	–	–	–	–	–
Selectmen, ...	1	Selectmen	–	–	–
Miscellaneous, . . .	2	Town Clerk	1780–1885	No	Good

[1] The first volume was rebound in 1839, a few torn leaves being replaced by copies.

[2] There is a copy also of the first volume.

[3] There is no record of marriages from 1762 to 1800.

[4] With the exception of the third volume.

[5] With the exception of the first volume.

[6] The records of assessors for ten years are missing, the years not being designated.

Town Records — Continued.

County of Hampden. Town of Montgomery — Con.

1780. Nov. 28. Part of that part of Westfield called the New Addition and parts of Norwich and Southampton established as Montgomery.

1792. Feb. 25. Parts of Montgomery and Westfield established as Russell.

1792. Mar. 6. Parts of Norwich and Southampton annexed to Montgomery.

County of Hampden. Town of Palmer.

Kind of Records.	Number of Volumes	In Keeping of —	Years Covered	Whether Indexed	Condition
Town proceedings, . . .	4	Town Clerk	1732–1885[1]	No	Good
Births, marriages, and deaths,	5	Town Clerk	1848–1885	Yes	Good
Selectmen and Assessors, .	6	Town Clerk	–	–	–
Proprietors, ...	2 {	E. B. Gates	1732–1750[1]	No	Good
		J. H. Temple	1716–1732[1]		

1752. Jan. 30. Prov. Laws, Vol. III., p. 599. The plantation called The Elbows established as the district of Palmer.

1763. Feb. 7. Prov. Laws, Vol. IV., p. 362. Bounds of Palmer definitely established.

1775. Aug. 23. Prov. Laws, Vol. V., p. 419. District of Palmer made the town of Palmer by this general act.

1828. Feb. 8. Bounds between Palmer and Monson established.

1831. Feb. 7. Part of Western annexed to Palmer.

County of Hampden. Town of Russell.

Kind of Records.	Number of Volumes	In Keeping of —	Years Covered	Whether Indexed	Condition
Town proceedings, . . .	4	Town Clerk	1804–1885[2]	No	Good
Births, marriages, and deaths,	4	Town Clerk	1804–1885[2]	No	Good
Selectmen and Assessors, .	36	Selectmen	1828–1885[3]	–	–
Miscellaneous, . . .	5	Town Clerk	1832–1885	Partially	Good

1792. Feb. 25. Part of that part of Westfield called the New Addition and part of Montgomery established as Russell.

1809. Feb. 22. Bounds established between Blandford and Russell.

[1] The records prior to 1841 are incomplete; those from 1807 to 1818 were burned. O. P. Allen has a copy of the records from 1732 to 1807.

[2] The records prior to 1804 were not bound, and the loose sheets being moved from one place to another were lost.

[3] The records of the selectmen and assessors prior to 1828 are lost.

Town Records — Continued.

County of Hampden. Town of Southwick.

KIND OF RECORDS.	Number of Volumes	In Keeping of —	Years Covered	Whether Indexed	Condition
Town proceedings, . . .	5	Town Clerk	{ 1777–1819[1] 1834–1885 }	No	Good
Births, ...	2	Town Clerk	1845–1885	No	Good
Marriages, ...	1	Town Clerk	1859–1885	No	Good
Deaths, ...	1	Town Clerk	1877–1885	No	Good
Selectmen and Assessors, .	55	Selectmen	–	–	–
Soldiers in the Rebellion, .	1	Town Clerk	1861–1865	No	Good
Miscellaneous, . . .	1	Town Clerk	1843–1885	Yes	Good

1770. **Nov.** 7. Prov. Laws, Vol. V., p. 75. Part of Westfield established as the district of Southwick.

1775. **Aug.** 23. Prov. Laws, Vol. V., p. 419. District of Southwick made the town of Southwick by this general act.

1779. **Oct.** 6. Part of Westfield annexed to Southwick.

1837. **Mar.** 20. Bounds between Southwick and Westfield established.

County of Hampden. City of Springfield.

KIND OF RECORDS.	Number of Volumes	In Keeping of —	Years Covered	Whether Indexed	Condition
Town proceedings, . . .	7	City Clerk	1636–1852[2]	Partially	Good
City proceedings, . . .	8	City Clerk	1852–1885	Yes	Good
Births, marriages, and deaths (town), . . .	1[3]	City Clerk	1640–1728	Yes	Good
(city), . . .	1[3]	City Clerk	1843–1849	Yes	Good
Births (town), . . .	2	City Clerk	1728–1843	Yes	Good
(city), . . .	5	City Clerk	1850–1885	Yes	Good
Marriages (town), . . .	2	City Clerk	1728–1844	Yes	Good
(city), . . .	6	City Clerk	1850–1885	Yes	Good
Deaths (town), . . .	1	City Clerk	1728–1844	Yes	Good
(city), . . .	4	City Clerk	1850–1885	Yes	Good
Assessors, ...	265	Assessors	–	–	–
Selectmen, ...	6	City Clerk	–	–	–
Proprietors, ...	6[4]	City Clerk	1650–1813	Yes	Good
Miscellaneous, . . .	112	City Clerk	–	Partially	Good

1641. **June** 2. Mass. Rec., Vol. I., p. 320. A letter from the General Court to Mr. Pinchen and others of " Agawam now Springfeild."

1647. **Nov.** 11. Mass. Rec., Vol. II., p. 224. Woronoko to be a part of Springfield.

1648. **Mar.** —. Mass. Rec., Vol. II., p. 227. Certain common lands annexed to Springfield.

1669. **May** 19. Mass. Rec., Vol. IV., Part 2, p. 432. Part of Springfield called Woronoake established as Westfield.

1670. **May** 31. Mass. Rec., Vol. IV., Part 2, p. 459. Bounds between Springfield and Westfield established.

1684. **May** 17. Mass. Rec., Vol. V., p. 444. Bounds established.

1685, **June** 4. Mass. Rec., Vol. V., p. 481. Bounds between Springfield and Northampton established.

---

[1] A volume of records covering the years from 1819 to 1834 is missing.

[2] The records from 1664 to 1681 are incomplete.

[3] There is also a copy.   [4] There are copies also of the first four volumes.

Town Records — Continued.

County of Hampden. City of Springfield — Con.

1763. June 15. Prov. Laws, Vol. IV., p. 644. Part of Springfield established as Wilbraham.
1774. Feb. 23. Prov. Laws, Vol. V., p. 335. Part of Springfield established as West Springfield.
1774. Feb. 28. Prov. Laws, Vol. V., p. 337. Part of Springfield established as Ludlow.
1783. Oct. 13. Part of Springfield established as Longmeadow.
1799. June 11. Part of Springfield annexed to Wilbraham.
1830. June 5. Bounds between Springfield and Ludlow established.
1848. April 29. Part of Springfield established as Chicopee.
1852. April 12. Springfield incorporated as a city.
1852. April 21. Act accepted by the town.

County of Hampden. Town of Tolland.

Kind of Records.	Number of Volumes	In Keeping of —	Years Covered	Whether Indexed	Condition
Town proceedings, . . .	3	Town Clerk	1810–1885	No	–
Births, marriages, and deaths,	4	Town Clerk	1810–1885	No	–
Assessors, ...	35	Town Clerk			–
Miscellaneous, ...	5	Town Clerk	1810–1885	No	–

1810. June 14. Part of Granville established as Tolland.
1853. May 4. Bounds between Tolland and Sandisfield established.
1855. May 15. Bounds between Tolland and Sandisfield established.

County of Hampden. Town of Wales.

Kind of Records.	Number of Volumes	In Keeping of —	Years Covered	Whether Indexed	Condition
Town proceedings, . . .	5	Town Clerk	1790–1885	No	Good
Births, marriages, and deaths,	4	Town Clerk	1790–1885	Yes	Good
Selectmen and Assessors, .	7	Town Clerk	1790–1885	–	–
Miscellaneous, ...	4	Town Clerk	1790–1885	No	Good

1828. Feb. 20. The name of the town of South Brimfield[1] changed to Wales.

County of Hampden. Town of Westfield.

Kind of Records.	Number of Volumes	In Keeping of —	Years Covered	Whether Indexed	Condition
Town proceedings, . . .	8	Town Clerk	1675–1762 / 1766–1885	–	Good
Births, marriages, and deaths,	2	Town Clerk	–	–	Good
Births, ...	1	Town Clerk	–	–	Good
Marriages, ...	3	Town Clerk	–	–	Good
Deaths, ...	1	Town Clerk	–	–	Good
Assessors, ...	42	Assessors	–	–	–
Selectmen, ...	2	Selectmen	–	–	–
Proprietors, ...	2	Town Clerk	1667–1830	–	Good
Miscellaneous, ...	3	Town Clerk	1823–1885	–	Good

[1] For legislation concerning the town of South Brimfield, see "Extinct Cities, Towns, and Districts."

Town Records — Continued.

County of Hampden. Town of Westfield — Con.

1669. May 19. Mass. Rec., Vol. IV., Part 2, p. 432. Part of Springfield called Woronoake established as Westfield.
1670. May 31. Mass. Rec., Vol. IV., Part 2, p. 459. Bounds between Westfield and
Springfield established.
1770. Nov. 7. Prov. Laws., Vol. V., p. 75. Part of Westfield established as the
district of Southwick.
1779. Oct. 6. Part of Westfield annexed to Southwick.
1780. Nov. 28. Parts of Westfield, Norwich, and Southampton established as Montgomery.
1792. Feb. 25. Parts of Westfield and Montgomery established as Russell.
1802. Mar. 3. Part of Westfield annexed to West Springfield.
1837. Mar. 20. Bounds between Westfield and Southwick established.

County of Hampden. Town of West Springfield.

Kind of Records.	Number of Volumes	In Keeping of—	Years Covered	Whether Indexed	Condition
Town proceedings, . . .	7	Town Clerk	1774–1885	No	Fair
Births, marriages, and deaths,	7[1]	Town Clerk	1774–1885	Yes	Fair
Assessors, ...	23	Town Clerk	–	–	–
Miscellaneous, ...	6	Town Clerk	1774–1885	No	Fair

1774. Feb. 23. Prov. Laws, Vol. V., p. 335. Part of Springfield established as West
Springfield.
1802. Mar. 3. Part of Westfield annexed to West Springfield.
1850. Mar. 14. Part of West Springfield established as Holyoke.
1855. May 17. Part of West Springfield established as Agawam.

County of Hampden. Town of Wilbraham.

Kind of Records.	Number of Volumes	In Keeping of—	Years Covered	Whether Indexed	Condition
Town proceedings, . . .	6	Town Clerk	1740–1885	No	Good
Births, ...	1	Town Clerk	1763–1885	Yes	Good
Marriages, ...	1	Town Clerk	1763–1885	Yes	Good
Births and deaths, . .	1	Town Clerk	1763–1885	Yes	Good
Marriage intentions, . .	1	Town Clerk	1763–1885	Yes	Good
Assessors, ...	89	Assessors	–	–	–
Selectmen, ...	11	Selectmen	–	–	–
Miscellaneous, ...	7	Town Clerk	1740–1885	No	Good

1763. June 15. Prov. Laws, Vol. IV., p. 644. Part of Springfield established as Wilbraham.
1799. June 11. Part of Springfield called The Elbows annexed to Wilbraham.
1878. Mar. 28. Part of Wilbraham established as Hampden.

[1] The records of births, marriages, deaths, and marriage intentions from 1774 to 1796 have
been copied.

TOWN RECORDS — Continued.

COUNTY OF HAMPSHIRE. TOWN OF AMHERST.

KIND OF RECORDS.	Number of Volumes	In Keeping of—	Years Covered	Whether Indexed	Condition
Town proceedings, . . .	4[1]	Town Clerk	1735–1885	–	Good
Births, marriages, and deaths,	5	Town Clerk	1735–1885	–	Good
Assessors, ...	–	Town Clerk	1777–1885	–	–

1759. Feb. 13. Prov. Laws, Vol. IV., p. 173. Part of Hadley established as the district of Amherst.

1775. Aug. 23. Prov. Laws, Vol. V., p. 419. District of Amherst made the town of Amherst by this general act.

1789. Jan. 15. Part of Hadley annexed to Amherst.

1811. Feb. 28. Part of Hadley annexed to Amherst.

1812. Feb. 18. Part of Hadley annexed to Amherst.

1814. Feb. 17. Part of Hadley annexed to Amherst.

1815. Mar. 1. Bounds between Amherst and Hadley established and part of each town annexed to the other town.

COUNTY OF HAMPSHIRE. TOWN OF BELCHERTOWN.

KIND OF RECORDS.	Number of Volumes	In Keeping of—	Years Covered	Whether Indexed	Condition
Town proceedings, . . .	5	Town Clerk	1740–1885	No	–[2]
Births, marriages, and deaths,	1	Town Clerk	1844–1856	–	–
Births, ...	2	Town Clerk	1784–1844 / 1856–1885	No / Yes	–
Marriages, ...	2	Town Clerk	1784–1844 / 1856–1885	No / Yes	–
Deaths, ...	2	Town Clerk	1784–1844 / 1856–1885	No / Yes	–
Marriage intentions, . .	1	Town Clerk	–	Yes	–
Assessors, ...	73	Assessors	1797–1885[3]	–	–
Miscellaneous, ...	4	Town Clerk	1841–1885	No	Good

1761. June 30. Prov. Laws, Vol. IV., p. 464. The plantation called Cold Spring established as "Belcher's Town."

1771. June 22. Prov. Laws, Vol. V., p. 155. Part of Belchertown annexed to Greenwich.

1788. June 16. Part of Belchertown annexed to Pelham.

1816. Feb. 15. Parts of Belchertown and Greenwich established as Enfield.

COUNTY OF HAMPSHIRE. TOWN OF CHESTERFIELD.

KIND OF RECORDS.	Number of Volumes	In Keeping of—	Years Covered	Whether Indexed	Condition
Town proceedings, ...	5	Town Clerk	1762–1885	No	Fair
Births, marriages, and deaths, .	3	Town Clerk	1762–1885	–	Fair
Assessors, ...	–	–	–	–	–
Selectmen, ...	1	Selectmen	–	–	–
Parish, ...	1	Town Clerk	1847–1865	–	–
Miscellaneous, ...	6	Town Clerk	1762–1885	No	Fair

[1] There is a copy also of the records from 1735 to 1788.

[2] A part of the records prior to 1800 are in poor condition and some of the pages are missing.

[3] The records of the assessors for 1804 are missing.

TOWN RECORDS — Continued.

COUNTY OF HAMPSHIRE.   TOWN OF CHESTERFIELD — Con.

1762. June 11. Prov. Laws, Vol. IV., p. 573. The new plantation called New Hingham established as Chesterfield.
1763. Jan. 31. Prov. Laws, Vol. IV., p. 625. Certain common lands called the Second Addition to the township called Number Four annexed to Chesterfield.
1789. June 8. Part of Goshen annexed to Chesterfield.
1794. Feb. 22. Part of Norwich annexed to Chesterfield.
1795. June 24. Bounds between Chesterfield and Williamsburg established.
1797. Feb. 7. Bounds between Chesterfield and Williamsburg established.
1810. Feb. 16. Bounds between Chesterfield, Goshen, and Williamsburg established.

COUNTY OF HAMPSHIRE.   TOWN OF CUMMINGTON.

KIND OF RECORDS.	Number of Volumes	In Keeping of—	Years Covered	Whether Indexed	Condition
Town proceedings, . . .	4	Town Clerk	1762–1885	No	Good
Births, marriages, and deaths,	3	Town Clerk	1762–1885	Yes	Good
Assessors, ...	–	Assessors	–	–	–
Selectmen, ...	3	Selectmen	–	–	–
Parish, ...	1	Town Clerk	1833–1845	No	Good
Proprietors, ...	1[1]	Town Clerk	1762–1804	No	Good
Miscellaneous, ...	4	Town Clerk	1762–1885	Yes	Good

1779. June 23. Prov. Laws, Vol. V., p. 1072. Part of the plantation called Number Five established as Cummington.
1785. Mar. 16. Part of Cummington established as the district of Plainfield.
1788. Mar. 21. Certain common lands called Murrayfield Grant and Minot's Grant, and a gore of 2200 acres "lately sold by the Commonwealth," all lying between Ashfield, Chesterfield, Cummington, and Goshen, annexed to Cummington.
1794. Feb. 4. Part of Cummington annexed to Plainfield.

COUNTY OF HAMPSHIRE.   TOWN OF EASTHAMPTON.

KIND OF RECORDS.	Number of Volumes	In Keeping of—	Years Covered	Whether Indexed	Condition
Town proceedings, . . .	5	Town Clerk	1785–1885	No	Fair
Births, marriages, and deaths,	1	Town Clerk	1844–1864	No	Fair
Births, ...	1	Town Clerk	1865–1885	No	Fair
Marriages, ...	1	Town Clerk	1865–1885	No	Fair
Deaths, ...	1	Town Clerk	1865–1885	No	Fair
Selectmen and Assessors, .	–	–	–	–	–
Soldiers in the Rebellion, .	1	Town Clerk	1862–1864	No	Fair

1785. June 17. Parts of Northampton and Southampton established as the district of Easthampton.
1809. June 16. District of Easthampton made the town of Easthampton.
1828. Feb. 1. Bounds between Easthampton and Southampton established.
1841. Mar. 13. Part of Southampton annexed to Easthampton.
1850. April 4. Part of Southampton annexed to Easthampton.
1862. Feb. 21. Bounds between Easthampton and Southampton established.
1872. Mar. 12. Bounds between Easthampton and Westhampton established.

---

[1] There is also a copy.

Town Records — Continued.

County of Hampshire. Town of Enfield.

KIND OF RECORDS.	Number of Volumes	In Keeping of —	Years Covered	Whether Indexed	Condition
Town proceedings, ...	4	Town Clerk	1816–1885	No	Fair
Births, marriages, and deaths,	1	Town Clerk	1844–1859[1]	No	Fair
Births, ...	1	Town Clerk	1874–1885	–	Fair
Marriages, ...	1	Town Clerk	1858–1885	–	Fair
Deaths, ...	1	Town Clerk	1858–1885	–	Fair
Assessors, ...	–			–	–
Selectmen, ...	2	Selectmen	1844–1885[2]	–	–
Miscellaneous, ...	7	Town Clerk	1816–1885	Partially	Fair

1816. Feb. 15. All the lands in Belchertown and Greenwich which are comprised within the South Parish of Greenwich, together with the farm of Robert Hathaway in said Greenwich, established as Enfield.

1818. June 12. Bounds between Enfield and Greenwich established and part of each town annexed to the other town.

County of Hampshire. Town of Goshen.

KIND OF RECORDS.	Number of Volumes	In Keeping of —	Years Covered	Whether Indexed	Condition
General, ...	3	Town Clerk	1781–1885	No	–
Births, marriages, and deaths,	2[3]	Town Clerk	1844–1885	Yes	–
Selectmen and Assessors, .	30	Selectmen	–	–	–
Miscellaneous, . . .	6	Town Clerk	1781–1885	No	–

1781. May 14. Part of Chesterfield and the plantation called Chesterfield Gore established as "Goshan."

1785. Feb. 9. Part of Conway annexed to Goshen.

1789. June 8. Part of Goshen annexed to Chesterfield.

1795. June 24. Bounds between Goshen and Williamsburg established.

1797. Feb. 7. Bounds between Goshen and Williamsburg established.

1810 Feb. 16. Bounds between Goshen, Chesterfield, and Williamsburg established.

County of Hampshire. Town of Granby.

KIND OF RECORDS.	Number of Volumes	In Keeping of —	Years Covered	Whether Indexed	Condition
Town proceedings, . . .	5	Town Clerk	1769–1885	–	–[4]
Births, ...	1	Town Clerk	1860–1885	–	–
Marriages, ...	1	Town Clerk	1860–1885	–	–
Deaths, ...	1	Town Clerk	1860–1885	–	–
Assessors, ...	–	Town Clerk	1850–1885	–	–
Proprietors, ...	2	Town Clerk	–	–	–

[1] The record of births is continued in this volume until 1874.

[2] Prior to 1844 the records were kept upon scraps of paper.

[3] There are a few omissions of years in the records of births, marriages, and deaths, but they are so scattered through the general records that the missing years cannot be given. A. B. Dresser has a diary containing a record of births, marriages, and deaths since 1868.

[4] The earlier volumes are in poor condition.

Town Records — Continued.

County of Hampshire. Town of Granby — Con.

1768. June 11. Prov. Laws, Vol. IV., p. 1011. Part of South Hadley established as Granby.
1781. June 28. Bounds between Granby and South Hadley established.
1792. Mar.   9. Part of South Hadley annexed to Granby.
1824. June 12. Bounds between Granby and South Hadley established.
1826. June 20. Bounds between Granby and South Hadley established.
1827. June 16. Bounds between Granby and South Hadley established.

County of Hampshire. Town of Greenwich.

Kind of Records.	Number of Volumes	In Keeping of—	Years Covered	Whether Indexed	Condition
Town proceedings, . . .	3	Town Clerk	1805–1885	No	Good
Births, marriages, and deaths,	3	Town Clerk	1805–1885	Yes	Good
Assessors, ...	–	–	–	–	–
Parish, ...	1	Town Clerk	1749–1782	No	Good
Proprietors, ...	1	Town Clerk	1733–1783	No	Good

1754. April 20. Prov. Laws, Vol. III., p. 730. The plantation called Quabin established as Greenwich.
1771. June 22. Prov. Laws, Vol. V., p. 155. Part of Belchertown annexed to Greenwich.
1801. Feb. 18. Parts of Greenwich, Hardwick, and Petersham established as Dana.
1811. June 19. Bounds between Greenwich and Dana established.
1816. Feb. 15. Parts of Greenwich and Belchertown established as Enfield.
1818. June 12. Bounds between Greenwich and Enfield established and part of each town annexed to the other town.

County of Hampshire. Town of Hadley.

Kind of Records.	Number of Volumes	In Keeping of—	Years Covered	Whether Indexed	Condition
Town proceedings, . . .	5[1]	Town Clerk	1661–1885	No	Good
Births, marriages, and deaths,	3[2]	Town Clerk	1661–1885	Yes	Good
Assessors, ...	–	–	–	–	–
Proprietors, ...	–[3]	Town Clerk	1689–1702	No	Good

1661. May 22. Mass. Rec., Vol. IV., Part 2, p. 11. The new plantation near Northampton established as Hadley.
1663. Oct. 21. Mass. Rec., Vol. IV., Part 2, p. 96. Bounds of Hadley established.
1664. May 18. Mass. Rec., Vol. IV., Part 2, p. 106. Certain common lands granted to Hadley.
1670. May ʼ31. Mass. Rec., Vol. IV., Part 2, p. 460. Part of Hadley established as Hatfield.
1673. May   7. Mass. Rec., Vol. IV., Part 2, p. 557. Certain common lands granted to Hadley.

---

[1] All the records prior to 1800 have been copied.

[2] A record of the births, marriages, and deaths in Hadley from 1655 to 1843 is in possession of the Town Clerk of Hatfield.

[3] There is a copy also in the Registry of Deeds at Northampton.

Town Records — Continued.

County of Hampshire. Town of Hadley — Con.

1683. **May** 16. Mass. Rec., Vol. V., p. 410. Certain common lands granted to Hadley.
1740. **Jan.** 2. Resolve. Bounds between Hadley and Sunderland established.
1753. **April** 12. Prov. Laws, Vol. III., p. 655. Part of Hadley made the district of South Hadley.
1759. **Feb.** 13. Prov. Laws, Vol. IV., p. 173. Part of Hadley established as the district of Amherst.
1789. **Jan.** 15. Part of Hadley annexed to Amherst.
1811. **Feb.** 28. Part of Hadley annexed to Amherst.
1812. **Feb.** 18. Part of Hadley annexed to Amherst.
1814. **Feb.** 17. Part of Hadley annexed to Amherst.
1815. **Mar.** 1. Bounds between Amherst and Hadley established and part of each town annexed to the other town.
1850. **April** 15. Part of Hadley annexed to Northampton.

County of Hampshire. Town of Hatfield.

Kind of Records.	Number of Volumes	In Keeping of —	Years Covered	Whether Indexed	Condition
Town proceedings, . . .	7	Town Clerk	1662–1885	No	–[1]
Births, marriages, and deaths,	4[2]	Town Clerk	1655–1885	No	–
Selectmen and Assessors, .	98	Selectmen	–	–	–
Proprietors, ...	2[3]	Town Clerk	1671–1767	No	–

1670. **May** 31. Mass. Rec., Vol. IV., Part 2, p. 460. Part of Hadley established as " Hattfeilds."
1672. **Oct.** 9. Mass. Rec., Vol. IV., Part 2, p. 540. Bounds of Hatfield established.
1771. **April** 24. Prov. Laws, Vol. V., p. 122. Part of Hatfield established as Whately.
1771. **April** 24. Prov. Laws, Vol. V., p. 125. Part of Hatfield and certain common lands established as the district of Williamsburg.
1845. **Mar.** 14. Bounds between Williamsburg and Hatfield established and part of each town annexed to the other town.
1846. **Mar.** 19. Bounds between Williamsburg and Hatfield established and part of each town annexed to the other town.

County of Hampshire. Town of Huntington.

Kind of Records.	Number of Volumes	In Keeping of —	Years Covered	Whether Indexed	Condition
Town proceedings, . . .	4	Town Clerk	1773–1885	No	Good
Births, marriages, and deaths,	6	Town Clerk	1773–1885	Yes	Good
Selectmen and Assessors,	66	Selectmen	–	–	–
Miscellaneous, ...	7	Town Clerk	1773–1885	No	Good

1855. **Mar.** 9. The name of the town of Norwich[4] changed to Huntington.

[1] The first volume, which is in poor condition, has been partly copied.
[2] There is one volume also of records of births, marriages, and deaths in Northampton, Hadley, and Hatfield from 1655 to 1843. Mrs. S. G. Hubbard has a private record of deaths from 1798 to 1885.
[3] There are copies also in the Registry of Deeds at Northampton, and a copy of one volume covering the years from 1712 to 1735 in possession of James M. Crafts of Whately.
[4] For legislation concerning the town of Norwich, see " Extinct Cities, Towns, and Districts."

TOWN RECORDS — Continued.

COUNTY OF HAMPSHIRE. TOWN OF MIDDLEFIELD.

KIND OF RECORDS.	Number of Volumes	In Keeping of —	Years Covered	Whether Indexed	Condition
Town proceedings, . . .	6	Town Clerk	1783–1885	No	Fair
Births, marriages, and deaths,	7	Town Clerk	1783–1885	Partially	Fair
Assessors, ...	25	Assessors	–	–	–
Miscellaneous, ...	4	Town Clerk	1783–1854	No	Fair

1783. Mar. 12. Parts of Becket, Chester, Partridgefield, Washington, and Worthington, and the common lands called Prescott's Grants, established as Middlefield.

COUNTY OF HAMPSHIRE. CITY OF NORTHAMPTON.

KIND OF RECORDS.	Number of Volumes	In Keeping of —	Years Covered	Whether Indexed	Condition
Town proceedings, . . .	8	City Clerk	1653–1883	No	Fair
City proceedings, . . .	3	City Clerk	1884–1885	Yes	Fair
Births, marriages, and deaths (town), ...	10	City Clerk	1653–1883	No	Fair
Births, marriages, and deaths (city), ...	3	City Clerk	1884–1885	Yes	Fair
Assessors, . . .	77	City Clerk and Assessors	–	No	–
Proprietors, . . .	3[1]	City Clerk	1653–1731 1757–1775 1800–1839	No	Fair
Miscellaneous, . . .	117	City Clerk	1654–1885	Partially	Fair

1656. May 14. Mass. Rec., Vol. IV., Part 1, p. 259. The towns of Springfield and North Hampton are mentioned.

1685. June 4. Mass. Rec., Vol V., p. 480. Bounds between Northampton and Springfield established.

1753. Jan. 5. Prov. Laws, Vol. III., p. 638. Part of Northampton established as Southampton.

1778. Sept. 29. Prov. Laws, Vol. V., p. 900. Part of Northampton established as Westhampton.

1778. Sept. 29. Prov. Laws, Vol. V., p. 901. Part of Northampton annexed to Southampton.

1785. June 17. Parts of Northampton and Southampton established as the district of Easthampton.

1850. April 15. Part of Hadley annexed to Northampton.

1872. Mar. 12. Bounds between Northampton and Westhampton established.

1883. June 23. Northampton incorporated as a city.

1883. Sept. 5. Act of incorporation accepted by the town.

---

[1] There are copies also in the Registry of Deeds at Northampton.

Town Records — Continued.

County of Hampshire. Town of Pelham.

Kind of Records.	Number of Volumes	In Keeping of —	Years Covered	Whether Indexed[1]	Condition
Town proceedings, . . .	6	Town Clerk	1738–1885	–	–[2]
Births, marriages, and deaths,	10	Town Clerk	1738–1885	–	–
Assessors, ...	–	–	–[3]	–	–
Selectmen, ...	2	Town Clerk	1862–1885[3]	–	–
Proprietors, ...	1	Town Clerk	1738–1767	–	–
Miscellaneous, ...	–	Town Clerk	1738–1885	–	–

1743. Jan. 15. Prov. Laws, Vol. III., p. 49. The common lands called New Lisburne established as Pelham.

1788. June 16. Part of Belchertown annexed to Pelham.

1822. Jan. 28. Parts of Pelham and New Salem established as Prescott.

County of Hampshire. Town of Plainfield.

Kind of Records.	Number of Volumes	In Keeping of —	Years Covered	Whether Indexed	Condition
Town proceedings, . . .	4	Town Clerk	1785–1885	Yes[4]	Good[5]
Births, marriages, and deaths,	6	Town Clerk	1845–1885	Yes	Good
Assessors, ...	52	Assessors			–
Soldiers in the Rebellion, .	1	Town Clerk	1861–1865	No	Good
Miscellaneous, ...	5	Town Clerk	1833–1885	No	Good

1785. Mar. 16. Part of Cummington established as the district of Plainfield.

1794. Feb. 4. Part of Cummington annexed to the district of Plainfield.

1803. June 21. Part of Hawley annexed to the district of Plainfield.

1807. June 15. District of Plainfield made the town of Plainfield.

County of Hampshire. Town of Prescott.[6]

Kind of Records.	Number of Volumes	In Keeping of —	Years Covered	Whether Indexed	Condition
Town proceedings, . . .	2	Town Clerk	1822–1885	No	Good
Births, marriages, and deaths,	5	Town Clerk	1822–1885	No	Good
Selectmen and Assessors, .	–	Selectmen			–
Miscellaneous, ...	2	Town Clerk	1822–1885	No	Good

1822. Jan. 28. Parts of Pelham and New Salem established as Prescott.

[1] A few volumes have been indexed.   [2] Some of the pages are missing.

[3] There are a few omissions of years in the records of selectmen and assessors.

[4] With the exception of the first volume.

[5] The first volume needs rebinding.

[6] See also "Prescott" under "Extinct Cities, Towns, and Districts."

Town Records — Continued.

County of Hampshire.   Town of South Hadley.

Kind of Records.	Number of Volumes	In Keeping of —	Years Covered	Whether Indexed	Condition
Town proceedings, . . .	2	Town Clerk	1753–1885	Yes	Fair
Births, marriages, and deaths,	7	Town Clerk	1753–1885	Yes	Fair
Assessors, ...	23	Town Clerk	–	–	–
Miscellaneous, ...	3	Town Clerk	1753–1885	Yes	Fair

1753. April 12. Prov. Laws, Vol. III., p. 655. Part of Hadley established as the district of South Hadley.

1768. June 11. Prov. Laws, Vol. IV., p. 1011. Part of the district of South Hadley established as Granby.

1775. Aug. 23. Prov. Laws, Vol. V., p. 419. District of South Hadley made the town of South Hadley by this general act.

1781. June 28. Bounds between South Hadley and Granby established.

1792. Mar. 9. Part of South Hadley annexed to Granby.

1824. June 12. Bounds between South Hadley and Granby established.

1826. June 20. Bounds between South Hadley and Granby established.

1827. June 16. Bounds between South Hadley and Granby established.

County of Hampshire.   Town of Southampton.

Kind of Records.	Number of Volumes	In Keeping of —	Years Covered	Whether Indexed	Condition
Town proceedings, . . .	6[1]	Town Clerk	1758–1885	Yes	Good[2]
Births, marriages, and deaths,	4[3]	Town Clerk	1758–1885	Yes	Good
Assessors, ...	25	Selectmen	1860–1885[4]	–	–
Selectmen, ...	3	Selectmen	–	–	–
Soldiers in the Rebellion, .	1	Town Clerk	1861–1865	Yes	Good
Miscellaneous, ...	3	Town Clerk	1758–1885	Yes	Good

1753. Jan. 5. Prov. Laws, Vol. III., p. 638. Part of Northampton established as the district of Southampton.

1775. Aug. 23. Prov. Laws, Vol. V., p. 419. District of Southampton made the town of Southampton by this general act.

1778. Sept. 29. Prov. Laws, Vol. V., p. 901. Part of Northampton annexed to Southampton.

1780. Nov. 28. Parts of Southampton, Norwich, and Westfield established as Montgomery.

1785. June 17. Parts of Southampton and Northampton established as the district of Easthampton.

1792. Mar. 6. Part of Southampton annexed to Montgomery.

1828. Feb. 1. Bounds between Southampton and Easthampton established.

1841. Mar. 13. Part of Southampton annexed to Easthampton.

1850. April 4. Part of Southampton annexed to Easthampton.

1862. Feb. 21. Bounds between Southampton and Easthampton established.

1872. Mar. 12. Bounds between Southampton and Westhampton established.

[1] There is a copy also of the first volume.

[2] With the exception of the first volume.

[3] Sardis Chapman has private records of births, marriages, and deaths.

[4] There are records of assessors prior to 1860, which are unbound.

TOWN RECORDS — Continued.
COUNTY OF HAMPSHIRE. TOWN OF WARE.

KIND OF RECORDS.	Number of Volumes	In Keeping of -	Years Covered	Whether Indexed	Condition
Town proceedings, . . .	5[1]	Town Clerk	1742–1885	No	Fair[2]
Births, marriages, and deaths,	4	Town Clerk	1742–1885	Yes	—[3]
Assessors, ...	55	Town Clerk	–	–	–
Selectmen, ...	2	Town Clerk	–	–	–
Miscellaneous, ...	2	Town Clerk	1837–1873	No	–

1761. Nov. 25. Prov. Laws, Vol. IV., p. 486. Ware-River Parish, so called, established as the district of Ware.

1775. Aug. 23. Prov. Laws, Vol. V., p. 419. District of Ware made the town of Ware by this general act.

1823. Feb. 8. Parts of Brookfield and Western annexed to Ware.

COUNTY OF HAMPSHIRE. TOWN OF WESTHAMPTON.

KIND OF RECORDS.	Number of Volumes	In Keeping of —	Years Covered	Whether Indexed	Condition
Town proceedings, . . .	4	Town Clerk	1778–1885	No	Fair
Births, marriages, and deaths,	10	Town Clerk	1808–1885[4]	Yes	Fair
Assessors, ...	54	Assessors	–	–	–
Miscellaneous, ...	4	Town Clerk	1841–1885	No	Fair

1778. Sept. 29. Prov. Laws, Vol. V., p. 900. Part of Northampton established as Westhampton.

1872. Mar. 12. Bounds between Westhampton and Easthampton, Northampton, and Southampton established.

COUNTY OF HAMPSHIRE. TOWN OF WILLIAMSBURG.

KIND OF RECORDS.	Number of Volumes	In Keeping of—	Years Covered	Whether Indexed	Condition
Town proceedings, . . .	5	Town Clerk	1771–1885	Yes	Fair
Births, marriages, and deaths,	4	Town Clerk	1771–1885	Yes	Fair
Assessors, ...	–	Town Clerk	1800–1885	–	–
Miscellaneous, ...	3	Town Clerk	1773–1885	Yes	Fair

1771. April 24. Prov. Laws, Vol. V., p. 125. Part of Hatfield and certain common lands adjoining established as the district of Williamsburg.

1775. Aug. 23. Prov. Laws, Vol. V., p. 419. District of Williamsburg made the town of Williamsburg by this general act.

[1] There is one copy of the first volume covering the years from 1742 to 1794 in possession of the Town Clerk, and one in possession of the Young Men's Library Association.

[2] The first volume is in certain portions nearly illegible.

[3] The records of births, marriages, and deaths prior to 1845 are imperfect.

[4] The records prior to 1808 have been destroyed, and those prior to 1844 are incomplete.

TOWN RECORDS — Continued.

COUNTY OF HAMPSHIRE.   TOWN OF WILLIAMSBURG — Con.

1795.	June 24.	Bounds between Williamsburg and Chesterfield and Goshen established.
1797.	Feb. 7.	Bounds between Williamsburg and Chesterfield and Goshen established.
1810.	Feb. 16.	Bounds between Williamsburg, Chesterfield, and Goshen established.
1845.	Mar. 14.	Bounds between Williamsburg and Hatfield established and part of each town annexed to the other town.
1846.	Mar. 19.	Bounds between Williamsburg and Hatfield established and part of each town annexed to the other town.
1849.	Feb. 2.	Resolve. Bounds between Williamsburg and Whately established.

COUNTY OF HAMPSHIRE.   TOWN OF WORTHINGTON.

KIND OF RECORDS.	Number of Volumes	In Keeping of —	Years Covered	Whether Indexed	Condition
Town proceedings, . . .	5	Town Clerk	1768–1885	No	–
Births, marriages, and deaths,	5	Town Clerk	1768–1885	Yes	–
Assessors, ...	–	Town Clerk	1785–1885	–	–
Miscellaneous, ...	15	Town Clerk	1768–1885	No	–

1768.	June 30.	Prov. Laws, Vol. IV., p. 1028. The new plantation called Number Three established as Worthington.
1783.	Mar. 12.	Parts of Worthington, Becket, Chester, Partridgefield, and Washington, and certain common lands, established as Middlefield.
1799.	June 21.	Part of Chester annexed to Worthington.

COUNTY OF MIDDLESEX.   TOWN OF ACTON.

KIND OF RECORDS.	Number of Volumes	In Keeping of —	Years Covered	Whether Indexed	Condition
Town proceedings, . . .	5	Town Clerk	1735–1885	No	–
Births, marriages, and deaths,	7[1]	Town Clerk	1735–1885[2]	No	–
Assessors, ...	–	–	–	–	–
Selectmen, ...	1	Selectmen	–	–	–
Selectmen, ...	1	Town Clerk	–	–	–
Miscellaneous, ...	5	Town Clerk	1803–1885	No	–

1735.	July 3.	Prov. Laws, Vol. II., p. 763. Part of Concord called " The Village," or " New Grant," with Willard's Farms, established as Acton.
1780.	April 28.	Parts of Acton, Billerica, Chelmsford, and Concord established as the district of Carlisle.

[1] There are indexed copies also of the first two volumes. Samuel Hosmer has private records of baptisms from 1737 to 1820.

[2] The record of marriages from 1735 to 1763 is omitted, but the marriage intentions for that period are recorded.

Town Records — Continued.

County of Middlesex. Town of Arlington.[1]

Kind of Records.	Number of Volumes	In Keeping of—	Years Covered	Whether Indexed	Condition
Town proceedings, . . .	5	Town Clerk	1807–1885	No	Fair
Births, marriages, and deaths,	4	Town Clerk	1807–1885	No	Fair
Assessors, ...	–	Town Clerk	–	–	–
Selectmen, ...	3	Selectmen	–	–	–

1867. April 13. The name of the town of West Cambridge[2] changed to Arlington.

1867. April 30. Act of April 13, 1867, took effect.

County of Middlesex. Town of Ashby.

Kind of Records.	Number of Volumes	In Keeping of—	Years Covered	Whether Indexed	Condition
Town proceedings, . . .	6[3]	Town Clerk	1767–1885	Since 1844	Fair
Births, marriages, and deaths,	4	Town Clerk	1767–1885	Since 1844	Fair
Assessors, ...	63	Selectmen	–	–	–

1767. Mar. 6. Prov. Laws, Vol. IV., p. 908. Parts of Ashburnham, Fitchburg, and Townsend established as Ashby.

1792. Nov. 16. Part of Ashburnham annexed to Ashby.

County of Middlesex. Town of Ashland.

Kind of Records.	Number of Volumes	In Keeping of—	Years Covered	Whether Indexed	Condition
Town proceedings, . . .	2	Town Clerk	1846–1885	No	Good
Births, ...	1	Town Clerk	1846–1885	Yes	Good
Marriages, ...	1	Town Clerk	1846–1885	Yes	Good
Deaths, ...	1[4]	Town Clerk	1846–1885	Yes	Good
Assessors, ...	40	Assessors	1846–1885	–	–
Selectmen, ...	1	Town Clerk	1885 –	–	–
Miscellaneous, . . .	15	Town Clerk	1846–1885	No	Good

1846. Mar. 16. Parts of Framingham, Holliston, and Hopkinton established as Ashland.

1853. April 28. Part of Ashland to be annexed to Hopkinton when a certain sum is paid by Hopkinton.

1853. May 2. Three hundred dollars paid by Hopkinton and the act of April 28, 1853, in effect.

---

[1] See also "the plantation of Arlington," in the notes to the town of Winchester, under "Extinct Cities, Towns, and Districts."

[2] For legislation concerning the town of West Cambridge, see "Extinct Cities, Towns, and Districts."

[3] The records prior to 1844 are being copied by the Town Clerk.

[4] There is also a copy.

TOWN RECORDS — Continued.

COUNTY OF MIDDLESEX. TOWN OF AYER.

KIND OF RECORDS.	Number of Volumes	In Keeping of—	Years Covered	Whether Indexed	Condition
Town proceedings, . . .	1	Town Clerk	1871–1885	Yes	Good
Births, ...	1	Town Clerk	1871–1885	Yes	Good
Marriages, ...	1	Town Clerk	1871–1885	Yes	Good
Deaths, ...	1	Town Clerk	1871–1885	Yes	Good
Selectmen and Assessors, .	15	Town Clerk	1871–1885	–	–
Miscellaneous, ...	4	Town Clerk	1871–1885	No	Good

1871. Feb. 14. Parts of Groton and Shirley established as Ayer.

COUNTY OF MIDDLESEX. TOWN OF BEDFORD.

KIND OF RECORDS.	Number of Volumes	In Keeping of—	Years Covered	Whether Indexed	Condition
Town proceedings, . . .	6	Town Clerk	1729–1885	No	Good
Births, marriages, and deaths,	4	Town Clerk	1729–1885	Since 1844	Good
Assessors,	74	Town Clerk	–	–	–
Selectmen, ...	2	Town Clerk	–	–	–
Selectmen, ...	1	Selectmen	–	–	–
Soldiers in the Rebellion, .	1	Town Clerk	–	No	Good
Miscellaneous, . . .	4	Town Clerk	1836–1885	No	Good

1729. Sept. 23. Prov. Laws, Vol. II., p. 527. Parts of Billerica and Concord established as Bedford.
1767. Feb. 26. Prov. Laws, Vol. IV., p. 906. Part of Billerica annexed to Bedford.

COUNTY OF MIDDLESEX. TOWN OF BELMONT.

KIND OF RECORDS.	Number of Volumes	In Keeping of—	Years Covered	Whether Indexed	Condition
General, ...	2	Town Clerk	1859–1885	Yes	Good
Births, ...	1	Town Clerk	1859–1885	Yes	Good
Marriages, ...	1	Town Clerk	1859–1885	Yes	Good
Deaths, ...	1	Town Clerk	1859–1885	Yes	Good
Assessors, ...	25	Assessors	1860–1885	–	–
Selectmen, ...	1	Selectmen	–	–	–
Miscellaneous, ...	1	Town Clerk	–	Yes	Good

1859. Mar. 18. Parts of Waltham, Watertown, and West Cambridge established as Belmont.
1861. Jan. 31. Bounds between Belmont and West Cambridge established.
1862. Feb. 25. Part of Cambridge annexed to Belmont and bounds established.
1880. April 19. Part of Belmont annexed to Cambridge.

TOWN RECORDS — Continued.

COUNTY OF MIDDLESEX. TOWN OF BILLERICA.

KIND OF RECORDS.	Number of Volumes	In Keeping of —	Years Covered	Whether Indexed	Condition
Town proceedings, . . .	12	Town Clerk	–	No	Good
Births, marriages, and deaths,	2	Town Clerk	–	No	Good
Selectmen and Assessors, .	50	Selectmen	–	–	–
Miscellaneous, ...	1	Town Clerk	–	No	Good

1655. May 29. Mass. Rec., Vol. IV., Part 1, p. 237. Certain proprietors and inhabitants of Shawshine granted a tract of land on Concord River, the name of the plantation to be " Billirikeyca."

1656. May 14. Mass. Rec., Vol. IV., Part 1, p. 263. " This court doth graunt the toune of Billirrikey eight thousand acres of land."

1657. May 15. Mass. Rec., Vol. IV., Part 1, p. 302. Lands granted to Billerica.

1658. May 26. Mass. Rec., Vol. IV., Part 1, p. 333. Bounds between Billerica and Andover established.

1661. June 7. Mass. Rec., Vol. IV., Part 2, p. 15. Four thousand acres of land granted to Billerica.

1666. Oct. 10. Mass. Rec., Vol. IV., Part 2, p. 325. Bounds between Billerica and Woburn established.

1729. Sept. 23. Prov. Laws, Vol. II., p. 527. Parts of Billerica and Concord established as Bedford.

1734. Dec. 17. Prov. Laws, Vol. II., p. 739. Part of Billerica established as Tewksbury.

1767. Feb. 26. Prov. Laws, Vol. IV., p. 906. Part of Billerica annexed to Bedford.

1780. April 28. Parts of Billerica, Acton, Chelmsford, and Concord established as the district of Carlisle.

COUNTY OF MIDDLESEX. TOWN OF BOXBOROUGH.

KIND OF RECORDS.	Number of Volumes	In Keeping of —	Years Covered	Whether Indexed	Condition
Town proceedings, . . .	4	Town Clerk	1783–1885	No	Good
Births, marriages, and deaths,	3	Town Clerk	1783–1885	Yes	Good
Assessors, ...	–	Assessors	–	–	–
Selectmen, ...	–	Selectmen	–	–	–
Miscellaneous, . . .	5	Town Clerk	1785–1885	No	Good

1783. Feb. 25. Parts of Harvard, Littleton, and Stow established as the district of Boxborough.

1794. Feb. 20. Bounds between Boxborough and Littleton established.

1836. May 1. District of Boxborough made the town of Boxborough by the provisions of chapter 15 of the Revised Statutes.

COUNTY OF MIDDLESEX. TOWN OF BURLINGTON.

KIND OF RECORDS.	Number of Volumes	In Keeping of —	Years Covered	Whether Indexed	Condition
Town proceedings, . . .	5	Town Clerk	1799–1885	No	Good
Births, marriages, and deaths,	5	Town Clerk	1799–1885	No	Good
Assessors, ...	–	Assessors	–	–	–
Selectmen, ...	1	Selectmen	–	–	–

1799. Feb. 28. Part of Woburn established as Burlington.

1800. Jan. 20. Part of Burlington annexed to Lexington.

TOWN RECORDS — Continued.

COUNTY OF MIDDLESEX. CITY OF CAMBRIDGE.

KIND OF RECORDS	Number of Volumes	In Keeping of —	Years Covered	Whether Indexed	Condition
Town proceedings, . . .	6[1]	City Clerk	1632–1845	No	Poor
City proceedings, . . .	18	City Clerk	1846–1885	Yes	Good
Births, marriages, and deaths,	18[2]	City Clerk	1632–1885	Yes	–
Assessors, ...	–	Assessors	–	–	–
Selectmen, ...	7	City Clerk	1769–1846	–	–
Proprietors, ...	1[3]	City Clerk	1634–1829	Yes	–
Soldiers in the Rebellion, .	1	City Clerk	1861–1866	No	–
Miscellaneous, ...	16[4]	City Clerk	1700–1885	No	–

1636.	Sept. 8.	Mass. Rec., Vol. I., p. 180. "Newe Towne[5] now called Cambridge."
1638.	May 2.	Mass. Rec., Vol. I., p. 228. "Ordered that Newetowne shall henceforward be called Cambridge."
1639.	Mar. 13.	Mass. Rec., Vol. I., p. 254. Bounds between Cambridge and Watertown established.
1641.	Oct. 7.	Mass. Rec., Vol. I., p. 342. Bounds between Cambridge and Boston established.
1659.	Nov 12.	Mass. Rec., Vol. IV., Part 1, p. 400. One thousand acres of land granted to Cambridge.
1664.	Oct. 19.	Mass. Rec., Vol. IV., Part 2, p. 138. The grant made November 12, 1659, renewed.
1712.	Mar. 20.	Resolve. Part of Cambridge established as Lexington.
1802.	Mar. 6.	Part of Charlestown annexed to Cambridge.
1807.	Feb. 27.	Part of Cambridge established as West Cambridge.
1820.	June 17.	Part of Charlestown annexed to Cambridge.
1846.	Mar. 17.	Cambridge incorporated as a city.
1846.	Mar. 30.	Act of incorporation accepted by the town.
1855.	April 27.	Part of Watertown annexed to Cambridge.
1856.	April 30.	Bounds between Cambridge and Somerville established and part of each place annexed to the other place.
1862.	Feb. 25.	Parts of Belmont and West Cambridge annexed to Cambridge, parts of Cambridge annexed to Belmont and West Cambridge, and bounds established.
1862.	April 29.	Bounds between Cambridge and Somerville established and part of each place annexed to the other place.
1880.	April 19.	Part of Belmont annexed to Cambridge.
1885.	Mar. 10.	Part of Watertown annexed to Cambridge.

COUNTY OF MIDDLESEX. TOWN OF CARLISLE.[6]

KIND OF RECORDS.	Number of Volumes	In Keeping of—	Years Covered	Whether Indexed	Condition
Town proceedings, . . .	9	Town Clerk	1755–1885	First 2 vols.	Good
Births, marriages, and deaths,	5	Town Clerk	1755–1885	No	Good
Selectmen and Assessors, .	27	Town Clerk	–	–	–

---

[1] There are copies also of the first three volumes.

[2] There is a copy also of the record of births, marriages, and deaths from 1632 to 1690. See foot-note to the records of births, marriages, and deaths in Boston.   [3] There is also a copy.

[4] One volume has been lost. There is a quantity of books, parts of books, and miscellaneous papers in the cellar of the City Hall.

[5] For legislation concerning the town of Newtowne, see "Extinct Cities, Towns, and Districts."

[6] For legislation concerning the first district of Carlisle, see "Extinct Cities, Towns, and Districts."

Town Records — Continued.

County of Middlesex. Town of Carlisle — Con.

1780. April 28. Parts of Acton, Billerica, Chelmsford, and Concord established as the district of Carlisle.

1780. Sept. 12. Part of the district of Carlisle annexed to Concord.

1783. Mar. 1. Part of the district of Carlisle annexed to Chelmsford.

1805. Feb. 18. District of Carlisle made the town of Carlisle.

1865. Feb. 17. Part of Chelmsford annexed to Carlisle and bounds established.

County of Middlesex. Town of Chelmsford.

Kind of Records.	Number of Volumes	In Keeping of—	Years Covered	Whether Indexed	Condition
Town proceedings, . . .	25	Town Clerk	1655–1885	Yes[1]	Good[1]
Births, marriages, and deaths,	3[2]	Town Clerk	1800–1885	Yes	Good
Assessors, ...	78	Town Clerk	–	–	–
Parish, ...	1	Town Clerk	1741–1872	Yes	Good
Miscellaneous, ...	10	Town Clerk	1867–1885	Yes	Good

1655. May 29. Mass. Rec., Vol. IV., Part 1, p. 237. A new plantation "the name thereof to be called Chelmsford" is mentioned.

1660. May 31. Mass. Rec., Vol. IV., Part 1, p. 430. Bounds between Chelmsford and the Indian plantation at Patucket established.

1729. Sept. 23. Prov. Laws., Vol. II., p. 528. Part of Chelmsford established as Westford.

1780. April 28. Parts of Chelmsford, Acton, Billerica, and Concord made the district of Carlisle.

1783. Mar. 1. Part of the district of Carlisle annexed to Chelmsford.

1826. Mar. 1. Part of Chelmsford established as Lowell.

1865. Feb. 17. Part of Chelmsford annexed to Carlisle and bounds established.

1874. May 18. Part of Chelmsford annexed to Lowell.

1874. June 23. Act of May 18, 1874, accepted by Lowell.

1874. Aug. 1. Act of May 18, 1874, took effect.

County of Middlesex. Town of Concord.

Kind of Records.	Number of Volumes	In Keeping of—	Years Covered	Whether Indexed	Condition
Town proceedings, . . .	9[3]	Town Clerk	1635–1885 / 1649–1693	1834–1885	–[4]
Births, marriages, and deaths,	3[5]	Town Clerk	1788–1850	No	–
Births, ...	1	Town Clerk	1850–1885	–	–
Marriages, ...	1	Town Clerk	1850–1885	–	–
Deaths, ...	1	Town Clerk	1850–1885	–	–
Marriage intentions, .	1	Town Clerk	1850–1885	–	–
Assessors, ...	89	Town Clerk	1796–1885	–	–
Selectmen, ...	1	Selectmen	1855–1885	–	–
Miscellaneous, . . .	6[6]	Town Clerk	–	Partially	–

[1] With the exception of the first volume, of which all that was legible was copied in 1741.

[2] There are three volumes also containing records of marriages and deaths from 1655 to 1800 copied from the records of town proceedings.

[3] One volume is being copied.   [4] The records from 1635 to 1696 are incomplete.

[5] See foot-note to records of births, marriages, and deaths in Boston. There are three volumes containing records of births, marriages, and deaths which were copied from the earlier records of town proceedings. There is a volume also containing the maiden names of married women, with a reference to the pages upon which their marriages are recorded. The Town Clerk has private records of births, marriages, and deaths.

[6] These include a copy of a volume containing records of divisions of lands from 16— to 17—.

TOWN RECORDS — Continued.

COUNTY OF MIDDLESEX.   TOWN OF CONCORD — Con.

1635.   Sept.   3.   Mass. Rec., Vol. I., p. 157.   "Ordered, that there shall be a plantation at Musketequid * * * and the name of the place is changed and hereafter to be called Concord."

1638.   June   8.   Mass. Rec., Vol. I., p. 230.   Bounds between Concord, Dedham, and Watertown established.

1729.   Sept. 23.   Prov. Laws, Vol. II., p. 527.   Parts of Concord and Billerica established as Bedford.

1735.   July   3.   Prov. Laws, Vol. II., p. 763.   Part of Concord with Willard's Farms established as Acton.

1754.   April 19.   Prov. Laws, Vol. III., p. 728.   Parts of Concord, Lexington, and Weston established as Lincoln.

1754.   April 19.   Prov. Laws, Vol. III., p. 729.   Part of Concord made the district of Carlisle.

1756.   Oct.   6.   Mass. Archives, Vol. CXVII., p. 206.   District of Carlisle annexed to Concord.

1780.   April 28.   Parts of Concord, Acton, Billerica and Chelmsford established as the district of Carlisle.

1780.   Sept. 12.   Part of the district of Carlisle annexed to Concord.

COUNTY OF MIDDLESEX.   TOWN OF DRACUT.

KIND OF RECORDS.	Number of Volumes	In Keeping of —	Years Covered	Whether Indexed	Condition
Town proceedings, . . .	8	Town Clerk	1711–1819[1] 1831–1885	No	Fair
Births, marriages, and deaths,	9	Town Clerk	1711–1885	No	Fair
Selectmen and Assessors, .	12	Selectmen	1769–1857	–	–
Proprietors, ...	1	Gayton M. Hall	1715–1733	–	–

1701.   Feb.   26.   Resolve. The tract of land called Dracut beyond Chelmsford established as Dracut.

1851.   Feb.   28.   Part of Dracut annexed to Lowell.

1874.   May   18.   Part of Dracut annexed to Lowell.

1874.   June   23.   Act of May 18, 1874, accepted by Lowell.

1874.   Aug.   1.   Act of May 18, 1874, took effect.

1879.   April   1.   Part of Dracut annexed to Lowell.

COUNTY OF MIDDLESEX.   TOWN OF DUNSTABLE.[2]

KIND OF RECORDS.	Number of Volumes	In Keeping of —	Years Covered	Whether Indexed	Condition
Town proceedings, . . .	5[3]	Town Clerk	1743–1885	No	–
Births, marriages, and deaths,	7	Town Clerk	1743–1885	Since 1844	–
Selectmen and Assessors, .	5	Town Clerk	–	–	–
Miscellaneous, . . .	5	Town Clerk	–	Since 1844	–

[1] One volume is lost.

[2] 1673. Oct. 17. Mass. Rec., Vol. IV., Part 2, p. 570. Certain men were empowered to begin a plantation beyond Chelmsford and Groton but no name is given to it. A marginal note in the record says " a plantation about Groaton, called Dunstable."

[3] There is also a copy.

Town Records — Continued.

County of Middlesex. Town of Dunstable — Con.

1680.	Oct.	13.	Mass. Rec., Vol. V., p. 295. Dunstable is mentioned in a military list.
1733.	Jan.	4.	Prov. Laws, Vol. II., p. 660. Part of Dunstable established as Nottingham (N. H.).
1735.	July	4.	Prov. Laws, Vol. II., p. 720. Part of Dunstable and certain common lands established as Litchfield (N. H.).
1789.	June	22.	Part of Dunstable established as the district of Tyngsborough.
1792.	Mar.	3.	Part of Dunstable annexed to the district of Tyngsborough.
1793.	Feb.	25.	Part of Groton annexed to Dunstable.
1796.	Jan.	26.	Part of Groton annexed to Dunstable.
1798.	Jan.	29.	Bounds between Dunstable and the district of Tyngsborough established.
1803.	June	18.	Part of Groton annexed to Dunstable.
1814.	June	10.	Bounds between Dunstable and Tyngsborough established.
1820.	Feb.	15.	Bounds between Dunstable and Groton established.

County of Middlesex. Town of Everett.

Kind of Records.	Number of Volumes	In Keeping of —	Years Covered	Whether Indexed	Condition
Town proceedings, . . .	3	Town Clerk	1870–1885	No	Good
Births, ...	1	Town Clerk	1870–1885	Yes	Fair
Marriages, ...	1	Town Clerk	1870–1885	Yes	Fair
Deaths, ...	1	Town Clerk	1870–1885	Yes	Fair
Assessors, ...	16	Town Clerk	1870–1885	–	–
Selectmen, ...	2	Town Clerk	1870–1885	–	–
Miscellaneous, . . .	4	Town Clerk	1870–1885	Yes	Good

1870.	Mar.	9.	Part of Malden established as Everett.
1875.	April	20.	Part of Everett annexed to Medford.

County of Middlesex. Town of Framingham.

Kind of Records	Number of Volumes	In Keeping of —	Years Covered	Whether Indexed	Condition
Town proceedings, . . .	7	Town Clerk	1701–1885	No	Good
Births, marriages, and deaths,	5	Town Clerk	1701–1885	Yes	Good
Assessors, ...	26	Assessors	–	–	–
Selectmen, ...	1	Selectmen	–	–	–
Miscellaneous, . . .	10	Town Clerk	1701–1885	Partially	Good

1675.	Oct.	13.	Mass. Rec., Vol. V., p. 56. "Fremingham" is mentioned in the Tax Act.
1700.	June	25.	Resolve. The plantation of Framingham established as Framingham.
1700.	July	5.	Resolve. Certain common lands annexed to Framingham.
1786.	Mar.	7.	Part of Framingham annexed to Southborough.
1791.	Feb.	23.	Part of Framingham annexed to Marlborough.
1833.	Feb.	11.	Part of Holliston annexed to Framingham.
1846.	Mar.	16.	Parts of Framingham, Holliston, and Hopkinton established as Ashland.
1871.	April	22.	Part of Natick annexed to Framingham.

TOWN RECORDS — Continued.

COUNTY OF MIDDLESEX. TOWN OF GROTON.

KIND OF RECORDS.	Number of Volumes	In Keeping of —	Years Covered	Whether Indexed	Condition
Town proceedings, . . .	8[1]	Town Clerk	1662–1885	Partially	–[2]
Births, marriages, and deaths,	8	Town Clerk	1662–1885[3]	No	Good
Selectmen and Assessors, .	28	Town Clerk	–	–	–
Proprietors, ...	5	Town Clerk	1683–1829	No	Good
Miscellaneous, ...	26	Town Clerk	1805–1885	No	Good

1655. May 29. Mass. Rec., Vol. IV., Part 1, p. 235. A plantation formerly called Petapawag established as "Groten."

1732. June 29. Prov. Laws, Vol. II., p. 644. Parts of Groton, Lancaster, and Stow established as Harvard.

1753. Jan. 5. Prov. Laws, Vol. III., p. 637. Part of Groton established as the district of Shirley.

1753. April 12. Prov. Laws, Vol. III., p. 652. Part of Groton made the district of Pepperell.

1793. Feb. 25. Part of Groton annexed to Dunstable.

1796. Jan. 26. Part of Groton annexed to Dunstable.

1798. Feb. 6. Part of Groton annexed to Shirley.

1803. Feb. 3. Part of Pepperell annexed to Groton.

1803. June 18. Part of Groton annexed to Dunstable.

1820. Feb. 15. Bounds between Groton and Dunstable established.

1857. May 18. Part of Groton annexed to Pepperell.

1871. Feb. 14. Parts of Groton and Shirley established as Ayer.

COUNTY OF MIDDLESEX. TOWN OF HOLLISTON.

KIND OF RECORDS.	Number of Volumes	In Keeping of —	Years Covered	Whether Indexed	Condition
Town proceedings, . . .	9	Town Clerk	1724–1885	Partially	Good
Births, marriages, and deaths,	6[4]	Town Clerk	1724–1885	–	Good
Assessors, ...	61	Assessors	–	–	–
Miscellaneous, ...	20	Town Clerk	1724–1885	–	Good

1724. Dec. 3. Prov. Laws, Vol. II., p. 340. Part of Sherborn established as Holliston.

1781. April 28. Part of Hopkinton annexed to Holliston.

1829. Mar. 3. Part of Medway annexed to Holliston and bounds established.

1833. Feb. 11. Part of Holliston annexed to Framingham.

1835. Mar. 27. Part of Holliston annexed to Milford.

1846. Mar. 16. Parts of Holliston, Framingham, and Hopkinton established as Ashland.

1859. April 1. Bounds between Holliston and Milford established.

---

[1] There are copies also of the first two volumes, and a copy of the first volume has been printed. Two volumes of town records covering the years from 1761 to 1826 have been discovered and obtained by Samuel A. Green, M.D., and deposited with the Town Clerk since the return made by him in 1885.

[2] The first three volumes are badly worn; the other volumes are in good condition.

[3] The records of marriages are omitted from 1775 to 1778.

[4] There are copies also of the earlier records.

TOWN RECORDS — Continued.

COUNTY OF MIDDLESEX. TOWN OF HOPKINTON.

KIND OF RECORDS.	Number of Volumes	In Keeping of —	Years Covered	Whether Indexed	Condition
Town proceedings, . . .	5[1]	Town Clerk	–	No	Fair
Births, marriages, and deaths,	4	Town Clerk	–	Partially	Fair
Assessors, ...	5	Assessors	–	–	–
Proprietors, ...	–	—[2]	–	–	–

1715. Dec. 13. Resolve. Certain common lands and the plantation called Moguncoy established as Hopkinton.

1735. June 14. Prov. Laws, Vol. II., p. 764. Parts of Hopkinton, Mendon, Sutton, and Uxbridge established as Upton.

1781. April 28. Part of Hopkinton annexed to Holliston.

1808. Mar. 8. Part of Hopkinton annexed to Upton.

1835. Mar. 27. Part of Milford annexed to Hopkinton, part of Hopkinton annexed to Milford, and bounds between Hopkinton, Holliston, and Milford established.

1846. Mar. 16. Parts of Hopkinton, Framingham, and Holliston established as Ashland.

1853. April 28. Part of Ashland to be annexed to Hopkinton when a certain sum is paid by Hopkinton.

1853. May 2. Three hundred dollars paid by Hopkinton and the act in effect.

COUNTY OF MIDDLESEX. TOWN OF HUDSON.

KIND OF RECORDS.	Number of Volumes	In Keeping of —	Years Covered	Whether Indexed	Condition
Town proceedings, . . .	1	Town Clerk	1866–1885	No	Good
Births, marriages, and deaths,	3	Town Clerk	1866–1885	Yes	Good
Assessors, ...	19	Town Clerk	1866–1885	–	–
Selectmen, ...	2	Town Clerk	1866–1885	–	–
Miscellaneous, ...	10	Town Clerk	1866–1885	Partially	Good

1866. Mar. 19. Parts of Marlborough and Stow established as Hudson.

1868. Mar. 20. Part of Bolton annexed to Hudson.

COUNTY OF MIDDLESEX. TOWN OF LEXINGTON.

KIND OF RECORDS.	Number of Volumes	In Keeping of —	Years Covered	Whether Indexed	Condition
Town proceedings, . . .	9[1]	Town Clerk	1692–1885	No	Fair
Births, marriages, and deaths,	5[3]	Town Clerk	1677–1885	No	Fair
Assessors, ...	10	Assessors	1820–1885[4]	–	–
Selectmen, ...	5	Selectmen	–	–	–
Miscellaneous, ...	15	Town Clerk	1749–1885	No	Fair

[1] There are copies also of the first two volumes.

[2] The proprietors records are deposited in the Registry of Deeds at East Cambridge.

[3] There is a copy also of the records of births, marriages, and deaths from 1677 to 1844. Henry G. Clark, M.D., Boston, has a private record kept by Rev. Jonas Clark, a former pastor of the First Church. [4] The records prior to 1820 are unbound.

TOWN RECORDS — Continued.

COUNTY OF MIDDLESEX.   TOWN OF LEXINGTON — Con.

1712.   Mar.   20.   Resolve. The North Precinct in Cambridge established as Lexington.
1754.   April 19.   Prov. Laws, Vol. III., p. 728. Parts of Lexington, Concord, and Weston
                     established as Lincoln.
1800.   Jan.   20.   Part of Burlington annexed to Lexington.
1853.   Feb.   28.   Bounds between Lexington and Lincoln established.

COUNTY OF MIDDLESEX.   TOWN OF LINCOLN.

KIND OF RECORDS.	Number of Volumes	In Keeping of—	Years Covered	Whether Indexed	Condition
Town proceedings, . . .	4	Town Clerk	1754–1885	No	Fair
Births, marriages, and deaths,	3[1]	Town Clerk	1754–1885	No	Fair
Assessors,	–	Assessors	–	–	–
Proprietors, ...	1	–	1747–1754	–	–
Miscellaneous, ...	10	Town Clerk	1754–1885	No	Fair

1754.   April 19.   Prov. Laws, Vol. III., p. 728. Parts of Concord, Lexington, and Weston
                     established as Lincoln.
1853.   Féb.   28.   Bounds between Lincoln and Lexington established.

COUNTY OF MIDDLESEX.   TOWN OF LITTLETON.

KIND OF RECORDS.	Number of Volumes	In Keeping of—	Years Covered	Whether Indexed	Condition
Town proceedings, . . .	5	Town Clerk	1715–1885	No	Fair
Births, marriages, and deaths,	7[2]	Town Clerk	1715–1885	No	Fair
Assessors, ...	40	Assessors	–	–	–
Proprietors.	1	Town Clerk	– 1715	No	Fair

1715.   Dec.   3.   Resolve. The ownership of a grant made November 2, 1714, is corrected,
                    and it is "ordered that the name of the township be henceforth
                    called Littleton."
1783.   Feb.   25.   Parts of Littleton, Harvard, and Stow established as the district of Box-
                     borough.
1794.   Feb.   20.   Bounds between Littleton and Boxborough established.

COUNTY OF MIDDLESEX.   CITY OF LOWELL.

KIND OF RECORDS.	Number of Volumes	In Keeping of—	Years Covered	Whether Indexed	Condition
Town proceedings, . . .	1	Town Clerk	1826–1836	Yes	Good
City proceedings . . .	14	Town Clerk	1836–1885	Yes	Good
Births, marriages, and deaths,	1	Town Clerk	1826–1843	Yes	Good
Births, ...	7	Town Clerk	1843–1885	Yes	Good
Marriages, ...	8	Town Clerk	1843–1885	Yes	Good
Deaths, ...	6	Town Clerk	1843–1885	Yes	Good
Assessors, ...	53	Assessors	1826–1885	–	–
Miscellaneous, ...	128	Town Clerk	1826–1885	Partially	Good

[1] There is a copy also of the first volume.

[2] There is an indexed copy also of the record of births, marriages, and deaths from 1700 to 1765.

TOWN RECORDS — Continued.

COUNTY OF MIDDLESEX.   CITY OF LOWELL — Con.

1826.	Mar. 1.	Part of Chelmsford established as Lowell.
1832.	Mar. 22.	Part of Tewksbury annexed to Lowell.
1834.	Mar. 29.	Part of Tewksbury annexed to Lowell.
1836.	April 1.	Lowell incorporated as a city.
1836.	April 11.	Act of incorporation accepted by the town.
1851.	Feb. 28.	Part of Dracut annexed to Lowell.
1874.	May 18.	Parts of Chelmsford and Dracut annexed to Lowell.
1874.	June 5.	Part of Tewksbury annexed to Lowell.
1874.	June 23.	Act of May 18, 1874, accepted by Lowell.
1874.	Aug. 1.	Act of May 18, 1874, took effect.
1879.	April 1.	Part of Dracut annexed to Lowell.
1888.	May 17.	Part of Tewksbury annexed to Lowell.

COUNTY OF MIDDLESEX.   CITY OF MALDEN.

KIND OF RECORDS.	Number of Volumes	In Keeping of —	Years Covered	Whether Indexed	Condition
Town proceedings, . . .	6	City Clerk	1678–1882[1]	No	–
City proceedings, . . .	2	City Clerk	1882–1885	No	–
Births, marriages, and deaths,	1[2]	City Clerk	1843–1861	No	–
Births, ...	2	City Clerk	1861–1885	Yes	–
Marriages, ...	2	City Clerk	1861–1885	Yes	–
Deaths, ...	2	City Clerk	1861–1885	Yes	–
Assessors, ...	40	Assessors	–	–	–
Selectmen, ...	10	Selectmen	–	–	–
Parish, ...	1	City Clerk	1758–1787	No	–
Miscellaneous, . . .	22	City Clerk	–	No	–

1649.	May 2.	Mass. Rec., Vol. II., p. 274. "Misticke side men" granted to be a town to be called "Mauldon."
1817.	June 10.	Part of Malden annexed to Medford.
1850.	May 3.	Part of Malden established as Melrose.
1870.	Mar. 9.	Part of Malden established as Everett.
1877.	April 20.	Part of Medford annexed to Malden.
1878.	Feb. 20.	Bounds between Malden and Medford established.
1881.	Mar. 31.	Malden incorporated as a city.
1881.	June 9.	Act of incorporation accepted by the town.

COUNTY OF MIDDLESEX.   TOWN OF MARLBOROUGH.

KIND OF RECORDS.	Number of Volumes	In Keeping of—	Years Covered	Whether Indexed	Condition
Town proceedings, . . .	9	Town Clerk	1656–1885	No	Fair
Births, marriages, and deaths,	19[3]	Town Clerk	1663–1885	Yes	Fair
Selectmen and Assessors, .	–	Selectmen	–	–	–
Parish, ...	1	Town Clerk	1808–1823	No	Fair
Proprietors, ...	3	Town Clerk	1699–1795	No	Fair
Miscellaneous, . . .	7	Town Clerk	1861–1885	No	Fair

[1] The first volume of town proceedings covering the years from 1649 to 1678 is lost.

[2] All the records of births, marriages, and deaths prior to 1835 have been copied.

[3] There is a copy also of the records of marriages from 1663 to 1843; of births from 1732 to 1845, and of deaths from 1663 to 1847.

Town Records — Continued.

County of Middlesex. Town of Marlborough — Con.

1660.	May	31.	Mass. Rec., Vol. IV., Part 1, p. 424. The grant to the Whip-sufferage planters confirmed, the name of the plantation to be "Marlborow."
1716.	Nov.	16.	Resolve. The title of a tract of land called Agaganquamasset confirmed to Marlborough.
1717.	Nov.	18.	Resolve. Part of Marlborough established as Westborough.
1727.	July	6.	Prov. Laws, Vol. II., p. 428. Part of Marlborough established as Southborough.
1784.	Mar.	16.	Parts of Marlborough and Bolton established as the district of Berlin
1791.	Feb.	23.	Part of Framingham annexed to Marlborough.
1807.	June	20.	Part of Marlborough annexed to Northborough and bounds established.
1829.	Feb.	11.	Part of Marlborough annexed to Bolton.
1838.	Mar.	16.	Bounds between Marlborough and Bolton established.
1843.	Mar.	24.	Part of Southborough annexed to Marlborough.
1866.	Mar.	19.	Parts of Marlborough and Stow established as Hudson.

County of Middlesex. Town of Maynard.

Kind of Records.	Number of Volumes	In Keeping of—	Years Covered	Whether Indexed	Condition
Town proceedings, . . .	1	Town Clerk	1872–1885	No	Good
Births, ...	1	Town Clerk	1872–1885	No	Good
Marriages, ...	1	Town Clerk	1872–1885	No	Good
Deaths, ...	1	Town Clerk	1872–1885	No	Good
Assessors, ...	–	–	–	–	–
Selectmen, ...	2	Selectmen	–	–	–
Miscellaneous, . . .	10	Town Clerk	1872–1885	No	Fair

1871.   April 19.   Parts of Sudbury and Stow established as Maynard.

County of Middlesex. Town of Medford.

Kind of Records.	Number of Volumes	In Keeping of—	Years Covered	Whether Indexed	Condition
Town proceedings, . . .	10[1]	Town Clerk	1670–1885[2]	No	Good
Births, marriages, and deaths,	11	Town Clerk	1630–1885	Since 1843	–
Assessors, ...	70	Assessors	–	–	–
Selectmen, ...	7	Selectmen	–	–	–
Miscellaneous, . . .	15	Town Clerk	1835–1885	No	Good

1630.	Sept.	28.	Mass. Rec., Vol. I., p. 77. "Meadford" is mentioned in a Tax Act.
1811.	June	21.	Part of Medford annexed to Charlestown.
1817.	June	10.	Part of Malden annexed to Medford.
1850.	April	30.	Parts of Medford, West Cambridge, and Woburn established as Winchester.
1875.	April	20.	Part of Everett annexed to Medford.
1877.	April	20.	Part of Medford annexed to Malden.
1878.	Feb.	20.	Bounds between Medford and Malden established.

[1] There is a copy also of the first volume.

[2] The records from 1630 to 1670 are missing.

TOWN RECORDS — Continued.

COUNTY OF MIDDLESEX. TOWN OF MELROSE.

KIND OF RECORDS.	Number of Volumes	In Keeping of —	Years Covered	Whether Indexed	Condition
Town proceedings, . . .	3	Town Clerk	1850–1885	Partially	Good
Births, ...	1	Town Clerk	1850–1885	–	Good
Marriages, ...	1	Town-Clerk	1850–1885	–	Good
Deaths, ...	1	Town Clerk	1850–1885	–	Good
Assessors, ...	–	Assessors	1850–1885	–	–
Selectmen, ...	–	Selectmen	–	–	–
Soldiers in the Rebellion, .	1	Town Clerk	–	No	Good
Miscellaneous, ...	7	Town Clerk	1850–1885	–	Good

1850. May 3. Part of Malden established as Melrose.
1853. Mar. 15. Part of Stoneham annexed to Melrose.

COUNTY OF MIDDLESEX. TOWN OF NATICK.

KIND OF RECORDS.	Number of Volumes	In Keeping of —	Years Covered	Whether Indexed	Condition
Town proceedings, . . .	5	Town Clerk	1745–1885	No	Fair
Births, marriages, and deaths,	8	Town Clerk	1745–1885	Since 1862	Fair
Assessors, ...	65	Assessors	–	–	–
Selectmen, ...	15	Selectmen	–	–	–
Proprietors, ...	4[1]	Town Clerk	1702–1790	No	Fair
Miscellaneous, ...	17[2]	Town Clerk	1720–1885	No	Fair

1679. April 16. Mass. Rec., Vol. V., p. 227. Exchange of land made between the plantation of Natick and Sherborn.
1679. May 30. Mass. Rec., Vol. V., p. 230. The exchange of land with Sherborn ratified by the General Court.
1745. June 28. Prov. Laws, Vol. III., p. 234. "The plantation of Natick, belonging to no particular town."
1762. Feb. 23. Prov. Laws, Vol. IV., p. 526. The Parish of Natick established as the district of Natick.
1781. Feb. 19. District of Natick made the town of Natick. [This act was confirmatory of the general act of August 23, 1775.]
1797. June 22. Bounds between Natick and Needham established and part of each town annexed to the other town.
1820. Feb. 7. Part of Sherborn annexed to Natick.
1850. April 26. Resolve. Bounds between Natick and Wayland established.
1871. April 22. Part of Natick annexed to Framingham.

[1] There is a copy also of the first volume.
[2] There is a copy of one volume which is written mostly in the Indian language.

TOWN RECORDS — Continued.

COUNTY OF MIDDLESEX.   CITY OF NEWTON.

KIND OF RECORDS.	Number of Volumes	In Keeping of—	Years Covered	Whether Indexed	Condition
Town proceedings, . . .	5	City Clerk	1706–1873[1]	No	Good
City proceedings, . . .	5	City Clerk	1874–1885	Yes	Good
Births, ...	5[2]	City Clerk	1669–1885	Yes	Good
Marriages, ...	9[2]	City Clerk	1669–1885	Yes	Good
Deaths, ...	11[2]	City Clerk	1669–1885	Yes	Good
Marriage intentions, . .	6	City Clerk	1669–1885	Yes	Good
Assessors, ...	60	Assessors	1790–1885	–	–
Selectmen, ...	4	City Clerk	–	–	–
Miscellaneous, . . .	35	City Clerk	1824–1885	–	Good

1691. Dec. 15. Mass. Archives, Vol. CXII., p. 421. Petition of inhabitants of "Cambridge Village sometimes called Little Cambridge" for a name for their town was granted, the name to be Newton and the town's brandmark to be N.

1803. June 21. An island in Charles River annexed to Newton.

1838. April 23. Part of Newton annexed to Roxbury.

1849. April 16. Part of Newton annexed to Waltham.

1873. June 2. Newton incorporated as a city.

1873. Oct. 13. Act of incorporation accepted by the town.

1875. May 5. Part of Boston annexed to Newton.

1875. June 23. Act of May 5, 1875, accepted by Newton.

1875. July 1. Act of May 5, 1875, took effect.

COUNTY OF MIDDLESEX.   TOWN OF NORTH READING.

KIND OF RECORDS.	Number of Volumes	In Keeping of—	Years Covered	Whether Indexed	Condition
Town proceedings, . . .	2	Town Clerk	1853–1885	No	Good
Births, ...	1	Town Clerk	1853–1885	No	Good
Marriages, ...	1	Town Clerk	1853–1885	No	Good
Deaths, ...	1	Town Clerk	1853–1885	No	Good
Assessors, ...	24	Assessors[3]	–	–	–
Selectmen, ...	1	Selectmen	–	–	–
Miscellaneous, . . .	3	Town Clerk	1853–1885	No	Good

1853. Mar. 22. Part of Reading established as North Reading.

1857. May 27. Bounds between North Reading and Lynnfield established and part of each town annexed to the other town, provided the act is accepted by both towns.

1858. Jan. 7. Act of May 27, 1857, accepted by North Reading. [Accepted by Lynnfield, November 3, 1857.]

---

[1] The records from 1828 to 1843 are incomplete.

[2] There is a copy also of the records of births, marriages, and deaths from 1669 to 1854.

[3] There are copies of the records of assessors in possession of the Town Clerk.

Town Records — Continued.

County of Middlesex. Town of Pepperell.

KIND OF RECORDS.	Number of Volumes	In Keeping of —	Years Covered	Whether Indexed	Condition
Town proceedings, . . .	6	Town Clerk	1742–1885	No	Good
Births, marriages, and deaths,	7	Town Clerk	1742–1885	Yes	Good
Selectmen and Assessors, .	41	Selectmen	1837–1885[1]	–	–
Miscellaneous, ...	14	Town Clerk	–	No	Good

1753. April 12. Prov. Laws, Vol. III., p. 652. Second Precinct of Groton made the district of "Pepperrell."

1775. Aug. 23. Prov. Laws, Vol. V., p. 419. District of Pepperell made the town of Pepperell by this general act.

1803. Feb. 3. Part of Pepperell annexed to Groton.

1857. May 18. Part of Groton annexed to Pepperell.

County of Middlesex. Town of Reading.

KIND OF RECORDS.	Number of Volumes	In Keeping of —	Years Covered	Whether Indexed	Condition
Town proceedings, . . .	5[2]	Town Clerk	1644–1885	Yes	Good
Births, ...	3[3]	Town Clerk	1644–1885	Yes	Good
Marriages, ...	3[3]	Town Clerk	1644–1885	Yes	Good
Deaths, ...	3[3]	Town Clerk	1644–1885	Yes	Good
Assessors, ...	25	Selectmen	–	–	–
Selectmen, ...	15	Selectmen	–	–	–
Proprietors, ...	1	Town Clerk	–	Yes	Good

1644. May 29. Mass. Rec., Vol. II., p. 73. "Linn Village shall be called Redding."

1644. May 29. Mass. Rec., Vol. II., p. 75. Bounds between Reading and Woburn established.

1730. Sept. 25. Prov. Laws, Vol. II., p. 556. Parts of Reading and Woburn established as Wilmington.

1812. Feb. 25. First or South Parish of Reading established as South Reading.

1813. June 16. Part of South Reading annexed to Reading.

1853. Mar. 22. Part of Reading established as North Reading.

1854. April 10. Bounds between Reading and Lynnfield established.

---

[1] The records of assessors between 1845 and 1855 are not dated separately for each year.

[2] There is a copy also of the first volume.

[3] There are copies also of the records of births, marriages, and deaths.

Town Records — Continued.

County of Middlesex.   Town of Sherborn.[1]

Kind of Records.	Number of Volumes	In Keeping of—	Years Covered	Whether Indexed	Condition
Town proceedings, . . .	7[2]	Town Clerk	1677–1885	No	Good[3]
Births, marriages, and deaths,	6[4]	Town Clerk	1663–1885	No	Good
Assessors, ...	–	Assessors	1808–1885	–	–
Proprietors, ...	1	Town Clerk	1681–1721	No	Good[5]
Proprietors, ...	1[4]	Town Clerk	1715–1730[6]	No	–
Miscellaneous, ...	12	Town Clerk	–	No	Good

1674. Oct.   7. Mass. Rec., Vol. V., p. 23. More land granted to the inhabitants and proprietors of the land at or near Boggestow, the place to be called Sherborne.

1679. April 16. Mass. Rec., Vol. V., p. 227. Exchange of land made with the plantation of Natick.

1679. May   30. Mass. Rec., Vol. V., p. 230. The exchange of land with the plantation of Natick ratified by the General Court.

1684. May   17. Mass. Rec., Vol. V., p. 443. The grant of land made to the inhabitants at or near Boggestow confirmed, the name of the town to be Sherborne.

1724. Dec.   3. Prov. Laws, Vol. II., p. 340. Part of Sherburn established as Holliston.

1792. Mar.   3. Bounds between Sherburne and Medway established.

1820. Feb.   7. Part of Sherburne annexed to Natick.

1852. May   3. The name of the town of Sherburne changed to Sherborn.

County of Middlesex.   Town of Shirley.

Kind of Records.	Number of Volumes	In Keeping of—	Years Covered	Whether Indexed	Condition
Town proceedings, . . .	5[7]	Town Clerk	1753–1885	Yes	Good
Births, marriages, and deaths,	6	Town Clerk	1753–1885	Yes	Good
Assessors, ...	–	Assessors	1753–1885	–	–

1753. Jan.   5. Prov. Laws, Vol. III., p. 637. Part of Groton established as the district of Shirley.

1775. Aug.   23. Prov. Laws, Vol. V., p. 419. District of Shirley made the town of Shirley by this general act.

1798. Feb.   6. Part of Groton annexed to Shirley.

1846. Mar.   3. Bounds between Shirley and Lunenburg established.

1848. April 25. Bounds between Shirley and Lunenburg established.

1871. Feb.   14. Parts of Shirley and Groton established as Ayer.

---

[1] See the town of Nantucket, and under "Extinct Cities, Towns, and Districts" see also "Sherburn." The spelling of the town name is given, in each instance, as found in the records.

[2] There are copies also of the records from 1674 to 1784. The records from 1683 to 1687 are in the first volume of the proprietors records.

[3] Some of the first pages are missing from the first volume.

[4] There are copies also of the records of births, marriages, and deaths from 1663 to 1845.

[5] The first six pages are missing.

[6] This is an attested copy; the original volume is missing.

[7] The first volume covering the years from 1753 to 1773 has been copied and indexed.

TOWN RECORDS — Continued.

COUNTY OF MIDDLESEX. CITY OF SOMERVILLE.

KIND OF RECORDS.	Number of Volumes	In Keeping of—	Years Covered	Whether Indexed	Condition
Town proceedings, . . .	2	City Clerk	1842–1872	Yes	Good
City proceedings, . . .	14	City Clerk	1872–1885	Yes	Good
Births, ...	3	City Clerk	1842–1885	Yes	Good
Marriages, ...	9	City Clerk	1842–1885	Yes	Good
Deaths, ...	2	City Clerk	1842–1885	Yes	Good
Assessors, ...	187	Assessors	1842–1885	–	–
Selectmen, ...	4	City Clerk	1842–1872	Yes	Good
Miscellaneous, . . .	75	City Clerk	1842–1885	No	Good

1842. Mar. 3. Part of Charlestown established as Somerville.
1856. April 30. Part of Cambridge annexed to Somerville and bounds established.
1862. April 29. Bounds between Somerville and Cambridge established and part of each place annexed to the other place.
1871. April 14. Somerville incorporated as a city.
1871. April 27. Act of incorporation accepted by the town.

COUNTY OF MIDDLESEX. TOWN OF STONEHAM.

KIND OF RECORDS.	Number of Volumes	In Keeping of—	Years Covered	Whether Indexed	Condition
Town proceedings, . . .	8[1]	Town Clerk	1725–1885	No	Good
Births, marriages, and deaths,	4[2]	Town Clerk	1725–1885	Yes	Good
Assessors, ...	8	Town Clerk	1799–1885	–	–
Selectmen, ...	1	Town Clerk	1859–1885	–	–
Miscellaneous, . . .	6	Town Clerk	1835–1885	No	Good

1725. Dec. 17. Prov. Laws, Vol. II., p. 369. Part of Charlestown established as Stoneham.
1853. Mar. 15. Part of Stoneham annexed to Melrose.
1856. April 5. Part of Stoneham annexed to South Reading.

COUNTY OF MIDDLESEX. TOWN OF STOW.

KIND OF RECORDS.	Number of Volumes	In Keeping of—	Years Covered	Whether Indexed	Condition
Town proceedings, . . .	6	Town Clerk	1683–1885	No	Fair
Births, marriages, and deaths,	4[3]	Town Clerk	1713–1885[4]	No	Fair
Assessors, ...	–	Town Clerk	1683–1885	–	–
Selectmen, ...	–	Town Clerk	1846–1885	–	–
Proprietors, ...	1[5]	Town Clerk	1722–1803	No	Fair
Miscellaneous, . . .	9	Town Clerk	1759–1863	No	Fair

1 There are copies also of the first two volumes covering the years from 1725 to 1821.
2 There are copies also of the records of births, marriages, and deaths to 1844.
3 There are copies also of the records of births, marriages, and deaths from 1713 to 1823.
4 The records prior to 1713 are destroyed.
5 There is also a copy.

TOWN RECORDS — Continued.

COUNTY OF MIDDLESEX. TOWN OF STOW — Con.

1683. May 16. Mass. Rec., Vol. V., p. 408. The plantation between Concord and Lancaster called Pompositticut established as Stow.
1732. June 29. Prov. Laws, Vol. II., p. 644. Parts of Stow, Groton, and Lancaster established as Harvard.
1783. Feb. 25. Parts of Stow, Harvard, and Littleton established as Boxborough.
1866. Mar. 19. Parts of Stow and Marlborough established as Hudson.
1871. April 19. Parts of Stow and Sudbury established as Maynard.

COUNTY OF MIDDLESEX. TOWN OF SUDBURY.

KIND OF RECORDS.	Number of Volumes	In Keeping of—	Years Covered	Whether Indexed	Condition
Town proceedings, . . .	10[1]	Town Clerk	1640–1885	No	Fair
Births, marriages, and deaths,	7[2]	Town Clerk	1640–1885	Yes	Fair
Assessors, ...	36	Assessors	–	–	–
Proprietors, ...	4	Town Clerk	1700–1780	No	Fair
Miscellaneous, ...	6	Town Clerk	1640–1885	No	Fair

1639. Sept. 4. Mass. Rec., Vol. I., p. 271. The new plantation by Concord to be called Sudbury.
1651. May 13. Mass. Rec., Vol. IV., Part 1, p. 54. Bounds between Sudbury and Watertown established.
1780. April 10. Part of Sudbury established as East Sudbury.
1871. April 19. Parts of Sudbury and Stow established as Maynard.

COUNTY OF MIDDLESEX. TOWN OF TEWKSBURY.

KIND OF RECORDS.	Number of Volumes	In Keeping of—	Years Covered	Whether Indexed	Condition
Town proceedings, . . .	5	Town Clerk	1734–1885	No	Good
Births, ...	3	Town Clerk	1734–1885	Yes	Good
Marriages, ...	2	Town Clerk	1844–1885	Yes	Good
Deaths, ...	3	Town Clerk	{ 1734–1829[3] 1844–1885	Yes	Good
Marriage intentions, . .	1	Town Clerk	1829–1885	Yes	Good
Assessors, ...	56	Assessors	–	–	–
Miscellaneous, ...	4	Town Clerk	1829–1885	Partially	Good

1734. Dec. 1. Prov. Laws, Vol. II., p. 739. Part of Billerica established as Tewksbury.
1832. Mar. 22. Part of Tewksbury annexed to Lowell.
1834. Mar. 29. Part of Tewksbury annexed to Lowell.
1874. June 5. Part of Tewksbury annexed to Lowell.
1888. May 17. Part of Tewksbury annexed to Lowell.

---

[1] The town of Wayland has a copy of the records of town proceedings prior to 1780.

[2] See foot-note to the records of births, marriages, and deaths in Boston. There are copies also of records of births, marriages, and deaths prior to 1840, indexed and arranged by families.

[3] The records of deaths from 1829 to 1844 were burned.

Town Records — Continued.

County of Middlesex. Town of Townsend.

KIND OF RECORDS.	Number of Volumes	In Keeping of —	Years Covered	Whether Indexed	Condition
Town proceedings, . . .	5	Town Clerk	1734–1885	No	Good
Births, ...	2[1]	Town Clerk	1843–1885	Yes	Good
Marriages, ...	2[1]	Town Clerk	1843–1885	Yes	Good
Deaths, ...	2	Town Clerk	1843–1885	Yes	Good
Assessors, ...	–	Assessors	1700–1885	–	–
Selectmen, ...	–	Selectmen	1734–1885	–	–
Proprietors, ...	–	Selectmen	–	–	–
Miscellaneous, ...	–	Town Clerk	–	–	–

1732. June 29. Prov. Laws, Vol. II., p. 643. The north part of Turkey Hills established as Townsend.

1767. Mar. 6. Prov. Laws, Vol. IV., p. 908. . Parts of Townsend, Ashburnham, and Fitchburg established as Ashby.

County of Middlesex. Town of Tyngsborough.

KIND OF RECORDS.	Number of Volumes	In Keeping of —	Years Covered	Whether Indexed	Condition
Town proceedings, . . .	5[2]	Town Clerk	1755–1885	No	Good
Births, marriages, and deaths,	4	Town Clerk	–	Yes	Good
Assessors, ...	29	Selectmen	–	–	–

1789. June 22. Part of Dunstable established as the district of Tyngsborough.

1792. Mar. 3. Part of Dunstable annexed to the district of Tyngsborough.

1798. Jan. 29. Part of Dunstable annexed to Tyngsborough and bounds established.

1809. Feb. 23. District of Tyngsborough made the town of Tyngsborough.

1814. June 10. Bounds between Tyngsborough and Dunstable established.

County of Middlesex. Town of Wakefield.

KIND OF RECORDS.	Number of Volumes	In Keeping of —	Years Covered	Whether Indexed	Condition
Town proceedings, . . .	6	Town Clerk	1812–1885	No	Good
Births, marriages, and deaths,	8[3]	Town Clerk	1812–1885	No	Good
Assessors, ...	24	Town Clerk	–	–	–
Miscellaneous, ...	1	Town Clerk	1852–1885	Yes	Good

1868. Feb. 25. Name of the town of South Reading[4] changed to Wakefield.

1868. June 30. Act of February 25, 1868, took effect.

---

[1] Two volumes of records of births and marriages from 1780 to 1810 are lost.

[2] There is a copy also of the first volume covering the years from 1755 to 1803.

[3] There are copies also of these records.

[4] For legislation concerning the town of South Reading, see "Extinct Cities, Towns, and Districts."

Town Records — Continued.

County of Middlesex. City of Waltham.

Kind of Records.	Number of Volumes	In Keeping of —	Years Covered	Whether Indexed	Condition
Town proceedings,[1] . .	7[2]	City Clerk	1737–1883	No	Good
City proceedings, . . .	1	City Clerk	1884–1885	No	Good
Births, marriages, and deaths,	9[3]	City Clerk	1737–1885	Yes	Good
Assessors, ...	70	City Clerk	–	–	–
Proprietors,[1]	1	City Clerk	1636–1742	–	–
Miscellaneous, ...	10	City Clerk	1828–1885	Yes	Good

1738. Jan.   4. Prov. Laws, Vol. II., p. 919. Part of Watertown established as Waltham.

1849. April 16. Part of Newton annexed to Waltham.

1859. Mar.   18. Parts of Waltham, Watertown, and West Cambridge established as Belmont.

1884. June   2. Waltham incorporated as a city.

1884. July   16. Act of incorporation accepted by the town.

County of Middlesex. Town of Watertown.

Kind of Records.	Number of Volumes	In Keeping of —	Years Covered	Whether Indexed	Condition
Town proceedings, . . .	13[4]	Town Clerk	1634–1885	Partially	–
Births, marriages, and deaths,[5]	7	Town Clerk	1630–1885	No	–
Assessors, ...	45	Town Clerk	–	–	–
Proprietors, ...	1[6]	Town Clerk	1644–1742	No	Good
Soldiers in the Rebellion, .	1	Town Clerk	1861–1865	No	Good

1630. Sept.   7. Mass. Rec., Vol. I., p. 75. " The town upon Charles River to be called Waterton."

1634. Sept. 25. Mass. Rec., Vol. I., p. 129. Part of New Towne to revert to Watertown, " if Mr. Hooker and his congregation shall remove hence."

1635. April   7. Mass. Rec., Vol. I., p. 144. Bounds between Watertown and New Towne established.

1638. Aug.   20. Mass. Rec., Vol. I., p. 230. Bounds between Watertown, Concord, and Dedham established.

1639. Mar.   13. Mass. Rec., Vol. I., p. 254. Bounds between Watertown and Cambridge established.

1639. May   22. Mass. Rec., Vol. I., p. 257. Bounds between Watertown and Dedham established.

---

[1] There are two volumes of copies of Watertown town records from 1630 to 1737 and one of Watertown proprietors records from 1636 to 1742.

[2] There are copies also of the first four volumes covering the years from 1720 to 1811.

[3] There is a copy also of the records of marriages and deaths from 1738 to 1815.

[4] There are copies also of six volumes which were in poor condition.

[5] See foot-note to the records of births, marriages, and deaths in Boston.

[6] There is also a volume relating to division of lands, containing copies of records found in the town records, the first date given being 1636. There is a copy also in possession of the City Clerk of Waltham.

Town Records — Continued.

COUNTY OF MIDDLESEX. TOWN OF WATERTOWN — Con.

1651. April 10. Mass. Rec., Vol. IV., Part 1, p. 54. Bounds between Watertown and Sudbury established.

1712. Jan. 1. Resolve. Part of Watertown established as Weston.

1738. Jan. 4. Prov. Laws, Vol. II., p. 919. Part of Watertown established as Waltham.

1855. April 27. Part of Watertown annexed to Cambridge.

1859. Mar. 18. Parts of Watertown, Waltham, and West Cambridge established as Belmont.

1885. Mar. 10. Part of Watertown annexed to Cambridge.

COUNTY OF MIDDLESEX. TOWN OF WAYLAND[1].

KIND OF RECORDS.	Number of Volumes	In Keeping of —	Years Covered	Whether Indexed	Condition
Town proceedings, . . .	4	Town Clerk	1780–1885	1 volume	Fair
Births, marriages, and deaths,	4	Town Clerk	1780–1885	No	Fair
Assessors, ...	–	Town Clerk	1780–1885	–	–
Miscellaneous, ...	6	Town Clerk	–	No	Fair

1835. Mar. 11. The name of the town of East Sudbury[2] changed to Wayland.

1850. April 26. Resolve. Bounds between Wayland and Natick established.

COUNTY OF MIDDLESEX. TOWN OF WESTFORD.

KIND OF RECORDS.	Number of Volumes	In Keeping of —	Years Covered	Whether Indexed	Condition
Town proceedings, . . .	8	Town Clerk	1726–1764 1768–1885	No	–[3]
Births, marriages, and deaths,	4[4]	Town Clerk	1728–1885	Yes	–
Assessors, ...	69	Town Clerk	–	–	–
Miscellaneous, ...	9	Town Clerk	1805–1885	Partially	–

1729. Sept. 23. Prov. Laws, Vol. II., p. 528. Part of Chelmsford established as "Wesford."

[1] There are copies of four volumes of records of the town of Sudbury in possession of the Town Clerk of Wayland.

[2] For legislation concerning the town of East Sudbury, see "Extinct Cities, Towns, and Districts."

[3] The records from 1727 to 1828 were damaged. Many of the older records are dilapidated.

[4] There is a volume also containing copies of the records of births from 1728 to 1840.

TOWN RECORDS — Continued.

COUNTY OF MIDDLESEX.   TOWN OF WESTON.

KIND OF RECORDS.	Number of Volumes	In Keeping of—	Years Covered	Whether Indexed	Condition
Town proceedings, . . .	5	Town Clerk	1746–1885	No	Good
Births, marriages, and deaths,	4[1]	Town Clerk	1713–1848	Yes	Good
Births, ...	1	Town Clerk	1848–1885	Yes	Good
Marriages, ...	1	Town Clerk	1848–1885	Yes	Good
Deaths, ...	1	Town Clerk	1848–1885	Yes	Good
Marriage intentions, . .	1	Town Clerk	1815–1885	Yes	Good
Assessors, ...	5[2]	Assessors	1820–1884	–	–
Selectmen, ...	2	Town Clerk	1754–1803	–	–
Soldiers in the Rebellion, .	1	Town Clerk	1861–1864	No	Good
Miscellaneous, ...	8	Town Clerk	1784–1885	No	Good

1712.   Jan.   1.   Resolve. West Precinct of Watertown established as Weston.
1754.   April 19.   Prov. Laws., Vol. III., p. 728. Parts of Weston, Concord, and Lexington established as Lincoln.

COUNTY OF MIDDLESEX.   TOWN OF WILMINGTON.

KIND OF RECORDS.	Number of Volumes	In Keeping of —	Years Covered	Whether Indexed	Condition
Town proceedings, . . .	6	Town Clerk	1730–1762[3] 1786–1885	No	Poor
Births, marriages, and deaths,	5	Town Clerk	1730–1885	No	Poor
Assessors, ...	63	Assessors	–	–	–
Miscellaneous, ...	5	Town Clerk	–	Partially	Poor

1730.   Sept. 25.   Mass. Rec., Vol. II., p. 556. Parts of Reading and Woburn established as Wilmington.

COUNTY OF MIDDLESEX.   TOWN OF WINCHESTER.[4]

KIND OF RECORDS.	Number of Volumes	In Keeping of—	Years Covered	Whether Indexed	Condition
Town proceedings, . . .	3	Town Clerk	1849–1885	Yes	Good
Births, marriages, and deaths,	3[5]	Town Clerk	1849–1885	Yes	Good
Assessors, ...	35	Assessors	1850–1885	–	–
Selectmen, ...	3	Selectmen	–	–	–
Miscellaneous, ...	–[6]	–	–	–	–

1850.   April 30.   Parts of Medford, West Cambridge, and Woburn established as Winchester.
1873.   May   12.   Part of Winchester annexed to Woburn.

[1] There are three volumes also containing copies of the records of births, marriages, and deaths from 1711 to 1849.

[2] There are incomplete records, unbound, from 1765 to 1820.

[3] The records from 1762 to 1786 are lost.

[4] See also "Winchester" under "Extinct Cities, Towns, and Districts."

[5] The Winchester Historical and Genealogical Society, formed in December, 1884, is collecting records of births, marriages, and deaths and has a small collection dating from 1630.

[6] There are no miscellaneous records, these records having been transferred to the Winchester Historical and Genealogical Society.

TOWN RECORDS — Continued.

COUNTY OF MIDDLESEX. TOWN OF WOBURN.

KIND OF RECORDS.	Number of Volumes	In Keeping of—	Years Covered	Whether Indexed	Condition
Town proceedings, . . .	22	Town Clerk	1640–1885	Last 2 vols.	Good
Births, marriages, and deaths,	31	Town Clerk	1640–1885[2]	1840–1885	Good
Assessors, ...	–	–	–	–	–
Selectmen, ...	6	Town Clerk	1640–1885	–	–
Proprietors, ...	1	Town Clerk	1738–1765	No	Good
Miscellaneous, ...	20	Town Clerk	1640–1885	No	Good

1642. Sept. 27. Mass. Rec., Vol. II., p. 28. "Charlestowne village is called Wooborne."

1644. May 23. Mass. Rec., Vol. II., p. 75. Bounds between Woburn and Reading established.

1664. Oct. 19. Mass. Rec., Vol. IV., Part 2, p. 138. Two thousand acres of land granted to Woburn.

1666. Oct. 10. Mass. Rec., Vol. IV., Part 2, p. 325. Bounds between Woburn and Billerica established.

1730. Sept. 25. Prov. Laws, Vol. II., p. 556. Parts of Woburn and Reading established as Wilmington.

1799. Feb. 28. Part of Woburn established as Burlington.

1850. April 30. Parts of Woburn, Medford, and West Cambridge established as Winchester.

1873. May 12. Part of Winchester annexed to Woburn.

1888. May 18. Woburn incorporated as a city.

1888. May 29. Act of incorporation accepted by the town.

COUNTY OF NANTUCKET. TOWN OF NANTUCKET.

KIND OF RECORDS.	Number of Volumes	In Keeping of—	Years Covered	Whether Indexed	Condition
Town proceedings, . . .	17	Town Clerk	1699–1753[3] 1784–1885	–	–
Births, marriages, and deaths,	2	Town Clerk	1662–1845	No	–
Births, marriages, and deaths,	1	Town Clerk	1844–1849	No	–
Births, ...	1	Town Clerk	1850–1885	Yes	–
Marriages, ...	1	Town Clerk	1850–1885	Yes	–
Deaths, ...	1	Town Clerk	1850–1885	Yes	–
Selectmen and Assessors, .	–	–	–	–	–
Proprietors, ...	6	Proprietors Clerk	1716–1885	–	–

1795. June 8. The name of the town of Sherburn[4] changed to Nantucket.

[1] See foot-note to the records of births, marriages, and deaths in Boston. There is a volume also containing copies of the records of births, marriages, and deaths from 1640 to 1840. This volume was copied by Rev. Samuel Sewall and contains also copies of all records of other births, marriages, and deaths which he was able to find in church and parish records.

[2] The records of marriages from 1708 to 1711 are omitted.

[3] One volume covering the years from 1754 to 1784 is missing.

[4] See also the town of Sherborn, and for legislation concerning the town of Sherburn, see "Extinct Cities, Towns, and Districts."

Town Records — Continued.

County of Norfolk. Town of Bellingham.

Kind of Records.	Number of Volumes	In Keeping of —	Years Covered	Whether Indexed	Condition
General, ...	6	Town Clerk	1720–1885	Yes	Good
Births, marriages, and deaths,	2	Town Clerk	–	–	–
Births and deaths, . . .	1	Town Clerk	–	–	–
Births, ...	1	Town Clerk	–	–	–
Marriages, ...	2	Town Clerk	–	–	–
Deaths, ...	1	Town Clerk	–	–	–
Assessors, ...	39	Assessors	–	–	–
Selectmen, ...	5	Selectmen	–	–	–
Proprietors, ...	1	Town Clerk	1713–1813	Yes	Good
Miscellaneous, ...	23	Town Clerk	1802–1885	Yes	Good

1719. Nov. 27. Resolve. Parts of Dedham, Mendon, and Wrentham established as Bellingham.

1832. Feb. 23. Bounds between Bellingham and Franklin established.

1872. Mar. 7. Bounds between Bellingham and Mendon established.

County of Norfolk. Town of Braintree.

Kind of Records.	Number of Volumes	In Keeping of —	Years Covered[1]	Whether Indexed	Condition
Town proceedings, . . .	6[2]	Town Clerk	1641–1885	–	Good
Births, marriages, and deaths,	8[2]	Town Clerk	1640–1885	Since 1851[3]	Good
Assessors, ...	45	Assessors	1792–1885	–	–
Selectmen, ...	2	Town Clerk	1688–1796	–	–
Selectmen, ...	2	Selectmen	1793–1885	–	Good
Miscellaneous, ...	18	Town Clerk	1792–1885	–	Good

1640. May 13. Mass. Rec., Vol. I., p. 291. Mount "Woollaston" to be a town called Braintree.

1792. Feb. 22. Parts of Braintree and Dorchester established as Quincy.

1793. Mar. 9. Part of Braintree established as Randolph.

1811. June 22. Certain estates in Braintree re-annexed to Randolph.

1856. April 24. Part of Braintree annexed to Quincy.

---

[1] The records for certain years prior to 1851, the years not being designated, are omitted.

[2] See foot-note to the records of births, marriages, and deaths in Boston. There is a copy also of the records of town proceedings, and of births, marriages, and deaths from 1640 to 1792, in possession of the Town Clerk of Quincy. A copy of the records of births, marriages, and deaths covering those years is in possession of Charles F. Adams of Quincy. Asa French has a copy of the records of the baptisms, marriages, and burials from 1711 to 1762 which were recorded by Rev. Samuel Niles.

[3] The records of births, marriages, and deaths prior to 1851 have been indexed by Samuel A. Bates and the index is in his private possession.

TOWN RECORDS — Continued.

COUNTY OF NORFOLK. TOWN OF BROOKLINE.

KIND OF RECORDS.	Number of Volumes	In Keeping of —	Years Covered	Whether Indexed	Condition
Town proceedings, . . .	9[1]	Town Clerk	1686–1885[2]	Yes	Fair[3]
Births, marriages, and deaths,	10	Town Clerk	1686–1885	Yes	Fair
Assessors, ...	37	Assessors	–	–	–
Selectmen, ...	2	Town Clerk	–	–	–
Selectmen, ...	4	Selectmen	–	–	–

1705. Nov. 13. Resolve. Muddy River, "a hamlet of Boston," established as "Brooklyn."
1825. Feb. 22. Bounds between Brookline and Boston confirmed.
1844. Feb. 24. Part of Roxbury annexed to Brookline.
1870. June 18. Part of Brookline annexed to Boston.
1870. Nov. 4. Act of June 18, 1870, accepted by Boston.
1872. April 27. Bounds between Brookline and Boston established.
1874. May 8. Part of Brookline annexed to Boston.

COUNTY OF NORFOLK. TOWN OF CANTON.

KIND OF RECORDS.	Number of Volumes	In Keeping of —	Years Covered	Whether Indexed	Condition
General, ...	12	Town Clerk	1797–1885	–	Good
Town proceedings, . . .	6[4]	Town Clerk	1797–1885	Partially	Good
Births, marriages, and deaths,	8[5]	Town Clerk	1797–1885	–	Good
Selectmen and Assessors, .	104[6]	Selectmen	–	–	–
Soldiers in the Rebellion, .	1	Town Clerk	–	–	Good
Miscellaneous, . . .	9	Town Clerk	1797–1885	–	Good

1797. Feb. 23. Part of Stoughton established as Canton.
1847. Mar. 31. Part of Canton annexed to Stoughton.

COUNTY OF NORFOLK. TOWN OF COHASSET.

KIND OF RECORDS.	Number of Volumes	In Keeping of —	Years Covered	Whether Indexed	Condition
Town proceedings, . . .	2[7]	Town Clerk	1770–1885	No	Good
Births, marriages, and deaths,	4[8]	Town Clerk	1770–1885	No	Good
Assessors, ...	–		–	–	–
Selectmen, ...	1	Town Clerk	1882–1885	–	–
Proprietors, ...	1	Town Clerk	1636–1813	No	Good
Miscellaneous, . . .	2	Town Clerk	1853–1885	No	Good

1 There is a copy also of the first volume covering the years from 1686 to 1753, and the records from 1686 to 1838 have been copied and printed.

2 The records from 1686 to 1697 are missing from the first volume.

3 With the exception of the first volume, which is very much worn and has some pages missing.

4 There are copies also of the records of town meetings from 1797 to 1885.

5 There are copies also covering the years from 1797 to 1843.

6 There are copies also of two volumes covering the years from 1727 to 1797.

7 There is a copy also of each volume.   8 There are copies also of the first two volumes.

TOWN RECORDS — Continued.

COUNTY OF NORFOLK. TOWN OF COHASSET — Con.

1770. April 26. Prov. Laws, Vol. V., p. 49. Part of Hingham established as the district of Cohasset.

1775. Aug. 23. Prov. Laws, Vol. V., p. 419. District of Cohasset made the town of Cohasset by this general act.

1823. June 14. Part of Scituate annexed to Cohasset.

1840. Mar. 20. Bounds between Cohasset and Scituate established.

COUNTY OF NORFOLK. TOWN OF DEDHAM.

KIND OF RECORDS.	Number of Volumes	In Keeping of —	Years Covered	Whether Indexed	Condition
General, ...	14¹	Town Clerk	1636–1885	Yes	Fair
Births, marriages, and deaths,	7¹	Town Clerk	1636–1885	Since 1875	Fair
Marriage intentions, . .	3	Town Clerk	1849–1885	Since 1875	Fair
Selectmen and Assessors, .	147	Selectmen	1738–1885	–	–
Proprietors, ...	1	Town Clerk	1636–1720	Yes	Fair
Miscellaneous, ...	20	Town Clerk	1832–1885	Since 1875	Fair

1636. Sept. 8. Mass. Rec., Vol. I., p. 179. The plantation to be settled above the falls of Charles River established as "Deddam."

1638. Aug. 20. Mass. Rec., Vol. I., p. 230. Bounds between Dedham, Concord, and Watertown established.

1650. May 22. Mass. Rec., Vol. IV., Part 1, p. 7. Part of Dedham called "the village" established as Medfield.

1711. Nov. 5. Resolve. Part of Dedham established as Needham.

1724. Dec. 10. Prov. Laws, Vol. II., p. 342. Part of Dedham established as Walpole.

1780. June 17. Part of Stoughton annexed to Dedham.

1784. July 7. Part of Dedham established as the district of Dover.

1791. Mar. 7. Bounds between Dedham and Dover established.

1831. June 17. Part of Dedham annexed to Dorchester.

1852. April 21. Part of Dedham annexed to West Roxbury upon payment of $400 by West Roxbury.

1852. April 30. Act of April 21, 1852, accepted by West Roxbury.

1852. April 30. Part of Dedham annexed to Walpole.

1853. July 4. $400 paid by West Roxbury to Dedham and act of April 21, 1852, in effect.

1868. April 22. Parts of Dedham, Dorchester, and Milton established as Hyde Park.

1868. May 1. Bounds fixed in the act of April 22, 1868, changed.

1872. Feb. 23. Parts of Dedham and Walpole established as Norwood.

COUNTY OF NORFOLK. TOWN OF DOVER.

KIND OF RECORDS.	Number of Volumes	In Keeping of—	Years Covered	Whether Indexed	Condition
General, ...	1	Town Clerk	1784–1885	No	Good
Town proceedings, . . .	3	Town Clerk	1784–1885	No	Good
Births, marriages, and deaths,	1²	Town Clerk	1844–1872	No	Good
Marriages, ...	1	Town Clerk	1872–1885	No	Good
Deaths, ...	1	Town Clerk	1872–1885	No	Good
Marriage intentions, . .	1	Town Clerk	1784–1844	No	Good
Selectmen and Assessors, .	–	–	–	–	–
Miscellaneous, ...	4	Town Clerk	1866–1885	No	Good

¹ There are copies also of the first two volumes. The Dedham Historical Society has records of deaths from about 1800 to 1840. See foot-note to the records of births, marriages, and deaths in Boston.

² The records of births are continued in this volume to 1885. There are copies also of the records of births, marriages, and deaths.

Town Records — Continued.

County of Norfolk. Town of Dover — Con.

1784.	July	7.	Part of Dedham established as the district of Dover.
1791.	Mar.	7.	Bounds between the district of Dover and Dedham established.
1836.	Mar.	31.	District of Dover made the town of Dover.
1836.	May	2.	Act of March 31, 1836, accepted by the district.
1872.	Feb.	27.	Bounds between Dover and Walpole established.

County of Norfolk. Town of Foxborough.

Kind of Records.	Number of Volumes	In Keeping of —	Years Covered	Whether Indexed	Condition
Town proceedings, . . .	12[1]	Town Clerk	1777–1885	Partially	Fair
Births, marriages, and deaths,	7[2]	Town Clerk	1777–1885	Partially	Fair[3]
Assessors,	42	Assessors	–	–	–
Selectmen, ...	12	Selectmen	–	–	–
Soldiers in the Rebellion,	2	Town Clerk	–	No	Fair
Miscellaneous, . . .	32	Town Clerk	1778–1885	No	Fair

1778.	June	10.	Prov. Laws, Vol. V., p. 875. Parts of Stoughton, Stoughtonham, Walpole, and Wrentham established as Foxborough.
1793.	Mar.	12.	Parts of Sharon and Stoughton annexed to Foxborough and bounds established.
1819.	Feb.	3.	Bounds between Foxborough and Wrentham established.
1831.	Feb.	7.	Part of Wrentham annexed to Foxborough.
1833.	Jan.	30.	Bounds between Foxborough and Sharon established and part of each town annexed to the other town.
1833.	Mar.	27.	Part of Foxborough annexed to Walpole.
1834.	Mar.	28.	Part of Foxborough annexed to Walpole.
1850.	Feb.	28.	Part of Sharon annexed to Foxborough.

County of Norfolk. Town of Franklin.

Kind of Records.	Number of Volumes	In Keeping of —	Years Covered	Whether Indexed	Condition
Town proceedings, . . .	3	Town Clerk	1778–1885	No	Fair
Births, marriages, and deaths,	5[4]	Town Clerk	1778–1885	Yes	Fair
Assessors, ...	53	Town Clerk	1825–1885	–	–
Selectmen, ...	1	Selectmen	–	–	–
Parish, ...	1	Town Clerk	1737–1778	No	Fair
Soldiers in the Rebellion,	1	Town Clerk	1861–1865	No	Fair
Miscellaneous, . . .	3	Town Clerk	–	No	Fair

1778.	Mar.	2.	Prov. Laws, Vol. V., p. 775. Part of Wrentham established as Franklin.
1792.	Nov.	13.	Bounds between Franklin and Medway established.
1832.	Feb.	23.	Bounds between Franklin and Bellingham and Medway established.
1839.	Mar.	13.	Bounds between Franklin and Medway established.
1870.	Feb.	23.	Parts of Franklin, Medway, Walpole, and Wrentham established as Norfolk.

---

[1] There is a copy also of the first volume.

[2] There are copies also of the first two volumes.

[3] Twelve pages are missing from the first volume.

[4] There are copies also of the records from 1778 to 1844.

Town Records — Continued.

County of Norfolk. Town of Holbrook.

Kind of Records.	Number of Volumes	In Keeping of —	Years Covered	Whether Indexed	Condition
Town proceedings, . . .	3	Town Clerk	1872–1885	Yes	Good
Births, ...	1	Town Clerk	1872–1885	Yes	Good
Marriages, ...	1	Town Clerk	1872–1885	Yes	Good
Deaths, ...	1	Town Clerk	1872–1885	Yes	Good
Assessors, ...	–	–	–	–	–
Selectmen, ...	2	Town Clerk	–	–	–

1872. Feb. 29. Part of Randolph established as Holbrook.

County of Norfolk. Town of Hyde Park.

Kind of Records.	Number of Volumes	In Keeping of—	Years Covered	Whether Indexed	Condition
Town proceedings, . . .	1	Town Clerk	1868–1885	No	Good
Births, ...	1	Town Clerk	1868–1885	–	Good
Marriages, ...	1	Town Clerk	1868–1885	–	Good
Deaths, ...	1	Town Clerk	1868–1885	–	Good
Assessors, ...	–	–	–	–	–
Selectmen, ...	1	Selectmen	–	–	–
Miscellaneous, . . .	6	Town Clerk	1868–1885	Partially	Good

1868. April 22. Parts of Dedham, Dorchester, and Milton established as Hyde Park.
1868. May   1. Act of April 22, 1868, amended and bounds changed.

County of Norfolk. Town of Medfield.

Kind of Records.	Number of Volumes	In Keeping of—	Years Covered	Whether Indexed	Condition
Town proceedings, . . .	7[1]	Town Clerk	1649–1859[2] 1675–1885	No	Good
Births, ...	2[3]	Town Clerk	1651–1885	1 volume	Good
Marriages, ...	3[3]	Town Clerk	1653–1885	1 volume	Good
Deaths, ...	2[3]	Town Clerk	1652–1885	1 volume	Good
Assessors, ...	10	Assessors	1829–1885	–	–
Selectmen, ...	1	Selectmen	–	–	–
Proprietors, ...	1	Town Clerk	1719–1800	No	Good
Miscellaneous, . . .	4	Town Clerk	1831–1885	No	Good

1650. May 22. Mass. Rec., Vol. IV., Part 1, p. 7. "At the request of the inhabitants of Dedham, the village there is by this Court named Meadfeild."
1659. May 28. Mass. Rec., Vol. IV., Part 1, p. 379. Land granted to Medfield.
1713. Oct. 24. Prov. Laws, Vol. I., p. 722. Part of Medfield established as Medway.

[1] There are copies also of the records from 1649 to 1788.
[2] One volume covering the years from 1860 to 1874 was burned.
[3] There are copies also of the records of births, marriages, and deaths from 1651 to 1876.

Town Records — Continued.

County of Norfolk. Town of Medway.

KIND OF RECORDS.	Number of Volumes	In Keeping of —	Years Covered	Whether Indexed	Condition
Town proceedings, . . .	9[1]	Town Clerk	1713–1885	No	Good[2]
Births, marriages, and deaths,	9[3]	Town Clerk	1713–1885	Yes	Good
Assessors, ...	50[4]	Town Clerk	–	–	–
Selectmen, ...	2	Town Clerk	–	–	–
Miscellaneous, . . .	9	Town Clerk	–	No	Good

1713. Oct. 24. Prov. Laws, Vol. I., p. 722. Part of Medfield established as Medway.
1792. Mar. 3. Bounds between Medway and Sherborn established.
1792. Nov. 13. Bounds between Medway and Franklin established.
1829. Mar. 3. Bounds between Medway and Holliston established and part of each town annexed to the other town.
1832. Feb. 23. Bounds between Medway and Franklin established.
1839. Mar. 13. Part of Franklin annexed to Medway and bounds established.
1870. Feb. 23. Parts of Medway, Franklin, Walpole, and Wrentham established as Norfolk.
1885. Feb. 24. Part of Medway established as Millis.

County of Norfolk. Town of Millis.

KIND OF RECORDS.	Number of Volumes	In Keeping of —	Years Covered	Whether Indexed	Condition
Town proceedings, . . .	1	Town Clerk	– 1885	–	Good
Births, ...	1	Town Clerk	– 1885	Yes	Good
Marriages, ...	1	Town Clerk	– 1885	Yes	Good
Deaths, ...	1	Town Clerk	– 1885	Yes	Good
Assessors, ...	1	Assessors	– 1885	–	Good
Miscellaneous, . . .	2	Town Clerk	– 1885	–	Good

1885. Feb. 24. Part of Medway established as Millis.

County of Norfolk. Town of Milton.

KIND OF RECORDS.	Number of Volumes	In Keeping of —	Years Covered	Whether Indexed	Condition
Town proceedings, . . .	8[5]	Town Clerk	1668–1885	Yes	Good[6]
Births, marriages, and deaths,	7[7]	Town Clerk	1668–1885	Yes	Good
Selectmen and Assessors, .	–		–	–	–
Miscellaneous, . . .	19	Town Clerk	–	–	Good

1662. May 7. Mass. Rec. Vol. IV., Part 2, p. 50. Part of Dorchester commonly called Uncataquissett established as Milton.
1868. April 22. Parts of Milton, Dedham, and Dorchester established as Hyde Park.
1868. May 1. Act of April 22, 1868, amended and bounds changed.
1885. April 16. Bounds between Milton and Quincy established and part of each town annexed to the other town.

---

[1] There is a copy also of the first volume.   [2] With the exception of the first volume.

[3] Some of the records were burned in 1870, but have since been copied from records at the State House.   [4] There are also assessors' lists which are imperfect for various years since 1800.

[5] There are copies also of the records from 1668 to 1729.

[6] The first volume is mutilated.   [7] There are copies also of the records from 1665 to 1843.

TOWN RECORDS — Continued.

COUNTY OF NORFOLK.   TOWN OF NEEDHAM.

KIND OF RECORDS.	Number of Volumes	In Keeping of —	Years Covered	Whether Indexed	Condition
Town proceedings, . . .	8	Town Clerk	1711–1885	No	–
Births, ...	2[1]	Town Clerk	1856–1885	Yes	–
Marriages, ...	2[1]	Town Clerk	1858–1885	Yes	–
Deaths, ...	2[1]	Town Clerk	1854–1885	Yes	–
Assessors, ...	–	Assessors	–	–	–
Selectmen, ...	–	Selectmen	–	–	–
Soldiers in the Rebellion, .	1	Town Clerk	1861–1865	No	–
Miscellaneous, ...	9	Town Clerk	1832–1885	No	–

1711.   Nov.   5.   Resolve. Part of Dedham established as Needham.
1797.   June   22.   Bounds between Needham and Natick established and part of Natick annexed to Needham.
1881.   April   6.   Part of Needham established as Wellesley.

COUNTY OF NORFOLK.   TOWN OF NORFOLK.

KIND OF RECORDS.	Number of Volumes	In Keeping of —	Years Covered	Whether Indexed	Condition
Town proceedings, . . .	1	Town Clerk	1870–1885	No	Good
Births, ...	1	Town Clerk	1870–1885	Yes	Good
Marriages, ...	1	Town Clerk	1870–1885	Yes	Good
Deaths, ...	1	Town Clerk	1870–1885	Yes	Good
Selectmen and Assessors, .	–	–	–	–	–
Parish, ...	1	Town Clerk	–	–	–

1870.   Feb.   23.   Parts of Franklin, Medway, Walpole, and Wrentham established as Norfolk.
1871.   April   19.   Bounds between Norfolk and Wrentham established.

COUNTY OF NORFOLK.   TOWN OF NORWOOD.

KIND OF RECORDS.	Number of Volumes	In Keeping of —	Years Covered	Whether Indexed	Condition
Town proceedings, . . .	1	Town Clerk	1872–1885	Yes	Good
Births, ...	1	Town Clerk	1872–1885	Yes	Good
Marriages, ...	1	Town Clerk	1872–1885	Yes	Good
Deaths, ...	1	Town Clerk	1872–1885	Yes	Good
Marriage intentions, . .	1	Town Clerk	1872–1885	Yes	Good
Assessors, ...	2	Selectmen	1872–1885	–	–
Selectmen, ...	13	Selectmen	1872–1885	–	–

1872.   Feb.   23.   Parts of Dedham and Walpole established as Norwood.

[1] There is a volume also of records of births, marriages, and deaths from 1711 to 1801, which have been copied from the records of town proceedings.

Town Records — Continued.

County of Norfolk. Town of Quincy.

Kind of Records.	Number of Volumes	In Keeping of—	Years Covered	Whether Indexed	Condition
Town proceedings, . . .	6	Town Clerk	1792–1885	Yes	Good
Births, marriages, and deaths,	4	Town Clerk	1792–1885	Yes	Good
Selectmen and Assessors, .	35	Selectmen	–	–	–
Parish, ...	2	Town Clerk	1643–1865	Yes	Good

1792. Feb. 22. Part of Braintree established as Quincy, and part of that part of Dorchester called Squantum and the Farms annexed to Quincy.
1814. Feb. 10. Part of that part of Dorchester called Squantum and the Farms annexed to Quincy.
1819. Feb. 12. Part of Dorchester annexed to Quincy.
1820. Feb. 21. Bounds between Quincy and Dorchester established, and part of that part of Dorchester called Squantum annexed to Quincy.
1855. May 2. Part of Dorchester at Squantum annexed to Quincy.
1856. April 24. Part of Braintree annexed to Quincy.
1885. April 16. Bounds between Quincy and Milton established and part of each town annexed to the other town.
1888. May 17. Quincy incorporated as a city.
1888. June 11. Act of incorporation accepted by the town.

County of Norfolk. Town of Randolph. *

Kind of Records.	Number of Volumes	In Keeping of—	Years Covered	Whether Indexed	Condition
Town proceedings, . . .	3	Town Clerk	1793–1885	–	–
Births, marriages, and deaths,	5[1]	Town Clerk	1793–1885	–	–
Selectmen and Assessors, .	29	Selectmen	–	–	–

1793. Mar. 9. Part of Braintree established as Randolph.
1811. June 22. Certain estates in Braintree re-annexed to Randolph.
1861. Mar. 21. Bounds between Randolph and Abington established.
1872. Feb. 29. Part of Randolph established as Holbrook.

County of Norfolk. Town of Sharon.

Kind of Records.	Number of Volumes	In Keeping of—	Years Covered	Whether Indexed	Condition
Town proceedings, . . .	8	Town Clerk	1740–1885	No	–
Births, marriages, and deaths,	5[2]	Town Clerk	1740–1885	–	–
Assessors, ...	65[2]	Town Clerk	–	–	–
Miscellaneous, ...	4[3]	Town Clerk	1832–1885	–	–

1783. Feb. 25. The name of the town of Stoughtonham[4] changed to Sharon.
1789. Feb. 16. Part of Stoughton annexed to Sharon.

[1] The heirs of Rev. Ebenezer Alden have private records of births, marriages and deaths.
[2] There are copies also of each volume.
[3] The records of the treasurer from 1850 to 1865 are missing.
[4] For legislation concerning the town of Stoughtonham, see "Extinct Cities, Towns, and Districts."

COUNTY OF NORFOLK.   TOWN OF SHARON — Con.

1792. Feb. 22. Part of Stoughton annexed to Sharon.
1793. Mar. 12. Bounds between Sharon and Foxborough established and parts of Sharon and Stoughton annexed to Foxborough.
1804. Feb. 28. Part of Sharon annexed to Walpole.
1811. June 21. Part of Sharon annexed to Walpole.
1833. Jan. 30. Bounds between Sharon and Foxborough established and part of each town annexed to the other town.
1850. Feb. 28. Part of Sharon annexed to Foxborough.
1864. Mar. 26. Part of Stoughton annexed to Sharon.
1874. May   1. Part of Sharon annexed to Walpole.

COUNTY OF NORFOLK.   TOWN OF STOUGHTON.

KIND OF RECORDS.	Number of Volumes	In Keeping of —	Years Covered	Whether Indexed	Condition
Town proceedings, . . .	8[1]	Town Clerk	1726–1885	No	Good
Births, marriages, and deaths,	11[1]	Town Clerk	1726–1885	Since 1844	Good
Selectmen and Assessors, .	25	Selectmen	–	–	–
Miscellaneous, ...	9[2]	Town Clerk	–	No	Good

1726. Dec. 22. Prov. Laws, Vol. II., p. 408. Part of Dorchester established as Stoughton.
1765. June 21. Prov. Laws, Vol. IV., p. 808. Part of Stoughton established as the district of Stoughtonham.
1770. Nov. 20. Prov. Laws, Vol. V., p. 116. Part of Stoughton annexed to Bridgewater.
1778. June 10. Prov. Laws, Vol. V., p. 875. Parts of Stoughton, Stoughtonham, Walpole, and Wrentham established as Foxborough.
1780. June 17. Part of Stoughton annexed to Dedham.
1789. Feb. 16. Part of Stoughton annexed to Sharon.
1792. Feb. 22. Part of Stoughton annexed to Sharon.
1793. Mar. 12. Parts of Stoughton and Sharon annexed to Foxborough.
1797. Feb. 23. Part of Stoughton established as Canton.
1798. Feb.   8. Part of Stoughton annexed to Bridgewater.
1847. Mar. 31. Part of Canton annexed to Stoughton.
1864. Mar. 26. Part of Stoughton annexed to Sharon.
1888. Feb. 21. Part of Stoughton established as Avon.

COUNTY OF NORFOLK.   TOWN OF WALPOLE.

KIND OF RECORDS.	Number of Volumes	In Keeping of —	Years Covered	Whether Indexed	Condition
Town proceedings, . . .	4	Town Clerk	1724–1885[3]	No	–[4]
Births, marriages, and deaths,	6	Town Clerk	1724–1885	No	Good
Assessors, ...	159	Assessors	1724–1885[5]	–	–[6]
Selectmen, ...	10	Selectmen	–	–	–
Miscellaneous, ...	14	Town Clerk	1724–1885	No	Good

[1] There are copies also of the earlier records.

[2] The volume of records of soldiers in the Rebellion, and a few other volumes, were burned.

[3] The records from 1776 to 1780 are missing from the first volume.

[4] The first two volumes are in poor condition, the first volume having pages missing.

[5] Five volumes covering the years from 1821 to 1825 are missing.

[6] The records prior to 1826 are in poor condition.

TOWN RECORDS — Continued.

COUNTY OF NORFOLK. TOWN OF WALPOLE — Con.

1724.	Dec.	10.	Prov. Laws, Vol. II., p. 342. Part of Dedham established as Walpole.
1778.	June	10.	Prov. Laws, Vol. V., p. 875. Parts of Walpole, Stoughton, Stoughton-ham, and Wrentham established as Foxborough.
1804.	Feb.	28.	Part of Sharon annexed to Walpole.
1811.	June	21.	Part of Sharon annexed to Walpole.
1833.	Mar.	27.	Part of Foxborough annexed to Walpole.
1834.	Mar.	28.	Part of Foxborough annexed to Walpole.
1852.	April	30.	Part of Dedham annexed to Walpole.
1870.	Feb.	23.	Parts of Walpole, Franklin, Medway, and Wrentham established as Norfolk.
1872.	Feb.	23.	Parts of Walpole and Dedham established as Norwood.
1872.	Feb.	27.	Bounds between Walpole and Dover established.
1874.	May	1.	Part of Sharon annexed to Walpole.

COUNTY OF NORFOLK. TOWN OF WELLESLEY.

KIND OF RECORDS.	Number of Volumes	In Keeping of —	Years Covered	Whether Indexed	Condition
Town proceedings,	1	Town Clerk	1881–1885	No	Good
Births, marriages, and deaths,	3	Town Clerk	1881–1885	Yes	Good
Assessors,	–	Assessors	–	–	–
Selectmen,	–	Selectmen	–	–	–
Miscellaneous,	1	Town Clerk	1881–1885	Yes	Good

1881. April 6. Part of Needham established as Wellesley.

COUNTY OF NORFOLK. TOWN OF WEYMOUTH.

KIND OF RECORDS.	Number of Volumes	In Keeping of —	Years Covered	Whether Indexed	Condition
Town proceedings,	8[1]	Town Clerk	1642–1885	No	Good
Births, marriages, and deaths,	13[2]	Town Clerk	1642–1885	Yes	Good
Marriage intentions,	3	Town Clerk	1642–1885	No	Good
Selectmen and Assessors,	–	Selectmen	–	–	–
Soldiers in the Rebellion,	1	Town Clerk	–	No	Good
Miscellaneous,	19	Town Clerk	1642–1885	No	Good

1635. Sept. 2. Mass. Rec., Vol. I., p. 156. The name of the plantation of Wessaguscus changed to "Waymothe."
1847. Mar. 31. Bounds between Weymouth and Abington established.

[1] There is a copy also of the first volume covering the years from 1642 to 1773.

[2] There are copies also of the records of births from 1644 to 1785, of marriages from 1655 to 1779, and of deaths from 1639 to 1844. The records of births from 1644 to 1654, of marriages from 1663 to 1700, and of deaths from 1642 to 1655, for 1657, and from 1661 to 1699, are missing.

TOWN RECORDS — Continued.

COUNTY OF NORFOLK.　TOWN OF WRENTHAM.

KIND OF RECORDS.	Number of Volumes	In Keeping of —	Years Covered	Whether Indexed	Condition
Town proceedings, . . .	10[1]	Town Clerk	1660–1885	No	Fair
Births, marriages, and deaths,	10	Town Clerk	1660–1885	–	Fair
Assessors, ...	35	Selectmen	–	–	–
Selectmen, ...	4	Selectmen	–	–	–
Proprietors, ...	4	Town Clerk	1662–1829	No	Fair
Miscellaneous, ...	11	Town Clerk	1794–1885	No	Fair

1673. Oct. 15. Mass. Rec., Vol. IV., Part 2, p. 569. Lands granted to the inhabitants of Wollonopaug and Wrentham established.

1778. Mar. 2. Prov. Laws, Vol. V., p. 775. Part of Wrentham established as Franklin.

1778. June 10. Prov. Laws, Vol. V., p. 875. Parts of Wrentham, Stoughton, Stoughtonham, and Walpole established as Foxborough.

1819. Feb. 3. Bounds between Wrentham and Foxborough established.

1830. Feb. 18. Bounds between Wrentham and Attleborough established and part of Attleborough annexed to Wrentham.

1831. Feb. 7. Part of Wrentham annexed to Foxborough.

1870. Feb. 23. Parts of Wrentham, Franklin, Medway, and Walpole established as Norfolk.

1871. April 19. Bounds between Wrentham and Norfolk established.

COUNTY OF PLYMOUTH.　TOWN OF ABINGTON.

KIND OF RECORDS.	Number of Volumes	In Keeping of —	Years Covered	Whether Indexed	Condition
General, ...	1[2]	Town Clerk	1712–1766	No	Good
Town proceedings, . . .	4	Town Clerk	1767–1885	No	Good
Births, marriages, and deaths,	2	Town Clerk	1749–1820	No	Good
Births and deaths, . .	1	Town Clerk	1821–1851	No	Good
Births, ...	2	Town Clerk	1851–1885	Yes	Good
Marriages, ...	4	Town Clerk	1821–1885	Yes	Good
Deaths, ...	2	Town Clerk	1851–1885	Yes	Good
Marriage intentions, . .	1	Town Clerk	1860–1885	Yes	Good
Assessors, ...	113	Assessors	–	–	–
Selectmen, ...	10	Selectmen	–	–	–
Soldiers in the Rebellion, .	1	Town Clerk	1861–1865	No	Good
Miscellaneous, . . .	15	Town Clerk	1824–1885	No	Good

1712. June 10. Resolve. Part of Bridgewater and certain lands adjoining established as "Abingdon."

1727. June 14. Prov. Laws, Vol. II., p. 429. Parts of Abington and Scituate established as Hanover.

1847. Mar. 31. Bounds between Abington and Weymouth established.

1861. Mar. 21. Bounds between Abington and Randolph established.

1861. Mar. 21. Bounds between Abington and Hingham established.

1874. Mar. 9. Part of Abington established as Rockland.

1875. Mar. 4. Parts of Abington and East Bridgewater established as South Abington.

---

[1] There is a copy also of the first volume.

[2] A part of the records of town proceedings, and of births, marriages, and deaths were copied by the town of Rockland.

TOWN RECORDS — Continued.

COUNTY OF PLYMOUTH. TOWN OF BRIDGEWATER.

KIND OF RECORDS.	Number of Volumes	In Keeping of —	Years Covered	Whether Indexed	Condition
Town proceedings, . . .	8[1]	Town Clerk	1656–1885	No	Good
Births, marriages, and deaths,	8[2]	Town Clerk	1656–1885	Partially	Good
Assessors, ...	5	Town Clerk	–	–	–
Selectmen, ...	2	Town Clerk	–	–	–
Proprietors, ...	4[3]	Town Clerk	1675–1827	No	Good
Miscellaneous, ...	–	Town Clerk	1656–1885	No	Good

1656. June 3. Ply. Col. Rec., Vol. III., p. 101. Duxburrow New Plantation established as Bridgewater.

1662. June 3. Ply. Col. Rec., Vol. IV., p. 18. Certain lands granted to Bridgewater.

1691. Feb. 11. Ply. Col. Rec., Vol. VI., p. 257. Lands between Bridgewater and Weymouth, called Foord's Farms, and lands adjoining, annexed to Bridgewater.

1712. June 10. Resolve. Part of Bridgewater and certain lands adjoining established as Abington.

1770. Nov. 20. Prov. Laws, Vol. V., p. 116. Part of Stoughton annexed to Bridgewater.

1798. Feb. 8. Part of Stoughton annexed to Bridgewater. ·

1821. June 15. Part of Bridgewater established as North Bridgewater.

1822. Feb. 16. Part of Bridgewater established as West Bridgewater.

1823. June 14. Part of Bridgewater established as East Bridgewater.

1824. Feb. 20. Part of Bridgewater annexed to Halifax.

1838. Feb. 23. Bounds between Bridgewater and East Bridgewater established.

1846. Mar. 20. Bounds between Bridgewater and East Bridgewater established and part of each town annexed to the other town.

COUNTY OF PLYMOUTH. CITY OF BROCKTON.

KIND OF RECORDS.	Number of Volumes	In Keeping of —	Years Covered	Whether Indexed	Condition
Town proceedings, . . .	3	Town Clerk	1821–1881	No	Good
City proceedings, . . .	2	Town Clerk	1882–1885	Yes	Good
Births, marriages, and deaths (town), ...	2	Town Clerk	1821–1881	–	Good
Births (city), ...	2	Town Clerk	1882–1885	–	Good
Marriages (city), . . .	2	Town Clerk	1882–1885	–	Good
Deaths (city), ...	2	Town Clerk	1882–1885	–	Good
Marriage intentions, . .	1	Town Clerk	–	–	Good
Assessors, ...	58	Assessors	–	–	–
Miscellaneous, ...	22	Town Clerk	–	Partially	Good

1874. Mar. 28. North Bridgewater[4] authorized to change its name.

1874. May 5. Brockton adopted as the name.

1875. April 24. Part of Brockton annexed to South Abington, and parts of East Bridgewater and South Abington annexed to Brockton.

1881. April 9. Brockton incorporated as a city.

1881. May 23. Act of April 9, 1881, accepted by the town.

---

[1] The first four volumes have been copied and indexed.

[2] Thomas Cushman and Mrs. Williams Latham have private records of births, marriages, and deaths.

[3] These are copies of the original records, and the town clerks of East Bridgewater and West Bridgewater have each a copy in their possession.

[4] For legislation concerning the town of North Bridgewater, see "Extinct Cities, Towns, and Districts."

TOWN RECORDS — Continued.

COUNTY OF PLYMOUTH. TOWN OF CARVER.

KIND OF RECORDS.	Number of Volumes	In Keeping of —	Years Covered	Whether Indexed	Condition
Town proceedings, . . .	5[1]	Town Clerk	1790–1885	Partially	Good
Births, marriages, and deaths,	8	Town Clerk	1790–1885[2]	Partially	Good
Selectmen and Assessors, .	30	Selectmen	1853–1885[3]	–	–
Soldiers in the Rebellion, .	1	Town Clerk	1861–1865	–	Good

1790. June 9. Part of Plympton established as Carver.
1827. Jan. 20. Part of Carver annexed to Wareham.
1849. Mar. 24. Bounds between Carver and Middleborough established.

COUNTY OF PLYMOUTH. TOWN OF DUXBURY.

KIND OF RECORDS.	Number of Volumes	In Keeping of—	Years Covered	Whether Indexed	Condition
Town proceedings, . . .	3	Town Clerk	1686–1885[4]	No	Fair
Births, marriages, and deaths,	6	Town Clerk	1645–1885	Yes	Fair
Assessors, ...	29	Selectmen	–	–	–
Selectmen, ...	3	Selectmen	–	–	–
Proprietors, ...	1	Town Clerk	1709–1730	No	Fair
Soldiers in the Rebellion, .	1	Town Clerk	–	No	Fair
Miscellaneous, ...	8	Town Clerk	–	Partially	Fair

1637. June 7. Ply. Col. Rec., Vol. I., p. 62. "Ducksburrow" made "a towneship, and to have the priviledges of a towne."
1641. Mar. 2. Ply. Col. Rec., Vol. II., p. 9. Bounds established.
1658. Mar. 2. Ply. Col. Rec., Vol. III., p. 133. Namassakeesett annexed to Duxbury.
1661. Mar. 5. Ply. Col. Rec., Vol. III., p. 209. Certain tract of land granted to Duxbury and Marshfield.
1670. July 5. Ply. Col. Rec., Vol. V., p. 44. Bounds between Duxbury and "the Major's purchase" established.
1678. June 5. Ply. Col. Rec., Vol. V., p. 258. Bounds established.
1683. Feb. 23. Ply. Col. Rec., Vol. VI., p. 155. Bounds between Duxbury and Marshfield established.
1712. Mar. 21. Prov. Laws, Vol. I., p. 684. Part of Duxbury and certain other lands established as Pembroke.
1813. June 14. Bounds between Duxbury and Marshfield established.
1857. April 14. Part of Duxbury annexed to Kingston.

[1] There are copies also of the first two volumes.
[2] The record of marriages for 1813 is missing.
[3] The records of selectmen and assessors from 1790 to 1853 are missing.
[4] One volume covering the years from 1640 to 1688 is lost.

Town Records — Continued.

County of Plymouth. Town of East Bridgewater.

Kind of Records.	Number of Volumes	In Keeping of—	Years Covered	Whether Indexed	Condition
Town proceedings, ...	3	Town Clerk	1823–1885	No	Good
Births, marriages, and deaths,	1	Town Clerk	1823–1844	–	Good
Births, ...	1	Town Clerk	1844–1885	Yes	Good
Marriages, ...	1	Town Clerk	1844–1885	Yes	Good
Deaths, ...	1	Town Clerk	1844–1885	Yes	Good
Selectmen and Assessors, .	58	Town Clerk	–	–	–
Proprietors, ...	1[1]	Town Clerk	1675–1827	–	–
Miscellaneous, ...	8	Town Clerk	1823–1885	No	Good

1823.	June 14.	Part of Bridgewater established as East Bridgewater.
1838.	Feb. 23.	Bounds between East Bridgewater and Bridgewater established.
1846.	Mar. 20.	Part of Bridgewater annexed to East Bridgewater and bounds established.
1857.	April 11.	Part of Halifax annexed to East Bridgewater and bounds established.
1875.	Mar. 4.	Parts of East Bridgewater and Abington established as South Abington.
1875.	April 24.	Part of East Bridgewater annexed to Brockton.

County of Plymouth. Town of Halifax

Kind of Records.	Number of Volumes	In Keeping of—	Years Covered	Whether Indexed	Condition
Town proceedings, . . .	5	Town Clerk	1735–1885	No	Good
Births, marriages, and deaths,	5	Town Clerk	1735–1885[2]	Yes	Good
Assessors, ...	–	Assessors	–	–	–
Selectmen, ...	4	Selectmen	–	–	–
Miscellaneous, ...	5	Town Clerk	1755–1885	No	Good

1734.	July 4.	Prov. Laws, Vol. II., p. 717. Parts of Middleborough, Pembroke, and Plympton established as "Halifax."
1824.	Feb. 20.	Part of Bridgewater annexed to Halifax.
1831.	Mar. 16.	Part of Plympton annexed to Halifax.
1857.	April 11.	Part of Halifax annexed to East Bridgewater and bounds established.
1863.	Feb. 6.	Part of Plympton annexed to Halifax and bounds established.

County of Plymouth. Town of Hanover.

Kind of Records.	Number of Volumes	In Keeping of—	Years Covered	Whether Indexed	Condition
Town proceedings, . . .	6	Town Clerk	1727–1885	No	Good
Births, marriages, and deaths,	7	Town Clerk	1727–1885	–	Good
Selectmen and Assessors, .	37	Assessors	–	–	–
Miscellaneous, . . .	13	Town Clerk	1727–1885	No	Good

[1] This is a copy of the records of the proprietors of Bridgewater.

[2] The records of births, marriages, and deaths from 1830 to 1840 are missing.

Town Records — Continued.

County of Plymouth. Town of Hanover — Con.

1727. June 14. Prov. Laws, Vol. II., p. 429. Parts of Abington and Scituate established as Hanover.

1835. Mar. 6. Bounds between Hanover and Pembroke established.

1857. May 15. Bounds between Hanover and South Scituate established.

1878. Feb. 11. Bounds between Hanover and South Scituate established and part of each town annexed to the other town.

1878. Mar. 23. Bounds between Hanover and Rockland established and part of each town annexed to the other town.

1885. April 23. Bounds between Hanover and Pembroke established.

County of Plymouth. Town of Hanson.

KIND OF RECORDS.	Number of Volumes	In Keeping of —	Years Covered	Whether Indexed	Condition
General, ...	3	Town Clerk	1820–1885	No	Fair
Births, marriages, and deaths,	5[1]	Town Clerk	1820–1885	4 volumes	–
Selectmen and Assessors, .	–	Selectmen	–	–	–
Miscellaneous, ...	5	Town Clerk	1820–1885	Partially	–

1820. Feb. 22. Part of Pembroke established as Hanson.

County of Plymouth. Town of Hingham.

KIND OF RECORDS.	Number of Volumes	In Keeping of —	Years Covered	Whether Indexed	Condition
Town proceedings, . . .	10[2]	Town Clerk	1635–1655 1657–1885	No	Good[3]
Births, marriages, and deaths,	9[4]	Town Clerk	1635–1885	Yes	Good
Deaths, ...	1[5]	Town Clerk	–	–	Good
Marriage intentions, . .	4[6]	Town Clerk	1700–1885	–	Good
Selectmen and Assessors, .	–	–	–	–	–
Proprietors, ...	2	Town Clerk	1635–1788	–	–
Miscellaneous, ...	5	Town Clerk	–	Partially	Good

1635. Sept. 2. Mass. Rec., Vol. I., p. 156. "The name of Barecove is changed and hereafter to be called Hingham."

1640. May 13. Mass. Rec., Vol. I., p. 290. Land at Conihasset granted to Hingham.

1770. April 26. Prov. Laws, Vol. V., p. 49. Part of Hingham established as the district of Cohasset.

1861. Mar. 21. Bounds between Hingham and Abington established.

[1] The records of marriages from 1837 to 1842 are missing, and the records of births and deaths for those years are very imperfect.

[2] There is an indexed copy also of the first volume and a partial copy of the second volume.

[3] With the exception of the first volume, from which some of the leaves are missing.

[4] Copies of the earlier volumes were made and are probably in the hands of the heirs of Solomon Lincoln. The heirs of Charles B. W. Lane, George Lincoln, Fearing Burr, and Reuben Hersey have private records of births, marriages, and deaths. See foot-note to the records of births, marriages, and deaths in Boston.

[5] This is a record of deaths of persons born in Hingham who died elsewhere.

[6] There is a package also of records of marriage intentions, unbound.

TOWN RECORDS — Continued.

COUNTY OF PLYMOUTH. TOWN OF HULL.

KIND OF RECORDS.	Number of Volumes	In Keeping of—	Years Covered	Whether Indexed	Condition
Town proceedings, . . .	7[1]	Town Clerk	} 1657–1793 1808–1885 {	} No {	Good[2]
Births, marriages, and deaths,	5[3]	Town Clerk	–	No	Good
Assessors, ...	25	Assessors	1860–1885	No	Good
Proprietors, ...	1[4]	Robert Gould[5]	–	–	–

1644. May 29. Mass. Rec., Vol. II., p. 74. The plantation of "Nantascot shall be called Hull."
1647. May 26. Mass. Rec., Vol. II., p. 189. Hull is mentioned as a town.

COUNTY OF PLYMOUTH. TOWN OF KINGSTON.

KIND OF RECORDS.	Number of Volumes	In Keeping of—	Years Covered	Whether Indexed	Condition
Town proceedings, . . .	7	Town Clerk	1719–1885	Yes	–
Births, marriages, and deaths,	6	Town Clerk	1719–1885	Yes	–
Selectmen and Assessors, .	6	–	–	–	–
Miscellaneous, . . .	23	Town Clerk	–	Yes	–

1726. June 16. Prov. Laws, Vol. II., p. 387. Part of Plymouth established as Kingston.
1857. April 14. Part of Duxbury annexed to Kingston.

COUNTY OF PLYMOUTH. TOWN OF LAKEVILLE.

KIND OF RECORDS.	Number of Volumes	In Keeping of—	Years Covered	Whether Indexed	Condition
Town proceedings, . . .	2	Town Clerk	1853–1885	No	Good
Births	1	Town Clerk	1853–1885	Yes	Good
Marriages, ...	1	Town Clerk	1853–1885	Yes	Good
Deaths, ...	1	Town Clerk	1853–1885	Yes	Good
Assessors, ...	–	–	–	–	–
Selectmen, ...	1	Selectmen	1853–1885	No	Good
Soldiers in the Rebellion, .	1	Town Clerk	1861–1865	No	Good
Miscellaneous, . . .	5	Town Clerk	1853–1885	No	Good

1853. May 13. Part of Middleborough established as Lakeville.
1867. June 1. Bounds between Lakeville and Taunton established.

---

[1] There are copies also of the first two volumes.
[2] With the exception of the first two volumes.
[3] There are records of baptisms, marriages, and deaths from 1726 to 1768, made by Rev. Ezra Carpenter and Rev. Samuel Veazie, and a diary of Zachariah Whitman from 1670 to 1726, in possession of Miss Sarah Jones, Hingham, copies of which are in possession of the Town Clerk.
[4] There are records of grants in the first volume of the town records which begins in 1657.
[5] East Cambridge.

TOWN RECORDS — Continued.

COUNTY OF PLYMOUTH. TOWN OF MARION.

KIND OF RECORDS.	Number of Volumes	In Keeping of—	Years Covered	Whether Indexed	Condition
Town proceedings, . . .	2	Town Clerk	1852–1885	1 volume	–
Births, marriages, and deaths,	3	Town Clerk	1852–1885	No	–
Selectmen and Assessors, .	3[1]	Selectmen	1880–1885	No	–
Proprietors, ...	1[2]	–	1679–1885	–	–
Miscellaneous, ...	3	Town Clerk	1852–1885	No	–

1852. May 14. Part of Rochester established as Marion.
1853. April 8. Bounds between Marion and Rochester established.
1859. Feb. 18. Bounds between Marion and Wareham established.
1866. Feb. 13. Bounds between Marion and Wareham established.

COUNTY OF PLYMOUTH. TOWN OF MARSHFIELD.

KIND OF RECORDS	Number of Volumes	In Keeping of—	Years Covered	Whether Indexed	Condition
Town proceedings, . . .	6[3]	Town Clerk	1643–1885	No	Good[4]
Births, marriages, and deaths,	6	Town Clerk	1843–1885	No	Good
Selectmen and Assessors, .	–	–	–	–	–
Proprietors, ...	–	Wendall A. Phillips[5]	–	–	–
Miscellaneous, ...	3	Town Clerk	–	No	Good

1642. Mar. 1. Ply. Col. Rec., Vol. II., p. 34. Marshfield is mentioned as one of the towns for which officers are chosen.
1643. Mar. 7. Ply. Col. Rec., Vol. II., p. 54. Bounds established.
1660. Mar. 5. Ply. Col. Rec., Vol. III., p. 209. Certain lands granted to Marshfield and Duxbury.
1683. Feb. 23. Ply. Col. Rec., Vol. VI., p. 155. Bounds between Marshfield and Duxbury established.
1787. Mar. 10. Part of Scituate annexed to Marshfield.
1813. June 14. Bounds between Marshfield and Duxbury established.
1887. May 11. Bounds between Marshfield and Scituate established.

COUNTY OF PLYMOUTH. TOWN OF MATTAPOISETT.

KIND OF RECORDS.	Number of Volumes	In Keeping of—	Years Covered	Whether Indexed	Condition
Town proceedings, . . .	1	Town Clerk	1857–1885	No	–
Births, marriages, and deaths,	4[6]	Town Clerk	1857–1885	Yes	–
Assessors, ...	28	Assessors	1857–1885	–	–
Selectmen, ...	2	Selectmen	1857–1885	–	–
Proprietors, ...	2[7]	–	16?9–1885	Yes	–
Miscellaneous, ...	2	Town Clerk	1857–1885	Yes	–

1857. May 20. Part of Rochester established as Mattapoisett.

[1] The records of the selectmen from 1852 to 1880 were burned.
[2] This is a copy of the records of the proprietors of Rochester.
[3] There is an indexed copy also of the first two volumes.
[4] With the exception of the first two volumes.   [5] East Marshfield.
[6] Noah Hammond has private records of deaths from 1822 to 1847.
[7] These are copies of the records of the proprietors of Rochester.

Town Records — Continued.

County of Plymouth. Town of Middleborough.

Kind of Records.	Number of Volumes	In Keeping of—	Years Covered	Whether Indexed	Cond tion
Town proceedings, . . .	9	Town Clerk	1669–1885	No	Good
Births, marriages, and deaths,	14[1]	Town Clerk	1669–1885	Yes	Good
Assessors, ...	25	Assessors	–	–	–
Proprietors, ...	1[2]	Town Clerk	1675–1704[3]	No	Good
Miscellaneous, . . .	12	Town Clerk	1708–1885	No	Good

1669. June 1. Ply. Col. Rec., Vol. V., p. 19. "Namassakett shall be a township and to be called by the name of Middleberry."

1680. Sept. 28. Ply. Col. Rec., Vol. VI., p. 51. Certain lands at Assowamsett Neck and places adjacent granted to Middleborough.

1734. July 4. Prov. Laws, Vol. II., p. 717. Parts of Middleborough, Pembroke, and Plympton established as Halifax.

1849. Mar. 24. Bounds between Middleborough and Carver established.

1853. May 13. Part of Middleborough established as Lakeville.

County of Plymouth. Town of Pembroke.

Kind of Records.	Number of Volumes	In Keeping of—	Years Covered	Whether Indexed	Condition
Town proceedings, . . .	5[4]	Town Clerk	1711–1885	No	Good
Births, marriages, and deaths,	6	Town Clerk	1711–1885[5]	Yes	Good
Selectmen and Assessors, .	67	Selectmen	–	–	–
Miscellaneous, ...	3	Town Clerk	1834–1885	No	Good

1712. Mar. 21. Prov. Laws, Vol. I., p. 684. Part of Duxbury called Mattakeeset, a tract of land known as the Major's Purchase, and the land called Marshfield Upper Lands at Mattakeeset, established as Pembroke.

1734. July 4. Prov. Laws, Vol. II., p. 717. Parts of Pembroke, Middleborough, and Plympton established as Halifax.

1820. Feb. 22. Part of Pembroke established as Hanson.

1835. Mar. 6. Bounds between Pembroke and Hanover established.

1885. April 23. Bounds between Pembroke and Hanover established.

County of Plymouth. Town of Plymouth.

Kind of Records.	Number of Volumes	In Keeping of—	Years Covered	Whether Indexed	Condition
Town proceedings, . . .	8[6]	Town Clerk	–	Yes	Fair
Births, marriages, and deaths,	10[7]	Town Clerk	–	Yes	Fair[8]
Selectmen and Assessors, .	–	–	–	–	–
Proprietors, ...	2	Town Clerk	1702–1713	Yes	Fair
Miscellaneous, . . .	9	Town Clerk	–	Yes	Fair

---

[1] There are also copies.

[2] There is also a copy.

[3] The earlier records are lost.

[4] There are copies also of the records from 1711 to 1735.

[5] The earlier records of births, marriages, and deaths, are incomplete.

[6] There are copies also of the first two volumes, at the court house.

[7] There is a copy also of the first volume, at the court house.

[8] With the exception of the first volume, from which three leaves are missing.

TOWN RECORDS — Continued.

COUNTY OF PLYMOUTH. TOWN OF PLYMOUTH — Con.

The first mention of the name of Plymouth in the records is in "Plimouth's great Book of Deeds of Lands Enrolled," under the date of 1620.

1670.   June   7.   Ply. Col Rec., Vol. V., p. 41. The bounds between Plymouth and Sandwich established January 19, 1663, not being recorded, were ordered to be entered on the records of the court.

1707.   June   4.   Resolve. Part of Plymouth established as Plympton.

1726.   June   16.   Prov. Laws, Vol. II., p. 387. Part of Plymouth established as Kingston.

1739.   July   10.   Prov. Laws, Vol. II., p. 992. Parts of Plymouth and Rochester established as Wareham.

1827.   Jan.   20.   Part of Plymouth annexed to Wareham.

COUNTY OF PLYMOUTH. TOWN OF PLYMPTON.

KIND OF RECORDS.	Number of Volumes	In Keeping of —	Years Covered	Whether Indexed	Condition
General, ...	13	Town Clerk	1707–1885	Yes	Good
Births, marriages, and deaths,	1[1]	Town Clerk	1841–1860	Yes	Good
Births, ...	1	Town Clerk	1857–1885	Yes	Good
Marriages, ...	1	Town Clerk	1852–1885	Yes	Good
Deaths, ...	1	Town Clerk	1860–1885	Yes	Good
Assessors, ...	30	Town Clerk	–	–	–

1707.   June   4.   Resolve. Part of Plymouth established as Plympton.

1734.   July   4.   Prov. Laws, Vol. II., p. 717. Parts of Plympton, Middleborough, and Pembroke established as Halifax.

1790.   June   9.   Part of Plympton established as Carver.

1831.   Mar.   16.   Part of Plympton annexed to Halifax.

1863.   Feb.   6.   Bounds between Plympton and Halifax established and part of each town annexed to the other town.

COUNTY OF PLYMOUTH. TOWN OF ROCHESTER.

KIND OF RECORDS.	Number of Volumes	In Keeping of —	Years Covered	Whether Indexed	Condition
Town proceedings, . .	15	Town Clerk	1697–1885	No	–[2]
Births, marriages, and deaths,	6	Town Clerk	1697–1885	Yes	Good
Selectmen and Assessors, .	30	–	–	–	–
Proprietors, . . .	1[3]	Town Clerk	1679–1885	No	Good
Miscellaneous, . . .	2	Town Clerk	1697–1885	No	Good

1686.   June   4.   Ply. Col. Rec., Vol. VI., p. 189. "Sippican, alias Rochester" made "a township with the privilidges of a town."

1739.   July   10.   Prov. Laws, Vol. II., p. 992. Parts of Rochester and Plymouth established as Wareham.

---

[1] There is a record of births, marriages, and deaths made by Lewis Bradford in keeping of William L. Soule of Cambridge.

[2] The earlier volumes are dilapidated.

[3] There are copies also in the Registry of Deeds at Plymouth and in possession of the Town Clerks of Marion and Mattapoisett.

TOWN RECORDS — Continued.

COUNTY OF PLYMOUTH. TOWN OF ROCHESTER — Con.

1836.	April	9.	Part of Rochester annexed to Fairhaven and bounds established.
1852.	May	14.	Part of Rochester established as Marion.
1853.	April	8.	Bounds between Rochester and Marion established.
1857.	May	20.	Part of Rochester established as Mattapoisett.
1864.	April	20.	Bounds between Rochester and Wareham established.
1866.	Feb.	15.	Bounds between Rochester and Wareham established.
1887.	June	3.	Bounds between Rochester and Wareham established.

COUNTY OF PLYMOUTH. TOWN OF ROCKLAND.

KIND OF RECORDS.	Number of Volumes	In Keeping of —	Years Covered	Whether Indexed	Condition
Town proceedings, . . .	2	Town Clerk	1874–1885	No	Good
Births, marriages, and deaths,	3	Town Clerk	1874–1885	Yes	Good
Selectmen and Assessors, .	17	Selectmen	–	–	–
Miscellaneous, ...	1	Town Clerk	1874–1885	No	Good

1874.	Mar.	9.	Part of Abington established as Rockland.
1878.	Mar.	23.	Bounds between Rockland and Hanover established and part of each town annexed to the other town.

COUNTY OF PLYMOUTH. TOWN OF SCITUATE.

KIND OF RECORDS	Number of Volumes	In Keeping of —	Years Covered	Whether Indexed	Condition
Town proceedings, . . .	9	Town Clerk	1665–1885	Partially	Good[1]
Births, marriages, and deaths,	8[2]	Town Clerk	1639–1885	Partially	Good
Selectmen and Assessors, .	185	Selectmen	–	–	–
Proprietors, ...	2[3]	Town Clerk	1648–1767	Partially	Good
Miscellaneous, ...	3	Town Clerk	1665–1885	Partially	Good

1633.	July	1.	Ply. Col. Rec., Vol. I., p. 13. "The brooke at Scituate" is mentioned.
1636.	Oct.	4.	Ply. Col. Rec., Vol. I., p. 44. "The towne of Scituate (viz' the purchasers and freemen)" was authorized to dispose of lands.
1640.	Nov.	30.	Ply. Col. Rec., Vol. I., p. 168. Land granted to Scituate.
1643.	Mar.	7.	Ply. Col. Rec., Vol. II., p. 54. Bounds established.
1727.	June	14.	Prov. Laws, Vol. II., p. 429. Parts of Scituate and Abington established as Hanover.
1787.	Mar.	10.	Part of Scituate annexed to Marshfield.
1823.	June	14.	Part of Scituate annexed to Cohasset.
1840.	Mar.	20.	Bounds between Scituate and Cohasset established and part of each town annexed to the other town.
1849.	Feb.	14.	Part of Scituate established as South Scituate.
1887.	May	11.	Bounds between Scituate and Marshfield established.

[1] Several leaves are missing from the fourth volume.

[2] The first volume is lost. Three of the volumes also contain other records.

[3] There is a copy also of the first volume in the Registry of Deeds at Plymouth.

Town Records — Continued.

County of Plymouth. Town of South Abington.

Kind of Records.	Number of Volumes	In Keeping of —	Years Covered	Whether Indexed	Condition
Town proceedings, . . .	1	Town Clerk	1875–1885	No	Good
Births, ...	1	Town Clerk	1875–1885	Yes	Good
Marriages, ...	1	Town Clerk	1875–1885	Yes	Good
Deaths, ...	1	Town Clerk	1875–1885	Yes	Good
Selectmen and Assessors, .	10	Selectmen	1875–1885	No	Good
Miscellaneous, . . .	7	Town Clerk	1875–1885	Partially	Good

1875. Mar. 4. Parts of Abington and East Bridgewater established as South Abington.
1875. April 24. Part of South Abington annexed to Brockton, and part of Brockton annexed to South Abington.
1886. Mar. 5. South Abington authorized to change its name.
1886. May 3. Whitman adopted as the name.

County of Plymouth. Town of South Scituate.

Kind of Records.	Number of Volumes	In Keeping of —	Years Covered	Whether Indexed	Condition
Town proceedings, . . .	2	Town Clerk	1849–1885	No	Good
Births, marriages, and deaths,	4	Town Clerk	1849–1885	Yes	Good
Assessors, ...	35	Assessors	1849–1885	No	Good
Selectmen, ...	9	Selectmen	1849–1885	No	Good

1849. Feb. 14. Part of Scituate established as South Scituate.
1857. May 15. Bounds between South Scituate and Hanover established.
1878. Feb. 11. Bounds between South Scituate and Hanover established and part of each town annexed to the other town.
1888. Feb. 27. South Scituate authorized to change its name.
1888. Mar. 5. Norwell adopted as the name.

County of Plymouth. Town of Wareham.

Kind of Records.	Number of Volumes	In Keeping of —	Years Covered	Whether Indexed	Condition
Town proceedings, . . .	4	Town Clerk	1739–1885	1 volume	–[1]
Births, marriages, and deaths,	7[2]	Town Clerk	1739–1885	–	–
Assessors, ...	36	Assessors	–	–	–
Miscellaneous, . . .	8	Town Clerk	1739–1885	–	–

1739. July 10. Prov. Laws, Vol. II., p. 992. Part of Rochester, and a plantation in Plymouth called Agawam, established as Wareham.
1827. Jan. 20. Parts of Carver and Plymouth annexed to Wareham.
1859. Feb. 18. Bounds between Wareham and Marion established.

[1] The first two volumes are in very poor condition, some of the pages being torn out and others mutilated.

[2] There are also copies.

TOWN RECORDS — Continued.

COUNTY OF PLYMOUTH. TOWN OF WAREHAM — Con.

1864. April 20. Bounds between Wareham and Rochester established.
1866. Feb. 13. Bounds between Wareham and Marion established.
1866. Feb. 15. Bounds between Wareham and Rochester established.
1887. June 3. Bounds between Wareham and Rochester established.

COUNTY OF PLYMOUTH. TOWN OF WEST BRIDGEWATER.

KIND OF RECORDS.	Number of Volumes	In Keeping of —	Years Covered	Whether Indexed	Condition
Town proceedings, . . .	3	Town Clerk	1823–1885	No	Good
Births, marriages, and deaths,	5	Town Clerk	1823–1885	Yes	Good
Selectmen and Assessors, .	61	Selectmen	–	–	–
Proprietors, ...	1[1]	Town Clerk	1675–1827	–	–
Miscellaneous, ...	9	Town Clerk	1823–1885	No	Good

1822. Feb. 16. Part of Bridgewater established as West Bridgewater.
1825. Jan. 26. Bounds between West Bridgewater and North Bridgewater established.

COUNTY OF SUFFOLK. CITY OF BOSTON.

KIND OF RECORDS.	Number of Volumes	In Keeping of —	Years Covered	Whether Indexed	Condition
Town proceedings, . . .	12	City Clerk	1674–1822	Yes	–
Board of Aldermen, . .	63	City Clerk	1822–1885	Yes	–
Common Council, . . .	46	City Clerk	1822–1885	Yes	–
Births, marriages, and deaths,	–[2]	–	–	–	–
Assessors, ...	6000[3]	Assessors	1780–1885[4]	–	–
Selectmen, ...	22	City Clerk	1701–1822	–	–
Parish, ...	–[5]	City Clerk	–	–	–
Proprietors, ...	2	City Clerk	1634–1728	–	–
Soldiers in the Rebellion, .	–	–	–	–	–
Miscellaneous, . . .	494	City Clerk	1706–1885	Partially	–

[1] This is a copy of the records of the proprietors of Bridgewater.

[2] There are in the office of the City Registrar 186 volumes of records of births, marriages, deaths, and marriage intentions. These include original volumes and copies, with indexes, containing records of births, marriages, deaths, and marriage intentions in Boston from 1630 to 1885. One volume, covering the years from 1630 to 1666, contains such records also for the following towns : Braintree, Cambridge, Charlestown, Concord, Dedham, Dorchester, Hingham, Medfield, Roxbury, Springfield, Sudbury, Watertown, Weymouth, and Woburn. There are also similar volumes containing the records of the births, marriages, and deaths, and marriage intentions in the cities and towns annexed to Boston, the number of volumes and the years covered by them being as follows : Brighton, 9 volumes from 1787 to 1873; Charlestown, 16 volumes from 1629 to 1873; Dorchester, 10 volumes from 1631 to 1869; Roxbury, 10 volumes from 1630 to 1867; and West Roxbury, 4 volumes from 1851 to 1873.

[3] These volumes include also records of the assessors of the cities and towns which have been annexed to Boston.

[4] The records prior to 1780 were destroyed by fire.

[5] There are in the office of the City Clerk several volumes of records, and various books and files of papers, placed there by officers of extinct parishes. There are in the office of the City Registrar 36 volumes of records of baptisms, christenings, deaths, marriages, burials, and church admission and dismissals. These records have been chiefly copied from records of various churches and are mostly indexed.

TOWN RECORDS — Continued.

COUNTY OF SUFFOLK. CITY OF BOSTON — Con.

1630.	Sept.	7.	Mass. Rec., Vol. I., p. 75. " Ordered that Tri-mountain shall be called Boston."
1632.	Nov.	7.	Mass. Rec., Vol. I., p. 101. " Ordered that the neck of land betwixt Powder Horne Hill and Pullen Poynte shall belong to Boston."
1634.	May	14.	Mass. Rec., Vol. I., p. 119. " Boston shall have convenient enlargement at Mount Wooliston " to be reported to the next General Court.
1634.	Sept.	3.	Mass. Rec., Vol. I., p. 125. " Ordered that Wynetsemit shall belong to Boston."
1634.	Sept.	25.	Mass. Rec., Vol. I., p. 130. " Boston shall have inlargement at Mount Wooliston and Rumney Marshe."
1635.	July	8.	Mass. Rec., Vol. I., p. 150. Bounds between Boston and Charlestown established.
1636.	Mar.	28.	Mass. Rec., Vol. I., p. 162. Bounds between Boston and Charlestown and Boston and Dorchester established.
1637.	Mar.	9.	Mass. Rec., Vol. I., p. 189. Noddles Island annexed to Boston.
1641.	Oct.	7.	Mass. Rec., Vol. I., p. 341. Bounds between Boston and Roxbury, at Muddy River, established.
1641.	Oct.	7.	Mass. Rec., Vol. I., p. 342. Bounds between Boston and Cambridge established.
1705.	Nov.	13.	Resolve. Part of Boston called Muddy River established as Brookline.
1739.	Jan.	10.	Prov. Laws, Vol. II., p. 969. Part of Boston called Winnissimet, Rumney Marsh, and Pullin Point, or otherwise called Number Thirteen (excepting Noddle's Island and Hog Island), established as Chelsea.
1804.	Mar.	6.	Part of Dorchester annexed to Boston.
1822.	Feb.	23.	Boston incorporated as a city.
1822.	Mar.	4.	Act of incorporation accepted by the town.
1825.	Feb.	22.	Bounds between Boston and Brookline established.
1834.	Mar.	25.	Thompson's Island set off from Dorchester and annexed to Boston while it shall be used for charitable purposes.
1836.	Mar.	16.	Bounds between Boston and Roxbury established.
1837.	April	19.	Bounds between Boston and Roxbury established.
1850.	May	3.	Part of Roxbury annexed to Boston and bounds established.
1855.	May	21.	Part of Dorchester annexed to Boston.
1860.	April	3.	Part of Roxbury annexed to Boston and bounds established, if the act is accepted by both cities.
1860.	April	16.	Act of April 3, 1860, accepted by Roxbury.
1860.	May	8.	Act of April 3, 1860, accepted by Boston.
1867.	June	1.	City of Roxbury annexed to Boston.
1867.	Sept.	9.	Act of June 1, 1867, accepted by Boston and Roxbury.
1868.	Jan.	5.	Act of June 1, 1867, took effect.
1869.	June	4.	Dorchester annexed to Boston.
1869.	June	22.	Act of June 4, 1869, accepted by Boston and Dorchester.
1870.	Jan.	3.	Act of June 4, 1869, took effect.
1870.	April	2.	Bounds between Boston and West Roxbury established.
1870.	June	18.	Part of Brookline annexed to Boston.
1870.	Nov.	4.	Act of June 18, 1870, accepted by Boston.
1872.	April	12.	Part of West Roxbury (Mount Hope Cemetery) annexed to Boston.
1872.	April	27.	Bounds between Boston and Brookline established.
1873.	May	14.	Charlestown annexed to Boston.
1873.	May	21.	Brighton annexed to Boston.
1873.	May	29.	West Roxbury annexed to Boston.
1873.	Oct.	7.	Acts of annexation accepted by Boston, Charlestown, Brighton, and West Roxbury.
1874.	Jan.	5.	Acts of annexation to Boston of Charlestown, Brighton, and West Roxbury took effect.

TOWN RECORDS — Continued.

COUNTY OF SUFFOLK. CITY OF BOSTON — Con.

1874. **May** 8. Part of Brookline annexed to Boston.
1875. **May** 5. Part of Boston annexed to Newton.
1875. **June** 23. Act of May 5, 1875, accepted by Newton.
1875. **July** 1. Act of May 5, 1875, took effect.

[The records of the following cities and towns which have been annexed to Boston, and the files of papers belonging with them, are in the possession of the City of Boston.]

Brighton.[1]

KIND OF RECORDS.	Number of Volumes	In Keeping of —	Years Covered	Whether Indexed	Condition
Town proceedings, . . .	5	City Clerk	1807–1874	Partially	–
Births, marriages, and deaths,	3	City Registrar	1787–1855	Yes	–
Births, ...	1	City Registrar	1855–1874	Yes	–
Marriages, ...	1	City Registrar	1855–1874	Yes	–
Deaths, ...	1	City Registrar	1855–1874	Yes	–
Marriage intentions, . .	3	City Registrar	1816–1873	Yes	–
Assessors, ...	–	Assessors	–	–	–
Selectmen, ...	3	City Clerk	1816–1874	No	–
Miscellaneous, ...	4	City Clerk	1817–1873	No	–

Charlestown.[2]

KIND OF RECORDS.	Number of Volumes	In Keeping of —	Years Covered	Whether Indexed	Condition
Town proceedings, . . .	14	City Clerk	1629–1847	Yes	Good
City proceedings, . . .	17	City Clerk	1847–1874	Yes	Good
Births, marriages, and deaths,	2[3]	City Registrar	1629–1843	No	Good
Births, ...	3	City Registrar	1843–1873	Yes	Good
Marriages, ...	3	City Registrar	1843–1873	Yes	Good
Deaths, ...	3	City Registrar	1843–1873	Yes	Good
Marriage intentions, . .	5	City Registrar	1725–1873	Yes	Good
Burials, ...	2	Board of Health	1863–1874	No	Good
Assessors, ...	–	Assessors	1721–1873	–	Good
Selectmen, ...	3	City Clerk	1795–1847	Yes	Good
Soldiers in the Rebellion, .	2	City Clerk	1861–1865	Yes	Good
Miscellaneous, . . .	60	City Clerk	1628–1874	No	Good

[1] For legislation concerning the town of Brighton, see "Extinct Cities, Towns. and Districts."

[2] For legislation concerning the town and city of Charlestown, see "Extinct Cities, Towns, and Districts."

[3] There are copies also of each volume, containing complete classified indexes.

The following presentation comprises a full and detailed statement concerning the town and city records and papers of Charlestown, including the years covered by each volume of archives. At the request of the Commissioner it has been furnished gratuitously for this report by Mr. HENRY H. EDES.

TOWN RECORDS — 1629–1647.

[The volume numbers (printed in capitals) which precede the kind of records apply to the volumes as numbered in the "Charlestown Archives" Series.]

I.	Births, marriages, and deaths, ...	1629–1800
II.	Births, marriages, and deaths, ...	1800–1843
	Marriages out of town. Returned under Chap. 84, Acts of 1857,	Prior to 1800
III.	Births, marriages, and deaths. A copy of volume I., with a complete classified index, ...	1629–1800
IV.	Births, marriages, and deaths, ...	1800–1843
	Marriages out of town. A copy of volume II., with a complete classified index, ...	Prior to 1800
V.	Births, ...	1843–1849
VI.	Births, ...	1849–1866
VII.	Births, ...	1867–1873
VIII.	Marriages, ...	1843–1848
IX.	Marriages, ...	1849–1862
X.	Marriages, ...	1862–1873
XI.	Deaths, ...	1843–1849
XII.	Deaths, ...	1849–1860
XIII.	Deaths, ...	1861–1873
XIV.	Marriage intentions, ...	1725–1826
XV.	Marriage intentions, ...	1826–1849
XVI.	Marriage intentions, ...	1849–1858
XVII.	Marriage intentions, ...	1858–1864
XVIII.	Marriage intentions, ...	1864–1873
	Index of marriage intentions, ...	1725–1873
	Index of births, ...	1843–1873
	Index of marriages, ...	1843–1873
	Index of deaths, ...	1843–1873

[These are entirely new and complete classified indexes.]

All of these records are in good order and condition and substantially bound, with the exception of volumes I. and II., which are now being repaired preparatory to being rebound.

The original marriage certificates and returns of deaths are kept in the City Registrar's office. They are substantially complete from 1847 to 1873, and there are preserved some certificates and returns of an earlier date than 1847.

Among the papers now being arranged, and which will be placed in the City Registrar's office when completed, are the following :

Three volumes of returns of marriages from 1788 to 1849, and returns of marriages out of town prior to 1800 made under Chap. 84, Acts of 1857.

One volume of returns of deaths from 1817 to 1846.

One volume of returns of births from 1833 to 1847; returns of deaths from 1846 to 1849; and records of families (mostly births) furnished to the town clerk.

[The above are in good condition but are not indexed. They are being chronologically arranged, except a part of the last volume, the arrangement of which will be alphabetical.]

In the office of the Board of Health are two volumes containing the records of the Superintendent of Burials in Charlestown from December 3, 1863, to January 7, 1874. These volumes are of very great value since the entries in them were made daily and because the record is fuller than that now in the City Registrar's office (Vol. xiii., referred to above), which is merely a monthly or quarterly compilation of undertakers' returns.

There is a complete classified index of all volumes of the Town Records, with the exception of volumes i., xvi., and xvii. Each volume is indexed separately; but all these indexes are bound together in one volume, with the exception of the index of " Greene's Transcript " which is bound in with the copy.

XLVI.	Treasury records, vol. xi.	1809-1825
XLVII.	Treasury records, vol. xii.	1825-1847
	[These two volumes contain receipts.]	
XLVIII.	Treasury records, vol. xiii. This volume contains bank deposit books, ...	1825-1833
XLIX.	Treasury records, vol. xiv. This volume contains sinking fund accounts and finance committee's records, ...	1818-1847
L.	Poor department, vol. i. This volume contains records of the board of overseers, ...	1807-1847
LI.	Poor department, vol. ii. This volume contains letter-books of overseers, ...	1790-1844
LII.	Poor department, vol. iii. This volume contains a register of paupers, ...	1813-1840
LIII.	Poor department, vol. iv.	1783-1815
LIV.	Poor department, vol. v.	1815-1830
LV.	Poor department, vol. vi.	1830-1847
	[The above three volumes contain accounts.]	
LVI.	Poor department, vol. vii. This volume contains the history of paupers, ...	1824-1857
LVII.	Record of beasts shipped to Barbadoes, Surinam, etc. This volume contains records of sales of beasts, strays impounded, and goods found, ...	1662-1799
LVIII.	List of inhabitants taken in February, ...	1789
LIX.	Estimate of losses by burning of the town, ...	June 17, 1775
LX.	Fire department, vol. i. This volume contains the records of the proceedings of the fire wards and the board of engineers, . .	1806-1853
LXI.	Fire department, vol. ii. This volume contains a register of members, ...	1827-1847
LXII.	Records of the board of health, ...	1819-1847
LXIII.	Lists of jurors, ...	1783-1844
LXIV.	Taxpayers who were voters. This volume contains the collectors' annual returns, ...	1826-1847
LXV.	Lists of voters, vol. i.	1802-1815
LXVI.	Lists of voters, vol. ii.	1816-1819
LXVII.	Lists of voters, vol. iii.	1820-1829
LXVIII.	Lists of voters, vol. iv.	1830-1836
LXIX.	Lists of voters, vol. v.	1837-1847

All of the foregoing records are in excellent condition and are substantially bound, with the exception of volume LVII., which is being repaired.

City Records — 1847-1874.

[For the various city records no numbers other than the original volume numbers are given, the city records not being given in the " Charlestown Archives " Series.]

Mayor and Aldermen's records (with full indexes):

Vol. i.	1847-1849	Vol. vi.	1861-1864
Vol. ii.	1849-1851	Vol. vii.	1865-1868
Vol. iii.	1851-1854	Vol. viii.	1868-1870
Vol. iv.	1854-1858	Vol. ix.	1870-1873
Vol. v.	1858-1861	Vol. x.	1873-1874

Common Council records (without indexes):

Vol. i.	1847-1850	Vol. v.	1866-1870
Vol. ii.	1850-1855	Vol. vi.	1870-1873
Vol. iii.	1855-1861	Vol. vii.	1873-1874
Vol. iv.	1861-1866		

Records of City Ordinances:

Vol. i.	1847-1869	Vol. ii.	1869-1874

Records concerning the public streets and lanes, compiled from the public records by order of the Mayor and Aldermen, by James K. Frothingham in 1849 and continued by the various city clerks, ... 1628-1873
Copies of deeds to and from the town and city recorded at Middlesex Southern District registry in Cambridge (with full index), ... 1800-1865
Records of corporations, ... 1866-1869

Records of ward officers (without indexes) :

Ward i.	.	.	.	.	1856-1873	Ward iii.	.	. . .	1856-1873
Ward ii.	.	.	.	.	1856-1873				

Record of personal mortgages (with indexes) :

Vol. i.	.	.	.	.	1832-1836	Vol. ix.	.	. . .	1858-1860
Vol. ii.	.	.	.	.	1836-1840	Vol. x.	.	. . .	1861-1864
Vol. iii.	.	.	.	.	1840-1844	Vol. xi.	.	. . .	1864-1867
Vol. iv.	.	.	.	.	1844-1847	Vol. xii.	.	. . .	1867-1868
Vol. v.	.	.	.	.	1847-1849	Vol. xiii.	.	. . .	1868-1870
Vol. vi.	.	.	.	.	1849-1852	Vol. xiv.	.	. . .	1870-1871
Vol. vii.	.	.	.	.	1852-1855	Vol. xv.	.	. . .	1871-1873
Vol. viii.	.	.	.	.	1855-1858	Vol. xvi.	.	. . .	1873-1874

Rebellion records (with indexes) :

Record of soldiers and officers in the military service, ... 1861-1865
Record of seamen and officers in the naval service, ... 1861-1865
[These rebellion records are in excellent condition but are very imperfect.]

PAPERS.

The papers during the town period are in process of arrangement by Mr. Henry H. Edes.

Besides the volumes already referred to as pertaining to the City Registrar's department, the following described volumes have been chronologically arranged :

Two volumes relating to fire matters from 1724 to 1847.

One volume relating to the church from 1726-7 to 1845.

Eleven volumes relating to the poor from 1725-6 to 1847.

Four volumes of warrants for town meetings from 1725-6 to 1847.

One volume of warrants to appraise strays and damages done by them from 1726-7 to 1847.

One volume of warrants to notify town officers of their election and to be sworn, and of certificates of oaths taken, from 1785 to 1847.

Two volumes relating to appointments and elections of town officers from 1727-8 to 1847.

Three volumes relating to innholders and retailers from 1728 to 1847.

Two volumes of writs of attachment from 1729 to 1846.

One volume of notifications of strangers, and history of paupers from 1727 to 1794.

Two volumes of war and military papers from 1744 to 1847.

Two volumes of estimates of losses June 17, 1775.

Two volumes of treasury papers from 1712 to 1800.

In addition to the above there are papers partially arranged, but not yet put into volumes, relating to highways, estates, and sewers from 1726 to 1847 ; deeds, leases, etc., from 1654 to 1847 ; petitions, orders of notice, etc., to the Legislature and County Commissioners from 1733 to 1825 ; schools, the treasury, and miscellaneous matters.

All of the town papers are in good condition and will eventually be accessible in folio volumes in the City Clerk's office in Boston.

The city papers, i. e., the files of the Board of Mayor and Aldermen and of the Common Council from 1847 to 1874, are preserved in good order and condition, in boxes in the City Clerk's office in Boston.

All of the Charlestown records and papers in the custody of the City Clerk of Boston are kept on shelves in the brick vault under his control in the basement of the City Hall.

TOWN RECORDS — Continued.

COUNTY OF SUFFOLK.   CITY OF BOSTON — Con.

Dorchester.[1]

KIND OF RECORDS.	Number of Volumes	In Keeping of—	Years Covered	Whether Indexed	Condition
Town proceedings, . . .	9[2]	City Clerk	{ 1633–1779 1809–1844 1852–1869 }	–[3]	Fair
Births, marriages, and deaths,	5	City Registrar	1646–1849	No	Fair
Births, ...	1	City Registrar	1850–1869	Yes	Fair
Marriages, ...	1	City Registrar	1850–1869	Yes	Fair
Deaths, ...	1	City Registrar	1850–1869	Yes	Fair
Marriage intentions, . .	2	City Registrar	1798–1869	Partially	Fair
Assessors, ...	–	Assessors	–	–	–
Selectmen, ...	2	City Clerk	1825–1869	Yes	Fair
Proprietors, ...	–	–[4]	1713–1793	–	–
Miscellaneous, ...	5	City Clerk	1827–1869	No	Fair

Roxbury.[5]

KIND OF RECORDS.	Number of Volumes	In Keeping of—	Years Covered	Whether Indexed	Condition
Town proceedings, . . .	4[6]	City Clerk	1647–1849	–	Fair
City proceedings, . . .	6	City Clerk	1849–1867	–	–
Births, marriages, and deaths,	4[7]	City Registrar	1630–1849	–	–
Births, ...	2	City Registrar	1849–1867	–	–
Marriages, ...	2	City Registrar	1849–1867	–	–
Deaths, ...	1	City Registrar	1849–1867	–	–
Marriage intentions, . .	1	City Registrar	1846–1867	–	–
Assessors, ...	–	Assessors	–	–	–
Selectmen, ...	1	City Clerk	1783–1784	–	–
Miscellaneous, ...	4	City Clerk	1806–1846	–	–

West Roxbury.[8]

KIND OF RECORDS.	Number of Volumes	In Keeping of —	Years Covered	Whether Indexed	Condition
Town proceedings, . . .	4	City Clerk	1851–1873	–	–
Births, marriages, and deaths,	1	City Registrar	1851–1873	–	–
Births, ...	1	City Registrar	1851–1873	–	–
Marriages, ...	1	City Registrar	1851–1873	–	–
Deaths, ...	1	City Registrar	1851–1873	–	–
Assessors, ...	–	Assessors	–	–	–

[1] For legislation concerning the town of Dorchester, see "Extinct Cities, Towns, and Districts."

[2] There is a copy also of the first volume. There is a volume also of copies of ancient papers collected by Rev. Thaddeus Mason Harris covering the years from 1638 to 1759.

[3] There is an index covering the records prior to 1725; the records since 1809 are also indexed.   [4] Registry of Deeds at Dedham.

[5] For legislation concerning the town and city of Roxbury, see "Extinct Cities, Towns, and Districts."   [6] There is a copy also of the first volume.

[7] There is a copy also of the records of births, marriages, and deaths from 1630 to 1867.

[8] For legislation concerning the town of West Roxbury, see "Extinct Cities, Towns, and Districts."

Town Records — Continued.

County of Suffolk. City of Chelsea.

Kind of Records.	Number of Volumes	In Keeping of—	Years Covered	Whether Indexed	Condition
Town proceedings,	6[1]	City Clerk	1738–1857	No	–
City proceedings,	16	City Clerk	1857–1885	Yes	–
Births, marriages, and deaths,	2	City Clerk	1738–1849	Partially	–
Births,	3	City Clerk	1850–1885	Yes	–
Marriages,	2	City Clerk	1849–1863 1877–1885	Yes	–
Deaths,	3	City Clerk	1850–1885	Yes	–
Marriage intentions,	1	City Clerk	1739–1843	No	–
	2	City Clerk	1850–1885	Partially	–
Assessors,	–		–	–	–
Selectmen,	2	City Clerk	1843–1857	No	–
Miscellaneous,	88	City Clerk	1738–1885	Partially	–

1739. Jan. 10. Prov. Laws, Vol. II., p. 969. Part of Boston called Winnissimet, Rumney Marsh, and Pullin Point, or otherwise called Number Thirteen (excepting Noddle's Island and Hog Island), established as Chelsea.
1841. Feb. 22. Part of Chelsea annexed to Saugus.
1846. Mar. 19. Part of Chelsea established as North Chelsea.

County of Suffolk. Town of Revere.

Kind of Records.	Number of Volumes	In Keeping of—	Years Covered	Whether Indexed	Condition
Town proceedings,	2	Town Clerk	1846–1885	No	Good
Births,	1	Town Clerk	1846–1885	No	Good
Marriages,	1	Town Clerk	1846–1885	No	Good
Deaths,	1	Town Clerk	1846–1885	No	Good
Selectmen and Assessors,	–	–	–	–	–

1871. Mar. 24. The town of North Chelsea[2] authorized to change its name.
1871. April 3. Revere adopted as the name.

County of Suffolk. Town of Winthrop.

Kind of Records.	Number of Volumes	In Keeping of—	Years Covered	Whether Indexed	Condition
Town proceedings,	2	Town Clerk	1852–1885	No	Good
Births,	1	Town Clerk	1852–1885	No	Good
Marriages,	1	Town Clerk	1852–1885	No	Good
Deaths,	1	Town Clerk	1852–1885	No	Good
Selectmen and Assessors,	7	Selectmen	–	–	–

1852. Mar. 27. Part of North Chelsea established as Winthrop.

[1] The first volume is made up of records copied from four old volumes.
[2] For legislation concerning the town of North Chelsea, see "Extinct Cities, Towns, and Districts."

Town Records — Continued.

County of Worcester. Town of Ashburnham.

KIND OF RECORDS.	Number of Volumes	In Keeping of—	Years Covered	Whether Indexed	Condition
Town proceedings, . . .	5	Town Clerk	–	No	Good
Births, marriages, and deaths,	5	Town Clerk	–	Yes	Good
Assessors, ...	96	Assessors	–	–	–
Proprietors, ...	1	Town Clerk	1736–1780	No	Good
Miscellaneous, ...	4	Town Clerk	1736–1885	No	Good

1765. Feb. 22. Prov. Laws, Vol. IV., p. 739. The plantation of Dorchester Canada established as Ashburnham.

1767. Mar. 6. Prov. Laws, Vol. IV., p. 908. Parts of Ashburnham and Fitchburg established as Ashby.

1785. June 27. Parts of Ashburnham, Templeton, Westminster, and Winchendon established as Gardner.

1792. Nov. 16. Part of Ashburnham annexed to Ashby.

1815. Feb. 16. Part of Gardner annexed to Ashburnham.

1824. Jan. 28. Part of Westminster annexed to Ashburnham.

County of Worcester. Town of Athol.

KIND OF RECORDS.	Number of Volumes	In Keeping of—	Years Covered	Whether Indexed	Condition
Town proceedings, . . .	6	Town Clerk	1762–1885	Partially	Good[1]
Births, marriages, and deaths,	4	Town Clerk	1843–1885	Yes	Good
Selectmen and Assessors, .	45	Selectmen	–	–	–
Proprietors, ...	2	Town Clerk	1749–1824[2]	Partially	Good
Miscellaneous, ...	9	Town Clerk	1762–1885	Partially	Good

1762. Mar. 6. Prov. Laws, Vol. IV., p. 534. The plantation called Payquage established as Athol.

1783. Oct. 15. Parts of Athol, Royalston, and Warwick, and Erving's Grant, established as the district of Orange.

1786. Oct. 20. Parts of Athol and Templeton established as Gerry.

1799. Feb. 26. Parts of Athol and Gerry annexed to Royalston.

1803. Mar. 7. Part of Athol annexed to Royalston.

1806. Feb. 28. Part of Gerry annexed to Athol.

1816. Feb. 7. Part of Orange annexed to Athol.

1829. June 11. Certain common lands annexed to Athol.

1830. Feb. 5. Part of New Salem annexed to Athol.

1837. Mar. 16. Part of New Salem annexed to Athol.

---

[1] With the exception of the first two volumes, which need rebinding.

[2] The records of the proprietors from 1734 to 1749 were carried away by the clerk.

TOWN RECORDS — Continued.

COUNTY OF WORCESTER. TOWN OF AUBURN.

KIND OF RECORDS.	Number of Volumes	In Keeping of —	Years Covered	Whether Indexed	Condition
Town proceedings, . . .	6	Town Clerk	1740–1885	No	Good
Births, marriages, and deaths,	5	Town Clerk	1740–1885	Yes	Good
Assessors, ...	38	Town Clerk	–	–	–
Selectmen, ...	2	Town Clerk	–	–	–
Soldiers in the Rebellion, .	1	Town Clerk	1861–1865	No	Good
Miscellaneous, . . .	3	Town Clerk	1832–1885	No	Good

1837. Feb. 17. The name of the town of Ward[1] changed to Auburn.
1851. May 24. Part of Auburn annexed to Millbury.

COUNTY OF WORCESTER. TOWN OF BARRE.

KIND OF RECORDS.	Number of Volumes	In Keeping of —	Years Covered	Whether Indexed	Condition
Town proceedings, . . .	5	Town Clerk	1762–1885[2]	Partially	Good
Births, marriages, and deaths,	8	Town Clerk	1762–1885	Partially	Poor[3]
Assessors, ...	24	Assessors	–	–	–
Selectmen, ...	15	Selectmen	–	–	–
Soldiers in the Rebellion, .	2	Town Clerk	1861–1865	No	Good
Miscellaneous, . . .	34	Town Clerk	1762–1885	Partially	Good

1776. Nov. 7. Prov. Laws, Vol. V., p. 592. The name of the town of Hutchinson[4] changed to Barre.

COUNTY OF WORCESTER. TOWN OF BERLIN.

KIND OF RECORDS.	Number of Volumes	In Keeping of —	Years[5] Covered	Whether Indexed	Condition
Town proceedings, . . .	4	Town Clerk	1784–1885	No	Good[6]
Births, ...	3[7]	Town Clerk	1739–1885	Yes	Good
Marriages, ...	3	Town Clerk	1763–1885[8]	Yes	Good
Deaths, ...	3[7]	Town Clerk	1781–1885	Yes	Good
Assessors, ...	32	Town Clerk	–	–	–
Selectmen, ...	1	Town Clerk	1861–1885	–	–
Soldiers in the Rebellion, .	1	Town Clerk	–	–	–
Miscellaneous, . . .	19	Town Clerk	1808–1885	No	Good

1784. Mar. 16. Parts of Bolton and Marlborough established as the district of Berlin.
1791. Feb. 8. Part of Lancaster annexed to the district of Berlin.
1812. Feb. 6. District of Berlin made the town of Berlin.

[1] For legislation concerning the town of Ward, see "Extinct Cities, Towns, and Districts."
[2] Part of the records prior to 1787 are supposed to have been burned.
[3] The records are being copied.
[4] For legislation concerning the town of Hutchinson, see "Extinct Cities, Towns, and Districts."
[5] The records for the years prior to 1784 are copies of the records of Bolton.
[6] With the exception of the first volume, which needs rebinding.
[7] There is one volume also of births and deaths arranged by families, and indexed.
[8] No records of marriages were kept from 1821 to 1824.

Town Records — Continued.

County of Worcester. Town of Blackstone.

Kind of Records.	Number of Volumes	In Keeping of —	Years Covered	Whether Indexed	Condition
Town proceedings, . . .	4	Town Clerk	1845–1885	–[1]	Fair
Births, marriages, and deaths,	4	Town Clerk	1845–1885	Yes	Fair
Marriage intentions, . .	2	Town Clerk	–	Yes	Fair
Assessors, ...	41	Assessors	–	–	–
Selectmen, ...	1	Selectmen	–	–	–
Miscellaneous, ...	25	Town Clerk	–	Partially	Fair

1845. Mar. 25. Part of Mendon established as Blackstone.

County of Worcester. Town of Bolton.

Kind of Records.	Number of Volumes	In Keeping of —	Years Covered	Whether Indexed	Condition
Town proceedings, . . .	7	Town Clerk	1738–1885	Partially	Good
Births, marriages, and deaths,	5[2]	Town Clerk	1738–1885	Yes	Good
Assessors, ...	23	Town Clerk	1852–1885[3]	–	–
Soldiers in the Rebellion, .	1	Town Clerk	–	Yes	Good
Miscellaneous, . . .	6	Town Clerk	–	Yes	Good

1738. June 24. Prov. Laws, Vol. II., p. 942. Part of Lancaster established as Bolton.
1784. Mar. 16. Parts of Bolton and Marlborough established as the district of Berlin.
1829. Feb. 11. Part of Marlborough annexed to Bolton.
1838. Mar. 16. Bounds between Bolton and Marlborough established.
1868. Mar. 20. Part of Bolton annexed to Hudson.

County of Worcester. Town of Boylston.

Kind of Records.	Number of Volumes	In Keeping of —	Years Covered	Whether Indexed	Condition
Town proceedings, . . .	6	Town Clerk	1786–1885	No	Good
Births, marriages, and deaths,	2	Town Clerk	1786–1866	Yes	Good
Births, ...	1	Town Clerk	1866–1885	Yes	Good
Marriages, ...	1	Town Clerk	1866–1885	Yes	Good
Deaths, ...	1	Town Clerk	1866–1885	Yes	Good
Marriage intentions, . .	1	Town Clerk	1835–1885	Yes	Good
Assessors, ...	6	Assessors	1797–1885	–	–
Selectmen, ...	7	Selectmen	1863–1885	–	–
Soldiers in the Rebellion, .	1	Town Clerk	1861–1865	No	Good
Miscellaneous, . . .	4	Town Clerk	1809–1885	Partially	Good

[1] One volume is partially indexed.

[2] The records of births and marriages from 1738 to 1885, and of deaths from 1844 to 1885 have been copied.

[3] Part of the records of assessors are supposed to have been burned in a fire which destroyed the Town Hall in 1852.

TOWN RECORDS — Continued.

COUNTY OF WORCESTER.   TOWN OF BOYLSTON — Con.

1786.	Mar.	1.	Part of Shrewsbury established as Boylston.
1808.	Jan.	30.	Parts of Boylston, Holden, and Sterling established as West Boylston.
1820.	Feb.	10.	Part of Boylston annexed to West Boylston.
1820.	June	17.	Part of Boylston annexed to West Boylston.

COUNTY OF WORCESTER.   TOWN OF BROOKFIELD.

KIND OF RECORDS.	Number of Volumes	In Keeping of—	Years Covered	Whether Indexed	Condition
Town proceedings, . . .	6	Town Clerk	1771–1885[1]	No	–
Births, marriages, and deaths,	7	Town Clerk	1771–1885	Yes	–
Assessors, ...	157	Town Clerk	–	–	–
Proprietors, ...	1	Town Clerk	1702–1767	–	–
Miscellaneous, . . .	5	Town Clerk	1771–1885	Partially	–

1673.	Oct.	15.	Mass. Rec., Vol. IV., Part 2, p. 568. Quobauge to be the town of "Brookefeild," when forty or fifty families shall have settled there.
1718.	Nov.	12.	Resolve. Brookfield invested with the privileges of a town.
1791.	June	10.	Bounds between Brookfield and New Braintree established and part of each town annexed to the other town.
1792.	Mar.	8.	Bounds between Brookfield and New Braintree established and part of each town annexed to the other town.
1812.	Feb.	28.	Part of Brookfield established as North Brookfield.
1823.	Feb.	8.	Part of Brookfield annexed to Ware.
1848.	Mar.	3.	Part of Brookfield established as West Brookfield.
1854.	April	15.	Part of North Brookfield annexed to Brookfield.

COUNTY OF WORCESTER.   TOWN OF CHARLTON.[1]

KIND OF RECORDS.	Number of Volumes	In Keeping of—	Years Covered	Whether Indexed	Condition
Town proceedings, . . .	4	Town Clerk	1780–1813 / 1830–1885	No	–
Births, ...	5	Town Clerk	1750–1885	Partially	–
Marriages, ...	5	Town Clerk	1750–1885	Partially	–
Deaths, ...	2	Town Clerk	1750–1885	Partially	–
Assessors, ...	42	Town Clerk	–	–	–
Soldiers in the Rebellion, .	1	Town Clerk	1861–1865	Yes	–
Miscellaneous, . . .	5	Town Clerk	1830–1885	Partially	–

1754.	Nov.	21.	Prov. Laws, Vol. III., p. 781. Part of Oxford established as the district of Charlton.
1775.	Aug.	23.	Prov. Laws, Vol. V., p. 419. District of Charlton made the town of Charlton by this general act.
1789.	Jan.	5.	Part of Charlton annexed to Oxford.
1792.	June	26.	Part of Charlton annexed to Sturbridge.
1809.	Feb.	23.	Part of Charlton annexed to Oxford.
1816.	Feb.	15.	Parts of Charlton, Dudley, and Sturbridge established as Southbridge.

[1] Part of the records prior to 1800 were burned; those saved were copied.

Town Records — Continued.

County of Worcester. Town of Clinton.

Kind of Records.	Number of Volumes	In Keeping of —	Years Covered	Whether Indexed	Condition
Town proceedings, . . .	4	Town Clerk	1850–1885	No	Good
Births, marriages, and deaths,	3	Town Clerk	1850–1885	Yes	Good
Marriage intentions, . .	3	Town Clerk	1850–1885	No	Good
Assessors, ...	35	Selectmen	–	–	–
Miscellaneous, ...	12	Town Clerk	1850–1885	No	Good

1850. Mar. 14. Part of Lancaster established as Clinton.

County of Worcester. Town of Dana.

Kind of Records.	Number of Volumes	In Keeping of —	Years Covered	Whether Indexed	Condition
Town proceedings, . . .	4	Town Clerk	1801–1885	No	Good[1]
Births, marriages, and deaths,	5	Town Clerk	1801–1885	–	Good
Assessors,	83	Town Clerk	1801–1885[2]	–	–
Selectmen, ...	2	Selectmen	1866–1885	–	–
Soldiers in the Rebellion, .	1	Town Clerk	1862–1865	No	Good
Miscellaneous, . . .	8	Town Clerk	1801–1885	No	Good

1801. Feb. 18. Parts of Greenwich, Hardwick, and Petersham established as Dana.
1803. Feb. 12. Bounds between Dana and Petersham established.
1811. June 19. Bounds between Dana and Greenwich established.
1842. Feb. 4. Parts of Hardwick and Petersham annexed to Dana.

County of Worcester. Town of Douglas.

Kind of Records.	Number of Volumes	In Keeping of —	Years Covered	Whether Indexed	Condition
Town proceedings, . . .	5	Town Clerk	1749–1885	No	–[3]
Births, marriages, and deaths,	6	Town Clerk	1749–1885	Partially	–
Selectmen and Assessors, .	–	–	–	–	–
Miscellaneous, . . .	6	Town Clerk	1749–1885	No	–

1746. June 5. Resolve. The district or precinct of New Sherburn "to be called by the name of Douglas."
1775. Aug. 23. Prov. Laws, Vol. V., p. 419. District of Douglas made the town of Douglas by this general act.
1841. Feb. 27. Bounds between Douglas and Webster established.
1864. April 25. Bounds between Douglas and Uxbridge established.

[1] With the exception of one volume.

[2] The records of assessors for 1808 are missing.

[3] The earlier records are imperfect.

TOWN RECORDS — Continued.

COUNTY OF WORCESTER. TOWN OF DUDLEY.

KIND OF RECORDS.	Number of Volumes	In Keeping of —	Years Covered	Whether Indexed	Condition
Town proceedings, . . .	5	Town Clerk	1732–1885	No	Good[1]
Births, marriages, and deaths,	7	Town Clerk	1732–1885	Partially	Good
Assessors, ...	4[2]	Town Clerk	1840–1885	–	–
Selectmen, ...	7	Selectmen	–	–	–
Miscellaneous, . . .	–	Town Clerk	1620–1885	No	Good

1732. Feb. 2. Prov. Laws, Vol. II., p. 626. Part of Oxford and certain common lands established as Dudley.

1794. June 25. Part of a gore of common land known as Middlesex Gore annexed to Dudley.

1816. Feb. 15. Parts of Dudley, Charlton, and Sturbridge established as Southbridge.

1822. Feb. 23. Part of Dudley annexed to Southbridge.

COUNTY OF WORCESTER. CITY OF FITCHBURG.

KIND OF RECORDS.	Number of Volumes	In Keeping of —	Years Covered	Whether Indexed	Condition
Town proceedings, . . .	5	City Clerk	1764–1872	No	Good[1]
City proceedings, . . .	6	City Clerk	1873–1885	No	Good
Births, marriages, and deaths,	15	City Clerk	1764–1885	–	Good
Assessors, ...	76	City Clerk	–	–	–
Proprietors, ...	–	_[3]	–	–	–
Miscellaneous, . . .	27	City Clerk	1774–1885	No	Good

1764. Feb. 3. Prov. Laws, Vol. IV., p. 685. Part of Lunenburg established as Fitchburg.

1767. Mar. 6. Prov. Laws, Vol. IV., p. 908. Parts of Fitchburg, Ashburnham, and Townsend established as Ashby.

1783. Feb. 26. Certain common lands annexed to Fitchburg.

1796. Feb. 27. Part of Fitchburg annexed to Westminster.

1813. Feb. 16. Part of Fitchburg annexed to Westminster.

1872. Mar. 8. Fitchburg incorporated as a city.

1872. April 8. Act of incorporation accepted by the town.

COUNTY OF WORCESTER. TOWN OF GARDNER.

KIND OF RECORDS.	Number of Volumes	In Keeping of —	Years Covered	Whether Indexed	Condition
Town proceedings, . . .	7[4]	Town Clerk	1785–1885	No	–
Births, marriages, and deaths,	5	Town Clerk	1785–1885	Yes	–
Assessors, ...	32	Assessors	–	–	–

[1] With the exception of the first volume.

[2] The records of assessors from 1777 to 1840 are unbound.

[3] The records are supposed to be in private possession in Lunenburg.

[4] There are copies also of the first volume.

Town Records — Continued.

County of Worcester.　Town of Gardner — Con.

1785.	June 27.	Parts of Ashburnham, Templeton, Westminster, and Winchendon established as Gardner.
1787.	Mar. 2.	Part of Gardner annexed to Winchendon.
1794.	Feb. 22.	Part of Winchendon annexed to Gardner.
1815.	Feb. 16.	Part of Gardner annexed to Ashburnham.
1851.	May 24.	Part of Winchendon annexed to Gardner.

County of Worcester.　Town of Grafton.

KIND OF RECORDS.	Number of Volumes	In Keeping of—	Years Covered	Whether Indexed	Condition
Town proceedings, . . .	10	Town Clerk	1735–1885	–	–[1]
Births, ...	5[2]	Town Clerk	1735–1885	–	Good
Marriages, ...	5[2]	Town Clerk	1735–1885	–	Good
Deaths, ...	5[2]	Town Clerk	1735–1885	–	Good
Assessors, ...	30	Town Clerk	–	–	–
Selectmen, ...	1	Selectmen	–	–	–
Proprietors, ...	1[3]	Town Clerk	1728–1742	–	Good
Miscellaneous, ...	10	Town Clerk	1735–1885	–	Good

1735.	April 18.	Prov. Laws, Vol. II., p. 743. The plantation of Hassanamisco established as Grafton.
1823.	June 14.	Certain common lands annexed to Grafton.
1826.	Mar. 3.	Part of Shrewsbury annexed to Grafton.
1842.	Mar. 3.	Part of Sutton annexed to Grafton.

County of Worcester.　Town of Hardwick.

KIND OF RECORDS.	Number of Volumes	In Keeping of—	Years Covered	Whether Indexed	Condition
Town proceedings, . . .	5[4]	Town Clerk	1734–1885	Partially	Good[5]
Births, marriages, and deaths,	7	Town Clerk	1734–1885	–	Good
Assessors, ...	65	Assessors	1825–1885	–	–
Proprietors, ...	1[6]	Town Clerk	1734–1739	–	–
Miscellaneous, ...	4	Town Clerk	1734–1885	–	Good

1739.	Jan. 10.	Prov. Laws, Vol. II., p. 971. The plantation of Lambstown established as Hardwick.
1751.	Jan. 31.	Resolve. The precinct of New Braintree and part of the town of Hardwick " erected into a district."
1801.	Feb. 18.	Parts of Hardwick, Greenwich, and Petersham established as Dana.
1814.	June 10.	Part of New Braintree annexed to Hardwick.
1831.	Feb. 7.	Certain common lands annexed to Hardwick.
1833.	Feb. 6.	Certain common land called Hardwick Gore annexed to Hardwick.
1842.	Feb. 4.	Part of Hardwick annexed to Dana.

[1] The first five volumes are in poor condition.

[2] There are copies also of the first two volumes.

[3] This is a copy of the original records, which are lost.

[4] The earlier records which were in manuscript have been copied, and the copies are bound in the first volume of town proceedings.

[5] With the exception of the second volume.

[6] This is a bound copy of the original manuscript, which is in possession of the Town Clerk.

Town Records — Continued.

County of Worcester. Town of Harvard.

KIND OF RECORDS.	Number of Volumes	In Keeping of —	Years Covered	Whether Indexed	Condition
Town proceedings, . . .	7	Town Clerk	1732–1885	Partially	Fair
Births, marriages, and deaths,	10	Town Clerk	1732–1885	Partially	Fair
Assessors, ...	–	Assessors	1726–1885	–	–
Miscellaneous, ...	5	Town Clerk	1732–1885	–	Fair

1732. June 29. Prov. Laws, Vol. II., p. 644. Parts of Groton, Lancaster, and Stow established as Harvard.

1783. Feb. 25. Parts of Harvard, Littleton, and Stow established as the district of Boxborough.

County of Worcester. Town of Holden.

KIND OF RECORDS.	Number of Volumes	In Keeping of —	Years Covered	Whether Indexed	Condition
Town proceedings, . . .	6	Town Clerk	1741–1885	No	Good
Births, marriages, and deaths,	5	Town Clerk	1741–1885	Partially	Good
Assessors, ...	98	Town Clerk	1787–1885[1]	–	–
Selectmen, ...	3	Town Clerk	–	–	–
Proprietors, ...	2	Town Clerk	1722 –	No	Good
Miscellaneous, ...	7	Town Clerk	1741–1885	Partially	Good

1741. Jan. 9. Prov. Laws, Vol. II., p. 1043. Part of Worcester called North Worcester established as Holden.

1793. Mar. 27. Bounds between Holden and Paxton established.

1808. Jan. 30. Parts of Holden, Boylston, and Sterling established as West Boylston.

1831. Mar. 19. Part of Paxton annexed to Holden.

1838. April 9. Part of Holden annexed to Paxton.

County of Worcester. Town of Hubbardston.

KIND OF RECORDS.	Number of Volumes	In Keeping of —	Years Covered	Whether Indexed	Condition
Town proceedings, . . .	6	Town Clerk	1767–1885	Partially	Good
Births, marriages, and deaths,	6[2]	Town Clerk	1767–1885	Partially	Good
Assessors, ...	28	Town Clerk	–	–	–
Soldiers in the Rebellion, .	1	Town Clerk	–	No	Good
Miscellaneous, ...	1	Town Clerk	–	Yes	Good

1767. June 13. Prov. Laws, Vol. IV., p. 953. Part of Rutland established as the district of Hubbardston.

1775. Aug. 23. Prov. Laws, Vol. V., p. 419. District of Hubbardston made the town of Hubbardston by this general act.

1810. Feb. 16. Part of Hubbardston annexed to Princeton.

---

[1] The records of assessors for the year 1885 relating to part of the town are missing.

[2] There is a copy also of the first volume.

Town Records — Continued.

County of Worcester. Town of Lancaster.

Kind of Records.	Number of Volumes	In Keeping of—	Years Covered	Whether Indexed	Condition
Town proceedings, . . .	7	Town Clerk	1653–1885[1]	No	Good
Births, marriages, and deaths,	6[2]	Town Clerk	1653–1885	Yes	Good
Assessors, ...	63	Town Clerk	–	–	–
Selectmen, ...	1	Town Clerk	–	–	–
Proprietors, ...	5	Town Clerk	1653–1818	No	Good
Miscellaneous, ...	18	Town Clerk	–	Partially	Good

1653. May 18. Mass. Rec., Vol. IV., Part 1, p. 139. "Nashaway" to be a township to be called Lancaster.

1672. Oct. 11. Mass. Rec., Vol. IV., Part 2, p. 545. Bounds established.

1732. June 29. Prov. Laws, Vol. II., p. 644. Parts of Lancaster, Groton, and Stow established as Harvard.

1738. June 24. Prov. Laws, Vol. II., p. 942. Part of Lancaster established as Bolton.

1740. June 23. Prov. Laws, Vol. II., p. 1023. Part of Lancaster established as Leominster.

1768. Feb. 27. Prov. Laws, Vol. IV., p. 991. Part of Shrewsbury annexed to Lancaster.

1781. Feb. 26. Part of Lancaster annexed to Shrewsbury.

1781. April 25. Part of Lancaster established as Sterling.

1791. Feb. 8. Part of Lancaster annexed to Berlin.

1793. Mar. 12. Bounds between Lancaster and Sterling established.

1837. Mar. 7. Part of Lancaster annexed to Sterling and bounds established.

1850. Mar. 14. Part of Lancaster established as Clinton.

County of Worcester. Town of Leicester.

Kind of Records.	Number of Volumes	In Keeping of—	Years Covered	Whether Indexed	Condition
Town proceedings, . . .	9	Town Clerk[3]	1713–1885	No	–[4]
Births, marriages, and deaths,	3	Town Clerk	1713–1885	Yes	Good
Assessors, ...	–	–	–	–	–
Proprietors, ...	2	Town Clerk	1714–1776	No	–[4]

1713. Feb. 15. Resolve. The petition of those who purchased lands at a place called Towtaid near Worcester confirmed, "the town to be named Leicester."

1753. April 12. Prov. Laws, Vol. III., p. 653. Part of Leicester made the district of Spencer.

1765. Feb. 12. Prov. Laws, Vol. IV., p. 734. Parts of Leicester and Rutland established as the district of Paxton.

1778. April 10. Prov. Laws, Vol. V., p. 796. The parish lately set off from Leicester, Oxford, Sutton, and Worcester established as Ward.

---

[1] The records from 1671 to 1717 are omitted.

[2] The records of births, marriages, and deaths from 1785 to 1825 have been copied.

[3] Two volumes are kept in the public library.

[4] Some of the pages are missing.

TOWN RECORDS — Continued.

COUNTY OF WORCESTER. TOWN OF LEOMINSTER.

KIND OF RECORDS.	Number of Volumes	In Keeping of —	Years Covered	Whether Indexed	Condition
Town proceedings, . . .	8[1]	Town Clerk	1740–1885	Partially	Good
Births, marriages, and deaths,	9	Town Clerk	1740–1885	Partially	Good
Assessors, ...	48	Assessors	–	–.	–
Selectmen, ...	6	Selectmen	–	–	–
Proprietors, ...	2	Town Clerk	1701–1847	Partially	Good
Miscellaneous, ...	31	Town Clerk	1701–1885	Partially	Good

1740. June 23. Prov. Laws, Vol. II., p. 1023. Part of Lancaster established as Leominster.

1838. April 13. Part of certain common lands called No Town annexed to Leominster.

COUNTY OF WORCESTER. TOWN OF LUNENBURG.

KIND OF RECORDS.	Number of Volumes	In Keeping of —	Years Covered	Whether Indexed	Condition
Town proceedings, . . .	9[1]	Town Clerk	1728–1885	No	–
Births, marriages, and deaths,	6	Town Clerk	1728–1885	–	–
Selectmen and Assessors, .	–	Selectmen	–	–	–
Proprietors, ...	1	Town Clerk	– 1728	No	–
Soldiers in the Rebellion, .	1	Town Clerk	–	No	–
Miscellaneous, ...	6	Town Clerk	1728–1885	No	–

1728. Aug. 1. Prov. Laws, Vol. II., p. 520. The south part of Turkey Hills established as Lunenburg.

1764. Feb. 3. Prov. Laws, Vol. IV., p. 685. Part of Lunenburg established as Fitchburg.

1846. Mar. 3. Bounds between Lunenburg and Shirley established.

1848. April 25. Bounds between Lunenburg and Shirley established.

COUNTY OF WORCESTER. TOWN OF MENDON.

KIND OF RECORDS.	Number of Volumes	In Keeping of —	Years Covered	Whether Indexed	Condition
Town proceedings, . . .	11[1]	Town Clerk	1662–1674 1681–1885	No	Good
Births, ...	4[1]	Town Clerk	1662–1885	Partially	Good
Marriages, ...	5[1]	Town Clerk	1662–1885	No	Good
Deaths, ...	3[1]	Town Clerk	1662–1885	Partially	Good
Assessors, ...	29	Town Clerk	–	–	–
Selectmen, ...	7	Town Clerk	–	–	–
Proprietors	3	Town Clerk	1708–1815	Partially	Good
Soldiers in the Rebellion, .	1	Town Clerk	–	No	Good
Miscellaneous, ...	41	Town Clerk	–	Partially	Good

[1] There is a copy also of the first volume.

TOWN RECORDS — Continued.

COUNTY OF WORCESTER. TOWN OF MENDON — Con.

1667. May 15. Mass. Rec., Vol. IV., Part 2, p. 341. Ordered that the name of Mendon be given to "the Court's grant to Qunstipauge, being the township of Qunshapage as it was laid out according to the grant of the General Court," and that Mendon be settled as a town.
1669. May 20. Mass. Rec., Vol. IV., Part 2, p. 434. Certain lands granted to Mendon.
1710. June 29. Resolve. Certain lands annexed to Mendon.
1727. June 27. Prov. Laws, Vol. II., p. 427. Part of Mendon established as Uxbridge.
1735. June 14. Prov. Laws, Vol. II., p. 764. Parts of Mendon, Hopkinton, Sutton, and Uxbridge established as Upton.
1770. April 24. Prov. Laws, Vol. V., p. 128. Part of Uxbridge annexed to Mendon.
1780. April 11. Part of Mendon established as Milford.
1845. Mar. 25. Part of Mendon established as Blackstone.
1872. Mar.   7. Bounds between Mendon and Bellingham established.

COUNTY OF WORCESTER. TOWN OF MILFORD.

KIND OF RECORDS.	Number of Volumes	In Keeping of—	Years Covered	Whether Indexed	Condition
Town proceedings, . . .	5[1]	Town Clerk	1780–1885	Yes	Good
Births, marriages, and deaths,	13	Town Clerk	1758–1885	Yes	Good
Assessors, ...	57	Selectmen	–	–	–
Selectmen, ...	1	Selectmen	–	–	–

1780. April 11. Part of Mendon established as Milford.
1835. Mar. 27. Bounds between Milford, Holliston, and Hopkinton established, parts of Holliston and Hopkinton annexed to Milford, and part of Milford annexed to Holliston.
1859. April 1. Bounds between Milford and Holliston established.
1886. April 7. Part of Milford established as Hopedale.

COUNTY OF WORCESTER. TOWN OF MILLBURY.

KIND OF RECORDS.	Number of Volumes	In Keeping of—	Years Covered	Whether Indexed	Condition
Town proceedings, . . .	3	Town Clerk	1813–1885	No	Good
Births, marriages, and deaths,	3	Town Clerk	1813–1885	–	Good
Assessors, ...	72	Town Clerk	1813–1885	No	Good

1813. June 11. Part of Sutton established as Millbury.
1851. May 24. Part of Auburn annexed to Millbury.

[1] There is a copy also of the records from 1780 to 1791.

TOWN RECORDS — Continued.

COUNTY OF WORCESTER. TOWN OF NEW BRAINTREE.

KIND OF RECORDS.	Number of Volumes	In Keeping of—	Years Covered	Whether Indexed	Condition
Town proceedings, . . .	4[1]	Town Clerk	1751–1885	No	—[2]
Births, marriages, and deaths,	6[3]	Town Clerk	1751–1885	First 2 vols.	Good
Assessors, ...	8[4]	Selectmen	—[4]	–	–
Selectmen, ...	10	Selectmen	–	–	–
Miscellaneous, . . .	6	Town Clerk	1800–1885	No[.]	Good

1751. Jan. 31. Resolve. "The precinct consisting of the lands called New Braintree, and part of the town of Hardwick is erected into a district."

1775. Aug. 23. Prov. Laws, Vol. V., p. 419. The above district [presumably] made the town of New Braintree by this general act.

1791. June 10. Bounds between New Braintree and Brookfield established and part of each town annexed to the other town.

1792. Mar. 8. Bounds between New Braintree and Brookfield established and part of each town annexed to the other town.

1814. June 10. Part of New Braintree annexed to Hardwick.

COUNTY OF WORCESTER. TOWN OF NORTHBOROUGH.

KIND OF RECORDS.	Number of Volumes	In Keeping of—	Years Covered	Whether Indexed	Condition
Town proceedings, . . .	5	Town Clerk	1744–1885	No	Good
Births, marriages, and deaths,	5[5]	Town Clerk	1744–1885	Yes	Good
Assessors, ...	23	Assessors	–	–	–
Selectmen, ...	2	Selectmen	–	–	–

1766. June 24. Prov. Laws, Vol. IV., p. 839. Part of Westborough established as the district of Northborough.

1775. Aug. 23. Prov. Laws, Vol. V., p. 419. District of Northborough made the town of Northborough by this general act.

1807. June 20. Part of Marlborough annexed to Northborough and bounds established.

COUNTY OF WORCESTER. TOWN OF NORTHBRIDGE.

KIND OF RECORDS.	Number of Volumes	In Keeping of —	Years Covered	Whether Indexed	Condition
Town proceedings, . . .	4	Town Clerk	1772–1885	—[6]	Good
Births, marriages, and deaths,	5	Town Clerk	1760–1885	–	Good
Assessors, ...	6	Town Clerk	–	–	Good
Selectmen, ...	3	Town Clerk	–	–	Good
Miscellaneous, . . .	7	Town Clerk	1788–1885	–	Good

[1] There is a copy of the mutilated parts of the first volume.

[2] With the exception of the first volume.

[3] There are private records of births, marriages, and deaths in possession of William Bowdoin and Mrs. Sarah Woods Peckham.

[4] The records prior to 1800 are incomplete; those for the years 1803, 1831, and 1851 are missing.

[5] Rev. Joseph Allen kept a private record of births, marriages, and deaths, which is in possession of his descendants.   [6] The earlier records have been copied and indexed.

Town Records — Continued.

County of Worcester. Town of Northbridge — Con.

1772. July 14. Prov. Laws, Vol. V., p. 198. Part of Uxbridge established as the district of Northbridge.
1775. Aug. 23. Prov. Laws, Vol. V., p. 419. District of Northbridge made the town of Northbridge by this general act.
1780. April 20. Part of Sutton annexed to Northbridge.
1801. Feb. 17. Part of Sutton annexed to Northbridge.
1831. June 15. Part of Northbridge annexed to Sutton.
1837. Mar. 7. Bounds between Northbridge and Sutton established.
1844. Mar. 16. Part of Sutton annexed to Northbridge.
1856. April 30. Bounds between Northbridge and Uxbridge established and part of each town annexed to the other town.

County of Worcester. Town of North Brookfield.

Kind of Records.	Number of Volumes	In Keeping of —	Years Covered	Whether Indexed	Condition
Town proceedings, . . .	3	Town Clerk	1862–1885[1]	No	Good
Births, marriages, and deaths,	3[2]	Town Clerk	1862–1885[1]	Yes	Good
Assessors, ...	24	Assessors	–	–	–
Selectmen, ...	5	Selectmen	–	–	–
Proprietors, ...	1[3]	Charles Adams, Jr.	1750–1812	–	–
Miscellaneous, ...	10	Town Clerk	1862–1885	Partially	Good

1812. Feb. 28. Part of Brookfield established as North Brookfield.
1854. April 15. Part of North Brookfield annexed to Brookfield.

County of Worcester. Town of Oakham.

Kind of Records.	Number of Volumes	In Keeping of —	Years Covered	Whether Indexed	Condition
Town proceedings, . . .	8	Town Clerk	1759–1885	No	Good
Births, marriages, and deaths,	7[4]	Town Clerk	1759–1885	–	Good
Assessors, ...	90	Assessors	–	–	–
Selectmen, ...	9	Selectmen	–	–	–
Miscellaneous, ...	5	Town Clerk	1759–1885	No	Good

1762. June 7. Prov. Laws, Vol. IV., p. 571. Part of Rutland established as the district of Oakham.
1775. Aug. 23. Prov. Laws, Vol. V., p. 419. District of Oakham made the town of Oakham by this general act.

[1] All records prior to 1862 were burned.
[2] There are copies also of the returns made to the Secretary of the Commonwealth from 1812 to 1863. Thomas Snell and Mrs. William H. Ayres have private records of births, marriages, and deaths.
[3] This is a copy only of the original records.
[4] Stephen Lincoln has private records of deaths from 1836 to 1885.

TOWN RECORDS — Continued.

COUNTY OF WORCESTER. TOWN OF OXFORD.[1]

KIND OF RECORDS.	Number of Volumes	In Keeping of —	Years Covered	Whether Indexed	Condition
Town proceedings, . . .	6	Town Clerk	1713-1752 / 1776-1885	No	Good
Births, marriages, and deaths,	7	Town Clerk	1713-1885	Yes	Good
Marriage intentions, . .	2	Town Clerk	1713-1885	Yes	Good
Assessors, ...	31	Town Clerk	–	–	–
Selectmen, ...	–	–	–	–	–
Miscellaneous, ...	20	Town Clerk	–	No	–

1693. May 31. Mass. Archives, Vol. VI., p. 278. Daniel Allen is recorded as Representative from Oxford.

1694. Sept. 14. Prov. Laws, Vol. I., p. 178. Oxford is mentioned in the Tax Act.

1732. Feb. 2. Prov. Laws, Vol. II., p. 626. Part of Oxford and certain common lands established as Dudley.

1754. Nov. 21. Prov. Laws, Vol. III., p. 781. Part of Oxford established as the district of Charlton.

1778. April 10. Prov. Laws, Vol. V., p. 796. The parish lately set off from Oxford, Leicester, Sutton, and Worcester established as Ward.

1789. Jan. 5. Part of Charlton annexed to Oxford.

1793. Feb. 18. Part of Sutton annexed to Oxford.

1807. Feb. 6. The Oxford South Gore annexed to Oxford.

1809. Feb. 23. Part of Charlton annexed to Oxford.

1838. Mar. 22. The Oxford North Gore annexed to Oxford.

COUNTY OF WORCESTER. TOWN OF PAXTON.

KIND OF RECORDS.	Number of Volumes	In Keeping of —	Years Covered	Whether Indexed	Condition
Town proceedings, . . .	5	Town Clerk	1765-1885	No	Good
Births, marriages, and deaths,	7[2]	Town Clerk	1765-1885	Yes	Good
Assessors, ...	34	Assessors	1821-1885	–	–
Selectmen, ...	1	Selectmen	1881-1885	–	–
Miscellaneous, ...	6	Town Clerk	1818-1885	Partially	Good

1765. Feb. 12. Prov. Laws, Vol. IV., p. 734. Parts of Leicester and Rutland established as the district of Paxton.

1772. July 14. Prov. Laws, Vol. V., p. 207. Part of Rutland adjudged to belong to the district of Paxton.

1775. Aug. 23. Prov. Laws, Vol. V., p. 419. District of Paxton made the town of Paxton by this general act.

1793. Mar. 27. Bounds between Paxton and Holden established.

1829. Feb. 20. Bounds between Paxton and Rutland established.

1831. Mar. 19. Part of Paxton annexed to Holden.

1838. April 9. Part of Holden annexed to Paxton.

1851. May 24. Part of Rutland annexed to Paxton.

[1] The records are very deficient in regard to the successive settlements of Oxford.

[2] There are copies also of the records from 1765 to 1843.

Town Records — Continued.

County of Worcester.   Town of Petersham.

Kind of Records.	Number of Volumes	In Keeping of—	Years Covered	Whether Indexed	Condition
Town proceedings, . . .	4	Town Clerk	1780–1885	No	Good
Births, marriages, and deaths,	2	Town Clerk	1754–1826[1] 1844–1854	,Yes	Good[2]
Births, ...	1	Town Clerk	1854–1885	Yes	Good
Marriages, ...	1	Town Clerk	1854–1885	Yes	Good
Deaths, ...	1	Town Clerk	1854–1885	Yes	Good
Assessors, ...	41	Assessors	–	–	–
Selectmen, ...	3	Selectmen	1841–1885[3]	–	–
Proprietors, ...	1	Selectmen	–	–	–
Miscellaneous, ...	7	Town Clerk	1832–1885	Partially	Good

1754. April 20. Prov. Laws, Vol. III., p. 731. The plantation of Nichewoag established as Petersham.

1801. Feb. 18. Parts of Petersham, Greenwich, and Hardwick established as Dana.

1803. Feb. 12. Bounds between Petersham and Dana established.

1842. Feb. 4. Part of Petersham annexed to Dana.

County of Worcester.   Town of Phillipston.

Kind of Records.	Number of Volumes	In Keeping of—	Years Covered	Whether Indexed	Condition
Town proceedings, ...	4	Town Clerk	1794–1885	Partially	Good
Births, marriages, and deaths,	4	Town Clerk	1794–1885	–	Good
Assessors, ...	29	Selectmen	–	–	–
Selectmen, ...	7	Selectmen	–	–	–
Miscellaneous, ...	4	Town Clerk	1794–1885	No	Good

1814. Feb. 5. The name of the town of Gerry[4] changed to Phillipston. ·

1837. Mar. 29. Bounds between Phillipston and Royalston established.

County of Worcester.   Town of Princeton.

Kind of Records.	Number of Volumes	In Keeping of—	Years Covered	Whether Indexed	Condition
Town proceedings, . . .	7	Town Clerk	1761–1885[5]	2 volumes	Good
Births, marriages, and deaths,	7[6]	Town Clerk	1757–1885	–	Good
Assessors, ...	78	Assessors	–	–	–
Selectmen, ...	1	Selectmen	–	–	–
Proprietors, ...	2	Town Clerk	1714–1770	No	Good
Soldiers in the Rebellion, .	1	Town Clerk	1861–1865	No	Good
Miscellaneous, ...	11	Town Clerk	1796–1885	No	Good

[1] One volume covering the years from 1826 to 1844 was burned.

[2] With the exception of the first volume.

[3] The records prior to 1841 were burned.

[4] For legislation concerning the town of Gerry, see "Extinct Cities, Towns, and Districts."

[5] The records from 1759 to 1761 have been missing for more than fifty years.

[6] There is a copy of the first volume covering the years from 1757 to 1842 in possession of the New England Historic Genealogical Society.

Town Records — Continued.

County of Worcester. Town of Princeton — Con.

1759. Oct. 20. Prov. Laws, Vol. IV., p. 266. Part of Rutland and certain common lands adjacent established as the district of " Prince-town."

1771. April 24. Prov. Laws, Vol. V., p. 124. District of Princeton and all lands adjacent not belonging to any town or district established as Princeton.

1773. Mar. 6. Prov. Laws, Vol. V., p. 238. All lands which did not belong to Princeton when it was a district are set off as they were before the passage of the act of April 24, 1771.

1810. Feb. 16. Part of Hubbardston annexed to Princeton.

1838. April 4. Part of the common lands of No Town annexed to Princeton.

1870. April 22. Part of Westminster annexed to Princeton.

County of Worcester. Town of Royalston.

KIND OF RECORDS.	Number of Volumes	In Keeping of —	Years Covered	Whether Indexed	Condition
Town proceedings, . . .	6[1]	Town Clerk	1765–1885	No	Good[2]
Births, marriages, and deaths,	7	Town Clerk	1798–1885	–	Good
Assessors, ...	78	Assessors	–	–	–
Selectmen, ...	8	Selectmen	–	–	–
Proprietors, ...	1	Town Clerk	1752–1787	No	Good
Soldiers in the Rebellion, .	1	Town Clerk	1861–1865	No	Good
Miscellaneous, ...	7	Town Clerk	1765–1885	No	Good

1765. Feb. 19. Prov. Laws, Vol. IV., p. 738. The tract of land called Royalshire established as Royalston.

1780. June 17. Part of Royalston annexed to Winchendon.

1783. Oct. 15. Parts of Royalston, Athol, and Warwick, and Erving's Grant, established as the district of Orange.

1799. Feb. 26. Parts of Athol and Gerry annexed to Royalston.

1803. Mar. 7. Part of Athol annexed to Royalston.

1837. Mar. 29. Bounds between Royalston and Phillipston established.

County of Worcester. Town of Rutland.

KIND OF RECORDS.	Number of Volumes	In Keeping of —	Years Covered	Whether Indexed	Condition
Town proceedings, . . .	7	Town Clerk	1720–1885	No	Fair
Births, marriages, and deaths,	8[3]	Town Clerk	1720–1885	Yes	Fair
Assessors, ...	3	Town Clerk	1832–1859	–	–
Assessors, ...	26	Assessors	1859–1885	–	–
Selectmen, ...	1	Town Clerk	1832–1859	–	–
Proprietors, ...	1	Town Clerk	1720–1797	No	Fair
Miscellaneous, ...	20	Town Clerk	1811–1870	No	Fair

1713. Feb. 23. Resolve. Certain common lands, " the name in general being Naquag," established as Rutland.

1722. June 18. Prov. Laws, Vol. II., p. 246. Rutland granted the privileges that other towns enjoy.

1 There is a copy also of the first volume covering the years from 1765 to 1798.

2 With the exception of the first volume.

3 There are private records in possession of Elias F. Meade.

TOWN RECORDS — Continued.

COUNTY OF WORCESTER. TOWN OF RUTLAND — Con.

1753. April 12. Prov. Laws, Vol. III., p. 654. Part of Rutland established as the Rutland District.
1759. Oct. 20. Prov. Laws, Vol. IV., p. 266. Part of Rutland established as Princeton.
1762. June 7. Prov. Laws, Vol. IV., p. 571. Part of Rutland established as the district of Oakham.
1765. Feb. 12. Prov. Laws, Vol. IV., p. 734. Parts of Rutland and Leicester established as Paxton.
1767. June 13. Prov. Laws, Vol. IV., p. 953. Part of Rutland established as Hubbardston.
1772. July 14. Prov. Laws, Vol. V., p. 207. Part of Rutland adjudged to belong to Paxton.
1829. Feb. 20. Bounds between Rutland and Paxton established.
1851. May 24. Part of Rutland annexed to Paxton.

COUNTY OF WORCESTER. TOWN OF SHREWSBURY.

KIND OF RECORDS.	Number of Volumes	In Keeping of —	Years Covered	Whether Indexed	Condition
Town proceedings, . . .	7	Town Clerk	1719–1885	No	Good
Births, marriages, and deaths,	4[1]	Town Clerk	1719–1885	Yes	Good
Assessors, ...	–	–	–	–	–
Proprietors, ...	1	Town Clerk	1718–1811	No	Good
Miscellaneous, ...	8	Town Clerk	–	No	Good

1720. Dec. 6. Resolve. A committee is paid for "running the lines of Whitehall Farm and Shrewsbury, * * * which service they performed in July, 1717."
1722. Aug. 16. Prov. Laws, Vol. II., p. 260. Shrewsbury is mentioned in a list of frontier towns.
1727. Dec. 19. Resolve. Shrewsbury endowed with equal powers with any other town in the province.
1768. Feb. 27. Prov. Laws., Vol. IV., p. 991. Part of Shrewsbury annexed to Lancaster.
1781. Feb. 26. Part of Lancaster annexed to Shrewsbury.
1786. Mar. 1. Part of Shrewsbury established as Boylston.
1793. Mar. 2. Part of Shrewsbury annexed to Westborough.
1826. Mar. 3. Part of Shrewsbury annexed to Grafton.

COUNTY OF WORCESTER. TOWN OF SOUTHBOROUGH.

KIND OF RECORDS.	Number of Volumes	In Keeping of—	Years Covered	Whether Indexed	Condition
Town proceedings, . . .	5	Town Clerk	1727–1885	No	Good
Births, marriages, and deaths,	9[2]	Town Clerk	1731–1885	Yes	Good[3]
Assessors, ...	67	Assessors	–	–	–
Soldiers in the Rebellion, .	1	Town Clerk	1861–1866	No	Good
Miscellaneous, ...	8	Town Clerk	1768–1885	No	Good

[1] There is a copy also of the records from 1717 to 1829.
[2] There is a copy also of the records from 1731 to 1788. There are private records of births, marriages, and deaths from 1689 to 1885 in possession of Daniel B. Johnson.
[3] With the exception of the first volume.

Town Records — Continued.

County of Worcester. Town of Southborough — Con.

1727. July 6. Prov. Laws, Vol. II., p. 428. Part of Marlborough established as Southborough.
1786. Mar. 7. Part of Framingham annexed to Southborough.
1835. Mar. 5. Bounds between Southborough and Westborough established.
1843. Mar. 24. Part of Southborough annexed to Marlborough.

County of Worcester. Town of Southbridge.

KIND OF RECORDS.	Number of Volumes	In Keeping of —	Years Covered	Whether Indexed	Condition
Town proceedings, . . .	4	Town Clerk	1816–1885[1]	No	Good
Births, marriages, and deaths,	12	Town Clerk	1816–1885	Yes	Good
Assessors, ...	28	Town Clerk	1857–1885	–	–
Selectmen, ...	2	Selectmen	1816–1885	–	–
Miscellaneous, ...	10	Town Clerk	1816–1885	No	Good

1816. Feb. 15. Parts of Charlton, Dudley, and Sturbridge established as Southbridge.
1822. Feb. 23. Part of Dudley annexed to Southbridge.
1839. April 6. Part of Sturbridge annexed to Southbridge.
1871. May 4. Bounds between Southbridge and Sturbridge established.

County of Worcester. Town of Spencer.

KIND OF RECORDS.	Number of Volumes	In Keeping of —	Years Covered	Whether Indexed	Condition
Town proceedings, . . .	7	Town Clerk	1744–1885	No	Fair
Births, marriages, and deaths,	5[2]	Town Clerk	1844–1885	–	Fair
Assessors, ...	85	Town Clerk	1800–1885	–	–
Miscellaneous, ...	3	Town Clerk	1800–1830	No	Fair

1753. April 12. Prov. Laws, Vol. III., p. 653. Part of Leicester established as the district of Spencer.
1775. Aug. 23. Prov. Laws, Vol. V., p. 419. District of Spencer made the town of Spencer by this general act.

County of Worcester. Town of Sterling.

KIND OF RECORDS.	Number of Volumes	In Keeping of —	Years Covered	Whether Indexed	Condition
Town proceedings, . . .	5	Town Clerk	1795–1885[3]	No	Good
Births, marriages, and deaths,	8	Town Clerk	1795–1885	Yes	Good
Assessors, ...	90	Town Clerk	1795–1885	–	–
Miscellaneous, ...	5	Town Clerk	1828–1885	Partially	Good

1781. April 25. Part of Lancaster established as Sterling.
1793. Mar. 12. Bounds between Sterling and Lancaster established.
1808. Jan. 30. Parts of Sterling, Boylston, and Holden established as West Boylston.
1837. Mar. 7. Bounds between Sterling and Lancaster established.

---

[1] The second volume of town proceedings is loaned.
[2] There are four volumes also of records of births, marriages, and deaths from 1744 to 1844 copied from the volumes of town proceedings. [3] All records prior to 1795 were burned.

TOWN RECORDS — Continued.

COUNTY OF WORCESTER. TOWN OF STURBRIDGE.

KIND OF RECORDS.	Number of Volumes	In Keeping of —	Years Covered	Whether Indexed	Condition
Town proceedings, . . .	6	Town Clerk	1738–1885	No	Good
Births, marriages, and deaths,	6[1]	Town Clerk	1738–1885	Yes	Good
Assessors, ...	34	Town Clerk	–	–	–
Proprietors, ...	1	Town Clerk	–	–	–
Miscellaneous, . . .	3	Town Clerk	1700–1885	No	Good

1738. June 24. Prov. Laws, Vol. II., p. 946. The tract of land called New-Medfield established as Sturbridge.
1792. June 26. Part of Charlton annexed to Sturbridge.
1794. June 25. Part of Middlesex Gore annexed to Sturbridge.
1816. Feb. 15. Parts of Sturbridge, Charlton, and Dudley established as Southbridge.
1839. April 6. Part of Sturbridge annexed to Southbridge.
1871. May 4. Bounds between Sturbridge and Southbridge established.

COUNTY OF WORCESTER. TOWN OF SUTTON.

KIND OF RECORDS.	Number of Volumes	In Keeping of —	Years Covered	Whether Indexed	Condition
Town proceedings, . . .	4	Town Clerk	1715–1885	No	Fair
Births, marriages, and deaths,	12[2]	Town Clerk	1715–1885	–	Fair
Assessors, ...	45	Assessors	1840–1885[3]	–	–
Selectmen, ...	–	Selectmen	–	–	–
Proprietors, ...	1	Town Clerk	1714–1809	No	Fair
Soldiers in the Rebellion, .	1	Town Clerk	–	No	Fair
Miscellaneous, . . .	30	Town Clerk	–	No	Fair

1714. Oct. 28. Resolve. " Voted a concurrence with the Representatives approving and confirming a survey and plat of the laying out of the township of Sutton."
1715. June 21. Resolve. Certain common lands allowed to the proprietors of Sutton.
1735. June 14. Prov. Laws, Vol. II., p. 764. Parts of Sutton, Hopkinton, Mendon, and Uxbridge established as Upton.
1778. April 10. Prov. Laws, Vol. V., p. 796. The parish lately set off from Sutton, Leicester, Oxford, and Worcester established as Ward.
1780. April 20. Part of Sutton annexed to Northbridge.
1789. June 5. A certain gore of land annexed to Sutton.
1793. Feb. 18. Part of Sutton annexed to Oxford.
1801. Feb. 17. Part of Sutton annexed to Northbridge.
1813. June 11. Part of Sutton established as Millbury.
1831. June 15. Part of Northbridge annexed to Sutton.
1837. Mar. 7. Bounds between Sutton and Northbridge established.
1842. Mar. 3. Part of Sutton annexed to Grafton.
1844. Mar. 16. Part of Sutton annexed to Northbridge.

---

[1] The records of births, marriages, and deaths from 1738 to 1816 have been copied and printed, and a manuscript copy of those from 1738 to 1844 is in the public library.

[2] There is also an indexed copy.

[3] The records prior to 1840 are unbound.

Town Records — Continued.

County of Worcester. Town of Templeton.

KIND OF RECORDS.	Number of Volumes	In Keeping of —	Years Covered	Whether Indexed	Condition
Town proceedings, . . .	6	Town Clerk	1762–1885	No	Good
Births, marriages, and deaths,	10[1]	Town Clerk	1762–1885	Yes	Good
Selectmen and Assessors, .	—[2]	Town Clerk	1763–1885	–	–
Proprietors, ...	3	Selectmen	1733 –	No	Good
Miscellaneous, . . .	6	Town Clerk	–	Partially	Good

1762.　Mar.　6.　Prov. Laws, Vol. IV., p. 533. The plantation called Narragansett Number Six established as "Templetown."

1785.　June 27.　Parts of Templeton, Ashburnham, Westminster, and Winchendon established as Gardner.

1786.　Oct.　20.　Parts of Templeton and Athol established as Gerry.

County of Worcester. Town of Upton.

KIND OF RECORDS.	Number of Volumes	In Keeping of —	Years Covered	Whether Indexed	Condition
Town proceedings, . . .	5[3]	Town Clerk	1735–1885	No	Good[4]
Births, marriages, and deaths,	6[5]	Town Clerk	1735–1885	–	Good
Assessors, ...	5	Town Clerk	–	–	–
Miscellaneous, . . .	15	Town Clerk	1735–1885	No	Good

1735.　June 14.　Prov. Laws, Vol. II., p. 764. Parts of Hopkinton, Mendon, Sutton, and Uxbridge established as Upton.

1808.　Mar.　8.　Part of Hopkinton annexed to Upton.

County of Worcester. Town of Uxbridge.

KIND OF RECORDS	Number of Volumes	In Keeping of —	Years Covered	Whether Indexed	Condition
Town proceedings, . . .	6	Town Clerk	1727–1885	No	–[6]
Births, marriages, and deaths,	4	Town Clerk	1730–1885	–	Good
Assessors, ...	28	Assessors	1821–1885	–	–
Selectmen, ...	4	Selectmen	1773–1885[7]	–	–
Miscellaneous, . . .	6	Town Clerk	1805–1884	No	Good

1727.　June 27.　Prov. Laws, Vol. II., p. 427. Part of Mendon established as Uxbridge.

1735.　June 14.　Prov. Laws, Vol. II., p. 764. Parts of Uxbridge, Hopkinton, Mendon, and Sutton established as Upton.

1770.　April 24.　Prov. Laws, Vol. V., p. 128. Part of Uxbridge annexed to Mendon.

---

[1] There is a copy also of the records from 1762 to 1841. The records of marriages from 1841 to 1844 are missing, but the marriage intentions for those years are recorded.

[2] The records prior to 1793 are unbound.

[3] There are indexed copies also of the first three volumes.

[4] With the exception of the first volume.

[5] The earlier records of marriages and marriage intentions have been copied. Velorous Taft has private records of deaths. From 1825 to 1851 the record of births and deaths was imperfectly kept, but the present Town Clerk has by personal investigation succeeded in supplying many of the omissions.　[6] The first three volumes are in poor condition.

[7] One volume covering the years from 1797 to 1824 is missing.

TOWN RECORDS — Continued.

COUNTY OF WORCESTER. TOWN OF UXBRIDGE — Con.

1772. July 14. Prov. Laws, Vol. V., p. 198. Part of Uxbridge established as the district of Northbridge.

1856. April 30. Part of Northbridge annexed to Uxbridge and bounds established.

1864. April 25. Bounds between Uxbridge and Douglas established.

COUNTY OF WORCESTER. TOWN OF WARREN.

KIND OF RECORDS.	Number of Volumes	In Keeping of—	Years Covered	Whether Indexed	Condition
Town proceedings, . . .	5[1]	Town Clerk	1741–1885	Partially	Good[2]
Births, marriages, and deaths,	5	Town Clerk	1835–1885	–	Good
Assessors, ...	94	Town Clerk	1788–1885[3]	–	–
Miscellaneous, ...	16	Town Clerk	1741–1885	No	Good

1834. Mar. 13. The name of the town of Western[4] changed to Warren.

COUNTY OF WORCESTER. TOWN OF WEBSTER.

KIND OF RECORDS.	Number of Volumes	In Keeping of—	Years Covered	Whether Indexed	Condition
General, ...	8	Town Clerk	–	Partially	Good
Births, marriages, and deaths,	7	Town Clerk	–	Yes	Good
Selectmen and Assessors, .	6	Town Clerk	–	No	Good

1832. Mar. 6. Certain common lands established as Webster.

1841. Feb. 27. Bounds between Webster and Douglas established.

COUNTY OF WORCESTER. TOWN OF WESTBOROUGH.

KIND OF RECORDS.	Number of Volumes	In Keeping of—	Years Covered	Whether Indexed	Condition
Town proceedings, . . .	6	Town Clerk	1722–1885	Yes	Good
Births, marriages, and deaths,	10[5]	Town Clerk	1722–1885	Yes	Good
Assessors, ...	–	–	–	–	–
Miscellaneous, . . .	12	Town Clerk	1722–1885	Yes	Good

1717. Nov. 18. Resolve. Part of Marlborough called Chauncy established as Westborough.

1766. Jan. 24. Prov. Laws, Vol. IV., p. 839. Part of Westborough established as the district of Northborough.

1793. Mar. 2. Part of Shrewsbury annexed to Westborough.

1835. Mar. 5. Bounds between Westborough and Southborough established.

---

[1] There is a copy also of the first volume.   [2] With the exception of the first volume.

[3] The records of assessors from 1741 to 1787 are missing.

[4] For legislation concerning the town of Western, see "Extinct Cities, Towns, and Districts."

[5] There is a copy also of the first volume. There is a record of births, marriages, and deaths in the diary of Rev. Ebenezer Parkman, part of which is in possession of the American Antiquarian Society and part in possession of Nahum Fisher.

TOWN RECORDS — Continued.

COUNTY OF WORCESTER. TOWN OF WEST BOYLSTON.

KIND OF RECORDS.	Number of Volumes	In Keeping of—	Years Covered	Whether Indexed	Condition
Town proceedings, . . .	4	Town Clerk	1808–1885	No	–
Births, marriages, and deaths,	9	Town Clerk	1808–1885	Yes	–
Assessors, ...	42	Town Clerk	–	–	–
Selectmen	16	Town Clerk	–	–	–
Miscellaneous, ...	9	Town Clerk	1808–1885	No	–

1808. Jan. 30. Parts of Boylston, Holden, and Sterling established as West Boylston.
1820. Feb. 10. Part of Boylston annexed to West Boylston.
1820. June 17. Part of Boylston annexed to West Boylston.

COUNTY OF WORCESTER. TOWN OF WEST BROOKFIELD.

KIND OF RECORDS.	Number of Volumes	In Keeping of —	Years Covered	Whether Indexed	Condition
Town proceedings, . . .	2	Town Clerk	1848–1885	No	Good
Births, ...	1	Town Clerk	1848–1885	Yes	Good
Marriages, ...	1	Town Clerk	1848–1885	Yes	Good
Deaths, ...	1	Town Clerk	1848–1885	Yes	Good
Marriage intentions, . .	1	Town Clerk	1848–1885	Yes	Good
Assessors, ...	33	Town Clerk	1848–1885[1]	–	–
Selectmen, ...	36	Town Clerk	1848–1885	–	–
Miscellaneous, ...	3	Town Clerk	1848–1885	Partially	Good

1848. Mar. 3. Part of Brookfield established as West Brookfield.

COUNTY OF WORCESTER. TOWN OF WESTMINSTER.

KIND OF RECORDS	Number of Volumes	In Keeping of–	Years Covered	Whether Indexed	Condition
Town proceedings, . . .	8	Town Clerk	1759–1885	No	Good
Births, marriages, and deaths,	4	Town Clerk	–	Yes	Good
Births, ...	1	Town Clerk	–	Yes	Good
Marriages, ...	1	Town Clerk	–	Yes	Good
Deaths, ...	1	Town Clerk	–	Yes	Good
Marriage intentions, . .	1	Town Clerk	–	Yes	Good
Assessors, ...	85	Town Clerk	–	–	–
Selectmen, ...	10	Town Clerk	–	–	–
Proprietors, ...	2[2]	Town Clerk	1728–1759	No	Good
Miscellaneous, ...	8	Town Clerk	1740–1820	Yes	Good

1759. Oct. 20. Prov. Laws, Vol. IV., p. 265. The plantation called Narragansett Number Two established as the district of Westminster.
1770. April 26. Prov. Laws, Vol. V., p. 50. District of Westminster made the town of Westminster.
1785. June 27. Parts of Westminster, Ashburnham, Templeton, and Winchendon established as Gardner.
1796. Feb. 27. Part of Fitchburg annexed to Westminster.
1813. Feb. 16. Part of Fitchburg annexed to Westminster.
1824. Jan. 28. Part of Westminster annexed to Ashburnham.
1838. April 10. Part of the common lands called No Town annexed to Westminster.
1870. April 22. Part of Westminster annexed to Princeton.

[1] The records for 1856, 1857, and 1858 are missing.

[2] There is a copy in possession of the Town Clerk, and one in possession of the Massachusetts Historical Society, at Boston.

TOWN RECORDS — Concluded.

COUNTY OF WORCESTER.   TOWN OF WINCHENDON.

KIND OF RECORDS.	Number of Volumes	In Keeping of —	Years Covered	Whether Indexed	Condition
Town proceedings, . . .	9	Town Clerk	1764–1885	No	Good[1]
Births, marriages, and deaths,	8	Town Clerk	1795–1885	Partially	Good[2]
Marriage intentions, . .	2	Town Clerk	1849–1885	No	Good
Assessors, ...	26	Assessors	1859–1885[3]	–	–
Selectmen, ...	–	Selectmen	1859–1885[3]	–	–
Proprietors, ...	1[4]	Town Clerk	1737–1797	No	Poor
Miscellaneous, ...	11	Town Clerk	1783–1885	Partially	Good

1764. June 14. Prov. Laws, Vol. IV., p. 721. The plantation called Ipswich-Canada established as Winchendon.

1780. June 17. Part of Royalston annexed to Winchendon, and the bounds of Winchendon extended to embrace all the lands on the north as far as the New Hampshire state line.

1785. June 27. Parts of Westminster, Ashburnham, and Winchendon established as Gardner.

1787. Mar. 2. Part of Gardner annexed to Winchendon.

1794. Feb. 22. Part of Winchendon annexed to Gardner.

1851. May 24. Part of Winchendon annexed to Gardner.

COUNTY OF WORCESTER.   CITY OF WORCESTER.

KIND OF RECORDS.	Number of Volumes	In Keeping of —	Years Covered	Whether Indexed	Condition
Town proceedings, . . .	7[5]	City Clerk	1722–1848	Yes	Good
City proceedings, . . .	18	City Clerk	1848–1885	Partially	Good
Births, ...	9[6]	City Clerk	1714–1885	Yes	Good
Marriages, ...	7	City Clerk	1795–1885	Yes	Good
Deaths, ...	7[6]	City Clerk	1714–1885	Yes	Good
Marriage intentions, . .	7	City Clerk	1796–1885	Yes	Good
Assessors, ...	40	City Clerk	–	–	–
Assessors, ...	61	Assessors	–	–	–
Proprietors, ...	1[7]	City Clerk	1667–1788	Yes	Good
Miscellaneous, ...	66	City Clerk	1790–1885	Yes	Good

1684. Oct. 15. Mass. Rec., Vol. V., p. 460. It was ordered that the "plantation" at Quansigamond be called Worcester and that the "town" brand mark be as is illustrated in the record.

1741. Jan. 9. Prov. Laws, Vol. II., p. 1043. Part of Worcester called North Worcester established as Holden.

1778. April 10. Prov. Laws, Vol. V., p. 796. The parish lately set off from Worcester, Leicester, Oxford, and Sutton established as Ward.

1785. June 14. Certain common lands annexed to Worcester.

1838. Mar. 22. Grafton Gore annexed to Worcester.

1848. Feb. 29. Worcester incorporated as a city.

1848. Mar. 18. Act of incorporation accepted by the town.

---

[1] With the exception of the first two volumes.

[2] With the exception of the first volume.   [3] The records prior to 1859 were burned.

[4] There is a copy of a part of the proprietors records in the private possession of the Town Clerk.

[5] There are copies also of the records from 1722 to 1783 which have been printed.

[6] There are copies also of the first two volumes of births and deaths.

[7] There is a copy also which has been printed by the Worcester Society of Antiquity.

TOWN RECORDS.

EXTINCT CITIES, TOWNS, AND DISTRICTS.

[This presentation comprises a summary of legislation relating to those cities, towns, and districts which have become extinct by change of name, annexation to cities or towns, or by uniting w:th a town to form a town under a new name. The districts which became towns and the towns which became cities without change of name are not considered as extinct and are not included, therefore, in this presentation. This summary of legislation is similar to that which follows the presentation for each city and town concerning "Town Records," and which is explained on page 149.]

Town of Bethlehem.[1]

1789.	June 24.	The North Eleven Thousand Acres, so called, established as the dist·ict of Bethlehem.
1809.	June 19.	District of Bethlehem and the town of Loudon united as the town of Loudon.
1810.	Mar. ·1.	Act of June 19, 1809, took effect.

District of Boston Corner.

1838.	April 14.	The tract of common land called Boston Corner established as the district of Boston Corner.
1847.	Mar. 12.	Bounds between the district of Boston Corner and Mount Washington established.
1853.	May 14.	District of Boston Corner ceded to the State of New York.

Town of Brighton.[2]

1807.	Feb. 24.	Part of Cambridge established as Brighton.
1816.	Jan. 27.	Part of Cambridge annexed to Brighton.
1873.	May 21.	Brighton annexed to Boston, if this act is accepted by both places.
1873.	Oct. 7.	Act of May 21, 1873, accepted by Brighton and Boston.
1874.	Jan. 5.	Act of May 21, 1873, took effect.

District of Carlisle.[3]

1754.	April 19.	Prov. Laws, Vol. III., p. 729. Part of Concord established as the district of Carlisle.
1756.	Oct. 6.	Mass. Archives, Vol. CXVII., p. 206. District of Carlisle annexed to Concord.

---

[1] See town of Loudon, also extinct.

[2] For the records of Brighton, see city of Boston, under "Town Records."

[3] See town of Carlisle, under "Town Records." Charles E. Clark, M.D., of Boston, has in his possession a volume of manuscript containing "The Book of Records of the District of Carlisle from January 7th, to July 8th, 1754"; "The Book of Accounts of the Selectmen of Carlisle District from January 7th, 1754, to Dec. 24, 1755," and a record of "sume deaths and tirths 1754–1755," there being, however, some earlier and later dates included. He has also a list of polls and real estate, dated October 14, 1754, and many files of papers.

EXTINCT CITIES, TOWNS, AND DISTRICTS — Continued.

City of Charlestown.[1]

1630.	Aug.	23.	Mass. Rec., Vol. I., p. 73. The first Court of Assistants was held at "Charlton."
1632.	Mar.	6.	Mass. Rec., Vol. I., p. 94. Bounds between Charlestown and Newe Towne established.
1635.	July	8.	Mass. Rec., Vol. I., p. 150. Bounds between Charlestown and Boston established.
1636.	Mar.	3.	Mass. Rec., Vol. I., p. 168. Bounds established "eight miles into the country from their meeting-house."
1636.	Mar.	28.	Mass. Rec., Vol. I., p. 162. Bounds between Charlestown and Boston established.
1636.	Oct.	28.	Mass. Rec., Vol. I., p. 183. "Lovels Iland is graunted to Charlestowne provided they imploy it for fishing by their own townsmen or hinder not others."
1640.	May	13.	Mass. Rec., Vol. I., p. 290. Certain common lands granted to Charlestown.
1640.	Oct.	7.	Mass. Rec., Vol. I., p. 306. Certain common lands granted to Charlestown.
1648.	Oct.	27.	Mass. Rec., Vol. II., p. 263. "The iland called Lovels Iland" granted to Charlestown "provided half the timber and firewood shall belong to the garrison at the Castle."
1659.	Nov.	12.	Mass. Rec., Vol. IV., Part 1, p. 400. One thousand acres of land granted to Charlestown.
1663.	Oct.	21.	Mass. Rec., Vol. IV., Part 1, p. 91. Certain common lands granted to Charlestown.
1664.	Oct.	19.	Mass. Rec., Vol. IV., Part 1, p. 138. The grant made November 12, 1659, renewed.
1725.	Dec.	17.	Prov. Laws, Vol. II., p. 369. Part of Charlestown established as Stoneham.
1802.	Mar.	6.	Part of Charlestown annexed to Cambridge.
1811.	June	21.	Part of Medford annexed to Charlestown.
1820.	June	17.	Part of Charlestown annexed to Cambridge.
1842.	Feb.	25.	Part of Charlestown annexed to West Cambridge.
1842.	Mar.	3.	Part of Charlestown established as Somerville.
1847.	Feb.	22.	Charlestown incorporated as a city.
1847.	Mar.	10.	Act of incorporation accepted by the town.
1873.	May	14.	Charlestown annexed to Boston if this act is accepted by both cities.
1873.	Oct.	7.	Act of May 14, 1873, accepted by Charlestown and Boston.
1874.	Jan.	5.	Act of May 14, 1873, took effect.

Town of Dorchester.[2]

1630.	Sept.	7.	Mass. Rec., Vol. I., p. 75. It was ordered that Mattapan be called Dorchester.
1636.	Mar.	28.	Mass. Rec., Vol. I., p. 162. Bounds established.
1641.	June	2.	Mass. Rec., Vol. I., p. 333. "Squantums Neck and Mennens Moone are layd to Dorchester."
1659.	Nov.	12.	Mass. Rec., Vol. IV., Part 1, p. 397. One thousand acres of common lands granted to Dorchester.
1662.	May	7.	Mass. Rec., Vol. IV., Part 1, p. 50. Part of Dorchester established as Milton.
1726.	Dec.	22.	Prov. Laws, Vol. II., p. 408. Part of Dorchester established as Stoughton.
1792.	Feb.	22.	Part of Dorchester annexed to Quincy.
1804.	Mar.	6.	Part of Dorchester annexed to Boston.
1814.	Feb.	10.	Part of Dorchester annexed to Quincy.

---

[1] For the records of Charlestown, see city of Boston, under "Town Records."

[2] For the records of Dorchester, see city of Boston, under "Town Records."

EXTINCT CITIES, TOWNS, AND DISTRICTS — Continued.

Town of Dorchester — Con.

1819.	Feb.	12.	Part of Dorchester annexed to Quincy.
1820.	Feb.	21.	Bounds between Dorchester and Quincy established.
1831.	June	17.	Part of Dedham annexed to Dorchester.
1834.	Mar.	25.	Thompson's Island set off from Dorchester and annexed to Boston while it shall be used for charitable purposes.
1855.	May	2.	Part of Dorchester annexed to Quincy.
1868.	April	22.	Parts of Dorchester, Dedham, and Milton established as Hyde Park.
1868.	May	1.	Act of April 22, 1868, amended and bounds changed.
1869.	June	4.	Dorchester annexed to Boston if this act is accepted by both places.
1869.	June	22.	Act of June 4, 1869, accepted by Dorchester and Boston.
1870.	Jan.	3.	Act of June 4, 1869, took effect.

Town of East Sudbury.[1]

1780.	April	10.	Part of Sudbury established as East Sudbury.
1835.	Mar.	11.	The name of the town of East Sudbury changed to Wayland.

Town of Gageborough.[2]

1771.	July	4.	Prov. Laws, Vol. V., p. 162. The new plantation called Number Four established as Gageborough.
1778.	Oct.	16.	Prov. Laws, Vol. V., p. 911. Part of the plantation called Number Five annexed to Gageborough, and the town of Gageborough, together with this annexed tract of land, to be a town by the name of Windsor.

Town of Gerry.[3]

1786.	Oct.	20.	Parts of Athol and Templeton established as Gerry.
1799.	Feb.	26.	Parts of Gerry and Athol annexed to Royalston.
1806.	Feb.	28.	Part of Gerry annexed to Athol.
1814.	Feb.	5.	The name of the town of Gerry changed to Phillipston.

Town of Hutchinson.[4]

1774.	June	17.	Prov. Laws, Vol. V., p. 389. Rutland District established as Hutchinson.
1776.	Nov.	7.	Prov. Laws, Vol. V., p. 592. The name of the town of Hutchinson changed to Barre.

Town of Loudon.[5]

1773.	Feb.	27.	Prov. Laws, Vol. V., p. 237. A tract of common land called Tyringham Equivalent established as "Loudun."
1809.	June	19.	Loudon and the district of Bethlehem united as the town of Loudon.
1810.	Mar.	1.	Act of June 19, 1809, took effect. Part of Loudon annexed to Becket.
1810.	June	13.	The name of the town of Loudon changed to Otis.

[1] For the records of East Sudbury, see town of Wayland, under "Town Records."

[2] For the records of Gageborough, see town of Windsor, under "Town Records."

[3] For the records of Gerry, see town of Phillipston, under "Town Records."

[4] For the records of Hutchinson and the district of Rutland, see town of Barre, under "Town Records."

[5] See district of Bethlehem, also extinct. For the records of Loudon and the district of Bethlehem, see town of Otis, under "Town Records."

EXTINCT CITIES, TOWNS, AND DISTRICTS — Continued.

Town of Murrayfield.[1]

1765.	Oct.	31.	Prov. Laws, Vol. IV., p. 837. The new plantation called Murrayfield established as Murrayfield.
1773.	June	29.	Prov. Laws, Vol. V., p. 297. Part of Murrayfield established as the district of Norwich.
1781.	May	8.	Part of Murrayfield annexed to Norwich.
1783.	Feb.	21.	The name of the town of Murrayfield changed to Chester.

Town of Nawsett.[2]

1643.	—.	—.	Ply. Col. Rec., Vol. VIII., p. 177. Nawsett is mentioned in the list of "towns" having freemen able to bear arms.
1645.	Mar.	3.	Ply. Col. Rec., Vol. II., p. 81. Certain common lands "lying between sea and sea" granted to those who go to dwell at "Nossett."
1646.	June	2.	Ply. Col. Rec., Vol. II., p. 102. Nawsett established as a township.
1651.	June	7.	Ply. Col. Rec., Vol. XI., p. 59. The name of the town of Nawsett changed to Eastham.

Town of Newtowne.[3]

1631.	July	26.	Mass. Rec., Vol. I., p. 90. "Charlton, Misticke, and the newe town" are mentioned.
1632.	Mar.	6.	Mass. Rec., Vol. I., p. 94. "Bounds between Charles-Towne and Newe Towne" established.
1636.	Sept.	8.	Mass. Rec., Vol. I., p. 180. "Newe Town now called Cambridge."
1638.	May	2.	Mass. Rec., Vol. I., p. 228. "It is ordered that Newtowne shall henceforward be called Cambridge."

Town of North Bridgewater.[4]

1821.	June	15.	Part of Bridgewater established as North Bridgewater.
1825.	Jan.	26.	Bounds between North Bridgewater and West Bridgewater established.
1874.	Mar.	28.	The town of North Bridgewater authorized to change its name.
1874.	May	5.	Brockton adopted as the name.

Town of North Chelsea.[5]

1846.	Mar.	19.	Part of Chelsea established as North Chelsea.
1852.	Mar.	27.	Part of North Chelsea established as Winthrop.
1871.	Mar.	24.	The name of the town of North Chelsea changed to Revere, if accepted within ninety days.
1871.	April	3.	Act of March 24, 1871, accepted.

Town of Norwich.[6]

| 1773. | June 29. | Prov. Laws, Vol. V., p. 297. Part of Murrayfield established as the district of Norwich. |
| 1775. | Aug. 23. | Prov. Laws, Vol. V., p. 419. District of Norwich made the town of Norwich by this general act. |

---

[1] For the records of Murrayfield, see town of Chester, under "Town Records."
[2] For the records of Nawsett, see town of Eastham, under "Town Records."
[3] For the records of Newtowne, see city of Cambridge, under "Town Records."
[4] For the records of North Bridgewater, see city of Brockton, under "Town Records."
[5] For the records of North Chelsea, see town of Revere, under "Town Records."
[6] For the records of Norwich, see town of Huntington, under "Town Records."

Extinct Cities, Towns, and Districts — Continued.

Town of Norwich — Con.

1780. **Nov. 28.** Parts of Norwich, Southampton, and Westfield established as Montgomery.

1781. **May 8.** Part of Murrayfield annexed to Norwich.

1792. **Mar. 6.** Part of Norwich annexed to Montgomery.

1794. **Feb. 22.** Part of Norwich annexed to Chesterfield.

1853. **May 25.** Parts of Blandford and Chester annexed to Norwich.

1855. **Mar. 9.** The name of the town of Norwich changed to Huntington.

Town of Parsons.[1]

1819. **Feb. 18.** Part of Newbury established as Parsons.

1820. **June 14.** The name of the town of Parsons changed to West Newbury.

Town of Partridgefield.[2]

1771. **July 4.** Prov. Laws, Vol. V., p. 164. The new plantation called Number Two established as Partridgefield.

1804. **June 21.** Part of Partridgefield established as Hinsdale.

1806. **June 19.** The name of the town of Partridgefield changed to Peru.

Town of Prescott.[3]

1653. **May 18.** Mass. Rec., Vol. III., p. 302. "Considering that there is already at Nashaway about 9 families * * * this court doth hereby give and grant them liberties of a township and at the request of the inhabitants do order it to be called Prescott." [The record is confusing in regard to Nashaway, which appears to have been made Prescott, West Towne, and Lancaster by one act.]

Town of Rexhame.[4]

1641. **Mar. 2.** Ply. Col. Rec., Vol. XI., p. 37. "It is enacted by the Court that Green's Harbour shall be a township * * * and that it shall be called by the name Rexhame."

1641. **Mar. 2.** Ply. Col. Rec., Vol. II., p. 9. "Rexame" is in the list of places for which constables were chosen.

1641. **June 1.** Ply. Col. Rec., Vol. II., p. 15. Rexhame is mentioned in a list of towns and the name then disappears from the records.

Town of Richmont.[5]

1765. **June 21.** Prov. Laws, Vol. IV., p. 817. The new plantation called Yokum Town and Mount Ephraim established as Richmont.

1767. **Feb. 26.** Prov. Laws, Vol. IV., p. 905. Part of Richmont established as the district of Lenox.

1785. **Mar. 3.** The name of the town of Richmont changed to Richmond.

---

[1] For the records of Parsons, see town of West Newbury, under "Town Records."

[2] For the records of Partridgefield, see town of Peru, under "Town Records."

[3] For the records of Prescott, see town of Lancaster, under "Town Records." See West Towne, also extinct.

[4] For the records of Rexhame, see town of Marshfield, under "Town Records." Nothing has been found in the records changing the name of the town of Rexhame to Marshfield. In the entry first above quoted, after the period which follows Rexhame, appear these words, "but now Marshfield." As Rexhame appears in a list of towns, June 1, 1641, it is probable that these words were not a part of the original entry and that the name Marshfield does not date from March 2, 1641, as is claimed.

[5] For the records of Richmont, see town of Richmond, under "Town Records."

EXTINCT CITIES, TOWNS, AND DISTRICTS — Continued.

City of Roxbury.[1]

1630. Sept. 28. Mass. Rec., Vol. I., p. 77. "Rocsbury" is mentioned in the list of plantations.

1633. Mar. 4. Mass. Rec., Vol. I , p. 103. Bounds between Roxbury and Boston established.

1635. April 7. Mass. Rec., Vol. I., p.144. Bounds between Roxbury and Newe Towne established.

1636. May 25. Mass. Rec., Vol. I., p. 176. Certain lands granted to Roxbury.

1638. May 2. Mass. Rec., Vol. I., p. 229. Certain lands granted to Roxbury.

1638. May 16. Mass. Rec., Vol. I., p. 230. Bounds between Roxbury and Dedham established.

1641. Oct. 7. Mass. Rec., Vol. I., p. 341. Bounds between Roxbury and Boston established.

1660. Oct. 16. Mass. Rec., Vol. IV., Part 1, p. 438. Certain lands granted to Roxbury.

1675. May 12. Mass. Rec., Vol. V., p. 38. Bounds between Roxbury and Dedham established.

1836. Mar. 16. Bounds between Roxbury and Boston established.

1837. April 19. Bounds between Roxbury and Boston established.

1838. April 23. Part of Newton annexed to Roxbury.

1844. Feb. 24. Part of Roxbury annexed to Brookline.

1846. Mar. 12. Roxbury incorporated as a city.

1846. Mar. 25. Act of incorporation accepted by the town.

1850. May 3. Bounds between Roxbury and Boston established.

1851. May 24. Part of Roxbury established as West Roxbury.

1860. April 3. Part of Roxbury annexed to Boston and bounds established, if the act is accepted by both cities.

1860. April 16. Act of April 3, 1860, accepted by Roxbury.

1860. May 8. Act of April 3, 1860, accepted by Boston.

1867. June 1. Roxbury annexed to Boston if this act is accepted by both cities.

1867. Sept. 9. Act of June 1, 1867, accepted by Roxbury and Boston.

1868. Jan. 5. Act of June 1, 1867, took effect.

District of Rutland.[2]

1753. April 12. Prov. Laws, Vol. III., p. 654. Part of the town of Rutland established as the Rutland District.

1774. June 17. Prov. Laws, Vol. V., p. 389. Rutland District established as Hutchinson.

Town of Saugus.[3]

1631. July 5. Mass. Rec., Vol. I., p. 89. The plantation of Saugus is mentioned in the Tax Act.

1635. Mar. 4. Mass. Rec., Vol. I., p. 141. Bounds between Saugus and Salem, and between Saugus and Marble Harbor, to be established.

1637. Nov. 20. Mass. Rec., Vol. I., p. 211. "Saugust is called Lin."

Town of Sherburn.[4]

1687. June 27. N. Y. Town Grants, Lib. VI., p. 254. "Sharborn" is mentioned.

1692. —. —. Prov. Laws, Vol. I., p. 9. By the Province Charter in 1692 the island of Nantucket was granted to the Province of Massachusetts Bay.

1795. June 8. The name of the town of Sherburn, in the county of Nantucket, changed to Nantucket.

---

[1] For the records of Roxbury, see city of Boston, under "Town Records."

[2] See town of Hutchinson, also extinct.

[3] See also the present town of Saugus, under "Town Records." For the records of the first town of Saugus, see city of Lynn, under "Town Records."

[4] See also the present town of Sherborn, under "Town Records." For the records of Sherburn, see town of Nantucket, under "Town Records."

Extinct Cities, Towns, and Districts — Continued.

Town of South Brimfield.[1]

1762. Sept. 18. Prov. Laws, Vol. IV., p. 601. Part of Brimfield established as the district of South Brimfield.
1766. Feb. 21. Prov. Laws, Vol. IV., p. 857. The district of South Brimfield divided into two parishes, the east and west.
1775. Aug. 23. Prov. Laws, Vol. V., p. 419. District of South Brimfield made the town of South Brimfield by this general act.
1783. July 5. The east parish of South Brimfield established as the district of Holland.
1796. Feb. 23. Bounds between South Brimfield and the district of Holland established.
1828. Feb. 20. The name of the town of South Brimfield changed to Wales.

Town of South Danvers.[2]

1855. May 18. Part of Danvers established as South Danvers.
1856. April 30. Part of Salem annexed to South Danvers and bounds established.
1856. May 31. Bounds between South Danvers and Danvers established.
1868. April 13. The name of the town of South Danvers changed to Peabody.
1868. April 30. Name of Peabody accepted by the town

District of Southfield.[3]

1797. June 19. The South Eleven Thousand Acres, so called, established as the district of Southfield.
1819. Feb. 8. District of Southfield and town of Sandisfield united as the town of Sandisfield.

Town of South Reading.[4]

1812. Feb. 25. Part of Reading established as South Reading.
1813. June 16. Part of South Reading annexed to Reading.
1856. April 5. Part of Stoneham annexed to South Reading.
1868. Feb. 25. The name of the town of South Reading changed to Wakefield.
1868. June 30. Act of February 25, 1868, took effect.

Town of Stoughtonham.[5]

1765. June 21. Prov. Laws, Vol. IV., p. 808. Part of Stoughton established as the district of Stoughtonham.
1775. Aug. 23. Prov. Laws, Vol. V., p. 419. District of Stoughtonham made the town of Stoughtonham by this general act.
1778. June 10. Prov. Laws, Vol. V., p. 875. Parts of Stoughtonham, Stoughton, Walpole, and Wrentham established as Foxborough.
1783. Feb. 25. The name of the town of Stoughtonham changed to Sharon.

Town of Troy.[6]

1804. June 18. The name of the town of Fall River changed to Troy.
1834. Feb. 12. The name of the town of Troy changed to Fall River.

[1] For the records of South Brimfield, see town of Wales, under "Town Records."
[2] For the records of South Danvers, see town of Peabody, under "Town Records."
[3] For the records of the district of Southfield, see town of Sandisfield, under "Town Records."
[4] For the records of South Reading, see town of Wakefield, under "Town Records."
[5] For the records of Stoughtonham, see town of Sharon, under "Town Records."
[6] For the records of Troy, see city of Fall River, under "Town Records."

EXTINCT CITIES, TOWNS, AND DISTRICTS — Continued.

Town of Ward.[1]

1778. April 10. Prov. Laws, Vol. V., p. 796. The parish lately set off from Leicester,
                   Oxford, Sutton, and Worcester established as Ward.
1837. Feb.   17. The name of the town of Ward changed to Auburn.

Town of Wellington.[2]

1814. June   9. Part of Dighton established as Wellington.
1824. Feb. 12. Part of Dighton annexed to Wellington.
1826. Feb. 22. Wellington and Dighton united as Dighton.

Town of West Cambridge.[3]

1807. Feb.   27. Part of Cambridge established as West Cambridge.
1842. Feb.   25. Part of Charlestown annexed to West Cambridge.
1850. April 30. Parts of West Cambridge, Medford, and Woburn established as Win-
                   chester.
1859. Mar.   18. Parts of West Cambridge, Waltham, and Watertown established as
                   Belmont.
1861. Jan.   31. Bounds between West Cambridge and Belmont established.
1862. Feb.   25. Part of Cambridge annexed to West Cambridge.
1867. April 13. The name of the town of West Cambridge changed to Arlington.
1867. April 30. Act of April 13, 1867, took effect.

Town of Western.[4]

1742. Jan.   16. Prov. Laws, Vol. II., p. 1088. Parts of Brimfield, Brookfield, and
                   Kingsfield established as Western.
1823. Feb.   8. Part of Western annexed to Ware.
1831. Feb.   7. Part of Western annexed to Palmer.
1834. Mar.   13. The name of the town of Western changed to Warren.

Town of West Roxbury.[5]

1851. May   24. Part of Roxbury established as West Roxbury.
1852. April 21. Part of Dedham annexed to West Roxbury.
1852. April 30. Act of April 21, 1852, accepted by West Roxbury.
1853. July   4. Four hundred dollars paid by West Roxbury to Dedham, and act of
                   April 21, 1852, in effect.
1870. April   2. Bounds between West Roxbury and Boston established.
1872. April 12. Part of West Roxbury (Mount Hope Cemetery) annexed to Boston.
1873. May   29. West Roxbury annexed to Boston if this act is accepted by both places.
1873. Oct.   7. Act of May 29, 1873, accepted by West Roxbury and Boston.
1874. Jan.   5. Act of May 29, 1873, took effect.

---

[1] For the records of Ward, see town of Auburn, under "Town Records."

[2] For the records of Wellington, see town of Dighton, under "Town Records."

[3] For the records of West Cambridge, see town of Arlington, under "Town Records."

[4] For the records of Western, see town of Warren, under "Town Records."

[5] For the records of West Roxbury, see city of Boston, under "Town Records."

Extinct Cities, Towns, and Districts — Concluded.

Town of West Towne.[1]

1653. May 18. Mass. Rec., Vol. III., p. 303. "The court taking the condition of Nash-away into further consideration do order, that it shall be cal.ed henceforth West Towne." [Under the same date Nashaway is made a township and is ordered to be called Prescott, and then Prescott is ordered to be called Lancaster, but no act has been found which abolishes the township of West Towne.]

Town of Winchester.[2]

1739. June 16. Prov. Laws, Vol. II., p. 990. The plantation of Arlington in the county of Hampshire established as the township of Winchester. [No act has been found abolishing the town of Winchester.]

---

[1] For the records of West Towne, see town of Lancaster, under "Town Records." See Prescott, also extinct.

[2] See also the present town of Winchester, in the county of Middlesex, under "Town Records."

COURT RECORDS.

[The establishing, abolishing, and reviving under the same or new names, of the various courts since 1636 has made it seem advisable for a better understanding of the "Court Records" to present chronologically the legislation by which the various changes were authorized.

The legislation concerning the establishment of courts is presented in two ways: First, by the original titles of courts, in the chronological order of establishment, with the reference to the establishing acts; second, by the present titles of courts, first presenting the legislation which may properly be called the original foundation of each court, this being followed by the successive legislation until the establishment of the court under its present title. Reference to volume and page is given in each instance until 1784, since which time the date of the act is deemed sufficient reference. Notes relating to many of the courts follow the references, in parentheses.

Special Courts of Oyer and Terminer were held in various places, by commissioners appointed by the Governor during the provincial period. As these courts were not established by acts of legislation, they are presented separately, although their records may be in the offices of the Clerks of the Courts.

From 1692 to 1699 many of the acts passed were disallowed by the Privy. Council in England, among them being several establishing courts. As these dates have been variously fixed by different writers, the legislation relating to these acts with the verified dates and references to the same are given. The compiling of the Province Laws and the indexing of many volumes of laws and records, in late years, have made this verification possible.]

ESTABLISHMENT OF COURTS: BY ORIGINAL TITLES.

QUARTER COURTS.

1636.   Mar.   3.   Mass. Rec., Vol. I., p. 169. To be held every quarter in Ipswich, Salem, Cambridge, and Boston. (There are no records reported of Quarter Courts, but as County Court records commence in 1636 they evidently include these courts.)

GREAT QUARTER COURTS.

1636.   Mar.   3.   Mass. Rec., Vol. I., p. 169. "Four Great Quarter Courts to be kept yearly at Boston." (No separate records are reported.)

COURTS OF ASSISTANTS.

1639.   ——.   Mass. Col. Laws, edit. 1660, p. 23. "Two Courts of Assistants yearly be kept at Boston." (The first Monthly Court or Court of Assistants in this country was holden August 23, 1630.)

COUNTY COURTS.

1639.   ——. Mass. Col. Laws, edit. 1660, p. 23. (See remarks under Quarter Courts.)

STRANGERS' OR MERCHANTS' COURTS.

1639.   ——. Mass. Col. Laws, edit. 1660, p. 24. (No records are reported.)

——.   ——. Mass. Col. Laws, edit. 1660, p. 24. Strangers were given liberty to enter actions in any court. (This was probably in 1650.)

COURTS OF CHANCERY.

1685. May 27. Mass. Rec., Vol. V., p. 475.

1687. Mar. 3. Mass. Archives, Vol. XL., p. 234.

1692. Nov. 25. Prov. Laws, Vol. I., p. 75. A High Court of Chancery. (Act disallowed by the Privy Council, August 22, 1695.[1])

SUPERIOR COURT OF JUDICATURE.

1687. Mar. 3. Mass. Archives, Vol. XL., p. 234.

1692. Nov. 25. Prov. Laws, Vol. I., p. 73. (Act disallowed by the Privy Council, August 22, 1695.[1])

COURTS OF SESSIONS.

1687. Mar. 3. Mass. Archives, Vol. XL., p. 234.

1808. Feb. 23. Mass. Laws. Name of the "Courts of General Sessions of the Peace" changed to "Courts of Sessions." (Powers and duties transferred to Courts of Common Pleas, June 19, 1809.)

1811. June 25. Mass. Laws. Act took effect September 1, 1811. (Abolished February 28, 1814, and powers and duties transferred to Circuit Court of Common Pleas, except for the counties of Dukes County, Nantucket, and Suffolk.)

1819. Feb. 20. Mass. Laws. (Abolished February 26, 1828.)

INFERIOR COURT OF COMMON PLEAS.

1687. Mar. 3. Mass. Archives, Vol. XL., p. 234.

1692. June 28. Prov. Laws, Vol. I., p. 37. Special terms until otherwise provided. (Act disallowed by the Privy Council, August 22, 1695.[1])

1692. Nov. 25. Prov. Laws, Vol. I., p. 73. (Act disallowed by the Privy Council, August 22, 1695.[1])

1697. June 19. Prov. Laws, Vol. I., p. 284. (Act disallowed by the Privy Council, November 24, 1698.[1])

1699. June 26. Prov. Laws, Vol. I., p. 369.

GENERAL SESSIONS OF THE PEACE.[2]

1692. June 28. Prov. Laws, Vol. I., p. 37. "General Sessions of the Peace ordered to be held and kept in each county" until other provision shall be made by the General Court. (Act disallowed by the Privy Council, August 22, 1695.[1])

COURT OF ASSIZE AND GENERAL GOAL DELIVERY.

1692. Nov. 25. Prov. Laws, Vol. I., p. 74. (Act disallowed by the Privy Council, August 22, 1695.[1])

---

[1] See page 309.   [2] See also "Courts of General Sessions of the Peace."

QUARTER SESSIONS OF THE PEACE.

1692. **Nov. 25.** Prov. Laws, Vol. I., p. 72. (Act disallowed by the Privy Council, August 22, 1695.[1])

SUPERIOR COURT OF JUDICATURE, COURT OF ASSIZE, AND GENERAL GOAL DELIVERY.

1697. **June 19.** Prov. Laws, Vol. I., p. 285. (Act disallowed by the Privy Council, November 24, 1698.[1])

1699. **June 26.** Prov. Laws, Vol. I., p. 370.

COURTS OF GENERAL SESSIONS OF THE PEACE.

1697. **June 19.** Prov. Laws, Vol. I., p. 284. (Act disallowed by the Privy Council, November 24, 1698.[1])

1699. **June 26.** Prov. Laws, Vol. I., p. 367.

1782. **July 3.** Perpet. Laws of Mass., edit. 1789, p. 92. (Name changed to Courts of Sessions, February 23, 1808.)

SUPREME JUDICIAL COURT.[2]

1781. **Feb. 20.** Perpet. Laws of Mass., edit. 1789, p. 89. Ordered to take cognizance of all matters cognizable before the late Superior Court of Judicature, Court of Assize, and General Goal Delivery.

1782. **July 3.** Perpet. Laws of Mass., edit. 1789, p. 90. (This act established the court, which had held terms and has records from February, 1781.)

---

[1] See page 309.

[2] An act to establish the Supreme Judicial Court was passed July 3, 1782 (Perpet. Laws of Mass., edit. 1789, p. 90), and that date is usually given as the date of establishment. There are records of the court, however, from February, 1781, in the office of the Clerk of the Supreme Judicial Court, in Boston, sessions having commenced probably under authority of the following act, passed February 20, 1781 (Perpet. Laws of Mass., edit. 1789, p. 89) :

" An Act empowering the Supreme Judicial Court to take Cognizance of Matters heretofore cognizable by the late Superior Court.

" Whereas by the Laws heretofore made by the General Assembly of the late Province, Colony and State of Massachusetts Bay, a Superior Court of Judicature, Court of Assize and General Goal Delivery was constituted, and sundry powers and Authorities are given to the same Court by Particular Laws. And whereas by the Constitution and Frame of Government of the Commonwealth of Massachusetts, the Style and Title of the same Court is now the Supreme Judicial Court of the Commonwealth of Massachusetts. And the Constitution aforesaid having provided that the Laws heretofore made and adopted, should continue and be in force until they shall be altered or repealed by the Legislature; whence some doubts may arise whether the Supreme Judicial Court shall have cognizance of those matters which by particular laws were expressly made cognizable by the Superior Court of Judicature, and General Goal Delivery :

Sect. 1. Be it therefore enacted by the Senate and House of Representatives in General Court assembled, and by Authority of the same, That the Court which hath been or shall be hereafter appointed and commissioned according to the Constitution as the Supreme Judicial Court of this Commonwealth, shall have cognizance of all such matters as have heretofore happened, or that shall hereafter happen, as by particular Laws were made cognizable by the late Superior Court of Judicature, Court of Assize and General Goal Delivery, unless where the Constitution and Frame of Government hath provided otherwise."

As the Constitution nowhere provides that " the Style and Title of the same Court is now the Supreme Judicial Court," the court by the strict letter of law did not exist under that particular title, until it had held sessions and kept records for a year and a half.

COURT OF COMMON PLEAS.

1782.   July   3.   Perpet. Laws of Mass., edit. 1789, p. 93.

1798.   June   27.   Mass. Laws. "Courts of Common Pleas" in the several counties. (Abolished September 1, 1811, by Act of June 25, 1811.)

1814.   Feb.   26.   Mass. Laws. To be holden at Boston. Act to take effect March 28, 1814. (Abolished February 14, 1821.)

1821.   Feb.   14.   Mass. Laws. (Abolished April 5, 1859.)

COURTS OF PROBATE.

1784.   Mar.   12.   Perpet. Laws of Mass., edit. 1789, p. 102. Supreme Judicial Court made Supreme Court of Probate by the same act.

1818.   Feb.   24.   Mass. Laws. Act to take effect July 1, 1818.

CIRCUIT COURT OF COMMON PLEAS.

1811.   June   21.   Mass. Laws. Established for all counties except Dukes County and Nantucket. (Abolished February 21, 1820.)

SUPERIOR COURT OF THE COUNTY OF SUFFOLK.

1855.   May   21.   Mass. Laws.

COURTS OF INSOLVENCY.

1856.   June   6.   Mass. Laws.

COURTS OF PROBATE AND INSOLVENCY.

1858.   Mar.   26.   Mass. Laws. Act to take effect July 1, 1858.

SUPERIOR COURT.

1859.   April   5.   Mass. Laws. (The Superior Court of the County of Suffolk, established by act of May 21, 1855, was abolished by this act.)

SPECIAL COURTS OF OYER AND TERMINER.[1]

[These courts were held, by commissioners appointed by the Governor on the dates following, for the special purposes named.]

1687.   Aug.   10.   Mass. Council Rec., Vol. II., p. 133. For the trial, at Ipswich, of persons committed on suspicion of piracy.

1688.   July   9.   Mass. Archives, Vol. CXXIX., p. 33. For the trial, at Rhode Island, "of any person or persons who shall knowingly entertain, harbour, conceal, trade or hold correspondence with, pirates."

1692.   May   27.   Mass. Council Rec., Vol. II., p. 176. To enquire of, hear and determine for this time, according to the law, and custom of England, and of this their majesties' province, all and all manner of crimes and offences had, made, done or perpetrated within the counties of Suffolk, Essex, Middlesex, and of either of them.

1692.   Oct.   22.   Mass. Council Rec., Vol. II., p. 196. To enquire of, hear and determine for this time, all and all manner of felonies, murders, homicides, manslaughters, and other offences, done and perpetrated within the county of York.

---

[1] The record of a special court of Oyer and Terminer, held at Boston August 19, 1686, for the trial of several persons for petty offences, is found in the first volume of the records of the Superior Court of Judicature, in the office of the clerk of the Supreme Judicial Court, at Boston, but the record of the appointment of the commissioners has not been found.

1696. Oct. 10. Mass. Council Rec., Vol. II., p. 419. For the trial of four Indians accused of murder near Hatfield, in the county of Hampshire.

1697. Oct. 14. Mass. Council Rec., Vol. II., p. 501. For the trial of an Indian, at Nantucket, accused of murder.

1698. Dec. 22. Mass. Council Rec., Vol. II., p. 569. For the trial, at Boston, of Jacob Smith for piracy and robbing upon the sea.

1703. Nov. 23. Mass. Council Rec., Vol. III., p. 494. For the trial, at Salem, of Mamoosin, an Indian, accused of murder.

1704. June 15. Mass. Council Rec., Vol. IV., p. 30. For the trial, at Nantucket, of an Indian for murder.

1707. Nov. 8. Mass. Council Rec , Vol. IV., p. 479. For the trial, at Kittery, of Joseph Gunnison, for the killing of Grace Wentworth.

1712. Mar. 7. Mass. Council Rec., Vol. V., p. 526. For the trial of Joseph Swaddell, commander of the ship Lake Frigate, of London, for the murder of John Johnston, one of his sailors.

1713. June 5. Mass. Council Rec., Vol. VI., p. 44. For the trial, at Barnstable, of two Indians for capital offences committed in the county of Barnstable.

1718. Dec. 3. Mass. Council Rec., Vol. VI., p. 631. For the trial, at Northampton, of Ovid Ruchbrock for counterfeiting.

1742. July 8. Mass. Council Rec., Vol. X., p. 644. For the trial, at Nantucket, of Harry Jude, an Indian, for murder.

1743. June 23. Mass. Council Rec., Vol. XI., p. 54. For the trial, at Nantucket, of Simeon Howsean, an Indian, "and any other capital offences."

1746. Aug. 9. Mass. Council Rec., Vol. XI., p. 652. For the trial, at Nantucket, of Jeremy Jude, an Indian, for murder.

ACTS DISALLOWED AND REVIVED.

1695. Aug. 22. Copies of the proceedings of the Privy Council in England, in the office of the Commissioner of the Province Laws, give under this date the record of the disallowance of the acts of 1692 establishing courts.

1696. July 13.[1] Mass. Council Rec., Vol. II., p. 403. The disallowance by the Privy Council of the acts of November 25, 1692, was read in Council.

1696. Sept. 17.[1] Mass. Archives, Vol. VI., p. 441. The Governor notified the legislature of a communication which he had received notifying him of the "allowance and confirmation" of, and the "repeal" of, "divers acts passed in 1692."

1696. Oct. 3. Mass. Archives, Vol. VI., p. 451. The legislature passed an act "reviving" the late acts for "Establishment of Judicatures and Courts of Justice," and continuing them until the end of the session in May, 1697.

1698. Nov. 24. Copies of the proceedings of the Privy Council in England, in the office of the Commissioner of the Province Laws, give under this date the record of the disallowance of the acts of June 19, 1697.

1699. April 27. S. J. Court, Suffolk County, Records. The records of the Superior Court of Judicature (Vol. 1686–1700, p. 256), in the office of the Clerk of the Supreme Judicial Court of Suffolk County, under date of April 27, 1699, say that the court being informed of the disallowance of the acts of June 19, 1697, ceased all further proceedings.

---

[1] These dates have been erroneously used by different writers as the dates of the disallowance of the acts of 1692 establishing courts (see reference to acts disallowed August 22, 1695).

1699. June 2.[1] Mass. Archives, Vol. VII., p. 5. The Earl of Bellamont, in his address, says, "I learn the Courts of Justice are fallen. I recommend your reviving them."

1699. June 2.[1] Mass. Archives, Vol. VII., p. 7. "The late act of Establishment of Courts, disallowed of by His Majesty, was read over, and ordered that there be a distinct and separate bill drawn."

1699. June 26. Prov. Laws, Vol. I., pp. 367–370. This act established the courts as they afterward existed until 1781.

ESTABLISHMENT OF COURTS: BY PRESENT TITLES.

SUPREME JUDICIAL COURT.

1639. ——. Mass. Col. Laws, edit. 1660, p. 23. In 1639, the month and day not being given, it was ordered that "Two Courts of Assistants yearly be kept at Boston."

1687. Mar. 3. Mass. Archives, Vol. XL., p. 234. "Superior Court of Judicature" was established.

1692. Nov. 25. Prov. Laws, Vol. I., p. 73. "Superior Court of Judicature" was established. A "Court of Assize and General Goal Delivery" was established at the same time.[2]

1697. June 19. Prov. Laws, Vol. I., p. 285. "Superior Court of Judicature, Court of Assize, and General Goal Delivery" was established.[3]

1699. June 26. Prov. Laws, Vol. I., p. 370. "Superior Court of Judicature, Court of Assize, and General Goal Delivery" was re-established.

1775. Sept. 19. Prov. Laws, Vol. V., pp. 420, 422. All court, and other officials, under the Royal Government ceased to hold office, but assumed their respective offices upon taking a new oath. (This act has been construed as an act abolishing the courts, which is evidently incorrect.)

1781. Feb. 20. Perpet. Laws of Mass., edit. 1789, p. 89. The Supreme Judicial Court was ordered to take cognizance of all matters cognizable before the late Superior Court of Judicature, Court of Assize, and General Goal Delivery.[4]

1782. July 3. Perpet. Laws of Mass., edit. 1789, p. 90. "Supreme Judicial Court" was established.[5]

1784. Mar. 12. Perpet. Laws of Mass., edit. 1789, p. 102. The Supreme Judicial Court was constituted the "Supreme Court of Probate."

---

[1] These dates have been erroneously used by different writers as the dates of the disallowance of the acts of June 19, 1697 (see reference to acts disallowed November 24, 1698).

[2] This act was disallowed by the Privy Council, August 22, 1695. See page 309.

[3] This act was disallowed by the Privy Council, November 24, 1698. See page 309.

[4] There is in the office of the Clerk of the Supreme Judicial Court, at Boston, a volume of records of this court, beginning February 20, 1781. See foot-note [2], p. 307.

[5] See foot-note [2], p. 307.

SUPERIOR COURT.

[The records, if existing, of the Quarter Courts, County Courts, Courts of Sessions, Courts of General Sessions of the Peace, Quarter Sessions of the Peace, Court of Common Pleas, Courts of Common Pleas, Inferior Court of Common Pleas, and Circuit Court of Common Pleas, are in the custody of the Clerks of the Superior Court in the several counties, and the acts establishing those courts is therefore given here. The term "Inferior" is sometimes used in the records of the Court of Common Pleas, at times when it was not a part of the title of the court.]

1636. Mar. 3. Mass. Rec., Vol. I., p. 169. Four courts were ordered "to be kept every quarter, 1 at Ipswich to which Newbury shall belong, 2 at Salem to which Saugus shall belong, 3 at Newtown" (now Cambridge) "to which Charlestown, Concord, Medford, and Watertown shall belong, 4 at Boston to which Roxbury, Dorchester, Weymouth, and Hingham shall belong." These courts were "to be kept by such magistrates as shall be dwelling in or near the said towns, and by such other persons of worth as shall be from time to time appointed by the General Court." Four "Great Quarter Courts" were ordered to be kept yearly at Boston.[1]

1639. ——. Mass. Col. Laws, edit. 1660, p. 23. In 1639, the month and day not being given, it was ordered that "County Courts" be established in each county; also "Strangers' or Merchants' Courts" were established.

1687. Mar. 3. Mass. Archives, Vol. XL., p. 234. "Courts of Sessions" and the "Inferior Court of Common Pleas" were established.

1692. June 28. Prov. Laws, Vol. I., p. 37. "Courts of General Sessions of the Peace" were ordered to be "held and kept in each county," until other provision should be made by the General Court. Special terms of the "Inferior Court of Common Pleas" were also ordered until other provision should be made.[2]

1692. Nov. 25. Prov. Laws, Vol. I., pp. 72, 73. "Quarter Sessions of the Peace" and the "Inferior Court of Common Pleas" were established.[2]

1697. June 19. Prov. Laws, Vol. I., p. 284. "Courts of General Sessions of the Peace" and the "Inferior Court of Common Pleas" were re-established.[3]

1699. June 26. Prov. Laws, Vol. I., pp. 367, 369. "Courts of General Sessions of the Peace" and the "Inferior Court of Common Pleas" were re-established.

1775. Sept. 19. Prov. Laws, Vol. V., pp. 420, 422. All court, and other officials, under the Royal Government ceased to hold office, but assumed their respective offices upon taking a new oath. (This act has been construed as an act abolishing the courts, which is evidently incorrect.)

1782. July 3. Perpet. Laws of Mass., edit. 1789, pp. 92, 93. "Courts of General Sessions of the Peace" and the "Court of Common Pleas" were established.

1798. June 27. Mass. Laws. "Courts of Common Pleas" in the several counties established.

1804. Mar. 9. Mass. Laws. The Courts of Common Pleas were ordered to exercise and perform the duties of Courts of General Sessions of the Peace, except as to certain county and town affairs.

1808. Feb. 23. Mass. Laws. "Courts of Sessions" were established by changing the name of "Courts of General Sessions of the Peace."

---

[1] No records of a court of this title are returned from any existing court.
[2] This act was disallowed by the Privy Council, August 22, 1695. See page 309.
[3] This act was disallowed by the Privy Council, November 24, 1698. See page 309.

1809. June 19. Mass. Laws. The powers and duties of Courts of Sessions were transferred to Courts of Common Pleas.

1811. June 21. Mass. Laws. "Circuit Court of Common Pleas" was established for all the counties except Dukes County and Nantucket.

1811. June 25. Mass. Laws. "Courts of Common Pleas" were abolished and "Courts of Sessions" were re-established, the act to take effect September 1, 1811.

1814. Feb. 26. Mass. Laws. A "Court of Common Pleas" to be holden at Boston was established, the act to take effect March 28, 1814.

1814. Feb. 28. Mass. Laws. "Courts of Sessions" were abolished and their powers and duties transferred to the "Circuit Court of Common Pleas," except for the counties of Dukes County, Nantucket, and Suffolk.

1819. Feb. 20. Mass. Laws. "Courts of Sessions" were re-established.

1820. Feb. 21. Mass. Laws. "Circuit Court of Common Pleas" was abolished and its powers and duties transferred to the "Courts of Sessions."

1821. Feb. 14. Mass. Laws. The "Court of Common Pleas" established February 26, 1814, to be holden at Boston, was abolished and the "Court of Common Pleas" was established.

1828. Feb. 26. Mass. Laws. "Courts of Sessions" were abolished.

1855. May 21. Mass. Laws. The "Superior Court of the County of Suffolk" was established.

1859. April 5. Mass. Laws. The "Superior Court of the County of Suffolk" and the "Court of Common Pleas" were abolished and the "Superior Court" was established.

RETURNS FOR THE SUPREME JUDICIAL COURT: BY COUNTIES.

BARNSTABLE COUNTY. (CLERK'S OFFICE AT BARNSTABLE.)

Volumes of records and dates of first entry in each volume:

    I. Oct. 23, 1827[1]   II. Jan. 18, 1855   III. May 3, 1881

Volumes Indexed. — Each volume has a strictly alphabetical index.

Condition of Records. — Good.

BERKSHIRE COUNTY. (CLERK'S OFFICE AT PITTSFIELD.)

Volumes of records and dates of first entry in each volume:

I. Oct. 3, 1797	IX. Sept. 8, 1835
II. May 18, 1802	X. May 14, 1839
III. Sept. 12, 1809	XI. May 16, 1843
IV. May 10, 1814	XII. Sept. 14, 1847
V. Sept. 8, 1818	XIII. Sept. 10, 1850
VI. May 13, 1823	XIV. May 13, 1851
VII. Sept. 11, 1827	XV. Sept. 13, 1859
VIII. Sept. 13, 1831	XVI. May 12, 1863

XVII. May 11, 1869
XVIII. May 9, 1876

Equity Records.
I. Sept. —, 1873
II. Feb. 10, 1882

Volumes Indexed. — The first eight volumes are indexed by the name of the plaintiff, and the other volumes both by the name of plaintiff and defendant.

Condition of Records. — Good.

---

[1] All volumes prior to 1827 were burned in the fire which destroyed the county buildings, October 22, 1827.

BRISTOL COUNTY. (CLERK'S OFFICE AT TAUNTON.)

Volumes of records and dates of first entry in each volume:

I.	Nov. 2, 1797	VIII.	April 2, 1851	XV.	Nov. 16, 1877
II.	Oct. 25, 1809	IX.	Nov. 11, 1856	XVI.	Nov. 11, 1879
III.	Oct. 25, 1814	X.	April 15, 1862	XVII.	April 19, 1881
IV.	Oct. 1, 1818	XI.	April 21, 1868	XVIII.	April 17, 1883
V.	April 18, 1829	XII.	April 18, 1871	XIX.	April 21, 1885
VI.	Oct. 1, 1837	XIII.	April 21, 1874		
VII.	Nov. 12, 1844	XIV.	April 18, 1876		

Volumes Indexed. — Each volume has an initial index.

Condition of Records. — Good.

COUNTY OF DUKES COUNTY.

[The terms of the Supreme Judicial Court for this county are held in Bristol County.]

ESSEX COUNTY. (CLERK'S OFFICE AT SALEM.)

Volumes of records and dates of first entry in each volume:

I.	Nov. 14, 1797	XII.	April 15, 1823	XXIII.	April 15, 1862
II.	Nov. 9, 1802	XIII.	April 26, 1825	XXIV.	April 17, 1866
III.	April 22, 1806	XIV.	May 1, 1827	XXV.	April 19, 1870
IV.	April 14, 1808	XV.	April 28, 1829	XXVI.	April 16, 1872
V.	April 24, 1810	XVI.	April 6, 1831	XXVII.	April 1, 1874
VI.	Nov. 5, 1811	XVII.	April 26, 1836	XXVIII.	April 18, 1876
VII.	Nov. 3, 1812	XVIII.	April 28, 1840	XXIX.	April 16, 1878
VIII.	April 26, 1814	XIX.	May 2, 1843	XXX.	April 20, 1880
IX.	April 22, 1817	XX.	May 2, 1848	XXXI.	April 18, 1882
X.	April 27, 1819	XXI.	May 2, 1854	XXXII.	April 15, 1884
XI.	April 17, 1821	XXII.	April 27, 1858		

Volumes Indexed. — Each volume has an initial index.

Condition of Records. — Good.

FRANKLIN COUNTY. (CLERK'S OFFICE AT GREENFIELD.)

Volumes of records and dates of first entry in each volume:

I.	May 21, 1816	V.	April 14, 1840	IX.	Sept. 15, 1862
II.	May 23, 1820	VI.	April 14, 1846	X.	April 9, 1872
III.	April 28, 1827	VII.	Sept. 13, 1853	XI.	Sept. 16, 1878
IV.	Sept. 13, 1834	VIII.	Sept. 8, 1857		

Volumes Indexed. — Each volume has an initial index.

Condition of Records. — Two of the earlier volumes need rebinding.

HAMPDEN COUNTY. (CLERK'S OFFICE AT SPRINGFIELD.)

Volumes of records and dates of first entry in each volume:

I.	April 23, 1816	VII.	Sept. 1, 1857	XII.	Sept. 25, 1882
II.	Sept. 15, 1829	VIII.	Sept. 26, 1859		
III.	Sept. 26, 1836	IX.	Sept. 29, 1866	*Equity Records.*	
IV.	April 27, 1847	X.	Feb. 10, 1873	I.	April 25, 1876[1]
V.	Sept. 4, 1851	XI.	April 23, 1878	II.	Sept. 6, 1881
VI.	May 1, 1855				

Volumes Indexed. — Each of the later volumes has an initial index by terms.

Condition of Records. — Good.

---

[1] Prior to April 25, 1876, the records of the equity proceedings of this court were not kept in separate volumes.

HAMPSHIRE COUNTY. (Clerk's Office at Northampton.)

Volumes of records and dates of first entry in each volume :

I.	Sept. 26, 1797	VI. Sept. 22, 1851	*Probate and Equity*
II.	April 23, 1805	VII. Feb. 6, 1865	*Records.*
III.	April 25, 1815	VIII. April 16, 1872	IX. April 16, 1872
IV.	May 1, 1821	X. April 16, 1878	XI. April 16, 1878
V.	April 22, 1834		

Volumes Indexed.—Volumes I., II., III., V., and VI. are imperfectly indexed; volume IV. is not indexed, and volumes VII. to XI. have each a strictly alphabetical index.

Condition of Records. — Good. The excessive heat to which the volumes are exposed is, however, injuring the binding.

MIDDLESEX COUNTY. (Clerk's Office at Cambridge.)

Volumes of records and dates of first entry in each volume :

I.	Oct. 31, 1797	X. Mar. 27, 1820	XIX. April 16, 1861
II.	April 14, 1801	XI. Mar. 28, 1825	XX. April 17, 1866
III.	April 10, 1804	XII. April 13, 1830	XXI. April 18, 1871
IV.	April 14, 1807	XIII. April 14, 1835	XXII. April 21, 1874
V.	April 12, 1808	XIV. April 10, 1838	XXIII. Mar. 16, 1878
VI.	April 10, 1810	XV. April 13, 1841	
VII.	April 1, 1812	XVI. April 13, 1847	*Probate Records.*
VIII.	April 5, 1814	XVII. April 8, 1851	I. Oct. 31, 1797
IX.	April 1, 1817	XVIII. April 10, 1858	

Volumes Indexed. — Each volume has an initial index.

Condition of Records. — Good.

NANTUCKET COUNTY.

[The terms of the Supreme Judicial Court for this county are held in Bristol County.]

NORFOLK COUNTY. (Clerk's Office at Dedham.)

Volumes of records and dates of first entry in each volume :

I.	Aug. 27, 1797[1]	IX. Feb. 15, 1831	XVII. Feb. 21, 1860
II.	Aug. 21, 1798	X. Feb. 19, 1834	XVIII. Feb. 16, 1864
III.	Mar. 3, 1807	XI. Feb. 21, 1837	XIX. Feb. 18, 1868
IV.	Mar. 5, 1811	XII. Feb. 18, 1840	XX. Feb. 18, 1873
V.	Feb. 20, 1816	XIII. Feb. 21, 1843	XXI. Feb. —, 1878
VI.	Feb. 16, 1819	XIV. Feb. 16, 1847	XXII. —— —, 1883
VII.	Feb. 18, 1823	XV. Feb. 18, 1851	
VIII.	Oct. 31, 1826	XVI. Feb. 20, 1855	

Volumes Indexed. — Each volume has a strictly alphabetical index.

Condition of Records. — Good.

PLYMOUTH COUNTY. (Clerk's Office at Plymouth.)

Volumes of records and dates of first entry in each volume :

I. May 5, 1798	III. Oct. 12, 1813	V. May 10, 1831
II. Oct. 16, 1810	IV. May 15, 1821	

Volumes Indexed. — Each volume has a strictly alphabetical index.

Condition of Records. — No volumes (with the exception of dockets) have been bound since 1843.

---

[1] The volumes of records for 1797 are imperfectly made up.

SUFFOLK COUNTY. (CLERK'S OFFICE AT BOSTON.)

Volumes of records and dates of first entry in each volume:

[From 1781 to 1797, during which time this was the only office of the Supreme Judicial Court.]

I.	Feb. 20, 1781	VIII.	Feb. 20, 1787	XIV.	Feb. 21, 1792
II.	Feb. 18, 1783	IX.	Feb. 19, 1788	XV.	Feb. 19, 1793
III.	Feb. 17, 1784	X.	Sept. 16, 1788	XVI.	Feb. 18, 1794
IV.	Feb. 16, 1785	XI.	May 19, 1789	XVII.	Feb. 17, 1795
V.	June 29, 1785	XII.	Feb. 16, 1790	XVIII.	Feb. 16, 1796
VI.	Feb. 21, 1786	XIII.	Feb. 15, 1791	XIX.	Feb. 21, 1797
VII.	June 20, 1786				

[After 1797, when offices were established for the other counties.]

I.	Feb. 20, 1798	XXXII.	Mar. 2, 1824	LXII.	Mar. 7, 1854
II.	Feb. 18, 1800	XXXIII.	Mar. 1, 1825	LXIII.	Mar. 6, 1855
III.	Feb. 22, 1803	XXXIV.	Mar. 7, 1826	LXIV.	Mar. 4, 1856
IV.	Mar. 12, 1805	XXXV.	Mar. 6, 1827	LXV.	Mar. 3, 1857
V.	Nov. 25, 1806	XXXVI.	Mar. 4, 1828	LXVI.	Mar. 2, 1858
VI.	Nov. 25, 1806	XXXVII.	Mar. 3, 1829	LXVII.	Mar. 1, 1859
VII.	Mar. 10, 1807	XXXVIII.	Mar. 2, 1830	LXVIII.	April 3, 1860
VIII.	Nov. 24, 1807	XXXIX.	Mar. 1, 1831	LXIX.	April 2, 1861
IX.	Mar. 8, 1808	XL.	Mar. 6, 1832	LXX.	April 1, 1862
X.	Nov. 22, 1808	XLI.	Mar. 5, 1833	LXXI.	April 7, 1863
XI.	Nov. 22, 1808	XLII.	Mar. 4, 1834	LXXII.	April 5, 1864
XII.	Mar. 14, 1809	XLIII.	Mar. 3, 1835	LXXIII.	April 4, 1865
XIII.	Nov. 28, 1809	XLIV.	Mar. 1, 1836	LXXIV.	April 3, 1866
XIV.	Mar. 13, 1810	XLV.	Mar. 7, 1837	LXXV.	April 2, 1867
XV.	Nov. 27, 1810	XLVI.	Mar. 6, 1838	LXXVI.	April 7, 1868
XVI.	Mar. 12, 1811	XLVII.	Mar. 5, 1839	LXXVII.	April 6, 1869
XVII.	Nov. 26, 1811	XLVIII.	Mar. 3, 1840	LXXVIII.	April 5, 1870
XVIII.	Mar. 10, 1812	XLIX.	Mar. 2, 1841	LXXIX.	April 4, 1871
XIX.	Nov. 24, 1812	L.	Mar. 1, 1842	LXXX.	April 2, 1872
XX.	Mar. 9, 1813	LI.	Mar. 7, 1843	LXXXI.	April 1, 1873
XXI.	Nov. 23, 1813	LII.	Mar. 5, 1844	LXXXII.	April 7, 1874
XXII.	Mar. 8, 1814	LIII.	Mar. 4, 1845	LXXXIII.	April 6, 1875
XXIII.	Mar. 14, 1815	LIV.	Mar. 3, 1846	LXXXIV.	April 4, 1876
XXIV.	Mar. 5, 1816	LV.	Mar. 2, 1847	LXXXV.	April 3, 1877
XXV.	Mar. 4, 1817	LVI.	Mar. 7, 1848	LXXXVI.	April 2, 1878
XXVI.	Mar. 3, 1818	LVII.	Mar. 6, 1849	LXXXVII.	April 1, 1879
XXVII.	Mar. 2, 1819	LVIII.	Mar. 5, 1850	LXXXVIII.	April 6, 1880
XXVIII.	Mar. 7, 1820	LIX.	Mar. 4, 1851	LXXXIX.	April 5, 1881
XXIX.	Mar. 6, 1821	LX.	Mar. 2, 1852	XC.	April 4, 1882
XXX.	Mar. 5, 1822	LXI.	Mar. 1, 1853	XCI.	April 3, 1883
XXXI.	Mar. 4, 1823				

Equity Records.

I.	Mar. —, 1838	XIV.	Oct. —, 1865	XXVII.	April —, 1877
II.	Nov. —, 1840	XV.	Oct. —, 1866	XXVIII.	Sept. —, 1877
III.	Nov. —, 1843	XVI.	Oct. —, 1867	XXIX.	April —, 1878
IV.	Mar. —, 1847	XVII.	Oct. —, 1868	XXX.	Sept. —, 1878
V.	Mar. —, 1850	XVIII.	Oct. —, 1869	XXXI.	April —, 1879
VI.	Nov. —, 1854	XIX.	April —, 1871	XXXII.	Sept. —, 1879
VII.	Nov. —, 1857	XX.	April —, 1872	XXXIII.	April —, 1880
VIII.	Oct. —, 1859	XXI.	April —, 1873	XXXIV.	Sept. —, 1880
IX.	Oct. —, 1860	XXII.	April —, 1875	XXXV.	April —, 1881
X.	April —, 1862	XXIII.	April —, 1875	XXXVI.	Sept. —, 1881
XI.	April —, 1863	XXIV.	Sept. —, 1875	XXXVII.	April —, 1882
XII.	April —, 1864	XXV.	April —, 1876	XXXVIII.	Sept. —, 1882
XIII.	April —, 1865	XXVI.	Sept. —, 1876	XXXIX.	April —, 1883

Volumes Indexed. — Each volume is indexed by the initial letter of the surname of the plaintiff.

Condition of Records. — Good.

WORCESTER COUNTY. (CLERK'S OFFICE AT WORCESTER.)

Volumes of records and dates of first entry in each volume:

I. Sept. 19, 1797	XII. April 14, 1846	XXIII. April 13, 1875
II. April 28, 1801	XIII. Oct. 2, 1849	XXIV. April 10, 1877
III. April 25, 1809	XIV. Oct. 5, 1852	XXV. Oct. 1, 1878
IV. April 12, 1814	XV. April 17, 1855	XXVI. April 13, 1880
V. April 6, 1819	XVI. April 15, 1856	XXVII. April 11, 1882
VI. April 15, 1823	XVII. April 14, 1857	
VII. April 17, 1827	XVIII. April 12, 1859	
VIII. April 13, 1830	XIX. April 8, 1862	*Probate Records.*
IX. April 16, 1833	XX. April 10, 1866	XXVIII. Sept. 18, 1798
X. April 18, 1837	XXI. April 12, 1870	XXIX. April 17, 1855
XI. April 13, 1841	XXII. April 8, 1873	

Volumes Indexed. — Each volume has an initial index.

Condition of Records. — Good.

MISCELLANEOUS RECORDS IN THE OFFICE OF THE SUPREME JUDICIAL COURT FOR THE COUNTY OF SUFFOLK.

[The following records relate to the proceedings of the Governor and Council, Court of Assistants, Superior Court of Judicature, Court of General Sessions of the Peace, and Supreme Judicial Court.]

COURT OF ASSISTANTS.

One volume, beginning with the session of March 3, 1673, and ending March 23, 1692. No index.

> [This volume contains records from 1673 to 1686, and from 1689 to 1692. The last date of 1686 is April 22, which is followed by three blank pages, the next record being of the session of December 24, 1689.
> This volume is marked on the back " E. R. S. 1673 to 1692 : 1673," and on the outside of the cover is written " Court of Assistants [yᵉ] second booke of Records beg[anne] the 3ʳᵈ of March, 1673." The first volume containing the records of this court prior to 1673 is lost.]

SUPERIOR COURT OF JUDICATURE.

Volumes of records and list of terms held for the several counties, with date of first day of term:

I. — Essex,	Jan. 3, 1693	Middlesex,	Jan. 26, 1694
Middlesex,	Jan. 31, 1693	Plymouth, Barnstable, and	
Suffolk,	April 25, 1693	Bristol,	Mar. 13, 1694
Essex,	May 12, 1693	Suffolk,	April 24, 1694
Middlesex,	July 25, 1693	Essex,	May 15, 1694
Plymouth, Barnstable, and		Middlesex,	July 31, 1694
Bristol,	Aug. 29, 1693	Plymouth, Barnstable, and	
Suffolk,	Oct. 31, 1693	Bristol,	Sept. 14, 1694
Essex,	Dec. 12, 1693	Suffolk,	Oct. 30, 1694

I. — Con.

Middlesex, . . .	Jan. 25, 1695
Plymouth, Barnstable,	
and Bristol, . .	Mar. 8, 1695
Suffolk, ...	April 26, 1695
Province of Maine (Kittery), . . .	May 16, 1695

Essex, ...	May 17, 1695
Middlesex, ...	July 26, 1695
Plymouth, Barnstable, and Bristol, . . .	Sept. 10, 1695
Suffolk, ...	Oct. 29, 1695

II. —

Essex, ...	Nov. 12, 1695
Middlesex, . . .	Jan. 28, 1696
Plymouth, Barnstable, Bristol, and Dukes County, . .	Mar. 10, 1696
Suffolk, . . .	April 28, 1696
Essex, . . .	May 19, 1696
Suffolk, . . .	Oct. 27, 1696
Essex, . . .	Nov. 10, 1696
Middlesex, . . .	Jan. 26, 1697
Plymouth, Barnstable, Bristol, and Dukes County, . .	Mar. 9, 1697
Suffolk, . . .	April 27, 1697
Essex, . . .	May 18, 1697
Middlesex, . . .	July 27, 1697
Bristol, Plymouth, Barnstable, and Dukes County, . .	Sept. 17, 1697
Suffolk, . . .	Oct. 26, 1697
Essex, . . .	Nov. 16, 1697
Middlesex, . . .	Jan. 25, 1698

Plymouth, Barnstable, Bristol, and Dukes County, . .	Mar. 8, 1698
Suffolk, ...	June 14, 1698
Essex, ...	June 25, 1698
Middlesex, ...	July 26, 1698
Hampshire, ...	Aug. 18, 1698
Plymouth, Barnstable, Bristol, and Dukes County, . .	Sept. 13, 1698
Suffolk, ...	Oct. 28, 1698
Essex, ...	Nov. 8, 1698
Boston (Oyer and Terminer), .	Jan. 18, 1699
Middlesex, ...	Jan. 31, 1699
Plymouth, Barnstable, Bristol, and Dukes County, . .	Mar. 14, 1699
Bristol, ...	Sept. 12, 1699
Suffolk, ...	April 25, 1699
Suffolk, ...	Nov. 7, 1699
Essex, ...	Nov. 14, 1699
Middlesex, ...	Jan. 30, 1700
Plymouth, Barnstable, and Dukes County, . .	Mar. 26, 1700

[This volume also contains the following records :

A " Speciall Court of Oyer and Terminer and generall Goale delivery holden at Boston," Aug. 19, 1686.

A " Court of Appeals, Grand Assize and generall Goal delivery holden at Boston in ye County of Suffolk in the territory and dominion of New England," Nov. 2, 1686.

" His Majesties Superiour Court, Assizes and generall Goal delivery holden at Boston for the County of Suffolk," April 26, 1687.

" His Majesties Superiour Court att Boston in New England," May 24, 1687.]

III. —

Suffolk, ...	May 7, 1700
York, . . .	May 16, 1700
Essex, . . .	May 21, 1700
Middlesex, . . .	July 30, 1700
Bristol, . . .	Sept. 10, 1700
Suffolk, . . .	Nov. 5, 1700
Essex, . . .	Nov. 26, 1700
Middlesex, . .	Jan. 28, 1701
Plymouth, Barnstable, and Dukes County, .	Mar. 25, 1701
Suffolk, . . .	May 6, 1701
York, . . .	July 10, 1701
Essex, . . .	July 15, 1701
Middlesex, . . .	July 29, 1701
Bristol, . . .	Sept. 9, 1701
Suffolk, . . .	Nov. 4, 1701
Essex, . . .	Nov. 11, 1701
Middlesex, . . .	Jan. 27, 1702
Plymouth, Barnstable, and Dukes County, .	Mar. 31, 1702
Suffolk, . . .	May 5, 1702
York, . . .	May 14, 1702
Essex, . . .	May 19, 1702
Bristol, . . .	Sept. 8, 1702

Suffolk, ...	Nov. 7, 1702
Essex, ...	Nov. 10, 1702
Middlesex, ...	Jan. 26, 1703
Plymouth, Barnstable, and Dukes County, . .	Mar. 30, 1703
Suffolk, ...	May 4, 1703
York, ...	May 13, 1703
Essex, ...	May 18, 1703
Middlesex, ...	July 27, 1703
Bristol, ...	Sept. 14, 1703
Suffolk, ...	Nov. 2, 1703
Essex, ...	Nov. 9, 1703
Middlesex, ...	Jan. 25, 1704
Plymouth, Barnstable, and Dukes County, .	Mar. 28, 1704
Suffolk, ...	May 2, 1704
Essex, ...	May 16, 1704
Middlesex, ...	July 25, 1704
Bristol, ...	Sept. 12, 1704
Suffolk, ...	Nov. 7, 1704
Essex, ...	Nov. 14, 1704
Middlesex, ...	Jan. 30, 1705
Plymouth, Barnstable, and Dukes County, . .	Mar. 27, 1705

III. — Con.

Suffolk, ...	May 1, 1705
Essex, ...	May 15, 1705
Middlesex, . . .	July 31, 1705
Bristol, ...	Sept. 22, 1705
Suffolk, ...	Nov. 6, 1705
Essex, ...	Nov. 13, 1705
Middlesex, . . .	Jan. 29, 1706
Plymouth, Barnstable, and Dukes County, .	Mar. 26, 1706
Suffolk, ...	May 7, 1706
Essex, ...	May 21, 1706
Middlesex, . . .	July 30, 1706
Bristol, ...	Sept. 12, 1706
Suffolk, ...	Nov. 5, 1706
Essex, ...	Nov. 12, 1706
Middlesex, . . .	Jan. 28, 1707
Plymouth, Barnstable, and Dukes County, .	Mar. 25, 1707
Suffolk, ...	May 6, 1707
Essex, ...	May 20, 1707
Middlesex, . . .	July 29, 1707
Bristol, ...	Sept. 9, 1707
Suffolk, ...	Nov. 4, 1707
Essex, ...	Nov. 11, 1707
Middlesex, . . .	Jan. 27, 1708
Plymouth, Barnstable, and Dukes County, .	April 20, 1708
Suffolk, ...	May 4, 1708
Essex, ...	May 8, 1708
Middlesex, . . .	July 27, 1708
Bristol, ...	Sept. 14, 1708
Suffolk, ...	Nov. 30, 1708
Essex, ...	Dec. 7, 1708
Middlesex, . . .	Jan. 25, 1709
Plymouth, Barnstable, and Dukes County, .	Mar. 29, 1709
Suffolk, ...	May 3, 1709
Essex, ...	May 21, 1709
Middlesex, . . .	July 26, 1709
Bristol, ...	Sept. 27, 1709
Suffolk, ...	Nov. 1, 1709
Essex, ...	Nov. 8, 1709
Middlesex, . . .	Jan. 31, 1710
Plymouth, Barnstable, and Dukes County, .	Mar. 28, 1710
Suffolk, ...	May 2, 1710
Essex, ...	May 16, 1710
Middlesex, ...	July 25, 1710
Bristol, ...	Sept. 12, 1710
Suffolk, ...	Nov. 7, 1710
Essex, ...	Nov. 14, 1710
Middlesex, ...	Jan. 30, 1711
Plymouth, Barnstable, and Dukes County, .	Mar. 27, 1711
Suffolk, ...	May 1, 1711
Essex, ...	May 15, 1711
Middlesex, ...	July 31, 1711
Bristol, ...	Sept. 11, 1711
Suffolk, ...	Nov. 6, 1711
Essex, ...	Nov. 13, 1711
Middlesex, ...	Jan. 26, 1712
Plymouth, Barnstable, and Dukes County, .	Mar. 25, 1712
Suffolk, ...	May 6, 1712
Essex, ...	May 20, 1712
Middlesex, ...	July 26, 1712
Bristol, ...	Sept. 9, 1712
Suffolk, ...	Nov. 4, 1712
Essex, ...	Nov. 11, 1712
Middlesex, ...	Jan. 27, 1713
Plymouth, Barnstable, and Dukes County, .	Mar. 31, 1713
Suffolk, ...	May 5, 1713
Essex, ...	May 19, 1713
Middlesex, ...	July 28, 1713
Bristol, ...	Sept. 8, 1713
Suffolk, ...	Nov. 3, 1713
Essex, ...	Nov. 10, 1713
Middlesex, ...	Jan. 26, 1714
Plymouth, Barnstable, and Dukes County, .	Mar. 30, 1714
Suffolk, ...	May 4, 1714
York, ...	May 14, 1714
Essex, ...	May 18, 1714
Middlesex, ...	July 31, 1714
Bristol, ...	Sept. 14, 1714
Suffolk, ...	Dec. 7, 1714
Essex, ...	Nov. 9, 1714
Middlesex, ...	Jan. 29, 1715

**IV. — **

Plymouth, Barnstable, and Dukes County, .	Mar. 26, 1715
Suffolk, ...	May 3, 1715
York, . . .	Aug. 24, 1715
Essex, . . .	May 17, 1715
Bristol, ...	Sept. 13, 1715
Middlesex, . . .	July 26, 1715
Suffolk, . . .	Nov. 1, 1715
Essex, . . .	Nov. 8, 1715
Middlesex, . . .	Jan. 31, 1716
Plymouth, Barnstable, and Dukes County, .	Mar. 27, 1716
Suffolk, ...	May 1, 1716
York, ...	May 10, 1716
Essex, ...	May 15, 1716
Middlesex, . . .	July 28, 1716
Hampshire, . .	Aug. 30, 1716
Bristol, ...	Sept. 11, 1716
Suffolk, ...	Nov. 6, 1716
Essex, ...	Nov. 13, 1716
Middlesex, ...	Jan. 29, 1717
Plymouth, Barnstable, and Dukes County, .	April 23, 1717
Suffolk, ...	May 7, 1717
York, ...	May 16, 1717
Essex, ...	May 21, 1717
Middlesex, ...	July 30, 1717
Bristol, ...	Sept. 10, 1717
Suffolk, ...	Nov. 5, 1717
Essex, ...	Nov. 12, 1717
Middlesex, ...	Jan. 25, 1718
Plymouth, Barnstable, and Dukes County, . .	April 29, 1718
Suffolk, ...	May 6, 1718

IV. — Con.

York, ...	May 15, 1718
Essex, ...	May 20, 1718
Middlesex, . . .	July 29, 1718
Bristol, ...	Sept. 9, 1718
Hampshire, . . .	Sept. 18, 1718
Suffolk, ...	Dec. 6, 1718
Essex, ...	Dec. 16, 1718
Middlesex, . . .	Jan. 31, 1719
Plymouth, Barnstable, and Dukes County, .	April 28, 1719
Suffolk, ...	May 5, 1719
York, ...	May 14, 1719
Essex, ...	May 19, 1719
Plymouth, Barnstable, and Dukes County, .	July 22, 1719
Middlesex, . . .	July 28, 1719
Bristol, ...	Sept. 8, 1719
Hampshire, ...	Sept. 17, 1719
Suffolk, ...	Nov. 3, 1719
Essex, ...	Dec. 15, 1719
Middlesex, ...	Jan. 26, 1720
Plymouth, Barnstable, and Dukes County, .	April 26, 1720
Suffolk, ...	May 3, 1720
York, ...	May 12, 1720
Essex, ...	May 17, 1720
Middlesex, ...	July 26, 1720
Bristol, ...	Sept. 13, 1720
Hampshire, ...	Sept. 27, 1720
Essex, ...	Oct. 25, 1720
Suffolk, ...	Nov. 1, 1720
Middlesex, ...	Jan. 31, 1721
Plymouth, Barnstable, and Dukes County, .	April 25, 1721
Suffolk, ...	May 2, 1721

V. — York, ... May 10, 1721

Essex, ...	May 16, 1721
Middlesex, . . .	July 25, 1721
Bristol, ...	Sept. 12, 1721
Hampshire, . . .	Sept. 26, 1721
Essex, ...	Oct. 31, 1721
Plymouth, . . .	April 24, 1722
Suffolk, ...	May 1, 1722
York, ...	May 9, 1722
Essex, ...	May 15, 1722
Middlesex, . . .	July 31, 1722
Bristol, ...	Sept. 11, 1722
Hampshire, . . .	Sept. 25, 1722
Essex, ...	Oct. 30, 1722
Suffolk, ...	Nov. 6, 1722
Middlesex, . . .	Jan. 29, 1723
Plymouth, Barnstable, and Dukes County, .	April 30, 1723
Suffolk, ...	May 7, 1723
York, ...	May 15, 1723
Essex, ...	May 21, 1723
Middlesex, ...	July 30, 1723
Bristol, ...	Sept. 10, 1723
Hampshire, ...	Oct. 15, 1723
Essex, ...	Oct. 29, 1723
Suffolk, ...	Nov. 5, 1723
Middlesex, ...	Jan. 28, 1724
Plymouth, Barnstable, and Dukes County, .	April 28, 1724
Suffolk, ...	May 5, 1724
York, ...	May 14, 1724
Essex, ...	May 19, 1724
Middlesex, ...	July 28, 1724
Bristol, ...	Sept. 8, 1724
Hampshire, ...	Sept. 22, 1724
Essex, ...	Oct. 27, 1724
Suffolk, ...	Nov. 3, 1724
Middlesex, ...	Jan. 26, 1725
Suffolk, ...	Feb. 9, 1725
Plymouth, Barnstable, and Dukes County, .	April 27, 1725

VI. — York, ... May 12, 1725

Essex, ...	May 18, 1725
Suffolk, ...	Aug. 10, 1725
Middlesex, . . .	Jan. 25, 1726
Suffolk, ...	Feb. 8, 1726
Middlesex, . . .	July 26, 1726
Bristol, ...	Sept. 13, 1726
Hampshire, . . .	Sept. 27, 1726
Essex, ...	Oct. 25, 1726
Plymouth, Barnstable, and Dukes County, .	April 25, 1727
York, ...	May 10, 1727
Essex, ...	May 16, 1727
Suffolk, ...	Aug. 8, 1727
Middlesex, ...	Jan. 30, 1728
Suffolk, ...	Feb. 13, 1728
Middlesex, ...	July 30, 1728
Bristol, ...	Sept. 10, 1728
Hampshire, ...	Sept. 24, 1728
Essex, ...	Oct. 29, 1728
Barnstable and Dukes County,	April 22, 1729
Plymouth, ...	April 29, 1729
York, ...	May 14, 1729
Essex, ...	May 20, 1729
Suffolk, ...	Aug. 12, 1729
Middlesex, ...	Jan. 27, 1730
Suffolk, ...	Feb. 10, 1730

VII. — Middlesex, . . . July 27, 1725

Bristol, ...	Sept. 14, 1725
Hampshire, . . .	Sept. 28, 1725
Essex, ...	Oct. 26, 1725
Plymouth, . . .	April 26, 1726
York, ...	May 11, 1726
Essex, ...	May 17, 1726
Suffolk, ...	Aug. 9, 1726
Middlesex, ...	Jan. 31, 1727
Suffolk, ...	Feb. 14, 1727
Middlesex, ...	July 25, 1727
Bristol, ...	Sept. 12, 1727

VII. — Con.

Hampshire, . . .	Sept. 26, 1727	
Essex, ...	Oct. 31, 1727	
Barnstable and Dukes County, . . .	April 23, 1728	
Plymouth, . . .	April 30, 1728	
York, ...	May 15, 1728	
Essex, ...	May 21, 1728	
Suffolk, . . .	Aug. 13, 1728	
Middlesex, . . .	Jan. 28, 1729	
Suffolk, ...	Feb. 11, 1729	
Middlesex, ...	July 29, 1729	
Bristol, ...	Sept. 9, 1729	
Hampshire, ...	Sept. 23, 1729	
Essex, ...	Oct. 28, 1729	
Barnstable and Dukes County,	April 21, 1730	
Plymouth, ...	April 28, 1730	
York, ...	May 13, 1730	
Essex, ...	May 19, 1730	
Suffolk, ...	Aug. 11, 1730	

VIII. — Middlesex, . . . July 28, 1730
Bristol, . . . Sept. 8, 1730
Hampshire, . . . Sept. 22, 1730
Essex, ... Oct. 27, 1730
Barnstable and Dukes County, . . . April 20, 1731

Plymouth, ... April 27, 1731
York, ... May 13, 1731
Essex, ... May 18, 1731
Suffolk, ... Aug. 10, 1731

IX. — Middlesex, . . . Jan. 26, 1731
Suffolk, . . . Feb. 9, 1731
Middlesex, . . . July 28, 1731
Bristol, . . . Sept. 14, 1731
Worcester, . . . Sept. 22, 1731
Hampshire, . . . Sept. 28, 1731
Essex, ... Oct. 26, 1731
Barnstable and Dukes County, . . . April 18, 1732
Plymouth, . . . April 25, 1732

York, ... May 10, 1732
Essex, ... May 16, 1732
Nantucket, . . . June 14, 1732
Suffolk, ... Aug. 8, 1732
Middlesex, ... Jan. 30, 1733
Suffolk, ... Feb. 13, 1733
Middlesex, ... July 31, 1733
Bristol, ... Sept. 11, 1733
Worcester, . . . Sept. 19, 1733
Worcester, . . . Sept. 17, 1734

X. — Hampshire, . . . Sept. 25, 1733
Essex, ... Oct. 30, 1733
Middlesex, . . . Jan. 29, 1734
Plymouth, . . . April 23, 1734
Barnstable and Dukes County, . . . April 30, 1734
Suffolk, . . . Aug. 13, 1734
Hampshire, . . . Sept. 24, 1734
Suffolk, . . . Oct. 22, 1734
Suffolk, . . . Feb. 11, 1735

Essex, ... May 13, 1735
York, ... June 18, 1735
Middlesex, ... July 29, 1735
Bristol, ... Sept. 9, 1735
Essex, ... Oct. 28, 1735
Middlesex, ... Jan. 27, 1736
Plymouth, ... April 17, 1736
Barnstable and Dukes County, April 27, 1736
Worcester, . . . Sept. 22, 1736
Hampshire, . . . Sept. 28, 1736

XI. — Suffolk, . . . Aug. 10, 1736
Suffolk, . . . Feb. 8, 1737
Essex, . . . May 10, 1737
York, ... June 15, 1737
Middlesex, . . . July 26, 1737
Bristol, . . . Oct. 31, 1737

Essex, ... Nov. 8, 1737
Middlesex, ... Jan. 31, 1738
Plymouth, ... April 18, 1738
Barnstable and Dukes County, April 25, 1738
Suffolk, ... Aug. 8, 1738
Worcester, . . . Sept. 19, 1738

XII. — Essex (in two folds of six and eight leaves, respectively, without covers), Nov. 14, 1738

XIII. — Plymouth, . . . April 17, 1739
Barnstable and Dukes County, . . . April 24, 1739
Suffolk, . . . Aug. 14, 1739
Worcester, . . . Sept. 18, 1739
Hampshire, . . . Sept. 25, 1739

Suffolk, ... Feb. 12, 1740
Essex, ... May 13, 1740
York, ... June 18, 1740
Middlesex, ... July 29, 1740
Bristol, ... Oct. 22, 1740

XIV.—Essex,	.	.	.	Nov. 11, 1740	Suffolk,	.	.	.	.	Feb. 9, 1742
	Middlesex,	.	.	Jan. 27, 1741	Essex,	.	.	.	.	May 11, 1742
	Plymouth,	.	.	April 14, 1741	York, .	.	.	.	.	June 16, 1742
	Barnstable and Dukes				Middlesex, .	.	.	.	.	Aug. 3, 1742
	County, .	.	.	April 28, 1741	Bristol,	.	.	.	.	Oct. 27, 1742
	Suffolk, .	.	.	Aug. 11, 1741	Essex,	.	.	.	.	Nov. 16, 1742
	Worcester,	.	.	Sept. 15, 1741	Middlesex, .	.	.	.	.	Jan. 25, 1743
	Hampshire,	.	.	Sept. 22, 1741						

XV.—Suffolk,	.	.	.	Aug. 12, 1740	Suffolk,	.	.	.	.	Aug. 21, 1744
	Worcester,	.	.	Sept. 16, 1740	Bristol,	.	.	.	.	Oct. 24, 1744
	Hampshire,	.	.	Sept. 23, 1740	Middlesex, .	.	.	.	.	Jan. 29, 1745
	Suffolk, .	.	.	Feb. 10, 1741	York, .	.	.	.	.	June 19, 1745
	Essex,	.	.	May 12, 1741	Middlesex, .	.	.	.	.	Aug. 6, 1745
	York,	.	.	June 17, 1741	Worcester,	.	.	.	.	Sept. 17, 1745
	Middlesex,	.	.	July 28, 1741	Hampshire,	.	.	.	.	Sept. 24, 1745
	Plymouth,	.	.	July 10, 1744	Essex,	.	.	.	.	Nov. 12, 1745
	Barnstable and Dukes				Suffolk,	.	.	.	.	Feb. 18, 1746
	County, .	.	.	July 17, 1744						

XVI.—Plymouth,	.	.	July 12, 1743	Essex,	.	.	.	.	May 14, 1745
	Barnstable and Dukes				Plymouth, .	.	.	.	.	July 9, 1745
	County, .	.	.	July 19, 1743	Barnstable and Dukes County,	July 16, 1745
	Suffolk, .	.	.	Aug. 16, 1743	Suffolk,	.	.	.	.	Aug. 20, 1745
	Worcester,	.	.	Sept. 20, 1743	Bristol,	.	.	.	.	Oct. 23, 1745
	Hampshire,	.	.	Sept. 27, 1743	Middlesex, .	.	.	.	.	Jan. 28, 1746
	Suffolk, .	.	.	Feb. 21, 1744	Essex,	.	.	.	.	June 3, 1746
	Essex,	.	.	May 8, 1744	York, .	.	.	.	.	June 10, 1746
	York,	.	.	June 20, 1744	Middlesex, .	.	.	.	.	Aug. 5, 1746
	Middlesex,	.	.	Aug. 7, 1744	Worcester,	.	.	.	.	Sept. 16, 1746
	Worcester,	.	.	Sept. 18, 1744	Hampshire,	.	.	.	.	Sept. 23, 1746
	Hampshire,	.	.	Sept. 25, 1744	Essex,	.	.	.	.	Nov. 11, 1746
	Essex,	.	.	Nov. 13, 1744	Suffolk,	.	.	.	.	Feb. 16, 1747
	Suffolk,	.	.	Feb. 19, 1745	Plymouth, .	.	.	.	.	July 14, 1747

XVII.—Barnstable and Dukes				Essex,	.	.	.	.	Oct. 18, 1748
	County, .	.	.	July 21, 1747	Middlesex, .	.	.	.	.	Jan. 31, 1749
	Suffolk, .	.	.	Aug. 18, 1747	Suffolk,	.	.	.	.	Feb. 21, 1749
	Bristol,	.	.	Oct. 28, 1747	Bristol,	.	.	.	.	May 9, 1749
	Middlesex,	.	.	Jan. 26, 1748	Essex,	.	.	.	.	June 6, 1749
	Suffolk, .	.	.	Feb. 16, 1748	York, .	.	.	.	.	June 13, 1749
	Bristol,	.	.	May 10, 1748	Plymouth, .	.	.	.	.	July 11, 1749
	Essex,	.	.	June 7, 1748	Barnstable and Dukes County,	July 18, 1749
	York,	.	.	June 16, 1748	Middlesex, .	.	.	.	.	Aug. 1, 1749
	Plymouth,	.	.	July 12, 1748	Suffolk,	.	.	.	.	Aug. 15, 1749
	Barnstable and Dukes				Worcester,	.	.	.	.	Sept. 19, 1749
	County, .	.	.	July 19, 1748	Hampshire,	.	.	.	.	Sept. 26, 1749
	Middlesex,	.	.	Aug. 2, 1748	Essex,	.	.	.	.	Oct. 17, 1749
	Suffolk,	.	.	Aug. 16, 1748	Middlesex, .	.	.	.	.	Jan. 30, 1750
	Worcester,	.	.	Sept. 20, 1748	Suffolk,	.	.	.	.	Mar. 8, 1750
	Hampshire,	.	.	Sept. 24, 1748	Bristol,	.	.	.	.	May 8, 1750

XVIII.—Essex,	.	.	.	June 5, 1750	Hampshire,	.	.	.	.	Sept. 25, 1750
	York,	.	.	June 12, 1750	Essex,	.	.	.	.	Oct. 16, 1750
	Plymouth,	.	.	July 10, 1750	Middlesex, .	.	.	.	.	Jan. 29, 1751
	Barnstable and Dukes				Suffolk,	.	.	.	.	Feb. 19, 1751
	County, .	.	.	July 17, 1750	Bristol,	.	.	.	.	May 14, 1751
	Middlesex,	.	.	Aug. 7, 1750	Essex,	.	.	.	.	June 4, 1751
	Suffolk, .	.	.	Aug. 22, 1750	Plymouth, .	.	.	.	.	July 9, 1751
	Worcester,	.	.	Sept. 18, 1750	York, .	.	.	.	.	June 11, 1751

XVIII.— Con.

Barnstable and Dukes County,	. . .	July 16, 1751
Middlesex,	. .	Aug. 6, 1751
Suffolk,	. . . . .	Aug. 20, 1751
Worcester,	. . . .	Sept. 17, 1751
Hampshire,	. . . .	Sept. 24, 1751
Essex,	. . . . .	Oct. 15, 1751

XIX.— Middlesex, . . . Jan. 28, 1752

Suffolk,	. . .	Feb. 18, 1752
Bristol,	. .	May 12, 1752
Essex,	. .	June 2, 1752
York,	. .	June 9, 1752
Plymouth,	. .	July 14, 1752
Barnstable and Dukes County,	. . .	July 21, 1752
Middlesex,	. .	Aug. 4, 1752
Suffolk,	. . .	Nov. 14, 1752
Worcester,	. . .	Sept. 19, 1752
Hampshire,	. . .	Sept. 26, 1752
Essex,	. . . .	Oct. 17, 1752
Middlesex,	. . . .	Jan. 30, 1753
Suffolk,	. . . .	Feb. 20, 1753
Essex,	. . . .	June 5, 1753
York,	. . . .	June 12, 1753
Bristol,	. . . .	July 10, 1753
Plymouth,	. . . .	July 17, 1753
Barnstable and Dukes County,		July 24, 1753

XX.— Suffolk, . . . Aug. 21, 1753

Middlesex,	. .	Aug. 7, 1753
Worcester,	. .	Sept. 18, 1753
Hampshire,	. .	Sept. 25, 1753
Essex,	. .	Oct. 16, 1753
Middlesex,	. .	Jan. 29, 1754
Suffolk,	. .	Feb. 9, 1754
Essex,	. .	June 11, 1754
York,	. .	June 18, 1754
Bristol,	. . . .	July 9, 1754
Plymouth,	. . . .	July 16, 1754
Barnstable and Dukes County,		July 23, 1754
Middlesex,	. . . .	Aug. 6, 1754
Suffolk,	. . . .	Aug. 20, 1754
Worcester,	. . .	Sept. 17, 1754
Hampshire,	. . .	Sept. 24, 1754
Essex,	. . . .	Oct. 15, 1754

XXI.— Middlesex, . . . Jan. 28, 1755

Suffolk,	. .	Feb. 18, 1755
Essex,	. .	July 1, 1755
York,	. .	June 17, 1755
Plymouth,	. .	July 15, 1755
Bristol,	. .	July 29, 1755
Barnstable and Dukes County,	. .	July 22, 1755
Middlesex,	. .	Aug. 5, 1755
Suffolk,	. .	Aug. 19, 1755
Worcester,	. .	Sept. 16, 1755
Hampshire,	. .	Sept. 28, 1755
Essex,	. .	Oct. 21, 1755
Middlesex,	. . . .	Jan. 27, 1756
Suffolk,	. . . .	Feb. 17, 1756
Essex,	. . . .	June 8, 1756
York,	. . . .	June 15, 1756
Bristol,	. . . .	July 13, 1756
Plymouth,	. . . .	July 20, 1756
Barnstable and Dukes County,		July 27, 1756
Middlesex,	. . . .	Aug. 3, 1756
Suffolk,	. . . .	Aug. 17, 1756
Worcester,	. . .	Sept. 21, 1756
Hampshire,	. . .	Sept. 28, 1756
Essex,	. . . .	Oct. 19, 1756

XXII.— Middlesex, . . . Jan. 25, 1757

Suffolk,	. .	Feb. 15, 1757
Essex,	. .	June 14, 1757
York,	. .	June 21, 1757
Plymouth,	. .	July 19, 1757
Barnstable and Dukes County,	. .	July 26, 1757
Middlesex,	. .	Aug. 2, 1757
Suffolk,	. .	Aug. 16, 1757
Worcester,	. .	Sept. 20, 1757
Hampshire,	. .	Sept. 27, 1757
Bristol,	. .	Oct. 11, 1757
Essex,	. .	Oct. 18, 1757
Middlesex,	. .	Jan. 31, 1758
Suffolk,	. .	Feb. 21, 1758
Barnstable and Dukes County,	. .	May 3, 1758
Plymouth,	. .	May 9, 1758
Essex,	. .	June 13, 1758
York,	. . . .	June 20, 1758
Middlesex,	. . .	Aug. 1, 1758
Suffolk,	. . .	Aug. 15, 1758
Worcester,	. . .	Sept. 19, 1758
Hampshire,	. . .	Sept. 26, 1758
Bristol,	. . .	Oct. 10, 1758
Essex,	. . . .	Oct. 17, 1758
Middlesex,	. . . .	Jan. 30, 1759
Suffolk,	. . . .	Feb. 21, 1759
Plymouth,	. . . .	April 24, 1759
Barnstable and Dukes County,		May 1, 1759
Essex,	. . . .	June 12, 1759
York,	. . . .	June 19, 1759
Middlesex,	. . . .	Aug. 7, 1759
Suffolk,	. . . .	Aug. 21, 1759
Worcester,	. . .	Sept. 18, 1759
Hampshire,	. . .	Sept. 25, 1759
Essex,	. . . .	Oct. 23, 1759
Bristol,	. . . .	Oct. 30, 1759

XXIII.—Middlesex,	.	. Jan. 29, 1760	Cumberland and Lincoln,	.	June 23, 1761
Suffolk, .	.	. Feb. 19, 1760	Middlesex, .	. . .	. Aug. 4, 1761
Plymouth,	.	. April 29, 1760	Suffolk,	. . .	. Aug. 18, 1761
Barnstable and Dukes			Worcester,	. .	. Sept. 15, 1761
County,	.	. May 6, 1760	Hampshire,	. . .	. Sept. 22, 1761
Essex,	.	. June 24, 1760	Bristol,	. . .	. Oct. 13, 1761
York,	.	. July 1, 1760	Essex,	. . .	. Oct. 20, 1761
Middlesex,	.	. Aug. 5, 1760	Middlesex, .	. .	. Jan. 26, 1762
Suffolk, .	.	. Aug. 19, 1760	Suffolk,	. . .	. Feb. 16, 1762
Worcester,	.	. Sept. 16, 1760	Plymouth, .	. .	. April 27, 1762
Hampshire,	.	. Sept. 23, 1760	Barnstable and Dukes County,	May 4, 1762
Bristol, .	.	. Oct. 15, 1760	Essex,	. . .	. June 8, 1762
Essex,	.	. Oct. 21, 1760	York, .	. .	. June 15, 1762
Middlesex,	.	. Jan. 27, 1761	Cumberland and Lincoln,	. June 22, 1762
Suffolk, .	.	. Feb. 17, 1761	Middlesex, .	. .	. Aug. 3, 1762
Plymouth,	.	. May 12, 1761	Suffolk,	. . .	. Aug. 17, 1762
Barnstable and Dukes			Worcester,	. .	. Sept. 21, 1762
County,	.	. May 7, 1761	Hampshire,	. .	. Sept. 28, 1762
Essex,	.	. June 9, 1761	Bristol,	. . .	. Oct. 12, 1762
York,	.	. June 16, 1761	Essex,	. . .	. Oct. 19, 1762

XXIV.—Middlesex,	.	. Jan. 25, 1763	Worcester,	. .	. Sept. 20, 1763
Suffolk, .	.	. Feb. 15, 1763	Hampshire and Berkshire,	. Sept. 27, 1763
Plymouth,	.	. April 26, 1763	Bristol,	. .	. Oct. 11, 1763
Barnstable and Dukes			Essex,	. .	. Oct. 18, 1763
County,	.	. May 3, 1763	Suffolk,	. .	. Feb. 21, 1764
Suffolk, .	.	. July 6, 1763	Middlesex, .	. .	. April 17, 1764
Essex,	.	. June 14, 1763	Plymouth, .	. .	. April 24, 1764
York,	.	. June 21, 1763	Barnstable and Dukes County,	May 1, 1764
Cumberland and			Essex,	. .	. June 12, 1764
Lincoln,	.	. June 28, 1763	York, .	. .	. June 19, 1764
Middlesex,	.	. Aug. 2, 1763	Cumberland and Lincoln,	. June 26, 1764
Suffolk, .	.	. Aug. 16, 1763	Middlesex, .	. .	. Aug. 7, 1764

XXV.—Worcester,	.	. Sept. 18, 1764	Essex,	. .	. June 18, 1765
Hampshire and			Cumberland and Lincoln,	. June 25, 1765
Berkshire, .	.	. Sept. 25, 1764	York, .	. .	. July 2, 1765
Bristol, .	.	. Oct. 9, 1764	Suffolk,	. .	. Aug. 27, 1765
Essex,	.	. Oct. 16, 1764	Worcester,	. .	. Sept. 17, 1765
Suffolk, .	.	. Aug. 22, 1764	Hampshire and Berkshire,	. Sept. 24, 1765
Suffolk, .	.	. Mar. 12, 1765	Bristol,	. .	. Oct. 8, 1765
Middlesex,	.	. April 9, 1765	Middlesex, .	. .	. Oct. 29, 1765
Plymouth,	.	. May 21, 1765	Essex,	. .	. Nov. 5, 1765
Barnstable and Dukes					
County,	.	. May 15, 1765			

XXVI.—Suffolk, .	.	. Mar. 11, 1766	Hampshire and Berkshire,	. Sept. 23, 1766
Middlesex,	.	. April 8, 1766	Bristol,	. .	. Oct. 14, 1766
Barnstable and Dukes			Middlesex, .	. .	. Oct. 28, 1766
County,	.	. May 14, 1766	Essex,	. .	. Nov. 4, 1766
Plymouth,	.	. May 20, 1766	Suffolk,	. .	. Mar. 11, 1767
Essex,	.	. June 17, 1766	Middlesex, .	. .	. April 14, 1767
Cumberland and			Barnstable and Dukes County,	May 13, 1767
Lincoln,	.	. June 24, 1766	Plymouth, .	. .	. May 19, 1767
York,	.	. July 1, 1766	Essex,	. .	. June 16, 1767
Suffolk, .	.	. Aug. 26, 1766	Cumberland and Lincoln,	. June 23, 1767
Worcester,	.	. Sept. 16, 1766	York, .	. .	. June 30, 1767

XXVII.—Worcester,	.	. Sept. 15, 1767	Middlesex, .	. .	. Oct. 27, 1767
Hampshire and			Essex,	. .	. Nov. 3, 1767
Berkshire, .	.	. Sept. 22, 1767	Suffolk, .	. .	. Aug. 25, 1767
Bristol,	.	. Oct. 13, 1767	Suffolk,	. .	. Mar. 8, 1768

XXVII.— Con.

Middlesex, . .	April 12, 1768
Barnstable and	
Dukes County, .	May —, 1768
Nantucket, . .	May 4, 1768
Plymouth, . .	May 17, 1768
Essex, . . .	June 21, 1768
Cumberland and	
Lincoln, . .	June 28, 1768

York, ...	July 5, 1768
Worcester, ...	Sept. 20, 1768
Hampshire and Berkshire,	Sept. 27, 1768
Bristol, ...	Oct. 11, 1768
Middlesex, ...	Oct. 25, 1768
Essex, ...	Nov. 1, 1768
Suffolk, ...	Aug. 30, 1768

XXVIII.— Suffolk, . .

Suffolk, . . .	Mar. 15, 1769
Middlesex, . .	April 11, 1769
Essex, . . .	June 20, 1769
Cumberland and	
Lincoln, . .	June 27, 1769
York, . .	July 18, 1769
Worcester, . .	Sept. 19, 1769
Hampshire and	
Berkshire, . .	Sept. 26, 1769

Bristol, ...	Oct. 10, 1769
Barnstable and Dukes County,	May —, 1769
Plymouth, ...	May 16, 1769
Middlesex, ...	Oct. 31, 1769
Essex, ...	Nov. 7, 1769
Suffolk, ...	Aug. 29, 1769

XXIX.— Suffolk, . .

Suffolk, . . .	Mar. 13, 1770
Suffolk, . . .	Aug. 28, 1770
Middlesex, . .	April 10, 1770
Barnstable and	
Dukes County, .	May 9, 1770
Plymouth, . .	May 15, 1770
Essex, . . .	June 19, 1770

York, ...	June 26, 1770
Cumberland and Lincoln,	July 3, 1770
Worcester, . . .	Sept. 18, 1770
Hampshire and Berkshire,	Sept. 25, 1770
Bristol, ...	Oct. 9, 1770
Middlesex, ...	Oct. 30, 1770
Essex, ...	Nov. 6, 1770

XXX.— Suffolk, . .

Suffolk, . . .	Feb. 19, 1771
Barnstable and	
Dukes County, .	May 8, 1771
Plymouth, . .	May 21, 1771
Middlesex, . .	April 9, 1771
Worcester, . .	April 23, 1771
Hampshire and	
Berkshire, . .	April 30, 1771
Essex, . . .	June 18, 1771

York, ...	June 25, 1771
Cumberland and Lincoln,	July 2, 1771
Worcester, . . .	Sept. 17, 1771
Hampshire and Berkshire,	Sept. 24, 1771
Bristol, ...	Oct. 8, 1771
Middlesex, ...	Oct. 29, 1771
Essex, ...	Nov. 5, 1771
Suffolk, ...	Aug. 27, 1771

XXXI.— Suffolk, . .

Suffolk, . . .	Feb. 18, 1772
Middlesex, . .	April 14, 1772
Worcester, . .	April 28, 1772
Hampshire and	
Berkshire, . .	May 5, 1772
Plymouth, . .	May 19, 1772
Barnstable and	
Dukes County, .	May 26, 1772
Essex, . . .	June 16, 1772

York, ...	June 23, 1772
Suffolk, ...	Aug. 25, 1772
Worcester, ...	Sept. 15, 1772
Hampshire and Berkshire,	Sept. 22, 1772
Cumberland and Lincoln,	June 30, 1772
Bristol, ...	Oct. 13, 1772
Middlesex, ...	Oct. 27, 1772
Essex, ...	Nov. 3, 1772

XXXII.— Suffolk, . .

Suffolk, . . .	Feb. 16, 1773
Middlesex, . .	April 6, 1773
Worcester, . .	April 20, 1773
Hampshire and	
Berkshire, . .	April 27, 1773
Plymouth, . .	May 18, 1773
Barnstable and	
Dukes County, .	May 12, 1773
Essex, . . .	June 15, 1773
York, . . .	June 22, 1773
Cumberland and	
Lincoln, . .	June 29, 1773
Suffolk, . .	Aug. 31, 1773

Worcester, . . .	Sept. 21, 1773
Hampshire and Berkshire,	Sept. 28, 1773
Bristol, ...	Oct. 12, 1773
Middlesex, ...	Oct. 26, 1773
Essex, ...	Nov. 2, 1773
Suffolk, ...	Feb. 15, 1774
Middlesex, ...	April 5, 1774
Worcester, . . .	April 19, 1774
Essex, ...	June 21, 1774
York, ...	June 28, 1774
Cumberland and Lincoln,	July 5, 1774
Suffolk, ...	Aug. 30, 1774

XXXIII.—Suffolk, . . .	Feb. 21, 1775
Essex, . . .	June 18, 1776
York, . . .	June 25, 1776
Cumberland and Lincoln, . .	July 2, 1776
Suffolk, . . .	Sept. 10, 1776
Worcester, . .	Sept. 17, 1776
Hampshire and Berkshire, .	Sept. 24, 1776
Bristol, . . .	Oct. 8, 1776
Barnstable and Dukes County, .	Oct. 16, 1776
Plymouth, . .	Oct. 22, 1776
Middlesex, . .	Oct. 29, 1776
Essex, . . .	Feb. 4, 1777
Suffolk, . . .	Feb. 18, 1777
Middlesex, . .	April 15, 1777
Worcester, . .	April 22, 1777
Hampshire and Berkshire, .	April 29, 1777
Barnstable and Dukes County,	May 14, 1777
Essex, ...	June 17, 1777
York, ...	June 24, 1777
Cumberland and Lincoln, .	July 1, 1777
Suffolk, ...	Aug. 26, 1777
Worcester, . . .	Sept. 16, 1777
Hampshire and Berkshire, .	Sept. 23, 1777
Bristol, ...	Oct. 13, 1777
Plymouth, ...	May 20, 1777
Middlesex, ...	Oct. 28, 1777
Essex, ...	Nov. 4, 1777
Suffolk, ...	Feb. 17, 1778
Middlesex, ...	April 14, 1778
Worcester, . . .	April 21, 1778
Hampshire and Berkshire, .	April 27, 1778
Barnstable and Dukes County,	May 13, 1778
Plymouth, ...	May 19, 1778
Essex, ...	June 16, 1778
York, ...	June 23, 1778
Cumberland and Lincoln, .	June 30, 1778

XXXIV.— Suffolk, . . .	Aug. 25, 1778
Worcester, . .	Sept. 15, 1778
Hampshire and Berkshire, .	Sept. 22, 1778
Bristol, . . .	Oct. 13, 1778
Middlesex, . .	Oct. 27, 1778
Essex, . . .	Nov. 3, 1778
Suffolk, . . .	Feb. 16, 1779
Middlesex, . .	April 3, 1779
Worcester, . .	April 20, 1779
Hampshire and Berkshire, .	April 27, 1779
Essex, . . .	June 15, 1779
York, . . .	June 22, 1779
Cumberland and Lincoln, . .	June 29, 1779
Suffolk, . . .	Aug. 31, 1779
Worcester, . .	Oct. 5, 1779
Bristol, . .	Oct. 12, 1779
Essex, ...	Nov. 16, 1779
Barnstable and Dukes County,	Aug. 24, 1779
Plymouth, ...	Oct. 19, 1779
Middlesex, ...	Nov. 23, 1779
Suffolk, ...	Feb. 15, 1780
Middlesex, ...	April 11, 1780
Worcester, . . .	April 18, 1780
Hampshire and Berkshire, .	May 2, 1780
Barnstable and Dukes County,	May 17, 1780
Plymouth, ...	May 23, 1780
Essex, ...	June 20, 1780
York, ...	June 27, 1780
Cumberland and Lincoln, .	July 4, 1780
Suffolk, ...	Aug. 29, 1780
Worcester, . . .	Sept. 19, 1780
Hampshire and Berkshire, .	Sept. 26, 1780
Bristol, ...	Oct. 10, 1780
Essex, ...	Nov. 7, 1780
Middlesex, ...	Nov. 14, 1780

Maritime Records :

[The terms held after 1780 were of the Supreme Judicial Court.]

XXXV.—Essex, . . .	June 15, 1779
Suffolk, . .	Aug. 31, 1779
Suffolk, . .	Feb. 15, 1780
York, . .	June 27, 1780
Suffolk, . .	Aug. 29, 1780
Essex, . .	Nov. 7, 1780
Middlesex, . .	Nov. 14, 1780
Middlesex, . .	April 10, 1781
Essex, . . .	June 19, 1781
Cumberland and Lincoln, . .	July 3, 1781
Suffolk, . .	Aug. 28, 1781
Bristol, . . .	Oct. 16, 1781
Essex, . .	Nov. 6, 1781
Suffolk, ...	Feb. 19, 1782
Barnstable and Dukes County,	May 16, 1782
York, ...	June 25, 1782
Cumberland, . . .	July 4, 1782
Suffolk, ...	Nov. 19, 1782
Middlesex, ...	Dec. 10, 1782
Suffolk, ...	Feb. 18, 1782
Middlesex, ...	April 8, 1782
Plymouth, ...	May 20, 1782
Essex, ...	June 17, 1782
Suffolk, ...	Aug. 26, 1782
Bristol, ...	Nov. 25, 1782
Middlesex, ...	April 13, 1784
Bristol, ...	Oct. 21, 1788

Volumes Indexed.— Each volume is indexed by the initial letter of the surname of the plaintiff.

Minute Books (with list of terms held for the several counties).

[Terms held after 1780 are of the Supreme Judicial Court.]

I. — " Minutes of Salem Court, November 10, 1702." Three sheets stitched together without covers, and containing the full minutes of the November term for Essex County, beginning November 10, 1702.

II. — " Essex County Minutes for His Majesty's Superior Court of Judicature, Court of Assize, and General Goal Delivery, holden at Salem, November 13, 1716." Five sheets stitched together without covers, and containing the full minutes of the said term.

III. — Plymouth, Barnstable, and Dukes County: April, 1719; April, 1720; April, 1721; April, 1722; April, 1723; April, 1724; April, 1725; April, 1726; April, 1727. Plymouth: April, 1728; April, 1729. Barnstable and Dukes County: April, 1728; April, 1729.

IV. — Suffolk: May and Nov., 1719; May and Nov., 1720; May, 1721; May and Nov., 1722; May and Nov., 1723.

V. — Essex: May and Dec., 1719; May and Oct., 1720; May and Oct., 1721; May and Oct., 1722; May and Oct., 1723; May and Oct., 1724; May and Oct., 1725; May, 1726. York: May, 1719; May, 1720; May, 1721; May, 1722; May, 1723; May, 1724; May, 1725; May, 1726.

VI. — Middlesex: July, 1719, and Jan., 1720; July, 1720, and Jan., 1721; July, 1721; July, 1722, and Jan., 1723; July, 1723, and Jan., 1724; July, 1724, and Jan., 1725; July, 1725, and Jan., 1726; July, 1726, and Jan., 1727; July, 1727, and Jan., 1728; July, 1728.

VII. — Bristol: Sept., 1719; Sept., 1720; Sept., 1721; Sept., 1722; Sept., 1723; Sept., 1724; Sept., 1725; Sept., 1726; Sept., 1727. Hampshire: Sept., 1719; Sept., 1720; Sept., 1721, Sept., 1722; Oct., 1723; Sept., 1724; Sept., 1725; Sept., 1726; Sept., 1727.

VIII. — Essex: Oct., 1726; Oct., 1727; May and Oct., 1728, May and Oct., 1729; May and Oct., 1730. York: May, 1728; May, 1729; May, 1730.

IX. — York: One leaf containing the last part of the May term, 1727.

X. — Essex: May, 1727.

XI. — Suffolk: Feb. (last part of), 1727; Aug., 1728, and Feb., 1729; Aug., 1729, and Feb., 1730.

XII. — Bristol: Sept., 1728; Sept., 1730; Sept., 1732; Sept., 1734. Hampshire: Sept., 1728; Sept., 1730; Sept., 1732. Suffolk: Oct., 1728. Worcester: Sept., 1732.

XIII. — Hampshire: Sept., 1728.

XIV. — Middlesex: Jan., 1728; July, 1729, and Jan., 1730; July, 1730, and Jan., 1731; July, 1738, and Jan., 1739; July, 1739.

XV. — Barnstable and Dukes County. April, 1729. Plymouth: April, 1729.

XVI. — Bristol: Sept., 1729.

XVII. — Barnstable and Dukes County: April, 1731; April, 1732; April, 1734; April, 1735; April, 1736; April, 1738; April, 1740. Plymouth: April, 1731; April, 1732; April, 1734; April, 1735; April, 1736; April, 1738; April, 1740.

XVIII. — York: May, 1731.
  Essex: May, 1731.

  XIX. — Suffolk: Aug., 1731, and Feb., 1732; Aug., 1733.

  XX. — Middlesex· Jan., 1731; July, 1732; Jan., 1733; July, 1734, and Jan., 1735; Mar., 1736; July, 1736.

  XXI. — Suffolk: Aug., 1732, and Feb., 1733; Aug., 1734; Oct., 1734.

  XXII. — Essex: Oct., 1732; May, 1733; May and Oct., 1734; May and Oct., 1736; May and Nov., 1738.
  York: May, 1733; June, 1734; June, 1736.

  XXIII. — Barnstable and Dukes County: April, 1733.
  Plymouth: April, 1733.

  XXIV. — Essex: Oct., 1733; May and Oct., 1735; May and Oct., 1737; May and Nov., 1739.
  York: June, 1735.

  XXV. — Suffolk: Feb., 1733; Aug., 1735.

  XXVI. — Suffolk: Feb., 1734; Aug., 1736, and Feb., 1737; Aug., 1738, and Feb., 1739.

  XXVII. — Barnstable and Dukes County: April, 1735; April, 1737.
  Plymouth: April, 1735; April, 1737.

  XXVIII. — Worcester: Sept., 1735.
  Hampshire: Sept., 1735.

  XXIX. — Middlesex: Jan., 1735; July, 1737, and Jan., 1738; Jan., 1739; July, 1741.

  XXX. — Suffolk: Feb., 1735; Nov., 1737.

  XXXI. — Bristol: Sept., 1736; Oct., 1738.

  XXXII. — Worcester: Sept., 1736; Sept., 1738; Sept., 1740; Sept., 1742.

  XXXIII. — York: June, 1737; June, 1739; June, 1741; June, 1743; June, 1745; June, 1747.
  Essex: June and Nov., 1747.

  XXXIV. — Worcester: Sept., 1737.
  Hampshire: Sept., 1737.

  XXXV. — Bristol: Oct., 1737; Oct., 1739.

  XXXVI. — Suffolk: Feb., 1737.

XXXVII. — York: June, 1738.

XXXVIII. — Hampshire: Sept., 1738; Sept., 1740; Sept., 1742.

  XXXIX. — Plymouth: April, 1739; April, 1741; July, 1743.
  Barnstable and Dukes County: April, 1739; April, 1741; July, 1743.

  XL. — Suffolk: Aug., 1739, and Feb., 1740; Aug., 1741, and Feb., 1742.

  XLI. — Worcester: Sept., 1739; Sept., 1741; Sept., 1743; Sept., 1744; Sept., 1746.
  Hampshire: Sept., 1739; Sept., 1741; Sept., 1743; Sept., 1744; Sept., 1746.

  XLII. — Essex: May and Nov., 1740; May and Nov., 1742; May and Nov., 1744; May, 1745; June, 1746.

  XLIII. — York: June, 1740; June, 1742; June, 1744; June, 1746.

  XLIV. — Middlesex: July, 1740, and Jan., 1741; Aug., 1742, and Jan., 1743; Aug., 1744; Jan., 1745; Aug., 1746; Jan., 1747; Aug., 1748.

XLV.—Suffolk: Aug., 1740, and Feb., 1741; Aug., 1742, and Feb., 1743; Aug., 1744; Feb., 1745; Aug., 1746.

XLVI.—Bristol: Oct., 1740; Oct., 1742; Oct., 1745; Oct., 1747; May, 1749.

XLVII.—Bristol: Oct., 1741; Oct., 1743; Oct., 1744; Oct., 1746; May, 1748; May, 1750; May, 1751; May, 1752; July, 1753.

XLVIII.—Middlesex: Jan., 1741; Aug., 1743, and Jan., 1744; Jan., 1744; Aug., 1745; Jan., 1746; Aug., 1747; Jan., 1748; Aug., 1749, and Jan., 1750; Aug., 1750, and Jan., 1751; Aug., 1751; Jan., 1752.

XLIX.—Plymouth: July, 1742; July, 1744; July, 1746.
Barnstable and Dukes County: July, 1742; July, 1744; July, 1746.

L.—Essex: May and Nov., 1743; Nov., 1745.

LI.—Suffolk: Feb., 1744; Aug., 1745.

LII.—Plymouth: July, 1745; July, 1747.
Barnstable and Dukes County: July, 1745; July, 1747.

LIII.—Worcester: Sept., 1745; Sept., 1747.

LIV.—Hampshire: Sept., 1745; Sept., 1747.

LV.—Essex: Nov., 1746.

LVI.—Suffolk: Feb., 1746; Aug., 1747.

LVII.—Suffolk: Feb., 1747, Aug., 1748, and Feb., 1749.

LVIII.—York: June, 1748; June, 1749; June, 1750.
Essex: June and Oct., 1748; June and Oct., 1749; June, 1750.

LIX.—Hampshire: Sept., 1748; Sept., 1749.
Worcester: Sept., 1748; Sept., 1749.

LX.—Barnstable and Dukes County: July, 1748; July, 1749; July, 1750.
Plymouth: July, 1748; July, 1749; July, 1750.

LXI.—Suffolk: Aug., 1749, and Mar., 1750; Aug., 1750, and Feb., 1751; Aug., 1751; Feb., 1752.

LXII.—Worcester: Sept., 1750; Sept., 1751.
Hampshire: Sept., 1750; Sept., 1751.

LXIII.—York: June, 1751; June, 1752; June, 1753.
Essex: Oct., 1750; June and Oct., 1751; June and Oct., 1752; June and Oct., 1753.

LXIV.—Plymouth: July, 1751; July, 1752; July, 1753; July, 1754; July, 1755; July, 1756.
Barnstable and Dukes County: July, 1751; July, 1752; July, 1753; July, 1754; July, 1755; July, 1756.
Bristol: July, 1754; July, 1755; July, 1756.

LXV.—Middlesex: Aug., 1752; Jan. and Aug., 1753; Jan. and Aug., 1754; Jan. and Aug., 1755; Jan., 1756.

LXVI.—Worcester: Sept., 1752; Sept., 1753; Sept., 1754; Sept., 1755; Sept., 1756; Sept., 1757.
Hampshire: Sept., 1752; Sept., 1753; Sept., 1754; Sept., 1755; Sept., 1756; Sept., 1757.

LXVII.—Suffolk: Nov., 1752; Feb. and Aug., 1753; Feb., 1754.

LXVIII.—Essex: June and Oct., 1754; July and Oct., 1755; June and Oct., 1756; June and Oct., 1757.
York: June, 1754; June, 1755; June, 1756; June, 1757.

LXIX.—Suffolk: Aug., 1754; Feb. and Aug., 1755; Feb. and Aug., 1756.

LXX.—Middlesex: Aug., 1756; Jan. and Aug., 1757; Jan. and Aug., 1758; Jan. and Aug., 1759; Jan. and Aug., 1760; Jan and Aug., 1761; Jan., 1762.

LXXI.—Suffolk: Feb. and Aug., 1757; Feb. and Aug., 1758; Feb. and Aug., 1759.

LXXII.—Plymouth: July, 1757; May, 1758; April, 1759; April, 1760; May, 1761; April, 1762; April, 1763; April, 1764.
Barnstable and Dukes County: July, 1757; May, 1758; May, 1759; May, 1760; May, 1761; May, 1762; May, 1763; May, 1764.

LXXIII.—Bristol: Oct., 1757; Oct., 1758; Oct., 1759; Oct., 1760; Oct., 1761; Oct., 1762; Oct., 1763; Oct., 1764; Oct., 1765.

LXXIV.—Essex: June and Oct., 1758; June and Oct , 1759; June and Oct., 1760; June and Oct., 1761.
York: June, 1758; June, 1759; July, 1760.

LXXV.—Worcester: Sept., 1758; Sept., 1759; Sept., 1760; Sept., 1761; Sept., 1762.
Hampshire: Sept., 1758; Sept., 1759; Sept., 1760.
Hampshire and Berkshire: Sept., 1761; Sept., 1762.

LXXVI.—Cumberland and Lincoln: June, 1761; June, 1762; June, 1763; June, 1764; June, 1765; June, 1766.
York: June, 1761; June, 1762; June, 1763; June, 1764; July, 1765; July, 1766.

LXXVII.—Essex: June and Oct., 1762; June and Oct., 1763; June and Oct., 1764; June and Nov., 1765; June, 1766.

LXXVIII.—Middlesex: Aug., 1762; Jan. and Aug., 1763; April and Aug., 1764; April and Oct., 1765; April and Oct., 1766; April, 1767.

LXXIX.—Suffolk: Aug., 1762; Feb. and Aug., 1763; Feb. and Aug., 1764.

LXXX.—Worcester: Sept., 1763; Sept., 1764; Sept., 1765.
Hampshire and Berkshire: Sept., 1763; Sept., 1764; Sept., 1765.

LXXXI.—Suffolk: Mar. and Aug., 1765; Mar. and Aug., 1766.

LXXXII.—Plymouth: May, 1765; May, 1766; May, 1767; May, 1768; May, 1769; May, 1770.
Barnstable and Dukes County: May, 1765; May, 1766; May, 1767; May, 1768; May, 1769; May, 1770.
Nantucket: May, 1768.

LXXXIII.—Worcester: Sept., 1766; Sept., 1767; Sept., 1768.
Hampshire and Berkshire: Sept., 1766; Sept., 1767; Sept., 1768.

LXXXIV.—Bristol: Oct., 1766; Oct., 1767; Oct., 1768; Oct., 1769; Oct., 1770; Oct , 1771; Oct., 1772.

LXXXV.—Essex: Nov., 1766; June and Nov., 1767; June and Nov., 1768; June and Nov., 1769; June, 1770.

LXXXVI.—Suffolk: Mar. and Aug., 1767; Mar. and Aug., 1768.

LXXXVII.—Cumberland and Lincoln: June, 1767; June, 1768; June, 1769.
York: June, 1767; July, 1768; July, 1769.

LXXXVIII.—Middlesex: Oct , 1767; April and Oct , 1768; April and Oct., 1769; April and Oct., 1770; April and Oct., 1771.

LXXXIX. — Suffolk : Mar. and Aug., 1769.

XC. — Worcester : Sept., 1769; Sept., 1770; April and Sept., 1771.
Hampshire and Berkshire : Sept., 1769; Sept., 1770; April and Sept., 1771.

XCI. — Suffolk : Mar. and Aug., 1770; Feb., 1771.

XCII. — Cumberland and Lincoln · July, 1770; July, 1771; June, 1772.
York : June, 1770; June, 1771; June, 1772.

XCIII. — Essex : Nov., 1770; June and Nov., 1771; June and Nov., 1772; June and Nov., 1773.

XCIV. — Plymouth : May, 1771; May, 1772; May, 1773; May, 1774; Oct., 1776; May, 1777; May, 1778; Oct., 1779; May, 1780; May, 1781.
Barnstable and Dukes County : May, 1771; May, 1772; May, 1773; May, 1774; Oct., 1776; May, 1777; May, 1778; Aug., 1779; May, 1780; May, 1781.

XCV. — Suffolk : Aug., 1771; Feb. and Aug., 1772.

XCVI. — Middlesex : April and Oct., 1772; April and Oct., 1773; April and Oct., 1774; Oct., 1776; April, 1777.

XCVII. — Worcester : April and Sept., 1772; April and Sept., 1773.
Hampshire and Berkshire : May and Sept., 1772; April and Sept., 1773.

XCVIII. — Suffolk : Feb. and Aug., 1773; Feb. and Aug., 1774.

XCIX. — Cumberland and Lincoln : June, 1773; July, 1774; July, 1776; July, 1777.
York : June, 1773; June, 1774; June, 1776; June, 1777.

C. — Bristol : Oct., 1773; Oct., 1774; Oct., 1776; Oct., 1777; Oct., 1778; Oct., 1779; Oct., 1780; Oct., 1781; Nov., 1782; Nov., 1783; Oct., 1784.

CI. — Worcester : April, 1774; Sept., 1776; April and Sept., 1777; April, 1778.
Hampshire and Berkshire : April, 1774; Sept., 1776; April and Sept., 1777; April, 1778.

CII. — Essex : June, 1774; June, 1776; Feb., 1777; June and Nov., 1777; June and Nov., 1778; June and Nov., 1779.

CIII. — Suffolk : Aug., 1776; Feb. and Aug., 1777; Feb. and Aug., 1778.

CIV. — Middlesex : Oct., 1777; April and Oct., 1778; April and Nov., 1779.

CV. — Cumberland and Lincoln : June, 1778; June, 1779; July, 1780; July, 1781; July, 1782.
York : June, 1778; June, 1779; June, 1780; June, 1781; June, 1782.

CVI. — Worcester : Sept., 1778; April and Oct., 1779; April and Sept., 1780.
Hampshire and Berkshire : Sept., 1778; April, 1779; May and Sept., 1780.

CVII. — Middlesex : April and Nov., 1780; April and Oct., 1781; April and Dec., 1782; April, 1783.

CVIII. — Essex : June and Nov., 1780; June and Nov., 1781; June and Nov., 1782; June, 1783.

CIX. — Suffolk : Feb. and Aug., 1779; Feb. and Aug., 1780; Feb. and Aug., 1781.

Appeals from Maritime Court.

CX. — Essex,	. . .	June, 1779	York, ...	June, 1782
Suffolk,	. . .	Aug., 1779	Cumberland and Lincoln, .	July, 1782
Suffolk,	. . .	Feb., 1780	Essex, ...	Nov., 1782
York,	. . .	June, 1780	Suffolk, ...	Nov., 1782
Suffolk,	. . .	Aug., 1780	Middlesex, ...	Dec., 1782
Essex,	. . .	Nov., 1780	Suffolk, ...	Feb., 1783
Middlesex,	. .	Nov., 1780	Middlesex, ...	April, 1783
Middlesex,	. .	April, 1781	Barnstable and Dukes County,	May, 1783
Essex,	. .	June, 1781	Plymouth, ...	May, 1783
Cumberland	and		Essex, ...	June, 1783
Lincoln, .	. . .	July, 1781	Suffolk, ...	Aug., 1783
Suffolk, .	. .	Aug., 1781	Bristol, ...	Nov., 1783
Bristol,	. . .	Oct., 1781	Suffolk, ...	Feb., 1784
Middlesex,	. .	Oct., 1781	Middlesex, ...	April, 1784
Essex,	. . .	Nov., 1781	Barnstable and Dukes County,	May, 1785
Suffolk,	. . .	Feb., 1782	Barnstable and Dukes County,	May, 1786
Middlesex,	. .	April, 1782	Barnstable and Dukes County,	June, 1787
Barnstable,	. .	May, 1782	Bristol, ...	Oct., 1788

Volumes Indexed. — The Minute Books are not indexed.

Partitions, Executions, etc.

[The volumes marked with an asterisk (*) are records of the Supreme Judicial Court. Subsequent records of partitions are in the general records of that court.]

I. — 1716 to 1727.	V. — 1750 to 1767.	IX. — 1784 to 1791.
II. — 1726 to 1732.	VI. — 1767 to 1771.	X. — 1791 to 1818.
III. — 1732 to 1749.	VII. — 1771 to 1783.	*XI. — 1819 to 1834.
IV. — 1736 to 1758.	VIII. — 1783 to 1785.	*XII. — 1834 to 1856.

COURT OF GENERAL SESSIONS OF THE PEACE.

Volumes of records and time covered by each volume:

[The first volume containing the records of this court from 1692 to 1701 is lost. There are no records of the court since 1732 in the Clerk's Office, with the exception of the minute books and fragmentary records described on pages 326–329.]

I. — From July 4, 1702, to July 15, 1712.   III. — From Jan. 5, 1719, to July 26, 1725.
II. — From Oct. 7, 1712, to Oct. 26, 1719.   IV. — From Sept. 29, 1725, to Oct. 30, 1732.

Volumes Indexed. — Each volume is indexed by the initial letter of the surname of the plaintiff.

Notaries Public.

One volume made by Samuel Cooper, for the County of Suffolk, covering the years from 1795 to 1804. This volume has no index.
One volume made by Samuel Cooper, for the County of Suffolk, covering the years from 1798 to 1801. This volume is indexed by the initial letter of the surname.

GOVERNOR AND COUNCIL.

Volumes of records and time covered by each volume:

One volume marked "Divorce 1760–1786" beginning April 22, 1760, and ending February 8, 1786. This volume is indexed by the initial letter of the surname.

SUPREME JUDICIAL COURT.

Probate Records.

Volumes of records and time covered by each volume :

I.— From Feb. 9, 1760, to Mar. 2, 1830.

> [From 1760 to 1783 these are records of the Governor and Council; from 1784 to 1830 of the Supreme Judicial Court. See dates 1760, Feb. 9, and 1784, Mar. 12, on page 366.]

II.— From Mar. 4, 1834, to Oct. —, 1870.

III.— From April term, 1871, to September term, 1879.

IV. — From April term, 1880, to ———.

Rules of the Supreme Judicial Court and Records of Admissions to the Bar.

Volumes of records and time covered by each volume :

I.— From Feb. 16, 1779, to Aug. 27, 1836.   III.— From Jan. 20, 1885, to ———.

II.— From Aug. 27, 1836, to Jan. 6, 1885.

Fragmentary Miscellaneous Records.

A fragmentary record or minute book, being a fold of six sheets, containing the following records :

Last part of the October term, 1738;

First part of the January term, 1739 (last date, January 29);

All of the July term, 1739;

First part of the October term, 1739 (last date, October 29).

A detached sheet, containing part of the record of the January term, 1762, viz.: A session held by adjournment at Braintree, February 2, and also the first part of the April term, 1762, held at Boston, April 6.

Ten detached leaves as follows :

I. — The record of the April term, 1776, held at Braintree, April 16, 1776.

II. and III.— A record of the July term, 1776, held at Dedham, July 2, 1776, and the first part of the record of the October term, 1776, held at Braintree, October 1, 1776.

IV.— The last part of the record of the January term, 1777.

V. and VI.— The record of the April term, 1777, held at Boston, April 15, 1777.

VII. and VIII.— The record of the July term, 1777, held at Boston, July 8, 1777.

IX.— One page containing " Account of the Attendance and travel of the Justices," with their receipts, from the April term, 1776, to the January term, 1777.

X.— The same account from July term, ——, to July term, 1780.

A fold of eleven sheets without covers, containing records of the Court of General Sessions of the Peace from October 7, 1777, to July 11, 1780; also one page of the term beginning October 3, 1780.

Minute Books as follows :

One volume from January 3, 1743, to May 15, 1749.

One volume marked on the outside, " Minute Book of the Court of General Sessions of the Peace, Began July, 1749, Ended [February] 1754." From July 4, 1749, to February 18, 1754.

One volume marked on the outside, " Sessions Book, begun April 1754, Ended ———." From April 3, 1754, to August 28, 1758.

> [The last five leaves have been almost wholly torn off and on what remains there appears in the margin, " Order issᵈ Septʳ 7 " and " Order [issᵈ] Novʳ, ———."]

One volume marked on the outside, " Suffolk ss. Minute Book of the Court of General Sessions of the Peace, for the County of Suffolk, begun January, 1769, and ended by adjournment on the first Tuesday of August, Anno Domini, 1773." From January 3, 1769, to August 3, 1773.

Condition of Records. —

The volume of records of Court of Assistants should be copied and rebound.

The first volume of records of Superior Court of Judicature should be copied.

The fragments of records of Court of General Sessions of the Peace and also of Superior Court of Judicature for Essex County, 1738, should be repaired and bound.

Many of the dockets or " minute books " of the courts before 1800 need repairing.

RETURNS FOR THE SUPERIOR COURT: BY COUNTIES.

BARNSTABLE COUNTY. (Clerk's Office at Barnstable.)

Volumes of records and date of first entry in each volume:

County Court.

[All volumes were burned in the fire which destroyed the county buildings, October 22, 1827.]

Inferior Court of Common Pleas.

[All volumes were burned in the fire which destroyed the county buildings, October 22, 1827.]

Court of Sessions.

I. Jan. 29, 1828.

Court of General Sessions of the Peace.

[All volumes were burned in the fire which destroyed the county buildings, October 22, 1827.]

Circuit Court of Common Pleas.

[All volumes were burned in the fire which destroyed the county buildings, October 22, 1827.]

Court of Common Pleas.[1]

I. Sept. 4, 1827	III. April 2, 1844	V. April 7, 1857
II. April 4, 1837	IV. April 6, 1852	

Superior Court.

I. July 2, 1859	III. Sept. 3, 1867	V. April 5, 1881
II. April 2, 1861	IV. Oct. 13, 1874	VI. April 7, 1885

Marriages.

[There are no records of marriages in the Clerk's Office.]

Notaries Public.

[There are no volumes of records kept by Notaries Public in the Clerk's Office, but there are scattering notarial papers.]

Miscellaneous.

[There are no miscellaneous records in the Clerk's Office.]

Volumes Indexed. — Each volume has an initial index.

Condition of Records. — Good.

BERKSHIRE COUNTY. (Clerk's Office at Pittsfield.)

Volumes of records and date of first entry in each volume:

County Court.

[Berkshire County was not established at the time of the existence of County Courts. The records, if any, for this jurisdiction would be in the Hampshire County records.]

---

[1] All volumes prior to 1827 were burned in the fire which destroyed the county buildings, October 22, 1827.

BERKSHIRE COUNTY. (Clerk's Office at Pittsfield.) — Con.

Inferior Court of Common Pleas.

I.	July 13, 1761	IV.	Sept. 4, 1770	II.	April 10, 1781[2]
II.	April 30, 1765	V.	Aug. 18, 1772[1]	III.	Feb. 26, 1782
III.	Sept. 1, 1767	VI.	Nov. 30, 1773		

Court of Sessions.

—.[3]	April 11, 1808	—.[5]	Sept. 28, 1819	*Records of Commissioners*
—.[4]	Dec. 30, 1811	III.	Sept. —, 1822	*of Highways.*
				A. — —, 1826

Court of General Sessions of the Peace.

I.[1]	Sept. 1, 1761	II.[6]	Dec. 29, 1806

Circuit Court of Common Pleas.

XXX.	Aug. 26, 1811	XXXV.	April 15, 1816	XXXIX.	Oct. 26, 1818
XXXI.	Sept. 21, 1812	XXXVI.	Feb. 24, 1817	XL.	June 28, 1819
XXXII.	April 12, 1813	XXXVII.	June 23, 1817	XLI.	June 26, 1820
XXXIII.	April 11, 1814	XXXVIII.	Feb. 23, 1818	XLII.	Feb. 26, 1821
XXXIV.	Sept. 25, 1815				

Court of Common Pleas.

IV.	Feb. 25, 1783	XXVI.	Dec. 26, 1808	LIX.	Feb. 27, 1837
V.	Feb. 3, 1784	XXVII.	Aug. 28, 1809	LX.	Feb. 26, 1838
VI.	Sept. 14, 1784	XXVIII.	April 9, 1810	LXI.	Feb. 25, 1839
VII.	May 10, 1785	XXIX.	Dec. 31, 1810	LXII.	Feb. 24, 1840
VIII.	Sept. 12, 1785			LXIII.	Feb. 22, 1841
IX.	Feb. 7, 1786	—.[7]	June 25, 1821	LXIV.	Feb. 28, 1842
X.	Sept. 9, 1788	XLIII.	Oct. 22, 1821	. LXV.	Feb. 27, 1843
XI.	Feb. 1, 1791	XLIV.	Feb. 24, 1823	LXVI.	Feb. 26, 1844
XII.	Sept. 11, 1792	XLV.	Feb. 23, 1824	LXVII.	Feb. 24, 1845
XIII.	April 15, 1794	XLVI.	Feb. 28, 1825	LXVIII.	Feb. 23, 1846
XIV.	Sept. 8, 1795	XLVII.	Feb. 27, 1826	LXIX.	Feb. 22, 1847
XV.	Sept. 12, 1796	XLVIII.	Feb. 26, 1827	LXX.	Feb. 28, 1848
XVI.	Sept. 11, 1797	XLIX.	Oct. 22, 1827	LXXI.	Feb. 26, 1849
XVII.	Dec. 31, 1798	L.	Oct. 27, 1828	LXXII.	Feb. 25, 1850
XVIII.	Sept. 9, 1799	LI.	Oct. 26, 1829	LXXIII.	Feb. 24, 1851
XIX.	Jan. 5, 1801	LII.	June 28, 1830	LXXIV.	Feb. 23, 1852
XX.	Oct. 11, 1802	LIII.	Feb. 28, 1831	LXXV.	Feb. 28, 1853
XXI.	Jan. 2, 1804	LIV.	Feb. 27, 1832	LXXVI.	Feb. 26, 1855
XXII.	Jan. 7, 1805	LV.	Feb. 25, 1833	LXXVII.	Feb. 25, 1856
XXIII.	Aug. 26, 1805	LVI.	Feb. 24, 1834	LXXVIII.	Feb. 23, 1857
XXIV.	Aug. 25, 1806	LVII.	Feb. 23, 1835	LXXIX.	Feb. 22, 1858
XXV.	Dec. 28, 1807	LVIII.	Feb. 22, 1836	LXXX.	Feb. 28, 1859

[1] In volume I., of the Court of General Sessions of the Peace, page 105, there is the record of a term February 25, 1772 and of all of the May term, 1772.

[2] No court was held from the May term of 1774 to the April term of 1781, when a new series of records was commenced with Vol. II.

[3] In volume II. of the Court of General Sessions of the Peace, page 30.

[4] In volume II. of the Court of General Sessions of the Peace, page 162.

[5] In volume II. of the Court of General Sessions of the Peace, page 357.

[6] From 1765 to 1796 the records are not extended in this volume, but the dockets for those years have a full and complete record, which is in fact a court record.

[7] In volume XLII. of the Circuit Court of Common Pleas, page 239.

BERKSHIRE COUNTY (CLERK'S OFFICE AT PITTSFIELD.) — Con.

Superior Court.

I.	Oct. 24, 1859	VI.	Feb. 25, 1867	XI.	Feb. 27, 1876
II.	Feb. 25, 1861	VII.	Feb. 22, 1869	XII.	June 26, 1877
III.	Feb. 24, 1862	VIII.	Feb. 27, 1871	XIII.	Feb. 24, 1879
IV.	Feb. 23, 1863	IX.	Feb. 25, 1872	XIV.	June 28, 1881
V.	Feb. 27, 1865	X.	Feb. 23, 1874		

Marriages.

One volume covering the period from May, 1788, to June, 1795, and including records of the following towns :

Adams,	Lanesborough,	Tyringham,
Cheshire,	Lenox,	West Stockbridge,
Dalton,	Mount Washington,	Williamstown,
Egremont,	Pittsfield,	Windsor.
Great Barrington,		

Notaries Public.

[There are no records of Notaries Public in the Clerk's Office.]

Miscellaneous.

One volume of records of Executions covering the years from 1767 to 1787, indexed by the name of the plaintiff.

Seven volumes of records of Naturalization of Aliens, commencing in 1856.

One volume of records of Variations of Surveyors' Compasses, commencing in 1871.

One volume of records of Pedlers' Licenses, commencing May 1, 1880.

Volumes Indexed. — Prior to 1781 there are no indexes; from 1781 to 1785 the records of the Court of Common Pleas are indexed by the names of the plaintiffs, and from 1786 each volume has an alphabetical index of the names of both plaintiffs and defendants. In the records of the Court of Sessions the highways are indexed by towns.

Condition of Records. — Good.

BRISTOL COUNTY. (CLERK'S OFFICE AT TAUNTON.)

Volumes of records and date of first entry in each volume :

County Court.

[There are no records in the Clerk's Office.]

Inferior Court of Common Pleas.

I.	Oct. 10, 1702	V.	Mar. 8, 1740	VIII.	Dec. 14, 1762
II.	July 11, 1724	VI.	Dec. 8, 1744	IX.	Nov. 8, 1767
III.	July 11, 1730	VII.	Sept. 10, 1754	X.	Mar. 9, 1773
IV.	June 11, 1737				

Court of Sessions.

—.[1]

Court of General Sessions of the Peace.

I.	April 12, 1702	III.	Mar. 13, 1738	V.	Sept. 9, 1777
II.	Oct. 9, 1714	IV.	Dec. —, 1746	VI.	Mar. 7, 1801

[1] In volume VI. of the Court of General Sessions of the Peace. No return is made of the Commissioners of Highways; the records are probably contained in the records of the Court of Sessions.

BRISTOL COUNTY.   (Clerk's Office at Taunton.) — Con.

Circuit Court of Common Pleas.

I.	Dec. 9, 1811	IV. Dec. 12, 1814	VII. June 14, 1819
II.	June 8, 1812	V. Dec. —, 1815	VIII. Sept. 10, 1821
III.	Mar. 14, 1814	VI. June 9, 1817	

Court of Common Pleas.

I. Mar. 11, 1783	XIV. Dec. 8, 1828	XXVII. Dec. 12, 1842
II. Mar. 8, 1785	XV. Dec. 14, 1829	XXVIII. June 10, 1844
III. Sept. 13, 1791	XVI. Mar. 14, 1831	XXIX. June 8, 1846
IV. April 18, 1797	XVII. Mar. 12, 1832	XXX. Sept. 13, 1847
V. April 14, 1800	XVIII. Sept. 9, 1833	XXXI. Mar. 12, 1849
VI. Dec. 12, 1803	XIX. June 9, 1834	XXXII. June 10, 1850
VII. July 3, 1807	XX. Mar. 9, 1835	XXXIII. Sept. 8, 1851
VIII. Mar. 14, 1808	XXI. Mar. 14, 1836	XXXIV. June 13, 1853
IX. Dec. —, 1809	XXII. Dec. 12, 1836	XXXV. Feb. 5, 1855
X. Dec. 10, 1821	XXIII. Dec. 11, 1837	XXXVI. Mar. 10, 1856
XI. Sept. 8, 1823	XXIV. Dec. 10, 1838	XXXVII. Mar. 9, 1857
XII. Mar. 14, 1825	XXV. Dec. 9, 1839	XXXVIII. June 14, 1858
XIII. Mar. 12, 1827	XXVI. Mar. 8, 1841	XXXIX. Mar. 14, 1859

Superior Court.

I. Dec. 5, 1859	VIII. Sept. 9, 1872	XV. Dec. 9, 1878
II. June 10, 1861	IX. Dec. 8, 1873	XVI. Dec. 1, 1879
III. Mar. 14, 1864	X. Dec. 14, 1874	XVII. Sept. 6, 1880
IV. Mar. 12, 1866	XI. Dec. 13, 1875	XVIII. June 6, 1881
V. June 8, 1868	XII. Sept. 11, 1876	XIX. Sept. 4, 1882
VI. Dec. 13, 1869	XIII. Mar. 12, 1877	XX. Mar. 3, 1884
VII. Mar. 13, 1871	XIV. Dec. 14, 1877	

Marriages.

One volume covering the period from May —, 1783, to —, 1795, and containing records of the following towns:

Attleborough,	Mansfield,	Somerset,
Berkley,	New Bedford,	Swansea,
Dartmouth,	Norton,	Taunton.
Easton,	Rehoboth,	

Notaries Public.

One volume made by George F. Baker for the Fall River district, covering the years 1874 and 1875. In good condition.

One volume made by Simeon Borden, Jr., for the Fall River district, covering the years from 1854 to 1860. In good condition.

Two volumes made by Benjamin T. Congdon for the New Bedford district, covering the following years: 1843 to 1845; 1846 to 1851. In good condition.

Two volumes made by Charles Drew for Fairhaven, covering the following years: 1865 to 1872; 1872 to 1879. In good condition.

Twelve volumes made by Benjamin Earle for the Fall River district, covering the following years: 1853 to 1856; 1856 to 1857; 1857 to 1860; 1860 to 1865; 1865 to 1870; 1870 to 1872; 1873; 1873 to 1874; 1874 to 1876; 1876 to 1878; 1878 to 1879; 1879 to 1882. In good condition.

One volume made by Thomas D. Elliot for the New Bedford district, covering the years from 1839 to 1849. In good condition.

One volume made by H. H. Fisher for the Fall River district, covering the years from 1848 to 1852. In good condition.

One volume made by John A. Hawes for Fairhaven, covering the years from 1853 to 1863. In good condition.

One volume made by Thomas Adam Mason for the New Bedford district, covering the years from 1846 to 1849. In good condition.

BRISTOL COUNTY (Clerk's Office at Taunton.) — Con.

Notaries Public — Con.

One volume made by Walter Mitchell for the New Bedford district, covering the years from 1853 to 1855. In good condition.

One volume made by Joseph Ricketson for the New Bedford district, covering the years from 1832 to 1833. In good condition.

One volume made by John B. Smith for the New Bedford district, covering the years from 1832 to 1833. In good condition.

Miscellaneous.

Record of Attachments of Real Estate :

    I. 1836 to 1856   II. 1856 to 1861   III. 1862 to 1871

Volumes Indexed. — Each volume has a strictly alphabetical index, with the exception of one volume of records of County Commissioners.

Condition of Records. — Good.

COUNTY OF DUKES COUNTY. (Clerk's Office at Edgartown.)

Volumes of records and date of first entry in each volume :

County Court.

[There is one large volume of miscellaneous records, chiefly court records, the date of the first entry being 1665 and the last 1715, no day or month being given. It contains the record of three terms of a court called "Court of Sessions," held December 28, 1680, June 28, 1681, and July 22, 1684. These records are for the island of Martha's Vineyard for eighteen years before the County of Dukes County was established by the legislature of New York.]

Inferior Court of Common Pleas.

I. Mar. 31, 1722	IV. Oct. 28, 1755	VII. Oct. 26, 1802
II. Oct. 31, 1736	V. Oct. 25, 1763	VIII. May 19, 1807
III. Oct. 25, 1740	VI. Oct. 30, 1798	IX. Nov. 9, 1809

Court of Sessions.[1]

I. May 18, 1808	III. Nov. 10, 1819	IV. May —, 1823
II. Nov. 5, 1811		

Court of General Sessions of the Peace.

I. May 15, 1687	III. Oct. 27, 1801	IV. Nov. —, 1807
II. Oct. 30, 1798		

Circuit Court of Common Pleas.

X. May 13, 1814	XI. Nov. 10, 1817

Court of Common Pleas.

XII. May 20, 1822	XIV. Sept. 28, 1829	XVI. May 25, 1840
XIII. May 31, 1826	XV. May 16, 1836	XVII. July 31, 1851

Superior Court.

I. July 2, 1859	III. Sept. 9, 1874	IV. May 26, 1885
II. May 25, 1868		

---

[1] The records of Commissioners of Highways are contained in the records of this court.

COUNTY OF DUKES COUNTY. (CLERK'S OFFICE AT EDGARTOWN.) — Con.

Marriages.

[There are no records of marriages in the Clerk's Office.]

Notaries Public.

One volume made by William Athearn for the Edgartown district. The date of the first entry is Dec. 14, 1807.

One volume made by John Cooke for the Edgartown district. The date of the first entry is Sept. 21, 1810.

Three volumes made by Thomas Dunham for the Edgartown district. The date of the first entry in each volume is as follows: Aug. 23, 1806; Aug. 7, 1810; Feb. 14, 1833.

One volume by Cornelius Marchant for the Edgartown district. The date of the first entry is Oct. 5, 1808.

The condition of the records of the several Notaries Public is not given.

Miscellaneous.

[There are no miscellaneous records in the Clerk's Office.]

Volumes Indexed. — All the records since 1840 are properly indexed.

Condition of Records. — Good, with the exception of the records for the Court of Common Pleas prior to 1840, which were very poorly kept.

ESSEX COUNTY. (CLERK'S OFFICE AT SALEM.)

Volumes of records and date of first entry in each volume:

County Court.

I.	Jan. 20, 1636	XIX.	June 18, 1672	XXXVII.	Dec. 10, 1680
II.	Mar. 1, 1651	XX.	June 11, 1673	XXXVIII.	April 30, 1682
III.	Mar. 27, 1655	XXI.	Jan. 28, 1673	XXXIX.	Nov. 2, 1682
IV.	Mar. 24, 1657	XXII.	June 27, 1674	XL.	May 10, 1682
V.	Mar. 29, 1659	XXIII.	Mar. 18, 1674	XLI.	Mar. 4, 1684
VI.	Sept. 25, 1660	XXIV.	Nov. 22, 1675	XLII.	June 24, 1684
VII.	Nov. 10, 1661	XXV.	June 22, 1676	XLIII.	Nov. 20, 1684
VIII.	June 8, 1662	XXVI.	Nov. 23, 1676	XLIV.	May 9, 1685
IX.	May 5, 1663	XXVII.	Jan. 5, 1676	XLV.	June 2, 1685
X.	Dec. 24, 1663	XXVIII.	Mar. 26, 1678	XLVI.	Sept. 9, 1686
XI.	Sept. 26, 1665	XXIX.	April 28, 1678	XLVII.	Mar. 19, 1686
XII.	Sept. 12, 1666	XXX.	Nov. 5, 1678	XLVIII.	Feb. 27, 1689
XIII.	Nov. 19, 1667	XXXI.	Dec. 13, 1678	XLIX.	June 4, 1690
XIV.	June 29, 1668	XXXII.	Sept. 30, 1679	L.	May 15, 1690
XV.	Sept. 28, 1669	XXXIII.	July 8, 1679	LI.	June 30, 1691
XVI.	June 12, 1670	XXXIV.	Sept. 15, 1680	LII.	Mar. 3, 1691
XVII.	Mar. 22, 1670	XXXV.	Mar. 24, 1680	LIII.	— —, 1634[1]
XVIII.	Nov. 6, 1671	XXXVI.	May 11, 1681		

Inferior Court of Common Pleas.

I.[2]	Dec. 27, 1692	VI.[3]	Sept. 26, 1704	XI.	July 10, 1770
II.	Dec. 31, 1695	VII.[4]	Mar. 28, 1749	XII.	Sept. 28, 1773
III.	Dec. 27, 1698	VIII.	Dec. 25, 1753	XIII.	Mar. 28, 1780
IV.	Dec. 27, 1692	IX.	Sept. 13, 1760		
V.	July 14, 1719	X.	Sept. 30, 1766		

[1] Volume LIII. contains a collection of miscellaneous court papers covering the years from 1634 to 1693.

[2] There are also two volumes made up of mutilated leaves of old records of the Inferior Court of Common Pleas and other records, one volume covering the time from March 13, 1688, to March 15, 1689, and the other volume covering the time from 1692 to 1695.

[3] This volume is composed of the remnants of old volumes.

[4] There were no records kept between the years 1726 and 1749 other than in dockets.

ESSEX COUNTY. (CLERK'S OFFICE AT SALEM.) — Con.

Court of Sessions.

—.[1] May 10, 1808   —.[2] Oct. 8, 1811   —.[3] Oct. 12, 1819
I.[4] Jan. 8, 1827

Court of General Sessions of the Peace.

I.	June 27, 1693	VI. July 10, 1744	XI. May 4, 1779
II.	Dec. 29, 1696	VII. Mar. 28, 1749	XII. July 12, 1796
III.	Dec. 27, 1709	VIII. Dec. 29, 1761	XIII. June 28, 1803
IV.	Mar. 17, 1718	IX. Mar. 27, 1764	XIV. Oct. 13, 1807
V.	Sept. 27, 1726	X. Mar. 31, 1778	XV. Oct. 12, 1819

Circuit Court of Common Pleas.

I.	Dec. 30, 1811	VIII. Sept. 19, 1814	XV. Mar. 16, 1818
II.	Mar. 30, 1812	IX. Mar. 20, 1815	XVI. Sept. 21, 1818
III.	June 29, 1812	X. Sept. 18, 1815	XVII. Mar. 15, 1819
IV.	Dec. 21, 1812	XI. Mar. 18, 1816	XVIII. Sept. 20, 1819
V.	Mar. 15, 1813	XII. Sept. 16, 1816	XIX. Mar. 21, 1820
VI.	Sept. 20, 1813	XIII. Mar. 17, 1817	XX. Sept. 18, 1820
VII.	Mar. 21, 1814	XIV. Sept. 15, 1817	XXI. Mar. 19, 1821

Court of Common Pleas.

XIV.	Dec. 3, 1782	XI. Sept. 18, 1826	XLV. Sept. 18, 1843
XV.	April 6, 1784	XII. Mar. 19, 1827	XLVI. Mar. 18, 1844
XVI.	April 6, 1785	XIII. Sept. 17, 1827	XLVII. Sept. 16, 1844
XVII.	Sept. 26, 1786	XIV. Mar. 17, 1828	XLVIII. Mar. 17, 1845
XVIII.	Sept. 30, 1788	XV. Sept. 15, 1828	XLIX. Sept. 15, 1845
XIX.	July 13, 1790	XVI. Mar. 16, 1829	L. Mar. 16, 1846
XX.	Sept. 25, 1792	XVII. Sept. 21, 1829	LI. Sept. 21, 1846
XXI.	Oct. 7, 1794	XVIII. Mar. 15, 1830	LII. Mar. 15, 1847
XXII.	April 4, 1797	XIX. Sept. 20, 1830	LIII. Sept. 20, 1847
XXIII.	Oct. 2, 1798	XX. Mar. 21, 1831	LIV. Mar. 20, 1848
XXIV.	July 8, 1800	XXI. Sept. 19, 1831	LV. Sept. 18, 1848
XXV.	Sept. 28, 1802	XXII. Mar. 19, 1832	LVI. Mar. 19, 1849
XXVI.	Dec. 27, 1803	XXIII. Sept. 17, 1832	LVII. Sept. 17, 1849
XXVII.	Mar. 26, 1805	XXIV. Mar. 18, 1833	LVIII. Mar. 18, 1850
XXVIII.	Mar. 31, 1806	XXV. Sept. 16, 1833	LIX. Sept. 16, 1850
XXIX.	Mar. 30, 1807	XXVI. Mar. 17, 1834	LX. Mar. 17, 1851
XXX.	Mar. 28, 1808	XXVII. Sept. 15, 1834	LXI. Sept. 15, 1851
XXXI.	Sept. 26, 1808	XXVIII. Mar. 15, 1835	LXII. Mar. 15, 1852
XXXII.	Mar. 27, 1809	XXIX. Sept. 21, 1835	LXIII. Sept. 16, 1851[5]
XXXIII.	Sept. 25, 1809	XXX. Mar. 21, 1836	LXIV. Sept. 20, 1852
XXXIV.	Sept. 24, 1810	XXXI. Sept. 19, 1836	LXV. Mar. 21, 1853
XXXV.	Mar. 26, 1810	XXXII. Mar. 20, 1837	LXVI. Sept. 19, 1853
XXXVI.	Mar. 25, 1811	XXXIII. Sept. 18, 1837	LXVII. Mar. 20, 1854
		XXXIV. Mar. 19, 1838	LXVIII. Sept. 18, 1854
I.	Sept. 17, 1821	XXXV. Sept. 17, 1838	LXIX. Mar. 19, 1855
II.	Mar. 18, 1822	XXXVI. Mar. 18, 1839	LXX. Sept. 17, 1855
III.	Sept. 18, 1822	XXXVII. Sept. 16, 1839	LXXI. Mar. 17, 1856
IV.	Mar. 17, 1823	XXXVIII. Mar. 16, 1840	LXXII. Sept. 15, 1856
V.	Sept. 15, 1823	XXXIX. Sept. 21, 1840	LXXIII. Mar. 16, 1857
VI.	Mar. 15, 1824	XL. Mar. 15, 1841	LXXIV. Sept. 21, 1857
VII.	Sept. 20, 1824	XLI. Sept. 20, 1841	LXXV. Mar. 15, 1858
VIII.	Mar. 21, 1825	XLII. Mar. 21, 1842	LXXVI. Sept. 20, 1858
IX.	Sept. 19, 1825	XLIII. Sept. 19, 1842	LXXVII. Mar. 21, 1859
X.	Mar. 20, 1826	XLIV. Mar. 20, 1843	

---

[1] In volume XIII. of the Court of General Sessions of the Peace.
[2] In volume XIII. of the Court of General Sessions of the Peace.
[3] In volume XIV. of the Court of General Sessions of the Peace.
[4] This volume contains records of the Commissioners of Highways only.
[5] This volume covers the time until the June term of 1852.

ESSEX COUNTY. (CLERK'S OFFICE AT SALEM). — Con.

Superior Court.

I.	Sept.	5, 1859	XVIII.	Mar.	2, 1868	XXXV.	Sept.	4, 1876
II.	Mar.	5, 1860	XIX.	Sept.	7, 1868	XXXVI.	Mar.	5, 1877
III.	Sept.	3, 1860	XX.	Mar.	1, 1869	XXXVII.	Sept.	2, 1877
IV.	Mar.	4, 1861	XXI.	Sept.	6, 1869	XXXVIII.	Mar.	4, 1878
V.	Sept.	2, 1861	XXII.	Mar.	7, 1870	XXXIX.	Sept.	2, 1878
VI.	Mar.	3, 1862	XXIII.	Sept.	5, 1870	XL.	Mar.	3, 1879
VII.	Sept.	1, 1862	XXIV.	Mar.	6, 1871	XLI.	Sept.	1, 1879
VIII.	Mar.	2, 1863	XXV.	Sept.	4, 1871	XLII.	Mar.	1, 1880
IX.	Sept.	7, 1863	XXVI.	Mar.	4, 1872	XLIII.	Sept.	6, 1880
X.	Mar.	7, 1864	XXVII.	Sept.	2, 1872	XLIV.	Mar.	7, 1881
XI.	Sept.	5, 1864	XXVIII.	Mar.	3, 1873	XLV.	Sept.	5, 1881
XII.	Mar.	6, 1865	XXIX.	Sept.	1, 1873	XLVI.	Mar.	6, 1882
XIII.	Sept.	4, 1865	XXX.	Mar.	2, 1874	XLVII.	Sept.	4, 1882
XIV.	Mar.	5, 1866	XXXI.	Sept.	7, 1874	XLVIII.	Mar.	5, 1883
XV.	Sept.	3, 1866	XXXII.	Mar.	1, 1875	XLIX.	Sept.	3, 1883
XVI.	Mar.	4, 1867	XXXIII.	Sept.	6, 1875	L.	Mar.	3, 1884
XVII.	Sept.	2, 1867	XXXIV.	Mar.	6, 1876	LI.	Sept.	1, 1884

Criminal.[1]

I.	May	8, 1849	XI.	Jan.	28, 1867	XXVIII.	Jan.	2, 1877
II.	Jan.	26, 1852	XIII.	Jan.	27, 1868	XXIX.	Jan.	26, 1878
III.	Jan.	23, 1854	XV.	Jan.	25, 1869	XXXI.	Jan.	27, 1879
IV.	Jan.	28, 1856	XVI.	Jan.	24, 1870	XXXII.	Jan.	26, 1880
V.	Jan.	25, 1858	XVII.	Jan.	23, 1871	XXXIII.	Oct.	4, 1880
VI.	Oct.	24, 1859	XVIII.	Jan.	22, 1872	XXXIV.	Jan.	24, 1881
VII.	Jan.	28, 1861	XX.	Jan.	27, 1873	XXXV.	Jan.	23, 1882
VIII.	Jan.	26, 1863	XXII.	Jan.	26, 1874	XXXVII.	Jan.	22, 1883
IX.	Jan.	23, 1865	XXIV.	Jan.	25, 1875	XXXVIII.	Jan.	28, 1884
X.	Oct.	8, 1866	XXVI.	Jan.	24, 1876	XL.	Feb.	2, 1885

Marriages.

One volume[2] covering the period from ——, 1654, to ——, 1691, and containing records of the following towns

Andover,	Merrimack Village [now	Salisbury,
Boxford,	Bradford],	Topsfield,
Haverhill,	Newbury,	Wenham.
Ipswich,	Rowley,	

One volume[3] covering the period from April —, 1681, to March —, 1786, and containing records of the following towns :

Amesbury,	Gloucester,	Newbury,
Andover,	Haverhill,	Newburyport,
Beverly,	Ipswich,	Rowley,
Boxford,	Lynn,	Salem,
Bradford,	Manchester,	Salisbury,
Chebacco [now Essex],	Marblehead,	Topsfield,
Danvers,	Methuen,	Wenham.

---

[1] The volumes missing from this series contain records of Naturalization of Aliens. See page 342.

[2] This is a volume of the Ipswich court series, and contains also a record of births and deaths. There is a copy also which has an initial index.

[3] There is a copy also which has an initial index.

ESSEX COUNTY. (CLERK'S OFFICE AT SALEM.) — Con.

Marriages — Con.

One volume covering the period from ——, 1776, to ——, 1795, and containing records of the following towns :

Amesbury,	Ipswich,	Middleton,
Andover,	Lynn,	Newbury,
Beverly,	Lynnfield,	Newburyport,
Boxford,	Manchester,	Rowley,
Danvers,	Marblehead,	Salem,
Gloucester,	Merrimack Village [now	Salisbury,
Hamilton,	Bradford],	Topsfield,
Haverhill,	Methuen,	Wenham.

One volume[1] covering the period from November —, 1631, to April —, 1791, and containing records of the following towns :

Andover,	Newbury,	Topsfield,
Merrimack Village [now	Rowley,	Wenham.
Bradford],	Salem,	

Notaries Public.

One volume made by Thomas Bancroft for Salem, covering the period from June 15, 1799, to April 2, 1803. In good condition.

Two volumes made by Stephen Cross for Newburyport, covering the following periods : July 11, 1806, to Jan. 22, 1808 ; Aug. 5, 1807, to Feb. 10, 1808. In good condition, but in paper covers and need binding.

One volume made by John Cook for Newburyport, covering the period from June 2, 1837, to May 12, 1848. In good condition.

Three volumes made by John Cook for Salem, covering the following periods : May 25, 1848, to Dec. 11, 1854 ; Dec. 9, 1854, to May 25, 1860 ; May 31, 1860, to Aug. 31, 1863. In good condition.

One volume made by William Fabens for Marblehead, covering the period from Oct. 2, 1874, to June 1, 1883. In good condition.

One volume made by J. S. O. Frothingham for Newburyport, covering the period from Mar. 3, 1842, to Feb. 6, 1849. In good condition.

One volume made by Thomas Garney for Marblehead, covering the period from May 20, 1875, to July 21, 1883. In good condition.

One volume made by J. G. Gould for Lawrence, covering the period from Dec. 10, 1872, to Aug. 11, 1874. In good condition.

One volume made by James Gregory for Marblehead, covering the period from Aug. 21, 1844, to Aug. 18, 1874. In good condition.

Four volumes made by Michael Hodge for Newburyport, covering the following periods : Feb. 13, 1792, to May 3, 1796 ; May 20, 1796, to Aug. 14, 1799 ; June 14, 1805, to June 19, 1806 ; June 20, 1808, to Nov. 19, 1810. In good condition.

Seven volumes made by William Howland for Lynn, covering the following periods : Oct. 1, 1858, to Oct. 31, 1868 ; June 29, 1868, to Sept. 26, 1870 ; Oct. 3, 1870, to May 6, 1872 ; May 10, 1872, to April 6, 1874 ; April 8, 1874, to Dec. 24, 1877 ; Jan. 2, 1878, to Sept. 18, 1878 ; Nov. 12, 1861, to Dec. 6, 1879. The condition is not stated.

Three volumes made by E. Norris for Salem, covering the following periods : Mar. 10, 1783, to Dec. 1, 1794 ; Feb. 4, 1794, to Dec. 11, 1797 ; June 30, 1797, to Oct. 19, 1803. In good condition.

Five volumes made by John Prince for Salem, covering the following periods : Feb. 8, 1804, to May 31, 1806 ; July 12, 1808, to April 16, 1811 ; Mar. 30, 1812, to May 17, 1824 ; July 3, 1824, to Mar. 2, 1831 ; Jan. 31, 1815, to June 4, 1832. In good condition.

Two volumes made by John Punchard for Salem, covering the following periods : June 5, 1806, to April 29, 1808 ; Oct. 20, 1810, to May 13, 1813. In good condition.

Two volumes made by Robert Rantoul for Beverly, covering the following periods : Mar. 3, 1806, to April 22, 1811 ; July 19, 1811, to May 20, 1826. The condition is not stated.

Three volumes made by A. Rhodes for Lynn, covering the following periods : Dec. 22, 1849, to Sept. 13, 1859 ; Mar. 11, 1858, to Mar. 1, 1862 ; Mar. 3, 1862, to April 21, 1868. The condition is not stated.

---

[1] This is a copy of the original records ; the original records are missing.

ESSEX COUNTY. (CLERK'S OFFICE AT SALEM.) — Con.

Notaries Public — Con.

One volume made by Ezekiel Savage for Salem, covering the period from Feb. 1, 1804, to June 2, 1806. In good condition.

One volume made by Stephen Sewall for Salem, covering the period from Feb. 9, 1657, to Aug. 20, 1722. The condition is not stated.

One volume made by A. Thorndyke for Beverly, covering the period from Nov. 23, 1831, to May 19, 1837. The condition is not stated.

Two volumes made by Enoch Titcomb for Newburyport, covering the following periods : April 13, 1804, to Mar. 24, 1806; June 19, 1807, to May 23, 1811. In good condition.

One volume made by Ichabod Tucker for Salem, covering the period from June 8, 1803, to Feb. 14, 1806. In good condition.

Two volumes made by Stephen P. Webb for Salem, covering the following periods : Nov. 20, 1833, to Aug. 6, 1846; July 27, 1846, to Feb. 18, 1852. In good condition.

Four volumes made by William Woart for Newburyport, covering the following periods : June 10, 1808, to June 22, 1810; June 16, 1810, to Aug. 28, 1811; June 11, 1812, to April 27, 1829; June 3, 1829, to Jan. 20, 1841. In good condition.

Three volumes made by Wallace W. Wright for Lynn, covering the following periods : April 1, 1873, to Oct. 15, 1873; Oct. 16, 1873, to Aug. 1, 1877; Dec. 3, 1877, to Oct. 12, 1883. The condition is not stated.

Miscellaneous.

Ten volumes of records of Naturalization of Aliens, the first date in each volume being as follows :

XII. Oct. 14, 1867	XXIII. Jan. 26, 1874	XXX. Oct. 2, 1878
XIV. Oct. 12, 1868	XXV. Jan. 25, 1875	XXXVI. Jan. 23, 1882
XIX. May 13, 1872	XXVII. Jan. 24, 1876	XXXIX. May 12, 1884
XXI. Jan. 27, 1873		

Thirteen volumes of records of Attachments of Real Estate, covering the following periods :

I. May 3, 1836, to Dec. 4, 1838	VIII. Jan. 3, 1854, to Dec. 31, 1856
II. Jan. 1, 1839, to Dec. 30, 1841	IX. Jan. 1, 1857, to Dec. 29, 1859
III. Jan. 1, 1842, to Dec. 27, 1843	X. Jan. 2, 1860, to Dec. 30, 1862
IV. Jan. 6, 1844, to Dec. 29, 1846	XI. Jan. 1, 1863, to Dec. 27, 1865
V. Jan. 1, 1847, to Dec. 25, 1848	XII. Jan. 1, 1866, to Dec. 28, 1868
VI. Jan. 1, 1849, to Dec. 21, 1850	XIII. Jan. 1, 1869, to Jan. 14, 1870
VII. Jan. 2, 1851, to Dec. 30, 1853	

Two volumes of old papers relating to trials for witchcraft, most of which bear date of 1692.

One volume of Norfolk County court papers in fragments, pasted on to the leaves of the volume, covering the period from May 24, 1654, to ——, 1679. Many of the papers are without date.

Three volumes of records of Executions, covering the following periods : Oct. —, 1686, to Dec. 30, 1757; Feb. 21, 1758, to Oct. 29, 1783; Mar. 29, 1783, to Oct. 25, 1787.

Eleven volumes, without date, of plans and descriptions of the Eastern Railroad.

One volume, without date, of plans and descriptions of the Boston, Revere Beach, and Lynn Railroad.

Seven volumes, without date, of plans and descriptions of the Boston and Lowell Railroad.

Ten volumes, without date, of plans and descriptions of the Boston and Maine Railroad.

One volume of records of the Quarter Court, held at Salem, covering the period from Oct. 25, 1836, to ——, 1641.

One volume of records of Liquor Licenses, covering the period from Aug. 1, 1868, to Dec. 13, 1868.

Three volumes[1] containing a list of persons in the several towns in Essex County, licensed as innholders and retailers to sell liquor, covering the following periods : July —, 1799, to July 3, 1809; June 19, 1809, to July —, 1830; July 10, 1832, to July —, 1868.

Volumes Indexed. — None of the volumes have strictly alphabetical indexes. The records of the Court of General Sessions of the Peace are all indexed.

Condition of Records. — The first three volumes of the Inferior Court of Common Pleas are merely fragments of books. The records are generally in good condition.

---

[1] There are many volumes of records of innholders' licenses, etc., stored in the attic of the court house, which are not accessible.

FRANKLIN COUNTY. (CLERK'S OFFICE AT GREENFIELD.)

Volumes of records and date of first entry in each volume:

County Court.

[Franklin County was not established at the time of the existence of County Courts. The records, if any, for this jurisdiction would be in the Hampshire County records.]

Inferior Court of Common Pleas.

[Franklin County was not established at the time of the existence of the Inferior Court of Common Pleas. The records, if any, for this jurisdiction would be in the Hampshire County records.]

Court of Sessions.[1]

I. Mar. 5, 1812

Court of General Sessions of the Peace.

[Franklin County was not established at the time of the existence of the Court of General Sessions of the Peace. The records, if any, for this jurisdiction would be in the Hampshire County records.]

Circuit Court of Common Pleas.

I. Mar. 12, 1812	III. Aug. 9, 1819	IV. Aug. 20, 1820
II. Aug. 12, 1815		

Court of Common Pleas.

V. Aug. 13, 1821	XII. Mar. 21, 1836	XIX. Mar. 18, 1850
VI. Nov. 10, 1823	XIII. Nov. 18, 1837	XX. Mar. 23, 1852
VII. April 7, 1826	XIV. Oct. 31, 1839	XXI. Nov. 13, 1854
VIII. Oct. 1, 1827	XV. Mar. 15, 1841	XXII. Aug. 11, 1856
IX. Mar. 1, 1829	XVI. Mar. 25, 1844	XXIII. Nov. 9, 1857
X. Nov. 13, 1830	XVII. Mar. 28, 1846	
XI. Mar. 18, 1833	XVIII. Mar. 20, 1848	

Superior Court.

I. Aug. 8, 1859	V. Mar. 20, 1871	IX. Aug. 13, 1877
II. Nov. 11, 1861	VI. Mar. 17, 1873	X. Nov. 11, 1878
III. Mar. 20, 1865	VII. Mar. 15, 1875	XI. Aug. 9, 1880
IV. Mar. 16, 1868	VIII. Mar. 20, 1876	

Marriages.

[There are no records of marriages in the Clerk's Office.]

Notaries Public.

Two volumes made by George L. Barton for Montague, covering the following periods: Nov. 2, 1872, to Jan. 30, 1874; Dec. 29, 1873, to Sept. 13, 1875. The condition is not stated.

One volume made by E. S. Francis for Shelburne, covering the period from Feb. 15, 1861, to Feb. 19, 1864. The condition is not stated.

Nine volumes made by Charles H. Grinnell for Greenfield, covering the following periods: Jan. 2, 1857, to Dec. 29, 1860; Jan. 2, 1861, to Aug. 23, 1862; July 26, 1862, to Dec. 31, 1864; Feb. 25, 1865, to Dec. 19, 1867; Jan. 6, 1868, to Sept. 17, 1869; Sept. 21, 1869, to Nov. 21, 1871; Nov. 27, 1871, to Jan. 8, 1873; Jan. 8, 1873, to Feb. 18, 1874; Feb. 21, 1874, to July 6, 1874. The condition is not stated.

---

[1] The records of Commissioners of Highways are contained in the records of this Court.

FRANKLIN COUNTY. (CLERK'S OFFICE AT GREENFIELD.) — Con.

Miscellaneous.

Five volumes of records of Attachments of Real Estate covering the following years:

I. 1836 to 1842	III. 1851 to 1863	V. 1874 to 1885
II 1842 to 1851	IV. 1864 to 1874	

Volumes Indexed — Each volume has an initial index.

Condition of Records. — Good, with the exception of two of the older volumes which need rebinding.

HAMPDEN COUNTY. (CLERK'S OFFICE AT SPRINGFIELD.)

Volumes of records and date of first entry in each volume:

County Court.

[Hampden County was not established at the time of the existence of County Courts. The records, if any, for this jurisdiction should be in the Hampshire County records. A few records of County Courts prior to 1700 are in the Registry of Deeds at Springfield.]

Inferior Court of Common Pleas.

I. June 6, 1693	II. May 17, 1720	III. Aug. 25, 1724

Court of Sessions.

I. Sept. 14, 1812	I Aug. 19, 1819	*Records of Commissioners of Highways.* I. Aug. 8, 1826

Court of General Sessions of the Peace.

I. Sept. 25, 1694	II. Aug. 30, 1720	III. Dec. 25, 1724

Circuit Court of Common Pleas.

A. Aug. 31, 1812	II. Aug. 26, 1816	V. Nov. 27, 1818
B. April 10, 1815	III. Nov. 30, 1816	VI. Nov. 27, 1819
I. Sept. 7, 1814	IV. Nov. 29, 1817	VII. Dec. 1, 1819

Court of Common Pleas.

Civil and Criminal.

VIII. Aug. 21, 1821	XIII. Mar. 20, 1830	XVIII. Nov. 9, 1839
IX. Aug. 29, 1822	XIV. Oct. 14, 1831	XIX. April 3, 1841
X. Aug. 27, 1824	XV. Oct. 22, 1834	XX. April 25, 1843
XI. Sept. 22, 1826	XVI. Feb. 20, 1836	XXI. Jan. 22, 1844
XII. Nov. 26, 1828	XVII. Feb. 24, 1838	

Civil.

XXII. June 21, 1845	XXVI. June 22, 1850	XXX. Dec. 3, 1853
XXIII. Oct. 23, 1846	XXVII. Mar. 29, 1851	XXXI. Nov. 7, 1855
XXIV. June 24, 1848	XXVIII. Nov. 19, 1851	XXXII. Jan. 13, 1857
XXV. June 23, 1849	XXIX. Oct. 28, 1852	XXXIII. April 12, 1859

Criminal.

I. May 19, 1845	III. June 9, 1855	IV. Jan. 1, 1858.
II. May 30, 1851		

HAMPDEN COUNTY.   (CLERK'S OFFICE AT SPRINGFIELD.) — Con.

Superior Court.

I.	Oct.	3, 1859	VI.	Mar. 13, 1871	XI.	Mar. 26, 1878
II.	Oct.	7, 1861	VII.	June 9, 1873	XII.	July 1, 1879
III.	Oct.	5, 1863	VIII.	Mar. 8, 1875	XIII.	Nov. 26, 1880
IV.	June	11, 1866	IX.	April 7, 1876	XIV.	Mar. 28, 1882
V.	Oct.	26, 1868	X.	May 1, 1877	XV.	June 24, 1883

Criminal.

I.	Dec.	5, 1859	V.	Dec. 17, 1874	IX.	Jan. 5, 1883
II.	June	30, 1866	VI.	Dec. 24, 1875	X.	Dec. 1, 1884
III.	June	3, 1870	VII.	Jan. 11, 1878			
IV.	Dec.	1, 1873	VIII.	May 22, 1880			

Marriages.

[There are no records of marriages in the Clerk's Office.]

Notaries Public.

One volume made by Richard Bliss mostly for Springfield, covering the years from 1837 to 1843. In good condition.

Two volumes made by Theodore Bliss mostly for Springfield, covering the years from 1842 to 1844. In good condition.

Three volumes made by L. D. Pelton mostly for Springfield, covering the years from 1850 to 1854. In good condition.

One volume made by George W. Rice mostly for Springfield, covering the years 1855 and 1356. In good condition.

Two volumes made by Henry K. Simons mostly for Springfield, covering the years from 1869 to 1873. In good condition.

One volume made by Addison Ware mostly for Springfield, covering the years from 1847 to 1850. In good condition.

One volume made by John R. Warriner mostly for Holyoke, covering the years from 1852 to 1853. In good condition.

Miscellaneous.[1]

Twenty-four volumes of records of Naturalization of Aliens, covering the years from 1853 to 1885, and including the records of all courts in this county having jurisdiction in naturalization cases during said period.

Sixteen volumes of maps of Locations of Railroad Companies.

One volume of records of Liquor Licenses, commencing in 1868.

One volume of tracings of Locations of Highways.

One volume of records of Variations of Surveyors' Compasses.

One volume of records of Investment of Hampden County Sinking Fund.

Seven volumes of records of Attachments of Real Estate.

Four volumes of returns of the U. S. Census, 1880.

One volume of records of By-laws approved by the Superior Court.

Volumes Indexed. — None of the records have strictly alphabetical indexes. The more recent records of the Court of Common Pleas and Superior Court are indexed for each term by the first letter of the surname of the parties alphabetically arranged.

All the records of the courts between 1692 and 1730 have imperfect indexes. The records of the Attachments of Real Estate prior to 1867 are imperfectly indexed.

Condition of Records. — Good, with the exception of portions of the records of the Court of General Sessions of the Peace and Inferior Court of Common Pleas from 1710 to 1730, which need to be both copied and rebound.

---

[1] Henry Morris of Springfield has in his possession the early records of the Magistrates for this jurisdiction, commencing about 1636 and called the " Pynchon Records."

HAMPSHIRE COUNTY. (CLERK'S OFFICE AT NORTHAMPTON.)

Volumes of records and date of first entry in each volume:

County Court.

I. Sept. 25, 1677

Inferior Court of Common Pleas.[1]

—.	Mar.	7, 1726	E.	Feb.	14, 1758	K.	Feb.	9, 1773
A.	Mar.	4, 1728	F.	May	4, 1762	M.	Nov.	12, 1777
B.	Sept.	2, 1735	G.	Sept.	4, 1764	N.	April	9, 1782
C.	May	14, 1741	H.	Nov.	11, 1766			
D.	Nov.	11, 1746	I.	Nov.	30, 1770			

Court of Sessions.

I.	Jan.	1, 1800	II.	Mar. —, 1824	*Records of Commissioners of*
					Highways.
					—.[2] Sept. —, 1826

Court of General Sessions of the Peace.[1]

A.	Mar.	4, 1728	E.	Feb.	14, 1758	M.	Nov.	12, 1771
B.	Sept.	2, 1735	F.	May	4, 1762	L.	May	7, 1776
C.	May	14, 1741	G.	Sept.	4, 1764	R.	Feb.	9, 1790
D.	Nov.	11, 1746	—.	Aug.	26, 1766	I.	Jan.	1, 1800

Circuit Court of Common Pleas.

XV.	Nov.	4, 1811	XVIII.	Nov.	18, 1816	XX.	Mar. —, 1819
XVI.	Aug.	16, 1813	XIX.	Nov.	17, 1817	XXI.	Nov.	22, 1820
XVII.	Nov.	23, 1815						

Court of Common Pleas.[1]

O.	Aug.	26, 1783	VI.	May	16, 1803	XXIV.	Nov.	17, 1828
P.	Aug.	3, 1784	VII.	May	21, 1804	XXV.	Mar.	26, 1830
Q.	Aug.	30, 1785	VIII.	May	26, 1805	XXVI.	Nov.	24, 1832
R.	Feb.	9, 1790	IX.	May	19, 1806	XXVII.	Aug.	17, 1835
S.	Nov.	11, 1791	X.	May	18, 1807	XXVIII.	Aug.	20, 1838
T.	May	17, 1794	XI.	May	21, 1808	XXIX.	Aug.	16, 1841
I.	May	13, 1798	XII.	June	9, 1809	XXX.	Aug.	19, 1845
II.	June	7, 1799	XIII.	June	8, 1810	XXXI.	Oct.	24, 1846
III.	June	13, 1800	XIV.	Nov.	5, 1810	XXXII.	Feb.	19, 1849
IV.	June	19, 1801	XXII.	Nov.	17, 1823	XXXIII.	June	2, 1851
V.	May	24, 1802	XXIII.	Aug.	21, 1826			

Civil.

I.	Feb.	20, 1854	II.	Oct.	19, 1857

Superior Court.

II.	Oct.	17, 1859	VII.	Feb.	16, 1874	XII.	Feb.	17, 1879
III.	Sept.	20, 1865	VIII.	Feb.	15, 1875	XIII.	June	7, 1880
IV.	Feb.	15, 1869	IX.	Feb.	21, 1876	XIV.	Oct.	17, 1881
V.	Feb.	20, 1871	X.	Feb.	19, 1877	XV.	June	4, 1883
VI.	Oct.	21, 1872	XI.	Feb.	18, 1878			

---

[1] Volumes A, B, C, D, E, F, and G contain records of the Inferior Court of Common Pleas, Court of General Sessions of the Peace, and Court of Common Pleas.

[2] In volume II. of the Court of Sessions.

HAMPSHIRE COUNTY. (CLERK'S OFFICE AT NORTHAMPTON.) — Con.

Superior Court — Con.

Criminal.

I. June 14, 1852	IV. June 12, 1871	VII. June 9, 1879
II. Dec. 19, 1864	V. June 9, 1873	VIII. June 12, 1882
III. Dec. 20, 1869	VI. June 12, 1876	

Marriages.

There are no separate volumes containing marriages, but among the records of the General Sessions of the Peace between the years 1786 and 1790, contained in volume L, there are a few marriages recorded, for the following towns :

Belchertown,	Hadley,	Southampton,
Bernardston,	Hatfield,	Sunderland,
Charlemont,	Monson,	Wendell,
Deerfield,	Northampton,	Westhampton.
Greenfield,	Orange,	

Notaries Public.

One volume made by Henry II. Bond for Hampshire County, covering the period from Aug. 25, 1868, to June 25, 1878. In good condition.

One volume made by James W. Boyden for Hampshire County, covering the period from July 6, 1853, to Sept. 23, 1853. In good condition.

One volume made by I. F. Conkey for Hampshire County, covering the period from Jan. 12, 1865, to Aug. 2, 1875. In good condition.

Three volumes made by Charles Delano for Hampshire County, covering the period from July 16, 1870, to Aug. 16, 1878. In good condition.

One volume made by Gordon R. Hall for Hampshire County, covering the period from Feb. 14, 1874, to June 19, 1874. In good condition.

Two volumes made by James Hibben for Hampshire County, covering the period from Jan. 29, 1839, to Aug. 27, 1858. In good condition.

One volume made by William H. Moseley for Hampshire County, covering the period from Jan. 26, 1830, to Mar. 4, 1833. In good condition.

One volume made by Albert D. Sanders for Hampshire County, covering the period from July 3, 1877, to June 22, 1883. In good condition.

Two volumes made by Daniel Stebbins for Hampshire County, covering the period from Sept. 16, 1813, to Aug. 29, 1846. In good condition.

Two volumes made by William E. Turner for Hampshire County, covering the period from Dec. 10, 1859, to Jan. 20, 1868. In good condition.

Miscellaneous.

[There are no miscellaneous records in the Clerk's office.]

Volumes Indexed. — The information is not given.

Condition of Records. — Good. The excessive heat to which the volumes are exposed is, however, injuring the binding.

MIDDLESEX COUNTY. (CLERK'S OFFICE AT CAMBRIDGE.)

Volumes of records and date of first entry in each volume :

County Court.[1]

| I.[2] Oct. 30, 1649 | IV.[2] April 5, 1681 | —.[3] Oct. 1, 1689 |
| III.[2] Oct. 4, 1671 | | |

---

[1] Volume II. of the records of the County Court is lost.

[2] There is a copy also of this volume.

[3] This volume also contains records of the Inferior Court of Common Pleas.

MIDDLESEX COUNTY.   (CLERK'S OFFICE AT CAMBRIDGE.) — Con.

Inferior Court of Common Pleas.

—.[1]	Oct.	4, 1692	V.	May	20, 1740	IX.	Dec.	12, 1758
I.	Dec.	12, 1699	VI.	Mar.	13, 1743	X.	Dec.	11, 1764
II.	Mar.	12, 1723	VII.	Dec.	11, 1750	XI.	Nov.	27, 1770
III.	May	18, 1731	VIII.	May	21, 1754	XII.	Nov.	28, 1780
IV.	Dec.	13, 1737						

Court of Sessions.

—.[2]	Sept.	20, 1808	—.[4]	Sept.	17, 1811	II.	Jan.	1, 1822
I.[3]	Jan.	3, 1809	—.[5]	Sept.	21, 1819	*Records of Commissioners of Highways.*[6]		

Court of General Sessions of the Peace.

I.	July	19, 1692	IV.	May	17, 1748	VII.[7]	Sept.	14, 1790
II.	Oct.	8, 1723	V.	May	19, 1761	VIII.[8]	May	18, 1801
III.	Mar.	9, 1735	VI.	Sept.	3, 1771			

Circuit Court of Common Pleas.

—.[9]	Dec.	16, 1811	VII.	Mar.	13, 1815	XIV.	Sept.	14, 1818
I.	Mar.	16, 1812	VIII.	Sept.	11, 1815	XV.[10]	Mar.	8, 1819
II.	Sept.	14, 1812	IX.	Mar.	11, 1816	XVI.	Sept.	13, 1819
III.	Mar.	8, 1813	X.	Sept.	9, 1816	XVII.	Mar.	13, 1820
IV.	Sept.	13, 1813	XI.	Mar.	10, 1817	XVIII.	Sept.	11, 1820
V.	Mar.	14, 1814	XII.	Sept.	8, 1817	XIX.	Mar.	12, 1821
VI.	Sept.	12, 1814	XIII.	Mar.	9, 1818			

Court of Common Pleas.

I.	June	7, 1783	XI.	Mar.	17, 1800	XXI.	Mar.	16, 1807
II.	Mar.	8, 1785	XII.	Mar.	16, 1801	XXII.	June	1, 1807
III.	Mar.	11, 1788	XIII.	Mar.	15, 1802	XXIII.	Sept.	7, 1807
IV.	Sept.	14, 1790	XIV.	Mar.	14, 1803	XXIV.	Dec.	14, 1807
V.	Sept.	12, 1792	XV.	Mar.	19, 1804	XXV.	Mar.	14, 1808
VI.	Mar.	17, 1795	XVI.	Mar.	18, 1805	XXVI.	June	6, 1808
VII.	Mar.	15, 1796	XVII.	Sept.	9, 1805	XXVII.	Sept.	12, 1808
VIII.	Mar.	20, 1797	XVIII.	Dec.	16, 1805	XXVIII.	Mar.	20, 1809
IX.	Mar.	19, 1798	XIX.	Mar.	17, 1806	XXIX.[11]	June	5, 1809
X.	Mar.	18, 1799	XX.	Sept.	8, 1806	XXX.	Dec.	18, 1809

---

[1] In the volume of records of the County Court which begins Oct. 1, 1689.

[2] In volume VIII. of the Court of General Sessions of the Peace, page 430.

[3] This volume also contains records of the Court of Common Pleas.

[4] In volume I. of the Court of Sessions, page 187.

[5] In volume I. of the Court of Sessions, page 457.

[6] In the records of the Court of Sessions.

[7] There is one volume also which appears to be a memorandum record or docket, covering the period from Mar. 15, 1796, to Dec. 21, 1799.

[8] This volume also contains records of the Court of Sessions. There is one volume also which appears to be a memorandum record or docket, covering the period from Mar. 17, 1800, to Nov. 20, 1802.

[9] In volume XL. of the Court of Common Pleas, page 249.

[10] In volume I. of the Court of Sessions, page 449, there is a record of a session of this court held Mar. 8, 1819.

[11] In volume I. of the Court of Sessions, pages 17 to 186, there are records of sessions of the above court, which appear to be terms held by special justices for trial of cases concerning highways. The record says these are held under authority of the statute authorizing two extra terms. The dates of the several terms are as follows: July 11, 1809; Aug. 1, 1809; Sept. 11, 1809; Dec. 18, 1809; Mar. 19, 1810; June 4, 1810; Sept. 10, 1810; Dec. 17, 1810; Mar. 18, 1811; June 3, 1811.

MIDDLESEX COUNTY. (CLERK'S OFFICE AT CAMBRIDGE.) — Con.

Court of Common Pleas — Con.

XXXI.	Mar. 19, 1810	LV.	Sept. 13, 1830	LXXIX.	Sept 13, 1841
XXXII.	June 4, 1810	LVI.	Mar. 14, 1831	LXXX.	Sept. 12, 1842
XXXIII.	Dec. 17, 1810	LVII.	Sept. 12, 1831	LXXXI.	Feb. 14, 1842
XXXIV.	Mar. 18, 1811	LVIII.	Mar. 12, 1832	LXXXII.	Feb. 13, 1843
XXXV.	June 3, 1811	LIX.	Sept. 10, 1832	LXXXIII.	Mar. 11, 1844
XXXVI.	Sept. 9, 1811	LX.	Mar. 11, 1833	LXXXIV.	Mar. 10, 1845
XXXVII.	Sept. 10, 1821	LXI.	Sept. 9, 1833	LXXXV.	Mar. 9, 1846
XXXVIII.	Mar. 11, 1822	LXII.	Dec. 9, 1833	LXXXVI.	Mar. 8, 1847
XXXIX.	Sept. 9, 1822	LXIII.	Mar. 10, 1834	LXXXVII.	Mar. 13, 1848
XL.[1]	Mar. 10, 1823	LXIV.	Sept. 8, 1834	LXXXVIII.	Mar. 12, 1849
XLI.	Sept. 8, 1823	LXV.	Dec. 8, 1834	LXXXIX.	Sept. 3, 1849
XLII.	Mar. 8, 1824	LXVI.	Mar. 9, 1835	XC.	Mar. 11, 1850
XLIII.	Sept. 13, 1824	LXVII.	Sept. 14, 1835	XCI.	Sept. 2, 1850
XLIV.	Mar. 14, 1825	LXVIII.	Mar. 14, 1836	XCII.	Mar. 10, 1851
XLV.	Sept. 12, 1825	LXIX.	Sept. 12, 1836	XCIII.	Sept. 1, 1851
XLVI.	Mar. 13, 1826	LXX.	Mar. 13, 1837	XCIV.	Mar. 8, 1852
XLVII.	Sept. 11, 1826	LXXI.	Sept. 11, 1837	XCV.	Sept. 6, 1852
XLVIII.	Mar. 12, 1827	LXXII.	Mar. 12, 1838	XCVI.	Mar. 14, 1853
XLIX.	Sept. 10, 1827	LXXIII.	Sept. 10, 1838	XCVII.	Mar. 13, 1854
L.	Mar. 10, 1828	LXXIV.	Mar. 11, 1839	XCVIII.	Mar. 12, 1855
LI.	Sept. 8, 1828	LXXV.	Sept. 9, 1839	XCIX.	Mar. 10, 1856
LII.	Mar. 2, 1829	LXXVI.	Feb. 10, 1840	C.	Mar. 9, 1857
LIII.	Sept. 14, 1829	LXXVII.	Sept. 14, 1840	CI.	Mar. 8, 1858
LIV.	Mar. 8, 1830	LXXVIII.	Feb. 8, 1841	CII.[2]	Mar. 14, 1859

Criminal.

I.	Feb. 12, 1844	IV.	Feb. 12, 1855	VII.	Feb. 8, 1858
II.	Feb. 11, 1850	V.	Mar. 11, 1856	VIII.[3]	Feb. 14, 1859
III.	Feb. 14, 1853	VI.	Mar. 9, 1857		

[There is one volume with the following title, "Proceedings and Judgments in actions entered in the Court of Common Pleas on the return days provided for by the Statute of 1851, Chap. 233, and not placed on the Trial Calendar of this Court," covering the period from October, 1851, to June, 1852.]

Superior Court.

—.[4]	Sept. 5, 1859	IX.	Mar. 9, 1868	XVIII.	Mar. 12, 1877
I.	Mar. 14, 1860	X.	Mar. 8, 1869	XIX.	Mar. 11, 1878
II.	Mar. 11, 1861	XI.	Mar. 14, 1870	XX.	Mar. 10, 1879
III.	Mar. 10, 1862	XII.	Mar. 13, 1871	XXI.	Mar. 8, 1880
IV.	Mar. 9, 1863	XIII.	Mar. 11, 1872	XXII.	Mar. 14, 1881
V.	Mar. 14, 1864	XIV.	Mar. 10, 1873	XXIII.	Mar. 13, 1882
VI.	Mar. 13, 1865	XV.	Mar. 9, 1874	XXIV.	Mar. 12, 1883
VII.	Mar. 12, 1866	XVI.	Mar. 8, 1875	XXV.	Mar. 10, 1884
VIII.	Mar. 11, 1867	XVII.	Mar. 13, 1876		

Criminal.

—.[5]	Feb. 13, 1860	VII.	Feb. 13, 1871	XIII.	Feb. 12, 1877
I.	Feb. 11, 1861	VIII.	Feb. 12, 1872	XIV.	Feb. 11, 1878
II.	Feb. 8, 1864	IX.	Feb. 10, 1873	XV.	Feb. 10, 1879
III.	Feb. 12, 1866	X.	Feb. 9, 1874	XVI.	Feb. 9, 1880
IV.	Feb. 11, 1867	XI.	Feb. 8, 1875	XVII.	Feb. 14, 1881
V.	Feb. 10, 1868	XII.	Feb. 14, 1876	XVIII.	Feb. 13, 1882
VI.	Feb. 14, 1870				

[1] This volume also contains records of the Circuit Court of Common Pleas.
[2] This volume also contains records of the Superior Court.
[3] This volume also contains criminal records of the Superior Court.
[4] In volume CII. of the Court of Common Pleas.
[5] In volume VIII. of the criminal records of the Court of Common Pleas.

MIDDLESEX COUNTY.   (CLERK'S OFFICE AT CAMBRIDGE.) — Con.

Births, Marriages, and Deaths.

One volume ("Liber 3") covering the period from 1651[1] to 1677, and containing records of the following towns:

Billerica,	Framingham	Mendon,
Cambridge,	Groton,	Reading,
Charlestown,	Lancaster,	Sudbury,
Chelmsford,	Malden,	Watertown,
Concord,	Marlborough,	Woburn.

This volume needs rebinding.

One volume ("Liber 4") covering the period from 1678 to 1745, and containing records of the following towns:

Auburn,	Lancaster,	Stow,
Billerica,	Lexington,	Sudbury,
Cambridge,	Malden,	Townsend,
Charlestown,	Marlborough,	Waltham,
Chelmsford,	Medford,	Watertown,
Concord,	Natick,	Westborough,
Dunstable,	Newton,	Weston,
Framingham,	Reading,	Worcester.
Groton,	Sherborn,	
Holliston,	Shrewsbury,	

This volume needs rebinding.

One volume (Volume I.).   This is a copy of "Liber 1," which is bound in at the end of the first volume of Deeds in the Registry of Deeds at Cambridge, covering the period from 1632 to 1678, and containing records of the following towns:

Billerica,	Framingham,	Mendon,
Cambridge,	Groton,	Reading,
Charlestown,	Lancaster,	Sudbury,
Chelmsford,	Malden,	Watertown,
Concord,	Marlborough,	Woburn.

In good condition.

One volume (Volume II.).   This is a copy of "Liber 2," which is bound in at the end of the first volume of Wills and Inventories in the Registry of Probate at Cambridge, covering the period from 1678 to 1745, and containing records of the following towns:

Auburn,	Lancaster,	Shrewsbury,
Billerica,	Lexington,	Stow,
Cambridge,	Malden,	Sudbury,
Charlestown,	Marlborough,	Townsend,
Chelmsford,	Medford,	Waltham,
Concord,	Mendon,	Watertown,
Dunstable,	Natick,	Westborough,
Framingham,	Newton,	Weston,
Groton,	Reading,	Worcester.
Holliston,	Sherborn,	

[There are also three folios which are copies of records of births, marriages, and deaths in the following towns:

Billerica,	Groton,	Stow,
Boston,	Malden,	Sudbury,
Cambridge,	Medford,	Watertown,
Charlestown,	New Cambridge,[2]	Woburn.
Chelmsford,	Reading,	
Concord,	Sherborn,	

The dates are in various years from 1687 to 1696, which are covered by "Liber 4," but these entries with a few exceptions are not included in that volume. The originals from which these records were copied cannot be found, nor has any information in regard to them been obtained.]

---

[1] The date 1645 appears in this volume, but it is in connection with the record of two births in England.

[2] Now Newton, probably, although according to the Mass. Archives "Cambridge Village sometimes called Little Cambridge" was established as Newton.

Marriages.

One volume (Volume I.) covering the period from 1733 to 1793, and containing records of the following towns:

Acton,	Holliston,	Stow,
Bedford,	Lexington,	Sudbury,
Billerica,	Lincoln,	Tewksbury,
Cambridge,	Littleton,	Townsend,
Charlestown,	Malden,	Waltham,
Chelmsford,	Marlborough,	Watertown,
Concord,	Medford,	Westford,
Dracut,	Natick,	Weston,
Dunstable,	Newton,	Wilmington,
East Sudbury [now Wayland],	Reading,	Woburn.
Framingham,	Sherborn,	
Groton,	Stoneham,	

In good condition.

One volume (Volume II.) covering the period from 1773 to 1793, and containing records of the following towns:

Bedford,	Groton,	Shirley,
Billerica,	Lexington,	Stoneham,
Boxborough,	Littleton,	Stow,
Cambridge,	Marlborough,	Sudbury,
Carlisle,	Medford,	Tewksbury,
Charlestown,	Natick,	Townsend,
Chelmsford,	Newton,	Waltham,
East Sudbury [now Wayland],	Reading,	Weston,
Framingham,	Sherborn,	Wilmington.

In good condition.

Notaries Public.

One volume made by Charles Hall Adams for Cambridge and vicinity, covering the period from Dec. 12, 1877, to Nov. 26, 1879. In good condition.

One volume made by George Stevens for Lowell, covering the period from Mar. 4, 1869, to April 18, 1874. In good condition.

Three volumes made by John C. Thurston for Cambridge, covering the following periods: Feb. 16, 1875, to June 7, 1878; April 16, 1878, to July 18, 1884; June 7, 1878, to Nov. 6, 1884. In good condition.

Miscellaneous.

One volume of Variation of Surveyors' Compasses, covering the period from Oct. 17, 1871, to ——, 1885.

Three volumes of records of Executions, covering the following periods: Dec. 9, 1721, to Mar. 6, 1756; June 7, 1757, to Dec. 26, 1767; Oct. 23, 1767, to July 4, 1785.

One volume of records of Executions and Partitions (Circuit Court of Common Pleas), covering the period from Sept. 27, 1785, to Sept. 12, 1814.

Two volumes of records of Partitions, covering the following years: 1815 to 1837; 1837 to 1856.

One volume of records of Partitions (Supreme Judicial Court), covering the years from 1800 to 1857.

One volume of records of Recognizances on Appeal, covering the period from Sept. 19, 1812, to Mar. 18, 1815.

Two volumes of records of Licenses, dated Sept. 13, 1791, and Sept. —, 1808.

Thirteen volumes of records of Naturalization of Aliens, covering the following years:

1842 to 1850	1858 to 1870	1870 to 1872
1842 to 1856	1860 to 1872	1872 to 1885
1850 to 1860	1864 to 1871	1872 to 1885
1850 to 1867	1867 to 1871	1872 to ——
1856 to 1860		

Forty-three volumes of plans of Locations of Railroads.

Volumes Indexed. — Each volume has an initial index.

Condition of Records. — Good.

NANTUCKET COUNTY. (CLERK'S OFFICE AT NANTUCKET.)

Volumes of records and date of first entry in each volume :

County Court.

[There are no records in the Clerk's Office.]

Inferior Court of Common Pleas.

I.   Oct.   3, 1721

Court of Sessions.

[There are no records in the Clerk's Office.]

Court of General Sessions of the Peace.

I.   Oct.   3, 1721   II.   Mar.   28, 1786   III.   Mar.   4, 1803

Circuit Court of Common Pleas.

[There are no records in the Clerk's Office.]

Court of Common Pleas.

II. Mar. 28, 1786	V. Nov. 5, 1821	VIII. Oct. 2, 1837
III. Oct. 5, 1802	VI. May 16, 1823	IX. June 5, 1847
IV. Mar. 24, 1807	VII. Mar. 25, 1829	

Superior Court.

I.   Oct.   3, 1859

Marriages.

Two volumes covering the period from Feb. 6, 1766, to Mar. 22, 1790, containing records of the town of Nantucket.

Notaries Public.

One volume made by William Barney for Nantucket, covering the period from Aug. 27, 1850, to Mar. 21, 1855. The condition is not stated.

One volume made by James M. Bunker for Nantucket, covering the period from Mar. 25, 1854, to Sept. 24, 1862. The condition is not stated.

One volume made by George Cobb for Nantucket, covering the period from Nov. 12, 1861, to Feb. 17, 1874. The condition is not stated.

One volume made by Edward M. Gardner for Nantucket, covering the period from June 3, 1852, to Sept. 5, 1870. The condition is not stated.

One volume made by George W. Jenks for Nantucket, covering the period from Sept. 6, 1876, to Mar. 30, 1880. The condition is not stated.

One volume made by William H. Macy for Nantucket, covering the period from Sept. 20, 1874, to July 5, 1876. The condition is not stated.

One volume made by Charles K. Whitman for Nantucket, covering the period from Aug. 14, 1840, to Dec. 10, 1850. The condition is not stated.

Miscellaneous.

[There are no miscellaneous records in the Clerk's Office.]

Volumes Indexed. — Each volume has an initial index.

Condition of Records. — Good.

NORFOLK COUNTY. (CLERK'S OFFICE AT DEDHAM.)

Volumes of records and date of first entry in each volume:

County Court.

[Norfolk County was not established at the time of the existence of County Courts. The records for this jurisdiction are in the Suffolk County records.]

Inferior Court of Common Pleas.

I.	Sept. 24, 1793	IV.	Jan. 1, 1805	VII.	April 24, 1809
II.	April 4, 1798	V.	Sept. 15, 1806	VIII.	April 23, 1810
III.	April 27, 1802	VI.	April 25, 1808	IX.	April 22, 1811

Court of Sessions.

—.[1]	April 25, 1808	—.	April —, 1819	*Records of Commissioners of Highways.*
—.	Sept. 16, 1811			—. July 6, 1826

Court of General Sessions of the Peace.

I.[2] June 20, 1793

Circuit Court of Common Pleas.

X.	April 22, 1812	XIII.	April 24, 1815	XVI.	April 27, 1818
XI.	April 26, 1813	XIV.	April 22, 1816	XVII.	April 26, 1819
XII.	April 25, 1814	XV.	April 28, 1817	XVIII.	April 24, 1820

Court of Common Pleas.

XIX.	April 23, 1821	XXXII.	April 28, 1834	XLV.	April 26, 1847
XX.	April 27, 1822	XXXIII.	April 25, 1835	XLVI.	April 24, 1848
XXI.	April 28, 1823	XXXIV.	April 25, 1836	XLVII.	April 23, 1849
XXII.	April 26, 1824	XXXV.	April 24, 1837	XLVIII.	April 22, 1850
XXIII.	April 25, 1825	XXXVI.	April 28, 1838	XLIX.	April 28, 1851
XXIV.	April 24, 1826	XXXVII.	April 22, 1839	L.	April 26, 1852
XXV.	April 23, 1827	XXXVIII.	April 27, 1840	LI.	April 25, 1853
XXVI.	April 28, 1828	XXXIX.	April 26, 1841	LII.	April 24, 1854
XXVII.	April 27, 1829	XL.	April 25, 1842	LIII.	April 23, 1855
XXVIII.	April 26, 1830	XLI.	April 24, 1843	LIV.	April 28, 1856
XXIX.	April 25, 1831	XLII.	April 22, 1844	LV.	April 27, 1857
XXX.	April 23, 1832	XLIII.	April 28, 1845	LVI.	April 26, 1858
XXXI.	April 22, 1833	XLIV.	April 27, 1846		

Superior Court.

LVII.	April 25, 1859	LXVI.	April 27, 1868	LXXV.	April 23, 1877
LVIII.	April 23, 1860	LXVII.	April 26, 1869	LXXVI.	April 22, 1878
LIX.	April 27, 1861	LXVIII.	April 25, 1870	LXXVII.	April 28, 1879
LX.	April 28, 1862	LXIX.	April 24, 1871	LXXVIII.	April 26, 1880
LXI.	April 27, 1863	LXX.	April 22, 1872	LXXIX.	April 25, 1881
LXII.	April 25, 1864	LXXI.	April 28, 1873	LXXX.	April 24, 1882
LXIII.	April 24, 1865	LXXII.	April 27, 1874	LXXXI.	April 23, 1883
LXIV.	April 23, 1866	LXXIII.	April 26, 1875	LXXXII.	April 28, 1884
LXV.	April 22, 1867	LXXIV.	April 24, 1876		

[1] In volume I. of the Court of General Sessions of the Peace.

[2] This volume also contains records of the Court of Sessions.

NORFOLK COUNTY. (CLERK'S OFFICE AT DEDHAM.) — Con.

Marriages.

One volume covering the period from Nov. 25, 1793, to June 7, 1795, and containing records of the following towns :

Bellingham,	Foxborough,	Randolph,
Braintree,	Franklin,	Roxbury,
Brookline,	Medfield,	Sharon,
Cohasset,	Medway,	Stoughton,
Dedham,	Milton,	Walpole,
Dorchester,	Needham,	Weymouth,
Dover,	Quincy,	Wrentham.

Notaries Public.

One volume made by Charles Howe and Abraham Noyes for the towns of Norfolk County, covering the years from 1849 to 1858. In fair condition.

Two volumes made by A. A. Russegue for Franklin and the towns in the vicinity, covering the period from April 10, 1869, to Aug. 6, 1881. In fair condition.

Five volumes made by Joshua Seaver for Roxbury, covering the period from Nov. —, 1855, to Sept. 4, 1863. In fair condition.

Miscellaneous.

[There are no miscellaneous records in the Clerk's Office.]

Volumes Indexed. — Each volume has a strictly alphabetical index.

Condition of Records. — Good.

PLYMOUTH COUNTY. (CLERK'S OFFICE AT PLYMOUTH.)

Volumes of records and date of first entry in each volume :

County Court.

I.[1] Sept. 25, 1686

Inferior Court of Common Pleas.

I. June 20, 1702	VI.[3] May 18, 1736	XI. May 20, 1755
II. June 16, 1724	VII.[3] Dec. 19, 1738	XII. April 29, 1760
III.[2] — —, —	VIII. Mar. 3, 1740	XIII. Jan. 1, 1765
IV. Mar. 5, 1727	IX. May 15, 1744	XIV. Oct. 3, 1769
V. Sept. 18, 1733	X. Sept. 20, 1749	XV. April 13, 1773

Court of Sessions.

VI. Mar. 15, 1808	VII. April 6, 1818	*Records of Commissioners of Highways.* —.[4] Oct. 9, 1827

Court of General Sessions of the Peace.

I. Sept. 15, 1730	II. Mar. 4, 1749	IV. April 9, 1782
—. May 17, 1733	III. Oct. 7, 1760	V. Nov. 22, 1791

---

[1] This volume is called "Quarter Sessions."

[2] Volume III. is omitted, but the time is covered by other volumes.

[3] This volume also contains records of the Court of Sessions.

[4] In volume VII. of the Court of Sessions.

PLYMOUTH COUNTY. (Clerk's Office at Plymouth.) — Con.

Circuit Court of Common Pleas.

XXIV. Nov. 23, 1812	XXVI. April 8, 1816	XXVIII.[1] April 10, 1820
XXV. Aug. 15, 1814	XXVII. April 13, 1818	

Court of Common Pleas.

XVI. Oct. 7, 1783	XXII. April 14, 1807	XXXIII. April 13, 1835
XVII. Jan. 10, 1785	XXIII. April 4, 1810	XXXIV. April 9, 1838
XVIII. Aug. 9, 1791	XXIX.[2] Aug. 11, 1823	XXXV. April 12, 1841
XIX. Nov. 15, 1796	XXX. Aug. 8, 1825	XXXVI.[3] April 13, 1846
XX. Nov. 19, 1799	XXXI. April 14, 1828	
XXI. Nov. 15, 1803	XXXII. April 11, 1831	

Superior Court.

[The records of this court since 1850, with the exception of the Dockets, are in sheets, which are unbound.]

Births, Marriages, and Deaths.

These records are contained in volume II. of the Inferior Court of Common Pleas, and volumes I., II., III., and IV. of the Court of General Sessions of the Peace. They cover the period from 1724 to 1788, and contain records of the following towns:

Abington,	Kingston,	Plympton,
Bridgewater,	Marshfield,	Rochester,
Duxbury,	Middleborough,	Scituate,
Halifax,	Pembroke,	Wareham.
Hanson,	Plymouth,	

Notaries Public.

One volume made by James F. Cox for Abington, covering the period from April 7, 1877, to Oct. 10, 1884. The condition is not stated.
Two volumes made by David Harding for Hingham, covering the following periods: June 26, 1834, to Jan. 26, 1841; May 5, 1841, to Oct. 31, 1857. The condition is not stated.
One volume made by Ephraim Spooner for Plymouth, covering the period from May 22, 1770, to Oct. 2, 1817. The condition is not stated.
One volume made by John Thomas for Plymouth, covering the period from June 26, 1819, to Nov. 1, 1830. The condition is not stated.
One volume made by Edward Winslow for Plymouth, covering the period from April 3, 1768, to May 8, 1770. The condition is not stated.

Miscellaneous.

[There are no miscellaneous records in the Clerk's Office.]

Volumes Indexed. — Each volume prior to 1841 has a strictly alphabetical index. Each volume of Docket Records has a strictly alphabetical index.

Condition of Records. — Some of the earlier volumes need rebinding. The manuscript records should be bound and indexed.

---

[1] The records are continued in volume XXIX. of the Court of Common Pleas to November 18, 1822.
[2] This volume also contains records of the Circuit Court of Common Pleas.
[3] Subsequent records of this court are in sheets, which are unbound.

SUFFOLK COUNTY.

(CIVIL SESSION. CLERK'S OFFICE AT BOSTON.)

Volumes of records and date of first entry in each volume :

County Court.

I.	April 27, 1680	II.	July 26, 1692

Inferior Court of Common Pleas.

I.	July 27, 1686	XIII.	July 6, 1725	XXVIII.	Oct. 3, 1738
II.	July 30, 1689	XIV.	Oct. 4, 1726	XXIX.	Oct. 2, 1739
		XV.	Oct. 3, 1727	XXX.	July 1, 1740
I.	July 26, 1692	XVI.	Oct. 1, 1728	XXXI.	Mar. 17, 1740
II.	April 4, 1699	XVII.	Oct. 7, 1729	XXXII.	Mar. 16, 1741
III.	Jan. 6, 1701	XVIII.	July 7, 1730	XXXIII.	July 5, 1743
IV.	Jan. 7, 1706	XIX.	April 6, 1731	XXXIV.	Jan. 1, 1744
V.	Jan. 2, 1710	XX.	April 4, 1732	XXXV.	Jan. 6, 1746
VI.	April 6, 1714	XXI.	Jan. 2, 1732	XXXVI.	Oct. 4, 1748
VII.	Jan. 3, 1715	XXII.	July 3, 1733	XXXVII.	Jan. 2, 1749
VIII.	July 1, 1718	XXIII.	July 2, 1734	XXXVIII.[1]	July 2, 1751
IX.	April 5, 1720	XXIV.	April 1, 1735	XXXIX.	April 16, 1776
X.	July 4, 1721	XXV.	Jan. 6, 1735	XL.	Jan. 4, 1780
XI.	Jan. 1, 1722	XXVI.	Oct. 5, 1736	XLI.	Jan. 3, 1782
XII.	April 7, 1724	XXVII.	Oct. 4, 1737		

Court of Sessions.

I.	Nov. 22, 1808	II.	Oct. 1, 1811	III.	Mar. 2, 1819

Court of General Sessions of the Peace

I.	April 21, 1796	III.	July 2, 1805
II.	Oct. 7, 1800	IV.	Jan. 18, 1808

Circuit Court of Common Pleas.

I.	Nov. 30, 1810	XVIII.	May 2, 1815	XXXV.	Sept. 29, 1818
II.	Jan. 7, 1812	XIX.	Mar. 14, 1815	XXXVI.	Nov. 1, 1818
III.	Mar. 12, 1812	XX.	Oct. 1, 1815	XXXVII.	Jan. 5, 1819
IV.	April 21, 1812	XXI.	Jan. 2, 1816	XXXVIII.	Jan. —, 1819
V.	July 7, 1812	XXII.	April 2, 1816	XXXIX.	April 6, 1819
VI.	Oct. 21, 1812	XXIII.	July 2, 1816	XL.	July 6, 1819
VII.	Sept. 29, 1812	XXIV.	Oct. 1, 1816	XLI.	Oct. 5, 1819
VIII.	Jan. 20, 1813	XXV.	Oct. 1, 1816	XLII.	Jan. 4, 1820
IX.	Mar. 23, 1813	XXVI.	Jan. 7, 1817	XLIII.	Jan. 5, 1820
X.	June 29, 1813	XXVII.	Jan. 20, 1817	XLIV.	April 3, 1820
XI.	Sept. 28, 1813	XXVIII.	April 1, 1817	XLV.	July 4, 1820
XII.	Dec. 28, 1813	XXIX.	July 1, 1817	XLVI.	Oct. 3, 1820
XIII.	May 3, 1814	XXX.	Oct. 7, 1817	XLVII.	Jan. 2, 1821
XIV.	July 5, 1814	XXXI.	Jan. 6, 1818	XLVIII.	April 3, 1821
XV.	Nov. 1, 1814	XXXII.	April 7, 1818	XLIX.	July 3, 1821
XVI.	Jan. 9, 1815	XXXIII.	July 7, 1818	L.	Oct. 2, 1821
XVII.	July 4, 1815	XXXIV.	Sept. 20, 1818		

---

[1] The records from 1751 to 1776 are supposed to have been carried off by the Tories in 1776.

SUFFOLK COUNTY — Con.

(CIVIL SESSION. CLERK'S OFFICE AT BOSTON.) — Con.

Court of Common Pleas.

XLII.	Jan.	—, 1783	XCVII.	Jan.	1, 1811	XLVIII.	Jan.	7, 1834
XLIII.	Oct.	4, 1783	XCVIII.	Jan.	28, 1811	XLIX.	April	1, 1834
XLIV.	July	6, 1784	XCIX.	April	16, 1811	L.	July	1, 1834
XLV.	July	5, 1785	C.	July	2, 1811	LI.	Oct.	7, 1834
XLVI.	April	18, 1786	CI.	July	9, 1811	LII.	Jan.	6, 1835
XLVII.	Jan.	2, 1787	CII.	Oct.	1, 1811	LIII.	April	7, 1835
XLVIII.	Jan.	1, 1788	CIII.	Nov.	7, 1811	LIV.	July	7, 1835
XLIX.	July	7, 1789				LV.	Oct.	6, 1835
L.	July	6, 1790	I.	Jan.	1, 1822	LVI.	Jan.	5, 1836
LI.	July	5, 1791	II.	April	2, 1822	LVII.	April	5, 1836
LII.	Jan.	1, 1793	III.	July	2, 1822	LVIII.	July	5, 1836
LIII.	Jan.	7, 1794	IV.	Oct.	1, 1822	LIX.	Oct.	6, 1836
LIV.	April	20, 1795	V.	Jan.	7, 1823	LX.	Jan.	3, 1837
LV.	April	19, 1796	VI.	April	1, 1823	LXI.	April	4, 1837
LVI.	April	18, 1797	VII.	July	1, 1823	LXII.	July	5, 1837
LVII.	Oct.	3, 1797	VIII.	Oct.	7, 1823	LXIII.	Oct.	3, 1837
LVIII.	April	17, 1798	IX.	Jan.	6, 1824	LXIV.	Oct.	3, 1837
LIX.	Oct.	2, 1798	X.	April	6, 1824	LXV.	Jan.	2, 1838
LX.	April	16, 1799	XI.	July	6, 1824	LXVI.	April	3, 1838
LXI.	Jan.	7, 1800	XII.	Oct.	5, 1824	LXVII.	July	3, 1838
LXII.	Oct.	7, 1800	XIII.	Jan.	4, 1825	LXVIII.	Oct.	2, 1838
LXIII.	July	7, 1801	XIV.	April	5, 1825	LXIX.	Jan.	1, 1839
LXIV.	July	6, 1802	XV.	Oct.	4, 1825	LXX.	April	2, 1839
LXV.	April	19, 1803	XVI.	Jan.	3, 1826	LXXI.	July	2, 1839
LXVI.	Jan.	3, 1804	XVII.	April	4, 1826	LXXII.	Oct.	1, 1839
LXVII.	July	3, 1804	XVIII.	July	5, 1826	LXXIII.	Jan.	7, 1840
LXVIII.	Oct.	2, 1804	XIX.	Oct.	3, 1826	LXXIV.	April	7, 1840
LXIX.	Jan.	1, 1805	XX.	Jan.	2, 1827	LXXV.	July	7, 1840
LXX.	April	16, 1805	XXI.	April	3, 1827	LXXVI.	Jan.	5, 1841
LXXI.	July	2, 1805	XXII.	July	3, 1827	LXXVII.	Jan.	4, 1842
LXXII.	Oct.	1, 1805	XXIII.	Oct.	2, 1827	LXXVIII.	Jan.	3, 1843
LXXIII.	Jan.	7, 1806	XXIV.	Jan.	1, 1828	LXXIX.	Jan.	2, 1844
LXXIV.	April	15, 1806	XXV.	April	1, 1828	LXXX.	Jan.	7, 1845
LXXV.	July	1, 1806	XXVI.	July	1, 1828	LXXXI.	Jan.	6, 1846
LXXVI.	Oct.	7, 1806	XXVII.	Oct.	7, 1828	LXXXII.	July	7, 1846
LXXVII.	Jan.	6, 1807	XXVIII.	Jan.	6, 1829	LXXXIII.	Jan.	5, 1847
LXXVIII.	April	20, 1807	XXIX.	April	7, 1829	LXXXIV.	July	6, 1847
LXXIX.	July	7, 1807	XXX.	July	7, 1829	LXXXV.	Jan.	4, 1848
LXXX.	Oct.	6, 1807	XXXI.	Oct.	6, 1829	LXXXVI.	July	5, 1848
LXXXI.	Jan.	5, 1808	XXXII.	Jan.	5, 1830	LXXXVII.	Jan.	2, 1849
LXXXII.	April	19, 1808	XXXIII.	April	6, 1830	LXXXVIII.	July	3, 1849
LXXXIII.	June	6, 1808	XXXIV.	July	6, 1830	LXXXIX.	Jan.	1, 1850
LXXXIV.	July	5, 1808	XXXV.	Oct.	5, 1830	XC.	July	2, 1850
LXXXV.	Oct.	4, 1808	XXXVI.	Jan.	4, 1831	XCI.	Jan.	7, 1851
LXXXVI.	Jan.	3, 1809	XXXVII.	April	5, 1831	XCII.	July	1, 1851
LXXXVII.	Mar.	11, 1809	XXXVIII.	July	5, 1831	XCIII.	Jan.	6, 1852
LXXXVIII.	April	18, 1809	XXXIX.	Oct.	4, 1831	XCIV.	Oct.	5, 1852
LXXXIX.	July	4, 1809	XL.	Jan.	3, 1832	XCV.	Mar.	—, 1852
XC.	Oct.	3, 1809	XLI.	April	3, 1832	XCVI.	Jan.	4, 1853
XCI.	Jan.	2, 1810	XLII.	July	3, 1832	XCVII.	July	5, 1853
XCII.	April	17, 1810	XLIII.	Oct.	2, 1832	XCVIII.	Jan.	3, 1854
XCIII.	July	3, 1810	XLIV.	Jan.	1, 1833	XCIX.	July	5, 1854
XCIV.	May	11, 1810	XLV.	April	2, 1833	C.	Jan.	2, 1855
XCV.	Oct.	2, 1810	XLVI.	July	2, 1833	CI.	April	3, 1855
XCVI.	Nov.	9, 1810	XLVII.	Oct.	1, 1833	CII.	July	3, 1855

SUFFOLK COUNTY — Con.

(CIVIL SESSION. CLERK'S OFFICE AT BOSTON.) — Con.

Superior Court of the County of Suffolk.[1]

I.	Nov.	6, 1855	VII.	Mar.	3, 1857	XIII.	May	4, 1858
II.	Jan.	7, 1856	VIII.	May	5, 1857	XIV.	July	6, 1858
III.	May	6, 1856	IX.	Sept.	1, 1857	XV.	Nov.	2, 1858
IV.	Sept.	4, 1856	X.	Nov.	3, 1857	XVI.	Jan.	4, 1859
V.	Nov.	4, 1856	XI.	Jan.	5, 1858	XVII.	Mar.	1, 1859
VI.	Jan.	6, 1857	XII.	Mar.	2, 1858			

Superior Court.

I.	July	5, 1859	XXX.	July	7, 1868	LIX.	July	4, 1876
II.	Oct.	4, 1859	XXXI.	Jan.	5, 1869	LX.	Oct.	3, 1876
III.	Jan.	3, 1860	XXXII.	April	6, 1869	LXI.	Oct.	3, 1876
IV.	Jan.	3, 1860	XXXIII.	Oct.	5, 1869	LXII.	Jan.	2, 1877
V.	April	3, 1860	XXXIV.	Jan.	4, 1870	LXIII.	Jan.	2, 1877
VI.	July	3, 1860	XXXV.	April	5, 1870	LXIV.	April	3, 1877
VII.	Oct.	2, 1860	XXXVI.	Oct.	4, 1870	LXV.	July	3, 1877
VIII.	Jan.	1, 1861	XXXVII.	Jan.	3, 1871	LXVI.	Oct.	2, 1877
IX.	April	2, 1861	XXXVIII.	April	4, 1871	LXVII.	Jan.	1, 1878
X.	Oct.	1, 1861	XXXIX.	Oct.	3, 1871	LXVIII.	April	2, 1878
XI.	Jan.	7, 1862	XL.	Jan.	2, 1872	LXIX.	July	2, 1878
XII.	April	1, 1862	XLI.	April	2, 1872	LXX.	Oct.	1, 1878
XIII.	Oct.	7, 1862	XLII.	July	2, 1872	LXXI.	Jan.	7, 1879
XIV.	Jan.	6, 1863	XLIII.	Jan.	7, 1873	LXXII.	April	1, 1879
XV.	April	7, 1863	XLIV.	April	1, 1873	LXXIII.	July	1, 1879
XVI.	Oct.	6, 1863	XLV.	July	1, 1873	LXXIV.	Jan.	6, 1880
XVII.	Jan.	5, 1864	XLVI.	Jan.	6, 1874	LXXV.	April	6, 1880
XVIII.	April	5, 1864	XLVII.	April	7, 1874	LXXVI.	July	6, 1880
XIX.	July	5, 1864	XLVIII.	Oct.	6, 1874	LXXVII.	Jan.	4, 1881
XX.	Jan.	3, 1865	XLIX.	Oct.	6, 1874	LXXVIII.	April	5, 1881
XXI.	July	4, 1865	L.	Jan.	5, 1875	LXXIX.	July	5, 1881
XXII.	Jan.	2, 1866	LI.	Jan.	5, 1875	LXXX.	Jan.	3, 1882
XXIII.	April	3, 1866	LII.	April	6, 1875	LXXXI.	April	4, 1882
XXIV.	Oct.	2, 1866	LIII.	April	6, 1875	LXXXII.	July	4, 1882
XXV.	Jan.	1, 1867	LIV.	July	6, 1875	LXXXIII.	Jan.	2, 1883
XXVI.	April	2, 1867	LV.	Oct.	5, 1875	LXXXIV.	April	3, 1883
XXVII.	July	2, 1867	LVI.	Jan.	4, 1876	LXXXV.	July	3, 1883
XXVIII.	Jan.	6, 1868	LVII.	Jan.	4, 1876	LXXXVI.	Jan.	7, 1884
XXIX.	April	7, 1868	* LVIII.	April	4, 1876			

Notaries Public.

There are in the cellar of the Court House eleven chests filled with volumes of records of Notaries Public. The chests are labelled and purport to contain records of the following notaries: Charles B. F. Adams, Charles Hall Adams, Adams Bailey, Samuel Barrett, Adolphus Bates, Prescott Bigelow, Alden Bradford, Duncan Bradford, William Breck, Thomas Brown, Henry Clark, Samuel Cooper, Daniel Everett, John Gardner, Charles Hayward, Edward Jones, John I. Loring, J. Thomas Needham, M. S. Parker, J. J. Prescott, John W. Quincy, Robert Rogers, Nathaniel Seaver, Daniel Sharp, William Stevenson, D. McBurney Thaxter, and E. W. Whittemore.

---

[1] The powers and duties of this court were transferred to the "Superior Court" (of the Commonwealth) upon its establishment in 1859.

SUFFOLK COUNTY — Con.

(CIVIL SESSION. CLERK'S OFFICE AT BOSTON.) — Con.

Miscellaneous.

There are several hundred volumes of dockets with indexes; also many volumes of Motion books, List of Appealed Cases, etc., and thousands of files of papers belonging to cases entered in the several courts from very early dates to the present time.

One volume of records of Licensed Inn-holders and Retailers, covering the years from 1812 to 1822.

Ten volumes of records made by the Justices of the Peace for the County of Suffolk who held the Court of General Sessions of the Peace, covering various years between 1787 and 1806.

Six volumes of records of Partitions and Executions, dated as follows.

I.	1782 to 1803	III.	1825 to 1828	V.	1849 to 1882
II.	1803 to 1824	IV.	1827 to 1850	VI.	1882 to ——

One volume of records of Proceedings and Judgments in Actions, covering the period from Oct. —, 1851, to Oct. —, 1852.

There are three chests containing population returns of the U. S. Censuses of 1850, 1860, and 1880.

Volumes Indexed. — There are initial indexes covering all volumes, with the exception of the records of the Court of General Sessions of the Peace and Court of Sessions. The Miscellaneous records are partially indexed.

Condition of Records. — The want of sufficient room makes it impossible to have the records of this court in order for convenient reference. It has been necessary to store many of the old books in the cellar of the building.

(CRIMINAL SESSION. CLERK'S OFFICE AT BOSTON.)

Volumes of records and date of first day of term:

I.	July 5, 1859	XXIX.	Nov. 6, 1865	LVII.	April 6, 1868
II.	Oct. 3, 1859	XXX.	Dec. 4, 1865	LVIII.	April 6, 1868
III.	Jan. 2, 1860	XXXI.	Jan. 1, 1866	LIX.	May 4, 1868
IV.	April 4, 1860	XXXII.	Mar. 5, 1866	LX.	Aug. 3, 1868
V.	July 2, 1860	XXXIII.	May 7, 1866	LXI.	Oct. 5, 1868
VI.	Oct. 1, 1860	XXXIV.	May 7, 1866	LXII.	Nov. 2, 1868
VII.	Jan. 7, 1861	XXXXV.	May 7, 1866	LXIII.	Dec. 7, 1868
VIII.	April 1, 1861	XXXVI.	June 4, 1866	LXIV.	Jan. 4, 1869
IX.	July 1, 1861	XXXVII.	July 2, 1866	LXV.	Mar. 2, 1869
X.	Oct. 7, 1861	XXXVIII.	Aug. 6, 1866	LXVI.	May 3, 1869
XI.	Jan. 6, 1862	XXXIX.	Sept. 3, 1866	LXVII.	Aug. 2, 1869
XII.	April 7, 1862	XL.	Oct. 1, 1866	LXVIII.	Oct. 4, 1869
XIII.	July 7, 1862	XLI.	Nov. 5, 1866	LXIX.	Dec. 6, 1869
XIV.	Oct. 6, 1862	XLII.	Dec. 3, 1866	LXX.	Jan. 3, 1870
XV.	Jan. 5, 1863	XLIII.	Jan. 7, 1867	LXXI.	Mar. 7, 1870
XVI.	April 6, 1863	XLIV.	Feb. 4, 1867	LXXII.	May 2, 1870
XVII.	July 6, 1863	XLV.	Mar. 4, 1867	LXXIII.	Aug. 1, 1870
XVIII.	Oct. 5, 1863	XLVI.	April 1, 1867	LXXIV.	Nov. 7, 1870
XIX.	Jan. 4, 1864	XLVII.	June 3, 1867	LXXV.	Jan. 2, 1871
XX.	April 5, 1864	XLVIII.	June 3, 1867	LXXVI.	April 3, 1871
XXI.	July 5, 1864	XLIX.	July 1, 1867	LXXVII.	July 3, 1871
XXII.	Oct. 3, 1864	L.	Sept. 2, 1867	LXXVIII.	Oct. 2, 1871
XXIII.	Jan. 2, 1865	LI.	Sept. 2, 1867	LXXIX.	Jan. 1, 1872
XXIV.	April 3, 1865	LII.	Sept. 2, 1867	LXXX.	April 1, 1872
XXV.	July 3, 1865	LIII.	Oct. 7, 1867	LXXXI.	July 1, 1872
XXVI.	Oct. 2, 1865	LIV.	Jan. 6, 1868	LXXXII.	Oct. 7, 1872
XXVII.	Oct. 2, 1865	LV.	April 6, 1868	LXXXIII.	Dec. 2, 1872
XXVIII.	Nov. 6, 1865	LVI.	April 6, 1868	LXXXIV.	Jan. 6, 1873

SUFFOLK COUNTY — Con.

(CRIMINAL SESSION. CLERK'S OFFICE AT BOSTON.) — Con.

LXXXV.	Mar.	3, 1873	CVIII.	Oct.	2, 1876	CXXXI.	Sept.	6, 1880
LXXXVI.	May	5, 1873	CIX.	Oct.	2, 1876	CXXXII.	Jan.	3, 1881
LXXXVII.	July	7, 1873	CX.	Oct.	2, 1876	CXXXIII.	April	4, 1881
LXXXVIII.	Oct.	6, 1873	CXI.	Nov.	6, 1876	CXXXIV.	Sept.	5, 1881
LXXXIX.	Dec.	1, 1873	CXII.	Dec.	4, 1876	CXXXV.	Nov.	7, 1881
XC.	Jan.	5, 1874	CXIII.	Jan.	1, 1877	CXXXVI.	Jan.	2, 1882
XCI.	Mar.	2, 1874	CXIV.	Feb.	5, 1877	CXXXVII.	April	3, 1882
XCII.	June	1, 1874	CXV.	Mar.	5, 1877	CXXXVIII.	July	3, 1882
XCIII.	Aug.	3, 1874	CXVI.	April	2, 1877	CXXXIX.	Sept.	4, 1882
XCIV.	Oct.	5, 1874	CXVII.	June	4, 1877	CXL.	Nov.	6, 1882
XCV.	Dec.	7, 1874	CXVIII.	Oct.	1, 1877	CXLI.	Jan.	1, 1883
XCVI.	Jan.	4, 1875	CXIX.	Dec.	3, 1877	CXLII.	April	2, 1883
XCVII.	Mar.	1, 1875	CXX.	Jan.	7, 1878	CXLIII.	July	2, 1883
XCVIII.	May	3, 1875	CXXI.	April	1, 1878	CXLIV.	Oct.	1, 1883
XCIX.	July	5, 1875	CXXII.	Aug.	5, 1878	CXLV.	Dec.	3, 1883
C.	Sept.	6, 1875	CXXIII.	Oct.	7, 1878	CXLVI.	Jan.	7, 1884
CI.	Nov.	1, 1875	CXXIV.	Dec.	2, 1878	CXLVII.	Mar.	4, 1884
CII.	Jan.	3, 1876	CXXV.	Jan.	6, 1879	CXLVIII.	May	5, 1884
CIII.	Feb.	7, 1876	CXXVI.	April	7, 1879	CXLIX.	July	7, 1884
CIV.	Mar.	7, 1876	CXXVII.	Aug.	4, 1879	CL.	Sept.	1, 1884
CV.	May	1, 1876	CXXVIII.	Nov.	3, 1879	CLI.	Nov.	3, 1884
CVI.	June	5, 1876	CXXIX.	Jan.	5, 1880			
CVII.	Aug.	7, 1876	CXXX.	April	5, 1880			

Volumes Indexed. — There is an initial index for each year covering all the volumes of that year.

Condition of Records. — Good. All the old dockets which were in confusion have been classified and conveniently arranged for reference by the present clerk.

[There are in the office 119 volumes of the records of the " Municipal Court of the Town (afterwards City) of Boston," beginning June 2, 1800.]

WORCESTER COUNTY. (CLERK'S OFFICE AT WORCESTER.)

Volumes of records and date of first entry in each volume :

County Courts.

[Worcester County was not established at the time of the existence of County Courts. The records, if any, for this jurisdiction would be in the records of Hampshire or Suffolk counties.

Inferior Court of Common Pleas.

I.	Aug.	14, 1731	V.	Nov.	2, 1756	IX.	Feb.	9, 1773
II.	Aug.	20, 1737	VI.	Aug.	17, 1762	X.	Sept.	7, 1779
III.	Nov.	3, 1744	VII.	May	13, 1766	XI.	Dec.	3, 1782
IV.	Aug.	21, 1753	VIII.	Jan.	2, 1770			

Court of Sessions.

—.	Feb.	23, 1808	—.	Mar.	8, 1819	*Records of Commissioners*
—.	Sept.	9, 1811	—.	Sept.	11, 1827	*of Highways.*
						IX. Sept. 11, 1827

Court of General Sessions of the Peace.

I.	Aug.	12, 1731	IV.	May	10, 1768	VI.	Mar.	24, 1795
II.	Aug.	16, 1737	V.	Sept.	5, 1780	VII.	Sept.	2, 1805
III.	Feb.	7, 1758						

WORCESTER COUNTY (CLERK'S OFFICE AT WORCESTER.) — Con.

Circuit Court of Common Pleas.

XLII.	June 17, 1816	XLVI.	Mar. 9, 1818	L.	Mar. 13, 1820
XLIII.	Dec. 9, 1816	XLVII.	Aug. 31, 1818	LI.	Sept. 4, 1820
XLIV.	Mar. 10, 1817	XLVIII.	Mar. 8, 1819		
XLV.	Sept. 1, 1817	XLIX.	Aug. 30, 1819		

Court of Common Pleas.

XII.	June 8, 1784	LXVIII.	Mar. 2, 1829	CI.	Sept. 4, 1844
XIII.	Dec. 6, 1785	LXIX.	Aug. 1, 1829	CII.	Mar. 3, 1845
XIV.	Sept. 2, 1788	LXX.	Dec. 7, 1829	CIII.	Mar. 2, 1846
XV.	Mar. 22, 1791	LXXI.	Mar. 1, 1830	CIV.	Mar. 1, 1847
XVI.	Dec. 3, 1793	LXXII.	June 21, 1830	CV.	Dec. 6, 1847
XVII.	Dec. 1, 1795	LXXIII.	Dec. 6, 1830	CVI.	Mar. 6, 1848
XVIII.	Mar. 26, 1798	LXXIV.	June 20, 1831	CVII.	Dec. 4, 1848
XIX.	June 10, 1799	LXXV.	Mar. 5, 1832	CVIII.	Mar. 5, 1849
XX.	June 8, 1801	LXXVI.	Sept. 3, 1832	CIX.	Dec. 3, 1849
XXI.	Mar. 1, 1803	LXXVII.	Mar. 4, 1833	CX.	Mar. 4, 1850
XXII.	Dec. 4, 1804	LXXVIII.	Sept. 2, 1833	CXI.	Sept. 2, 1850
XXIII.	Mar. 25, 1806	LXXIX.	Mar. 3, 1834	CXII.	Dec. 2, 1850
XXIV.	Sept. 2, 1806	LXXX.	Sept. 1, 1834	CXIII.	Mar. 3, 1851
XXV.	June 8, 1807	LXXXI.	Dec. 1, 1834	CXIV.	Sept. 1, 1851
XXVI.	Dec. 1, 1807	LXXXII.	Mar. 2, 1835	CXV.	Dec. 1, 1851
XXVII.	June 13, 1808	LXXXIII.	Aug. 31, 1835	CXVI.	Mar. 1, 1852
		LXXXIV.	Mar. 7, 1836	CXVII.	Dec. 6, 1852
LII.	Mar. 12, 1821	LXXXV.	Mar. 29, 1836	CXVIII.	Dec. 31, 1852
LIII.	Sept. 3, 1821	LXXXVI.	Mar. 1, 1837	CXIX.	Mar. 7, 1853
LIV.	Mar. 17, 1822	LXXXVII.	Sept. 4, 1837	CXX.	Dec. 5, 1853
LV.	Sept. 2, 1822	LXXXVIII.	Mar. 5, 1838	CXXI.	Mar. 6, 1854
LVI.	Mar. 10, 1823	LXXXIX.	Sept. 3, 1838	CXXII.	Dec. 4, 1854
LVII.	Sept. 21, 1823	XC.	Mar. 4, 1839	CXXIII.	Mar. 5, 1855
LVIII.	Mar. 8, 1824	XCI.	Sept. 2, 1839	CXXIV.	Sept. 3, 1855
LIX.	Aug. 13, 1824	XCII.	Mar. 2, 1840	CXXV.	Mar. 3, 1856
LX.	Mar. 14, 1825	XCIII.	Aug. 31, 1840	CXXVI.	Oct. 27, 1856
LXI.	Aug. 29, 1825	XCIV.	Mar. 1, 1841	CXXVII.	Feb. 2, 1857
LXII.	Mar. 13, 1826	XCV.	Aug. 30, 1841	CXXVIII.	Aug. 31, 1857
LXIII.	Sept. 4, 1826	XCVI.	Mar. 7, 1842	CXXIX.	Feb. 1, 1858
LXIV.	Mar. 12, 1827	XCVII.	Aug. 29, 1842	CXXX.	Aug. 30, 1858
LXV.	Sept. 3, 1827	XCVIII.	Mar. 6, 1843	CXXXI.	Mar. 7, 1859
LXVI.	Mar. 3, 1828	XCIX.	Sept. 4, 1843		
LXVII.	Sept. 1, 1828	C.	Mar. 4, 1844		

Criminal.

I.	—, 1835	IV.	—, 1851	VI.	—, 1856
II.	—, 1845	V.	—, 1854	VII.	—, 1857
III.	—, 1850				

Superior Court.

I.	July 2, 1859	IX.	Mar. 2, 1868	XVII.	Dec. 11, 1876
II.	June 11, 1860	X.	Aug. 13, 1869	XVIII.	Dec. 10, 1877
III.	Mar. 4, 1861	XI.	Nov. 14, 1870	XIX.	Sept. 1, 1879
IV.	Mar. 9, 1862	XII.	Mar. 4, 1872	XX.	Nov. 8, 1880
V.	Nov. 10, 1862	XIII.	June 9, 1873	XXI.	Dec. 12, 1881
VI.	Dec. 14, 1863	XIV.	June 8, 1874	XXII.	Mar. 12, 1883
VII.	Mar. 6, 1865	XV.	June 15, 1875		
VIII.	Nov. 12, 1866	XVI.	Mar. 6, 1876		

Criminal.

I.	—, 1859	VI.	—, 1870	X.	—, 1877
II.	—, 1862	VII.	—, 1871	XI.	—, 1878
III.	—, 1865	VIII.	—, 1873	XII.	—, 1879
IV.	—, 1867	IX.	—, 1874	XIII.	—, 1880
V.	—, 1868				

WORCESTER COUNTY. (Clerk's Office at Worcester.) — Con.

Marriages.

Two volumes covering the years from 1746 to 1794, and containing records of the following towns:

Ashburnham,	Hubbardston,	Shrewsbury,
Athol,	Lancaster,	Southbridge,
Barre,	Leicester,	Spencer,
Berlin,	Leominster,	Sterling,
Bolton,	Lunenburg,	Stockbridge,
Boylston,	Mendon,	Sutton,
Brookfield,	Milford,	Templeton,
Charlton,	New Braintree,	Upton,
Douglas,	Northborough,	Uxbridge,
Dudley,	Northbridge,	Ward (now Auburn),
Fitchburg,	Oakham,	Westborough,
Gardner,	Oxford,	Western (now Warren),
Gerry (now Phillipston),	Paxton,	Westminster,
Grafton,	Petersham,	Winchendon,
Hardwick,	Princeton,	Worcester.
Harvard,	Royalston,	
Holden,	Rutland,	

Notaries Public.

One volume made by Joel C. Allen for Worcester County, covering the period from Mar. 17, 1880, to April 25, 1884. The condition is not stated.

One volume made by John B. D. Coggswell for Worcester district, covering the period from June 23, 1856, to Nov. 2, 1857. The condition is not stated.

Three volumes made by Samuel Jameson for Worcester district, covering the following periods: Feb. 15, 1842, to Aug. 5, 1846; Nov. 23, 1842, to Feb. 21, 1851; Sept. 7, 1846, to Mar. 3, 1849. The condition is not stated.

One volume made by Samuel Jameson for Worcester County, covering the period from Feb. 24, 1851, to Mar. 18, 1852. The condition is not stated.

Four volumes made by Nathaniel Richardson for Worcester district, covering the following periods: May 6, 1857, to Jan. 27, 1869; Mar. 4, 1869, to Feb. 24, 1873; Feb. 24, 1873, to Jan. 5, 1877; Jan. 5, 1877, to Dec. 23, 1882. The condition is not stated.

One volume made by John S. Scammell for Worcester County, covering the period from Jan. 12, 1850, to Dec. 25, 1854. The condition is not stated.

One volume made by Daniel Stearns for Fitchburg district, covering the period from Mar. 3, 1862, to Dec. 3, 1867. The condition is not stated.

One volume made by Isaac Stevens for Worcester district, covering the period from Nov. 26, 1856, to Aug. 5, 1864. The condition is not stated.

Four volumes made by G. A. Trumbull for Worcester County and district, covering the following periods: April 29, 1831, to July 12, 1839; Aug. 26, 1841, to April 28, 1846; Dec. 25, 1845, to June 11, 1849; April 17, 1849, to Oct. 10, 1850. The condition is not stated.

Three volumes made by Joseph Trumbull for Worcester County and district, covering the following periods: Jan. 1, 1852, to Jan. 22, 1853; Jan. 25, 1853, to Oct. 21, 1854; Mar. 8, 1858, to Sept. 9, 1860. The condition is not stated.

Miscellaneous.

Three volumes of records of Partitions of Real Estate, covering the following periods: Jan. 24, 1816, to Aug. 6, 1828; Dec. 2, 1828, to Aug. 10, 1840; Jan. 12, 1841, to June 16, 1849.

Nine volumes of records of Attachments of Real Estate, covering the following years:

I. 1836 to 1850	IV. 1862 to 1867	VII. 1873 to 1878
II. 1850 to 1858	V. 1868 to 1872	VIII. 1878 to 1882
III. 1858 to 1861	VI. 1872 to 1873	IX. 1882 to 1885

WORCESTER COUNTY. (Clerk's Office at Worcester.) — Con.

Miscellaneous — Con.

Twenty-nine volumes of records of Naturalization of Aliens, covering the following years:

I.	1837 to 1848	XI.	1875 to 1876	XXI.	1883 to 1884	
II.	1849 to 1856	XII.	1876 to 1878	XXII.	1884	
III.	1856 to 1859	XIII.	1878			
IV.	1859 to 1866	XIV.	1878 to 1879	I.	1836 to 1848	
V.	1866 to 1867	XV.	1879 to 1880	II.	1848 to 1858	
VI.	1867 to 1868	XVI.	1880 to 1881	III.	1858 to 1867	
VII.	1868 to 1871	XVII.	1882	IV.	1868 to 1871	
VIII.	1871	XVIII.	1882	V.	1871 to 1873	
IX.	1872	XIX.	1882 to 1883	VI.	1873 to 1880	
X.	1873 to 1874	XX.	1883	VII.	1881 to 1883	

Two volumes of records of Sheriffs' Bonds, covering the following years: 1864 to 1877; 187⁻ to 1885.

One volume entitled Index of Roads.

One volume of By-Laws and City Ordinances.

One volume of records of Stray Beasts, covering the years from 1750 to 1776.

One volume of records of Variations of Surveyors' Compasses, covering the years from 1871 to 1885.

Volumes Indexed. — Each volume has an initial index. The first volume of records of Marriages and the volume of records of Stray Beasts have imperfect indexes.

Condition of Records. — Good, with the exception of volumes III., IV., V., VI., and VII. of the Court of Sessions, which need rebinding.

COUNTY RECORDS.

ESTABLISHMENT OF PROBATE COURTS AND REGISTRIES OF PROBATE.

[Although the Registry of Probate is the recording office of the Probate Court and for that reason the presentation in regard to probate records might appear appropriately under the title "Court Records," the fact that the recording of wills and similar documents far antedates the establishment of the Probate Court, and the character of the office is so nearly allied to that of the Registry of Deeds, it has seemed best to present the returns in regard to the Registries of Probate under the title "County Records."]

1633. July 1. Ply. Col. Laws, edit. 1836, p. 32. Wills were ordered to be proved before the Governor and Council.

1639. Sept. 9. Mass. Rec., Vol. I., p. 276. Records were ordered to be kept of all wills, administrations, and inventories within this jurisdiction, and "Mr. Stephen Winthrop was chosen to record things at Boston."

1649. ——. ——. Mass. Col. Laws, edit. 1660, p. 80. It was ordered that any executor who does not make probate of the will at the next Court of the County shall be fined.

1652. Oct. ——. Mass. Col. Laws, edit. 1660, p. 81. "Recorders or Clerks of County Courts" were ordered to record wills.

1657. May 6. Mass. Rec., Vol. IV., Part 1, p. 287. Fees were fixed for the "Recorder or Clerk" of any County Court, for the entry of "wills and inventories, with sixpence apiece for filing of the original and safe keeping thereof."

1685. May 27. Mass. Rec., Vol. V., p. 478. County Courts were authorized to hear and determine all cases relating to wills and administrations of estates.

1685. Oct. 14. Mass. Rec., Vol. V., p. 503. The act of May 27, 1685, was perfected.

1686. Feb. 16. Mass. Rec., Vol. V., p. 508. Executors were required "to make and exhibit into the Registry of the Court" [County] "a just and true inventory." The act of October 14, 1685, was repealed.

1687. June 1. Taken from the original parchment in the office of the Secretary of the Commonwealth. All wills and letters of administration were henceforth to be probated by the Governor or such persons as he shall commission.

1691. Oct. 7. Prov. Laws, Vol. I., p. 15. By the provisions of the Province Charter, the Governor and Council were to probate wills and grant letters of administration.

1692. June 18. Council Rec., Vol. II., p. 179. Judges and Registers of Probate were appointed by the Governor under powers conferred by the charter.

1692. Nov. 1. Prov. Laws, Vol. I., p. 44. Wills were to be proved before "Judges of Probate," and "Registers for the Counties" were to record them.

1760. Feb. 9. Taken from a volume called " Supreme Court of Probate," in the office of the Secretary of the Commonwealth. At a Court of Probate held by the Governor and Council or Assistants, the Governor laid before the Council a communication calling attention to the fact that the court had long existed " without a seal, records and rules, or even the common formalities of a Judicial Court," and it was ordered that a Register be appointed by this court to enter all determinations and proceedings therein; that a seal be provided, and that a Supreme Court of Probate be held twice in each year.

1763. Feb. 25. Prov. Laws, Vol. IV., p. 618. The several " Registers of Probate " are mentioned.

1784. Mar. 12. Perpet. Laws of Mass., edit. 1789, p. 102. Courts of Probate within the several counties were established, and the Supreme Judicial Court was constituted the " Supreme Court of Probate." " Registers of Wills " within the several counties were to be appointed, who should " have the care, custody, and keeping of all files, papers, and books to the Probate Office belonging." Inventories were " to be exhibited into the Registry of the Court of Probate."

1784. Nov. 6. Perpet. Laws of Mass., edit. 1789, p. 79. " Suitable persons to be appointed in the manner the Constitution directs for Judge and Register of said Court" [of Probate].

1818. Feb. 24. Mass. Laws. Courts of Probate within the several counties were established, and by this act Judges of Probate and Registers [of wills] were to be appointed. This act was to take effect July 1, 1818, and repealed all previous acts relating to Probate Courts.

1856. June 6. Mass. Laws. Courts of Insolvency were established.

1858. Mar. 26. Mass. Laws. Courts of Probate and Insolvency were established, the act to take effect July 1, 1858.

RETURNS FOR REGISTRIES OF PROBATE.

BARNSTABLE COUNTY. (REGISTRY AT BARNSTABLE.)

Number of volumes of records, ... 141
Date of earliest entry, ... July 19, 1686
Volumes lost or destroyed, ... 2

[Two volumes, numbers XXIX. and XLIV., were burned by the fire which destroyed the county buildings, October 22, 1827. Volume XXIX. is supposed to have been an index; volume XLIV. contained some miscellaneous records from 1821 to 1825.]

Volumes Indexed. — A general alphabetical index covers all volumes to 1840. Since 1840 each volume has a separate index.

Condition of Records. — Good.

Probate Court Files. — Files are complete since 1827. All files previous to that time are supposed to have been burned by the fire of 1827.

Supreme Court of Probate Decrees. — Decrees are filed.

County Court Proceedings prior to 1692. — Proceedings were probably burned by the fire of 1827.

BERKSHIRE COUNTY. (REGISTRY AT PITTSFIELD.)

Number of volumes of records, ... 182
Date of earliest entry, ... July 30, 1761
[Records prior to 1761, for the towns comprising this county, are at the Hampshire County Registry of Probate, at Northampton.]
Volumes lost or destroyed, ... None
[The records are complete from the organization of the county.]

Volumes Indexed. — Each volume has an alphabetical index.

Condition of Records. — Good.

Probate Court Files. — Files are complete.

Supreme Court of Probate Decrees. — Decrees are filed.

County Court Proceedings prior to 1692. — Proceedings for the towns comprising this county are at the Hampshire County Registry of Probate, at Northampton.

BRISTOL COUNTY. (REGISTRY AT TAUNTON.)

Number of volumes of records, ... 241
Date of earliest entry, ... —, 1686
Volumes lost or destroyed, ... None

Volumes Indexed. — Each volume has an alphabetical index. An index in three volumes, covering volumes I. to CCXXX., has been recently made.

Condition of Records. — Good. Fifteen volumes need rebinding.

Probate Court Files. — Files are complete.

Supreme Court of Probate Decrees. — Decrees are filed.

County Court Proceedings prior to 1692. — Proceedings are in the Registry.

COUNTY OF DUKES COUNTY. (REGISTRY AT EDGARTOWN.)

Number of volumes of records, ... 38
[As originally made there are 38 volumes, but several of the oldest volumes which were unbound have been bound together.]
Date of earliest entry, ... July 14, 1697
Volumes lost or destroyed, ... None

Volumes Indexed. — All volumes since 1852 are indexed.

Condition of Records. — Good.

Probate Court Files. — Files are complete.

Supreme Court of Probate Decrees. — Decrees are filed and recorded.

County Court Proceedings prior to 1692. — Proceedings are not in the Registry.

ESSEX COUNTY. (REGISTRY AT SALEM.)

Number of volumes of records, ... 443
Date of earliest entry, ... —, 1671
Volumes lost or destroyed, ... None

Volumes Indexed. — All volumes have strictly alphabetical indexes recently made, the indexes to the oldest volumes having been imperfect.

Condition of Records. — Good. The first ten volumes, covering the years from 1671 to 1700, should be copied.

Probate Court Files. — Files are complete.

ESSEX COUNTY. (REGISTRY AT SALEM.)— Con.

Supreme Court of Probate Decrees. — Decrees are filed. There are also records of the Supreme Court of Probate among the records in the earlier volumes.

County Court Proceedings prior to 1692. — Proceedings are not in the Registry. Copies covering the proceedings from 1638 to 1691, in three volumes, with strictly alphabetical indexes, are in the Registry.

Miscellaneous Records. — Copies of unrecorded papers belonging to the files were made in book form, about 1866, by order of the County Commissioners. They are unbound, and contain inaccuracies, not having been attested by the Register.

FRANKLIN COUNTY. (REGISTRY AT GREENFIELD.)

Number of volumes of records, ... 133
Date of earliest entry, ... April 7, 1812
    [Records prior to 1812, for the towns comprising this county, are at the Hampshire County Registry of Probate, at Northampton.]
Volumes lost or destroyed, ... None

Volumes Indexed. — Each volume has an alphabetical index.

Condition of Records. — Good.

Probate Court Files. — Files are complete and indexed.

Supreme Court of Probate Decrees. — Decrees are filed and recorded.

County Court Proceedings prior to 1692. — Proceedings for the towns comprising this county are at the Hampshire County Registry of Probate, at Northampton.

HAMPDEN COUNTY. (REGISTRY AT SPRINGFIELD.)

Number of volumes of records, ... 154
Date of earliest entry, ... August 11, 1812
    [Records prior to 1812, for the towns comprising this county, are at the Hampshire Registry of Probate, at Northampton. Some Probate records are at the Registry of Deeds for this county.]
Volumes lost or destroyed, ... None

Volumes Indexed. — Each volume has an alphabetical index. There is also an alphabetical index covering all volumes.

Condition of Records. — Good.

Probate Court Files. — Files are complete.

Supreme Court of Probate Decrees. — Decrees are filed.

County Court Proceedings prior to 1692. — Proceedings for the towns comprising this county are at the Hampshire County Registry of Probate, at Northampton, with the exception of a few which are at the Hampden County Registry of Deeds, at Springfield.

HAMPSHIRE COUNTY. (REGISTRY AT NORTHAMPTON.)

Number of volumes of records, ... 146
Date of earliest entry, ... March 27, 1660
Volumes lost or destroyed, ... None

Volumes Indexed. — Volumes LXI. to LXV. have strictly alphabetical indexes. All other volumes have incomplete indexes.

Condition of Records. — Fifteen volumes need rebinding.

Probate Court Files. — Files are complete.

Supreme Court of Probate Decrees. — Decrees are filed and recorded.

County Court Proceedings prior to 1692. — Proceedings are in the Registry, and include those relating to the towns afterwards comprising Berkshire, Franklin, Hampden, and Hampshire counties.

COUNTY RECORDS.

MIDDLESEX COUNTY. (Registry at Cambridge.)

Number of volumes of records, ... **474**

[There are also copies of the first fourteen volumes. The second volume relating to births, marriages, and deaths in the towns in Middlesex County, from 1678 to 1745, which should be in the office of the Clerk of the Courts, is bound in at the end of the first volume relating to "Wills and Inventories." A copy of this volume is in the office of the Clerk of the Courts.]

Date of earliest entry, ... May 14, 1654

Volumes lost or destroyed, ... 1

[One volume was lost about 1849, when the records were removed during repairs to the court house.]

Volumes Indexed. — Each volume has an initial index.

Condition of Records. — Twenty-two of the oldest volumes have been rebound. About ten pages of the records of wills recorded in 1654 are mutilated.

Probate Court Files. — Files are substantially complete.

Supreme Court of Probate Decrees. — Decrees are filed, and since 1861 are indexed.

County Court Proceedings prior to 1692. — Proceedings are not in the Registry.

NANTUCKET COUNTY. (Registry at Nantucket.)

Number of volumes of records, ... 28

Date of earliest entry, ... September 27, 1706

Volumes lost or destroyed, ... None

Volumes Indexed. — Each volume has an initial index.

Condition of Records. — Good.

Probate Court Files. — Files are complete.

Supreme Court of Probate Decrees. — There are none in the Registry.

County Court Proceedings prior to 1692. — Proceedings are not in the Registry.

NORFOLK COUNTY. (Registry at Dedham.)

Number of volumes of records, ... 153

Date of earliest entry, ... August 22, 1793

Volumes lost or destroyed, ... None

Volumes Indexed. — Each volume has an alphabetical index.

Condition of Records. — Good.

Probate Court Files. — Files are complete.

Supreme Court of Probate Decrees. — Decrees are filed.

County Court Proceedings prior to 1692. — Proceedings are not in the Registry.

PLYMOUTH COUNTY. (Registry at Plymouth.)

Number of volumes of records, ... 199

Date of earliest entry, ... May 14, 1686

Volumes lost or destroyed, ... None

Volumes Indexed. — Each volume has an alphabetical index.

Condition of Records. — Twenty-five of the older volumes need rebinding.

Probate Court Files. — Files are complete.

Supreme Court of Probate Decrees. — Decrees are filed and recorded.

County Court Proceedings prior to 1692. — Proceedings from 1685 to 1692 are in the Registry. The records of estates of deceased persons prior to 1685 are in the Plymouth Colony Records, in the Registry of Deeds at Plymouth.

SUFFOLK COUNTY. (Registry at Boston.)

Number of volumes of records, ... 567

[In the earlier volumes, there are records of estates of residents of Salem mixed in with the records of resident estates for this county.]

Date of earliest entry, ... —, 1636

Volumes lost or destroyed, ... -

[Some volumes have undoubtedly been lost.]

Volumes Indexed. — A strictly alphabetical index, in six volumes, has been made. Until 1862 each volume had an initial index.

Condition of Records. — A few of the earliest volumes have pages missing and are badly worn.

Probate Court Files. — Many papers belonging to the files are lost. About 1854 many papers were placed in the cellar of the Probate Court Building, without any regard to order, and many of these papers were carried away.

Supreme Court of Probate Decrees. — Decrees are filed and indexed.

County Court Proceedings prior to 1692. — Proceedings are not in the Registry.

WORCESTER COUNTY. (Registry at Worcester.)

Number of volumes of records, ... 428

Date of earliest entry, ... July 12, 1731

Volumes lost or destroyed, ... None

Volumes Indexed. — Each volume has an initial index.

Condition of Records. — Good.

Probate Court Files. — Files are complete.

Supreme Court of Probate Decrees. — Decrees are filed.

County Court Proceedings prior to 1692. — Proceedings are not in the Registry.

ESTABLISHMENT OF REGISTRIES OF DEEDS.

1634. April 1. Mass. Rec., Vol. I., p. 116. " A constable and four or more of the chief inhabitants of every town chosen by all the freemen at some meeting, with the advice of some one or more of the next assistants, shall make a survey of all improved or enclosed land of every free inhabitant there and shall enter the same in a book (fairly written in words at length and not in figures) with the several bounds, and quantities by the nearest estimation, and shall deliver a transcript into the court, and the same so entered and recorded shall be a sufficient assurance to every free inhabitant of such estate or inheritance as they shall have in any such lands or frank tenements."

1637. Aug. 1. Mass. Rec., Vol. I., p. 201. Ordered, "That some course be taken to cause men to record their lands, or to fine them that neglect."

1639. Sept. 9. Mass. Rec., Vol. I., p. 276. Ordered, "To record all men's houses and lands, being certified under the hands of the men of every town, deputed for the ordering of their affairs." "Mr. Stephen Winthrop was chosen to record things at Boston."

1640. Oct. 7. Mass. Rec., Vol. I., pp. 306, 307. Ordered, "That after the end of this month, no mortgage, bargain, sale or grant made of any houses, lands, rents or other hereditaments shall be of force against any other person except the grantor and his heirs, unless the same be recorded."

1642. —— ——. Mass. Col. Laws, edit. 1660, p. 21. The clerk of every shire town was to enter deeds.

1657. May 6. Mass. Rec., Vol. IV., Part 1, p. 287. Fees were fixed for the "Recorder or Clerk of any County Court, for entry of a mortgage or sale of houses or lands."

1685. —— ——. Ply. Col. Laws, edit. 1836, pp. 295, 296. Conveyances of land were to be recorded in the county where the land lay, by the "County Recorder." The clerk of the County Court was to be "County Recorder."

1697. Oct. 30. Prov. Laws, Vol. I., p. 299. Clerks of the Inferior Court in each county were to be registers of deeds.

1715. July 26. Prov. Laws, Vol. II., p. 8. Registers of deeds in each county were to be chosen by freeholders for five years, and a public office was to be kept in the shire town of each county for the registering of deeds.

1720. Nov. 17. Prov. Laws, Vol. II., p. 187. Registers of deeds were to be chosen *every* five years and to keep the office open daily and therein keep books, records, files, and papers thereto belonging.

RETURNS FOR REGISTRIES OF DEEDS.

BARNSTABLE COUNTY. (REGISTRY AT BARNSTABLE.[1])

Number of volumes of records, ... 206
    Barnstable County Records, ... 204
    Marshpee Records, ... 2
    [One volume of the Marshpee Records is a copy of the list made by commissioners appointed to make partition of the common land of the District of Marshpee, dated June 4, 1842.]
Date of earliest entry, ... October 24, 1827
Volumes lost or destroyed, ... 93
    [Ninety-three out of ninety-four volumes were burned in the fire which destroyed the county buildings, October 22, 1827. Thirty-two of the present volumes contain records of deeds which were returned and re-recorded after the fire.]

Volumes Indexed. — Each volume has an alphabetical index.

Condition of Records. — Good. A few volumes have been recently repaired.

---

[1] No act has been found establishing this registry.

BERKSHIRE COUNTY.

[Berkshire County is divided into three districts for the registry of deeds. Prior to the incorporation of Berkshire County in 1761, deeds for the towns in this county were recorded at Springfield. From June 30, 1761, to June 18, 1788, the Registry for the whole of Berkshire County was at Pittsfield.]

BERKSHIRE NORTHERN DISTRICT. (REGISTRY AT ADAMS. ESTABLISHED JUNE 18, 1788.)

[The towns of Adams, Cheshire, Clarksburg, Florida, Hancock, Lanesborough, New Ashford, North Adams, Savoy, Williamstown, and Windsor constitute the Berkshire Northern District. The records for these towns from 1761 to 1789 are in the Registry of Deeds at Pittsfield.]

Number of volumes of records, ... 181
Date of earliest entry, ... March 24, 1789
Volumes lost or destroyed, ... None

Volumes Indexed. — Each volume since 1880 has a strictly alphabetical index, and arrangements are being made for a similar index for previous volumes.

Condition of Records. — Volumes I., II., and V. need rebinding.

BERKSHIRE MIDDLE DISTRICT. (REGISTRY AT PITTSFIELD. ESTABLISHED JUNE 18, 1788.)

[The towns of Becket, Dalton, Hinsdale, Lee, Lenox, Otis, Peru, Pittsfield, Richmond, Stockbridge, Tyringham, and Washington constitute the Berkshire Middle District.]

Number of volumes of records, ... 263
Date of earliest entry, ... August 8, 1761
Volumes lost or destroyed, ... None

Volumes Indexed. — Each volume since January 1, 1871, has a strictly alphabetical index, and a similar index is being prepared for previous volumes.

Condition of Records. — Six volumes need rebinding.

BERKSHIRE SOUTHERN DISTRICT. (REGISTRY AT GREAT BARRINGTON. ESTABLISHED JUNE 18, 1788.)

[The towns of Alford, Egremont, Great Barrington, Monterey, Mount Washington, New Marlborough, Sandisfield, Sheffield, and West Stockbridge constitute the Berkshire Southern District. The records for these towns from 1761 to 1790 are in the Registry of Deeds at Pittsfield.]

Number of volumes of records, ... 138
Date of earliest entry, ... June 23, 1790
Volumes lost or destroyed, ... None

Volumes Indexed. — Prior to 1845 the indexes are imperfect; from 1845 to 1860 each town has a separate index, and since 1860 each volume has a strictly alphabetical index.

Condition of Records. — A few of the older volumes need rebinding.

BRISTOL COUNTY.

[Bristol County is divided into two districts for the registry of deeds. From June 2, 1685, to July 1, 1837, the Registry for the whole of Bristol County was at Taunton.]

BRISTOL NORTHERN DISTRICT. (REGISTRY AT TAUNTON.[1])

[The cities of Fall River and Taunton and the towns of Attleborough, Berkley, Dighton, Easton, Freetown, Mansfield, Norton, Raynham, Rehoboth, Seekonk, Somerset, and Swansea constitute the Bristol Northern District.]

Number of volumes of records, ... 439
There are also the following volumes of records:
    Town of Fall River, Rhode Island, ... 3
    Proprietors of Taunton (copies), ... 6
    Tiverton, R. I., lands, now in Fall River (copies), ... 8
Date of earliest entry, ... September 14, 1686
Volumes lost or destroyed, ... None

Volumes Indexed. — Each volume has an index, the indexes to the later volumes being strictly alphabetical.

Condition of Records. — About twenty of the older volumes need copying or rebinding.

BRISTOL SOUTHERN DISTRICT. (REGISTRY AT NEW BEDFORD. ESTABLISHED JULY 1, 1837.)

[The city of New Bedford and the towns of Acushnet, Dartmouth, Fairhaven, and Westport constitute the Bristol Southern District. The records for these towns from June 2, 1685, to July 1, 1837, are in the Registry of Deeds at Taunton.]

Number of volumes of records, ... 114
[There are two volumes of copies of Dartmouth Land Records made by order of the County Commissioners, in accordance with an act passed May 24, 1867.]
Date of earliest entry, ... July 1, 1837
Volumes lost or destroyed, ... None

Volumes Indexed. — Each volume has a strictly alphabetical index.

Condition of Records. — Good.

COUNTY OF DUKES COUNTY. (REGISTRY AT EDGARTOWN.[1])

Number of volumes of records, ... 76
[There are four volumes of copies made by authority of the County Commissioners.]
Date of earliest entry, ... 1686
Volumes lost or destroyed, ... None

Volumes Indexed. — Each volume has a strictly alphabetical index.

Condition of Records. — Good.

---

[1] No act has been found establishing this Registry.

ESSEX COUNTY.

[Essex County is divided into two districts for the registry of deeds. Prior to 1869 the Registry for the whole of Essex County was at Salem.]

ESSEX NORTHERN DISTRICT. (REGISTRY AT LAWRENCE. ESTABLISHED OCTOBER 1, 1869.)

[The city of Lawrence and the towns of Andover, Methuen, and North Andover constitute the Essex Northern District.]

Number of volumes of records, ... 83
Date of earliest entry, ... October 1, 1869
Volumes lost or destroyed, ... None

Volumes Indexed. — Each volume has a strictly alphabetical index.

Condition of Records. — Good.

ESSEX SOUTHERN DISTRICT. (REGISTRY AT SALEM.[1])

[The cities of Gloucester, Haverhill, Lynn, Newburyport, and Salem and the towns of Amesbury, Beverly, Boxford, Bradford, Danvers, Essex, Georgetown, Groveland, Hamilton, Ipswich, Lynnfield, Manchester, Marblehead, Merrimac, Middleton, Nahant, Newbury, Peabody, Rockport, Rowley, Salisbury, Saugus, Swampscott, Topsfield, Wenham, and West Newbury constitute the Essex Southern District.]

Number of volumes of records, ... 1,227
[There are also eleven volumes of copies. There are three series of records : the Ipswich series, beginning in 1640 and ending in 1694; the old County of Norfolk series, beginning in 1637 and ending in 1714, and the Salem or present series beginning in 1640.]
Date of earliest entry, ... —, 1640
Volumes lost or destroyed, ... None

Volumes Indexed. — Most of the volumes have strictly alphabetical indexes, and an index is being prepared for the other volumes.

Condition of Records. — Good. As volumes have become worn they have been copied or rebound.

FRANKLIN COUNTY. (REGISTRY AT GREENFIELD. ESTABLISHED DECEMBER 2, 1811.)

[March 1, 1787, three Registries of Deeds were established in Hampshire County : one at Northampton for twenty-two towns, which are named in the Act ;[2] one at Deerfield "for towns north of the above," and one at Springfield " for towns south of the above." The " towns north of the above " at that time, and consequently within the jurisdiction of the Registry at Deerfield, were probably Ashfield, Bernardston, Buckland, Charlemont, Colrain, Conway, Deerfield, Greenfield, Heath, Leverett, Leyden, Montague, New Salem, Northfield, Orange, Rowe, Shelburne, Shutesbury, Sunderland, Warwick, Wendell, and Whately. The records for these towns prior to 1787, are in the Registry of Deeds at Springfield.]

Number of volumes of records, ... 385
Date of earliest entry, ... June 2, 1787
Volumes lost or destroyed, ... None

Volumes Indexed. — Each volume has a strictly alphabetical index.

Condition of Records. — Good.

---

[1] No act has been found establishing this Registry.
[2] See head-note for Hampshire County Registry of Deeds.

HAMPDEN COUNTY. (REGISTRY AT SPRINGFIELD. ESTABLISHED AUGUST 1, 1812.)

[March 1, 1787, three Registries of Deeds were established in Hampshire County: one at Northampton for twenty-two towns, which are named in the Act;[1] one at Deerfield "for towns north of the above," and one at Springfield "for towns south of the above." The "towns south of the above" at that time, and consequently within the jurisdiction of the Registry at Springfield at that time, were probably Blandford, Brimfield, Granville, Holland, Longmeadow, Ludlow, Monson, Montgomery, Palmer, South Brimfield (now Wales), Southwick, Springfield, Tolland, Westfield, West Springfield, and Wilbraham.

The Registry at Springfield was the Registry for the original county of Hampshire, which comprised the present county of Berkshire until 1761, the present county of Franklin until 1811, the present county of Hampden until 1812, certain towns afterward in the present county of Worcester, and the towns of Somers and Suffield now in the State of Connecticut.]

Number of volumes of records, ... 451
Date of earliest entry, ... April 12, 1673
Volumes lost or destroyed, ... None

Volumes Indexed. — Each volume has a strictly alphabetical index, with the exception of one volume of executions which has an initial index.

Condition of Records. — Volumes are repaired as often as is necessary to keep them in good condition.

HAMPSHIRE COUNTY. (REGISTRY AT NORTHAMPTON. ESTABLISHED MARCH 1, 1787.)

[March 1, 1787, a Registry was established at Northampton for the following-named towns: Amherst, Belchertown, Chester, Chesterfield, Cummington, Easthampton, Goshen, Granby, Greenwich, Hadley, Hatfield, Middlefield, Northampton, Norwich (now Huntington), Pelham, Plainfield, Southampton, South Hadley, Ware, Westhampton, Williamsburg, and Worthington. The records for these towns prior to 1787 are in the Registry of Deeds at Springfield.]

Number of volumes of records, ... 413

[There are four volumes of copies of Proprietors Records for Amherst, Easthampton, Hadley, Hatfield, Northampton, Pelham, Prescott, Southampton, South Hadley, and Williamsburg.]

Date of earliest entry, ... August 30, 1787
Volumes lost or destroyed, ... None

Volumes Indexed. — Volumes prior to 1869 do not have strictly alphabetical indexes; since 1869 each volume has a strictly alphabetical index.
Condition of Records. — Volumes I. to XXX. need rebinding and certain volumes should be copied. The older indexes are badly faded, and owing to insufficiency of room the volumes are subjected to unnecessary wear.

MIDDLESEX COUNTY.

[Middlesex County is divided into two districts for the registry of deeds. Prior to 1855 the Registry for the whole of Middlesex County was at Cambridge.]

MIDDLESEX NORTHERN DISTRICT. (REGISTRY AT LOWELL. ESTABLISHED JULY 1, 1855.)

[The city of Lowell and the towns of Billerica, Carlisle, Chelmsford, Dracut, Dunstable, Tewksbury, Tyngsborough, Westford, and Wilmington constitute the Middlesex Northern District. From June 1, 1856, to June 1, 1860, the town of Littleton was in this district. The records for these towns from 1649 to 1855 are in the Registry at Cambridge.]

Number of volumes of records, ... 177
Date of earliest entry, ... July 2, 1855
Volumes lost or destroyed, ... None

Volumes Indexed. — Each volume has a strictly alphabetical index.

Condition of Records. — Good.

---

[1] See head-note for Hampshire County Registry of Deeds.

MIDDLESEX COUNTY — Concluded.

MIDDLESEX SOUTHERN DISTRICT.   (REGISTRY AT CAMBRIDGE.[1])

[The cities of Cambridge, Malden, Newton, Somerville, and Waltham and the towns of
Acton, Arlington, Ashby, Ashland, Ayer, Bedford, Belmont, Boxborough, Bur-
lington, Concord, Everett, Framingham, Groton, Holliston, Hopkinton, Hudson,
Lexington, Lincoln, Littleton (from June 1, 1856, to June 1, 1860, in the Middlesex
Northern District), Marlborough, Maynard, Medford, Melrose, Natick, North Read-
ing, Pepperell, Reading, Sherborn, Shirley, Stoneham, Stow, Sudbury, Townsend,
Wakefield, Watertown, Wayland, Weston, Winchester, and Woburn constitute
the Middlesex Southern District.]

Number of volumes of records, ... 1,724
[There are copies of the first two volumes. There is a series of sixteen volumes called
"Deeds of Hopkinton and Upton." There is also one volume called "Littleton
Records," which is a copy of records in the Middlesex Northern District, of lands in
Littleton. The first volume of births, marriages, and deaths in Middlesex County,
from 1632 to 1678, which should be in the office of the Clerk of the Courts, is bound
in at the end of the first volume relating to deeds. A copy is in the office of the
Clerk of the Courts.]
Date of earliest entry, ... June 14, 1649
Volumes lost or destroyed, ... None

Volumes Indexed. — Each volume until about 1800 has an initial index; since 1800 each volume
has a strictly alphabetical index.

Condition of Records. — Many volumes need rebinding.

NANTUCKET COUNTY.   (REGISTRY AT NANTUCKET.[1])

Number of volumes of records, ... 70
[There are six volumes of records of Proprietors of the Common and Undivided Lands,
from 1716 to 1885.]
Date of earliest entry, ... February —, 1659
Volumes lost or destroyed, ... None

Volumes Indexed. — Each volume has an initial index.

Condition of Records. — Good.   Thirty volumes have been rebound.

NORFOLK COUNTY.   (REGISTRY AT DEDHAM.[1])

[The records of old Norfolk County are in the Essex Southern District Registry at
Salem.]

Number of volumes of records, ... 572
[There are records of the Common and Undivided Lands of the Townships of Dor-
chester and Stoughton, between 1713 and 1793.]
Date of earliest entry, ... September 24, 1793
Volumes lost or destroyed, ... None

Volumes Indexed. — Many of the earlier volumes have initial indexes.   A strictly alphabetical
index covers all volumes.

Condition of Records. — Volume XX. is being copied; a few of the other volumes need copying.
Several volumes have been rebound.

---

[1] No act has been found establishing this Registry.

PLYMOUTH COUNTY. (Registry at Plymouth.[1])

Number of volumes of records, ...	536
Plymouth Colony Records,.	6
Plymouth County Records, ...	530
There are also the following volumes of records :	
Births, marriages, and deaths, ...	1
Commissioners of the United Colonies, ...	2
Court actions, ...	1
Court orders, ...	6
Laws, ...	1
Wills, ...	6
Date of earliest entry :	
Plymouth Colony Records, ...	July 3, 1630
Plymouth County Records, ...	July 20, 1700
Volumes lost or destroyed, ...	None

Volumes Indexed. — All the volumes are indexed. The Plymouth County Records have classified indexes.

Condition of Records. — Good. Two volumes in which the ink had eaten through the paper have been copied by order of the County Commissioners.

SUFFOLK COUNTY. (Registry at Boston.[1])

Number of volumes of records, ...	1,698
[There are six volumes of copies, three volumes of which have been printed by the Boston Record Commissioners.]	
Date of earliest entry, ...	—, 1639
Volumes lost or destroyed, ...	2

[Volume CXII., covering the time from January to July, 1768, and volume CXIV., covering January, February, and March, 1769, were lost, probably in moving the records to Dedham as authorized by the General Court, February 8, 1776. (Prov. Laws, Vol. V., p. 456.)]

Volumes Indexed. — Many volumes have separate indexes, but all are covered by strictly alphabetical indexes contained in three hundred volumes. From 1800 to 1885 the indexes are classified and contain a brief description of the premises described in the deed.

Condition of Records. — Good. Volumes are copied or rebound as often as required.

WORCESTER COUNTY.

[Worcester County is divided into two districts for the registry of deeds. Prior to August 1, 1884, the Registry for the whole of Worcester County was at Worcester.]

WORCESTER DISTRICT. (Registry at Worcester.[1])

[The city of Worcester and the towns of Athol, Auburn, Barre, Berlin, Blackstone, Bolton, Boylston, Brookfield, Charlton, Clinton, Dana, Douglas, Dudley, Gardner, Grafton, Hardwick, Harvard, Holden, Hubbardston, Lancaster, Leicester, Mendon, Milford, Millbury, New Braintree, Northborough, Northbridge, North Brookfield, Oakham, Oxford, Paxton, Petersham, Phillipston, Princeton, Royalston, Rutland, Shrewsbury, Southborough, Southbridge, Spencer, Sterling, Sturbridge, Sutton, Templeton, Upton, Uxbridge, Warren, Webster, Westborough, West Boylston, West Brookfield, and Winchendon constitute the Worcester District.]

Number of volumes of records, ...	1,211
Date of earliest entry, ...	—, 1731
Volumes lost or destroyed, ...	None

Volumes Indexed. — Each volume has an initial index. Indexes of grantors from 1731, and of grantees from 1840, are strictly alphabetical; the grantees prior to 1840 are also being alphabetically indexed.

Condition of Records. — Good.

---

[1] No act has been found establishing this Registry.

WORCESTER .COUNTY — Concluded.

WORCESTER NORTHERN DISTRICT. (REGISTRY AT FITCHBURG. ESTAB-
LISHED AUGUST 1, 1884.)

[The city of Fitchburg and the towns of Ashburnham, Leominster, Lunenburg, and
Westminster constitute the Worcester Northern District. The records from August
1, 1864, to August 1, 1884, in the Registry of Deeds at Worcester, relating to land in
the city of Fitchburg and the towns in this district, are being copied into volumes
to be kept in this Registry.]

Number of volumes of records, ... 11
Date of earliest entry, ... August —, 1884
Volumes lost or destroyed, ... None

Volumes Indexed. — Each volume has a strictly alphabetical index.

Condition of Records. — Good.

ESTABLISHMENT OF COUNTY COM-MISSIONERS.

[Until the act of March 4, 1826, the Courts of Sessions and Courts of Common Pleas had
powers in matters relating to county buildings, county accounts, and highways.]

1826. Mar. 4. "Commissioners of Highways" were established for all the counties
except Nantucket and Suffolk. They were to make return of their
doings to the Courts of Sessions, to be there recorded.

1828. Feb. 26. "County Commissioners" were established for all the counties except
Nantucket and Suffolk, and "Commissioners of Highways" and
the "Courts of Sessions" were abolished. The clerks of the Courts
of Common Pleas were made clerks of the County Commissioni
in their respective counties.

1857. Feb. 5. The clerks of the Supreme Judicial Court and Court of Common Pleas
were made clerks of the County Commissioners in their respective
counties.

1859. Apr. 5. The clerks of the Superior Court were made clerks of the County Commissioners in their respective counties.

1860. Feb. 2. The assistant clerks of the Superior Court were made assistant clerks
of the County Commissioners in their respective counties.

RETURNS FOR COUNTY COMMISSIONERS.

[The records of the County Commissioners are in the offices of the Clerks of the Courts in their respective counties.]

COUNTIES AND VOLUMES OF RECORDS.	Date of Earliest Entry	COUNTIES AND VOLUMES OF RECORDS.	Date of Earliest Entry	COUNTIES AND VOLUMES OF RECORDS.	Date of Earliest Entry
BARNSTABLE.		FRANKLIN.		MIDDLESEX —Con.	
I.	April 9, 1828	I.[3]	—— ——	VIII.	Jan. 3, 1830
II.	April 9, 1839	II.	June 9, 1829	IX.	Jan. 2, 1836
III.	Oct. 12, 1852	III.	Mar. 5, 1839	X.	Jan. 5, 1839
IV.	Jan. 2, 1865	IV.	July 17, 1847	XI.	Jan. 2, 1872
V.	Feb. 13, 1877	V.	Dec. 14, 1852	XII.	Jan. 6, 1874
		VI.	Dec. 13, 1859	XIII.	Jan. 5, 1876
		VII.	Dec. 10, 1872		
BERKSHIRE.		VIII.	Dec. 15, 1882	NORFOLK.	
III.[1]	April 29, 1828			I.	April 15, 1828
IV.	April 26, 1831			II.	April 2, 1833
V.	May 11, 1838	HAMPDEN.		III.	April 13, 1836
VI.	Jan. 3, 1843	I.	May 13, 1828	IV.	April 27, 1843
VII.	July 3, 1849	II.	Sept. 28, 1830	V.	April 16, 1850
VIII.	Jan. 4, 1859	III.	Dec. 2, 1839	VI.	April 18, 1854
IX.	April 6, 1869	IV.	Oct. 6, 1846	VII.	April 21, 1857
X.	April 3, 1877	V.	June 12, 1850	VIII.	April 21, 1863
		VI.	Feb. 8, 1854	IX.	April 21, 1868
		VII.	June 17, 1859	X.	April —, 1873
BRISTOL.		VIII.	Mar. 30, 1867	XI.[6]	April 17, 1877
I.	Sept. 21, 1830	IX.	June 25, 1873		
II.	Sept. 17, 1850	X.	Sept. 17, 1878	PLYMOUTH.	
III.	Mar. 22, 1870			—[7]	—— —, 1828
		HAMPSHIRE.		—[8]	Jan. 6, 1840
DUKES CO.		II.[4]	Mar. —, 1828		
I.	Nov. 14, 1838	III.	June 6, 1837	WORCESTER.	
II.	May 21, 1856	IV.	Sept. 2, 1844	IX.	May 13, 1828
III.	Jan. 6, 1869	V.	Mar. 3, 1852	X.	Mar. 27, 1832
IV.	Jan. 7, 1880	VI.	Dec. 4, 1861	XI.	Mar. 22, 1836
		VII.	Mar. 3, 1868	XII.	Mar. 26, 1839
		VIII.	Sept. 5, 1871	XIII.	Mar. 22, 1842
ESSEX.[2]		IX.	Mar. 7, 1876	XIV.	Mar. 25, 1845
I.	June 10, 1828	X.	Mar. 1, 1881	XV.	Dec. 26, 1848
II.	July 12, 1831			XVI.	Sept. 11, 1849
III.	April 11, 1837	MIDDLESEX.		XVII.	Dec. 23, 1851
IV.	April 13, 1841	—[5]		XVIII.	Mar. 28, 1854
V.	April 13, 1847	I.	May 13, 1828	XIX.	Sept. 9, 1856
VI.	April 13, 1852	II.	Sept. 20, 1831	XX.	Mar. 22, 1859
VII.	April 13, 1858	III.	May 12, 1835	XXI.	Dec. 22, 1863
VIII.	April 9, 1867	IV.	Jan. 4, 1842	XXII.	Mar. 26, 1867
IX.	April 9, 1872	V.	Sept. 1, 1846	XXIII.	Mar. 22, 1870
X.	July 11, 1876	VI.	Jan. 2, 1849	XXIV.	Mar. 26, 1872
XI.	April 11, 1880	VII.	Jan. 1, 1856	XXV.	Mar. 24, 1874
XII.	April 8, 1884			XXVI.	Dec. 28, 1880

[1] In volume III. of Court of Sessions, page 164.

[2] All the volumes are indexed.

[3] This volume is missing.

[4] In volume II. of Court of Sessions.

[5] In volume II. of Court of Sessions, page 255.

[6] There are later records which are unbound.

[7] In volume VII. of Court of Sessions.

[8] These records, and others in dockets, are unbound.

Recommended Reading
from NEHGS

Pioneers of Massachusetts, 1620–1650
By Charles Henry Pope
foreword by Scott C. Steward
NEHGS • 6 x 9 pbk, 574 pp. • $29.95

New England Marriages Prior to 1700
By Clarence Almon Torrey
NEHGS • 8 1/2 x 11, 2,400 pp. in 3 vols • $84.95 pbk, $124.95 hcvr

The Original Lists of Persons of Quality, 1600–1700
By John Camden Hotten, foreword by Robert Charles Anderson, FASG
NEHGS • 6 x 9 pbk, 616 pp. • $27.95

The Founders of New England
Originally Collected for and Published in
The New England Historical and Genealogical Register
By Samuel G. Drake
foreword by Henry B. Hoff, CG, FASG
NEHGS • 6 x 9 pbk, 272 pp. • $21.95

New Englanders in the 1600s
A Guide to Genealogical Research
Published Between 1980 and 2010
EXPANDED EDITION
By Martin E. Hollick
NEHGS • 6 x 9 pbk, 272 pp. • $21.95

The Great Migration Study Project
Books • Quarterly Newsletter • Tours
By Robert Charles Anderson, FASG
www.AmericanAncestors.org/great-migration-store